Digital Media and Democracy

Digital Media and Democracy

Tactics in Hard Times

edited by Megan Boler

The MIT Press
Cambridge, Massachusetts
London, England

First MIT Press paperback edition, 2010
© 2008 Massachusetts Institute of Technology

For information about special quantity discounts, please email special_sales@mitpress.mit.edu

This book was set in Stone Sans and Stone Serif by SNP Best-set Typesetter Ltd., Hong Kong. Printed and bound in the United States of America.

Library of Congress Cataloging-in-Publication Data

Digital media and democracy : tactics in hard times / edited by Megan Boler.
  p. cm.
Includes bibliographical references and index.
ISBN 978-0-262-02642-0 (hardcover : alk. paper)—978-0-262-51489-7 (pb. : alk. paper)
1. Mass media—Political aspects. 2. Digital media—Political aspects. 3. Democracy.
I. Boler, Megan.
P95.8.D54   2008
302.23′1—dc22
                                                    2007032258

10 9 8 7 6 5 4 3 2

To the worlds grown smaller
In tribute to the life and work of Ricardo Rosas, 1969–2007

And to worlds grown bigger
Dedicated to the countless who persist in speaking up through the media

Contents

Acknowledgments

I conceived this collection in the collegial space of a six-week Cyberdisciplinarity Institute, hosted at the Dartmouth Center for the Humanities by Dr. Mark Williams in the spring of 2005. I am particularly grateful to those who offered comments on my Introduction: Nathalie Magnan, Marcia McKenzie, Carly Stasko, Trevor Norris, Graham Meikle, Catherine Burwell, Stephen Turpin, Jane Sooby, Mark Lipton, and D. Travers Scott. Special thanks to those who worked on editing interviews: Andréa Schmidt, Deetje Boler, Catherine Burwell, Stephen Turpin, and Chikako Nagayama. Enormous awe and gratitude to Andréa Schmidt for her expert consultation on almost all interview questions, and for her thorough and skillful work transcribing the interviews with Deepa Fernandes, Amy Goodman, Hassan Ibrahim, and Shaina Anand. Thank you to Lisa Gitelman for sharing her wisdom all along the way, and to Carol Burch Brown and Melisande Charles for consultation on images and design. My heartfelt thanks to Jennie McKnight, who provides ever-curious willingness to engage and parry ideas, labor-intensive reproduction of daily life, and a cheerful, steady ballast. A special thanks to Education Commons (Alfredo Chow and others) at OISE/University of Toronto who always extend my e-mail server storage, and who fielded my slightly frantic call during the final hours of this manuscript preparation: "Why have I stopped receiving e-mails?!" Alfredo calls me back: "Megan, the system only handles 1,200 and you have over 5,000 e-mails in your inbox." Finally, thank you to the dynamic intellectual environment created by the team of researchers engaged in my Canadian Social Science and Humanities Research Council–funded project "Rethinking Media, Democracy and Citizenship" from 2005 to the present—Catherine Burwell, Jennifer Kayahara, Chantelle Oliver, Laura Pinto, Alessandra Renzi, Andréa Schmidt, and Stephen Turpin.

Introduction

Megan Boler

"A lie can be halfway around the world before the truth has its boots on" becomes doubly true with today's technologies.
—Donald Rumsfeld, February 17, 2006

As an unnamed Bush official told reporter Ron Suskind, "We're an empire now, and when we act, we create our own reality. And while you're studying that reality—judiciously, as you will— we'll act again, creating other new realities, which you can study too, and that's how things will sort out. We're history's actors . . . and you, all of you, will be left to just study what we do."
—Eric Alterman, *The Nation*, April 21, 2005

Moyers: I do not know whether you are practicing an old form of parody and satire . . . or a new form of journalism.
Stewart: Well then that either speaks to the sad state of comedy or the sad state of news. I can't figure out which one. I think, honestly, we're practicing a new form of desperation . . .
—Bill Moyers interview of Jon Stewart, on Public Broadcasting Service, July 2003

On a cold March night in southwestern Virginia in 2003, one week prior to the United States invasion of Iraq, I filed into a packed auditorium of 2,000 students, including the entire corps of Virginia Tech military cadets dressed in white pants, white gloves, and navy blue hats. Tim Russert, host of *Meet the Press*, a weekly news magazine that airs on U.S. network television, was to speak on the topic of the impending U.S.-led invasion of Iraq. A professor at this university at the time, I was in the midst of con- ducting research for a Web site that had been launched on September 11, 2002, enti- tled, "Critical Media Literacy in Times of War." For over a year, my team of talented graduate students and I had been immersed in an examination of how and what dif- ferent news sources were reporting on the effect of sanctions, civilian casualties, and number of persons reported at war protests in relationship to recent events in Afghani- stan and Iraq. I was steeped in international press coverage related to Bush's threatened war, and as the talk progressed, it became evident that Russert was omitting central arguments against the preemptive attacks that had been widely published in most international and some domestic news media in early 2003. Describing his talk as an "objective evaluation" of the bipartisan views represented in news media, Russert concluded his speech by saying that, given journalism's objective work reporting the facts, Bush's proposed invasion was justified and warranted.

I was first to the microphone for the question and answer period. As Russert spoke, I had written down carefully worded remarks identifying key facts reported in respected news sources that he had neglected to mention.[1] Outlining these omitted arguments, I asked Russert if he read any international news sources and suggested that he seemed extremely partisan in his selection of news coverage and consequent appraisal of the situation. His face turning red, Russert shouted that I had no right to claim to be a professor given my misreading of the facts. Cheering on Russert's cowardly attack, the audience began hissing and booing at me when I attempted a reply, and I was forced to retreat to my seat, genuinely afraid. As I left the auditorium, I feared I would be accosted, and was grateful for the few people who thanked me on my way out.[2]

It was at that moment that I realized the potency of the active silencing of dissent, and how distorted myths of journalistic objectivity could be used to justify something as devastating as the bombing of a nation and its people. Of course, my experience was not unusual—this was during a post-9/11[3] period in the United States when academics deemed "unpatriotic" were being "blacklisted" by such right-wing organizations as CampusWatch.[4]

The university newspaper reported the sparks that flew:[5]

After Russert's lecture, questions were taken from various audience members; one of whom was a professor who engaged Russert in a heated debate.

She accused Russert of not presenting objective journalism and of having a pro-war stance on Iraq, sentiments to which a small portion of the audience applauded.

Russert rebutted by saying he presented the views of the administration and was objective and that she needed to reexamine her facts.

The majority of audience members said they thought Russert's lecture was objective.

... Russert closed his lecture with a patriotic appeal. "Never underestimate our ability as a nation," he said. (March 13, 2003, *Collegiate Times*, Blacksburg, VA)[6]

Less than a year later, in early 2004, Tim Russert grilled George W. Bush on *Meet the Press*. When I read that Russert accused Bush of misleading the public and congress with stories about weapons of mass destruction (WMD), I felt a familiar anger—the anger at the number of politically powerful people who have adopted a revisionist story of their views on Bush's preemptive invasion. Just one of the many turncoats.[7] And this about-face of opinion—from supporting invasion to opposing the war—was enacted by so many politicians, in so many media outlets, and through the "evidence" of public opinion polls that one is simply left in a twilight zone of desperation. Who has the power to define reality? The question of what is required to counter the sophisticated operations of dominant media in this era of unparalleled public perception management merely leads to the next question in the hall of mirrors:[8] How is it that the changing whims of media and politicians are able, through censorship, omission, explicit suppression of dissent, and perverse manipulation of facts, to manipulate publics; which leads in turn to the question, what determines how and when the dominant media adopt an investigative rather than parroting role? In one sense Jodi Dean's chapter throws down the gauntlet: "How does one make sense of the phenomenon that, in the face of power, no amount of 'facts,' arguments, or rational counterpoints impact decisions being made by 'elected' officials?"[9]

My exchange with Tim Russert is emblematic of how the media functions in terms of truth and power. The auditorium is a public sphere; Mr. Russert, paid to stand at the podium with his hand on the microphone, epitomizes the power of media. The professor plays the role of merely one citizen, whose "opinions" (not facts) cannot possibly be right. (Where was Colbert's "truthiness" in 2003?) *And playing the part of media aptly, Russert would never admit in that public sphere that he was possibly wrong for excluding internationally recognized, credible arguments that countered his view.* When public perception of the facts changes, and it is safe for dominant media to take a more dissenting position, media tend not to accept responsibility for harm already

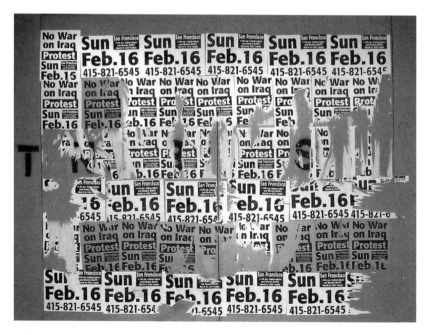

Figure 0.1
San Francisco, February 16, 2003. Photo by Dave Glass

Figure 0.2
London, February 15, 2003. Photo by Genny Bove

done. There are rare exceptions: both the *New York Times* and National Public Radio in February 2003 had to correct their underreporting of the number of antiwar protestors at demonstrations around the world on February 15, which in fact comprised the largest international antiwar movement in history. In 2005, the *New York Times* offered a feeble mea culpa for their role in disseminating false information about WMD.

As I travel and speak internationally, people frequently ask, "Is there a public in the United States that disagrees with the Bush Administration's policies? If there is, we don't see it reported here [in Canada, France, England, New Zealand, Australia, the Netherlands, Belgium]." Even progressive scholars do not seem to dig farther than headline bytes to recognize the fact of the largest international anti-war movement in history.[10]

Even if we debate what will constitute "truth," there is no doubt that battles are being fought because of what has been passed off as truth, and fought over the larger questions of what counts as truth. And media—whether corporate-owned or the smallest intervention posted through uses of the World Wide Web, Web 2.0[11]—traffics in truths and power.

No wonder, by 2005, we were all desperate for comedic interventions, including Stephen Colbert's popularization of the term "truthiness" to "describe things that a person claims to know intuitively, instinctively, or 'from the gut' without regard to evidence, logic, intellectual examination, or actual facts." We face an unparalleled crisis of public faith in media and politician's rhetorical claims and bytes, well illustrated by the top-cited media event in the blogosphere in 2004: Jon Stewart's appearance on *Crossfire* and his demand for media accountability (paralleled perhaps only by Colbert's 2006 performance at the White House Press Correspondent's Dinner and Colbert's popularization of "truthiness"; chap. 17, this volume). One cannot miss the irony of the "most trusted name in fake news" making the call for responsible journalism. It is this sort of paradox that sparks my current research, a three-year Social Science and Humanities Research Council (SSHRC)-funded project titled "Rethinking Media and Democracy: Digital Dissent after September 11."[12] Our research reveals how digital dissent (political blogs, viral videos, online discussion of Jon Stewart's appearance on *Crossfire*, MoveOn.org's Bush in 30 Seconds Contest) expresses simultaneously a demand for truthfulness, alongside a contradictory "postmodern" sensibility that "all the world's a fiction" (Boler 2006a; Boler 2006b).

Figure 0.3
Antiwar protest, New York City, February 15, 2003. Photo by Sara Bethell

Figure 0.4
Iraq War protest, San Francisco, February 15, 2003. Photo by Michael Seaman

These crises of truth coincide with increased sociable uses of the World Wide Web (also referred to by many as uses of Web 2.0, by others as sociable media, groupware, participatory Web—I will use the term social Web to refer most generally to the diverse uses addressed in this book, and Web 2.0 when I refer more specifically to the corporate resonance of the technology and its users). In fact, one might suggest that the "intercreative" possibilities of social Web practices are leading to different kinds of representations and constructions of truth (a focus of this book; but see specifically Meikle, chap. 16 this volume, on remix). For example, there are no public archives of broadcast news, so previously (e.g., during the Persian Gulf War in 1991) one could not "evidence" the deceptions of television news spin very easily. Now however, because much footage is accessible in digital form (whether through official news sites or individuals posting footage), we have a new way of "constructing" accounts to assuage our sense of having been lied to but having few ways to "prove" it. As Mark Lipton notes, "One can argue that the sociability of new Web processes are producing new pathways for 'truth.' The construction of truth, then, will probably follow two modes: the 'Truth' as propagated as fact by corporate media and 'truth' as ideas that emerge from the sociability of new pathways of sharing knowledge."[13]

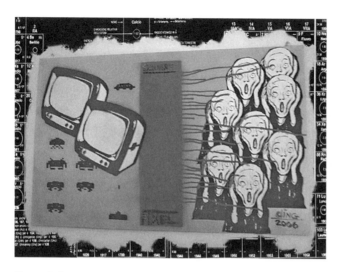

Figure 0.5
"Square Pixel—War, Lies and Media." *Source*: ding, http://www.flickr.com/photos/d1ng/

This desire and longing for truth expressed by public demands for media account-ability is in tension with the coexisting recognition of the slipperiness of meaning. In a landmark work titled *Virtual Geography* in which he addresses how corporate media represented the Persian Gulf War, McKenzie Wark defines the convergent landscape of print/digital/broadcast as the "media vector." "The paradox of the media vector [is that] the technical properties are hard and fast and fixed . . . but it is an oxymoronic relay system: a rigorous indeterminacy; a determinate imprecision; a precise ambigu-ity; and ambiguous determinism." (1994: 12) The media vector describes in part then the desire to "grasp for facts" in the face of elusive "electric mobility" of media. The combination of "horizontal mass media flows" and the affective circulation across binary definitions produces new tensions that are deeply understood and felt.

Semiotics cannot be distinguished from actual bodies when propaganda is literally dropped from planes and the returned gaze of the camera from the ground rapidly blurs distinctions between producer and consumer. In the shift to "user-generated content"—the same people who "consume" what is on the Web increasingly produce it—there is no longer the distinction so central to media and communication studies between producers and consumers, nor between authors and audience. We are pressed to describe not only new subjective formations but new theories of how power, dis-course, and poesis circulate in relation to the combinatory function and apparatus of digital distribution.[14] Alongside this slipperiness, there are moments when we need certainty. Now, in the early twenty-first century, we arguably have new sources of media democracy, new means for fact checking, as many of the chapters in this book debate. As Hassan Ibrahim reiterates in his interview here, our best hope for accuracy in media is double-sourcing. Perhaps that is what truth has come to—and it could be worse.

In my current research of four sites of digital dissent, this paradox has been reiterated and corroborated through thirty-five interviews with bloggers and independent viral video producers. Yet, despite the mistrust, people are using new media approaches to intervene in public debate and to try to gain a seat at the table. Central to this has been the introduction of the sociable web, including Web 2.0 collaborative Web-authoring software. The use of these digital dissent media suggest a double-edged contradiction of an awareness that all truths are constructed, alongside an affective desire for truth and an urgent political need for accuracy and responsible reporting. These concerns about "truth" even lead renowned scholar Bruno Latour to question his entire lifetime of scholarship that sought to question how facts are constructed:

Figure 0.6
"Empty Lies," July 14, 2006. Photo by Adam Kitzmann

"What has become of critique, I wonder, when the *New York Times* runs the following story?" He describes how renowned Republican lobbyist and paid spinmeister Fred Luntz[15] advises the Republicans how to redirect the increasing scientific (and, hence, public) understanding of global warming as caused by man-made pollutants. Luntz is in fact worried that science is winning the debate on global warming and advises Washington to divert public attention by emphasizing in the press that "the evidence is not complete. 'Should the public come to believe that the scientific issues are settled,' he writes, 'their views about global warming will change accordingly. Therefore, you need to continue to make the *lack of scientific certainty* a primary issue.'"

Alarmed by how public relations is working so directly to challenge science through political purchase of press spin of "scientific facts," Latour questions whether his entire lifetime of scholarship, which sought to question how facts are constructed, has backfired:

Figure 0.7
"Weather Report #14 Global Lying and Opining," by Melisande Charles (ongoing artist postcard series)

April 2003

"Naturally, the common people don't want war,
but after all, it is the leaders of a country who
determine the policy, and it is always a simple matter
to drag the people along whether it is a democracy,
or a facistic dictatorship, or a parliament, or a
communist dictatorship. Voice or no voice, the people
can always be brought to do the bidding of the leaders.
This is easy: All you have to do is to is tell them they
are being attacked and denounce the pacifists for lack
of patriotism and exposing the country to danger. It
works the same in every country."

Herman Goering
Hitler's Reich-Marshall
Nuremberg Trials, WWII

Figure 0.8
Text accompanying "Weather Report #14 Global Lying and Opining," by Melisande Charles

Should I reassure myself by simply saying that bad guys can use any weapon at hand, naturalized facts when it suits them and social construction when it suits them? Should we apologize for having been wrong all along? Should we rather bring the sword of criticism to criticism itself and do a bit of soul-searching here: What were we really after when we were so intent on showing the social construction of scientific facts? Nothing guarantees, after all, that we should be right all the time. There is no sure ground even for criticism. Is this not what criticism intended to say: that there is no sure ground anyway? But what does it mean, when this lack of sure ground is taken out from us by the worst possible fellows as an argument against things we cherished?[16]

This is surely a critical juncture, when the science of perception management and fact-marketing uses the media to create public doubts about scientific certainties. As Walter Benjamin once said, "It is hardly possible to write a history of information separately from a history of the corruption of the press." (1985: 28) It is at this historical turning point of public crises of faith, and resulting sea change in media studies, journalism, and media activism that I offer this collection of work by cross-disciplinary scholars, journalists, and tactical interventionists. It is my hope that through our collective insight, we spark further interrogation and intervention precisely around the question of whether and how diverse types of media interventions challenge dominant media, what new forms tactical interventions take in these hard times, and where precisely lies public interest and its representation in media in the face of oligarchies and media moguls. If our best hopes are televised court jesters who use satire to speak truth to power, with truthiness replacing scientific evidence of global warming—well, let's practice our new forms of desperation. Desperate times require desperate measures.

Media and Power

The story of my exchange with Tim Russert highlights two key challenges about media and power addressed across the essays in this book: (1) how to alter the axes of domination so that those with little or no power have a seat at the table, and (2) how to conceive of media (whether dominant, grassroots, or tactical) with the capacity to intervene at the level of public perception, and that can challenge the perverse manipulation of "facts" about something like global warming. As Graham Meikle notes addressing remix in chapter 16, "'Reality', James Carey once argued, 'is a scarce resource'—one which people compete to control. In the digital era, this competition remains fierce, but the raw material is no longer in short supply. Defining reality, carving up and exploiting that resource, is one of the central phenomena of the media."

In a version of the oft-cited maxim the "pen is mightier than the sword," Amy Goodman stated in an interview that "media is more powerful than any bomb."

Figure 0.9
American newsroom, MSNBC. Photo © Sean Hemmerle 2005

Figure 0.10
Baghdad, February 15, 2003. Photo by Martin Sasse

Is it?[17] I posed this question to both Amy Goodman and Hassan Ibrahim, two internationally recognized journalists who broadcast to tens of thousands, and in the latter case, sometimes millions, daily.

Goodman responded to my question, "But the people who are being impacted, the people who are having the bombs dropped on them—something happens to pave the way for the bombs. That's what the media does. It manufactures consent for war. That's what it's about. The bomb doesn't just happen in one day."

When I asked Hassan Ibrahim whether he believes the media to be more powerful than any bomb, he quickly replied:

Well, of course it is. Of course it is. And I'll give you an example of an Al Jazeera mistake. When the second Intifada erupted in 1999, one of our reporters mistakenly reported that the Israelis had declared a curfew in Ramallah. He misheard the Hebrew message. And the program on the radio was an analytical program that was using examples from the first Intifada. So the Al Jazeera reported on this fraud curfew in Ramallah. People rushed to get their kids from school to bring them home before curfew. And there was huge crowding in the streets and three people died trying to get to their kids. That's a small example of what the media can do to people—especially if you have a credible news outlet, people believe you and what you say is gospel truth. And if you get it wrong, then people get it wrong.

Exploring these questions about the relationship of media to public interests, which have come into particularly acute focus since 2001, and perhaps most especially after 2003 with uses of social Web challenging mainstream media muzzling of dissent, this book grapples with media tactics in hard times.[18] I would argue that 2003–04 is the pinnacle of the clash of media war, with such widespread viral video productions as the "Bush in 30 Seconds" contest and Jon Stewart's rising popularity and October 2004 appearance on *Crossfire*. Russert's challenge to my facts and impugning of my authority is but one small glimpse of where and how the questions surrounding media resonate: all have to do with issues of power and knowledge and with who gets to construct dominant narratives that shape global events. Wark describes the need to accept stupidity as an inevitable kernel:

French semiotician Roland Barthes pointed to something in this respect: "From a musical game heard on FM and which seemed 'stupid' to him, he realises this: stupidity is a hard and indivisible kernel, a primitive: no way of decomposing it scientifically (if a scientific analysis of TV were possible, TV would entirely collapse)." Rather than attempt to penetrate to the kernel of the media event, I treat it here as a primitive, an ineluctable core. One could attempt to exhaust the Gulf war as an event with analysis, but the resulting analysis, like most which approach their objects with the suspicion that the truth lies hidden in them somewhere, will be interminable. Perhaps theory needs to find a pace and a style that allows it to accompany the event, but without pretending to master it." (Wark 1994: 8)

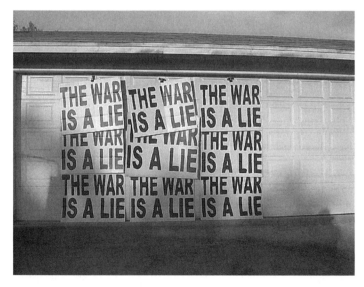

Figure 0.11
"The War is a Lie," July 3, 2006, El Cajon, California. *Source:* Beachblogger.net

A surreal twilight zone threatens to drive many mad with irrational logics, manipulations, and spin. Sometimes one thinks this sense of living in paradox is the nature of social Web, creating aporia through networks of communication that overlay one another becoming a blur of ambiguous bits and bytes—all in an effort to find correspondence between "media" and "reality."

When we do challenge these dominant media, political strategies, and hyperreal uses of public relations that manipulate public perception, we are often accused of being paranoid conspiracy theorists. Yet this is the challenge we face: the media traffic in power and do not give many a seat at the table to voice their views at the grand scale; political and corporate powers have developed ways of making us doubt even the most basic "facts."

How do we begin to understand the contradictions of proliferation (access to production, circulation, expression), alongside the rigid coordination of political, corporate, and media institutions? The conversations represented through these pages are crucial at this historical turning point, in part because of two things that by chance occurred at the same moment: (1) a radical democratization of knowledge and multiplication of sources and voices afforded by digital media—("Web 2.0 challenges dominant media!!"); and (2) blatant and outrageous instances of falsified national intelligence shielded from scrutiny ("National Press Falls into Lockstep with Bush Administration over Falsified Facts about WMD!!"). This conjunction of uses of social Web alongside the post-9/11 muzzling of press and stunning propaganda creates a dizzying labyrinth for those interested in how political decisions are made—and a crucial point of investigation for studies in media, communication, journalism, digital technologies, and social movements.

In terms of uses of media forms, it is hard to tell left from right.[19] Examples include conservatives offering training camps to bloggers; mainstream media adopting official bloggers to augment their behind-the-times print news; progressive bloggers redefining the dominant news agenda through investigation and muckraking; enemies of progressives eager to be lambasted by Jon Stewart, or vice versa; and viral video being used for savvy public relations and advertising. These uses of "Web 2.0" distinguish our current predicament from the questions posed regarding the last Persian Gulf War and the United States Pentagon's unidirectional and highly controlled media display of smart bombs in "Desert Storm."

Yet the efforts of the Pentagon to control the media remain: banning photos of returning military coffins; carefully controlled press briefings; selling the "rescue" of Private Jessica Lynch;[20] embedding journalists in Iraq; White House Press Briefings parroted to the public by cowed journalists; silencing of dissent through legislation such as the Patriot Act—this is but a brief list of egregious strategies used by the political oligarchy in the United States. All of these reveal the propaganda science and

Figure 0.12
"20,000 Volts in Your Pocket." Photo by Brian McConnell

public perception management capacities of political administrations that use news networks to create spin that shapes our perception and understanding of global events.

At the same time, some of the hype about democratization of media may be true: witness the meteoric rise of social network platforms and citizen journalism— with examples ranging from leaked photos of Abu Ghraib to a cellphone video of Saddam's hanging leaked to the public despite military and White House efforts at PR control.

Previously unimaginable and now ubiquitous access to media production and distribution is available through blogs, videoblogs, digital transmissions, and YouTube. "As U.S. President, Bush not only occupies the paramount position in U.S. electoral politics," writes Meikle in his chapter, "but he is also a symbol at the heart of a burgeoning activist participatory culture: one which manifests itself by, among other things, creating and circulating remixes, mash-ups, and subverted texts and imagery of all kinds." Amplifying the question of the power of such tactics as remix, my last three years of research evidence an interesting difference between the experience of bloggers and viral video/independent producers such as those whose work Meikle references: compared to viral video producers or tactical media artists, bloggers have a greater sense of community, belief that they are impacting dominant news agenda, and sense of being heard—which raises interesting questions about the difficulty of tracking the kinds of networks of circulation and forms of communication of viral video (online videos, animations, etc., which circulate widely with unpredictable popularity), whose "effects," trails, and links are harder to trace.

I asked Hassan Ibrahim, "Do you have any comments about this new hybrid form that combines classic TV with Web-based digital media?" He replied, "It's a revolution. It's a revolution because for the first time an average human walking down the streets of Jakarta, New York, or Khartoum, or Darfur, can actually pick up the phone and dial a number and report what they see—you're recruiting journalists from all over the world, people who know nothing about the secrets of the trade, of the industry, but they just saw something and they want to report it. And that's a revolution, when you have millions and millions of reporters around the world." In Europe, recent conferences such as the World Information Summit and the Italian San Precario[21] movement represent scholars and activists interested in tactical media focused on questions of perception and propaganda; tactics for getting diverse perspectives onto the public agenda; and the semantic, semiotic, and visual wars fought to try to exclude the smaller voices and hence prevent other collective imaginings.

Figure 0.13
Not In My Name sign, London, February 15, 2003. Photo by Ron Rademaker

Figure 0.14
London antiwar march sign, February 15, 2003. Photo by Pete Ashton

These complexities come across in the interview with Deepa Fernandes, who explains the significance of "hyperlocal" community radio as a more accessible and feasible medium than the overly hyped fantasy of democracy through the Internet. Fernandes is the host of Wakeup Call, WBAI's New York Pacifica flagship morning program, and an award-winning journalist whose work has appeared regularly on BBC World Service and across the Pacifica Network. Fernandes expressed a very tempered view on questions of access:

MB: Do you feel that the kinds of access to production and distribution that have been made possible through digital media such as blogging, YouTube, MySpace represent possibilities for the kind of participatory media you envision?
DF: Yes and no. I think the reality is that low-income communities and communities of color do not have access even to Internet in the way that those who—they don't have access to not only just computers but also to Internet. So in terms of uploading to YouTube—what's the difference in speed between uploading and downloading, and who has access to that? Do we even know the answer to that question? And do we even know that there's a difference?

And in the communities where we live, how much are we paying, which makes it impossible for some of us to have that kind of access?

So it continues to lock out a large amount of people.

Aware of such complexities, this collection as a whole addresses the convergence of three areas previously not found in developed conversation: are digital media and social Web use redefining the public sphere, and if so how and for whom? How are

Figure 0.15
Rome, February 15, 2003. Photo by Simone Ramella

digital media redefining journalistic practices? How do diverse media interventions and practices function as media activism, reform, or social movements? This book brings together the forces of academic scholarship in media alongside radical tactical media that emerged in the 1990s. Media scholars, tactical media activists, and journalists engage side-by-side to interrogate the changes effected at the turning point of the coincidental convergence of wartime media with the radical rise in public uses of digital media to question dominant media control of public life.

Debates about Media and Democracy within the Digital Media Landscape

Despite the magnitude of the challenge, the activists and journalists and scholars included here do address the sites of resistance and hope, however dark and twisted the road does seem. We are at a new crossroads in which the potential of media democratization allows us to challenge some lies and manipulations. Distortions by politicians and corporate media are by no means new. What is new is the explosion of public and citizen access to digital media during a moment when civil liberties and freedom of expression have been severely curtailed by the unilateral policies of the U.S. oligarchy. However, the kinds of hopes that have circulated since the turn of this century about the promise of the democratization of media are tempered by the views expressed overall in this collection.[22] My own sense of possibilities about democratization of media and practices of sociable web was less shaky when I commenced this volume in 2005, as demonstrated in my interview with Geert Lovink. The volume taken together reflects a tempered view about the potential of media to alter patterns of communication and to create more robust forms of democracy.

One way to read these chapters is as a sustained analysis and debate about the potential of digital media communications to revitalize the public sphere.[23] The tension is perhaps epitomized in this volume by Jodi Dean's pessimistic vision of the public sphere and its foreclosure by what she calls communicative capitalism, on the one hand, and, on the other, the explicit optimism of journalists like Amy Goodman and Hassan Ibrahim.

Figure 0.16
Barcelona antiwar protest, March, 2003. Photo by Andy Miah

Jodi Dean argues that:

In the United States today . . . there is a significant disconnect between politics circulating as content and official politics. Today, the circulation of content in the dense, intensive networks of global communications relieves top-level actors (corporate, institutional, and governmental) from the obligation to respond. Rather than responding to messages sent by activists and critics, they counter with their own contributions to the circulating flow of communications, hoping that sufficient volume (whether in terms of number of contributions or the spectacular nature of a contribution) will give their contributions dominance or stickiness. *Instead of engaged debates, instead of contestations employing common terms, points of reference, or demarcated frontiers, we confront a multiplication of resistances and assertions so extensive that it hinders the formation of strong counterhegemonies. The proliferation, distribution, acceleration, and intensification of communicative access and opportunity, far from enhancing democratic governance or resistance, results in precisely the opposite, the postpolitical formation of communicative capitalism.* (Jodi Dean, chap. 3, this volume, emphasis added)

Ron Deibert echoes Dean's pessimism: "For those concerned with global democratic communications, mostly this is a rather pessimistic story. If we start from any ideal perspective on what the communications infrastructure should look like for global civic networks and democracy to flourish . . . the current reality offers a fairly bleak picture" (chap. 5, this volume).

Sophie Statzel's chapter on Stormfront, a white nationalist group using tactical media for effective social mobilization of a movement, also offers a stringent warning: "The tactical mobilization of racial sentiments on Stormfront gives us caution about the continued existence of nationalist imaginaries even through new media which provide the possibility of more liberatory politics and imaginaries. This continuation of nationalist sentiments and subjectivities should challenge our thinking about our understandings of political agency as it is expressed through various political engagements, including tactical media." The pessimism and warnings of these authors is countered by the analyses of tactical media and tactical media activists (Renzi, Anand, Rosas), by Susan Moeller's hopes for the fourth estate, and to some extent by the analyses of Axel Bruns on "gate-crashing" and citizen journalism and by Chris Atton's analyses of alternative media processes. Even Deibert counters his own pessimism, noting the "substantial set of social forces combining to bring questions of access, privacy, and diversity to the principles . . . and technologies that configure global communications," including, of course, interventions of the Citizen Lab and the OpenNet Initiative projects.

It is useful to note briefly some common views on the relationship of media to democracy. In her chapter titled "Media and Democracy," Moeller outlines one classic view of the relationship of the press to democracy, the fourth estate: "Democracy . . . effectively argued, needs the media to report the news, without 'fear or favor.'

Figure 0.17
CNN newsroom. Photo © Sean Hemmerle 2006

Citizens need to know what the government is doing; the press needs the freedom to tell them. . . . Only a news organization that bravely reports what it knows, rather than what it is told is acceptable to say, can act as a check on government."

Practitioners engaged in political communication also evidence the vibrant engagements that shape the public sphere or perhaps most aptly the many counterpublics. When I asked Robert McChesney, "Could you describe the particular vision of democracy that underlies a project like the media reform movement or Free Press?" he didn't hesitate in his reply: "I think that the vision is actually pretty elementary—this movement doesn't require a very elaborate one. Self government is impossible without a viable press, and this is not a controversial idea, this is a foundation of the democratic theory, and it's foundational to progressive, liberal, mainstream, it's just right there, it's unavoidable. And it's also foundational to *anti-democratic* theory that you need a press system that manipulates people, keeps them in their place." The other optimists include people like Hassan Ibrahim and Amy Goodman, who, despite bearing witness to world events and horrors, day in and day out, maintain almost unfathomable energy and persistence in their public work of journalism. "I aspire for Al Jazeera to become a true voice of the people, a place where diversity can be expressed freely," states Ibrahim.

Susan Moeller offers in this volume an argument that ends on an optimistic note about media's power to redefine political agendas.[24] Moeller sums up the necessity of the fourth estate:

Despite their at times crucial failures, there is still no group better equipped than traditional journalists—whatever their journalistic platform—to ask the tough questions: of politicians and scientists, of corporate executives and social workers, of the military and of doctors, of academics and of children. There is still no group better equipped than traditional journalists—whatever their platform—to find the hidden crises. "My guess is that while serious reporting may not be delivered as often on paper made from trees," agreed Sydney Schanberg, "it will nonetheless live long and contribute to democracy in other delivery forms. This is so because it will always be propelled by abuses of power—and abuses of power are everlasting."[25] The need for a vital, aggressive, independent Fourth Estate remains.

And as Fernandes aptly situates the particularities of such challenges of the fourth estate: "Especially in youth communities, and in communities of color which are particularly targeted by media outlets and resold the images of people of color as criminals, and of youth as violent offenders, I think what we need to do is take what works and what we like from that and let that help us make the kind of media with the messages that we want for our communities."

So, while many of the chapters do not share extreme pessimism, one will not find in this volume any unbridled celebration. In fact, it seems that my studies of satire are among the most optimistic—though for those who believe that the press is closely linked to the functioning of democracy in contemporary contexts, there is irony in the fact that irony and satire are among our best salvations.

Viewers of Jon Stewart's *The Daily Show* and Stephen Colbert's *The Colbert Report* rank number 1 in the category of "best informed American public": "The six news sources cited most often by people who knew the most about current events were: 'The Daily Show' and 'The Colbert Report' (counted as one), tied with Web sites of major newspapers; next came 'News Hour with Jim Lehrer'; then 'The O'Reilly Factor,' which was tied with National Public Radio; and Rush Limbaugh's radio program" (*New York Times*, April 16 2007).[26] Satire speaking truth to power is a central place of optimism in political discourse—even if, as Amy Goodman told me about her interview on *The Colbert Report*, "You know what they tell you—just imagine yourself speaking to a drunk in a bar. That's what his producers tell you for talking to Mr. Stephen Colbert."[27]

It is not a coincidence that political satire is popular during times of political repression and censorship. People respond to satire because it pokes holes in the edifice of lies that have been built, as Goodman remarks in her interview in chapter 7. Some

Figure 0.18
Stewart/Colbert '08

blame *The Daily Show* for causing cynicism in American voters; others lament in opinion editorials that we are laughing our way into doomsday using irony as therapy for the world's horrors.[28] My studies indicate the contrary: the court jesters of our dark times translate into far more than chitchat. For starters, the quality political satire of comedians and parodists such as Stewart and Colbert give airtime—and often longer segments of airtime—to topics largely unmentioned by any other media—with the other crucial aim of holding media accountable to the public. On February 12, 2007, for example, Colbert devoted "The Word" to a story buried or unreported by almost all other news: the latest Defense Department report that evidences Defense Undersecretary Douglas Feith's "prewar report fabricating a link between Saddam and al Qaeda . . . Putting al Qaeda in Iraq may have taken some imagination back then, but thanks to inappropriateness [Feith] made it a reality." Colbert provided more than three minutes of time to a crucial story of precisely who manipulated intelligence and how it was done. (Any online search for this report will yield only the slightest coverage, beginning with a confusing AP version, with most stories headlining Feith's self-defense rather than the critical report.) Or how about April 18, 2007 when interviewing author Ali Allawi, Jon Stewart commented to Allawi with uncharacteristic seriousness—and much against the grain of mainstream media spectacle—that in the course of watching and being part of the nation grieving those massacred at Virginia Tech on April 16, 2007, he realized this level of casualties occurs on a daily basis in Iraq.[29] Yet, Stewart continued, making no jokes, the American media offer almost no coverage and certainly no humanizing stories of the grief of that nation.

A second reason perhaps for the currency of political satire is because the fair-use shield of parody allows these court jesters to report on politician's lies and corruption, as well as launch major critiques of media and press failures to hold politicians accountable.[30] In contrast to the notion of digital publics being only so much "chatter," across thirty-five interviews with bloggers and online video producers as part of my research project "Rethinking Media, Democracy and Citizenship," my research team and I discovered that Web-based communities sparked by political commentary like *The Daily Show* are vibrant and translating into action.[31] Our survey of 159 producers evidences that more than half agree that, "My online political activity has caused me to take action in my local community (e.g., protest, boycott, etc.)." A majority, 60 percent, say that "My online participation in political forums has led me to join at least one political gathering or protest." Since becoming active online, 29 percent are "more active in 'offline' political activities," and 63 percent "spend about the same amount of time in 'offline' political activities."

The question is no longer a simple one of laughter versus action, or online versus offline. Similarly misleading is the headline and implication of Jennifer Earl's Washingtonpost.com commentary (February 4, 2007, B01): "Where have all the protests gone? Online." This is simply not true. While the Internet is being used extensively for organizing, as our research shows online activists remain active offline—and more important, the protests against U.S. invasion of Iraq on January 27, 2007, were attended by hundreds of thousands (despite misrepresentation by hundreds of mainstream newspapers using the inaccurate AP assessment of the crowd as numbering in the "thousands").

These concepts about how and where media are being used to revitalize the public sphere offer a partial counterargument to Dean's pessimism. I would suggest further that to counter her argument we need a thorough theoretical inquiry into the nature of viral communication. Instead of reading the "multiplication of resistances" as leading nowhere—and merely representing what Dean calls "communicative capitalism"—it is more productive to recognize the contradictory nature of viral communications. In an age of spectacle and complicity, tactical interventions are often simultaneously recuperated by dominant power while still functioning to shift and modulate perceptions and representations within the dominant culture. As Wark described in 1994 in *Virtual Geography*, "The criticisms, even good ones, are part of the same matrix of relations as produced the spectacle of the Gulf War in the first place. . . . Both the dangers and our ability to do anything about it tie in to our everyday experience of the vector" (1994: 6). Form and content are inseparable, as are producer and consumer. While the impact of interventions cannot always be easily measured, this does not mean they are only or merely absorbed into a model of communicative capitalism. For these reasons, viral communications (and especially the interrelationship of irony, spectacle, and complicity as explored in chap. 17, this volume) are a crucial area of investigation.

By reading together political theory, social movement theory, semiotics, and cyberculture studies, perhaps we can push for new accounts of viral communication that suggest the possibility of a visible rupture between capital and commodity that would change the spectacle.[32] Viral communications redefine the public sphere through mutations of corporate-owned spectacles at the same time that profit is gained from user-generated content. In what ways do viral communications—the potential of a form that can be capitalized by any user—disrupt our understandings of commodity spectacle? No doubt, in contradictory predictability, both consolidation *and* rupture of dominant power takes place even with the most tactical interventions. As Brian Holmes notes, "Nothing yet shows that viral marketing has in any way overcome or demeaned the rather magical experience of throwing an idea or an image or any other creation out into the public realm, and watching it proliferate and spread. That's a viable mode of distribution today, no question. But I think to lay too much emphasis on such small miracles is imprudent. It can also become a form of mysticism, flourishing in the face of general despondency and lack of wider perspectives" (chap. 19, this volume).

Lovink too might at times be seen to support Dean, when he dismisses many of the online interventions I highlighted in discussion with him: "Content comes and goes and we shouldn't really pay too much attention to the production of content as such" (chap. 4, this volume). However, he emphasizes instead the importance of developing dense networks and the counterpublics formed through journalistic and tactical work such as those featured in this collection.

On the question of how tactical media activists shift their tactics to meet the moment, Shaina Anand in her interview comments, "Like Jodi Dean says in her essay, there is all this circulation of content, but it is all mainstream. Arundhati Roy says it in a recent essay: 'The information is out there, it is just going nowhere.' I think my tactical media practice has therefore shifted, it has moved into the generation of micromedia. It has developed by harvesting or claiming resources, and it is not necessarily events but everyday life and embedded politics with which you dirty your hands and respond" (chap. 13, this volume).

Despite some of the doubts that arise in the electronic world of information overload and what rises into a visible field or has force, I remain hopeful about the kinds of counterpublics and networks formed, for example, through the online networks that circulate interventions and critical commentary from *The Daily Show* and *The Colbert Report*, and through the blogging practices that trace their presence in ways that build a sense of solid community. These networked counterpublics work alongside community radio, as well as other sources ranging from *Democracy Now!* to *Al Jazeera English*. The interplay of all these media—and their convergence through Web-based circulation—pushes us to trace tactics and interventions, to understand the interplay between sources, which is, in essence, a field of viral communications.

Flooding, Intervening, Reforming . . . Tactics and Spaces of Media Intervention

The interviews and chapters in this book illustrate media interventions which take a range of different forms: media reform or "flooding"—seeking to change the very structures of media policy and legislation; media watchdog/gatewatching—critical analysis of media and the profession of journalism; media justice—creating alternative channels ranging from global-scale *Al Jazeera English* to smaller scale community radio, while others create smaller or more temporal interventions such as those represented by tactical media. All are interested in challenging and intervening in dominant media structures, and in cutting across modes of distribution with aims of resisting the messages and form of dominant media. As Fernandes puts it quite directly, "I think the question becomes, how much do we drive agendas, and potentially use the tactics of the mainstream media, like the slick production of MTV? 'Cause we need the slick production of MTV to win over all our highschoolers. They're not going to sit back and listen to someone on a soap box preaching about how Bush should have done this and that." Alternative media seeks to feature the voices of the public, of communities, those not usually represented in corporate media. In Amy Goodman's words,

People are experts on their own lives. And that's the power of [grassroots media]. That's when people take hope. I always find it amazing, in the most difficult situations we cover, that people feel hopeful. They don't get overwhelmed by it. But there's something about hearing about someone doing something about something—it's not just about the problem, it's about how people are responding to it, that ultimately is hopeful.

Deepa Fernandes frames it more specifically,

I think there's also a tendency in community media to kind of make a platform for the most often heard voices on the Left or in progressive communities. And that's very important and we absolutely need that because in some way they're the leaders on this side. But we also just need to hear from regular ordinary people living what's going on, and who might not have the savvy media training, or the Ph.D., or be able to frame it the way—they can just talk from their heart. So I think it's always trying to balance those kinds of things. Because the other thing, really, is that if you're flicking through the dial and you hear someone who sounds like you, maybe that will be an incentive to keep listening.

Interventions take myriad forms. While it can be tempting to privilege certain tactics or approaches over others, to imagine we can measure the "effects" of some better

Figure 0.19
"Weather Report #30 The Yellow Cake Road." (Judith Miller is depicted.) Artwork by Melisande Charles

Judy, Judy, Judy

She just loves to cook up WMD stews and
to bake yellow cakes for her boys to enjoy.

She keeps recipes secret and prefers to go
directly to jail rather than divulge any
ingredients.

A true domestic diva who can also whip up
a wicked batch of the Lying Virus and can
launch it under the cover of All the News
That's Fit to Print.

With Phlame in mind, will Fitzgerald go for
the top bad boys?

What a woman! She visits congress to plead
for legislation to cover future deeds.
Will she ever truthfully memoir us?

Can't wait for the next installment of
"Desperate Reporters", better yet

"Desperate Republicans".
OCTOBER 2005

Figure 0.20
Text accompanying "Weather Report #30 The Yellow Cake Road" (text by Melisande Charles)

than others, I am increasingly convinced that tracing effects is part of a deceptive
science usually conflated with the pseudoscience of public polls. Instead, it is crucial
to understand process and form as increasingly interconnected and to see the diversity
of interventions taken up for different purposes.

The modes of interventions analyzed and represented here include:

· Challenging media ownership concentration with media reform (in the U.S. context,
through federal policies of the FCC and legislative movements such as "Save the
Internet")
· Participating in "first" tier "dominant" media structures—e.g., establishing Al Jazeera
as major broadcast alternatives
· Establishing alternative media outlets and spaces
· Engaging tactical media interventions
· Broadcasting independently owned, community radio/online/Web-based broad-
casts
· Producing and accessing the social Web
· Posting blogs
· Engaging in citizen journalism

The Goals of Media Studies within Twenty-First-Century Politics

There are numerous goals and related challenges faced in trying to get a glimpse of the state of media within the contemporary digital landscape beginning with the very problem of calling them "new" media. One of the greatest challenges and goals of conducting media studies at this historical moment is to keep apace with the *rapidly changing face of media use, production, and practices,* both corporate and independent. A graduate student recently expressed this frustration. She had completed a literature review on media convergence, returned to teaching media in an English high school classroom for one semester. She returned to university to finish writing her comps only to discover the landscape of media ownership entirely shifted in four months. "I'm freaking out!" she exclaimed. "All my research in interactivity suddenly seems obsolete—YouTube wasn't really happening six months ago! My students say 'I watched *x* on YouTube' and I say 'You watched what?' I have to spend twelve hours a day tracking YouTube to keep up." (By the time you read this—many months after the completion of the manuscript, illustrating ironically the severe challenges of print in our 24/7 daily changing mediascape—who knows what the new digital-use phenomena will look like?)

A second goal is to find *a balance of theory and practice.* We need more than new theoretical frameworks and concepts to help us understand what is happening and how to intervene. We also need to know what interventions are happening and how they are working. Simply examining a question such as "journalism after September 11" frames the question fairly narrowly and risks making theorizations obsolete rather quickly. At the same time, theory needs to examine the practices, experiences, and cultural productions that constitute the object of study. To address the need for analyses of practice as well as theory, I have included in this book the voices of media activists and practicing journalists to augment scholarly theory.

The strategies of practice that are studied or exemplified here include: (a) reform —changing media policy and legislation around ownership and concentration, in order to limit the monopolization of media and exclusion of diversity within public agenda setting; (b) establishment of grassroots, independent news channels and networks such as Pacifica, Democracy Now!, and Al Jazeera English; (c) temporal interventions, tactical strategies such as those of The Yes Men[33] who managed to get onto the BBC as imposters of Dow Chemical to raise public awareness about media silencing of environmental disasters; and (d) the odd case of public expressions of progressive views through such "floodcasts" as cable or broadcast news shows as Keith Obermann of MSNBC and Jon Stewart and Colbert of Comedy Central, a cable network, which are then available online to even more vast audiences through Quicktime, Windows Media Player (WMP), or other Web-streaming files or torrents.

We might follow one of Renzi's concluding directions: "Academic work on spaces of resistance . . . can have a double effect: first, it can acknowledge that social attempts should not only be analyzed in terms of their achieved aims but rather in the light of the processes/practices set in motion in certain spaces. Second, in-depth case studies of single instances can help reveal the elements that hinder or facilitate the sustainability of some actions, thereby contributing to future, more-enduring projects" (Renzi, chap. 2, this volume).

A third goal is to offer *cross- and multidisciplinary answers*. To that end, I have brought into conversation people who engage different approaches and strategies for intervention. How can we effect social change through media interventions and what interventions in the past have been effective? What are the best kinds of tactics for reforming, revolutionizing, or otherwise making a media system more accountable to the diverse constituents it claims to represent? This answer will not come from any one area of expertise—not solely media studies scholarship or from a conference organized to strategize the latest forms of culture jamming. These answers will come from sharing diverse disciplinary and professional and guerilla approaches and sparking the next generation—the "You" recognized by *Time* magazine as Person of the Year in 2006: those creating the user-generated content that simultaneously profits Google and represents a potential of democracy and media.

In existing literatures one finds several distinct fields: cutting-edge work on journalism after 9/11; pioneering work on cyberactivism; communication studies of digital media and journalism; and theoretical studies of the public sphere, often in relation to mass media. In this volume, at least four disciplines meet to discuss the processes of media democracy—journalism, communication and media studies, political theory, and cyberstudies (cyberactivism studies: critical theories of cyberculture and sociology/social movement theory), yielding a cross-disciplinary and cross-tactical conversation of insight and analyses not found elsewhere.

The fourth goal is *the challenge of understanding the relationship between audiences, media, and political representation and actions*. How does media shape public perception? How do we grasp the perverse phenomenon Latour describes, which caused him to question his entire life's work and shook the foundation of his research? How do we begin to understand, much less challenge, the science of manipulating the public to achieve corporate or political aims? Classical communication studies in the American tradition have spent generations of scholarship analyzing media effects, while those in a cultural studies tradition have given up on tracing media effects. Yet, we want to know how to identify effects, of course! This volume further challenges dominant perspectives through its cross- and multidisciplinary approaches.

A fifth goal is to understand the unexplored *affective dimensions involved in the construction of publics and counterpublics*. What mobilizes social movements? How does the representation (or lack of representation) of these movements in press and popular imaginary shape participants' sense of a social movement's efficacy? Another aspect of the affective dimension of the public sphere is, quite simply, how to maintain hope in the face of what can feel like an overdetermined world of corporate-controlled media and politics. As Statzel (chap. 18, this volume) points out,

questions about race, passions, agency, and media mobilizations rarely emerge in new media theory. While the trend in cyberstudies literature is to theorize the Internet as a postracial space, the Internet itself seems to be employed to do the opposite. There is also a gaping lack of applied tactical interventions on the Internet with the power to counter the messages of Stormfront and the hundreds of other racist and neo-Nazi websites currently in operation. This lack of antiracist theory and practice in contradistinction to the organizing savvy of the white nationalist movement leave the playing field of cyberspace tilted toward the success of conservative and white supremacist organizing.

It is helpful, no matter what we study, to keep in mind the epiphany McChesney experienced in the 1980s that pushed him on to author or coauthor seventeen books and help establish Free Press as one major arm of the media reform movement.

I had an epiphany and it occurred to me what I needed to study: I shouldn't assume that commercial media was a *natural* American system that was embraced all the time and that there was never any qualms about it . . . [and people resonated with this question:] "You mean it didn't have to be this way? We don't have to have this media system?" For a surprising number of people it was *like the sky had opened for them—the idea that the media is not a natural system you were stuck with like the Rocky Mountain range.* (McChesney, chap. 1, this volume)

This denaturalizing critique is crucial to developing alternative visions of media and its role in democracy. At every turn we can challenge the spectacularly insidious ways in which media appears to be pregiven—assumed in its "naturalized" current commercial form to be best suited to serving public interests.

Contradictions will be central to all we study.

Conclusion

Represented here are international voices of scholars and journalists who share a passion and commitment to questions about how media as a space of access to representation, communication, and distribution can be shared by diverse voices and visions and not dominated by media conglomerates. Many authors may be skeptical of how to define democracy or whether and how it may be achieved. The writers and journalists disagree on effective models of social change. But each has a vision of media playing a central and defining role in the constitution of publics and social change, and each author and approach represents a unique political, cultural, and strategic perspective.

Figure 0.21
Free Josh Wolf demonstration in San Francisco. Photo by Bill Carpenter

There are two concluding observations I can make about the chorus of voices here. One, they are quite tempered in their vision of how radical change can happen in the mediascape, and tempered in the evaluation of how and whether practices of the social Web may radically shift what counts as democracy. In short, these scholars and journalists do not buy the hype of democratization that often characterizes discourses around digital media. My own contrasting optimism is maintained in part because I focus my research on satire as a form of salvation from the bitter realities of what we call media and democracy. Some lament that satire and humor are among the most effective ways to communicate critiques of media and politics today. As McChesney states, "If we had a legitimate or decent media you wouldn't have to put on a clown suit to get noticed." Despite this, the court jesters and satirists speaking truth to power give me hope. Second, each author sees a space for change and resistance—but each person's vision of change, tactics, and actors is shaped by how they outline the problem and where they focus their analysis. Each has a different and varying sense of hope. And, third, everyone here understands media ownership concentration as the beast we face.

Without a doubt, questions of media ownership concentration are front and center. Amy Goodman expresses her hope and direction: "But I do have hope, because people are hungry for information. And we don't really have a choice. We have to fight at the policy level to ensure . . . equal access to media, to the Internet—I agree with Bill Moyers when he says we have to come up with a better term than *Net neutrality*." Responding to my query, "What is the biggest concern we face?" Goodman reiterates:

"Media consolidation. Media concentration. It's a tremendous threat. The more radio stations and TV stations that are owned by just a few corporations—that is the greatest threat to a democratic society. . . . The Clear Channeling of America has to be challenged. They own over 1,200 radio stations in the United States and sponsored pro-war rallies."

Fernandes emphasizes *media justice*:

We don't only need to work on simply taking media out of corporate hands. Because simply taking it out of corporate hands means that we'll most likely fall into elite white hands. And that doesn't bring in the huge diversity that exists, that is what we actually need. . . . At People's Production House, we see it as a three-pronged approach. [First], we build, in our own communities, strong, powerful journalists [who] learn the art and the craft of telling stories. . . . The second part of it is that we fight like hell for access. . . . The third part is that corporate media is not going to go away over night. . . . And so we learn the skills of being able to watch, listen, read, and analyze, and then hold accountable that media.

Fernandes goes on to describe her hope in the face of media concentration:

My dad once told me, "When things seem tough, and you walk into a room and the door's closed, and you can't get out, look for that tiny window. Look up. Look around. Maybe it's underneath. But find that window." And I feel like that analogy is where we're at today in terms of making an impact mediawise. Because, yes, we're losing to the big Tel Cos. Yes the big Tel Cos are steamrolling us in many ways. But there is that window—all we need to do is find it and begin to climb through it, and then the sky is ours.

If we can bring that vision to people in low-income communities and in communities of color, in youth communities and immigrant communities, to actually dream about how this could be possible, that's a strong constituency of people who will stand up for and demand something a hell of a lot better than they have now.

So, where do we go from here? At the moment of this writing, I think the questions that remain outstanding and which need to be further explored include these:

• We will benefit from developing further the existing theories of "virality" to catch up with the media practices discussed here.[34] Such theorizations will attend to how the logic of capitalism functions and is disrupted through distributions.
• We need a better understanding of how affect shapes the formation of counterpublics.[35] Warner's 2002 essay "Publics and Counterpublics" doesn't address the "affective glue" that helps constitute counterpublics. How do online communities develop around particular concerns, and what is the relationship between their correlative offline communities? For example, how does humor, and specifically parody and satire, constellate political and critical inquiry and potential action (Boler, chap. 17, this volume)? How do we understand the affective dimensions of the formation of the on- and offline dimensions of the white nationalist organization Stormfront discussed by Statzel (chap. 18, this volume)?

· We need to watch how new networks such as Al Jazeera English continue to increase viewership, and when and how the power of interventions like these will be curtailed through forces of advertising.

· We will have to work hard either to establish nonproprietary, noncommercial Internets and/or ensure that the existing Internet is not legislated into a two-tiered system that severely curtails access, thereby limiting the kinds of production and distribution we are seeing through a variety of social networking and video-streaming sites.

Finally, there is the ever-pressing question of where we turn—in an information-saturated economy of attention drawn between 57 million blogs and thousands of uploads to YouTube each day—to reconceptualize that elusive desire for "truth," accuracy, fairness, or balance. Stuart Hall once said to us: "I turn to theory when I'm stuck." So here, I suggest we turn to Donna Haraway: "We are also bound to seek perspective from those points of view, which can never be known in advance, which promise something quite extraordinary, that is, knowledge potent for constructing worlds less organized by axes of domination. In such a viewpoint, the unmarked category would *really* disappear—quite a difference from simply repeating a disappearing act" (Haraway 1991: 192).

Can we begin to envision knowledge and media that recognize the inevitability of point of view but are still faithful to a sense of justice and "no-nonsense responsibility" to the planet? Can those who are writing the stories that shape the world's future recognize the responsibility of their point of view—rather than "repeating the disappearing act"? Is it possible to be organized by something other than axes of domination? These are questions that we and our media face in this lifetime.

And if all of that seems too tall an order, I take to heart Mr. Ibrahim's response to the million-dollar question: "What are the terms you would use to describe good journalism?" "I would say accuracy. You need to be accurate. I remember my former mentor at the BBC said to me: we don't need to get it fair, but we need to get it right."

Glossary

The following definitions are extracted from the chapters in this book in order to give readers an overview of key terms. More extensive debates and literature about nomenclature and definitions can be found within the articles and in their footnotes and references.

Corporate/Dominant/Mainstream Media

Deepa Fernandes distinguishes the varied use of the terms *mainstream* and *corporate*:

Actually, I like to define it more in terms of who owns it. So I call it corporate media. Mainly because I think *we* are the mainstream. Not that I'd necessarily call us the mainstream media, and I think it's easy to use that term from time to time. But the more correct term is to define it as the people who own it—so we are community media, we're owned by the community, and corporate media is owned by corporations—just because it doesn't let us forget that. I think it's too easy to forget or just not think about why news is being produced. And for the most part news is being produced for profit motive. (Fernandes, chap. 9, this volume)

Media Reform

Freedom of the press requires carefully crafted and thoroughly debated public policies that provide the foundation for a pluralistic and well-funded free press. Without such policies, democracy would be impossible. Not surprisingly, Madison and Jefferson, arguably the most brilliant of the founders, wrote the most on this subject. They both championed government subsidies for newspapers through printing subsidies and heavily subsidized postal rates to encourage a broad range of publications, among other measures. Without these policies, U.S. democracy would have never developed to the level it did.

The U.S. media system to this day is based on government subsidies, monopoly franchises, and regulations. All of the largest media firms are built on government sanctioned monopoly rights, either through cable franchises, broadcast channel licenses, and/or copyright. The government doesn't just set the terms of competition—it helps pick the winners.

The problem today is that these immense government-granted privileges are made in the most corrupt manner possible, behind closed doors with minimal public participation. Controlling interests do everything in their power to see that this is the case because they know if the general public had any idea how these corrupt policies are made, they would never stand for it. (Free Press Media Reform Movement, http://www.freepress.net/content/faqs#question11, retrieved April 26, 2007)

Media Justice

Maybe the simplest way for me to explain the difference between media reform and media justice is with an analogy I have heard made to the environmental movement. You can look at "Save the Trees," "Save the Air," and "Save the Whales," as part of an environmental call that is critically important. We need that. But then particular communities, especially communities of color, began to say, but what about our communities? We are living in the path of polluting industries. Isn't that an environmental issue? And it changed from environmentalism to environmental justice. And I think that in some ways the analogy works for the media reform movement. Saying that, yes, the media right now is not serving our communities. But the media reform movement harkens back to some golden age of the media that we need to take back. And for many of our communities, that did not exist. When was that time? When was there a truly participatory media?

We need to work on more than simply taking media out of corporate hands. It is so much broader than that. Simply taking it out of corporate hands means that it will most likely fall into elite white hands. And that does not bring in the huge diversity that exists, which is actually what we need. How do we have any guarantee that our communities will be any better served by a media that's simply not owned by corporations? (Fernandes, chap. 9, this volume)

Alternative Media

Whereas mainstream media make extensive use of members of elite groups as sources . . . alternative media offer access to a much wider range of voices. These often include members of local communities, protesters and activists: 'ordinary' voices compared to the 'privileged' voices of elites. (Atton, chap. 8, this volume)

Perhaps alternative media is best conceived not merely in terms of its content but its "place" in a landscape. As Deepa Fernandes described when I asked, "How do you decide what is worth covering on your show each morning, and how might you say this differs substantively from corporate radio agenda setting?":

I like to think of us as the place—'cause WBAI is 99.5, and it's right in the middle of the dial in New York. Maybe not so much now because most people have digital radios. But the point is, some people do still turn the dial, and when you actually have to turn the dial, you have to go through BAI all the time, just to get to either side of it. And that's the power that we have that we need to take advantage of. (Fernandes, chap. 9, this volume)

An emphasis on the independence of alternative media can blind us to the relationship between alternative media and mass media. . . . While social movement theories might explain the role of alternative media in constructing collective identity, they do little to help us explain alternative media as communication. If we consider alternative media as "ways of going on within journalism," then we may ask: Where do alternative media practices come from? Where do alternative media practitioners learn to practice? By linking theories of alternative media with those of journalism studies we might develop models of alternative media to deal with the norms and means of media practice as well as with "empowerment" and identity. (Atton, chap. 8, this volume)

Tactical Media (TM)

In general, TM are expressions of dissent that rely on artistic practices and do-it-yourself (DIY) media created from readily available, relatively cheap technology and means of communication (e.g., radio, video, and the Internet). They are described by Patricia Aufderheide as "projects that people do opportunistically—seizing temporarily available or unclaimed resources" (Aufderheide in VCB 2002). Gregg Bordowitz adds that they are a "constantly evolving set of approaches . . . collectively produced" (Bordowitz in VCB 2002). Above all, it is the slippery character of TM, with its potential to resist characterization in dominant terms, which renders them peculiar. (Renzi, chap. 2, this volume)

Web 2.0/Social Web

The phrase "Web 2.0" was coined by Tim O'Reilly. Web 2.0 is . . . not a replacement for the Web that we know and love, but rather a way of using existing systems in a new way: to bring people together creatively. O'Reilly has described it as "harnessing collective intelligence." The spirit of Web 2.0 is that individuals should open themselves to collaborative projects instead of seeking to make and protect their "own" material (David Gauntlett 2007).[36]

Initially, people were mystified about the exact meaning of the concept, and O'Reilly's blog essay "What is Web 2.0?" was supposed to address that problem. In this text, he proposes a versioning of the Web and suggests that what we are currently experiencing is version number two. The first (think: old) version of the Web is characterized by listing a set of static browser-based applications and components including Ofoto, Brittanica Online, personal Web sites, sites like evite, broadcast-type publishing, content management systems, and taxonomies.

Subsequently, O'Reilly distinguishes Web 2.0 by associating it with folksonomies (user-generated taxonomies), blogging, wikis, and syndication and—more specifically—sites like Flickr, BitTorrent, Napster, Wikipedia, Upcoming.org, and Google AdSense. Techniques and technologies include AJAX, API, XML, and RSS. . . .

[But] the Web has always been social. Its first incarnation, ARPANET, was rapidly taken over by email exchanges. Blogging, another supposed argument for the novelty of Web 2.0, was some ten years old at the moment of the conception of Web 2.0. . . . User-generated content did not just suddenly appear in 2004. Forms of self-publishing are as old as Amazon.com, which allowed users to write reviews and consumer guides since its launch in 1995. An additional, often repeated feature of Web 2.0 is that now users have a voice. David Weinberger reminds us that, "No, back from the very beginning what drove people onto the net was not so that people can shop. . . . Weblogs and all that have made it way, way easier but the Web has always been about voice and conversation" (Trebor Scholz, http://www.collectivate.net/journalisms/2007/10/3/the-web-20-ideology.html).

What all of these, including Web 2.0, are pointing to is the erosion of the fundamental break between producers and audiences. Such developments illustrate what Tim Berners-Lee, creator of the Web, termed in 1999 "intercreativity"—collaborative creative work made possible through the adoption of digital media technologies. For Berners-Lee, the Web was never intended to be about delivering content to passive audiences, but to be about shared creativity. Twentieth-century media were pretty much produced in one place by some people and consumed in other places by other people. For the most part, you didn't go to CNN's studios to watch the news, and for the most part, they didn't come to your place to produce the news. What's distinctive about the emerging forms—user-generated content, etc.—is the blurring of the line between producer and consumer. So to a certain extent, it doesn't matter what we call it, as long as we recognize the new blurring of producer and consumer. Then again, there is also a sense in which it *does* matter and that's the McLuhan rearview mirror sense in which the metaphors we use to describe things ("horseless carriage") can blind us to the distinctive features of the new. (Meikle, correspondence, April 28, 2007)[37]

Blogs

Originally known as web logging, blogging content ranged from bloggers' diaries and self-promotional musings to highly personalized real-time news coverage and analysis. After blogging's "big bang" in September 1999 with the release of Pyra Labs' software application Blogger, blogging spread beyond the technological elite with steadily increasing adoption. . . . This process was facilitated by point-and-click Web-publishing software that required no detailed knowledge of HTML authoring, and RSS applications for outgoing content syndication and incoming personalized aggregation. Current events drove adoption as well, such as the September 11, 2001, U.S. terrorist attacks and the Iraq war. . . . In 2002, Blogger's registered users reached over 970,000 and online behemoth Google acquired the company. A 2003 survey (Perseus Development Corporation 2003) measured 4.12 million total blogs online, although only 1.4 million were active.

. . . Meanwhile, the medium evolved to incorporate photography, video, audio, satellite positioning, and mobile technologies. (Scott, chap. 11, this volume)

Citizen Journalism

Citizen journalism is inspired by the positive ideas to emerge from the *Indymedia* experience—the coverage of nonmainstream themes and topics, and the open debate of issues that does not inherently privilege any one participant. Such journalism is focused not on the mere provision of "facts" as determined by a small group of journalists and editors, but instead highlights the discursive, dialogic, and even deliberatory nature of public engagement with the news. . . .

Citizen journalism . . . is positioned as an alternative and a corrective to the first, mainstream tier of the news media, but no longer stands in fundamental opposition to it, as the perspectives expressed in that tier have a valid role to play in public debate as well. Instead, it engages those "mainstream" perspectives, and (where appropriate) debunks them as the views of individual political and lobby groups, think tanks, and news proprietors rather than as representative for a more diverse range of societal views, values, and beliefs. (Bruns, chap. 10, this volume)

Gatewatchers

Some of the most active news bloggers and participatory journalism contributors of present-day second-tier media forms engage predominantly in what we can describe as *gatewatching*: the observation of the output gates of first-tier news organizations as well as of primary sources. These practitioners are watching out for material passing through those gates that is relevant to their own audience's interests and concerns and introduce it into their own coverage of news and current events. Often, they combine and contrast the coverage of a number of mainstream news organizations in order to highlight differences in emphasis or interpretation and thus point to political bias or substandard journalistic handiwork. If through a recombination and reconsideration of existing materials such coverage produces compelling new insights previously overlooked by the first-tier media, it offers a means to reintroducing alternative viewpoints into first-tier media debates. (Bruns, chap. 10, this volume)

Independent Media

Independent media . . . oh my god! That's so difficult. Bloggers are probably the only independent media providers in the world. Because they're basically individuals or a group of individuals who are using a very affordable means to broadcast a message. (Ibrahim, chap. 12, this volume)

An example of this is the network of collectives that make up Indymedia. Local groups make up this network and decision-making mostly operates at this local level. These independent, self-managed 'nodes' in a network are examples of democratic, non-corporate media. Organizationally they are quite different from the hierarchical structures of the mass media of western democracies. (Atton, chap. 8, this volume)

Accuracy in Media

MB: The question of what constitutes accuracy, or objectivity are widely debated. Given the risks of how Al Jazeera can be perceived, how does Jazeera make decisions on sources and content in terms of the political perception?

Hassan Ibrahim: It can take hours to answer that! In a nutshell, when we evaluate the political content of the message, you need to satisfy certain criteria. Number one: Newsworthiness. Authenticity. Value to the audience. I mean if someone sent to me a report about a mosque collapsing in a remote village in Thailand, it wouldn't really be on top of my agenda ahead of a Bin Laden or a Zawahiri tape. But even a Bin Laden tape or Zawahiri tape is screened for political worthiness. We have at least ten or twelve Bin Laden tapes that were not fit for broadcast because they contained no political message whatsoever; it's the same rantings and ravings and a few lines of poetry and advice—so you don't broadcast that. There is no value, there is nothing new in that.

When you deal with the Palestinian–Arab-Israeli conflict, the pivotal topic for the Middle East, again you have to exercise editorial control and air what is newsworthy world wide, rather than a news item that would be fit for a domestic Palestinian agenda. I wouldn't worry that much about a cabinet reshuffle in the Sudan because that happens every other weekend, but I would worry about the Sudanese government's response to the UN over the issue of Darfur for example. That type of thing—you have to exercise your judgment based on certain criteria.

MB: You've stressed double sourcing as the way to ensure fairness and accuracy—are those terms you would use? What are the terms you would use to describe good journalism?

Hassan Ibrahim: I would say accuracy. You need to be accurate. I remember my former mentor at the BBC said to me: we don't need to get it fair, but we need to get it right. (Ibrahim, chap. 12, this volume)

Participatory Media

What does participatory journalism mean? Participatory media is something that will make our democracy healthy and functioning. Because we're not at a place in this country where we're instantly going to begin doing the varied actions that a participatory democracy requires, that are happening in local communities in Venezuela, and that are happening in local communities around the world that actively participate in the running and the governing of their local communities.

But I think we can achieve that with media. And I think they go hand in hand. If we could have a participatory media, that would be one of the most concrete steps to impacting the community we want to live in and how our community functions. . . .

I think to me it means that Wake Up Call on WBAI every morning is more of an interchange between the people who are on the program, the people who make the program, the people who listen to the program. So it doesn't become an elitist institution as well, whereby I'm the host and I get to sit up here and look at all of you, and report on all of you and tell you all what to think. No. That is just repetitive and mimicking the very structures of the media that don't allow for participation in democracy. And hopefully, I have just as much to learn from you as you have to learn from me.

It doesn't mean we all have to go out there and be journalists, it doesn't mean we all are going to turn into a TV news anchor. But what it means is that we are players in a circle that allows for ideas to be circular, rather than to be top-down. (Fernandes, chap. 9, this volume)

Participatory . . . that hype around Web 2.0! I would not bandy that word around too much. It sometimes has too happy a veneer of sharing and democracy around it that often does not exist. In my own work, the "conception" has not been participatory in that sense at all. Of course the projects themselves are about the involvement, co-operation of a number of people. (Anand, chap. 13, this volume)

Notes

1. Specifically, I stated the following to Russert before being shouted down: "Your comments reflect a U.S. nationalistic bias. All international press that I have been researching sees the U.S. as more of a threat than Saddam. The U.S. has weapons of mass destruction and is about to use them. You did not address: (1) that preemptive strike is illegal and defies international law; (2) that there is not international support for Bush's decision, a decision which will result in increased terrorist threats to U.S. and the rest of world far worse than any atrocities committed by Saddam Hussein; and (3) you claimed that a democracy must 'respect a duly elected president and honor his decisions.' This is not accurate—democracy involves checks and balances, and Bush has unilaterally ignored domestic and international requests to cease threats of war, instead prioritizing his own moral and economic motives over concern for Middle East stability or 'homeland security.'" (Boler, written notes that I read publicly to Tim Russert, March 12, 2003)

2. One person walked out after me to find me as I left before the crowd, and thanked me; and I received one e-mail the next day from another who shared my views.

3. The term *post-9/11* is highly problematic. In this instance, there is a coincidence of access and use of social Web when after 2001 the Internet becomes an increasingly accessible form not only of communication but also representing an increase of one-to-many broadcast. Thus while *post 9/11* begs many questions about what conditions one claims exist *after* 9/11 that didn't exist before—one coincidence of cultural shift post 9/11 is the exponential increase in uses of social Web in a sense peaking, as I suggest, in 2003–2004.

4. In 2002 Campus Watch came into the public eye when it created an online "blacklist" of questionable professors: "Campus Watch Lists 108 Academics Supporting Apologists for Terrorism (October 21, 2002, Philadelphia)—The Middle East Forum posted a new page today on www.campus-watch.org, a site launched last month to monitor the campus-based Middle East specialists. The new page lists more than 100 academics from North American institutions who requested to be listed on the site in solidarity with eight academics identified as apologists for Palestinian violence or militant Islam" (http://www.campus-watch.org/article/id/269, retrieved April 30, 2007).

Campus Watch, a program initiated by the Middle East Forum founded by Daniel Pipes, was forced by public pressure to remove this online blacklisting. One now finds on their site a more nuanced interface inviting anyone to "keep us informed" (about unAmerican and "terrorist" professors among other things). According to their current Web site, Campus Watch is an organization that "gathers information on Middle East studies from public and private sources and makes this information available on its website, www.Campus-Watch.org; produces analyses of institutions, individual scholars, topics, events, and trends; makes its views known through the media—newspaper op-eds, radio interviews, television interviews; invites student complaints of abuse, investigates their claims, and (when warranted) makes these known" (http://www.campus-watch.org/about.php, retrieved April 30, 2007).

5. There is no public record of the content of his speech nor of the actual flier that drew me to the event billing it as a pro and con debate and analysis of media coverage of Iraq. One college record announced the talk in January 2003, headlined "Political Analyst Russert to Speak on Campus," (Sookhan Ho, *Spectrum Magazine*, 25, Jan. 31, 2003). Some might suggest I should have been more wary of speaking out at a talk billed as "An Inside View of Washington," sponsored by the Virginia Tech Corps of Cadets' Cutchins Distinguished Lecture. However, the event was not publicized as such in the fliers that drew me there.

6. "Russert: Citizens Should Back Troops," by Aaron Blackwell, *Collegiate Times*, March 14, 2003, http://collegiatetimes.com/archive/2003-3/1/898.html. *The Roanoke Times* also ran a short story about the scheduled talk, which does refer to it indeed as a Virginia Tech Corps of Cadets' Cutchins Distinguished Lecture, with Russert's talk titled "An Inside View from Washington" (March 13, 2003, *Roanoke Times*).

7. In Bill Moyers' 2007 documentary, *Buying the War*, there seems to be a question of whether or not Russert was a shill for the U.S. administration. Moyers pointedly asks Tim Russert about the timing of Russert scheduling Vice President Dick Cheney on *Meet the Press* the day after the story of aluminum tubes (now seen as totally misleading) as evidence of WMD in Iraq. Russert turns a bit red as well in this interview with Moyers and looks away as he claims that it was

simply happenstance that Cheney was on his show—i.e., Russert claims to have had no prior knowledge of the Bush Administration's story that would have just broken in the *New York Times* the day before. The April 2007 transcript reads as follows:

Bill Moyers: Was it just a coincidence in your mind that Cheney came on your show and others went on the other Sunday shows, the very morning that that story appeared?

Tim Russert: I don't know. The *New York Times* is a better judge of that than I am.

Moyers: No one tipped you that it was going to happen?

Russert: No, no. I mean—

Moyers: The—the Cheney—office didn't make any—didn't leak to you that there's gonna be a big story?

Russert: No. No. I mean, I don't—I don't have the—this is, you know, on *Meet the Press*, people come on and there are no ground rules. We can ask any question we want. I did not know about the aluminum-tube story until I read it in the *New York Times*.

Moyers: Critics point to September 8, 2002, and to your show in particular, as the classic case of how the press and the government became inseparable. Someone in the administration plants a dramatic story in the *New York Times* and then the Vice President comes on your show and points to the *New York Times*. It's a circular, self-confirming leak.

(From transcript of *"Buying the War,"* http://www.pbs.org/moyers/journal/btw/transcript1.html, retrieved April 28, 2007.)

On a more general note about the swinging press pendulum, in her chapter Susan Moeller notes, "Since the late summer of 2003, after the hunt for the Iraqi WMD came up empty, and accelerated in 2006 by the rising death toll in Iraq of both American troops and Iraqi civilians and the related plummeting poll numbers of President Bush, the U.S. media have been less reticent to challenge the administration's messages on the war in Iraq and the larger 'War on Terror'."

8. Again, with my stacks of "archival" videotapes of broadcast news from 2001–2003, I am acutely aware that, aside from the increasingly common "remixes" of digital recordings of news made possible through people streaming news segments online, we do not have public access to broadcast news archives.

9. When I spoke around the world about my work with the Web site Critical Media Literacy in Times of War, people would always ask: "If you can only read one thing, what should it be?" We need, unfortunately, more than one source—which is why something like Ibrahim's emphasis on double-sourcing is so key. I do recommend www.truthout.org, which compiles daily a range of news stories most often buried in AP, corporate-owned, and alternative news, which allows one to receive a daily culling of key stories from diverse sources. But other equally important questions include: Where do we turn for accounts that make sense? To what extent can the interventions of millions of citizen journalists from around the world, of tactical media activists, of on- and offline social movements, counter the unapologetic purchase of much press by political power? How do we offer media criticism without being dismissed as conspiracy theorists? And what filters can we count on in a media-saturated environment? Do we aggregate 300 RSS feeds? Yet sources are so concentrated (i.e., so much of the news we read emanates from one AP

story, or spins a version of one dominant media source), it becomes easy to fall into paranoia. Where do we turn?

10. One finds dozens of links to news coverage of these protests, and videos, through Wikipedia as one source of diverse international news reports of protests around the world. "The February 15, 2003, anti-war protest was a coordinated day of protests across the world against the imminent invasion of Iraq. Millions of people protested in approximately 800 cities around the world. According to BBC News, between six and ten million people took part in protests in up to sixty countries over the weekend of the 15th and 16th; other estimates range from eight million to thirty million. The biggest protests took place in Europe. The protest in Rome involved around 3 million people and is listed in the 2004 *Guinness Book of World Records* as the largest anti-war rally in history. Opposition to the war was highest in the Middle East, although protests there were relatively small. Mainland China was the only major region not to see any protests" (Wikipedia, "February 15, 2003 anti-war protest," retrieved April 30, 2007).

11. At the time of this writing, there is some heated debate about terms and definitions to describe social uses of the Internet and Web: whether to use the term *Web 2.0, sociable Web media* (used by the MIT Sociable Media Group), *groupware*, or others. Trebor Scholz strongly advocates the term *social Web*, to counter the commercialized and corporatized aspects of *Web 2.0*. In his essay titled "Against Web 2.0," he states "The term Web 2.0 is yet another fraudulent bubble designed to trick investors with pretended newness" (http://www.collectivate.net/journalisms/2006/5/26/against-web-20.html). As evidence of these debates, the following are threads of the conversation I had with authors as I tried to determine which vocabulary to use. [D. Travers] Scott originally weighed in saying, 'what is most important is the *how* of Web 2.0 and not the *what* . . . but use Web 2.0 for widest recognition." But the next day he amended: "No, changed my mind, for your purposes Web 2.0 invokes too much of a corporate sensibility, go with 'sociable media' or 'participatory web.'" Nathalie Magnan insisted on "uses of Web 2.0" and not "Web 2.0" because it is not a thing but a set of uses. Meikle referred to Gauntlett's summary: "the phrase 'Web 2.0' was coined by Tim O'Reilly. 'Web 2.0' is . . . not a replacement for the Web that we know and love, but rather a way of using existing systems in a new way: to bring people together creatively. O'Reilly has described it as 'harnessing collective intelligence'." The spirit of "Web 2.0" is that individuals should open themselves to collaborative projects instead of seeking to make and protect their "own" material (www.theory.org/uk/mediastudies2.htm. February 24, 2007, David Gauntlett). However, as Scott notes, "the term's origins are firmly in marketing, but its social implications grew to overshadow this. The tension between the (at least two) meanings may actually be productive, pointing to a process, illustrating *how* Web 2.0 is rather than *what* it is." I have elected to use *social Web* to distinguish it from the connotations of *Web 2.0*.

12. Our key research questions included: How are digital media being used to create communicative networks for political debate and social activism? What are users' and producers' motivations for engaging in online political engagement? Do online participants feel they have a public voice and/or political efficacy? To what extent is/was frustration with mainstream media a motivation to blogging or other forms of digital production? During year one (2005–2006), we analyzed four Web-based networks of circulated dissent: (1) The 150 finalists of MoveOn's Bush in 30 Seconds

campaign, 30-second Quicktime movies that address a range of political concerns; (2) Web logs that engage political discussion of media representation of U.S. foreign policy, particularly with respect to the invasion of Iraq ; (3) Online discussions (threads, blogs, comments posted to blogs) that address Jon Stewart and *The Daily Show*, with particular focus on Stewart's 2004 appearance on the CNN talk show Crossfire; (4) Independently produced viral videos that address diverse political issues related to U.S. policy. We developed a validated survey using nonprobabilistic convenience sampling and administered the seventy-question survey to 159 bloggers and viral video producers. During year two, we conducted 35 semistructured interviews. We are now in the process of data analysis and dissemination. This research was made possible thanks to the funding of the Canadian Social Science and Humanities Research Council.

13. Personal correspondence, April 29, 2007.

14. *Virality* describes a twentyfirst-century mode of communication that relies on digital transmissions. Features of virality include:

• Lack of distinction between producer/consumer, author/audience, production/reception, characterized in part by user-generated content
• Convergence of old and new media, old and new conceptions of biopolitics, power, and discourses
• Genealogies that recognize the blurring of host/body and virus/inorganic, not for a simple invocation of hybrid or cyborg but rather for an understanding of how network transmissions simultaneously rely on what we think of as "bodies," "persons," and "subjects" that also establish lives of their own
• Multidirectionality: to engage a soundbite for purposes of intervention almost necessarily requires reappropriation of that which one resists. Likewise, as soon as this independent transmission is produced it is, through digital circulation, commodified and co-opted. Yet this process cannot be argued to detract from intervention or tactics in a simple sense
• Blurred boundaries between intervention-insurgence-tactics with more familiar circulation of capital and corporate information

The works of Brian Massumi and McKenzie Wark provide useful directions for exploring viral communications. Wark's 1994 term *media vector* aptly describes how different directions and sources of information collide and relationally inform and shape one another, a problem that is echoed by Massumi in *Parables for the Virtual*. As Wark describes, "There is no 'fact' or 'object' to be located. . . . One deals less with the object of a media event than with its trajectory. . . . In the Gulf War, the object caught both journalism and critical analysis off-guard because it was never where it was supposed to be. Modes of discourse which still want to 'grasp' the facts, or get 'to the bottom' of 'things' have a hard time with objects endowed with electric mobility. Hence the need for an analysis which does not 'look' at 'things,' either factually or critically" (Wark 1994: 28). Echoing this affective relationship to the gap between content and effect, Massumi writes, "It may be noted that the primacy of the affective is marked by a gap between *content* and *effect*: it would appear that the strength or duration of an image's effect is not logically connected to the content in any straightforward way. . . . The event of image reception is multilevel, or at least bi-level" (2002: 24).

15. One of my favorite performances by Samantha Bee is her interview of Luntz for *The Daily Show*. You can find a partial transcription of this phenomenal demonstration of the emperor with no clothes in my paper, "Mediated Publics and the Crises of Democracy," www.ovpes. org/2006/Boler.pdf, keynote address published in the 2006 Ohio Valley Philosophy of Education Proceedings.

16. Bruno Latour, "Why Has Critique Run Out of Steam? From Matters of Fact to Matters of Concern," *Critical Inquiry* 30, no. 2, 2004.

17. "What bears thinking about is whether this media vector is part of what killed people, what led to the starvation and misery of the Kurdish refugees, or Iraqi people dying from cholera and dysentery in shattered hospitals. Not the technical vector alone, but the vector and the networks and structures of social, political, economic, and cultural power it connects across are at the centre of this event. . . . In terms of vectoral power in general, the media are part of the problem of power, not merely a separate space of reportage or critique of emergent forms of power that exist elsewhere" (Wark 1994: 13).

18. There is a key space of resistance within media that is not addressed in this collection, and that is independently produced documentaries that are in fact major players in the politics of representation. Yale film scholar Charles Musser in 2006 gave a talk at University of Toronto, arguing that since 2002 there is a new genre of political documentaries that deal with this desire for "truth." He focused particularly on the work of Robert Greenwald (director of *Outfoxed*, among many other crucial documentaries), significant for going direct to DVD access and simply using the Web for circulation rather than for the usual theatrical and commercial distribution time-suck—an interview with Greenwald would complement this volume. I also recommend a new German film (in English, curiously enough), *The Big Sellout* (dir. Florian Opitz, 2007) for an excellent, humanizing portrait of privatization, useful in a pedagogical context, not to mention its amazing cinematography and beautiful editing. *The Big Sellout* (which could be screened along with *Manufacturing Consent* and *The Corporation* to offer a larger portrait) features four individuals who resist the following privatization efforts in their countries: Bolivia's water; South Africa's electricity; Britain's railway system; and health care in the Phillipines.

19. As Statzel states, "Exploring the political passions which steer the white nationalist movement increases our understanding of the limitations and possibilities of new media and political activism. Exploring the relations between these two imagined revolutions is actually productive in attempting to understand both. Though "the 'Internet' revolution may be over, there is far less consensus as to the nature and impacts of this revolution. Has it provided a rupture with or extension of previous political forms and identities? Does it divert or enhance democratic potential? Are new identities and publics produced through computer-mediated communication or are off-line identities reinforced in online play and practice? While often seen in binary or potentially oppositional terms, the distinction between 'the real world' and 'virtual reality' is often actually quite blurred. And, when it comes to questions of 'power, politics, and structural relations' it is argued that 'cyberspace is as real as it gets.'" (chap. 18, this volume)

20. Lynch again recently testified again to a hearing about the spectacle of mistruths circulated by the early Pentagon control of U.S. media held by the House Committee on Oversight and Government Reform (April 25, 2007, *New York Times*).

21. Renzi, Alessandra, and Stephen Turpin, "Nothing Fails Like Prayer, or Why San Precario Is More Dangerous Than Religion," *FUSE Magazine* 30, no. 1, (2007) pp. 25–35.

22. For further reading see Michael Schudson's essay "Was There Ever a Public Sphere? If So, When? Reflections on the Habermas and the Public Sphere" (Cambridge, MA: MIT Press, 1992), McChesney, *The Problem of the Media* (New York: Monthly Review Press, 2004), and Timothy Cook, *Governing with the News: The News Media as a Political Institution* (Chicago: University of Chicago Press, 1998).

23. Statzel challenges Dean in chapter 19 when she notes, "Stormfront highlights another reading of the possibilities of tactical engagements of new media. To appreciate this, politics requires a rethinking of how we actually understand the political. Jodi Dean quotes Shirkley, writing on the disparity between Howard Dean's on- and off-line campaign success, 'When you're communing with like-minded souls, you *feel* [emphasis in original] like you're accomplishing something by arguing out the smallest details of your perfect future world, while the imperfect and actual world takes no notice, as is its custom' (Dean, chap. 3, this volume). Yet, this emphasis on *feeling* takes on new significance when considering a cyber-supremacist online community as opposed to the online dimension of a political campaign, where the mobilization of sentiments creates imagined worlds as its politics." This offers nuance to the model of politics that animates Dean's described public sphere of communicative capitalism.

24. I shall mention here that she expresses this hope in spite of her rigorous and intensive scholarship on the politics of news media, as represented in her books *Compassion Fatigue: How the Media Sell Disease, Famine, War and Death* and *Shooting War: Photography and the American Experience of Combat* and of major reports such as "Media Coverage of Weapons of Mass Destruction". See NSF-funded study through the Center for International and Security Studies, University of Maryland, http://www.cissm.umd.edu/papers/display.php?id=32.

25. http://www.villagevoice.com/news/0548,schanberg,70452,6.html

26. Seelye, Katharine Q., "Best-Informed Also View Fake News, Study Says," *New York Times,* April 16, 2007.

27. But Goodman immediately went on to stress the value of that airtime. "I also knew how many people watch this, and how important it was to get out information and not waste the moment. So just to give out information with a smile. And to show the appreciation of the venue, and what he was doing . . . but also, every minute on the air—the airwaves are a national treasure—is an awesome responsibility."

28. See Schmidt and Boler, February 20 2007, "Will New Media Save Democracy?" http://www. commondreams.org/views07/0222-29.htm and Boler, "Changing the World, One Laugh at a Time: The Daily Show and Political Activism," February 2007, http://www.counterpunch.org/ boler02202007.html.

29. This segment is featured in Bill Moyers' April 2007 interview of Jon Stewart.

30. An important direction of analysis is how laws around parody and fair use instruct us further about questions of open access and share, share widely, creative commons, and copyright/copyleft.

31. I interviewed an established blogger who began streaming TDS clips when his Macintosh wouldn't interface with the Comedy Central site, and decided it would be a service to other Mac users to post clips in Quicktime format. As a result, he unexpectedly began to get voluminous traffic from readers around the globe. I asked him if he thought that his site resulted in any action. It was a surprise to me to hear him report that, in fact, as he learns from the ongoing conversations and comments posted on his Web site, as a result of viewing and discussing *The Daily Show* many members of this progressive community have been led to activism. Another blogger was inspired to go join Cindy Sheehan's protest in Crawford because of the conversations engaged through his *Daily Show* postings. For more, see www.meganboler.net.

32. See Meikle, chapter 16 this volume, for discussion of Debord and the Situationists in relation to tactical media.

33. Known to many as the ultimate tactical media activists, "The Yes Men have impersonated some of the world's most powerful criminals at conferences, on the Web, and on television, in order to correct their identities." See their Web site, http://www.theyesmen.org/, for news reports of their "pranks" and links to videos of their appearances on BBC and at conferences. See also their film *The Yes Men* (United Artists, 2004, dir. Dan Ollman, Sarah Price, and Chris Smith).

34. In addition to Wark (1994), I am thinking here of the work of Brian Massumi, "Fear (The Spectrum Said)," *positions: east asia cultures critique* 13, no. 1 (Spring 2005), pp. 31–48, and Massumi, *Parables for the Virtual: Movement, Affect, Sensation*, Duke University Press, 2002; Mark B. N. Hansen, "Digitizing the Racialized Body or The Politics of Universal Address," *SubStance* 104 (2004): 107–133, 127; and *Bodies in Code: Interfaces with New Media*, New York: Routledge, 2006. For example, Massumi's notion of modulation helps describe a different way to understand "effects" in the context of political media landscapes. In *Parables for the Virtual* he notes that the "networkability of event transmission must be seen as pertaining not only to mass-media images but to information in general, to commodities, and to money: to any sign whose basic operation is to flow. . . . All of these transmitters carry a high charge of indeterminacy, of unrealized . . . potential" (2002: 87). What would a theory of virality look like that interrogated the inevitable recuperation of tactical interventions in communication, alongside our affective need for certainty at particular junctures and the ways in which affect produces the possibility of seeing otherwise despite the overdeterminations of spectacle and complicity?

35. The works cited in these footnotes—Warner (2002), Wark (1994), and Massumi (2002 and 2005)—suggest different conceptual directions regarding media, publics, and affect that could be read alongside my own theoretical analyses of emotion and power (Boler 1999) to begin outlining more rigorously the role of affect in shaping social movements and the cultural imaginaries produced within the user-producer subjectivities and interactivity of digital media convergence.

36. See http://www.theory.org.uk/mediastudies2.htm, February 24, 2007, David Gauntlett.

37. See Meikle's useful discussion of these debates in his commentary published on the Australian Broadcasting Corporation online: http://www.abc.net.au/news/opinion/items/200702/s1844193. htm. Also see, D. Travers Scott, "Bubble 2.0: Online Organized Critique of Web 2.0," conference paper presented at Media in Transition 5, MIT, April 2007.

Bibliography

Benjamin, Walter. 1985. *Charles Baudelaire: A Lyric Poet in the Era of of High Capitalism*. London: Verso Press.

Boler, Megan. 1999. *Feeling Power: Emotions and Education*. New York: Routledge.

Boler, Megan. February 2007. "Changing the World, One Laugh at a Time: The Daily Show and Political Activism," http://www.counterpunch.org/boler02202007.html

Haraway, Donna. 1991. *Simians, Cyborgs and Women: The Reinvention of Nature*. New York: Routledge.

Hansen, Mark B. N. 2006. *Bodies in Code: Interfaces with New Media*. New York: Routledge.

Latour, Bruno. 2004. "Why Has Critique Run out of Steam?" *Critical Inquiry* 30 (Winter): 238–239.

Massumi, Brian. 2002. *Parables for the Virtual: Movement, Affect, Sensation*. Durham: Duke University Press.

Massumi, Brian. 2005. "Fear (The Spectrum Said)." *positions: east asia cultures critique* 13, 1 (Spring): 31–48.

Schmidt, Andrea, and M. Boler. 2007. "Will New Media Save Democracy?" http://www.common-dreams.org/views07/0222-29.htm

Wark, McKenzie. 1994. *Virtual Geography*. Bloomington: Indiana University Press.

Warner, Michael. 2002. "Publics and Counterpublics," *Public Culture* 14, 1 (Winter): 49–90.

I   The Shape of Publics: New Media and Global Capitalism

1 The State of the Media: An Interview with Robert McChesney

Megan Boler

Robert W. McChesney is Professor in the Department of Communication at the University of Illinois at Urbana-Champaign. He is the cofounder and president of Free Press, the media reform organization (www.freepress.net). McChesney also hosts the Media Matters weekly radio program every Sunday afternoon on WILL-AM radio. He has written or edited seventeen books, including *Communication Revolution: Critical Junctures and the Future of Media* (New Press, 2007); *The Political Economy of the Media: Enduring Issues, Emerging Dilemmas* (Monthly Review Press, 2007); *The Problem of the Media* (Monthly Review Press, 2004), the award-winning *Telecommunications, Mass Media, and Democracy: The Battle for the Control of U.S. Broadcasting, 1928–1935* (Oxford University Press, 1993); *Corporate Media and the Threat to Democracy* (Seven Stories Press, 1997); with Edward S. Herman, *The Global Media: The New Missionaries of Corporate Capitalism* (Cassell, 1997; multiple award-winning *Rich Media, Poor Democracy: Communication Politics in Dubious Times* (New Press, 2000) and, with John Nichols, *Tragedy and Farce: How American Media Sell Wars, Spin Elections and Destroy Democracy* (New Press, 2005). He is presently at work on *Communication and Monopoly Capital*, with John Bellamy Foster (New Press), and *Freedom of the Press: America's Gift to the World* (Yale University Press). This interview took place by telephone in February 2007.

Megan Boler: In your 2004 book *The Problem of the Media* you pose the question, "Is the media system a democratic force?" This focus frames the questions I'll be asking today and I'm excited to get an update from you on this crucial topic. You're a scholar with expertise in many areas—history, policy analysis, and communications—and I've been indebted to your work for many years. To begin, I thought I'd ask about your intellectual and political roots—about your background, your vision of change, your thoughts on democracy and its future. Who do you recall reading in your early formative years and who do you look to now for inspiration?

Robert McChesney: I graduated from high school in 1971 and was deeply influenced by the social movements of the times. I was also a bit of a hippie. I dropped out of college for a year, and when I returned in 1973, I was committed to studying economics—mainstream economics—to understand how capitalism works from a capitalist perspective. I also wanted to study history and politics: I was very serious about understanding the world. This was a very different moment historically from anything subsequently. It was a time in which radical social theory and critical scholarship were really increasing in importance in universities across the world, so there was a space opened for critical work. I went to college exactly at this moment and used it as an opportunity to really immerse myself in social theory, history, and economics in a very productive manner.

There were many authors I read during that period who have been the foundation of everything I've done since then. I discuss this period at length in my new book, *Communication Revolution*. I had the privilege of reading Marx thoroughly and pretty systematically after doing a study in European history and classical economics and philosophy. It was exhilarating to read him and Engels, and then later to study the twentieth century Marxists. You know I've never quoted Marx, he's never really played a noticeable role in my subsequent research but that experience was so extraordinary intellectually. It certainly had an effect on me, on how I put things together and think about the world. Specific authors that I read then that really stuck with me include C. B. MacPherson and C. Wright Mills, the legendary American sociologist. His books *The Power Elite* and *The Sociological Imagination* were two cornerstones of my development. Mills was an active scholar in the '50s, and he was a genuine public intellectual long before that term was in vogue. Mills was the sort of figure I was familiar with in high school. I think it would be unusual for a scholar of that nature to be known to high school students today. That says something about the times as much as it does about C. Wright Mills.

The most important intellectuals forced upon me during that period were the economists Paul Sweezy, Leo Huberman, Paul Baran, Harry Magdoff, and Harry Braverman. They were loosely called the Monthly Review School, after their magazine, the *Monthly Review*. I stumbled across their work when I was a college dropout in 1972 and living with friends in a dump over some bar in Cambridge, Massachusetts. I was browsing in a bookstore when I came across their books. I think I was working as a night watchman at a Christmas tree stand that winter and I had plenty of time to read. It was the first time I gained a coherent understanding of capitalism that avoided left-wing jargon and posturing but did not water down the critique. It was empirically driven. I devoured those books, and they really changed everything in terms of how I view capitalism, history, scholarship, and politics. There is no question that the education I received from them was a foundation that's been central to my work, the scholarship you talk about, and my understanding of the world.

MB: That's a fascinating description of how you came to some of the major theory—your training in economics isn't often commented upon but it definitely shows up in much of the focus of your work. Is there anything you'd like to say about your early experiences in media production?

RM: Well, I've been working hands-on in media going back to 1962 when I became a paper deliverer for the *Cleveland Plain Dealer*. Then I worked, of course, on school and college papers. I also worked at my college radio station, as the news anchor! When I moved to Seattle in the late '70s I worked as a volunteer in the local alternative newspaper for a while, and I worked on the paper of the Tenants' Union in Seattle—it was a pretty significant movement in the '70s in the USA. I was always doing media-related stuff—it was something I gravitated to fairly naturally.

In fact I didn't go to graduate school until I was 30, and I spent a good five years in my 20s working in commercial media. Following in my father's footsteps, I started selling advertising for a weekly alternative paper in Seattle in 1979. And events being what they were at that time, within six months I was made the publisher. That was the middle of 1979, and then the following year a bunch of us who worked in the paper broke off and started a monthly rock and roll magazine, *The Rocket*. I did that for several years in Seattle. It was actually a very extraordinary experience for me and very helpful for my later research because I was in charge of running a magazine. By the time I left that in '83 to go to graduate school, I think we had a staff of seven or eight, a fairly large payroll, and we were a significant and recognized force in Seattle and the Puget Sound area. Later, when I was going through graduate school and studying political economy, this experience informed my thinking because some of the questions I was asking I had first-hand experience addressing—they weren't abstract issues to me.

MB: Questions, for example, around how advertising shapes content or how business shapes publication?

RM: Absolutely. How advertising shapes content was a central issue I had to deal with directly as a publisher. One of the big issues for us as a publication—and this isn't something I'm especially proud of but I'm not going to run from it—was that the central advertiser was cigarette companies. My general manager, Greg Feise, and I spent an inordinate amount of time cultivating the big tobacco companies and their ad agencies to get them to make ad buys, because if we could get a contract with them it would make us economically solvent. We had a shot at getting their accounts because they weren't permitted to advertise on radio and television and we were delivering exactly the market they wanted. My skin crawls as I say these words. I mean, I was delivering teenage eyeballs to this death industry. But that's the context I worked in, and it gave me a rich appreciation for real business situations, real markets, and how people ethically deal with these situations.

I remember how triumphant Greg and I were when we finally got R. J. Reynolds to sign a huge, year-long contract for something like four full page ads in every issue, in full color no less. That meant we would get to use full color throughout the entire magazine, paid for by R. J. Reynolds. Upon hearing the news, one of our editors, Karrie Jacobs, said, "OK, now it's time for *The Rocket* to do a cover story on the harmful effects of cigarette smoking." She was serious. I looked at her like she was absolutely insane, when in fact she was the only sane person in an absurd situation, and I said,

"Of course we're not going to do that. If we do the contract is void and we may go out of business." That's the dilemma—a real world dilemma—I faced. There were scores of incidents like this. As a result, I have been very critical of how the system is set up while being sympathetic to the people doing their best within that system.

MB: Indeed, a central contradiction of capitalism. I wonder if that perhaps leads to the question of how you came to establish a media reform movement through Free Press?

RM: My work as a scholar crystallized when I stumbled across my dissertation topic in the mid '80s, which eventually became my first book. I say stumbled because I was just reading Ben Bagdikian's *Media Monopoly* and I sort of had an epiphany and it occurred to me what I needed to study. I realized that commercial media was not a natural American system that was embraced all the time without any qualms. My dissertation and the resulting book addressed the movement in the United States in the early 1930s to oppose commercial broadcasting and to establish a much stronger nonprofit, noncommercial media. I didn't realize it at the time, but it became clear that selecting that topic had put my career on a certain trajectory.

Telecommunications, Mass Media and Democracy came out in 1993, and it got a lot of popular public interest, even though of all my books it was the most academic. Because when people heard about the book and then read it, the response was always the same: "You mean it didn't have to be this way?" For a surprising number of people, it was like the sky had opened for them—the idea that media wasn't a natural system you were stuck with like the Rocky Mountain range.

I ended up giving lots of public talks, and doing more media than many professors get to do. Invariably people were asking me questions like, "How does this relate to today, when journalism has collapsed and our democracy is struggling?" I used my historical training to look at more contemporary issues. Everything I've done since then has fallen pretty much into that category, and that was because the moment of that first book demanded it. I didn't think it was right for me to say, "I'm the historian—you figure it out. I'm going back to the archives. See you later." I wrote that first book because I was concerned about today; I didn't write the book because I only cared about 1932. And so I felt I had to come up with answers. I had to partici-pate in that discussion. I needed to talk to many people and draw people into this conversation—to make it a public issue.

The argument that I made in my books and articles in the '90s was that the media system wasn't natural, it was the result of policies and extensive subsidies. And that the problem in the United States was that these subsidies and policies had been made in the public's name but without the public's support and consent. I used the example of the 1930s as a case study to show how that has worked historically and the type of journalism we get as a result. The whole unavoidable conclusion is that we need to have some sort of political campaign to increase participation in these policy decisions. The argument received a great deal of momentum with the emergence of the Internet, which again drew attention to the key role of policies. The Internet forced a rethinking of regulations and rules surrounding media structure. For some, especially those on the political right or those who had commercial interests, the emergence of the Internet simply signified that technology was running supreme and we could let free markets do their magic. But that was really more a rhetorical ploy. In the real world of media it actually forced a whole number of important policy questions to the fore, questions about how industry is structured, what sort of subsidies are given, and what sort of regulations apply.

So the issues that I was interested in would be coming to the fore no matter what, because of the technological revolution and because of a deep concern about the quality of journalism and the quality of the cultural content being delivered by the corporate media system. You put those two things together and throughout the 1990s you saw a tremendous increase in popular dissatisfaction with the media status quo. This was an issue that people needed to organize around; they wanted to win, it was that important. But for people to organize around media issues was an extraordinarily difficult thing to do compared to most other issues. It was very difficult to get popular attention for an issue when you had to rely on the news media to organize for you, because this was not an issue that the media were going to cover. Or if they were going to cover media policy-making, they would do so in a way that would fit the interests of the dominant media firms that had a stake in the outcome of these media policy debates. That was one of the factors explaining why the people lost in the 1930s and why it was difficult to get something up and running in the 1990s.

So my work naturally led to the idea that there had to be a movement to do this. There had to be an organized campaign to draw people in, to link up to other organized groups, to put grassroots heat on policy-makers to actually serve the public interest and not the corporate interest. There was a recognition that this would be extraordinarily difficult to do because of the power of lobbyists and their control over the media. This made it hard to get more than a very small fraction of the population to understand that it was their right, and I would argue, their duty, to engage in media policy.

By the beginning of this decade I think we saw a qualitative shift. I think the crucial factor was that I was contacted by a campaign finance organizer, Josh Silver, in 2002, and we got together and began discussions with my friend and journalist John Nichols about starting a group that would organize public support for media reform. It would be called Free Press and Josh would run it and John and I would be on the Board and lend what support we could. And when we started it we thought this was going to be a long slow ramp up. We thought it was going to take us 10 or 15 or 20 years to make this a really big issue, and we'd have a lot of digging to do and a lot of seeds to plant, so to speak.

Then in December 2002, I think, Josh was sleeping in a closet in Massachusetts somewhere—we have almost no budget—and this media ownership fight hits the United States. The Federal Communications Commission decided to revisit its media ownership rules, which it had to do by law, and the Republican majority was expressly committed to getting rid of the rules or relaxing them as much as possible. It was a blatant giveaway to the big media companies. The corruption was so thick it was impossible not to see, and we came in just as this was taking place. And you know I think my initial response, and most people's response, was that the fix was in, the Republicans were going to get this change through, and we were screwed. They were going to allow one company to own most of the media in any given town around the country, with all that that would suggest for the quality of journalism and community involvement in media.

And then the anticoncentration in media ownership movement just exploded. I'd like to say Free Press was responsible for it, but it wasn't. Free Press was still just getting started; there were a lot of existing public interest groups in Washington that played a crucial role. Consumers Union media project, Jeff Chester's operation, really did a lot of the heavy lifting to the extent that a number of other groups got involved for the first time, like Common Cause, the National Rifle Association, and MoveOn, and this thing just took off. It was astonishing. For those of us at Free Press, it collapsed what we thought would have taken ten years to do into one year. It showed us that we actually had an issue you could organize heterogeneous communities around. You could take what seemed like complex issues and draw popular attention to them, and people genuinely cared—the soil was very fertile.

By the end of 2003 we had our first media conference. It was really great to get everyone with interest in this issue together in one room, talk things through, and get a sense of what sort of movement we had. We planned this conference in January of 2003, and we thought we might get 200 people. Well, thanks to the ownership fight, the conference exploded like a volcano. We had 1,700 people there, we had to close down registration, and it was extraordinary—it was like a Woodstock type event for us. For everyone it was just a revelation to have this conference. So by the end of 2003, it was clear there was actually a movement. It has continued to grow ever since through our next two conferences, and moved into a wider range of important policy issues. Now, in April 2007, we have a staff of 25 to 30, almost 400,000 members, and we've really developed a lot of skills and the ability to do stuff. I'm not on the staff—I'm a board member, and I'm the president—but I'm still quite pleased and delighted and shocked by the success. It's not just the group, though, it's really about the movement. The stars were aligned and the timing was just perfect. There are a number of other activists outside of Free Press working on this issue who are the heart and soul of this movement—we're just one part of it—and it's an extraordinary movement.

MB: Having attended the most recent Media Reform conference (Memphis, January 2007), I can say that it seemed to me it was a record turnout and an historic event. My experience on the ground was that there was a wide-ranging group of media activists, journalists, and policy-makers on hand—primarily, if not all, from the U.S.—but with quite diverse agendas. I wonder about your experience there in Memphis, and the evidence that you're part of building a movement. Does it give you some sense of hope?

RM: Oh, it can't help but give me hope. The politics of this movement are different from a lot of social movements and it produces very interesting outcomes as a result. It makes the politics easier and trickier at the same time. What I mean is that media reform is both a nonpartisan movement and it's a progressive movement. It's nonpartisan in the sense that the sort of reforms we're working for are not, for example, to censor certain types of political speech and enhance others, or to air our viewpoint more than other viewpoints. That's not at all what this movement is about. This movement is about building a media system that does justice to the democratic needs of a self-governing people. We just want to expand the range and quality of media, not favor one group over the other in a zero-sum game. It's not about censorship. So almost all the reforms we work on—network neutrality, media ownership, public broadcasting, getting rid of government propaganda—are nonpartisan issues and apply to Republican, Democrat, liberal, conservative. They aren't meant to favor one group over another. This is about expanding the range and quality of the media system so that it's not in the service of a relatively small number of commercial interests. What we found in issue after issue is that when you are out of Washington and away from the party bosses, we have immense support from rank-and-file Republicans on a lot of these issues. They don't like their kids' brains marinated in advertising, they don't like political advertising on TV, they don't want one company to own all the media in their community, they don't want their cable and phone company to privatize the Internet and determine which Web sites they can and can't see. What we found is that these issues cut across the political spectrum. In that way this movement is similar to voting reform groups or campaign finance reform or electoral reform groups who are simply trying to make the system work more efficiently and have a viable democracy.

On the other hand, though, this isn't purely a nonpartisan movement, it's very much a progressive movement. Despite the rhetoric that you hear from people in power in the United States or in other countries, not everyone really wants democracy. Not everyone in this country wants to make it easier for people without property to have influence over policies. There are people, or interests, who currently have significant power in our government and our society who like the status quo. They don't want an informed, participating population. To Thomas Jefferson, the press system was necessary because unless poor people had information to govern their lives, they were left with a corrupt system that couldn't be democratic. Because the wolves, as we call them, will eat the sheep, the rich will plunder the poor. I think that's why so many of the people associated with this movement come from liberals, progressive ranks, the political left, because that's what gets you into the movement, that's what gets you fired up.

MB: What vision underlies the *kinds* of change you've been part of? Your work evidences a commitment to legislation and policy as one front for change, and I wonder how you came to decide on those as a focus for the social movement?

RM: Well, I think the media reform movement actually has four different components. Working on policies is one of them and that's the one we focus on at Free Press. I think it's the most important one for social and political organizing, and the most important overall. The next two are doing independent media, which is especially important in the digital era, and providing media education and critique. This is something that we have a lot of skill at from years of academia and being on the outside looking in. Groups like Fairness and Accuracy in Reporting and the tremendous media literacy movement are making people informed about how the media system works so they can participate in changing it. And criticism of bias in the news from groups like Media Matters for America is another component of critique. A fourth component is the movement among media producers, especially workers, journalists, and creative people. Their interest in taking a larger role in the media process could just shift some of the power from Wall Street, from advertisers, managers, and corporate interests. That's the fourth leg of the table.

And I think all four parts work together, and I've argued this at length in *Tragedy and Farce*, the book I wrote with John Nichols. They really aren't competing approaches to solving the problem; they're entirely complementary and need each other. None of them can succeed without the other. Now we put most emphasis at Free Press on legislation and policy for a number of reasons, but the primary one is that our media system is not a natural free market system. It is a system that's created through policies and subsidies by the government and has been that way since the beginning. It's a profit-motivated system, but it's not a free market system. United States media firms—and I think this is pretty much true in every major nation, I'm sure it's true in Canada—receive extraordinary subsidies from the government, way beyond what other traditional industries receive. Every private firm gets benefits from the government: they get to use the roads, the water system, public education; they get employees who are trained by the state. Media firms get those same benefits and, theoretically, they pay taxes to earn those benefits. But what I'm talking about in terms of subsidies for media firms goes way beyond that. Media firms are receiving direct and indirect subsidies from the U.S. government, especially the federal government and also state and local governments, totaling in the tens of billions of dollars every year. These include monopoly franchises to radio and TV stations, and cable and telephone systems; copyright provisions that protect content providers and give them monopoly markets; government postal subsidies; government work to enhance sales overseas; and subsidies for audiovisual productions. You put all these things together, and you have an enormous public subsidy. These subsidies are made in the public's name without the public's informed consent. That's really what drives the policy side. The government created this media system to no small extent, and it's done so based on policies that the public's played no role in drafting, but they're paying for out of their wallets. So to me that's really where the rubber hits the road in this movement. Ultimately, we have to change the system and that means going through the policies. I'm not opposed to subsidies, by the way, I just think the public should get something in return for these enormous gifts. I think we have to consider all the options for how we must deploy our resources, and maybe giving monopoly privileges to AT&T to run the Internet isn't such a smart idea.

MB: That's a good segue to my next question. Your scholarship and movement with the Free Press reflect to me a combination of conviction and principles, alongside a kind of pragmatism in your choice of where to push for media democracy. Which does leave me with the question: What about the micro level? For example, where do small-scale initiatives such as pirate TV or community radio fit into the vision you've just described of challenging corporate media?

RM: Well, one of the pleasant surprises of the last five years is that unlike other social movements, the media reform movement doesn't have one goal that you either get or you don't get. For example, in the United States the election campaign finance reform movement, which took off in the 1990s, has pretty much died off. It has died off not because the issue is no longer important—the issue is more important today than ever—but because the organizers realized either you win publicly funded elections or whatever reform you have will leave a crack in the edifice that will allow big money to come in and take it over and destroy the spirit of your initial reform.

In the media reform movement, what you have are a broad range of areas that you can work in and you can win tangible discrete victories that can't be taken away. That's what gives it a lot of its vibrancy. For example, you raised the issues of community radio or TV; you know, we're going to have hundreds and hundreds of new low power FM radio stations in the United States due to a large extent to public activism forcing Washington to deliver these signals. New stations are going up around the country. They're getting licensed now as a result of this activism and these stations can't be taken away—it's a real victory. There are a number of instances like this. The micro stuff is a very important part of the big picture. It's not just about winning some huge fight. Although there are huge policies, like network neutrality, that are absolute thumbs up or thumbs down for the whole media system, where we need all hands on deck.

MB: Let me follow up on that question about small scale developments with some examples. I'm wondering if you have any thoughts about say, for example, Andy Bichlbaum and The Yes Men's interventions, and how they managed to get significant airtime on the BBC about the otherwise unreported Bhopal disaster by adopting the identity of Jude Finisterra, spokesman for Dow Chemical. Tactical media intervention is one of the themes of this book. How do you see these types of activities? Are they effective? Do you see them as part of media reform or not?

RM: Oh, they're good, The Yes Men are terrific. We're big believers in using humor and creative mechanisms to draw attention to our movement because it's not like the news media are racing out to cover our story. There's going to be a study done at some point about media coverage of this movement compared to similar movements in size and magnitude. I think it will be an interesting study because my sense is that the news media run from the media reform story for a variety of reasons. And I think what that means is that it puts the onus upon us to come up with creative ways to communicate with the public.

One of the things that this movement's done has been to use new media—podcasting, blogging, YouTube, MySpace—to popularize the issues and to bypass the traditional media. We've really worked on this in the last year with the Save the Internet campaign, and in some ways, the media reform movement has been among the pioneers of developing the Internet as a grassroots organizing tool. It really goes back to 2003 when e-mail and the Internet were so crucial to organizing the media ownership campaign. We've gone through a whole new phase today of how we work that, but a lot of it is putting together catchy, entertaining, informative podcasts and video that then go viral and get communicated outside those channels. And if they're powerful enough they might get picked up by the traditional media and noticed. So I think that one of the things that this movement works on is creative ways to use media to publicize issues, and going back to The Yes Men, creative ways to get attention. While The Yes Men aren't talking about media issues per se—oftentimes they talk about issues of social justice—I think their existence is a testament to the fact that our media system has fundamental problems.

But let me let me tell you one story about that. I heard a talk Ralph Nader gave about two years ago. He was running for president in 2000 and he was being introduced by Michael Moore, who gave a great talk to introduce Nader. He was very funny, he told jokes, everyone was jumping up and down and laughing. And then Nader comes up to talk. And you know Nader isn't going to win any stand-up awards as a comedian—he's a very serious guy. Nader says, "Isn't it great to have someone like Michael Moore giving this great political talk to introduce me?" And everyone agrees. And then he says, "You know we should really think about that for a second—the only critical ideas that our media systems get out and circulate are funny ideas. There are comedians—you know Bill Maher, Michael Moore—but there are no serious voices." Nader said he once traveled in the Soviet Union in the 1960s as a young man and he was struck by the fact that it had the best political humor he'd ever seen. There was an underground political humor that was simply off the charts. That didn't mean they had a healthy society or healthy media systems—the official media system was actually so atrocious that humor was the only way people could survive. And I think he was trying to make a point that this is the situation we have in our society, that the official media is so atrocious as a rule, that the only way you can get in edgewise is through satire and humor. And that while that is an understandable approach, we shouldn't romanticize it, because it really points to the fundamental crisis. If we had a legitimate or decent media you wouldn't have to put on a clown suit to get noticed. You could just talk about an issue and be taken seriously—you wouldn't be automatically dispelled to the lunatic fringe.

MB: I want to pick up on an argument in your book *The Problem of the Media*, which I heard you reiterate at a journalism education conference in Toronto in 2005. I was going to say, at that panel in 2005, "Bob, can you say more about your lack of faith in the uses of Web 2.0 as an intervention? Don't they in any way offer viable alternatives or challenges to corporate media?" Ironically, it was small-scale uses of Web 2.0 that made the Save the Internet campaign successful. But overall, I hear you express very little faith in the promise of the Internet as an alternative to corporate owned media. Is that accurate?

RM: The way I would frame it is this: Can the technology offered by the Internet be sufficient to unleash popular power such that the system can be overturned independent of any other policy actions? There are some who actually believe that now that the Internet exists we can all go out and blog and do our thing and we're going to take over, the corporate interests are doomed, and we're going to have a much better media system. I don't agree with that. I just don't buy it. That doesn't mean those microactions aren't very important, but their importance is part of a broader movement that works on a number of different fronts.

Unleashing the free market with the magic of the Internet does not magically produce great journalism. The technology does a lot of great things, as I've talked about already. We used the Internet and new technologies with our organizing, and they're a foundation of our success. But I have no illusion that that means that you can just go online and have great journalism. Journalism requires resources and skilled people getting paid salaries. It requires institutional support so that if you offend someone in power you will have support and you won't get hassled or arrested. These things don't happen magically just by having the Internet, they require public decisions, distribution of resources, creation of systems. In the United States, it's clear that merging profit seeking with the Internet has not done anything to improve our journalism, or very little. If anything it's part of the process of seeing it continue to unravel.

And so we need to come up with constructive policies to take advantage of these technologies, in order to create community journals and community media. It won't happen organically on its own and that's really my argument. Now that doesn't mean you don't do the little stuff, it just means you don't have the illusion that the little stuff is sufficient and therefore you can let the big guys continue to get the ten billion dollar subsidies, privatize the Internet, run everything. That's my argument.

MB: Following up on that, I think about the examples that exist despite the fact that we haven't achieved our ends yet necessarily. You've written that "good journalism and good media requires money and institutional support," but what about the exceptions to this: Pacifica, Democracy Now, Indy Media. I assume that given your lack of optimism about poorly funded interventions, you see some limitations to these independent media?

RM: Oh, absolutely there are limitations. For one thing, let's take community radio stations like Pacifica. These stations depend upon federal support. I'm in Madison now, and WORT, a wonderful community station, maybe the most popular radio station in this community, gets 20 percent of its money from the federal government. It gets as much of its money from the government in broadcasting subsidy as does any NPR station in the United States. It desperately needs that money or it can't survive—it's already hanging on by the skin of its teeth despite its popularity. You know we need enlightened policy so that stations that are this popular actually can have equipment that doesn't look like it was air-shipped out of London after the Blitzkrieg of 1943. And so I think the examples you gave are exactly why we do need coherent policies in addition to independent media.

MB: Turning to the broader landscape outside of North America, do you have any thoughts about the recent launching of Al Jazeera English?

RM: Well, not specifically because I haven't seen it.

MB: Which is another interesting aspect of new media—how and if it is known, where it is and isn't broadcast, and all of these questions of visibility and distribution. I think it is very significant that access to the Web now allows many in the international community to access Al Jazeera in English. That is one example that stands out in terms of the significant difference that Web-based communication has helped establish.

RM: I think in the next three to five years the really interesting developments are going to be at the global level. In every country and region around the world, people are battling with these issues, and they're really the same issues everywhere. There are differences between countries and concerns are different, but there's so much common ground and there are so many issues now, like Internet governance, which transcend national governments. I think the next stage is going to be drawing people together, like the Memphis conference, but also people from around the world, in some sort of global summit to put pressure on leaders and global institutions to serve the public. The problem we see in the United States with corruption is only magnified at the global level where institutions are even one step further removed from grassroots pressure.

MB: Picking up on the Save the Internet campaign: I was talking to some colleagues who work in these areas and they noted that people working in open source and open access movements have been inspired by your critiques—but they are also concerned to develop an alternative, networked information economy. I wonder if you have any thoughts on the possibilities of a nonproprietary, nonmarket information economy to see possibilities of democratic politics and economy online.

RM: My belief right from the beginning of seeing digital communication was that there's a fundamental conflict between the potential and logic in digital communications systems and the sort of traditional, intellectual property/copyright rules that really increasingly butt up against and make no sense with the new technologies. This is exactly why we need an enlightened policy-making to pursue policies that don't just serve the entrenched interests of commercial powerhouses but that actually go beyond that to what sort of policies regarding information are needed to encourage a more vibrant market media system. The one thing I know for sure though is that winning that fight, especially in the United States, is going to be really hard because there's so much money on the other side of the table. And the key to getting there is building up popular awareness and support, it's the only way you're going to win that fight.

MB: So this is a huge question, but I know you're up to it, given the historian and philosopher that you are. I wondered if you could say something about the particular vision of democracy that underlies a project like the media reform movement or Free Press?

Oops. Cut off. (Line goes dead.)

RM: Hello.

MB: Which corporation do you owe your money to? (*Laughs.*)

RM: I don't know what happened.

MB: Just dropped the signal, I don't know. . . . so yes, I was asking you about visions of democracy.

RM: I think that the vision is actually pretty elementary—this movement doesn't require a very elaborate one. Self-government is impossible without a viable press, and this is not a controversial idea, this is a foundation of the democratic theory. And it's also foundational to *antidemocratic* theory that you need a press system that manipulates people, keeps them in their place. You don't really have to have much more of an understanding beyond that to know the importance of this movement and of these issues.

MB: And do you see democracy as a strictly formal process or would you want to say something about democracy as a way of life, a right to know, that's broader than formal process?

RM: Well, I think the way democracy has evolved in the United States, and arguably in other nations to an extent as well, it has become a formal entity in which the actual participation of citizens is pretty minimal. In fact, MacPherson's work that I referred to earlier was very instrumental in helping me to grasp this understanding of democracy and its limitations. What we need to do is try to invigorate public life, to put people in a position to actively participate in their communities and their world—as governors, not simply as consumers going through formal bouts of voting every three years for candidates and parties over which they don't have very much control and about which they know very little. That form of democracy is better than nothing to a certain extent, but it's not sufficient. And the media is part of that problem in that it's become so hollow that public life has been largely demoralized.

MB: Do you see new platforms such as YouTube, Facebook, blogging, and other kinds of tactical media interventions, as part of that kind of invigorated participation, as showing signs of impacting what is counting as democratic process?

RM: It seems to me the evidence so far is very positive about the ability of the new technologies to help generate popular awareness that wouldn't be there otherwise and get people engaged and involved, but at this point still I'm uncomfortable extrapolating because I think we're still early in the game. We're doing everything we can to push that, but I think there's a tendency to get so tied to a technology that it's like when you fall in love with someone—you don't see their warts for a few days. I think there's an element of that with the fascination with YouTube and Facebook and things like that, which doesn't mean there isn't any reason to fall in love, but rather that we have to always be careful not to jump into the deep end—to make sure there's enough water in there.

MB: In *The Problem of the Media* you address the hype that the Internet will set us free and you write, "In one sense this is a blatant ideological ploy by powerful media firms to distract attention if they gobble up more media so they may be better poised to crush competition generated by new technologies." [2004: 217]

RM: There is no question about that, it isn't even a debatable point. I mean the Internet is this enormous propaganda device employed by industry and their PR people and their lackeys. Every time they want to do anything, they wave the Internet flag, and say, "Well, there is always new content on the Internet so you've got to do whatever we want, everything's changing, you can't regulate it, you have to keep giving us subsidies on our terms, you have to do whatever we tell you because of the Internet." There's no question that's going on. There's not an issue we're dealing with where we don't get that argument—argument number 1A that's used by industry at every turn in the United States.

MB: And what's the logic there?

RM: Well, the logic is that with the Internet now here every market is blasted off, open, it's completely competitive. So you don't have to worry about whether one company owns all the radio stations, TV stations, and newspapers in the community because you know people can go online and blog to their heart's content. You don't get that argument in Canada? Your capitalists ought to come down here for a PR lesson.

MB: Well, I'm a native of San Francisco, and I've only been here a few years, but a big bone I have to pick is that there is even less attention to media ownership concentration here in Canada than there is in the U.S. It's nearly impossible to find an accurate visual map of Canada's media ownership concentrations. In terms of concentration, I would say we are nearly worse off in Canada than in the States, and there's less public input about regulation.

And then I get students who, even after spending a long while deconstructing notions of objectivity, fairness, and balance, will say, "Well, at least there's the CBC and the CBC is objective." What do you say to that?

RM: Yeah, the CBC plays a big role in my historical research. It looks good today by comparison to the sort of horse manure that's served up by the balance of the press system. But that's like saying someone is the best ice hockey player in Malaysia. You've got to look at the context. I think the value of looking at something like the CBC is that you see, as Marc Raboy puts it in the title of his famous book, *Missed Opportunities*—what it could be that it isn't, what's been lost over the years. And in that context, you know, the possibilities are much greater than the realities.

MB: We actually haven't talked about your feelings about government role in media. What are your thoughts on the BBC and CBC, and on Public Broadcasting Service and Corporation for Public Broadcasting in the U.S., in terms of content, and in terms of your hopes for media democracy?

RM: I'm a believer in public media as a big part—not the only part, but a big part—of a vibrant media system. By public media I mean subsidized through the public, noncommercial, nonprofit media. There's been so much frustration by progressives around the world with their own domestic public services, frustration with the content, the bureaucracy, the lack of democracy, that there have been schools of thought saying, "Let's just throw them all under the train, we don't need them anymore, we'll just go online and blog each other. We don't need those guys." I think that's the anarchism of fools, so to speak. I would argue that with the new technologies what we now have is an opportunity to have a much more heterogeneous structure for a noncommercial, nonprofit media than we've had in the past. We should view it as an opportunity to expand and radically enhance nonprofit, noncommercial media so that it's not a centralized operation with one institution controlling the entire thing, but rather you have local community media, some national media, but competitive nonprofit media. Multiple nonprofit, noncommercial media operating independently.

But I do think the need for public funding to support media, which has been the premise of the process in the United States since 1791, is not going away and one of the great campaigns in the United States today is to find resources and funding to enhance noncommercial, nonprofit media into the digital area and build vibrant institutions that can be accountable, that can serve the public. And so I'm a big believer in public media, and the need to make that a central issue in our organizing.

MB: What might be the kinds of questions that are most important to you as you teach the next generation of communications studies students? What's most important to you to convey to them or get them to engage in?

RM: My experience is that at the undergraduate level, most students are pretty much ignorant of everything that you and I have just been talking about.

When they hear about this and learn about it and read about it and talk about it, it's sort of a litmus test for them. The vast majority of them get really interested and really engaged, and it's very exciting as a teacher to see this process take place. I see it every year, and it makes me really enjoy going into the classroom. I see these students who are starved to engage with this world, who are frustrated with the sort of corporate culture that they're immersed in, and when they get some perspective on it and can see some of the limitations and some of the alternatives, they get energized and excited.

MB: I was giving a talk at a major university on some of my work in the area of media and philosophy and democracy, and somebody in this audience of top education scholars asked with hostility, "What does media have to do with conventional education?" I have to say I was a bit taken aback because where does one begin in answering that question? What might your response be to a question like that?

RM: Well, for me, media is the number one department of education in the world today. So I think a better question would be, What does school have to do with education? I'd turn it around because for a lot of people coming of age in the United States today, their education is coming through media on fundamental matters and issues as much as through schools. I think I can understand why you would find the question bizarre since the connections between the two institutions are so strong, as are the premises of education and media. To no small extent the media is the educational system of our society, certainly as much as school if not more. To view it as divorced from education is to me a very formalistic view of education that is not connected to the actual lived experiences of people on this planet.

MB: I wanted to ask you about the recent headlines about the satellite company merger and any thoughts you had on that?

RM: Well, we're still formulating our response to that. What is lost often times in the shuffle is that we have two satellite radio companies instead of ten or twenty, not because the market per se can only have two, but because there's only enough spectrum right now allocated to have two. It's a government-created duopoly in effect and now the two players are saying considering that the government created a duopoly, this could be turned into a government-sanctioned monopoly. By *sanctioned* I mean that, if the merger does go through, it would be impossible for a new competitor to start up, not just for economic reasons, it's tough enough to go against a monopoly, but because there wouldn't be spectrum to do it.

The firms are going to argue of course that they'll go broke unless they can have this monopoly, they can't survive otherwise. And, traditionally, in the United States, the way issues like this are then resolved, is that the merger goes through, they allow the monopoly, and then in exchange the monopoly is supposed to do all sorts of public service stuff. The public gets squeezed because the corporate lobbyists are one hundred times stronger, and the politicians and regulators are really half-hearted in their efforts to represent the public. We aren't strong enough now, I don't think, to stop this merger necessarily, but we'll see if we're strong enough to at least put much stronger terms in the merger proposal, much greater teeth than would be there otherwise. It's going to be an interesting test of the strength of our movement.

MB: Shifting again the focus to the micro: as you describe corporate capitalism as it defines and shapes the potential of media and democracy, I want to return once again to the question of where the individual fits in this scheme of change?

RM: The question is how one regards his or her role as an individual. Do you regard yourself as sort of a solo operator who basically came out of the woods one hundred thousand years ago, on your own, and made contracts with all the other people who came out of the woods, so you're basically a single unit on your own? Or do you regard yourself as part of an evolving social organism with tremendous dependency on others for survival? And I view the human condition as very much the latter. I view us as fundamentally social creatures where the individual exists and is defined by relationship to other people, and in that sense then the key is to look at what seem like individual problems to try and see if there's a social link there. There might not be for every issue, but for many issues, lots of people have similar concerns and if they try to treat them all individually, they won't really find satisfactory results. But if they come together and treat them socially, they can actually solve the problems.

And those are the sort of problems we're dealing with in media reform. Everyone can sit around and whine about the fact they don't like all the advertising in media, they don't like the crappy journalism, but they think it's an individual problem—they've just got a problem with the media personally, and then they just try to solve it by finding a Web site to go to and they can do their thing. That's really not ultimately a satisfactory solution, a rational solution. A much smarter solution is for all those individuals to find their common interests and ground, understand how the system works, and create a system that works to their satisfaction. That's called media reform.

Figure 1.1
Robert McChesney, Media Reform Conference. Photo credit Free Press

2 The Space of Tactical Media

Alessandra Renzi

Tactical media are media of crisis, criticism and opposition. This is both the source [of] their power, ("anger is an energy": John Lydon), and also their limitation. Their typical heroes are: the activist, Nomadic media warriors, the pranxter, the hacker, the street rapper, the camcorder kamikaze, they are the happy negatives, always in search of an enemy. But once the enemy has been named and vanquished it is the tactical practitioner whose turn it is to fall into crisis.
—Garcia and Lovink, The ABC of Tactical Media

Defining the Hype

At the center of the tactical media site "Virtual Casebook Project at NYU" (VCB), an interactive box asks the question, "What is tactical media?" Although media tacticians themselves offer an explanation, when looking at the list of contributions, one is still left to wonder what exactly *tactical media* means. A close look shows that despite some threads running through the texts, a clear definition of the phenomenon is not given. Rather, the reader is provided with some recurring tendencies, including temporality, use of available resources, collective work, polymorphism, wit, overlapping of art and politics, and so forth.

In general, tactical media (TM) are expressions of dissent that rely on artistic practices and "do it yourself" (DIY) media created from readily available, relatively cheap technology and means of communication (e.g., radio, video and Internet). They are described by Patricia Aufderheide as "projects that people do opportunistically— seizing temporarily available or unclaimed resources" (Aufderheide, in VCB 2002). Gregg Bordowitz adds that they are a "constantly evolving set of approaches . . . collectively produced" (Bordowitz, in VCB 2002). Above all, it is the slippery character of TM, with its potential to resist characterization in dominant terms, which renders them peculiar: "As with other cultures of exile and migration, practitioners of tactical media have studied the techniques by which the weak become stronger than their oppressors by scattering, by becoming centreless, by moving fast across the physical and virtual landscapes. 'The hunted must discover the ways to become the hunter'"(Garcia, in VCB 2002).

Another way of describing TM has been to highlight the distinction between tactics and strategies, separating TM from other kinds of political activism. This dichotomy goes back to Michel de Certeau's work, in which the former concept of tactics describes short-term actions, while the latter deals with more future-oriented work (de Certeau 1984). This distinction surfaces as a reference in the TM manifesto "The ABC of Tactical Media" (Garcia and Lovink 1997), yet when taken too literally, it has often resulted in some restrictive definitions that automatically exclude any project or action that is long-lasting or that creates the conditions for lasting networks.[1] In fact, the main obstacle for researchers attempting to study this phenomenon is that, lacking an identifiable enemy and using very heterogeneous tactics, TM do not allow for a pre-definition of their work, which is continuously reshaped by actors and contexts. At the same time, TM practices also trouble those who attempt to define and represent them by constantly reframing their tactics and by explicitly avoiding definitions: TM elude representation to preserve their autonomy (Wilson 1997).

In order to make sense of these practices, the "post-oppositional character" of TM (Lovink 2002) should be located within an economy of power relations where resistance is never outside of the field of forces but is, rather, its indispensable element. Indeed, the existence of power relationships depends on a multiplicity of points of resistance (Foucault 1978: 95). In this context, TM as a form of resistance can be seen as mobile and transitory points of struggle, "producing cleavages in a society that shift about, fracturing unities and effecting regroupings, furrowing across individuals themselves, cutting them up and remoulding them, marking off irreducible regions in them, in their bodies and minds" (Foucault 1978: 96).[2] In my view, TM's avoidance of essentialized identity is the manifestation of a differentiating minoritarian position that allows groups to exercise a critique of the system as well as self-criticism—with the aim of developing new experiments.[3] These practices are fundamental for a constant reinvention of the tactics that expose cracks in the system where action can take place. By so doing, the pragmatic, shifty character of TM allows actors to engage with the changing, normalizing forces they oppose and to drop tactics that have lost their effect. However, since the social sciences strongly rely on classification strategies as an analytical and descriptive tool—and TM cannot easily be classified—scholars often ignore or dismiss TM as not being a form of resistance *in their own right*.

In general, sociologically oriented approaches to TM are not much different from studies of other social movements, which are mainly characterized by two tendencies: first, they concentrate on groups as definable entities and according to their assessable political impact; second, they tend towards a taxonomic dissection of their discourses and practices in order to understand the dynamics of their visible effects (or failures).[4] To be fair, most macroanalytical studies are always confronted with the problem of leaving out important aspects from their findings in order to provide a coherent description of the *object* of study. Yet, when looking at how knowledge production is indissolubly tied to social representations and visibility of social and political actors, it becomes important to recognize the impact of academic classification or of the need for (now, qualitative) generalizing claims in silencing certain phenomena.[5] In fact, although it cannot be denied that some classification principles have allowed new insights into many social and cultural phenomena, they indeed rely on a need to represent interaction though a uniform system for the sake of consistency, excluding what cannot be classified.

On a more fundamental level, this reminds us of the "mutual relation between systems of truth and modalities of power" (Foucault, in Couzens Hoy 1986: 224), thereby exposing an intersection that shows us the power struggle between conceptual frames reflecting different stakes and positions in the academic field(s). On one front, there are those who claim that social descriptions are merely tools to "understand" practices—they promote a "neutral" stance for the researcher, whose role is to explain the world around us. To paraphrase Bourdieu, this approach often applies to practice a mode of thinking that brackets practical necessity—and uses instruments of thought against practice for the sake of producing scientific knowledge (Bourdieu 1990). As a consequence, it poses knowledge production as detached from social change, and it denies any responsibilities for researchers as agents in this process. On the other front, there are those who are politically engaged due to their critical stance toward issues of social justice, or simply because they provide visibility for certain silenced actors. However, there may also be a problem with the theoretical frameworks of academic work of this kind. In fact, many studies often sacrifice the properly strategic dimensions, the contradictory and problematic aspects of the practices rooted in the uncertainties of daily struggles in order to yield a coherent picture of the phenomena described. For the same reason, the discrepancies between diverse discourses circulating within the studied sites, as well as present conflicts and power relations within activist groups, are seldom granted any space in sociological studies. The resulting pictures are useful to expose those struggles that would otherwise go unnoticed, yet they fall short of offering the ground for a constructive critique that can become a useful tool for activists themselves.[6]

Researchers who want to find an alternative framework to look at TM, while also offering an instrument of information and critique to the groups studied, are thus faced with two key obstacles. On the one hand, they have to overcome already well-established attitudes with respect to taxonomic and classifying approaches and success-driven evaluation of activist enterprises. On the other, they are confronted with gatekeeping attitudes of activist-theorists themselves, skeptical about the role of academics, who are perceived as outsiders. One way out of these structural impasses is to adopt a praxis-logical approach rather than an ontological one and to focus on the spaces of aggregation and on the communicative processes set in motion within TM spaces. In fact, perhaps, the question What is TM? is a poorly posed question.

Alternatively, one could ask about the function served by the articulation of the concept—Who has put it forward? Under what circumstances? To accomplish what? How does it work? Where and how does it come into being? How does it circulate? This series of questions can be used to conceptualize the political significance[7] of TM as a form of social struggle by exposing many aspects that are ignored in most studies on contemporary forms of activism.

It would bring to a scholarly perspective a conceptual frame that can be helpful for studying emergent forms of resistance within globalizing capitalism. These forms of activism challenge "traditional" definitions of social movements in the twenty-first century with a definite enemy and a clearly articulated group identity (Castells 2004; Melucci 1996). Instead of making their claims for social change through institutional politics, they focus on prepoliticizing or politicizing their audiences and on developing strategies to escape power acting on people's innermost sense of individuality. At the same time, they are strategically and transversally linked (often at a global level) with other forms of resistance (such as open source movement, squatters, hackers, etc.), forming *ad hoc* temporary alliances around various issues and campaigns.

More precisely, in today's economies the creation of wealth emphasizes more and more the commercialization of social life itself. The production of subjects within western societies is no longer solely aimed at governing citizens from the field of politics but increasingly also at creating consuming subjects for the economic marketplace[8] This way of controlling and administering life turns life itself into the new object of power. At the same time, though, life also becomes the new object of resistance: "Life becomes resistance to power when power takes life as its object" (Deleuze 1988: 92). Many dissenting groups active in the world today function within such a diagram. It is important to keep this new site of resistance in mind if we are to notice emerging struggles against forms of power and control that are characteristic of hypermodernity.

In addition to this, a praxis-logical approach to TM engenders a politically engaged, constructive, and contextualized analysis that can eventually help make such projects more effective. It can (re)invent the relationship between activists and researchers to offer not only reciprocal symbolic force but also practical advice for projects to come. In Guattari's words, this new form of cooperation can offer a " 'collective assemblage of enunciation'—that gives this discourse its unity, its gesture, its meaning, as a seat of its coherence" (Guattari 1996: 180).

In this overview of TM, I demonstrate the need for different lenses to look at emergent forms of social struggles, too slippery to be defined in conventional terms of identity and objectives. I also call for an effort on the part of the researcher to construct the object of study differently, i.e., to ask different questions, even though the results may not always conform to the prescribed rules within universities. Future case studies that follow this path will have the advantage of portraying the polyvocality of the actors involved in each struggle, as opposed to producing generalizations based on the official discourses of some selected sites. Therefore, in this chapter, I look at TM not as a movement or a practice but as a space where "tactical things" happen. I rely on Doreen Massey's (1994) theories of space and on Arjun Appadurai's (1996) ideas of global cultural flows and the role of the imagination. This framework is instrumental in showing how social relations within TM spaces come to enable the circulation and appropriation of cultural images that articulate new discourses and subject positions. Subsequently, I map TM spaces into a broader cartography of social struggle using Michael Warner's notion of counterpublics. This brings to the fore the function of TM spaces as sites for ongoing experimentation of discourses and practices that in turn flow into and are taken up in other spaces. Moreover, it highlights the dynamics of structural affiliation, exploring how different solidarities and pedagogies engage subjects and function as discursive frames to connect them within TM spaces—while eluding established forms of knowledge and dominant forms of power (Deleuze 1995: 176). In order to provide some empirical evidence of how TM spaces function, I refer to examples of actions and projects, events and communication means,[9] and look at the construction of narratives, at the work of politics, and of "minor knowledge production" in TM actions (Deleuze and Guattari 2000).

Hubs, Flows, and Contact Zones

Networks versus Networked Spaces

After narrating the history of the World Wide Web in *The Internet Galaxy* (Castells 2001), Manuel Castells describes how information networks relying on the Internet can be used as powerful interaction tools. He analyzes the cultural discourses produced by actors such as hackers, dotcom entrepreneurs, and members of online communities. However, Castells' book is more concerned with the "new sociotechnical pattern" emerging from their interaction (Castells 2001: 5) than with documenting the work of such groups. A more detailed study of activism and resistance is provided in the second volume of *The Power of Identity* (Castells 2004), where the author looks, for instance, at the "anti" globalization movement, the Zapatistas, and the environmental movements. These movements are portrayed by Castells as networked forms of organization at the transnational level. At the same time, the Internet and other new communication means are present as an argument to reinforce the picture of the "network society"—they are a technology, a tool, more than a plane of interaction.[10] In this context, the concept of identity as a way of articulating cohesion and political mandates is pivotal for the analysis of such groups, as it links them to the broader sociohistorical, economic, and political contexts of the network society in general.

Building on Castells' research, scholars are considering the implications of networks as a framework for the analysis of activism in general.[11] However, the model of the network society, in particular, its reliance on identity models, seems less suitable to look at TM. Social movements, NGOs, or social justice organizations usually exist in function of a clearly articulated objective and mobilize to alter preexisting conditions caused by a definite enemy—for example, corporations, poverty, racism. The articulation of their discourses is generally based on a dualistic description of identity that opposes communal identity to individualism and also contrasts what Castells calls "resistance identity" (Castells 2004) of transnational movements to the nation-state. Conversely, TM are characterized by the lack of an ultimate identity or goal: "If tactical media were to ever attain their legitimate objectives they would immediately become redundant" (Garcia in VCB 2002).[12] This means that in TM, resistance identities are not necessarily articulated in opposition to dominant ones; rather, that there is the possibility for alternative subjectivities to develop through different practices. This is the case for *Telestreet,* an Italian network of illegal microbroadcasters. For many of these pirate televisions, programming is not solely aimed at challenging Berlusconi's monopoly of mainstream media but especially at experimenting with the medium of television as a communication space (Verna 2005). The actors involved in this media-making project perceive themselves as cultural producers, video or community activists, and so forth, according to the context in which they work—for instance, at festivals, demonstrations, or educational events (see also Anand, chap. 13, in this volume).

In TM, we are dealing with individuals and nonprofit groups of artists/activists working with DIY media who are constantly reconfiguring and reshaping their work and objectives (Lovink 2003). Matters are often complicated further because media tacticians cross more than one boundary and subject positions, in particular, the very controversial one between politics and art,[13] between being an artist and being an activist. TM are not an organized group that can be located within a sociopolitical landscape, as in the case of Castells' nodes and networks. Neither can they be isolated, described, and then positioned as a unity with respect to other groups in the networked society. A focus on the space of social interaction rather than the identity of actors enables an analysis of TM without having to rely on a defining collective identity; it concentrates on the communicative practices, organizational dynamics, and creative processes rather than on shooting a group picture. Framing TM as a socially constructed space also foregrounds the voluntary, and often temporary, self-positioning of its actors instead of the absolute definition of the group. Thus, I see TM not as a homogeneous movement within a network, but as "networked spaces"— discursive spaces where resistance discourses and subjectivities are constantly produced and dropped once they become redundant.

"A network is a set of interconnected nodes" (Castells 2001: 1), hence, the network model implies a degree of homogeneity that allows researchers to describe each node (e.g., identity). On the contrary, my term "networked space" can be used as a theoretical construct for thinking through TM as a set of social relations among actors that articulate the notion of a network in structure and practice. Hence, the notion of networked spaces highlights how the networked character is consciously constructed through communication means and especially how its function goes beyond simply increasing efficiency—as I show in the following sections, it is the socially constructed field of action itself. For the same reason, the idea of networked space also has the advantage of including the in-between spaces—ignored in the network model—by considering them also as spaces where discourses circulate. More precisely, the TM spaces are apprehended as "contact zones." They represent the space for agency itself, they also include the infrastructure that allows both the construction of such spaces and the action within them. This conceptualization of contact zones allows me to focus, for example, on how the encounter of activists and artists from different countries at a festival or on a mailing list can produce new TM projects. Three elements are fundamental to map TM spaces: the idea of space as socially constructed, the concept of flows of ideas, and the role of the imagination in the construction of subjectivities.

Topology versus Typology

In *Space, Place and Gender*, feminist geographer Doreen Massey maintains that "what is at issue is not social phenomena in space but both social phenomena and space as constituted out of social relations, the spatial is social relations 'stretched out'" (Massey 1994: 2). Furthermore, "social relations are inevitably and everywhere imbued with power and meaning and symbolism" (Massey 1994: 3); hence, power and signification cannot be separated from this ever-shifting social geometry. Starting from these considerations, it is possible to map the existence of spaces such as TM into a geography of social struggles. More precisely, the act of forming TM contact zones that enable communication between actors in itself can already be contextualized as a practice of resistance within such a landscape. At a general level, it illustrates how power itself may be obtained and flagged through a reterritorialization and resignification of space. At a specific level, the value of these zones does not only lie in the fact that they allow the development of new tactics but also in their ability to function as sites for new modes of organization and new kinds of political practice.

TM spaces are constructed through interaction that takes place online and offline—but they also encompass the discursive space created by TM cooperations and transnational projects. These networked spaces are socially constructed sites where actors, technology, and practices interact, not as a preexisting dimension but as an ongoing process. My emphasis on the networked aspect is necessary to piece together the various dimensions, such as the transnational aspect of some TM work and the circulation of knowledge. TM spaces are constituted primarily through (1) Web sites, (2) social software,[14] and (3) organized events.

Web Sites More specifically, this mix of events, practices, and technology becomes the medium of social relations themselves. In the case of Web sites, apart from those that can be strictly seen as TM projects, such as Voteauction.net,[15] TM Web sites also function as hubs of information on upcoming and past events and projects, and as repositories of theoretical texts.[16] An illustrative example is the Next Five Minutes (N5M4) Web site, which contains information on an international festival for TM, taking place in Amsterdam, and is linked to the N5M4 journal. Participants in these projects include media tacticians, members of Indymedia, media centers in Eastern European countries offering technical infrastructure and education, and European organizations which provide ICT assistance to less developed countries (Richardson 2002). This site is also linked to the *Nettime* mailing list, where theory and practice are discussed and new ideas are explored. Both the festival and the journal can be seen as showcases for experiments in new media, bringing together people of different backgrounds around what Geert Lovink calls "issues of a critical techno-culture" (Lovink 2002: 11). These issues range from open content licenses and bandwidth policy to developing viable forms of interaction that allow for diversity and pluralism.

Directly linked to the N5M4 Web site is the *Virtual Casebook* (VCB), the result of the workshop "Tactical Media: The Impact of New Media on Cultural Activism and Political Engagement."[17] This site contains a series of contributions on the definition of TM, yet it should not only be considered for its archival quality but also as tactical work in itself. The virtual casebook was created after 11 September "to focus [this VCB] on understanding, reporting, exhibiting, and archiving the responses of those who had extreme close-up views of Ground Zero in a physical sense" (VCB 2002: introduction), and whose narratives and actions had been ignored or dismissed by the mainstream media. In this sense, the tactical aspect is that of creating a space distinct from the mainstream media to reflect on and rethink the role of activism and the media after the attack on the World Trade Center. Also worth mentioning are the work-in-progress character and the interactive aspect of the site. These underscore the polymorphisms of TM space in general "Because tactical media practices (see definitions) are inherently responsive, interactive, and constantly evolving, we chose a format that would make it possible to capture the specificity of such developments in different political and cultural contexts" (VCB 2002: introduction). Furthermore, the sections on the definitions of TM and the other projects mentioned create a direct connection with other TM sites. As I will discuss shortly, it is the flow of such discourses and practices, more than the Networked structure of the Net itself, which create the element of continuity that maps the spaces of TM.

TM meetings often produce a journal that reports on the event, so that, like the VCB and the N5M4 journal, many other TM Web sites contain essays on theoretical and practical issues.[18] These event-driven (web)journals attempt to "bridge the real and virtual by building in interactive elements between online audiences and the actual site" (Lovink 2002: 249) and emphasize the multiplicity of sites involved. They use video, audio, sound, and text tools and allow participation before, during, and after the event. The structure and characteristics of the meetings deserve a closer look since they play an important role in structuring the way media tacticians interact with each other and with the audience.

Social Software TM actors lay considerable weight on face-to-face encounters to foster cooperation and create an environment of familiarity and trust: "Conferences function foremost to gain motivation in order to continue with the neverending patchwork, requiring both creativity and persistence" (Lovink 2002: 241). The theory discussed at the meetings is an attempt to "bridge the divide between new technologies and old powers" (Lovink 2002: 242). Further, these conferences are attended by artists, curators, consultants, academics, designers, programmers, and activists, who debate cultural policies, art, design, and the media. At the same time, their format tries to overcome the limitations of traditional conferences, which rely mainly on lectures and offer little dialogue. Instead, TM conferences try to rearrange and question the relation between speakers and audience (Lovink 2002: 245). They are not aimed a creating consensus and avoid long papers, preferring moderation of roundtables and audiovisual material contributions through Webcams, chatrooms, and video conferencing.

"Temporary media labs" (TML) are an important space where consistent international exchange takes place. TM labs can be part of well-established art and new media exhibitions or festivals like the Documenta in Kassel and the Transmediale in Berlin, or they can be part of events set up in other areas to start fostering transnational cooperation and media user empowerment. TML introduce the field to new audiences, they aim at producing content, and often result in "long term initiatives and transnational cooperation" that "experiment with social interfaces, visual languages and cultural/political processes" (Lovink 2002: 249). One important aspect of these labs is that they create a space for negotiation and experimentation by bringing people together, such as the case of a TML set up in Sao Paulo. This lab was organized as a response to a N5M4 call for Latin American countries interested in starting a TM project, the "organization's attempt to both broaden its geographical compass and decentralize its editorial process" (Garcia 2005). According to one of the organizers, Ricardo Rosas, this event had "both a cultural impact (an artistic/activist intervention of social and political relevance) and a practical one (creation of devices and tools for the use of groups that intend to act in the public sphere with a sense of social responsibility)" (Rosas 2004).

The Sao Paulo project brought together "grassroots undertakings of bridging the digital gap by working with computer recycling and using Linux," artists/activists collectives, independent media, and "the institutional segment that work with the access of marginalized and poor people to the digital age (the 'Telecentros')" (Rosas 2004b). By so doing, it created a network of Brazilians who had not previously met, and it laid the conditions both for the organization of the event and for future collaborations. Another effect of the TML in Brazil was that it attracted mainstream media attention and created awareness of the phenomenon in the country.[19]

The format itself was inspired by the N5M4 festival, a model for setting up both spaces for theory and practice of TM in many possible forms. It combined conferences, exhibitions, discussion spaces, performance, and other kinds of activities like workshops and parties. Rosas remarks that "in a way, we tried to follow Lovink and Garcia's varieties of tactical media as mentioned in "The ABC of Tactical Media", and for that reason we created something which included from art/activist groups and collectives to djs and street theatre performances [*sic*]" (Rosas 2004b).

As I explain in the following section, there are some recurring concepts circulating in the TM space that are consistently taken up and readapted by the actors. For instance, the formats of TM festivals, with TML or TAZ areas,[20] are often a common feature to events around the world. To a certain extent, it can be argued that the strength of TM meetings does not necessarily lie in the size of their audience but in what happens once the people have met. In fact, these kinds of events have a double effect: on the one hand, they make the concept of TM known to a wider audience, thereby creating the possibility for more work. On the other, they bring people of different backgrounds together to discuss and exchange knowledge and concepts. Hence, the act of communicating as "critiquing subjects" consolidates these spaces as sites for sustained reflection on our world. TM events play an important role in creating flows of "images" that enable the development of active critical work. In this sense, TML also offer the space for consolidating the tactical into more stable projects.

Organized Events   A third spatial dimension of TM interaction is related to the use of social software. Social software is a subset of software—such as blogs, wikis, listservs, and RSS feeds (a program that informs users when Web sites have been updated)—that enable many-to-many communication.[21] In particular, I will concentrate on the use of the Nettime mailing list because it has played an important role in TM spaces for a long time, although other tools, like blogs, message boards, and Web sites that facilitate social networking and the exchange of resources are also used. Mailing lists are consistently used to exchange information (internationally) or to organize events and to discuss theoretical and practical issues.

Nettime—"mailing lists for networked cultures, politics, and tactics" (Nettime 2004)—was founded in 1995 to discuss "the cultural politics of the net" (Lovink 2002: 68). Among other things, it was a forum for the production of critical texts about culture and art on the Internet from a variety of perspectives (art, cultural policy, activism, computer science, media theory). It was aimed at producing "Net criticism"—a body of theory on the Net that goes beyond mere enthusiasms and demonizations (Lovink 2002: 22). The list later branched out into parallel lists in various languages and its texts are all archived by content on the Web,[22] creating a common context for its users and for the public. At the same time, many contributions have also been printed in publications and readers, and they are now part of an institutionalized body of theory. Moreover, it is worth mentioning that many of the texts are translated and posted on other mailing lists, allowing their discourses to flow into different spaces.

Nettime was born as a reaction to the kind of "religious quality of technology, and passion for techno-Darwinism" of magazines like *Wired, Mondo 2000,* and *Virtual* (Lovink 2002: 77), an attitude that already presaged the corporate influence on the Net. Its members define it as an

effort to formulate an international, networked discourse that neither promotes a dominant euphoria (to sell products) nor continues the cynical pessimism, spread by journalists and intellectuals in the "old" media who generalize about "new" media with no clear understanding of their communication aspects. We have produced, and will continue to produce books, readers, and web sites in various languages so an "immanent" net critique will circulate both on- and offline . . . is a way to reach a large group of active cultural producers. . . . a forwarding channel, a social text filter, for own texts, found texts, requests, announcements.—Nettime 2002.

The list uses its networked structure to form a discursive space that enables transnational interaction and discussion of theoretical issues from an insider's perspective, offering knowledge to boost new and DIY media production. Many Nettime subscribers are established writers, artists or critics, often part of institutional or independent organizations. In this respect, the list functions as testing ground to post ideas and texts that will be published as essays. It creates a new flow of ideas that are both freshly formulated by these tacticians and drawn and reelaborated from other fields and authors. They produce new discourses on art, politics, and culture and a common context for constant innovation.

Analyzing Tactical Media: Flows and the Imagination

Appadurai's (1996) concept of global cultural flows seems particularly useful in describing this transnational cultural traffic. More precisely, the relationship between two dimensions of cultural flows, the *mediascapes* and *ideoscapes*[23]—"closely related landscapes of images"[24] (Appadurai 1996: 35)—aptly describes the role of images and discourses circulating the TM space. *Mediascape* refers to both the electronic means to disseminate information and to "the images of the world created by these media," whereas *ideoscapes* are concatenations of images/ideas/terms with a more political or ideological character (Appadurai 1996: 33–36). In this context, TM can be seen as (re)claimed spaces inhabited "by the historically situated imaginations of persons and groups around the globe" (Appadurai 1996:33) and constructed by the flow of discourses on media, politics, and culture. More precisely, TM spaces constitute the contact zones—local points of intersection—where "groups and individuals who feel aggrieved by or excluded from the wider culture" (Garcia and Lovink 1997) come together around issues of power and social change. Here, the various flows of discourses on art, new media, technology, and knowledge commons intersect with local histories, cultures, and imaginaries, thereby constructing resistance as a localized, ongoing invention of practices. These practices focus on the colonized internal spaces of individuals as well as the external ones. Thus, TM spaces become the breeding grounds for the construction of creative tools and strategies to contest dominant values (such as subject positions as passive consumer of cultural goods), while also producing flows into and from other spaces. Here, in turn, ideas will be transformed according to the context—for instance, in the more generic field of activist social movements, or into the cultural mainstream, where tactics are co-opted and marketed to consumers.[25] A simple—and rather superficial—instance of how such flows function is the recurring presence on numerous Web sites, mailing lists, and blogs of Garcia and Lovink's "The ABC of Tactical Media,"[26] one of the first introductory texts in the field. This manifesto has worked as an inspiration for groups outside the Netherlands, where it was first written in 1997 for the opening of the Web site of the Tactical Media Network, hosted by De Waag, the Society for Old and New Media. As Ricardo Rosas explains in his report (Rosas 2004b), this was a formative text in the creation of the TML in Sao Paulo.

One aspect that is particularly relevant to the TM context of flows is how ideas are shaped in different places, where different sets of communicative genres may be valued in different ways. Again, in the case of the TML in Brazil, the challenge had been to adapt the tactics to the Brazilian environment. As Rosas notes in his report, much weight was placed on the use and manipulation of mass media (radio and, especially, television), since these tools (and spaces) play a major role in shaping the Brazilian imaginary. Moreover, due to the economic gap between sectors of the population, the TML placed considerable emphasis on the low-tech character of the equipment, so as to enable participation of economically disadvantaged groups (Rosas 2004b). The TM project later evolved into the "Autolabs"—permanent (tactical) media labs in free software in the favelas of the city—where young people are offered the tools and the training to work creatively with technology. Following Appadurai, it could be argued that the *ideoscapes* and *mediascapes* of TM have introduced certain keywords—one of which is *midia tatica* (tactical media)—to Sao Paulo, where the Brazilians construct their own meaning through the work of the imagination as much as through the available theoretical and historical background. In fact, *midia tatica* developed their own version of practices: "Digitofagia" (Digitophagy). The concept goes back to ancient Brazilian cannibalistic rituals and to an artistic movement from the 1920s that recuperated the concept as a metaphor for "catching foreign information, and, by 'digesting' it and mixing with the local circumstances, transform the results into something original" (Rosas 2004*a*). The keyword TM itself, by not being defined and by travelling across (national and cultural) borders works like a "loosely structured synopticon of politics" (Appadurai 1996: 36) whose semantic field is continuously reinvented. At a time when so much analysis focuses on the homogenizing potential of globalization, this aspect emphasizes a more subtle and active relationship between the local and the global. By the same token, reports and reflections on the local situations also circulate and become part of this discursive space and can be taken on and resignified in other contexts. In this way, the *ideoscapes* and *mediascapes* of TM are continuously being shaped and imagined in the attempt to keep alive the possibilities of the imagination by combining it with more critical approaches to theory and practice. This also includes the potentials for practicing self-critique and of developing new approaches once the old ones have become ineffective.

The work of the imagination as a "space of contestation" (Appadurai 1996: 4) plays a fundamental role in the agency of TM, whose work often consists of creative, short-lived interventions that trouble commonly held beliefs about art, politics, and everyday life. For instance, in practices of "culture jamming," action often takes place through the creative use of language that borrows from art, politics, and consumerism, but is never fixed on any of these fields. TM language's most striking characteristic is indeed its imaginative and disruptive capacity. Here, messages are subverted through stunts and pranks, such as linguistic sabotage or *detournement*,[27] which involve an appropriation of the language and discourses of their political target. In other words, the subversion of symbolic codes is achieved by using a language that is familiar to the nonactivist audience and that pushes the audience to question its legitimacy. This is the case of many cloned Web sites that look like the official sites of institutions and organizations but contain subversive messages, like the George Bush Web site[28] set up by the Yes Men. This stunt prompted Bush to announce on television that "there ought to be limits to democracy." TM language draws on and reframes known discourses, thereby causing recognition of their limits. It creates temporary reversal of the flows of power by exposing hidden and transparent areas where strategies of domination are at work. According to TM group Critical Art Ensemble, "We try to exploit those areas with participatory cultural practice. From the perspective of the status quo a minor (in the Deleuzian sense of the term) movement cannot be anything other than an organization that tears" (McKenzie and Schneider 2000: 138). In this context, TM practices can be seen as providing the space for encounters that can trigger the development of different modes of subjectification.

More precisely, the chance to briefly hijack the dominant language of power—especially that of the media, which plays such an important role in the creation of

identities today—creates a potentially shared discourse that can offer alternative subjectivities as active producers of symbols rather than merely passive consumers. An
example of how the relationship between different subject positions can be temporarily thrown off balance is the work of RustleTV, a three-day-long media event in a public
market in Bangalore.[29] Here, the passersby and shopkeepers from the market were
invited to take part in the production of video material—which was then broadcasted
within their closed-circuit TV. On the one hand, this project managed to open up a
media space for the people of the Russell Market, which is usually closed to them. In
fact, although they often feature in reports about the popular venue, they are usually
the "objects" rather than the "subjects" of such features. With RustleTV, they became
active subjects by acting, dancing, and interacting with the cameras.[30] It created a
different relationship between the producers and the users. On the other hand, for
the film students taking part in the workshop, the project exposed and troubled the
"politics of the gaze" and the power relationship between those who hold the camera
and the "object" of their work (Anand et al. 2005; and chap. 13, in this volume).

Imagining New Subjects

Arjun Appadurai's ideas about the role of the imagination in shaping social and political subjectivities (Appadurai 1996) can help us see what happens in local projects
where individuals and groups speak for themselves, to each other, and to other groups
with the means and technologies made available. An example is the case of DiscovolanteTV, a microbroadcaster from the *Telestreet* network (Renzi 2006). Discovolante's
staff is composed mainly by disabled people, who, through their artwork and journalistic reports, managed to open some cracks in the Italian media and social systems.
First of all, by running their own microTV station, the group successfully makes itself
more visible in the community, thereby starting a dialogue with its members. Second,
by appearing on television both as "disabled" bodies and as "unskilled" cultural producers, they push the audience to question what is "supposed" to be on TV. Finally,
with an award-winning documentary on architectonic barriers, they forced the local
authorities to tackle and solve logistical problems for wheelchairs. Most importantly,
on a personal level, DiscovolanteTV also becomes the space where actors reflect on
and elaborate subject positions. Due to little data collected so far, I have not yet been
able to provide a detailed analysis of the ways in which these processes take place.
However, the material available online and several conversations I had with its
members can be taken as a starting point to explore some of the possible ways Discovolante experiments with different modes of subjectification.[31] For example, the actors
appropriate the language of television to tell their own stories, exposing their position
to the gaze of the other, while at the same time posing as communicating subjects
(Foucault 1997).[32] By tapping into old and new technology—into TM discourses and

into their own local reality—Discovolante's crew imaginatively create new narratives as self-defined subjects within the Italian mediascape.[33] Moreover, DIY television fosters questioning, if only in the process of comparing it with what are considered to be the norms and standards of production and the "right" choice of what is supposed to be broadcasted. Thus, the resulting critical mode is also a way in which Telestreet actors are "forced" to act upon at the very instant they take on the responsibility of becoming active in the process of cultural production. On a more general level, a critiquing subject refers to the act through which subjects reflect on the rules of government that constitute them for what they are. It implies a constructive process through which these modes of subjectification are evaluated with the intention of developing alternatives to it (Butler 2005: 9). It is worth emphasizing how the role of culture in shaping of these subjectivities and in political agency has been clearly recognized by TM actors. In fact, by acknowledging the role of the media[34] and of the imagination in the construction of dynamic forms of individuation, TM underline the importance of alternative sources of flows for new political projects.

As stated above, Mouffe's distinction between *the political* and *politics* is useful here to understand political agency in an enlarged context outside of institutional forms of politics. This is because the idea of *the political* places power relations and antagonism at the center of human interaction. It highlights the antagonistic dimension of democracies, emphasizing the fact that "some existing rights have been constructed on the very exclusion or subordination of others" (Mouffe 2000: 20; see also Dean, chap. 3, in this volume). Acts of power are, thus, also in the realm of the social and are deeply implicated in the constitution of identities[35] (Mouffe 2000: 99–101). Therefore, the dimension of the political is a highly conflictual one, and it is played out on multiple levels of social interaction, including the formation of subjects. In this context, TM spaces are sites where explicit political acts of resistance take place through the fashioning of new subjectivities. While emphasizing the need to establish new cultural practices—both in the construction of new spaces and what is articulated within such spaces—TM directly call attention to the complexity of power structures. On the one hand, TM projects foreground the exclusion of certain voices in the debate about artistic standards, political action, and media representation. On the other, by empowering media users, TM work flies in the face of crystallized identities, as in the case of Discovolante. Thus, the boosting of dialogue by providing "imaginative" sources of identification seems to find an implementation in many TM projects (e.g., Brazilian tactical labs in the favelas, *Telestreet*), where activism, art (Mouffe 2001: 123), and empowerment through action are combined. This is because DIY media offers affordable tools to fight stereotypes, to elaborate new symbolic strategies of identification (Mouffe 2000: 148), and to foster participation in the communicative process. If, according to Butler, critique is also "that perspective on established and ordering ways of knowing which is not immediately assimilated into that ordering function" (Butler

2005: 5), then the fluid spaces of TM are also the sites where new modes of critique can be continuously developed and new subjectivities can be developed and cast off.

Spaces of Counterpublics

The idea of contact zones has been instrumental in approaching TM without classifying it as a homogenous movement. Yet, TM spaces should not be seen in isolation from the entire social field but rather as an integral part of it. Here, Michael Warner's (2002) notion of counterpublics can be useful to think through TM as spaces for the articulation of resistant practices and alternative modes of subjectification within a broader field of power relations. Specifically, what is useful about Warner's idea of counterpublics is that it allows me to avoid a normative definition of TM as publics and to focus on the constitutive and temporary processes at work, as well as to analyze the conditions that enable the existence of TM in interaction with other spaces. This approach shifts the emphasis from gauging TM as somewhat outmoded dissent to mapping them as sites for the continuous experimentation of alternative forms of solidarity and self-expression.

More precisely, Warner sees publics and counterpublics as a result, rather than a starting point, of communication between humans: a public is "understood as an ongoing space of encounter for discourse" (Warner 2002: 90). Publics are not static entities, they come into being through their self-creating, self-organizing capacities and through the reflexive circulation of discourses—but they disappear once these activities cease. Hence, the comparison of TM contact zones with counterpublics is not an attempt to articulate a definition; rather, it locates TM in the social field on the basis of the interaction taking place within their spaces and with other spaces.[36]

According to Warner, a counterpublic is also a public, albeit one that "maintains at some level, conscious or not, an awareness of its subordinate status" (Warner 2002: 119). This relationship also includes cultural codes, apart from political positions, and in TM it is articulated through a "minoritarian" position. Again, this means that the minority is not defined in terms of identity as an aggregate or state (Deleuze and Guattari 2000: 291) but as a presence that continuously deterritorializes the norms of the majority. In other words, TM gives difference a positive status as it puts itself in a minority position to question every form of power—even its own (Garcia and Lovink 1997). Thus, when considered as counterpublics, TM are not apprehended in absolute terms as opposed to the mainstream but as dynamic spaces of discourse that constantly refashion themselves through different projects in a dialogic relationship with their environment.

Publics not only communicate within themselves but also do so with other publics (Warner 2002). Because communication is verbal but also visual and textual, any form of TM action that is displayed publicly, potentially and automatically addresses everyone. This is especially the case when TM events make it to the mainstream media or to institutional sites of display such as art exhibitions or publications, starting a dialogue with other groups. Exposure may be due to the recognition of TM works' symbolic value but especially to truly tactical interventions that hijack public attention, as in the case of the cult of Saint Precario (Renzi and Turpin 2007).[37] At the same time, it is not the dialogue with the dominant power formations that I want to highlight in TM spaces. Instead, what is key to my argument is the formation of alliances with other oppositional forces. In this case, TM can be seen as intersecting with other spaces through collaborations with the *alter*-globalization movement, activists, artists, and other minority groups. This, however, not only takes place through dialogue, sharing of resources, and support of some campaigns but also simply due to the flow of new ideas and practices from TM into other sites of resistance.

Indeed, since "the tactical is also about reclaiming imagination and fantasy" (Garcia and Lovink 1999), TM practices are increasingly borrowed by social movements to stage their protests. This is because "classical TM, unlike agit-prop, are designed to invite discourse" (Garcia 2006); they plant the seeds for discussion by operating a fissure in what is considered to be "objective reality," leaving the receivers of the message to fill the tear with meaning. It can be argued that, in most cases, TM language tends to attract attention by causing an affective response[38] in their audience and requiring a form of engagement to decode their message: "The activists were 'wearing' a statement which required completion by others; to wear this logo was to draw people into conversation. Not a command but an invitation to discourse." (Broeckmann et al. 2002). Here again, Warner helps draw attention to what he calls "the poetic world-making" (2002: 122) of TM; that is, not only the poetic function of language and affect in general but also the idea of *poiesis* as creation and production. Through critical discourses as well as through cultural production, TM works prompt people to communicate, thereby facilitating the development of social solidarity. It is worth noting that cultural production does not only include projects and work but also shared practices of production and communication (Calhoun 2002).

Furthermore, as the case of Discovolante shows, reclaiming a space of discourse can offer individuals the ground to constitute themselves as subjects, while bypassing dominant norms of cultural production and other forms of power. For Warner, publics unite because of participation rather than common identity, and they are sites of learning because individuals come to understand themselves differently as members of a public. In this context, the forms of solidarity facilitated by TM are a fundamental element in the construction and maintenance of spaces where this kind of reflexivity can be kept alive, allowing a constant questioning of dominant discourses and experimentation with alternative forms of expression and resistance. More precisely, my approach to TM spaces underlines how individuals and groups are offered the tools to partake in such reflection. Indeed, the cultural traffic described above, as well as experiments like the TML or Culture Jamming workshops, locate learning, discussing, and cooperating as fundamental practices for the formation of solidarities—and, hence, of resistance.

TM alliances function precisely on the recognition of the need for tools and knowledge that are embedded in different cultures and social relations.[39] Thus, TM spaces are adapted to different realities, from Eastern Europe to India, paying attention to the local context and needs. In the best cases, favoring local solidarities and collective self-determination also advances connections across lines of cultural and social difference. These can develop a sense of commitment, mutual dependence, and exchange between and within groups. This can take place not only in the alliances between international actors but also at the local level in the transdisciplinary cooperation of different national groups, as in the case of Brazil. In this way, TM shapes new forms of solidarity across time and space, often sharing labor and knowledge and bringing new items to debate in the local public sphere. Still, one thing needs to be clarified. I am by no means painting a picture of a TM as a harmonious environment of productive alliances. Similar to any other social space, TM cooperation is often a matter of argument and struggle. As Geert Lovink describes in his case study of the Nettime mailing list, TM works within an environment of competition as much as of cooperation; it is marred by flame wars and gender and language discrimination, as well as sometimes by a lack of long-term mutual commitment (Lovink 2002, 2003). These aspects can be given more space and emphasis in case studies on single projects.

In sum, these various forms of solidarity are joined together across localities reinforcing the potential of TM as the site for the experimentation and construction of different modes of subjectification and expression. However, the question of how effective tactical, short-lived incursions as a form of struggle is often raised and hard to answer. Some actions have indeed had considerable effects, and they have established collaborations with institutions or organizations that are part of civil society.[40] The Autolabs, for instance have been taken up by the Telecentros an institutional program to breech the digital divide (Garcia 2005).[41] Others, like the Yes Men, are becoming a well-known media phenomenon.

In particular, given the temporary character of TM actions, one is often left to wonder how long these kinds of solidarities are going to last. As with many other social phenomena, this question can only be answered by considering the single cases. Because of its exploratory character, more than each single project, the relevant role of TM discourses is that they mantain the foundations and pedagogies to allow communication and new solidarities. At the same time, whereas the development of any valid theory on strengthening social solidarities can only help TM practitioners at an abstract level, a close analysis of different TM spaces and of longer-lasting projects could be instrumental in creating more solid grounds to join people together with enduring social relationships. Thus, while TM try to develop new forms of solidarities, social research could ask questions about how single TM projects may offer more promising frameworks for visualizing the central role that artistic and cultural practices can play in the pursuit of radical politics (Mouffe 2001: 118).[42]

Conclusion

I have shown how different levels of interactive zones, created by/for TM, can be seen as coming together in a dynamic space. TM, apprehended as contact zones, facilitate the encounter and development of discourses on resistance and new formulations of the self in relation to different collectivities. In particular, Web sites, public events, and social software set the conditions for the existence of such kaleidoscopic, transnational spaces. At the same time, the flows of images and discourses circulating are picked up by individuals and groups and resignified according to, and against, their local context. This produces a circulation of ideas and work where pedagogical approaches and critical theory mix with the power of the imagination and breed a fertile ground to engage local cultures and politics. Ultimately, TM occasion a new space for theorizing the relationship among tactics, duration, and that research should be regarded as an integral part of an ecology of power that is never neutral and where resistance is immanent, multiple, and diffused (Foucault 1978).

By conceptualizing TM as fluidly constructed spaces, I have also attempted to take into consideration the unstable construction of subjects that inhabit and interact within them, as opposed to relying on stable categories of identity. "The spatial organisation of society . . . is integral to the production of the social, and not merely its result. It is fully implicated in both history and politics" (Massey 1994: 4). Moreover, spaces play an active role in the very formation and transformation of subjects. Thus, it is important to look at resistance also as the practice of (re)claiming spaces in order to analyze power struggles where subjectivity itself is at stake. From this perspective, struggles do not necessarily need to be glamorous or revolutionary, they can also be about the daily act of maturing active subjects of resistance, as in the case of people involved in the welfare of their own local community or of those that begin to take part in cultural production or decoding—no matter on what scale. These subjectivities are never stable, they coexist with other ones and are mainly tied to the spaces inhabited at that moment.

Warner's notion of counterpublics (2002) has been instrumental in highlighting how transnational and local publics can temporarily form around common concerns rather than only on the basis of preexisting institutionalized issues of political life and group identities. Most importantly, this notion has indicated how TM offer the tools for a critical pedagogy that enables actors to partake in exchanges both within the TM space and across other spaces. On the one hand, the cultural traffic I have described above, as well as experiments like the TML, locate learning, cooperation, and creativity within practices of the formation of solidarities that keep these spaces from disappearing. On the other hand, I also see TM spaces as sites where explicit radical political acts of resistance take place through the constant questioning of what constitute "social objectivity" from a minoritarian position. TM actions call attention to the dynamics of exclusion and can help bring about social change through their experimentation and the flow of their discourses. It is through new cultural practices—both in the construction of new spaces and what is articulated within such spaces—that TM can elaborate new symbolic strategies of identification (Mouffe 2000: 148). It can also call attention to the very language that sustains discrimination by undermining the relationship between signifier and signified, through the use of innovative, affective language(s).

Furthermore, a definition of space as a social artifact foregrounds the fact that the public sphere is not a place of rational debate but one where the power struggle between different groups, cultures, and backgrounds of actors takes place. At the same time, another issue also becomes visible: political activity within and between publics and counterpublics is not limited to discourse but seems to extend to action, redefining in a sense the meaning of communication and cultural production as important sites of resistance.

As a site for minor politics, TM are situated on the margins of normal political and social boundaries and their ongoing change of tactics and forms of identification (which quickly become ways of being labeled and neutralized by neoliberal discourses) turn out to be a vital part of practices of resistance. It is in this creative attempt to shape new forms of communication, to do without normalized forms of representation, and to foster individual empowerment that the political strength of TM spaces resides, rather than always in their directly resulting actions.

This, however, is by no means always a simple or successful task and, as mentioned before, questions about the sustainability and effectiveness of TM projects remain open. In particular, one of the challenges that TM face is how to develop pedagogies that create more stable and durable forms of solidarity, or even how to create or maintain the conditions for their projects to thrive. Political opposition, lack of resources, and internal conflict are only a few of the obstacles for TM initiatives. In the line of true struggles, the challenge is ongoing, alternating success and failure and radically changing the face of the phenomenon as it develops. Consequently, the question of sustainability cannot be answered a priori, as these kinds of dynamics are part and parcel of the battle between various cultural and political formations. To return to Michael Warner once more, "publics act historically" (2002: 123). Indeed, publics and counterpublics form and dissolve, and their voices are raised and then fade away, hopefully only to be substituted by new energetic attempts.

To conclude, my choice of Massey's and Appadurai's visions of spaces that are constructed out of multiple social relations and flows brings to the fore an example of sites created through a tactical use of technologies. These practices and flows, in turn, may be shaping our cultural and political environment through the use of the imagination. Beyond providing some tools to specifically look at TM, this approach aimed at offering some guiding threads for a dynamic description of social interaction within power relations. In fact, scholars' insistence on taxonomic theories to understand social struggles by looking for common features and stable group features is not always suitable for an analysis of contemporary social phenomena.

All in all, for both theorist/activists and researchers, to inhabit chaotic spaces of resistance from a contingent, partial, and uncertain position seems to better fit the messiness of TM—and of contemporary social struggles as a whole. Hence, this chapter remains incomplete if one is to assume that it was supposed to transfix TM in a coherent picture, or to asses what kind of effects TM are having/will have on society at large. More realistically, along with TM spirit, it attempted to point to a weakness in scholarly research that ignores or flattens the vitality and contradictions of some forms of social struggle, for the sake of consistency. It also aimed to expose a crack in the system—both social and academic—where new challenges can be taken up. By and large, here, a clear picture of TM is not a priority anyway. Much more important is to draw attention to the fact that in our postindustrial, neoliberal society, the ephemeral and experimental character of TM is a valid tactic to create spaces of contestation. In this context, the kind of academic work on spaces of resistance described in this chapter can have a double effect: first, it can acknowledge that social attempts should not only be analyzed in function of their achieved aims but also in the light of the processes/practices set in motion within certain spaces. Second, indepth case studies of single instances can help reveal the elements that hinder or facilitate the sustainability of some actions, thereby contributing to future, more enduring projects.

Most important, reinventing the relationship between researcher and activist as one of mutual collaboration and exchange will not only lend symbolic force to activist work but it will also locate sociological work itself within a cartography of resistance. In this context, we do well to remember Foucault's statement:

the problems that I pose are always concerned with local and particular issues . . . because it seems to me that none of the major discourses that can be produced about society is so convincing that it may be trusted; and if one really wants to construct something new and different, or in any case if one wants the great systems to be open to certain real problems, it is necessary to look for the data and the questions in which they are hidden. And then I'm not convinced that intellectuals . . . can point to the essential problems of the society in which they live. On the contrary, one of the main opportunities for collaboration with "non-intellectuals" is in listening to their problems, and in working with them to formulate these problems. (1991: 151)

From this position, a praxis-logical approach to TM practices and their formation of relational assemblages within a broader public context engenders new potentialities in the interstitial spaces where theory and practice are both codependent and coproductive.

Notes

I would like to thank Stephen Turpin for the invaluable help and endless discussions that lead me to write this chapter. Many thanks also to Bob Hanke for his great comments and suggestions.

1. For example, Graham Meikle's *Future Active* has two whole chapters on TM/culture jamming where he analyzes "a particular kind of Net politics" (3). Meikle describes TM as hit-and-run guerrilla tactics to attract mainstream media attention on political issues. Although the book offers one of the best descriptions of TM, this dichotomy between short and long term practices already presupposes a specific assessment of the value of TM. In fact, despite his attempt to disentangle himself from rigid grids of analysis, Meikle still feels the need to define TM practices and to justify their success in terms of raising awareness on issues usually not or poorly covered by the mainstream media. See G. Meikle, *Future Active: Media Activism and the Internet*. (London: Routledge, 2002), and Meikle, chap. 16 in this volume.

2. Foucault's idea of "transversal struggles" is useful to describe the kind of resistant practices associated with TM. These are not limited to one country and target "power effects as such" (2000: 330)—i.e., they critique an uncontrolled exercise of power. Transversal struggles are "immediate" because they target instances of power closest to the actors, searching for the immediate enemy instead of the chief enemy and not expecting a solution. Moreover, as it will be explained shortly, "they are struggles that question the status of the individual" by claiming the right to be different, while at the same time attacking anything that splits up community life or ties to "identity in a constrained way" (Foucault 2000: 330). Finally, TM struggles oppose the effects of power "linked with knowledge, competence and qualification [. . .] and mystifying representations imposed on people" (Foucault 2000: 330).

3. Another possible way to approach TM—and hard to avoid due to recurring references throughout their texts—is through the lenses of Deleuze and Guattari's "minor politics." Here, the majority is seen as a construct that allows the normalization of dominant discourses. At the same time, minorities are the seeds "whose value is to trigger uncontrollable movements and deterritorialisations of the mean or majority" (Deleuze and Guattari 2000: 106). In this context, the postoppositional aspect of TM lies in taking the position of a minority not as an objectively definable state but as a mode of existing in the social field. Importantly, TM make no claims to win power by eventually becoming the majority (Deleuze and Guattari 2000: 106): "Once the enemy has

been named and vanquished it is the tactical practitioner whose turn it is to fall into crisis" (Garcia and Lovink 1997).

4. For example, Manuel Castells mentions tactical media in *The Internet Galaxy* when talking about the Dutch project "the digital city," in his chapter on online civil society (Castells 2001: 144–154).

5. Even studies that take a qualitative or poststructuralist approach often tend to fall into the same trap. One such example is the recent book on new social movements, Richard Day, *Gramsci Is Dead: Anarchist Currents in the Newest Social Movements.* (Toronto: Between the Lines, 2005). For a critique of Dei's position, see also A. K. Thompson, "Making Friends with Failure," *Upping the Anti: A Journal of Theory and Action* 3 (2006).

6. For an example of analysis that takes into consideration some contradictions within activist practices and provides some criticism, see Bob Hanke, "For a Political Economy of Indymedia Practice," *Canadian Journal of Communication* 30, no. 1 (2005).

7. Here, the *political* is helpfully understood to Chantal Mouffe's distinction between *political* and *politics*. The first term refers to the antagonism that is part of social relations, whereas *politics* is "the ensemble of practices, discourses and institutions which seek to establish a certain order . . . in conditions that are always potentially conflictual because they are affected by the dimension of the political" (Mouffe 2000*a*: 149).

8. To this purpose, culture and creativity are themselves commodified and become an economic resource. This is often a topic of discussion in TM circles. For instance, an essay by David Garcia and a response by Brian Holmes, appeared on the *Mute Magazine* website (Garcia 2006), raise the problem of a new split between artist and activists, precisely on the basis of the commercial cannibalization of creativity: "Neo-liberalism's effective capture of the rhetoric of 'freedom' and 'creativity,' has re-opened an old fault-line which the first wave of tactical media did so much to bridge; the fault-line dividing artists from political activists. Such an approach results in producing mere epiphenomena of communicative capitalism not only tolerated but consumed by it with relish." This, apparently, has the effect of depoliticizing and subtracting credibility from TM. Garcia tackles the issue by calling for a need to connect tactics with strategies of resistance: "It is not that cultural or information politics are not important, it is just that outside of a broader context and strategy of meaningful confrontations they are simply not enough." Holmes, on his part, comments on the lack of radical forms of both art and protest: "But what's mainly lacking . . . are not only audacious direct action stunts, and not only . . . forms of political engagement that can reach huge numbers of participants. . . . What's also missing are artworks that cut through the trendy flaky fashions, . . . to touch the core of the human quandry and help you transform your self and your relation to the others, at a moment when things go on getting worse and worse and worse" (Holmes 2006).

9. Before starting the analysis, some clarifications are in order: the choice of projects has been conditioned by the idea that the fuzziness of a self-imposed identity as "tactical media" can be the starting point for the analysis, thereby avoiding top-down, abstract definitions. Rather than boxing tactical media into a strict category, I am more concerned with looking at what kind of

spaces it creates and what kind of interaction takes place within them. Moreover, my analysis is an alternative overview from a spatial perspective and does not claim to be exhaustive in describing this phenomenon. Also, I have left out any kind of criticism concerning the mentioned projects and the drawbacks of tactical media practices, as they would have taken this essay in a different direction, one that is worth pursuing in future, individual case studies. Finally, for the sake of brevity I will not dwell on the history and background of TM, each of which have been extensively discussed by media tacticians themselves (e.g., see Lovink 2002, and chap. 4 in this volume).

10. Castells seems to approach communication means as marginal or instrumental to the development of the network society rather than as specifically developed or adopted by groups with certain purposes in mind.

11. For instances of studies of social movements see M. McCaughey and M. D. Ayers, eds. *Cyberactivism: Online Activism in Theory and Practice* (New York: Routledge, 2003), and W. van de Donk, B. D. Loader, et al., eds. *Cyberprotest: New Media, Citizens and Social Movements.* (London, Rutledge, 2004).

12. Indeed, resistance does not always necessarily mirror domination (Pile and Keith 1997), hence it can be seen as occupying and creating new spaces not always coupled with oppression. Importantly, as it will be hinted at later, the spaces constructed with the help of TM create the conditions not only for the antagonistic power struggle between dominant and dominated groups but they are also the ground where alternative forms of subjectivity thrive.

13. While sociologists have not paid much attention to this dimension of TM, practitioners themselves are producing a strong and useful body of work that reflects on their own work and that of others. This is often available from the archives of listservs such as the Nettime mailinglist. It has the advantage of providing firsthand experience, personal narratives, and also a consistent theoretical corpus backing up their discourses on art, culture, and politics. At the same time one cannot but be surprised at how small and omnipresent the circle of such theorists is. This issue is well worth further investigations to uncover the internal power dynamics of knowledge production and the inherent exclusions of the process. Such elements could be important, not so much to undermine the prestige of such theoretical contributions as to offer a commentary on TM's own limitations.

14. In this chapter I align myself with Coates' broad definition of social software, loosely defined as "software which supports, extends, or derives added value from, human social behaviour—message-boards, musical taste-sharing, photo-sharing, instant messaging, mailing lists, social networking" (http://www.plasticbag.org/archives/2005/01/an_addendum_to_a_definition_of_social_software.shtml).

15. http://www.vote-auction.net/. The project "[V]ote-auction—Bringing Democracy and Capitalism Closer Together" by the Vienna-based artist duo Ubermorgen. Voteauction offered U.S. citizens an opportunity to sell their presidential vote to the highest bidder during the presidential elections in 2000. Over 2,500 global and national news features in online media, print, television, and radio have been reported (including a 27 minute. CNN feature, "Burden of Proof"). In 2005

Ubermorgen.com received a Prix Ars Electronica "Award of Distinction" for Voteauction (http://www.hansbernhard.com/index_x.html). As a reaction to repeated attempts by the U.S. government to shut down the Web site, Ubermorgen also created "IP NIC The Injunction Simulator." This is another site where anyone who does not like a Web page can "auto-generate an 'INJUNCTION,' a standard court-order, claiming the target-website to operate on an illegal basis. This document will then be sent to the appropriate dns-registrar [dns = domain name service], to the owner of the web-site and to some journalists and lawyers for legal and public processing" (http://ipnic.org/intro.html).

16. I decided to pay some attention to Web sites and mailing lists because they are a precious source of information on TM projects and events, and they play an important role in determining how actors organize and interact. However, it should be clarified that my interest does not lie in focusing on the links between Web sites as the basis for the construction of networks.

17. Organized by The Center for Media, Culture, and History at New York University and funded by The Rockefeller Foundation through its Creativity and Culture Program, that took place in April 2001.

18. For instance, Subsol: http://subsol.c3.hu/subsol_2/index.html; the Net.congestion Archive: http://www.net-congestion.net/html/introduction.html; the Makeworlds Archive: http://www.makeworlds.org.

19. I take up the issue of communication across spaces of resistance and with the mainstream in the last section of this chapter.

20. Tactical Autonomous Zones. These are unprogrammed, open presentation spaces where participants can present their their work. Registration for the TAZ is open to all festival participants and works on a first come first serve basis (http://www.next5minutes.org/n5m/program.jsp?programid=Tactical%20Autonomous%20Zone).

21. My aim is not to discuss the function of social software but to look at what kind of cultural traffic it enables for TM. Social software seems to be presently enjoying a wave of hype, with consequent attention of scholars and mainstream media (e.g., J. Schofield, Social Climbers. "*The Guardian*, http://www.guardian.co.uk/online/story/0,3605,950918,00.html (2003). Both its definition and aim have given rise to animated debates (see the blogs *Plasticbag* and *many2many*).

22. For a case study of *Nettime*, including some problematic issues concerning interaction and moderation, see G. Lovink, *Dark Fibre* (Cambridge: MA, MIT Press, 2002).

23. Of course, one could as well look at other aspects, like the *ethnoscapes* and *technoscapes* in relation to TM.

24. Appadurai has explicitly chosen the suffix -*scape* to underscore the irregular shapes of these landscapes that originate from the disjuncture between economy, culture, and politics. He also stresses that these are "deeply perspectival constructs" that reside in the individual actor "who both experience and constitute larger formations, in part form their own sense of what these landscapes offer" (Appadurai 1996: 33).

25. TM tactics can be—and increasingly are—effectively used in political campaigns by activist groups as tools of protest. It is also worth pointing out that the direction of flows between TM and mainstream is not always one-directional. In fact, a lot of the language TM subverts has its origin (and target) precisely in the language of consumer society. E.g. range from RTMark Corporation—using corporate liability laws to take corporate ownership and responsibility for many TM projects—to Web sites like Google Will Eat Itself (GWEI). GWEI is a Web project that generates money by serving Google text advertisments on Web sites and then buys Google shares with the money earned. In turn, the shares are redistributed for public ownership though GTTP, Ltd. (Google To The People Public Company) with the aim of turning Google into a public service (http://www.gwei.org).

26. A Google search yielded 297 entries, many of which were in languages other than English.

27. A term first coined by Guy Debord and the Situationists.

28. GWBush.com was a clone of Bush's official website GeorgeWBush.com containing subversive information about Bush's motives to become president. For more information, see http://www. theyesmen.org/hijinks/bush/gwbushcom.shtml. The Yes Men are a group of actors who take the place of representatives of famous corporations and institutions like the WTO to subvert their messages in the mainstream media. See www.theyesmen.org.

29. "Rustle TV Live," a TV channel, went on air for three days inside Russell Market, Bangalore. "The market presented a microcosm of the real world. Over this was forced an idealistic 'utopia.' Commerce and authorship were absent, and the group performed in the service of the community. . . . The people in the market were clients, the 'stars' and also the primary audience. They had high level of participation and control over their media." This media arts intervention was designated as part of a workshop at "Force!" new media festival and directed by Shaina Anand, filmmaker and media artist from Mumbai" (Ars Electronica 2005, Linz, Austria, installation flyer).

30. It is significant that the choice was to let everyone interact with the cameras rather than handpick a few and teach them how to make films. This is because, realistically, those actors would not have the resources to continue the work (Anand et al., 2005).

31. Future case studies can fill this gap and help answer questions on how actors make use of TM spaces in different contexts. One issue that could also be useful to the activists themselves is to look at how individuals are empowered through TM. More precisely, what are the techniques and discourses used to transform individuals from passive spectators into TM practitioners? As Cruikshank puts it, "How is subjugation transformed into subjectivity?" (1999: 3).

32. Issues of representation are an important topic in TM spaces where it is recognized that self-definition is a fundamental element for individuals and groups to negotiate their position in society: "To believe that issues of representation are now irrelevant is to believe that the very real life chances of groups and individuals are not still crucially affected by the available images circulating in any given society" (Garcia and Lovink 1997).

33. Discovolante's films can be downloaded from http://www.viveresenigallia.it/modules. php?name=News&file=categories&op=newindex&catid=27.

34. In most cases, media does not only refer to mass media (television and radio)—although these are also targets and tools of TM actions—but any kind of means to communicate a message, ranging from fliers to T-shirts and buttons.

35. Mouffe talks about multiple possible identities and sees them as "political articulation, not merely the acknowledgment of empirical differences" (Mouffe 2000: 56). This kind of identity is not a fully constituted one and is present only in the form of multiple and competing forms of identifications.

36. While using the concept of counterpublics, I understand that this tool can only be instrumental to underscore the abovementioned communicative processes of TM, at the same time raising other issues. In particular, I am not entirely comfortable with the traditional associations that theories of publics and the public sphere carry with them (e.g., Habermas, Arendt). In most cases, these notions have been developed in the context of normative discussions of democracy and implicitly assume that publics are rational agents for democratic participation and citizenship. It is not my intention here to characterize TM as ideal spaces where citizens directly partake in the life of a democracy nor to contribute to public-sphere theory. Rather, I conceive of TM as sites of struggles that are part and parcel of broader power networks—since power itself depends on a multiplicity of points of resistance (Foucault 1978: 95). In this sense, I also see the public sphere as simply another arena of social struggle.

At the same time, Warner does not consider counterpublics as preexisting, rational, and abstract entities but as self-organized intertextual frameworks (in the broadest sense of "text") constituted in the very form of address they embody. This means that counterpublics are a fictional construct to describe a social space with a potential for social transformation rather than one for recognition or replication of opinions.

37. Saint Precario is the newly born patron saint of temp workers, and his statue often appears, followed by a procession of devotees, gate-crashing international events like the Venice Film Festival or Fashion Week in Milan. See http://www.globalproject.info/art-1894.html and http://www.sanprecario.info/logo.html#.

38. For Brian Massumi, affects are moments of intensity, which might resonate with linguistic expression but do not operate on the semantic or semiotic level. Massumi differentiates affect from emotion, which is "the point of insertion of intensity into semantically and semiotically formed progressions, into narrativazible action-reaction circuits" (Massumi 2002: 28). When decoding a message, affective responses primarily originate from a gap between content and effect. More precisely, if coupled with images, language amplifies the flow of images on another level. This creates a tension that may play itself out in any number of creative ways, causing a reconfiguration of the flow of meaning (Massumi 2002: 20–25). Drawing on Deleuze and Guattari's concept of "societies of control," Massumi maintains that we are witnessing a shift from normative power to affective power. In fact, market forces—but also governments—have started intensifying and diversifying affect to extract surplus value. For this reason, he argues, there is a need to resist this new form of power by learning to function on the level of affective modulation, using "a performative, theatrical or aesthetic approach to politics" (Zournazi 2002: 212). Although necessary, this kind of convergence between the dynamics of capitalist power and resistance paradoxically runs the danger of neutralizing the impact of forms of struggle like

TM—and TM practitioners should be particularly aware of it. It is in this context that the debate on the commodification of "political" art and the need for long-term commitments should be read. At the same time though, TM's role as a site to test viable "affective approaches to resistance" remains relevant, especially if situated in a broader context that connects such practices with other sites of struggles and strengthens their resources.

39. Here, Appadurai's idea of cultural global flows helps us see how the *ideoscapes* and the *mediascapes* of TM have an impact on the creation of publics at the local level. It is true that there is a global dimension to this flux of ideas, images, and people in the spaces I described above. Yet, the whole picture can only make sense if rooted in the locality of each project.

40. Whether this is always a positive step depends on the degree of autonomy each project can retain.

41. The relationship between counterpublics and institutions is a complex one and it often leads groups to make compromises between their oppositional stance and forms of agency and the dominant discourses. Warner maintains that "for many counter-publics, to do so is to cede the original hope of transforming not just policy but the space of public life itself" (Warner 2002: 124).

42. Elsewhere I take up the specific ontological and methodological questions related to the development of an activist sociology. See Alessandra Renzi, "Cartographies of Resistance: Knowledge Production within a Practical Sociology," paper presented at the ASCA International Workshop, *Inside Knowledge: (Un)doing Methodologies, Imagining Alternatives*. University of Amsterdam, March 28–30, 2007.

References

Anand, Shaina, OrfeoTV, and Alessandra Renzi. 2005. *Videoconversation* (unreleased video footage). Ars Electronica, Linz, Austria.

Appadurai, Arjun. 1996. *Modernity at Large: Cultural Dimensions of Globalization*. Minneapolis: University of Minnesota Press.

Bourdieu, Pierre. 1990. "The Scholastic Point of View." *Cultural Anthropology* 5 (4):380–391.

Broeckmann, Andreas, David Garcia, and Geert Lovink. 2002. "The GHI of Tactical Media." *Artnodes* (2):5. http://www.uoc.edu/artnodes/eng/art/broeckmann0902/broeckmann0902.html#.

Butler, Judith. 2005. "What is Critique? An Essay on Foucault's Virtue." http://www.law.Berkeley. edu/cenpro/kadish/what%20is%20critique%20J%20Butler.

Calhoun, Craig. 2002. "The Necessity and Limits of Cosmopolitanism." Paper read at UNESCO/ ISSC conference, "Identity and Difference in the Global Era" (20–23 May 2001), at Rio de Janeiro: EDUCAM.

Castells, Manuel. 2001. *The Internet Galaxy: Reflections on the Internet, Business, and Society*. Oxford University Press.

———. 2004. The *Power of Identity*. Vol. II, *The Information Age: Economy, Society and Culture*. London: Blackwell.

Couzens Hoy, David, ed. 1986. *Foucault: A Critical Reader*. Cambridge: Blackwell.

Cruikshank, Barbara. 1999. *The Will to Empower: Democratic Citizens and Other Subjects*. Ithaca, NY: Cornell University Press.

de Certeau, Michel. 1984, *The Practice of Everyday Life*. Berkeley: University of California Press.

Day, Richard J. F. 2005. *Gramsci Is Dead: Anarchist Currents in the Newest Social Movements*. Toronto: Between the Lines.

Deleuze, Gilles. 1988. *Foucault*. Edited by and translated by Seán Hand. London: Athlone.

———. 1995. *Negotiations*, 1972–1990. New York: Columbia University Press.

Deleuze, Gilles, and Félix Guattari. 2000. A *Thousand Plateaus: Capitalism and Schizophrenia*. Translated and introduced by Brian Massumi. Minneapolis: University of Minnesota Press.

Foucault, Michel. 1978. *The History of Sexuality: An Introduction*. Translated by R. J. Hurly. Harmondsworth: Penguin.

———. 1991. *Remarks on Marx*. Translated by R. James Goldstein and Duccio Trombadori. New York: Semiotext(e).

Garcia, David. 2005. "Autolabs: Critiquing Utopia." *Mute: Culture and Politics after the Net* (29): 28–30.

———. 2006. "Learning the Right Lessons." *Mute Beta: Culture and Politics after the Net*. http://www.metamute.org/en/Learning-the-Right-Lessons.

Garcia, David, and Geert Lovink. 1997. "The ABC of Tactical Media." http://www.debalie.nl/dossierartikel.jsp?dossierid=22375&articleid=1638.

———. 1999. "The DEF of Tactical Media." http://www.nettime.org/Lists-Archives/nettime-1-9902/msg00104.html.

Guattari, Felix. 1996. *The Guattari Reader* Edited by G. Genosko. Cambridge: Blackwell.

Hanke, Bob. 2005. "For a Political Economy of Indymedia Practice". *Canadian Journal of Communication* 30 (1):41–64.

Holmes, Brian. 2006. "Let's Have a Discussion." *Mute Beta: Culture and Politics after the Net*. http://www.metamute.org/en/Learning-the-Right-Lessons.

Lovink, Geert. 2002. *Dark Fibre*. Cambridge: MIT Press.

———. 2003. *My First Recession*. Rotterdam: V2_Publishing/NAi Publishers.

Massey, Doreen. 1994. *Space, Place and Gender*. Minneapolis: University of Minnesota Press.

Massumi, Brian. 2002. *Parables for the Virtual: Movement, Affect, Sensation*. Durham and London: Duke University Press.

McCaughey, Martha, and Michael D. Ayers, eds. 2003. *Cyberactivism: Online Activism in Theory and Practice*. New York: Routledge.

McKenzie, Jon, and Rebecca Schneider. 2000. "Interview. Critical Art Ensemble: Tactical Media Practitioners." *TDR: The Drama Review* 44 (4):136–150.

Meikle, Graham. 2002. *Future Active. Media Activism and the Internet*. London: Routledge.

Melucci, Alberto. 1996. *Challenging Codes: Collective action in the Information Age*. Cambridge: Cambridge University Press.

Mouffe, Chantal. 2000. "Politics and Passions: the Stakes of Democracy." *Ethical Perspectives* 7:146–150.

———. 2001. "Every Form of Art Has a Political Dimension." *Grey Room* 02:98–125.

Pile, Steve, and Michael Keith. 1997. *Geographies of Resistance*. London and New York: Routledge.

Richardson, Joanne. 2002. "The Language of Tactical Media." *Next 5 Minutes*. http://www.n5m4.org/journal5e2d.html?118+275+1410.

Rosas, Ricardo. 2004a. "Digitofagy." http://www.discordia.us/scoop/special/eadobbs/indexa15f.html?eaid=97.

———. 2004b. "Midia Tatica Brasil." http://www.midiatatica.org/mtb/mtb_ingles.htm.

Schofield, Jack. 2003. "Social climbers." *The Guardian*, Thursday May 8, 2003, http://www.guardian. co.uk/online/story/0,3605,950918,00.html.

Thompson, Andrew K. 2006. "Making Friends with Failure" *Upping the Anti: A Journal of Theory and Action* 3:77–92.

van de Donk, Wim, Brian D. Loader, Paul G. Nixon, and Dieter Ruch, eds. 2004. *Cyberprotest. New Media, Citizens and Social Movements*. London: Rutledge.

VCB. 2002. "Defining Tactical Media." *The Virtual Casebook Project*. http://www.nyu.edu/fas/projects/vcb/case_911_FLASHcontent.html.

Verna, Sandro. 2005. "Conversation with the Author." Sant'Agapito Film Festival, Sant'Agapito, Italy.

Warner, Michael. 2002. *Publics and Counterpublics*. New York: Zone Books.

Wilson, Peter Lamborn. 1997. "A Network of Castles." http://www.hermetic.com/bey/network-castles.html.

Zournazi, Mary. 2002. "Navigating Movements: Interview with Brian Massumi." In *Hope: New Philosophies for Change*, 210–243. Annandale: Pluto Press.

3 Communicative Capitalism: Circulation and the Foreclosure of Politics

Jodi Dean

No Response

Although mainstream U.S. media outlets provided the Bush administration with supportive, noncritical, and even encouraging platforms for making his case for invading Iraq, critical perspectives were nonetheless well represented in the communications flow of mediated global capitalist technoculture. Alternative media, independent media, and non-U.S. media provided thoughtful reports, insightful commentary, and critical evaluations of the "evidence" of weapons of mass destruction in Iraq. Amy Goodman's syndicated radio program, "Democracy Now," regularly broadcast shows intensely opposed to the militarism and unilateralism of the Bush administration's national security politicy. The *Nation* magazine offered detailed and nuanced critiques of various reasons introduced for attacking Iraq. Circulating on the Internet were lists with congressional phone and fax numbers, petitions, and announcements for marches, protests, and direct-action training sessions. As the march to war proceeded, thousands of bloggers commented on each step, referencing other media supporting their positions. When mainstream U.S. news outlets failed to cover demonstrations such as the September protest of 400,000 people in London or the October march on Washington when 250,000 people surrounded the White House, myriad progressive, alternative, and critical left news outlets supplied frequent and reliable information about the action on the ground. All in all, a strong antiwar message was out there.

But, the message was not received. It circulated, reduced to the medium. Even when the White House acknowledged the massive worldwide demonstrations of February 15, 2003, Bush simply reiterated the fact that a message was out there, circulating—the protestors had the right to express their opinions. He didn't actually respond to their message. He didn't treat the words and actions of the protestors as sending a message to him to which he was in some sense obligated to respond. Rather, he acknowledged that there existed views different from his own. There were his views and there were other views; all had the right to exist, to be expressed—but that in no way meant, or so Bush made it seem, that these views were involved with each other. So, despite the terabytes of commentary and information, there wasn't exactly a debate over the war. On the contrary, in the days and weeks prior to the U.S. invasion of Iraq, the antiwar messages morphed into so much circulating content, just like all the other cultural effluvia wafting through cyberia.

We might express this disconnect between engaged criticism and national strategy in terms of a distinction between politics as the circulation of content and politics as official policy. On the one hand, there is media chatter of various kinds—from television talking heads, radio shock jocks, and the gamut of print media to Web sites with RSS (Real Simple Syndication) feeds, blogs, e-mail lists, and the proliferating versions of instant text messaging. In this dimension, politicians, governments, and activists struggle for visibility, currency, and, in the now quaint term from the dot-com years, mindshare. On the other hand are institutional politics, the day-to-day activities of bureaucracies, lawmakers, judges, and the apparatuses of the police and national security states. These components of the political system seem to run independently of the politics that circulates as content.

At first glance, this distinction between politics as the circulation of content and politics as the activity of officials makes no sense. After all, the very premise of liberal democracy is the sovereignty of the people. And, governance by the people has generally been thought in terms of communicative freedoms of speech, assembly, and the press, norms of publicity that emphasize transparency and accountability, and the deliberative practices of the public sphere. Ideally, the communicative interactions of the public sphere, what I've been referring to as the circulation of content and media chatter—are supposed to impact official politics.

In the United States today, however, they don't, or, less bluntly put, there is a significant disconnect between politics circulating as content and official politics. Today, the circulation of content in the dense, intensive networks of global communications relieves top-level actors (corporate, institutional, and governmental) from the obligation to respond. Rather than responding to messages sent by activists and critics, they counter with their own contributions to the circulating flow of communications, hoping that sufficient volume (whether in terms of number of contributions or the spectacular nature of a contribution) will give their contributions dominance or stickiness. Instead of engaged debates, instead of contestations employing common terms, points of reference, or demarcated frontiers, we confront a multiplication of resistances and assertions so extensive that it hinders the formation of strong counterhegemonies. The proliferation, distribution, acceleration, and intensification of communicative access and opportunity, far from enhancing democratic governance or resistance, results in precisely the opposite, the postpolitical formation of communicative capitalism.

Needless to say, I am not claiming that networked communications never facilitate political resistance. One of the most visible of the numerous examples to the contrary is perhaps the experience of B92 in Serbia. Radio B92 used the Internet to circumvent governmental censorship and disseminate news of massive demonstrations against the Milosevic regime.[1] My point is that the political efficacy of networked media depends on its context. Under conditions of the intensive and extensive proliferation of media, messages are more likely to get lost as mere contributions to the circulation of content. What enhances democracy in one context becomes a new form of hegemony in another. Differently put, the intense circulation of content in communicative capitalism forecloses the antagonism necessary for politics. In relatively closed societies, that antagonism is not only already there but also apparent at and as the very frontier between open and closed.

My argument proceeds as follows. For the sake of clarity, I begin by situating the notion of communicative capitalism in the context of other theories of the present that emphasize changes in communication and communicability. I then move to emphasize specific features of communicative capitalism in light of the fantasies animating them. First, I take up the fantasy of abundance and discuss the ways this fantasy results in a shift in the basic unit of communication from the message to the contribution. Second, I address the fantasy of activity or participation. I argue that this fantasy is materialized through technology fetishism. Finally, I consider the fantasy of wholeness that relies on and produces a global both imaginary and Real. I argue that this fantasy prevents the emergence of a clear division between friend and enemy, resulting instead in the more dangerous and profound figuring of the other as a threat to be destroyed. My goal in providing this account of communicative capitalism is to explain why, in an age celebrated for its communications, there is no response.

In the months before the 2002 congressional elections, just as the administration urged congress to abdicate its constitutional responsibility to declare war to the president, mainstream media frequently employed the trope of "debate." Democratic "leaders," with an eye to this "debate," asserted that questions needed to be asked. They did not take a position or provide a clear alternative to the Bush administration's emphasis on preventive war. Giving voice to the ever-present meme regarding the White House's public relations strategy, people on the street spoke of whether Bush had "made his case." Nevertheless, on the second day of Senate debate on the use of force in Iraq, *no one* was on the floor—even though many were in the gallery. Why, at a time when the means of communication have been revolutionized, when people can contribute their opinions and access those of others rapidly and immediately, why has democracy failed? Why has the expansion and intensification of communication networks, the proliferation of the very tools of democracy, coincided with the collapse of democratic deliberation and, indeed, struggle? These are the questions the idea of communicative capitalism helps us answer.

Communicative Capitalism

The notion of communicative capitalism conceptualizes the commonplace idea that the market, today, is the site of democratic aspirations, indeed, the mechanism by which the will of the demos manifests itself. We might think here of the circularity of claims regarding popularity. McDonalds, Walmart, and reality television are depicted as popular because they seem to offer what people want. How do we know they offer what people want? People choose them. So, they must be popular.

The obvious problem with this equation is the way it treats commercial choices as the paradigmatic form of choice per se. But the market is not a system for delivering political outcomes—despite the fact that political campaigns are indistinguishable from advertising or marketing campaigns. Political decisions—to go to war, say, or to establish the perimeters of legitimate relationships—involve more than the mindless reiteration of faith, conviction, and unsupported claims (I'm thinking here of the Bush administration's faith-based foreign policy and they way it pushed a link between Iraq and Al Qaeda.) The concept of communicative capitalism tries to capture this strange merging of democracy and capitalism. It does so by highlighting the way networked communications bring the two together.

Communicative capitalism designates that form of late capitalism in which values heralded as central to democracy take material form in networked communications technologies.[2] Ideals of access, inclusion, discussion, and participation come to be realized in and through expansions, intensifications, and interconnections of global telecommunications. But instead of leading to more equitable distributions of wealth and influence, instead of enabling the emergence of a richer variety in modes of living and practices of freedom, the deluge of screens and spectacles undermines political opportunity and efficacy for most of the world's peoples.

Research on the impact of economic globalization makes clear how the speed, simultaneity, and interconnectivity of electronic communications produce massive concentrations of wealth.[3] Not only does the possibility of super-profits in the finance and services complex lead to hypermobility of capital and the devalorization of manufacturing, but financial markets themselves acquire the capacity to discipline national governments. In the United States, moreover, the proliferation of media has been accompanied by a shift in political participation. Rather than actively organized in parties and unions, politics has become a domain of financially mediated and professionalized practices centered on advertising, public relations, and the means of mass communication. Indeed, with the commodification of communication, more and more domains of life seem to have been reformatted in terms of market and spectacle. Bluntly put, the standards of a finance- and consumption-driven entertainment culture set the very terms of democratic governance today. Changing the system—organizing against and challenging communicative capitalism—seems to require strengthening the system: how else can one organize and get the message across? Doesn't it require raising the money, buying the television time, registering the domain name, building the Web site, and making the links?

My account of communicative capitalism is affiliated with Georgio Agamben's discussion of the alienation of language in the society of the spectacle and with Slavoj Žižek's emphasis on postpolitics. And, even as it shares the description of communication as capitalist production with Michael Hardt and Antonio Negri, it differs from their assessment of the possibilities for political change.

More specifically, Agamben notes that "in the old regime . . . the estrangement of the communicative essence of human beings was substantiated as a presupposition that had the function of a common ground (nation, language, religion, etc.)."[4] Under current conditions, however, "it is precisely this same communicativity, this same generic essence (language), that is constituted as an autonomous sphere to the extent to which it becomes the essential factor of the production cycle. What hinders communication, therefore, is communicability itself: human beings are being separated by what unites them." Agamben is pointing out how the commonality of the nation-state was thought in terms of linguistic and religious groups. We can extend his point by recognizing that the ideal of constitutional states, in theories such as Jürgen Habermas's, say, has also been conceptualized in terms of the essential communicativity of human beings: those who can discuss, who can come to an agreement with one another, at least in principle, can be in political relation to one another. As Agamben makes clear, however, communication has detached itself from political ideals of belonging and connection to function today as a primarily economic form. Differently put, communicative exchanges, rather than fundamental to democratic politics, are the basic elements of capitalist production.

Žižek approaches this same problem of the contemporary foreclosure of the political via the concept of "postpolitics." Žižek explains that postpolitics "emphasizes the need to leave old ideological divisions behind and confront new issues, armed with the necessary expert knowledge and free deliberation that takes people's concrete needs and demands into account."[5] Postpolitics thus begins from the premise of consensus and cooperation. Real antagonism or dissent is foreclosed. Matters previously thought to require debate and struggle are now addressed as personal issues or technical concerns. We might think of the ways that the expert discourses of psychology and sociology provide explanations for anger and resentment, in effect treating them as syndromes to be managed rather than as issues to be politicized. Or we might think of the probabilities, measures, and assessments characteristic of contemporary risk management. The problem is that all this tolerance and attunement to difference and emphasis on hearing another's pain prevent politicization. Matters aren't represented—they don't stand for something beyond themselves. They are simply treated in all their particularity, as specific issues to be addressed therapeutically, juridically, spectacularly, or disciplinarily rather than being treated as elements of larger signifying chains or political formations. Indeed, this is how third-way societies support global capital: they prevent politicization. They focus on administration, again, foreclosing the very possibility that things might be otherwise.

The postpolitical world, then, is marked by emphases on multiple sources of value, on the plurality of beliefs, and the importance of tolerating these beliefs through the cultivation of an attunement to the contingencies already pervading one's own values. Divisions between friends and enemies are replaced by emphases on all of us. Likewise, politics is understood as not confined to specific institutional fields but as a characteristic of all of life. There is an attunement, in other words, to a micropolitics of the everyday. But this very attunement forecloses the conflict and opposition necessary for politics.

Finally, Hardt's and Negri's description of the current techno-global-capitalist formation coincides with Agamben's account of communication without communicability and with Žižek's portrayal of a global formation characterized by contingency, multiplicity, and singularity. For example, they agree that "communication is the form of capitalist production in which capital has succeeded in submitting society entirely and globally to its regime, suppressing all alternative paths."[6] Emphasizing that there is no outside to the new order of Empire, Hardt and Negri see the whole of Empire as an "open site of conflict" wherein the incommunicability of struggles, rather than a problem, is an asset insofar as it releases opposition from the pressure of organization and prevents cooptation. This position, while inspiring, not only embraces the elision between the political and the economic, but in so doing cedes primacy to the economic, taking hope from the intensity and immediacy of the crises within Empire. The view I advocate is less optimistic insofar as it rejects the notion that anything is immediately political and instead prioritizes politicization as the difficult challenge of representing specific claims or acts as universal.[7] Specific or singular acts of resistance, statements of opinion, or instances of transgression are not political in and of themselves. Rather, they have to be politicized, that is, articulated together with other struggles, resistances, and ideals in the course or context of opposition to a shared enemy or opponent.[8] Crucial to this task, then, is understanding how communicative capitalism, especially insofar as it relies on networked communications, prevents politicization. To this end, I turn now to the fantasies animating communicative capitalism.

The Fantasy of Abundance: From Message to Contribution

The delirium of the dot-com years was driven by a tremendous faith in speed, volume, and connectivity. The speed and volume of transactions, say, was itself to generate new "synergies" and, hence, wealth. A similar belief underlies the conviction that enhanced communications access facilitates democracy. More people than ever before can make their opinions known. The convenience of the Web, for example, enables millions not simply to access information but to register their points of view, to agree or disagree, to vote, and to send messages. The sheer abundance of messages, then, is offered as an indication of democratic potential.

In fact, optimists and pessimists alike share this same fantasy of abundance. Those optimistic about the impact of networked communications on democratic practices emphasize the wealth of information available on the Internet and the inclusion of millions upon millions of voices or points of view into "the conversation" or "public sphere." Pessimists worry about the lack of filters, the data smog, and the fact that "all kinds of people" can be part of the conversation.[9] Despite their differing assessments of the value of abundance, then, both optimists and pessimists are committed to the view that networked communications are characterized by exponential expansions in opportunities to transmit and receive messages.

The fantasy of abundance covers over the way facts and opinions, images and reactions circulate in a massive stream of content, losing their specificity and merging with and into the data flow. Any given message is thus a contribution to this ever-circulating content. My argument is that a constitutive feature of communicative capitalism is precisely this morphing of message into contribution. Let me explain.

One of the most basic formulations of the idea of communication is in terms of a message and the response to the message.[10] Under communicative capitalism, this changes. Messages are contributions to circulating content—not actions to elicit responses. Differently put, the exchange value of messages overtakes their use value. So, a message is no longer primarily a message from a sender to a receiver. Uncoupled from contexts of action and application—as on the Web or in print and broadcast media—the message is simply part of a circulating data stream. Its particular content is irrelevant. Who sent it is irrelevant. Who receives it is irrelevant. That it need be responded to is irrelevant. The only thing that is relevant is circulation, the addition to the pool. Any particular contribution remains secondary to the fact of circulation. The value of any particular contribution is likewise inversely proportionate to the openness, inclusivity, or extent of a circulating data stream—the more opinions or comments that are out there, the less of an impact any one given one might make (and the more shock, spectacle, or newness that is necessary for a contribution to register or have an impact). In sum, communication functions symptomatically to produce its own negation. Or, to return to Agamben's terms, communicativity hinders communication.

Communication in communicative capitalism, then, is not, as Habermas would suggest, action oriented toward reaching understanding.[11] In Habermas's model of communicative action, the use value of a message depends on its orientation. In sending a message, a sender intends for it to be received and understood. Any acceptance or rejection of the message depends on this understanding. Understanding is thus a *necessary* part of the communicative exchange. In communicative capitalism, however, the use value of a message is less important than its exchange value, its contribution to a larger pool, flow, or circulation of content. A contribution need not be understood; it need only be repeated, reproduced, forwarded. Circulation is the context, the condition for the acceptance or rejection of a contribution. Put somewhat differently, how a contribution circulates determines whether it had been accepted or rejected. And, just as the producer, labor, drops out of the picture in commodity exchange, so does the sender (or author) become immaterial to the contribution. The circulation of logos, branded media identities, rumors, catch phrases, even positions and arguments exemplifies this point. The popularity, the penetration and duration of a contribution, marks its acceptance or success.

Thinking about messages in terms of use value and contributions in terms of exchange value sheds light on what would otherwise appear to be an asymmetry in communicative capitalism: the fact that some messages are received, that some discussions extend beyond the context of their circulation. Of course, it is also the case that many commodities are not useless, that people need them. But, what makes them commodities is not the need people have for them or, obviously, their use. Rather, it is their economic function, their role in capitalist exchange. Similarly, the fact that messages can retain a relation to understanding in no way negates the centrality of their circulation. Indeed, this link is crucial to the ideological reproduction of communicative capitalism. Some messages, issues, debates, are effective. Some contributions make a difference. But more significant is the system, the communicative network. Even when we know that our specific contributions (our messages, posting, books, articles, films, letters to the editor) simply circulate in a rapidly moving and changing flow of content, in contributing, in participating, we act as if we do not know this. This action manifests ideology as the belief underlying action, the belief that reproduces communicative capitalism.[12]

The fantasy of abundance both expresses and conceals the shift from message to contribution. It expresses the shift through its emphases on expansions in communication—faster, better, cheaper; more inclusive, more accessible; high-speed, broadband, etc. Yet even as it emphasizes these multiple expansions and intensifications, this abundance, the fantasy occludes the resulting devaluation of any particular contribution. Social network analysis demonstrates clearly the way that blogs, like other citation networks, follow a power law distribution. They don't scale; instead, the top few are much more popular than the middle few, and the middle are vastly more popular than the smaller. Some call this the emergence of an A-list or the 80/20 rule. As Clay Shirkey summarily puts it, "Diversity plus freedom of choice creates inequality, and the greater the diversity, the more extreme the inequality."[13] Emphasis on the fact that one can contribute to a discussion and make one's opinion known misdirects attention from the larger system of communication in which the contribution is embedded.

Put somewhat differently, networked communications are celebrated for enabling everyone to contribute, participate, and be heard. The form this communication takes, then, isn't concealed. People are fully aware of the media, the networks, even the surfeit of information. But, they act as if they don't have this knowledge, believing in the importance of their contributions, presuming, say, that there are readers for their blogs. Why? As I explain in the next section, I think it involves the way networked communications induce a kind of registration effect that supports a fantasy of participation.

The Fantasy of Participation: Technology Fetishism

In their online communications, people are apt to express intense emotions, intimate feelings, some of the more secret or significant aspects of their sense of who they are. Years ago, while surfing through Yahoo's home pages, I found the page of a guy who featured pictures of his dog, his parents, and himself fully erect in an s/m style harness. At the bottom of his site was the typical, "Thanks for stopping by! Don't forget to write and tell me what you think!" I mention this quaint image to point to how easy many find it to reveal themselves on the Internet. Not only are people accustomed to putting their thoughts online but also, in so doing, they believe their thoughts and ideas are registering—*write and tell me what you think*! Contributing to the infostream, we might say, has a subjective registration effect. One *believes* that it matters, that it contributes, that it means something.

Precisely because of this registration effect, people believe that their contribution to circulating content is a kind of communicative action. They believe that they are active, maybe even that they are making a difference simply by clicking on a button, adding their name to a petition, or commenting on a blog. Žižek describes this kind of false activity with the term "interpassivity." When we are interpassive, something else, a fetish object, is active in our stead.

Žižek explains: "You think you are active, while your true position, as embodied in the fetish, is passive."[14] The frantic activity of the fetish works to prevent actual action, to prevent something from really happening. This suggests to me the way activity on the Net, frantic contributing and content circulation, may well involve a profound passivity, one that is interconnected, linked, but passive nonetheless. Put back in terms of the circulation of contributions that fail to coalesce into actual debates, that fail as messages in need of response, we might think of this odd interpassivity as content that is linked to other content, but never fully connected.

Weirdly, then, the circulation of communication is depoliticizing, not because people don't care or don't want to be involved, but because we do! Or, put more precisely, it is depoliticizing because the form of our involvement ultimately empowers those it is supposed to resist. Struggles on the Net reiterate struggles in real life, but insofar as they reiterate these struggles, they displace them. And this displacement, in turn, secures and protects the space of "official" politics. This suggests another reason communication functions fetishistically today: as a disavowal of a more fundamental political disempowerment or castration. Approaching this fetishistic disavowal from a different direction, we can ask, if Freud is correct in saying that a fetish not only covers over a trauma but that in so doing it helps one through a trauma, what might serve as an analogous sociopolitical trauma today? In my view, in the United States a likely answer can be found in the loss of opportunities for political impact and efficacy. In the face of the constraining of states to the demands and conditions of global markets, the dramatic decrease in union membership and increase in corporate salaries and benefits at the highest levels, and the shift in political parties from person-intensive to finance-intensive organization strategies, the political opportunities open to most Americans are either voting, which increasing numbers choose not to do, or giving money. Thus, it is not surprising that many might want to be more active and might feel that action online is a way of getting their voice heard, a way of making a contribution.

Indeed, interactive communication technology corporations rose to popularity in part on the message that they were tools for political empowerment. One might think of Ted Nelson, Stewart Brand, the People's Computer Company, and their emancipatory images of computing technology. In the context of the San Francisco Bay Area's anti-war activism of the early seventies, they held up computers as the means to the renewal of participatory democracy. One might also think of the image projected by Apple Computers. Apple presented itself as changing the world, as saving democracy by bringing technology to the people. In 1984, Apple ran an ad for the Macintosh that placed an image of the computer next to one of Karl Marx. The slogan was, "It was about time a capitalist started a revolution." Finally, one might also recall the guarantees of citizens' access and the lure of town meetings for millions, the promises of democratization and education that drove Al Gore and Newt Gingrich's political rhetoric in the nineties as Congress worked through the Information and Infrastructure Technology Act, the National Information Infrastructure Act (both passing in 1993), and the 1996 Telecommunications Act. These bills made explicit a convergence of democracy and capitalism, a rhetorical convergence that the bills brought into material form. As the 1996 bill affirmed: "The market will drive both the Internet and the information highway."[15] In all these cases, driving the Net is the promise of political efficacy, of the enhancement of democracy through citizens' access and use of new communications technologies. But, the promise of participation is not simply propaganda. No, it is a deeper, underlying fantasy wherein technology functions as a fetish covering over our impotence and helping us understand ourselves as active. The working of such a fantasy is clear in discussions of the political impact of a new device, system, code, or platform. A particular technological innovation becomes a screen upon which all sorts of fantasies of political action are projected.

We might think here of peer-to-peer file-sharing, especially in light of the early rather hypnotic, mantra-like, appeals to Napster. Napster—despite that fact that it was a commercial venture—was heralded as a sea change; it would transform private property, bring down capitalism. More than piracy, Napster was a popular attack on private property itself. Nick Dyer-Witherford, for example, argues that Napster, and other peer-to-peer networks, present "real possibilities of market disruption as a result of large-scale copyright violation." He contends:

While some of these peer-to-peer networks—like Napster—were created as commercial applications, others—such as Free Net—were designed as political projects with the explicit intention of destroying both state censorship and commercial copyright. . . . The adoption of these celebratory systems as a central component of North American youth culture presents a grassroots expansion of the digital commons and, at the very least, seriously problematizes current plans for their enclosure.[16]

Lost in the celebratory rhetoric is the fact that capitalism has never depended on one industry. Industries rise and fall. Corporations like Sony and Bertelsmann can face declines in one sector and still make astronomical profits in other ones. Joshua Gamson's point about the legacy of Internet-philia is appropriate here: wildly displaced enthusiasm over the political impact of a specific technological practice results in a tendency "to bracket institutions and ownership, to research and theorize uses and users of new media outside of those brackets, and to 'newness' overshadow historical continuity."[17] Worries about the loss of the beloved paperback book to unwieldy e-books weren't presented as dooming the publishing industry or assaulting the very regime of private property. Why should sharing music files be any different?

It shouldn't—and that is my point. Napster is a technological fetish onto which all sorts of fantasies of political action are projected. Here, of course, the fantasy is one deeply held by music fans: music can change the world. And, armed with networked personal computers, the weapons of choice for American college students in a not-so-radical, oh-so-consumerist entertainment culture, the wired revolutionaries could think they were changing the world, comforted all the while that nothing would really change (or, at best, they could get record companies to lower the prices on compact disks).

The technological fetish covers over and sustains a lack on the part of the subject. That is to say, it protects the fantasy of an active, engaged subject by acting in the subject's stead. The technological fetish "is political" for us, enabling us to go about the rest of our lives relieved of the guilt that we might not be doing our part and secure in the belief that we are after all informed, engaged citizens. The paradox of the technological fetish is that the technology acting in our stead actually enables us to remain politically passive. We don't have to assume political responsibility because, again, the technology is doing it for us.

The technological fetish also covers over a fundamental lack or absence in the social order. It protects a fantasy of unity, wholeness, or order, compensating in advance for this impossibility. Differently put, technologies are invested with hopes and dreams, with aspirations to something better. A technological fetish is at work when one disavows the lack or fundamental antagonism forever rupturing (yet producing) the social by advocating a particular technological fix. The "fix" lets us think that all we need is to universalize a particular technology, and then we will have a democratic or reconciled social order.

Gamson's account of gay Web sites provides a compelling illustration of this fetish function. Gamson argues that in the United States, the Internet has been a major force in transforming "gay and lesbian media from organizations answering at least partly to geographical and political communities into businesses answering primarily to advertisers and investors."[18] He focuses on gay portals and their promises to offer safe and friendly spaces for the gay community. What he notes, however, is the way that these safe gay spaces now function primarily "to deliver a market share to corporations." As he explains, "community needs are conflated with consumption desires, and community equated with market."[19] Qua fetish, the portal is a screen upon which fantasies of connection can be projected. These fantasies displace attention from their commercial context.

Specifying more clearly the operation of the technological fetish will bring home the way new communications technologies reinforce communicative capitalism. I emphasize three operations: condensation, displacement, and foreclosure.

The technological fetish operates through *condensation*. The complexities of politics—of organization, struggle, duration, decisiveness, division, representation, etc.—are condensed into one thing, one problem to be solved and one technological solution. So, the problem of democracy is that people aren't informed; they don't have the information they need to participate effectively. Bingo! Information technologies provide people with information. This sort of strategy, however, occludes the problems of organizing and political will. For example, in the United States, as Mary Graham explains in her study of the politics of disclosure in chemical emissions, food labeling, and medical error policy, transparency started to function as a regulatory mechanism precisely at a time when legislative action seemed impossible. Agreeing that people had a right to know, politicians could argue for warning labels and more data while avoiding hard or unpopular decisions. Corporations could comply—and find ways to use their reports to improve their market position. "Companies often lobbied for national disclosure requirements," Graham writes. "They did so," she continues, "because they believed that disclosure could reduce the chances of tougher regulation, eliminate the threat of multiple state requirements, or improve competitive advantage. . . . Likewise, large food processing companies and most trade associations supported national nutritional labeling as an alternative to multiple state requirements and new regulations, or to a crackdown on health claims. Some also expected competitive gain from labeling as consumers, armed with accurate information, increased demand for authentically healthful productions."[20] Additional examples of condensation appear when cybertheorists and activists emphasize singular Web sites, blogs, and events. The MediaWhoresOnline blog might be celebrated as a location of critical commentary on mainstream and conservative journalism—but it is also so small that it doesn't show up on blog ranking sites like daypop or Technorati.

The second mode of operation of the technological fetish is through displacement. I've addressed this idea already in my description of Napster and the way that the technological fetish is political for us. But I want to expand this sense of displacement to account for tendencies in some theory writing to displace political energies elsewhere. Politics is displaced upon the activities of everyday or ordinary people—as if the writer and readers and academics and activists and, yes, even the politicians, were somehow extraordinary. What the everyday people do in their everyday lives is supposed to overflow with political activity: conflicts, negotiations, interpretations, resistances, collusions, cabals, transgressions, and resignifications. The Net—as well as cell phones, beepers, and other communications devices (though, weirdly, not the regular old telephone)—is thus teeming with politics. To put up a Web site, to deface a Web site, to redirect hits to other sites, to deny access to a Web site, to link to a Web site—this is construed as real political action. In my view, this sort of emphasis displaces political energy from the hard work of organizing and struggle. It also remains oddly one-sided, conveniently forgetting both the larger media context of these activities, as if there were not and have not been left and progressive print publications and organizations for years, and the political context of networked communications—the Republican party as well as all sorts of other conservative organizations and lobbyists use the Internet just as much, if not more, than progressive groups.

Writing on Many-2-Many, a group weblog on social software, Clay Shirkey invokes a similar argument to explain Howard Dean's poor showing in the Iowa caucuses following what appeared to be his remarkable successes on the Internet. Shirkey writes:

We know well from past attempts to use social software to organize groups for political change that it is hard, very hard, because participation in online communities often provides a sense of satisfaction that actually dampens a willingness to interact with the real world. When you're communing with like-minded souls, you *feel* [emphasis in original] like you're accomplishing something by arguing out the smallest details of your perfect future world, while the imperfect and actual world takes no notice, as is its custom.

There are many reasons for this, but the main one seems to be that the pleasures of life online are precisely the way they provide a respite from the vagaries of the real world. Both the way the online environment flattens interaction and the way everything gets arranged for the convenience of the user makes the threshold between talking about changing the world and changing the world even steeper than usual.[21]

This does not mean that web-based activities are trivial or that social software is useless. The Web provides an important medium for connecting and communicating, and the Dean campaign was innovative in its use of social software to build a vital, supportive movement around Dean's candidacy. But, the pleasures of the medium should not displace our attention from the ways that political change demands much, much more than networked communication and the way that the medium itself can and does provide a barrier against action on the ground. As the Dean campaign also demonstrates, without organized, mobilized action on the ground, without responses to and from caucus attendees in Iowa, say, Internet politics remain precisely that—a politics of and through new media, and that's all.

The last operation of the technological fetish follows from the previous ones: fore-closure. As I've suggested, the political purchase of the technological fetish is given in advance; it is immediate, presumed, understood. File-sharing *is* political. A Web site *is* political. Blogging *is* political. But this very immediacy rests on something else, on a prior exclusion. And, what is excluded is the possibility of politicization proper. Consider this breathless proclamation from Geert Lovink and Florian Schneider:

> The revolution of our age should come as no surprise. It has been announced for a long time. It is anticipated in the advantage of the open source idea over archaic terms of property. It is based on the steady decline of the traditional client-server architecture and the phenomenal rise of peer-to-peer-technologies. It is practiced already on a daily basis: the overwhelming success of open standards, free software and file-sharing tools shows a glimpse of the triumph of a code that will transform knowledge-production into a world-writable mode. Today revolution means the wikification of the world; it means creating many different versions of worlds, which every-one can read, write, edit and execute.[22]

Saying that "revolution means the wikification" of the world employs an illegitimate short-circuit. More specifically, it relies on an ontologization such that the political nature of the world is produced by particular technological practices. Struggle, conflict, and context vanish, immediately and magically. Or, put somewhat differently, they are foreclosed, eliminated in advance so as to create a space for the utopian celebration of open source.

To ontologize the political is to collapse the very symbolic space necessary for politi-cization, a space between an object and its representation, its ability to stand for something beyond itself. The power of the technological fetish stems from this fore-closure of the political. Bluntly put, a condition of possibility for asserting the imme-diately political character of something Web-radio or open-source code, say, is not simply the disavowal of other political struggles. Rather, it relies on the prior exclusion of the antagonistic conditions of emergence of Web-radio and open source, of their

embeddedness within the brutalities of global capital, of their dependence for existence on racialized violence and division. Technologies can and should be politicized.
They should be made to represent something beyond themselves in the service of a
struggle against something beyond themselves. Only such a treatment will avoid
fetishization.

The Fantasy of Wholeness: A Global Zero Institution

Thus far I've discussed the foreclosure of the political in communicative capitalism in
terms of the fantasy of abundance accompanying the reformatting of messages as
contributions and the fantasy of participation accompanying the technology fetishism. These fantasies give people the sense that our actions online are politically significant, that they make a difference. I turn now to the fantasy of wholeness further
animating networked communications. This fantasy furthers our sense that our contributions to circulating content matter by locating them in the most significant of
possible spaces—the global. To be sure, I am not arguing that the world serves as a
space for communicative capitalism analogous to the one the nation provided for
industrial capitalism. On the contrary, my argument is that the space of communicative capitalism is the Internet and that networked communications materialize specific
fantasies of unity and wholeness as the global. The fantasies in turn secure networked
transactions as the Real of global capitalism.

To explain why, I draw from Žižek's elucidation of a concept introduced by Claude
Levi-Straus, the zero-institution.[23] A zero-institution is an empty signifier. It has no
determinate meaning but instead signifies the presence of meaning. It is an institution
with no positive function—all it does is signify institutionality as such (as opposed to
chaos, say). As originally developed by Levi-Straus, the concept of the zero-institution
helps explain how people with radically different descriptions of their collectivity
nevertheless understand themselves as members of the same tribe. Žižek adds to the
Levi-Straussian idea insight into how both the nation and sexual difference function
as a zero-institutions. The nation designates the unity of society in the face of radical
antagonism, the irreconcilable divisions and struggles between classes; sexual difference, in contrast, suggests difference as such, a zero-level of absolute difference that
will always be filled in and overdetermined by contextually given differences.

In light of the nation's failing capacity to stand symbolically for institutionality, the
Internet has emerged as the zero-institution of communicative capitalism. It enables
myriad constituencies to understand themselves as part of the same global structure
even as they radically disagree, fail to co-link, and inhabit fragmented and discon-
nected network spaces. Differently put, the Internet is not a wide-open space, with
nodes and links to nodes distributed in random fashion such that any one site is
equally likely to get hits as any other site. This open, smooth, virtual world of endless

and equal opportunity is a fantasy. In fact, as Albert-Laszlo Barabasi's research on directness in scale-free networks makes clear, the World Wide Web is broken into four major "continents" with their own navigational requirements.[24] Following links on one continent may never link a user to another continent; likewise, following links in one direction does not mean that a user can retrace links back to her starting point. So despite the fact that its very architecture (like all directed networks) entails fragmentation into separate spaces, the Internet presents itself as the unity and fullness of the global. Here the global is imagined and realized. More than a means through which communicative capitalism intensifies its hold and produces its world, the Internet functions as a particularly powerful zero-institution insofar as it is animated by the fantasy of global unity.

The Internet provides an imaginary site of action and belonging. Celebrated for its freedoms and lack of boundaries, this imagined totality serves as a kind of presencing of the global. On the one hand, the Internet imagines, stages, and enacts the "global" of global capital. But, on the other, this global is nothing like the "world"—as if such an entity were possible, as if one could designate an objective reality undisturbed by the external perspective observing it or a fully consistent essential totality unruptured by antagonism.[25]

The oscillations in the 1990s debate over the character of the Internet can clarify this point. In the debate, Internet users appeared either as engaged citizens eager to participate in electronic town halls and regularly communicate with their elected representatives, or they appeared as Web-surfing, wastes-of-lives in dark, dirty rooms, downloading porn, betting on obscure Internet stocks, or collecting evidence of the U.S. government's work with extraterrestrials at Area 51. In other versions of this same matrix, users were either innocent children or dreadful, war-game playing, teenage boys. Good interactions were on Amazon. Bad interactions were underground and involved drugs, kiddie porn, LSD, and plutonium. These familiar oscillations remind us that the Net has always been particular and that struggles over regulating the Internet have been struggles over what kind of particularity would and should be installed. Rather than multiply far-reaching, engaging, and accessible, the Internet has been constituted in and through conflict over specific practices and subjectivities. Not everything goes.

We might even say that those who want to clean up the Internet, who want to get rid of or zone the porn and the gambling, who want to centralize, rationalize, and organize commercial transactions in ways more beneficial to established corporations than to mom and pop shops, express as a difference on the Internet what is actually the starker difference between societies traversed and mediated through electronic communications and financial networks and those reliant more on social, interpersonal, and extralegal networks. As Ernesto Laclau argues, the division between the social and the nonsocial, or between society and what is other to it, external and threatening, can only be expressed as a difference internal to society.[26] If capital today traverses the globe, how can the difference, between us and them be expressed? The oscillations in the Internet debate suggest that the difference is between those who are sexualized, undisciplined, violent, irrational, lazy, excessive, and extreme, on the one hand, and those who are civilized, mainstream, hard-working, balanced, and normal, on the other. Put in psychoanalytic terms, the other on the Internet is the Real other—not the other I imagine as like me and not the symbolic other to be recognized and respected through abstract norms and rights. That the other is Real brings home the fact that the effort to clean up the Internet was more than a battle of images and involved more than gambling and porn. The image of the Internet works as a fantasy of a global unity. Whatever disrupts this unity cannot be part of the global.

The particularity of the fantasies of the global animating the Internet is striking. For example, Richard Rogers' research on linking practices on the World Wide Web brings out the Web's localism and provincialism. In his account of the Dutch food safety debate, Rogers notes "little in the way of 'web dialogue' or linkage outside of small Dutch 'food movement.'"[27] Critics of personalized news as well as of the sheltered world of AOL click on a similar problem—the way the world on the Web is shrunken into a very specific image of the global.[28] How would fringe culture fans of blogs on incunabula.org or ollapodrida.org come into contact with sites providing Koranic instruction to modern Muslims—even if there were no language problems? And, why would they bother? Why should they? Indeed, as a number of commentators have worried for a while now, opportunities to customize the news and announcements one reads—not to mention the already undigestible amount of information available on topics in which one is deeply interested—contribute to the segmentation and isolation of users within bubbles of views and opinions with which they already agree.

The particularity of these fantasies of the global is important because this is what the global networked communications produce. Our networked interactions produce our specific worlds as the global of global capital. They create the expectations and effects of communicative capitalism, expectations and effects that necessarily vary according to one's context. And, precisely because the global is whatever specific communities or exchanges imagine it to be, anything outside the experience or comprehension of these communities either does not exist or is an inhuman, otherworldly alien threat that must be annihilated. So, if everything is out there on the Internet, anything I fail to encounter—or can't imagine encountering—isn't simply excluded (everything is already there), it is foreclosed. Admitting or accessing what is foreclosed destroys the very order produced through foreclosure. Thus, the imagined unity of the global, a fantasy filled in by the particularities of specific contexts, is one where there is no politics; there is already agreement. Circulating content can't effect change in this sort of world—it is already complete. The only alternative is the Real that ruptures my world, that it to say, the evil Other I cannot imagine sharing a world with. The very fantasy of a global that makes my networked interactions vital and important results in a world closed to politics, on the one hand, and threatened by evil, on the other.

Conclusion

A Lacanian commonplace is that a letter always arrives at its destination. What does this mean with respect to networked communications? It means that a letter, a message, in communicative capitalism is not really sent. There is no response because there is no arrival. There is just the contribution to circulating content.

Many readers will likely disagree. Some might say that the line I draw between politics as circulating content and politics as governance makes no sense. Dot-orgs, dot-coms, and dot-govs are all clearly interconnected and intertwined in their personnel, policies, and positions. But, to the extent that they are interconnected, identifying any impact on these networks by critical opponents becomes all the more difficult.

Other readers might bring up the successes of MoveOn. From its early push to have Congress censure Bill Clinton and "move on," to its presence as a critical force against the Iraq war, to recent efforts to prevent George W. Bush from acquiring a second term, MoveOn has become a presence in mainstream American politics and boasts over two million members worldwide. In addition to circulating petitions and arranging e-mails and faxes to members of Congress, one of MoveOn's best actions was a virtual sit-in: over 200,000 of us called into Washington, D.C. at scheduled times on the same day, shutting down phone lines into the capital for hours. In early 2004, MoveOn sponsored an ad contest: the winning ad would be shown on a major television network during the Super Bowl football game. The ad was great—but CBS refused to broadcast it.

As I see it, far from being evidence against my argument, MoveOn exemplifies technology fetishism and confirms my account of the foreclosure of the political. MoveOn's campaigns director, Eli Pariser, says that the organization is "opt-in, it's decentralized, you do it from your home."[29] No one has to remain committed or be bothered with boring meetings. Andrew Boyd, in a positive appraisal of the group, writes that "MoveOn's strength lies . . . in providing a home for busy people who may not want to be a part of a chapter-based organization with regular meetings. . . . By combining a nimble entrepreneurial style with a strong ethic of listening to its members—via online postings and straw polls—MoveOn has built a responsive, populist and relatively democratic virtual community."[30] Busy people can think they are active—the technology will act for them, alleviating their guilt while assuring them that nothing will change too much. The responsive, relatively democratic virtual community won't place too many (actually any) demands on them, fully aware that its democracy is the democracy of communicative capitalism—opinions will circulate, views will be expressed, information will be accessed. By sending an e-mail, signing a petition, responding to an article on a blog, people can feel political. And that feeling feeds communicative capitalism insofar as it leaves behind the time-consuming, incremental, and risky efforts of politics. MoveOn likes to emphasize that it abstains from ideology, from division. While I find this disingenuous on the surface—MoveOn's politics are progressive, anti-war, left-democratic—this sort of nonposition strikes me as precisely that disavowal of the political I've been describing: it is a refusal to take a stand, to venture into the dangerous terrain of politicization.

Perhaps one can find better reasons to disagree with me when one looks at alternative politics, that is, when one focuses on the role of the Internet in mass mobilizations, in connecting activists from all over the world, and in providing an independent media source. The February 15, 2003, mobilization of ten million people worldwide to protest the Bush administration's push for war against Iraq is perhaps the most striking example, but one might also mention MoveOn's March 16th candlelight vigil, an action involving over a million people in 130 countries. Such uses of the Internet are vitally important for political activists—especially given the increasingly all-pervasive reach of corporate-controlled media. Through them, activists establish social connections to one another—even if not to those outside their circles. But this does not answer the question of whether such instances of intense social meaning will drive larger organizational efforts and contribute to the formation of political solidarities with more duration. Thus, I remain convinced that the strongest argument for the political impact of new technologies proceeds in precisely the opposite direction, that is to say, in the direction of postpolitics. Even as globally networked communications provide tools and terrains of struggle, they make political change more difficult—and more necessary—than ever before. To this extent, politics in the sense of working to change current conditions may well require breaking with and through the fantasies attaching us to communicative capitalism.

Acknowledgments

I am grateful to John Armitage, Ryan Bishop, Kevin Dunn, and Lee Quinby for comments on earlier drafts of this paper. My thinking on this paper benefited greatly from exchanges with Noortje Marres, Richard Rogers, and Auke Towslager.

Notes

This essay was originally published in *Cultural Politics* 1, no. 1 (2005), 51–74.

1. Veran Matic and Drazen Pantic, "War of Words," *The Nation*, November 29, 1999, http://www.thenation.com/doc.mhtml?i=19991129&s=matic (accessed April 29, 2007).

2. See Jodi Dean, *Publicity's Secret: How Technoculture Capitalizes on Democracy* (Ithaca, NY: Cornell University Press, 2002) and "The Networked Empire: Communicative Capitalism and the Hope for Politics," in *Empire Strikes Back: Reading Hardt and Negri*, ed. Paul A. Passavant and Jodi Dean (New York: Routledge, 2004), 265–288.

3. Saskia Sassen, *Losing Control?* (New York: Columbia University Press, 1996).

4. Giorgio Agamben, *Means without End: Notes on Politics*, trans. Vincenzo Binetti and Cesare Casarino (Minneapolis: University of Minnesota Press, 2000), 115.

5. Slavoj Žižek, *The Ticklish Subject* (London: Verso, 1999), 198.

6. Michael Hardt and Antonio Negri, *Empire* (Cambridge: Harvard University Press, 2000), 347. See also, Dean, "The Networked Empire," 272–275.

7. See Ernesto Laclau, *Emancipations* (London: Verso, 1996), 56–64.

8. See Ernesto Laclau and Chantal Mouffe, *Hegemony and Socialist Strategy* (London: Verso, 1986), 188.

9. See Dean, *Publicity's Secret*, 72–73.

10. A thorough historical analysis of the contribution would spell out the steps involved in the uncoupling of messages from responses. Such an analysis would draw out the ways that responses to the broadly cast messages of television programs were configured as attention and measured in terms of ratings. Nielsen families, in other words, responded for the rest of us. Yet, as work in cultural studies, media, and communications has repeatedly emphasized, ratings are not responses and provide little insight into the actual responses of viewers. These actual responses, we can say, are uncoupled from the broadcast message and incorporated into other circuits of communication.

11. Jürgen Habermas, *The Theory of Communicative Action*, vol. 1, *Reason and the Rationalization of Society*, trans. Thomas McCarthy (Boston: Beacon Press, 1984).

12. See Slavoj Žižek, *The Sublime Object of Ideology* (London: Verso, 1989).

13. Clay Shirkey, "Power Laws, Weblogs, and Inequality," in Jodi Dean, Jon Anderson, and Geert Lovink, eds., *Reformatting Politics: Information Technology and Global Civil Society* (New York: Routledge, 2006), 35–42.

14. Slavoj Žižek, *The Plague of Fantasies* (London: Verso, 1997), 21.

15. Nick Dyer-Witheford, *Cyber-Marx* (Champaign: University of Illinois Press, 1999), 34–35.

16. Nick Dyer-Witheford, "E-Capital and the Many-Headed Hydra," in *Critical Perspectives on the Internet*, ed. Greg Elmer (Lanham, MD: Rowman and Littlefield, 2002), 142.

17. Joshua Gamson, "Gay Media, Inc.: Media Structures, the New Gay Conglomerates, and Collective Sexual Identities," in *Cyberactivism: Online Activism in Theory and Practice*, ed. Martha McCaughey and Michael D. Ayers (New York: Routledge, 2003), 259.

18. Gamson, 260.

19. Gamson, 270–271.

20. Mary Graham, *Democracy by Disclosure: The Rise of Technopopulism* (Washington, DC: The Brookings Institution, 2002), 140.

21. Clay Shirkey, "Is Social Software Bad for the Dean Campaign?" *Many-2-Many*. Posted January 26, 2004, accessed April 28, 2007. http://www.corante.com/many/archives/2004/01/26/is_social_software_bad_for_the_dean_campaign.php.

22. Geert Lovink and Florian Schneider, "Reverse Engineering Freedom," *Make Worlds* (2003, accessed April 28, 2007). http://www.makeworlds.org/?q=node/view/20. See also Jamie King, "The Packet Gang." *Mute* 27 (Winter/Spring 2004), www.metamute.com (accessed April 28, 2007).

23. Slavoj Žižek, *Enjoy Your Symptom!*, 2nd ed. (New York: Routledge, 2001), 221–223.

24. Albert-Laszlo Barabasi, *Linked* (New York: Plume, 2003), 161–178.

25. See Slavoj Žižek, "Lenin's Choice," afterword to *Revolution at the Gates: Selected Writings of Lenin from 1917* (London: Verso, 2002), 181.

26. Laclau, 38.

27. Richard Rogers, "The Issue Has Left the Building." Paper presented at the Annual Meeting of the International Association of Internet Researchers, Maastricht, the Netherlands (October 13–16, 2002).

28. Korinna Patelis, "E-Mediation by America Online," in *Preferred Placement: Knowledge Politics on the Web*, ed. Richard Rogers (Maastrict: Jan van Eyck Academie, 2004), 49–64.

29. Andrew Boyd, "The Web Rewires the Movement," *The Nation*, August 4, 2003, 14.

30. Boyd, 16.

4   Toward Open and Dense Networks: An Interview with Geert Lovink

Megan Boler

This interview with Geert Lovink took place in Hanover, Connecticut, in May 2005. At the time I was participating in a six-week Cyberdisciplinarity Institute at the Dartmouth Center for the Humanities hosted by Dr. Mark Williams, and as it happens I conceptualized this edited collection during those six weeks of tranquility. Geert Lovink was present as part of a two-day conference that crystallized the questions of surveillance, the digital body, how Internet studies connect to geography, how the Internet had been used in political campaigns, sociology of blogging, and critical cyberculture studies that frame this edited collection.[1]

I interviewed Geert directly after a meeting with Joe Trippi, the campaign manager of the Howard Dean presidential campaign, "Blog for America," which had been a site of great energy and Democratic party "hopes" in the buildup to the 2004 election. The Dean campaign in the United States was a turning point in uses of the Internet as a campaign tool. Most famous for its establishment of online "meet ups" around the country that afforded "new civic participation" at a populist level, the Dean campaign made its own history: vast online bandwidth through blogs and discussions and through official online networks of campaign. As a result, this Web-based hybrid movement/electoral campaign (somewhat like Linus Torwald's organizational management) harnessed the grassroots energy of a range of rural and urban, mostly white 20- to 35-year-old men from small towns alongside Silicon Valley media experts, the event capturing the American imaginary and garnering the front cover of the *New York Times Magazine* as poster child for a new model of campaign organizing with a grassroots, almost DIY model.[2] With hundreds from around the country lined up to work on the net-end of this campaign, the Dean campaign set groundbreaking records for online fundraising networks.

Joe Trippi was in the process of a book launch about his experience managing the Howard Dean campaign. Elements of Trippi's story and position in the media landscape captured our attention at times in the interview that follows. Throughout his presentation and in our conversation that followed, Trippi repeatedly expressed and embodied unbridled hope about people working on computers—"in their garage and changing the world!" A character with unique charisma and persuasive insider sensibility that gives the sense of a scoop, Trippi was also beyond the honeymoon as there had been a "falling out" between Dean and Trippi, which leant an aura of further drama to the entire landmark shift in campaign organizing. (As of April 2007, Trippi is the campaign manager for Democratic candidate John Edwards.)

By 2005, those like myself were beginning to stabilize after an intense period of propaganda, unveilings of Washington and press manipulations of intelligence, alongside the communicative shifts afforded by the Internet as a space for virtual publics to contest and challenge dominant media. I had spent several years engaged in a project, Critical Media Literacy in Times of War,[3] and had just been awarded a three-year funding grant to study digital dissent. I was in the midst of augmenting my years of cultural and social analyses, developing a working conceptual and "methodological" framework to study the online media productions of four different sites of dissent, all of which I had been observing closely since 2003. Lovink had just completed writing "The Principles of Notworking: Concepts in Critical Network Culture."

Megan Boler: I would like to begin by asking you about the talk we attended by Joe Trippi, the campaign manager for Howard Dean. Trippi has a very optimistic view regarding the potential of new media practices; he believes that everyone now has access, that there is no barrier to participation, and that with this access comes an incredible possibility for revolutionizing the world. During Trippi's talk, I was reminded of your cautious remarks in your interview with Rodrigo Garcia (February 2004), in which you said, "Social movements do not emerge out of technology." Given this statement, what would you say about Trippi's optimism?

Geert Lovink: Social movements can utilize technologies and have done so in the past. This is a really rich history, it is something to be proud of, and something that scholars, historians, and theorists can go back to time and again. But, it is not something that has ever really initiated movements. It has enhanced movements, but the question has never really been posed regarding whether technology is capable of generating social movements, and I think it is time to make this an issue. People know that technologies themselves are not going to spark political movements and they are not in themselves going to change democracy, the media landscape, or capitalism.

Trippi spoke about the enormous anxiety and real desire to change the Democratic Party, and I think he and his team have done a tremendous job. Indeed, they have gone through an almost religious experience of transformation. This is also why I think there is still excitement when you hear him talk, even if within the larger picture of American politics people still feel lost. However, he said something over lunch that worried me a great deal, namely, that the Republican Party is much more interested in his experiences than his fellow. Democratic Party members and so, in the end, these experiences will be used by them, which is a sad given.

But what I like and find important in the enthusiasm is the scale. The issue of scale is something that is really on my mind right now. From the side of social movements, there are similar questions about how to create a critical mass with all of the smaller groups working on varying topics. The potential for affinities can suddenly turn smaller groups into something much larger. So the scalability of issues and how protests can grow into larger social movements is really important, especially today when this can reach a global level using new media technologies.

That is an interesting phenomenon in itself, and I think Trippi's experiences tell us something about that process of transformation in which people who start something suddenly find themselves in a completely different dynamic. It's probably a similar dynamic, or transformation, that a lot of people went through during the protests in Seattle—the spark that initiates something with countless consequences that in turn spark off other events. But this goes back much more to the roots, because I'm talking about an event with a capital "E," the beginning of something, and this is what activists should really be looking at.

Of course, you can study the social techniques, the laws of weblogs, and the bigger mechanisms in the wikipediasphere, or even podcasting, you name it. In each case, the technology is offering new standards, platforms and ways of expression. So, we can study them and learn to better utilize them, but real change goes deeper and it comes from somewhere else.

MB: Given your familiarity with these technologies and their emergence, as I read your work I wondered if you have changed some of your thinking. Right now there is a huge amount of enthusiasm and people are talking about cyberactivism—I am thinking of Graham Meikle's book *Future Active* and Martha McCaughey's edited collection *Cyberactivism*. There is a kind of grassroots enthusiasm about access to technology and new practices, whether it is multimedia animation or blogging. Since you were at the beginning of Nettime,[4] you have witnessed the ebb and flow of this enthusiasm for some time. Do you feel that your own views have changed? Did you have a different sense of hope in the '90s than you have now?

GL: No, I have to say that in the '90s I was part of a current that really identified itself with the medium. But, with the other-globalization movement (as the antiglobalization was renamed), after about five years there is something else that emerges in its shadow, and it allows us to move beyond just technology issues. The enthusiasm is always present when there is a movement rising, and to be part of something that comes into being is a very special thing. As I say, it is almost a religious experience, and it cannot be repeated.

You can long for it and you can write about it, you can reconstruct it, you can go through it by looking at films or reading, etc., but that does not bring you any closer. Of course, you can study the mass psychology and look into the mechanisms of how these "smart mobs," as they are called these days, are gathering, and you will understand something. But what they are concerned with, the reasons for their discontent, cannot be discovered entirely through these histories or these technologies.

For instance, in the Howard Dean campaign, I think that the excitement was there because of the network technologies. But, the discontent that this was connected to was the completely dysfunctional democracy, the decision making, the whole corrupt atmosphere around presidential candidates, the way these campaigns had to be funded, etc. So, that discontent in society is really important, but the technology will not and cannot indicate this; technology cannot initiate that discontent. And, because people are living in fear, the discontent has not even really reached the surface yet. I certainly do not agree with the mechanical thinking that suggests technology leads to more democracy or that technology will be the cause of revolution.

MB: In your essay "The Principles of Notworking," you question the use of terms like *democracy* and *civil society*. Considering the widespread, popular usage of these terms and the "language" of democracy—*public sphere, civic participation, participatory democracy*, etc.—what do you see as the best conceptual framework to think about questions of engagement and mobilization?

GL: We cannot go back to the vocabulary of the nineteenth and twentieth centuries. I think many people believe that we will eventually not organize ourselves, for instance, through political parties. It is even questionable today whether or not the concept of social movements is adequately expressing what is happening around us. The "movement" is still a metaphor—it moves something, it has a direction—whereas we know from all our work that movements are deeply temporary and heterogeneous experiences, all geared toward creating a political event as an almost metaphysical statement. It can be easy to create media events, but they are not by definition political events, since they do not necessarily make much difference.

I think a lot of people would like to scale up and prolong that experience. That in itself is legitimate because it is special. These days it is not normal, though it has probably never been normal, to be in a revolutionary situation. The problem comes when we try to prolong these revolutionary moments, but the way is blocked, as in the case of the political party. People just won't go there anymore. You can say, "Oh, well, you're an anarchist, you're an autonomous thinker, you never liked political parties anyway," but I think there is really more going on than that. How you can prolong a situation, a shared concern, is really what is on the agenda, and this has to do with the fact that people want to organize themselves. But they do not and cannot commit themselves completely to this form of organization because it is not a religion, it is not a capital "C" cause that they're fighting for. People have really fairly complex lives these days; they have a multitude of identities, they have a multitude of concerns and quite often these concerns are conflicting even in a single person.

So we desire things that are clearly paradoxical and we have to face that. If you want to say that people have heterogeneous agendas, you are really suggesting that people want opposite things themselves without really or consciously being aware of this. But, I don't want to enlighten people about these paradoxes because I don't think this is a matter of enlightenment. These are the very concerns that lead to more important questions regarding possible sustainable forms of organization.

This is also why we are currently struggling with the whole notion of the network—the network seems to offer at least some relief because it allows for loose affiliations and relationships. The network is not like a political party or a church. It's not a marriage, it's not a lifelong commitment, it's not an ideology. We can have even loose ties in a group. We can have strong ties and collaborate, but it can also decompress. So it is these forms of organization that are of interest to me, and they always find a technological media expression.

MB: So do you see the technology as coming after the political impetus?

GL: This is complicated—I am a technological determinist in the sense that I believe that the infrastructure of the technology dictates the possible practices we can take up. But these days, because of the interactive nature of media, this whole idea of techno-determinism is shifting. However, I would argue that access still remains a very important issue. We don't have access to this camera, for instance, because we can't deconstruct it. Because many moments in our so-called networked lives are still largely prescribed by the architectures of the apparatuses that we work with, I remain something of a techno-determinist.

MB: In "The Principles of Notworking," you are really pushing strategists, political thinkers, and theorists to move beyond studies of users and how the technology is being used. You were arguing that theorists of Internet culture need to consider more important issues with respect to the network, and this seems related to what you're talking about in terms of deconstructing technologies. But, it also connects to the questions of sustainability that you're talking about. So, with respect to these concerns regarding organizational models and social change, do you think that social change can be provoked through the use of technology?

GL: In this sense my work is close to the concerns of organizational studies. I feel that the technology is leading us to the question of whether we can create new forms of organization that at times will be dictated by its architecture.

Maybe there are ways out through the imaginative use of free software and open source metaphors that we can transplant into other contexts and social environments and thus make situations more fluid and more open to change.

But the increasing role of technology also poses the threat that the architecture of technologies will dictate what practices we can develop. This leads back to the question about Trippi's optimism regarding new media technologies. For instance, I find blogs incredibly limiting because they are not social platforms and they are mainly used as a form of individual expression, with the tendency of bloggers to legitimize their positions by linking to news sources. Why would you link to news sources? The question really becomes one of commentary and production. Some people will contend that the blogger will eventually change the news, but can you really change the news if you take up the role of the news commentator within a collective body of commentary? No, we all know that this is not the case. We hope that through these commentaries we can change the nature, that is, the very the laws of the news organization themselves, but so far there is not really any indication that this is going to happen. Of course, there are cases where bloggers have some influence, and there is indeed a clash happening between journalists and bloggers. But is that really affecting the nature of news production itself? It seems that the whole world of blogging is still not addressing the long term issue of the deeply unequal and questionable ideological agendas of the news organizations. The whole organization of blogs is centered around an individual, an autonomous subject, who is usually a person writing in his or her home, then inviting others to comment. But we know that the amount of people visiting blogs is really, really very low for 99% of blogs, and, in that sense, there is a direct replication of the uneven world of the mainstream media. Then there is the other issue that blogs may include function of reply, which would differentiate them from the media, but we know there is often no comment or response because people are just not interested.

In that sense most of the blogs are more like what I have referred to in my previous work as "sovereign media," or media that talk to themselves. And, there is certainly a liberating aspect there, and I have been celebrating sovereign media, in some contexts, because of this power, but from an activist point of view, of course, they are completely useless.

MB: In your critique of sovereign media you draw on concepts of free cooperation and collaboration as marking the limitations of these sovereign practices. Can you suggest how critical Internet theorists might develop an understanding of networking that took into account free cooperation and collaboration in a way that could radically transform the platform? How would this transformation take place?

GL: I would strongly urge everyone to set up denser networks and suppress the typical urge to disperse. There is already so much fragmentation, and, although there is a liberating element in it, although there is a pleasure in dispersals, I think if you really want to go for that techno-event, as I call it, the technologically enhanced or enabled event, you really have to compress networks.

And we can't do that through the logic of political parties. So this compression has to be done through linking, through what we've been theorizing as a free cooperation. The compression needs to be done through free cooperation . . . but we can't continue to think that through growth into nowhere, we're going to get anywhere.

In terms of compression, what I want to stress is that networks can manifest a certain social density that is really important. I think all networks go through these times, usually in their beginning stages, but not always. Networks, just like anything else, can also just slumber. And they just go nowhere and then find their moment, why they exist. For instance, if they associate themselves with others, they might suddenly find that they're not working on certain things themselves and integrate into the larger picture.

MB: How does this connect to the desire for more prolonged or sustainable forms of organization?

GL: If the network is falling apart, for instance, it is not really useful, in some cases, to bring in the necessary forces that will repair it. But I am interested in exactly these social dynamics because I think if we really want to achieve something we have to study these very complex social behaviors of larger groups. Call them smart mobs, call them critical masses, call them social movements, it doesn't matter . . . call them networks. This is where I think activists should be focused, and activists really need to understand the limits and the possibilities of software and network architecture.

MB: On the question of fragmentation, I want to ask you about MoveOn.org's "Bush in 30 Seconds" contest.[5] It was a precise moment of intensification, and it has been very interesting to study the hundreds of people who are producing these viral videos with new media technologies. So many people were submitting them, watching them, voting on them, yet the issue remains whether such processes of engagement are sustainable. How do you see these types of do-it-yourself productions in terms of political commentary and political activism?

GL: This really doesn't concern me because the examples that you mention are just content, and since content comes and goes we shouldn't really pay too much attention to the production of content as such. We can write a great piece or we can make a wonderful documentary and, of course, we can be concerned about accessibility, but in general people are not thinking through content, just through one film, etc. You can't really achieve anything much looking exclusively at content. Instead we need to understand the underlying mechanisms there. That seems to be why I remain a follower of McLuhan—we have to understand the underlying media laws, whether McLuhan himself dreamed up the right ones or not is irrelevant. I mean we should go beyond the content of individual projects, so, in that sense, we can't expect much from a single 30-second film. What is important is the way you can engage people and create incredible excitement around a competition like this. It tells us also a lot about the positive aspect of competitions because they really engage people. You can appeal to a process that is not just about winning, because it is taking part in a social process with which they can identify. There are many examples like this of a process where we can ask how can we build new forms of the social in the media environment.

MB: As I watched these "Bush in 30 Seconds" ads and study parody and satire as forms of political commentary, particularly after September 11, what I noticed was a cultural contradiction or paradox. That is, on the one hand you have very media savvy, skeptical viewers who are aware that all truths are constructed. Yet, at the same time, there is a recurrent theme of demanding truthful accounts from media and politicians. At some point I realized that things have changed since 1983, when Frederic Jameson wrote that parody is dead.[6] Something has changed, certainly, and although it is perhaps problematic to use the term *desire* here, there is a desire for accountability. There is a sense of absolute certainty that we are being lied to, and there is a demand for some kind of accountability and that seems in tension with the skeptical, or postmodern concept of truth itself. That is, that desire for truthfulness seems in paradoxical tension with the simultaneous awareness that all truth is constructed.

GL: It's similar to what Peter Sloterdijk said in his first book on kynicism.[7] There is a difference between the normal kind of cynical approach that people have and the enlightened form of what he called *kynicism*, going back to the origins of the concept. There is an enlightenment moment in being cynical, and I think that's what we find a lot in these media commentaries . . . where through a process of deep cynical investigation people try to find something. And it's really questionable whether it is the truth that they tried to find. And very often political activists can't really laugh, or they laugh but feel a little bit uncomfortable with it . . .

It's the same kind of double move that you make: you want to deconstruct power and, on the other hand, you want to build up counterpower. Now how can you do these things simultaneously because they contradict themselves. In the media, and in networks, you have similar operations because you have to understand and really actively deconstruct the workings of networks, while at the same time you're very busy building them up.

MB: But what is the function of parody and satire in the United States right now? There is a particular pleasure in watching parody and that must be true at certain moments, historical moments and cultural moments. Do you have any thoughts about the different uses of satire or parody in tactical media?

GL: San Precario, the made-up saint of precarious workers in Italy, obviously using this parodic aspect in creating a new discourse around working conditions, labor, etc.[8] I think that it is a fantastic play. There's a lot of inspiration in Europe coming from Italy because people are actively using creative, imaginative new tactics. Whether this is satire or not, I don't think so. I think in Europe at the moment it's something else . . . In Europe, I think there is a strong belief that maybe new social formations can come into being because we can do something completely unique and imaginative and organize—not organize in the way people have done this in the nineteenth and twentieth century, but under a completely new set of paradoxical postmodern conditions.

MB: Yes—these new paradoxical postmodern conditions are I think aptly described in Claire Colebrook's *Irony*[8] in which she argues that the more sophisticated kinds of irony highlight contradiction. In the best instances irony doesn't function within a logical, binary order of either/or, but rather undermines our hope for truth by showing a "conflict of sense"—how two apparently oppositional assertions have equal force.

The Yes Men certainly seem to represent the possibilities of this kind of tactical media and irony. I was particularly impressed when they appeared on the BBC in 2004 as representatives of Dow Chemical and claimed responsibility for the Bhopal disaster. Do you think so?

GL: I think they are tactical media activists in the best sense because they understand the art of transforming yourself and what really distinguished them is that they make up new identities on the spot. In that sense, it is different from a long-term strategic plan where you just sit and work on the issues of Union Carbide and organize directly through a lengthy process. Of course, the Yes Men had to do this work, the research, etc., because they needed to know the specificity of the crimes Union Carbide had committed. In that sense, they profit from strategic, long-term, but often quite invisible work that other activists have done. But they give this work a special turn, and it is with this augmentation, it is that kind of work that is the work of media activism.

But there is still a lot of very basic knowledge that we need to communicate to fellow activists. What I find a little bit worrying is the whole idea of activists as the heroic technological forefront. Unfortunately, I think most activists are running behind, and there is some self-deception here. So the whole rhetoric around cyberactivism should be one of great worry because most activists don't understand anything about new media. The butcher around the corner is much more informed about what he or she can do with these new media, and what the neighbor next door is doing with media is usually much more interesting than what the average activist is doing, unfortunately.

MB: That speaks to a divide that frustrates me between critical theorists and people who are doing the IT work, the people who really understand the technology. The problem is that often these communities fail to interact or connect.

GL: No, and despite everything that happens, the whole Silicon Valley–Californian attitude towards technology is still superior at this moment, so despite everything that happened in the late '90s, I think that, for activists, this is still the place to look. And I think we should really try to overcome the kind of techno-hippy bashing that is happening there because a lot of the issues that are being dealt with there should really be of great interest for activists from all over the world. For instance, there are concerns with the issue of open networks, closed networks, mechanisms of trust, etc. These are things that are rooted deeply in the architecture of networks, and the kind of critical work that is being done on this will have an enormous impact on activist work over the next decade. There is a similar movement with respect to issues around censorship that became somewhat boring in the '90s with a focus on libertarian values.

But after 9/11, these issues have become really important again, and the deeply political concerns of censorship and cyber-rights within context of the war on terror should be a serious concern for all activists.

MB: You have said in an earlier article, "Let's face it: friction free capitalism is not in need of networks."[10] How would this connect with concerns about new media technologies and political activism? What concerns does it raise about the concept of the network?

GL: The whole idea of the networked society is something that's come from corporations, and it is really a very strange idea. But it is an inherent threat for all those in power when things begin to happen from below. There was, of course, the cutting edge, avant-garde business literature that presented itself as a kind of capitalist revolution in the '90s. These people have a really weird kind of hypercapitalist mentality combined with almost a necessary anticapitalist resentment. We have to understand that there are inherent power structures that cannot deal with networked environments because they pose an inherent threat to their interests. Of course, companies are introducing all these technologies, and now all companies are networked and have their own internal networks. Some would say these are productive frictions and will always be corporate issues, but there is a cynical logic as well that claims the frictions are always good because they indicate places where capitalism has not yet reached its optimal form of exploitation or abstraction of surplus value.

But there's an interesting case, for instance, where workers of different companies and even workers within different branches are starting to have conversations within or across firms that have no direct relationships. For me, that is an interesting idea because it indicates new forms of innovation. This certainly suggests a subversive potential within the new business logic and its entrepreneurial culture, although it may typically be understood simply as innovation.

MB: That's interesting, but I wonder how it connects to your claim that "tactical media set themselves up for exploitation in the same manner that modders[11] do in the game industry: they both dispense with their knowledge of loopholes in the system for free. They point out the problem, and then run away. Capital is delighted, and thanks the tactical media outfit or nerd-modder for the home improvement. But make no mistake . . . the emergence of organized networks amount to an articulation of info-war."[12] It seems like you are saying media activism must position itself within this info-war and that this is a core issue for you.

GL: I don't mean it in the way as it has been discussed in the late '90s when this idea was formally initiated by the Rand Corporation in one of their reports.[13] They were concerned about something emerging that threatened business and were afraid of hackers. But that's not what I'm pointing to because even if hacktivist tactics will continue, I find the discussion too centered on technology. It puts a lot of emphasis on this kind of technique, this software package. Targeting specific sites, the fact that one particular site is down for an hour or even a day, is simply a symbolic gesture, but it can't really go much beyond that. So I don't associate the info-war with those hacker techniques, but instead I think of it as a heightened tension around a topic. Where there is a buildup of social activity around a topic, an event, a candidate, a gathering . . .

MB: So would you say there are moments around the preemptive U.S. invasion of Iraq that you would consider moments of info-war or that are of particular interest to you?

GL: Not necessarily, but I think for a very long time people will remember February 15, 2003, as a global event. I think we've all been part of it. And it's strong, it really expressed something very powerful. And it will always be connected to this war, so no matter what stories or manipulations, etc., will happen, the fact that so many millions of people around the globe gathered at the same day to make this international demonstration is of great importance.

MB: It's interesting to me because I frequently refer to February 15th as the largest international antiwar movement in history, yet I am shocked at how many people in the United States do not seem to be fully aware of that date.[14] I wonder if it's different in Europe.

GL: No, because I see it as a global event, and the American antiwar movement has never been as strong or as vocal in its opposition. The significance here is that this day, this really very strong global-resistance day, is actually one month before the actual war, not three years after its beginning. In that sense, there is no Vietnam effect where only after five or so years of bloody conflict a strong war movement comes into being. For me, that is the significance of it, that people really anticipated and understood what was about to happen.

MB: What frustrates me is that the mainstream media did not even really cover that event. I still encounter people who were not aware of February 15, and I'm wondering if that counts as part of our info-war, the beleaguered moment. I constantly feel this cognitive dissonance between the fact of the event and the twilight zone created by the mainstream media news organizations that didn't cover it. It's as though the event didn't occur. This is my frustration as an activist. What does it mean for the event to have happened, with millions of participants, yet to remain completely obscure in terms of media coverage?

GL: I don't know what to do about that, but it also points to our present inability to organize new forms of collective memory. For instance, we could ask why you would focus only on that one day, it's only one day, and it's just 24 hours, right? But for us the meaning of that event goes way beyond this time scale, while for the news media there was only a possibility to report on it for a very short moment of time. So in order to capture that significance, we need to think of other ways of setting up sites and spaces for collective memory, memorial sites related to significant moments. Of course, there is a lot we can find on the Net about that day, but maybe we should think of more condensed, larger forms of organization for networked memorial sites, as in the work of Brewster Kahle in San Francisco, who set up this enormous project, Archive.org.

MB: Within my current research on new media, I'm interested in talking to the people who are writing blogs or producing multimedia virals to understand the role of the mainstream media in their production; that is, to what extent is frustration with mainstream media the impetus for engaging in these activities? I'm curious whether you think that's a valuable approach to the question or not, though I suspect you don't.

GL: No, I don't think so because the desire to have genuine exchanges and social experiences is much stronger than frustration with the media. So I think we should really approach this question from the side of desire, the desire to create new forms of social networks. I think that's where people start and that's where they make a difference. And, yes, intuitively, the frustration is the impetus, because it builds up over time. But there is also the question of whether people are really capable of, or even interested in, formulating a really profound media critique, and I don't think they are. One of the problems here is that the criticisms are often produced within a general sense of banality. What people tend to do is reproduce the kind of organized banality that they have been confronted with over decades . . . and I always wonder if that type of media critique is not really asking too much.

The problem is that it's a constant environment. Even the most conscious and attentive people are not really able to switch off this environment because it's a media ecology, in the worst sense of the term. So, in that sense, it's not an opinion, it's an environment, which makes a compelling and rigorous critique really difficult. What you see a lot with the bloggers, too, is a parasitic attitude toward the existing news organizations, which they ultimately depend on.

MB: What I wanted to conclude with is this: I have the sense that you are really pushing researchers to move beyond questions of use and rather to examine the potentials for different kinds of networks. If this is the case, where do you see research going in the future?

GL: Very much, because first of all, we should be more imaginative in the sense that we have incredible opportunities to open up new spaces of possibility. And I think the technology is in a new phase again, a phase of renaissance, and there is so much happening in the field of free software and open source. There is also the relatively unexpected way the wikipedias are becoming a new standard form for expressing and organizing common knowledge.

These are things that have happened over the past few years, but we can push this even further. We can invent similar forms and we should study how they come into being, study how a very small group that starts this Wikipedia is now setting a new standard for knowledge production. We need to redefine how open networks and closed networks interact with each other. We should not only withdraw into trusted closed networks but always take up the challenge of designing new open networks, which can be really difficult these days.

So if we want to grow, we always need to be thinking about how we can transform. We need to understand the mechanisms of growth, and what is important there is understanding how closed networks and open networks interact in a dynamic arrangement, and how these dynamics can be further expanded and utilized. Personally, I am a bit worried about the focus on cultures of use because, quite often, they're lagging behind, and even though they are important, they do not necessarily tell us where things are heading. I think it's much better to look at smaller and more innovative initiatives run by activists because they can tell us so much about potential metamorphoses.

Notes

1. The two-day Cyberdisciplinarity Conference in May 2005 at which Lovink and Trippi presented to our institute at Dartmouth included as well invited scholars Wendy Chun, Michael Curry, Eszter Hargitta, Michael Heim, Alan Liu, Lisa Nakamura, David Phillips, and Jeffrey Rosen. There were fourteen participants in the six-week Dartmouth Center for the Humanities Institute, and I am especially grateful to participants Lisa Gitelman, John Willinsky, Brenda Silver, Mark Williams, Denise Anthony, and Quintus R. Jett for insights on my research project.

2. As characterized in the December 7, 2003, *New York Times Magazine* cover story by Samantha Shapiro, "The (mostly) young people behind Howard Dean's campaign—the brokenhearted, the techno-utopians, the formerly apolitical—come together because they like the candidate. But they also come together because they like one another."

The *New York Times* feature profiles this "new age" of "new media" in relation to reinvigoration of public life:

"The latest holy grail of the tech industry is the idea that people can fuse the virtual communities and digital connections of the Internet with real, human life. Investors are pouring money into Web sites and software programs that claim to perform this function, like Friendster, which lets users visually represent their real friend networks online, and Meetup.com, the site that has helped build the Dean campaign. Meetup.com takes its inspiration from books like *Bowling Alone*, by Robert D. Putnam, about the decline of American public life; its founders claim that the regular monthly meetings arranged through its site (gathering any group from Wiccans to dachshund lovers to, more recently, supporters of political candidates) can help heal the disintegration of the American community."

3. Critical Media in Times of War, http://www.tandl.vt.edu/Foundations/mediaproject/, retrieved April 29, 2007.

4. Nettime is a mailing list that began in the fall of 1995 following an initial meeting, also called Nettime, that was organized in June 1995 at the Venice Biennale. The list describes itself as follows: "Nettime is not just a mailing list but an effort to formulate an international, networked discourse that neither promotes a dominant euphoria (to sell products) nor continues the cynical pessimism, spread by journalists and intellectuals in the "old" media who generalize about "new" media with no clear understanding of their communication aspects. We have produced, and will continue to produce books, readers, and web sites in various languages so an "immanent" net critique will circulate both on- and offline." See http://www.nettime.org/info.html.

5. The "Bush in 30 Seconds" contest was a project of the MoveOn.org Voter Fund, a new fund affiliated with MoveOn.org. The top ranked ads can be viewed online at http://www.bushin30seconds.org/.

6. Fredric Jameson, "Postmodernism and Consumer Society," in *The Anti-Aesthetic: Essays on Postmodern Culture*, ed. Hal Foster (Port Townsend, WA: Bay Press, 1983), pp. 111–125.

7. Peter Sloterdijk, *Kritik der Zynischen Vernunft* (Frankfurt: 1983).

8. Claire Colebrook, *Irony: The New Critical Idiom* (New York: Routledge, 2004).

9. For an introduction to the San Precario movement, see Alessandra Renzi and Stephen Turpin, "Nothing Fails Like Prayer; or, Why San Precario Is More Dangerous Than Religion," *FUSE Magazine* 30, no. 1 (2007): 25–35.

10. Geert Lovink, "The Principles of Notworking: Concepts in Critical Internet Culture," http://www.hva.nl/lectoraten/documenten/ol09-050224-lovink.pdf.

11. "Modders" refers to those who create video game modifications that circumvent proprietary software.

12. Geert Lovink, "The Principles of Notworking."

13. John Arquilla and David Ronfeldt, International Policy Department, Rand Corporation, "Cyberwar is Coming!," *Comparative Strategy* 12, no. 2 (Summer 1993): 141–165.

14. For a comprehensive description of this global protest, see *2/15: The Day the World Said No to War* (New York: Hello NYC Helló/Oakland: AK Press, 2003).

5   Black Code Redux: Censorship, Surveillance, and the Militarization of Cyberspace

Ronald J. Deibert

It has long been a conventional wisdom to believe that the Internet's material properties are biased toward openness, liberalization, democracy, freedom of speech, and communications. Its distributed architecture—a "network of networks" without central control—has been seen as a foundation for a global commons of information, a vehicle for the flourishing of transnational social movements, and a powerful force for democratization that authoritarian regimes worldwide could not resist. This conventional wisdom has, in turn, not only informed a vast array of development initiatives but global political theorizing as well. Underlying most of the many different theories of globalization and global civil society is an assumption about the "speed" and "global reach" of new information and communication technologies, and how these properties have begun to facilitate important changes in the architecture of world order away from a state-based toward a "network" society.[1]

Whatever the merits of that conventional wisdom, pressures from the security and commercial sectors to regulate and control the Internet are beginning to alter its basic material framework in ways that may undermine both the activities of global civic networks and an open global communications environment as well. In many ways these pressures to regulate the Internet reflect a natural maturation process that previous media, such as print, radio, and television, all experienced as they evolved out of unrestrained and experimental to tightly controlled and regulated environments. As new information and communication technologies move from the margins to permeate society, economics, and politics, the stakes become much higher and authorities—both public and private—take more of an active interest in how media are designed and secured.[2] Today's Internet is no exception. Whereas once questions of Internet governance were largely determined by technical experts and engineers, today they are increasingly decided by politicians, government officials, lawyers, and military personnel.

But in other ways, these pressures on Internet security and design issues can be seen as a ramification flowing in the wake of September 11, 2001 and the ensuing global war on terrorism. As will be described below, legislation has been passed in virtually every industrialized country and in many developing countries that expands the capacities of state intelligence and law enforcement agencies to monitor Internet communications. Even more ominous is the very real prospect of an arms race in cyberspace, led by the United States. When combined with the mounting pressures to regulate intellectual property on the Internet coming from the commercial sector, the forces impinging on and shaping the very foundations of global civic networks are formidable and grow daily.

One intent of this chapter is to provide an overview of the current state-of-play with regard to security and design pressures bearing down on the Internet. For those concerned with global democratic communications, mostly this is a rather pessimistic story. If we start from an ideal perspective on what the communications infrastructure should look like for global civic networks and democracy to flourish (and there is wide variation here to be sure), the current reality offers a fairly bleak picture. As the pressures in favor of military, intelligence, and commercial interests bear down on the Internet, I argue below, the prospects for civic networking and democratic communications become increasingly fragile. The paper concludes by outlining the prospects for contrary forces emerging to censorship, surveillance, and militarization. Here, the story is not entirely discouraging, as there is a substantial set of social forces combining to bring questions of access, privacy, and diversity to the principles, rules, and technologies that configure global communications. The interventions of the Citizen Lab and the OpenNet Initiative projects, upon whose research much of this chapter rests, are manifestations of such contrary forces.[3] I refer to these social forces as "civic networks." Although their challenges are formidable, civic networks have begun to create an alternative transnational paradigm of Internet security and design, oriented around shared values and technologies.[4]

A second, less explicit intent of this paper is more theoretical, and concerns the importance of taking "material" factors seriously in International Relations theorizing. By *material factors*, I mean not just those traditionally associated with the term, such as military capabilities and modes of production, but the very technologies through which we communicate as human beings as well. Elsewhere—drawing from a long line of theorizing in the so-called medium theory or media ecology tradition—I have argued that the media through which we communicate are not neutral or empty vessels but present specific constraints and opportunities for the nature and type of communications that can take place through them.[5] The biases of communication technologies, as Harold Innis referred to them, shape and constrain the environment within which communications take place.[6] Whatever their many differences, for those who study global politics from a broadly constructivist, discursive, and/or critical perspective, and in particular those who are normatively inclined toward supporting spaces for alternative voices, grassroots democracy, and civil society in its many different variations to flourish, the material properties of the communications environment have at best been taken for granted, and at worst been largely ignored.[7] As the

Internet changes, so too do the many consequences that have formed the basis for assumptions made about new communication technologies, including the flourishing of civic networks. Those interested in civic networks need to think seriously about the security and design of the communications infrastructure as a constitutive force and material reality, how those properties should be designed in ways that promote, rather than detract from, principles deemed important. At the very least, the communications environment cannot be taken for granted.

The Changing Architecture of the Internet

There was once a time, not that long ago, when serious claims could be made that the Internet was a lawless frontier immune to regulation and control by governments. Libertarian by nature, open in its architecture, the Internet was seen by many as encouraging democracy, freedom, and liberty around the world. Attempts by oppressive regimes to block information were futile. Thanks to this unstoppable, open, liberal architecture, citizens would be able to communicate and deliberate with each other, forming the basis for a single, vibrant global village polity.

As researchers have investigated how the Internet emerged and how it has been governed over the course of its evolution, however, this conventional wisdom has been increasingly called into question. Standing out as a landmark in this respect has been the work of the legal scholar Lawrence Lessig.[8] Although his central theoretical point—that code is not neutral or transparent but actively shapes what can be communicated and how—would not be considered novel by media ecologists, it has demonstrated convincingly to a wide audience that the architecture of the Internet should not be taken for granted. From this perspective, many of those prior conventional wisdoms about the open, liberal character of the Internet and its many attendant consequences reflect less some inherent nature than they do the properties of the technology at a specific moment in time. Media certainly facilitate, shape, and constrain the possibilities of human communication, but it is important to keep in mind that media themselves evolve over time as well. We are living through such a time today. Across several interrelated dimensions, it appears that Internet's "lawless frontier" is quickly closing. Taken individually, these changes eat away at some of the important foundations that would have to be incorporated into any communications infrastructure for global democratic governance, such as diversity, access, openness, and privacy. When combined, they present a rather bleak future indeed.

Censorship

Censorship is defined as the act or system of practice suppressing, limiting, or deleting objectionable or any other kind of speech. Although all political regimes engage in some forms of censorship, liberal democratic polities have distinguished themselves from illiberal polities on the basis of limitations on censorship and accompanying protections of free speech.[9] Freedom of speech is constitutionally enshrined in many liberal democratic states around the world, and it is one of the cornerstones of the United Nations Declaration of Human Rights (Article 19). The Internet has long been seen as providing a technological fortification for free speech. Citizens can publish their views to a worldwide audience, communicate in an unrestricted fashion with other citizens, and create new communities of interest. Social forces have emerged, however, that have begun to chip away at that technological fortification. The most direct assault comes from increasingly sophisticated forms of state content filtering, described below. A more unlikely source comes from intensifying pressures to regulate intellectual property and copyright.

Intellectual Property Protection as Commercial Censorship

As information has become increasingly digitized, so have a wide range of consumer products, including movies, music, and books. Although entertainment, software, and other commercial industries have sought to capitalize on new means of distributing their products through digital networks, they have had to face the problem of the theft of intellectual property and copyright violations. Once digitized and placed on distributed networks, information is easy to duplicate and distribute. Companies and their lobbyists in the affected industries, such as the Recording Industry Association of America (RIAA) and the Motion Picture Association of America (MPAA), have claimed large losses in potential sales, though determining figures with precision rests on questionable counterfactuals. To take one example, losses to the worldwide software industry caused by the use of unlicensed software were said to amount to US$34 billion in 2005, according the antipiracy organization Business Software Alliance (BSA).[10]

Not surprisingly, stakeholders of the new information economy have taken or supported increasingly strident measures to protect their property and preserve copyright in cyberspace. To be sure, there are good reasons to support intellectual property and copyright as a source of innovation, creativity, and, indeed, freedom of speech itself. Without a system of incentives to ensure appropriate recompense for expended resources and protections against theft and plagiarism, the circulation of ideas essential to a liberal democratic society could wither. However, the application of long-standing principles of intellectual property and copyright to "knowledge" and "information" has proven difficult in practice, leading to subtle (and not-so-subtle) restrictions of creativity and self-expression.[11] Approaches range from the introduction of new laws at both the domestic and international levels, new forms of industry practice, and, perhaps most consequentially, the development of new codes built directly into technologies themselves.

One of the more notorious of these measures is the Digital Millennium Copyright Act (DMCA), an act of U.S. Congress that was signed into law on October 28, 1998, by President Clinton, and whose purpose is to update U.S. copyright laws for the digital age. According to a study by the Electronic Frontier Foundation on *the Unintended Consequences of the DMCA*, the DMCA has been employed as a tool of anticompetition, has stifled legitimate research into cybersecurity and encryption technologies, and has undermined "fair use."[12] To give just a few egregious examples listed by the study, a garage door opener company has employed the DMCA to prevent rival companies from developing universal remote controls that operate on its system. Computer scientists working on encryption and filtering systems have been scared away from their research by legal threats from corporations manufacturing such systems.[13] The DMCA and other laws have also impinged on academic databases and the circulation of electronic journals, once one of the unmistakably positive elements of the Internet. Many believe the restrictions are leading to the suffocation of works in the public domain for scholarship and a wholesale erosion of the global commons of information.

The DMCA is but a piece of a larger trend that includes other legal measures with the same intent, including other national, regional, and international regulations. For example, the United States Trade Representative has pushed the DMCA in bilateral trade negotiations, and many of its main elements are manifest in treaties administered by the World Intellectual Property Organization (WIPO). In 2001, the European Union passed the EU Copyright Directive, similar in intent to the DMCA. Among other things, the internationalization of the DMCA has raised questions about the relationship between intellectual property, human rights, international trade, and development. Although there is good evidence that the introduction of strong intellectual property laws encourages foreign direct investment, some have begun to explore ways in which intellectual property laws create new forms of dependency, locking businesses into monopolistic chains of exchange, preventing local entrepreneurship, and sacrificing human rights concerning access to essential medicines, health care, and information in favor of intellectual property protections.[14]

Some of the limitations on free speech and access to information are emerging not through new laws but changes in industry practices and to the architecture of the Internet, including most importantly the advent of "tiered services." Historically, the development of the Internet's architecture has followed a trajectory following the principle of "network neutrality"—that is, the network should not discriminate on the basis of connecting hardware or content delivery.[15] In other words, all network devices and content should be treated equally from an architectural standpoint. Although in reality there has always been some measure of tiering in the Internet's architecture, neutrality has always been considered the underlying principle around which the Internet's design should evolve. Over the course of the Internet's evolution, however, this principle has been steadily eroding, and tiering deepened, codified, and extended. The biggest force behind these developments has been private broadband and telecom providers, who charge (or are proposing to charge) differential rates of connectivity for subscribers, or who arbitrarily set variable connectivity rates for content providers within the corporate-ownership family, as opposed to those competitors without.[16] Although the erosion of the "network neutrality" principle has met with stiff civic opposition, the proponents of tiered services represent a formidable constituency of telecommunications and Internet service providers, and the trend looks likely to persist.[17]

Perhaps of most concern are measures taken to protect intellectual property and copyright through technical means; in particular through the introduction of codes built into the software and hardware that structure permissible communications. A wide range of devices, from Apple's iPod to Playstation and Xbox, build into their products code to enforce digital rights management, so that software communicates securely with vendors. Once installed, the codes prevent applications other than those that fall within the trusted platform as a whole from working, building into the architecture a kind of software-based vertical integration. Apart from the restriction of choice and user innovation, such initiatives could create a new dependency around major vendors like Microsoft, especially for the developing world. More broadly, such initiatives foment a litigious environment around electronic communications that in turn could lead to self-censorship. You know something does not square properly for the notion of the public sphere when explicit consent must be given to lengthy legal documents before installing a piece of software, viewing a downloaded movie, or entering a chat room—now a commonplace part of the cyberspace experience.[18]

While directed at the illegal trading of software, music, and video files, legislation and activities such as those outlined above are having the unintended effect of overriding technologies and communicative practices that are used and should be considered vital to support civic networks, such as open source software, P2P network systems, and a global commons of information in the open public domain. What makes these new laws so draconian, as Lessig in particular has argued, is that their enforcement can now be implemented by code—in other words written into the very architecture of the Internet itself.[19] Such a shift in intellectual property regimes does not just affect a compartmentalized sphere of activity on the Internet or ensure that piracy is stemmed (although even that is debatable in a digital environment). Rather, it affects the very architecture of the Internet, corralling online communications into channels that support information consumption and the so-called knowledge economy, while stifling the democratic exchange of ideas and creative production.[20]

State Content Filtering as Internet Censorship

One of the conventional wisdoms about the Internet is that it is immune to state control. During the 1990s, many observers extrapolated far-reaching implications for state sovereignty tied to the properties of digital electronic communications, drawing inferences from the swift way in which banned content could be made available by "mirroring" the content on other Web sites. While global flows of communication have made state censorship difficult, to be sure, they have not made it impossible. Many states around the world, assisted by new software technologies, have put in place highly developed Internet content filtering systems that place controls on what type of information their citizens can access. When accompanied by contextual factors, such as severe regulations and stiff penalties imposed on user activities and ISPs, these tools have begun to carve out national censorship islands within the global flow of information.

Although state content filtering practices are growing and widespread, knowledge of them has tended to be limited. In part, this is a function of a lack of accountability and transparency about these practices. In part, it is a function of the lack of empirical evidence. Up until recently, the majority of reports on Internet censorship tended to emerge from users, news reports, or advocacy organizations. Not surprisingly, they have tended to be unsystematic, sometimes unreliable, and contradicted by states themselves. Moreover, because of the complex and varied ways in which filtering can be implemented, reports have occasionally been made in error or have contained contradictory information.

Overcoming this problem has been one of the main goals of the OpenNet Initiative (ONI), a collaborative project among researchers at the Universities of Toronto, Harvard, Cambridge, and Oxford, plus partner organizations worldwide.[21] The aim of the ONI has been to develop a systematic way to investigate empirically Internet filtering practices from behind national firewalls over an extended period of time to give an accurate picture of state content filtering practices. The ONI employs a unique methodology that combines in-field investigations by partners and associates who travel to or live in the countries concerned and a suite of technical interrogation tools that probe the Internet directly for forensic evidence of content filtering and filtering technologies, about which more will be said below. The aim of the ONI is to provide a comprehensive picture of Internet content filtering in a particular country by probing all aspects of the national information infrastructure (Internet cafés, ISPs, wireless networks, backbone gateways) and over an extended period of time, testing accessibility in both English and local languages.

Since 2002, the ONI has produced eleven country reports (Belarus, Yemen, Tunisia, Burma, Singapore, Iran, China, Bahrain, United Arab Emirates, Vietnam, and Saudi Arabia) and various bulletins and advisories. In 2006, the ONI conducted the first global survey of Internet censorship, running field tests in more than forty countries worldwide.[22] As the research makes clear, the scope, scale, and sophistication of Internet content filtering practices are on the rise worldwide. Furthermore, these practices are spreading in a largely unaccountable and nontransparent fashion.

Increasing Scope   At the start of the ONI project in 2002, only a handful of countries were known to actively engage in Internet content filtering practices, including China and Saudi Arabia. Over the course of the last four years, however, the number of countries has grown rapidly. As a reflection, the ONI has expanded its global testing regime from eleven to forty countries worldwide based on reports of Internet filtering. The type of countries engaged in filtering range from advanced industrialized countries, like Norway, the United Kingdom, Germany, France, Australia, the United States, and Canada to nondemocratic and authoritarian regimes like Tunisia, Iran, China, and Uzbekistan. There are many reasons for this increasing scope: growing securitization of information and communication policies since 9/11; the spread of "best practices" and imitation among states that censor; the increased sophistication of commercially available filtering technologies marketed to countries as "solutions" to economic, social, and political problems; concerns over access to material involving the sexual exploitation of children or "extremist" Web sites. Whatever the reasons, there can be no doubt that Internet content filtering is on the rise worldwide. States are recolonizing information environments within their territorial spaces and content filtering practices are becoming seen as legitimate tools to such ends.

Increasing Scale   The actual content and services that authorities are targeting for filtering is increasing, suggesting that states are reaching further down into the information and communications matrix to which their citizens have access. Typically, most states justify their content filtering practices in terms of blocking "culturally offensive" information, such as pornography. And pornography remains the single most common category of content that is blocked on the Internet across those categories tested by the ONI. However, once content filtering mechanisms are put in place and authorities are accustomed to the capabilities at their disposal, there is a temptation to further encroach upon access to information by blocking other types of content. In Pakistan, for example, the government started by filtering access to Web sites containing imagery offensive to Islam but now targets content relating to the Balochistan independence movement and a variety of extremist sites. Among the countries that the ONI examined, state content filtering targeted access to news, human rights information, opposition movements, local dissident groups, religious conversion Web sites, Web sites providing access to translation, anonymizer, privacy, and security enhancing tools, such as encryption systems and circumvention tools.

Increasing Sophistication   Not surprisingly, the methods used to do Internet content filtering have become more sophisticated, as states and the firms that sell censorship and surveillance technologies continually refine them. There are several examples of increasing sophistication. First, authorities are becoming increasingly adept at targeting newly developed modes of communication, such as blogs, SMS, chat, instant messaging protocols, and Voice-over-IP (VOIP) services. In the past, such newly devised methods of information sharing could be used as a means to circumvent Internet censorship. However, today, authorities are becoming more adept at targeting new media and developing methods particular to such services. Second, although content filtering is prone to overblocking and error, there are examples where authorities have been able to use such technologies with precision.

A good example is China's targeting of the specific string of codes embedded in the URL of the Google cache function.[23] The latter is a service provided by Google whereby users can connect to archived information from Web sites stored on Google's servers, rather than on the servers of the original Web site. The service was designed to provide a way to access information through redundancy, but it is also a very simple and effective way to get around content filtering. Since users connect to Google servers rather than to the blacklisted servers, they bypass the content filters. Upon learning of this technique, China implemented a blocked string on their backbone/gateway routers that prevented any use of the Google cache function from within China.

A third example of increasing sophistication of content filtering is the targeting of local languages and Web sites of opposition movements and dissidents particular to a particular national context. Figure 5.1 below shows the results of ONI tests from within China comparing the top 100 Google search results for keywords in English and Chinese. As the results show, a very significant disproportionate amount of keywords are filtered when they are searched for in Chinese as opposed to English.

Table 5.1 shows a similar set of test results from ONI research on Iran. In this case, many of the blocked Web sites in various categories had a higher percentage of inaccessibility in Farsi as opposed to English. Overall, 80 percent of the Farsi-language Web sites tested were inaccessible whereas 45 percent of English language sites were inaccessible. Such localization filtering—where "international" sources of information are left accessible while local variants are blocked—may at first seem counterintuitive. However, there are two potential explanations. First, localization filtering targets those groups that matter most to regime stability and power, such as local opposition movements and dissident groups presenting contentious information in languages spoken by citizens within the country. Second, the disproportionately open access to English language international sites can give the impression that access to global information

Figure 5.1
A comparison of Google search results of Chinese and English keywords. *Source:* OpenNet
Initiative, Internet Filtering in Chisandra, 2004–2005, http://opennet.net/studies/china/

Table 5.1
Inaccessible Sites—Iran

General Category	English Only			Available in Farsi		
	# Blocked	# Tested	%	# Blocked	# Tested	%
Blogs	5	5	100%	43	44	98%
Lifestyles	1	10	10%	3	5	60%
News	1	20	5%	13	26	50%
Opposition & Dissent	10	26	38%	15	36	42%
Political/Religious/Social (General)	7	7	100%	56	58	97%
Politics	9	9	100%	41	42	98%
Religion	0	15	0%	4	9	44%
Sex	6	6	100%	3	3	100%
Total (Includes non-categorized sites)	54	121	45%	199	250	80%

is wide open, particularly to foreign journalists who do not speak local languages. Authorities can point to contentious human rights and news sites in English and say that they allow access to information, while blocking relatively more obscure sites that matter most to local politics.

Accountability and Transparency Issues Related to Internet Content Filtering

In politics, accountability and transparency are seen as important components of good governance, particularly in liberal democratic states. Accountability is defined as identifying and holding public and private officials to account for their actions; transparency is defined as reliable, relevant, and timely information about the activities of public and private officials made available to the public. Both are seen as being important checks on the extent to which authorities can deviate from their permitted roles in governing. There has been a remarkable lack of accountability and transparency in the areas of Internet content filtering that the ONI has examined on the part of both states that filter and the corporations that provide the technologies used to do the filtering.

Secrecy Although there is no prima facie reason why states should withhold information about content filtering and surveillance, the area is shrouded in secrecy for two reasons. First, many states have tended to treat Internet censorship as a domain to be withheld from public scrutiny because of the connection to intelligence and national security. Historically, collection and interception of information and communications has been a closely guarded branch of state intelligence—among the most top secretive of all state activities. Within many countries, the methods and objects of content filtering are not disclosed because of the connections to intelligence gathering, both in terms of domestic and international contexts. Filtering technologies can and often are placed "beneath the surface" of a country's national information infrastructure, for all intents and purposes "hidden" from public scrutiny and not acknowledged as even existing.

Second, many of the states (though not all) that engage in Internet content filtering are not democratic states, and so make decisions about what information to release to citizens on the basis of regime power and national security interests, imposing uneven and largely arbitrarily defined levels of oversight and feedback. The result is a mixed range of openness and transparency among states that filter. For example, Saudi Arabia is relatively open about the fact that it engages in Internet filtering, going so far as to provide extensive documentation for public consumption about its Internet content filtering regime. It even makes some gestures toward public accountability by offering an online avenue for public complaints and feedback. When users visit a banned site in Saudi Arabia, a standard blocked page is returned to their browser with an option to register complaints or suggest further sites for filtering.

China, on the other, has at least once officially admitted to its Internet filtering practices, while at other times denying that it does so. Liu Zhengrong, an official with the Chinese government responsible for Internet filtering, defended the country Internet content filtering regime at a press conference in February 2006.[24] The official likened China's filtering practices to those of private companies in the United States, and said the brunt of its filtering is aimed at screening out child pornography. While the press conference was certainly a measure of some degree of transparency, China's filtering practices as a whole are almost entirely secretive. The very fact that such a press conference is a rare occurrence is suggestive of the lack of transparency and accountability. And while the Chinese official discussed some of the objects of content filtering, he was entirely misleading about others, such as blocking access to religious movements, human rights groups, and dissidents. More recently, a Chinese representative at the Internet Governance Task Force meetings in Athens claimed that the Internet is not censored at all by China.

The more filtering practices are withheld from public scrutiny and accountability, the more tempting it is for state authorities to employ these tools for illegitimate reasons, including stifling opposition and civil society networks. Working to bring these practices into the realm of public disclosure and oversight, however, is a function of broader issues relating to democratization and the rule of law within each of the countries concerned—a formidable problem beyond just the issues of Internet content filtering. This problem is exacerbated by the fact that censorship practices, when they are focused on democratic opposition movements, inhibit grassroots civil society organization and thus stifle those very groups who would likely push for greater openness and accountability among governments. The more that Internet content filtering is defined as an element of national security policy, the less likely it is to be treated as a function of statecraft open to accountability and transparency.

Corporate Accountabilty   As the scope, scale, and sophistication of Internet censorship has increased, so too has the market for the technologies employed for such ends. Many of the most advanced technologies of Internet censorship have been developed and marketed by multinational corporations whose home base is the United States. A second area of commercial involvement in Internet filtering is the collusion by companies with authorities in terms of providing archived information stored on their servers that is in turn used to arrest and imprison dissidents. The extent to which these corporations should be held accountable for their actions in these areas has become a matter of wide public debate, and in the United States, the subject of congressional inquiries and regulatory proposals.

ONI research has empirically verified the use of a range of commercial technologies in national filtering regimes around the world. For example, our research has documented the use of a product called SmartFilter, made by the U.S. company Secure

Computing, Inc., in the filtering systems of Kuwait, Oman, Saudi Arabia, Tunisia, the United Arab Emirates, and Iran. The company does not advertise that it sells filtering technologies to regimes that restrict access to information. Our research was able to ascertain the use of SmartFilter in these cases by a series of "forensic fingerprints"—categorization errors unique to the Smartfilter program and detailed analysis of http header information. The Iranian case was particularly troublesome for Secure Computing because U.S. regulations forbid the sale of technology products to Iran and the sale of SmartFilter would have presented a serious violation of those laws. Secure Computing denied that it sold the product to Iran, speculating that Iranian ISPs had somehow acquired an unregistered version of its product illegally.[25] In addition to the use of SmartFilter, our research has documented several other commercial products in the course of our research: The United States produced Netcache is often used in conjunction with filtering products like SmartFilter and is employed in Iran; the U.S. product Websense was used in Iran and is now used by Yemen; the U.S. product Fortinet is employed in Burma; Cisco routers filter at the backbone level in China; and Singapore uses the U.S. product SurfControl.[26]

A related corporate accountability and transparency issue concerns corporate practices around user information protection and sharing information with regimes that violate human rights. For example, the American Internet company Yahoo! turned over e-mail records to the Chinese government leading to the arrest of three people, Jiang Lijun, Shi Tao, and Li Zhi. In testimony before U.S. Congress, Yahoo said that they had no choice but to comply with the request, that "Yahoo! China was legally obligated to comply with the requirements of Chinese law enforcement" . . . or face the possibility of "criminal charges, including imprisonment." Ultimately U.S. Companies in China face a choice: comply with Chinese law, or leave. Concerning filtering of search engine results, Yahoo said that they were "deeply concerned by efforts of governments to restrict and control open access to information and communication . . . [and] . . . if we are required to restrict search results, we will strive to achieve maximum transparency to the user."[27] However the ONI's tests of the search engines operated and/or owned by Yahoo contradict these claims, revealing very little transparency.[28]

There are issues of accountability and transparency having to do with the proprietary nature of commercial filtering technologies. Filtering software works by having lists of categorized Web sites and keywords that can be activated by customers, and which are updated typically through online connections to databases operated by the companies. The companies themselves treat the lists as intellectual property and normally do not disclose what sites are included and/or how they are categorized. Although some companies, like Secure Computing, allow tests of their filtering software online, none of the companies openly discloses the contents of their lists to public scrutiny. The lack of openness—although understandable from a commercial perspective—has significant public policy implications when commercial filtering software is used at a national level to filter access to information on public networks, as happens in numerous countries around the world today.

Increasingly, the corporations who supply or are implicated in Internet filtering and surveillance have come under pressure from rights and advocacy organizations worldwide, and at least in one case—the United States—from their home governments. As mentioned above, U.S. Congressional hearings have been held, and at least one piece of legislation—the Global Internet Freedom Act—has been proposed that will restrict the sale of filtering and surveillance technologies to regimes that violate human rights. Outside of the U.S. context, however, there are presently no forums within which the activities of corporations selling filtering and surveillance technologies could be restricted. One possibility is that the corporations themselves will agree upon norms or codes of behavior to avoid legislation being imposed on them, but that seems unlikely in the present competitive environment and would be of questionable value considering the lack of an enforcement mechanism.

The picture that emerges from the ONI's research shows an Internet that is much more of a patchwork quilt than a borderless world of free-flowing information. Such censorship strategies, employed in many cases with Western commercial filtering technologies, restrict the capacity of civic networks to disseminate information both at home and abroad, harming information and education initiatives along with lobbying efforts and awareness campaigns. Furthermore, they constrain the researching, networking, and resource-sharing opportunities of NGOs and civic networks with other domestic and international NGOs by effectively blocking e-mail access, Web sites and other Internet services.

Electronic Surveillance

An important lever of modern state power has always been the ability to eavesdrop on and collect electronic information. During the Cold War, massive resources were directed to electronic espionage, including the creation of an international network of signals intelligence that included the United States, Canada, the United Kingdom, Australia, and New Zealand.[29] In liberal democratic states, regulations were enacted over time that restricted the type of information that could be collected and what could be done with it once collected, although some areas, particularly intelligence, operated with little oversight and control. At the least, most liberal democratic states maintained sharp divisions between domestic law enforcement and foreign surveillance and information collection as a way to check and constrain the centralization of power.

Since 9/11, however, these checks and constraints have been loosened and in some cases deliberately ignored. First, legislation has been adopted by many states around the world that paves the way for a far more permissive environment for electronic surveillance and the sharing of information among domestic law enforcement and foreign intelligence. Specific state legislation along these lines includes the United States Patriot Act, the United Kingdom Crime and Security Act, Canada's and Australia's Anti-Terrorism Acts, among others. At the international level, the Council of Europe's Cybercrime Treaty, while initiated prior to 9/11, has been beefed up significantly since. The Cybercrime Treaty has become a major legislative node that includes not only European powers, but potentially states outside Europe as well, such as Canada, Australia, South Africa, and the United States, all of whom will have to make domestic adjustments to its invasive provisions once ratified. Among other controversial elements, the treaty allows for intrusive wiretaps that allow for the real-time collection of traffic, forces individuals with knowledge of security methods related to data of concern to reveal them under force of law and places extraordinary responsibilities on ISPs to collect and archive content for "lawful access." Although each of these pieces of legislation differs, what they have in common is the introduction of a substantially more permissive environment for the use of electronic wiretaps, the collection of e-mail and Web surfing data, and the sharing of information between law enforcement and intelligence agencies, both domestically and internationally.

Electronic surveillance has been augmented not only by new regulations but also by new technologies, including video surveillance systems, biometric and facial recognition technologies, and "smart" identification cards. Both Australia and Canada, for example, have introduced controversial plans to keep security databases on travelers leaving and entering the country. Many of these new technologies have been introduced without accompanying regulations on usage. In the area of video surveillance, for example, many countries have no limits on what can be done with the data once collected. In some countries, like the United Kingdom, the data derived from public and private video surveillance technologies is already being actively integrated into intelligence collection operations.

One remarkable illustration of the extent to which state electronic surveillance has been enhanced has been the revelations of extralegal electronic surveillance undertaken by the Bush Administration and the United States National Security Agency. In 2005, the New York Times reported that the Bush Administration had ordered the National Security Agency to eavesdrop on phone calls of American citizens without warrants—an order that seems to violate U.S. laws prohibiting the collection of intelligence on U.S. citizens.[30] While the Bush administration has claimed the wiretaps are legal under executive order, most observers, and at least one judge ruling on the case, believes the actions are not. However the specific issue is resolved, the case underscores the extent to which constraints on electronic surveillance have eroded since 9/11.

So far, the surveillance outlined has been limited to that which takes place on behalf of law enforcement and intelligence. For decades, commercial organizations have been undertaking analogous surveillance practices targeting consumer purchasing and transaction habits both on and offline. From the use of cookies to track Web surfing to the collation of credit card purchases to the use of closed circuit television (CCTV) cameras in private and public space, corporations have gathered a wealth of information on individuals' habits from new ICTs. What makes them more troublesome today, however, is the prospect not only of the relaxation of privacy laws designed to restrain such practices but also the increased porosity of commercial and state databases due to post- 9/11 security legislation.

These measures fundamentally alter the environment within which Internet communications take place. NGOs and civil society networks, particularly in human rights and humanitarian areas and those working in repressive regimes or on behalf of resistance movements, are of course most immediately affected. But the intensification of surveillance practices raises much deeper concerns about the nature of electronic communications for the electronic public sphere. Much like freedom of speech, liberal democratic societies depend on and value strong protections for privacy. While at one time the Internet may have enabled privacy through anonymous communications, all signals today point to its rapid dissolution.

Militarization of Cyberspace

Accompanying electronic surveillance has been the largely overlooked militarization of cyberspace. A great deal of attention has focused on the question of cyberterrorism, particularly in the wake of 9/11 and fears of potential terrorist use of electronic networks. While some see the possibility of an "electronic Pearl Harbor" being unleashed by terrorists, skilled individuals and nonstate actors, many others believe these fears are largely overdrawn and ignore the redundancies built into the architecture of the Internet, as well as the relatively low payoff for groups whose ultimate aim is violence. In spite of the alarm, there are no empirical examples of cyberterrorism to date, unless the term is used so broadly as to encompass politically motivated hacks on Web sites and occasional inconveniences caused by denial of service attacks. Rather than tools of mass destruction, threats from terrorist actors employing the Internet to wreak violence appear to bode little more than periodic disruptions to Internet traffic.[31]

Whatever the ultimate nature of the threat, the debate has largely obscured a potentially more serious development: the quiet expansion and adoption of offensive information warfare capabilities by states. The military use of cyberspace operates on a new terrain, presenting many thorny legal and moral questions concerning the targeting of civilian infrastructures, and the boundaries between an armed assault, a probe, the collection of information, and the dissemination of propaganda.[32] Theory has definitely trailed behind practice in this case.

As in most areas of military capabilities, the United States leads the cyber arms race. The development of cyberwar tools can be seen as a natural evolution of the so-called Revolution in Military Affairs (RMA), the latter defined as a major change in the nature of warfare brought about by the innovative use of new technologies and organizational structures related to them; from advanced computing and communications technologies to remote sensors. Going back further, its roots can be found in the use of propaganda and psychological warfare techniques and electronic jamming that date to the Second World War: electromagnetic pulse bombs (EMPs) and the insertion of malicious codes and secret back doors in software for intelligence purposes during the Cold War.

Since 2001, however, these roots have solidified into a coherent doctrine around fighting and winning wars in cyberspace.[33] In mid-2006, the U.S. Department of Defense was well underway in preparing the country's first National Military Strategy for Operations in Cyberspace. While the details of the strategy are expected to remain classified, the identification of cyberspace as a distinct "domains of operations" equal to land, air, sea, and space, mark an acknowledgment of its importance to national military capabilities and national security. The strategy is expected to unify and expand the Computer Network Operations that are presently distributed among several separate commands (Joint Task Force—Computer Network Operations, 67th Network Warfare Wing, as well as dedicated resources of the National Security Agency and elsewhere). In December 2006, the U.S. Air Force announced the establishment of the U.S. Cyberspace Command (formally becoming the 8th Air Force), that is expected to become the global force provider for all U.S. cyberspace operations and will include both offensive and defense Computer Network Operations. The formal announcement of this capability is expected to accelerate the emergence of similar capabilities among other military powers. Already, both China and Russia have declared doctrines for pursing cyberspace operations. China's doctrine of "Integrated Network Electronic Warfare" for example, considers computer network attacks as essential to developing a first-strike capability. Special units consisting of reservists drawn from among China's research and computational elite have been formed within the People's Liberation Army, and since 2006, these units have reportedly participated in large-scale exercises. The entry of the United States and major regional superpowers into cyberspace operations is likely to spur an arms race as military establishments worldwide seek to develop both offensive and defensive capabilities.

The number of documented state cyberwar cases has risen in recent years as well. In spite of the greater penetration of these technologies in advanced industrialized countries, many of the more prominent examples of information warfare have occurred in the developing world. It is, of course, well known that radio networks were employed by Hutus militia to incite genocidal violence against Tutsi in Rwanda. Later, the Rwandan military regularly eavesdropped on insecure United Nations and humanitarian NGOs' communications networks, and, in at least one case, used the intelligence to hunt down and kill Hutu refugees. During the Russian campaign against Chechnya in the mid-1990s, Chechen commanders made efficient use of mobile phone networks and eavesdropped on insecure Russian radio networks to organize devastatingly successful military strikes. In 2000, an "inter-fada" erupted between Israeli and Lebanese hackers as each bombarded the other's networks in distributed denial of service attacks. In the 2002 reoccupation of Palestine by the Israeli Defence Forces (IDF), the IDF systematically targeted the communications and information infrastructure of the Palestinian Authority and other civil society groups in tactics ranging from removing hard drives to disabling telephone switchboards.[34] In 2005 and 2006, the ONI documented the use of denial of service attacks in Kyrgyszatan and Belarus against key opposition Web sites by authorities during critical election periods.[35]

What are the concerns for global civic networks of the militarization of cyberspace? In some respects, the threats may be exaggerated. Just as networked redundancies and distributed security practices constrain the potential ramifications of cyberterrorism, there may be natural limits to the type of havoc states can wreak on the global communications infrastructure. There are also rational, as well as technological, constraints. Much like the deterrent effect of nuclear weapons, states that are home to private corporations with assets spread transnationally throughout the world face strong financial incentives to preserve the security and seamless functioning of global communications networks that are the sinews of hypercapitalism. These constraints should not be overdrawn, however. Rational choice models of costs and benefits do not always translate neatly into the equations drawn for the use of force internationally. And even targeted attacks on infrastructures can cause enormous disruptions to the flows of information worldwide, as several recent worms and viruses have demonstrated.

More broadly for global democratic governance, however, is a theoretical question about the proper constitutive relationship between military and civilian spheres in liberal democratic polities, particularly as these bear on questions concerning the design of the public sphere. The Internet is much more than a simple appendage to other sectors of world politics—it is the forum or commons within which civic communications will take place. Preserving this commons from militarization is as essential to global democratic governance as is the judicial restraint on force in domestic political spheres. Given the race by states to develop offensive information warfare capabilities, and its potentially destructive and unforeseeable consequences, has the time come for a kind of cyberspace arms control? If so, what might that look like and how might it emerge? Though not described in terms of arms control per se, the following section offers a survey of the prospects.

Transnational Information Security and Global Civic Networks?

The time has long since passed when it would be beneficial for global civic networks to allow the Internet to evolve on its own. Although its initial open, liberal architecture provided an enormous boost to civic networks around the world, changes outlined above have begun to alter its root characteristics. As it stands to date, these changes overwhelmingly reflect the interests of businesses on the one hand and states' military and intelligence agencies on the other. These social forces have different conceptions of what constitutes a threat, what is to be protected, and what should be the prevailing design of the global communications infrastructure, and they have considerable resources at their disposal to bring those interests to fruition. Unless a transnational social movement arises to bring to bear on Internet governance the concerns of civic networks—an open commons of information, freedom of speech, privacy, and distributed grassroots communications—the prospect of building a communications infrastructure that supports, rather than detracts from, these basic human rights will become increasingly difficult.

While subject to assertions of power and attempts at control by states, civic networks have not sat by idly, responding and, in some cases, resisting these developments. Civic networks are pushing their strategic interests throughout the Internet environment, from codes and infrastructure to laws, norms, and ideas. Though lacking the formal legal authority and coercive power of states, or the structural market power of firms, civic networks are able to capitalize on the asymmetrical power resources conferred on them by the distributed technologies of the Internet itself. But are these asymmetric capacities enough to truly push back states and restore the Internet as an open environment of free expression and access to information? Are they enough to withstand the collateral impacts caused by state targeting of uncivil networks? The answers to these questions may not be apparent for many years to come. The following section outlines these efforts and offers an analysis of their prospects.[36]

Within a dynamic, technologically savvy sector of civic networks, a transnational social movement has emerged around what might be called "Internet protection"—that is, collective securitization action whose aim is to uphold the Internet as a forum of free expression and access to information through advocacy, training, policy development, and technological research and development. Though coming at the problem from different backgrounds, Internet protection advocates are beginning to network around a shared agenda of communications security and privacy, freedom of expression, equal access, the protection of an open public domain of knowledge, and the preservation of cultural diversity. The participants in this social movement include local, regional, and global nongovernmental organizations, activists, and policy networks, including major international rights organizations, such as Human Rights Watch and Amnesty International.

Critical to the constitution of this social movement has been the support provided by major, nonprofit research and advocacy foundations, such as the Ford Foundation, Markle Foundation, Open Society Institute, the MacArthur Foundation, and others. The support of these nonprofit foundations has included not only financial resources but also networking opportunities, venues for collaboration, and research and development coordination. To be sure, this type of support has had an important impact. However, the resources provided by these donor agencies do not rival the collective financial capacities that can be marshaled by states. Nor do they always come without unintended consequences. Scholars have noticed funding of this sort can promote the emergence of patron-client ties between donors and recipients, rather than horizontal links among civic networks. They may also create a hostile environment for civic networks due to the impression of outside interference and meddling—particularly if the NGOs are perceived as a thin vehicle for one state's foreign policy within the jurisdiction of another state. One recent study found that nineteen countries, concentrated mostly in Africa, the Middle East, and the Commonwealth of Independent States, have enacted or proposed laws that would in some way restrict the activities of civil society over the past five years.

One area where the pressures of the Internet protection social movement have been manifest, though to ambiguous effect, has been Internet governance. Internet governance is a complex affair, involving public and private actors at national, regional, and global levels of authority.[37] Although there is no single site of Internet governance, in recent years the United Nations, through the World Summit of the Information Society (WSIS) process and its follow-on, the Internet Governance Forum (IGF), has become an important center of gravity and an arena where numerous stakeholders, including civic networks, have coalesced. Over the course of the last several years, civic networks have helped press for inclusion of principles of "Internet protection" (privacy, freedom of expression, access to information) on the Internet governance agenda and achieved formal recognition as a stakeholder in the ongoing IGF process. The IGF process itself has served to both catalyze the civic network movement and serve as a global medium through which their collective values and interests can be legitimately expressed. From their mutual interaction, ideas are already beginning to emerge that give policy and technology focus to global civic networks, including creating zones of civic-run Internet access points and overlay networks designed to protect and preserve the public commons. At the IGF meeting in Athens in 2006, policy advocates proposed an Internet bill of rights. While admitting that the bill would have little meaningful impact on state policy in the short term, it is nonetheless a reflection of the extent to which civic networks are beginning to press the case of restraint on state activities in cyberspace. However, it is important to recall that the IGF lacks any rule-making or enforcement capacity that would affect state policy and certainly comes nowhere near impacting upon the assertions of state or corporate power outlined earlier in this chapter, which tend to be closely guarded tools of state military, intelligence, and law enforcement or backed up by strong intellectual property regimes.

None of this should diminish the norm-promoting and coordinating activities of the IGF, which are significant, particularly when considered in combination with other instances of awareness raising and advocacy undertaken by the Internet protection movement. Efforts by NGOs and rights organizations—including the OpenNet Initiative itself—have helped put a spotlight on Internet censorship and surveillance practices worldwide, as well as the technologies used to inform such practices. Although these efforts have not reigned in states or corporations entirely, they have forced some measure of accountability and transparency and have created a form of countersurveillance, or what media theorist Steve Mann has aptly called *sousveillance*.[38] Major Internet services companies, like Microsoft, Cisco, Yahoo, Google, and others, have had to answer for and even modify their practices in response to the sousveillance campaign of the Internet protection movement.

Hacktivism

One area where the asymmetric capacities of civic networks may be most tangibly felt is in building code, software, and other tools explicitly designed from an Internet protection perspective. From the outset, the Internet's character has been shaped not only by states and corporations but also by the distributed base of users themselves. Skilled computer geeks, hacktivists, and other individuals have been responsible for some of the most innovative Internet technologies, from open source/free software platforms to P2P networks and encryption systems. Although "Internet protection" technologies go back decades, in recent years there has been a more concerted and organized research and development effort, working in tandem with the policy/governance/awareness efforts described above. These efforts include tools to support anonymous communications online, such as the Tor system; tools that circumvent Internet censorship, such as psiphon or peacefire; and tools that support privacy online, such as PGP, ScatterChat, and others. These tools are, in turn, increasingly localized to different country contexts, distributed via non-governmental organizations and human rights networks, and built into training and advocacy workshops organized by the Internet protection civic networks described above.

It is difficult to determine the ultimate implications of the Internet protection efforts, particularly in the short run. Such civic networking and advocacy, like any civil rights movement, can take years to come to fruition and are a constant struggle. Certainly the Internet itself affords small, nonstate actors power resources that further their aims. But asymmetric capacities notwithstanding, it is clear that civic networks cannot hope to marshal the financial resources, legal authority, or even concerted policy direction that states can muster behind their strategic aims. These relative limitations can be seen, for example, in the sustainability problems surrounding the hacktivist tools described above. While one or another software project may puncture state control efforts, the momentum is presently in the opposition direction. Internet protection will require a long-term, globally distributed, and multilevel engagement, from code and infrastructure, to laws, norms, and ideas.

Conclusion

Generally speaking, theories of globalization, global civil society, and transnational networks have assumed a continuing trajectory of increasingly open and distributed communications. This trajectory in turn is gradually diminishing the power of the state while fuelling the rise of transnational nonstate networks. As the analysis above suggests, that assumption can no longer be taken for granted. Although the properties of the Internet may very well have been biased toward openness and decentralization in the past, it is important to remember that the Internet is not a fixed medium that will remain unchanged into the future and, as it changes, so too will its consequences. The Internet is, rather, a complex mix of technological systems in constant evolution, morphing in response to the pressures and technological choices of powerful actors able to influence its overall architecture. States—especially powerful ones like the United States—still constitute one of those major actors.

For those concerned with deepening and expanding the prospects for global civic networks, the evolving nature or architecture of the communications infrastructure should be, therefore, of vital concern. For all its many faults and digital divides, it is the Internet that is providing the means by which an increasing number of citizens around the world can and will deliberate, debate, and ultimately have an input into the rules of the game by which they are governed. While at one time the Internet, and in particular its characteristically liberal environment, could be taken for granted by civil society actors, that time has now passed. A formidable set of social forces is pushing regulations and technologies that, whatever their individual aims, collectively have the effect of taking that open, liberal architecture in a decidedly different direction. Global civic networks must now become dynamic participants in the politics of Internet design or risk having the power source for their activities increasingly unplugged.

To do so, however, international relations and media theorists—interested in and normatively in favor of opening up spaces for alternative voices, grassroots democracy, and global democratic governance to flourish—will have to pay greater attention to the material foundations upon which global communications take place. Doing so means qualifying notions of "ideas all the way down" and "worlds of our making" to acknowledge the extent to which material factors of communication, albeit socially constructed, present a formidable set of real constraints on the realm of the possible.

Quite naturally, those interested in such topics have been concerned primarily with moving away from older, positivist-materialist notions of state interaction to concerns about the circulation of ideas, the framing role of discourses, and processes of legitimation. But communication does not take place in a vacuum. It is anchored within and shaped by the material properties of the communications environment.

It is with some small measure of optimism, then, that one can look upon recent developments in the area of civic networks and Internet governance. Among the converging interests of NGO users, privacy advocates, computer scientists, and grassroots media, one can detect the emergence of a kind of epistemic community. Although principles have nowhere been formally codified, a constellation of values brings these groups together to help give shape to a common agenda. Bolstering this transnational social movement is the powerful ammunition of politically motivated research and development of civic technologies that feed into, and give concrete shape to, the Internet's basic structural design. Those material constraints, embedded in code, may in the long run provide the most important constitutional mechanisms to ensure that a communications infrastructure supports, rather than detracts from, basic human rights.

Notes

This chapter is a slightly revised and updated version of a previous article, Ronald J. Deibert, "Black Code: Censorship, Surveillance, and Militarization of Cyberspace," *Millenium: Journal of International Studies* 32, no. 3 (2003): 501–530. Among other changes, I have updated the empirical sections of the chapter to reflect the work of the Citizen Lab in the OpenNet Initiative project.

1. The landmark study in this respect is Manuel Castells, *The Rise of the Network Society*, vol. 1, *The Information Age: Economy, Society, and Culture* (Oxford: Blackwell, 1996).

2. See Herb Schiller, *Culture Inc.* (New York: Oxford University Press, 1989).

3. For the Citizen Lab, see http://www.citizenlab.org/. For the OpenNet Initiative, see http://opennet.net/.

4. For research on the "social construction of security," see Barry Buzan, Ole Wæver and Jaap de Wilde, *Security: A New Framework for Analysis* (Boulder, CO: Lynne Rienner Publishers, 1998) and Peter Katzenstein, ed., *The Culture of National Security: Norms and Identity in World Politics* (New York: Columbia University Press, 1996). I analyze in some depth different "paradigms" of Internet security in Ronald J. Deibert, "Circuits of Power: Security in the Internet Environment," in *Information Technologies and Global Politics: The Changing Scope of Power and Governance*, ed. J. P. Singh and James N. Rosenau (Albany, NY: SUNY Press, 2002), 115–142.

5. Ronald J. Deibert, *Parchment, Printing, and Hypermedia: Communication in World Order Transformation* (New York: Columbia University Press, 1997).

6. Harold A. Innis, *The Bias of Communication* (Toronto: University of Toronto Press, 1952).

7. See, for example, Michael A. Froomkin, "The Internet as Source of Regulatory Arbitrage," in *Borders in Cyberspace: Information Policy and the Global Information Infrastructure*, ed. Brian Kahin and Charles Nesson (Cambridge, MA: MIT Press, 1997), 129–163.

8. See in particular, Lawrence Lessig, *Codes and Other Laws of Cyberspace* (New York: Basic Books, 2000).

9. John Stuart Mill, *On Liberty*, Chapter 1: "This, then, is the appropriate region of human liberty. It comprises, first, the inward domain of consciousness; demanding liberty of conscience, in the most comprehensive sense; liberty of thought and feeling; absolute freedom of opinion and sentiment on all subjects, practical or speculative, scientific, moral, or theological." (New Haven: Yale University Press, 2003).

10. Third Annual BSA and IDC Global Software Piracy Study (May 2006; available at http://www.bsa.org/globalstudy/upload/2005%20Piracy%20Study%20%20Official%20Version.pdf).

11. For accessible discussions, see Siva Vaidhyanathan, Copyrights and *Copywrongs: The Rise of Intellectual Property and How It Threatens Creativity* (New York: New York University Press, 2001); and Lawrence Lessig, *The Future of Ideas: The Fate of the Commons in a Connected World* (New York: Random House, 2001).

12. Electronic Frontier Foundation, "Unintended Consequences: Three Years Under the DMCA" (May 3, 2002; available at http://www.eff.org/IP/DMCA/20020503_dmca_consequences.pdf).

13. Jonathan Band, "Congress Unknowingly Undermines Cyber-Security," SiliconValley.Com (December 16, 2002; http://www.siliconvalley.com/mld/siliconvalley/4750224.htm?template= contentModules/printstory.jsp). See also the Web site, http://chillingeffects.org/ for a detailed archive of such cases.

14. "Policy Brief on Intellectual Property, Development and Human Rights: How Human Rights Can Support Proposals for a World Intellectual Property Organization (WIPO) Development Agenda," Policy Brief 2 (February 2006; available online at http://www.3dthree.org/pdf_ 3D/3DPolBrief-WIPO-eng.pdf).

15. Tim Wu, "Network Neutrality, Broadband Discrimination," *Journal of Telecommunications and High Technology Law* 2 (2003: 141). Available online at SSRN, http://ssrn.com/abstract=388863. 141–175.

16. American Civil Liberties Union, "See No Competition: How Monopoly Control of the Broadband Internet Threatens Free Speech." ACLU White Paper, available at http://archive.aclu.org/ issues/cyber/NoCompetition.pdf.

17. An excellent resource is Tim Wu's "Network Neutrality" page, found at http://timwu.org/ network_neutrality.html.

18. For a nuanced discussion of the relationship between communicative capitalism, electronic networks, and the public sphere, see Jodi Dean's contribution to this volume.

19. See Lessig, *Code and Other Laws of Cyberspace*.

20. For a critique of global civil society from the perspective of communications and consumption, see Edward Comor, "The Role of Communication in Global Civil Society: Forces, Processes, Prospects," *International Studies Quarterly* 45, no. 3 (September 2001).

21. The principal investigators of the OpenNet Initiative project, apart from myself, are John Palfrey, Rafal Rohozinski, and Jonathan Zittrain.

22. See Ronald J. Deibert, John Palfrey, Rafal Rohozinski, and Jonathan Zittrain, *Access Denied: The Practice and Policy of Internet Content Filtering*, (Cambridge, MA: MIT Press, 2007). Unless where noted, the following section draws from the research of the ONI can be found in *Access Denied* or on the ONI's Web site.

23. See OpenNet Initiative Bulletin 006, "Google Search and Cache Filtering Behind China's Great Firewall," September 3, 2004, http://www.opennetinitiative.net/bulletins/006/.

24. See Joseph Kahn, "China Defends Internet Censorship," *New York Times*, February 15, 2006.

25. See http://www.itnews.com.au/newsstory.aspx?CIaNID=19195.

26. See http://www.opennetinitiative.net/modules.php?op=modload&name=Archive&file=index&req=viewarticle&artid=1.

27. Testimony of Michael Callahan, Senior Vice President and General Counsel, Yahoo! Inc., before the Subcommittees on Africa, Global Human Rights and International Operations, and Asia and the Pacific, February 15, 2006.

28. See OpenNet Initiative Bulletin 005, "Probing Chinese Search Engine Filtering," August 19, 2004, http://www.opennetinitiative.net/bulletins/005/.

29. James Bamford, *Body of Secrets: Anatomy of the Ultra Secret National Security Agency* (New York: Anchor Books, 2002); Matthew M. Aid and Cees Weibes, *Secrets of Signals Intelligence During the Cold War and Beyond* (London: Frank Cass, 2001).

30. James Risen and Eric Lichtblau, "Bush Lets U.S. Spy on Callers Without Courts," *New York Times*, December 16, 2005.

31. Of course, militant and extremist actors have been very capable adopters of Internet technologies for organizational and outreach purposes. Using the Internet to create violent disruptions to civilian targets, however, seems remote. See Evan F. Kohlmann, "The Real Online Terrorist Threat," *Foreign Affairs* 85, no. 5, 115.

32. William J. Bayles, "The Ethics of Computer Network Attack," *Parameters* (Spring 2001): 44–58.

33. The following section draws from Ronald Deibert and Rafal Rohozinski, *The Global Geopolitics of Internet Securitization* (forthcoming, 2008).

34. This section draws from Rafal Rohozinski, "Bullets to Bytes: Reflections on ICTs and 'Local' Conflict," in *Bombs, Bytes, and Bandwidth*, ed. Robert Latham (New York: New Press, 2003).

35. See http://www.opennetinitiative.net/studies/belarus/ONI_Belarus_Country_Study.pdf and http://opennet.net/special/kg/.

36. This section draws from Ronald Deibert and Rafal Rohozinski, "Good For Liberty, Bad for Security?" in Deibert et al., *Access Denied* (Cambridge, MA: MIT Press, 2007).

37. Milton Mueller et al., "Internet Governance: The State of Play," Internet Governance Project (2004), http://www.internetgovernance.org/pdf/ig-sop-final.pdf

38. http://wearcam.org/sousveillance/.

References

ACLU. No Competition: How Monopoly Control of the Broadband Internet Threatens Free Speech. July 7, 2002 White Paper available online at http://archive.aclu.org/issues/cyber/NoCompetition.pdf.

Aid, Matthew M., and Cees Weibes. 2001. *Secrets of Signals Intelligence during the Cold War and Beyond*. London: Frank Cass.

Bamford, James. 2002. *Body of Secrets: Anatomy of the Ultra Secret National Security Agency*. New York: Anchor Books.

Buzan, Barry, OleWæver, and Jaap de Wilde. 1998. *Security: A New Framework for Analysis*. Boulder, CO: Lynne Rienner.

Callahan, Michael. 2006. Senior Vice President and General Counsel, Yahoo! Inc. Testimony before the Subcommittees on Africa, Global Human Rights and International Operations, and Asia and the Pacific, February 15.

Castells, Manuel. 1996. *The Rise of the Network Society*, vol. 1, *The Information Age: Economy, Society, and Culture*. Oxford: Blackwell.

Comor, Edward. 2001. "The Role of Communication in Global Civil Society: Forces, Processes, Prospects," *International Studies Quarterly* 45, no. 3. 389–408.

Deibert, Ronald J. 1997. *Parchment, Printing, and Hypermedia: Communication in World Order Transformation*. New York: Columbia University Press.

———. 2002. "Circuits of Power: Security in the Internet Environment," in *Information Technologies and Global Politics: The Changing Scope of Power and Governance*, ed. J. P. Singh and James N. Rosenau, 115–142. Albany, NY: SUNY Press.

———. 2003. "Black Code: Censorship, Surveillance, and Militarization of Cyberspace," *Millenium: Journal of International Studies* 32, no. 3 (2003): 501–530.

Deibert, Ronald J., and John Palfrey, Rafal Rohozinski, and Jonathan Zittrain. 2007. *Access Denied: The Practice and Policy of Internet Content Filtering.* Cambridge, MA: MIT Press.

Deibert, Ronald J., and Rafal Rohozinski. 2007. "Good For Liberty, Bad for Security?" in *Access Denied,* ed. Deibert et al. Cambridge, MA: MIT Press.

———. *The Global Geopolitics of Internet Securitization* (manuscript in preparation).

Electronic Frontier Foundation. Unintended Consequences: Three Years under the DMCA. May 3, 2002. Available at http://www.eff.org/IP/DMCA/20020503_dmca_consequences.pdf.

Froomkin, Michael A. "The Internet as Source of Regulatory Arbitrage," in *Borders in Cyberspace: Information Policy and the Global Information Infrastructure,* ed. Brian Kahin and Charles Nesson, 129–163. Cambridge, MA: MIT Press.

Innis, Harold. 1952. *The Bias of Communication.* Toronto: University of Toronto Press.

Katzenstein, Peter, ed., *The Culture of National Security: Norms and Identity in World Politics.* New York: Columbia University Press.

Kohlmann, Evan F. 2006. "The Real Online Terrorist Threat," *Foreign Affairs,* 115–124.

Lessig, Lawrence. 2000. *Codes and Other Laws of Cyberspace.* New York: Basic Books.

———. 2001. *The Future of Ideas: The Fate of the Commons in a Connected World.* New York: Random House.

Mueller, Milton, et al., 2004. "Internet Governance: The State of Play." Internet Governance Project. Available at http://www.internetgovernance.org/pdf/ig-sop-final.pdf.

OpenNet Initiative Bulletin 006. "Google Search and Cache Filtering Behind China's Great Firewall." September 3, 2004. Available at http://www.opennetinitiative.net/bulletins/006/.

———. 005. "Probing Chinese Search Engine Filtering." August 19, 2004. Available at http://www.opennetinitiative.net/bulletins/005/.

Rohozinski, Rafal. 2003. "Bullets to Bytes: Reflections on ICTs and 'Local' Conflict," in *Bombs, Bytes, and Bandwidth,* ed. Robert Latham. New York: New Press.

Schiller, Herb. *Culture Inc.* New York: Oxford University Press.

Third Annual BSA and IDC Global Software Piracy Study (May 2006). Available at http://www.bsa.org/globalstudy/upload/2005PiracyStudy-OfficialVersion.pdf.

Vaidhyanathan, Siva. 2001. *Copyrights and Copywrongs: The Rise of Intellectual Property and How It Threatens Creativity.* New York: New York University Press.

Wu, Timothy. 2005. "Network Neutrality, Broadband Discrimination." *Journal of Telecommunications and High Technology Law* 3.23: 69–95.

II The Changing Face of News Media

6 Media and Democracy

Susan D. Moeller

The Rhetoric of "Democracy"

Shortly before Thanksgiving in November 2006, President George W. Bush embarked on a five-day trip to Asia. On his last stop, in Indonesia, several thousand protesters staged demonstrations against the White House's policies in Iraq. At a press conference at the presidential palace in Bogor, President Bush was asked how he would respond to the protesters "saying that your policy in the Middle East and Iraq and elsewhere is anti-Islamic." Bush answered:

Look, I applaud a society where people are free to come and express their opinion. And it's to Indonesia's credit that it's a society where people are able to protest and say what they think. . . . My answer to people about whether or not—how do you comfort people of the Muslim faith that our policies are open, is that I believe freedom is universal and democracy is universal. . . . I believe people desire to live in free societies, and I believe the vast majority of people want to live in moderation and not have extremists kill innocent people. And so, therefore, our policies are to promote that kind of form of government.[1]

During the Bush administration, "democracy," while a term comfortably familiar to all Americans, increasingly became part of the conservative foreign policy lexicon. The word "democracy" as used by President Bush signaled the White House's avowed commitment to exporting representative government, but it was often employed reflexively—especially in speeches with leaders of nations where democracy has been anything but certain, solid, or transparent—giving an air of wishful thinking to such moments. Oval Office meetings and state visits with presidents, prime ministers, and leaders of international institutions are formal ceremonies where little more than rhetorical pabulum is expected. But President Bush's usage of "democracy" on such public occasions helped abstract "democracy" from its civic meaning.[2]

As employed by the Bush White House, "democracy," like the words "family," "mother," and "child," became more of a political term used to stake a claim to an abstract foundational value than a word denoting something concrete. Democracy was one of the chief rhetorical weapons employed by the administration in the aftermath of September 11: "The war on terror is a struggle between freedom and tyranny, and . . . the path to lasting security is to defeat the hateful vision the terrorists are spreading with the hope of freedom and democracy," argued President Bush in a speech at George Washington University in Washington, D.C. in 2006.[3]

Here one sees President Bush characterizing democracy as a transcendent value—less of a governmental structure than an ideological weapon. Speaking to the Secretary General of NATO, in the Oval Office in October that same year, President Bush noted that the Secretary-General had "made NATO [into] a values-based organization that is capable of dealing with the true threats of the 21st century . . . I particularly appreciate the fact that you have led the 26 nations of NATO into Afghanistan to help this young democracy. You know what I know, that the real challenge for the future is to help people of moderation and young democracies succeed in the face of threats and attacks by radicals and extremists who do not share our ideology, have kind of a dark vision of the world.[4]

In this construction, "democracy" is the core political "value" that governments and security organizations such as NATO must use to counter the global extremist, terrorist agenda. As President Bush remarked in a speech in West Virginia in March 2006, "We're dealing with a group of folks that want to spread an ideology, and they see a problem developing in Iraq, and so they're heading into Iraq to fight us, because they can't stand the thought of democracy. Democracy trumps their ideology every time. Freedom and democracy represent hope; their point of view represents despair."[5] In 2006 the Bush administration planned deep cuts in antipoverty spending in order to reorient aid to promote democracy and fight terrorism. "A little-noticed statement on the Web site of the Agency for International Development," observed *The New York Times*, "says the goal is to 'focus all U.S. foreign assistance on helping to build and sustain democratic and well-governed states.'"[6]

The terrorists, President Bush argued, want to "stop democracy . . . democracy stands for the exact opposite of their vision. Liberty is not their credo. And they understand a defeat to their ideology by the establishment of a free Iraq will be a devastating blow for their vision."[7] "The advance of democracy is the terrorists' greatest fear," he noted on another occasion. "That's an interesting question, isn't it—why would they fear democracy? What is it about freedom that frightens these killers? What is it about a liberty that causes these people to kill innocent women and children?"[8]

In his speeches, President Bush detailed the terrorist agenda:

"The enemy we face is brutal and determined. The terrorists have an ideology. They share a hateful vision that rejects tolerance and crushes all dissent. They seek a world where women are oppressed, where children are indoctrinated, and those who reject their ideology of violence and extremism are threatened and often murdered.

The terrorists have aims. They seek to impose their heartless ideology of totalitarian control throughout the Middle East. They seek to arm themselves with weapons of mass murder. Their stated goal is to overthrow moderate governments, take control of countries, and then use them as safe havens to launch attacks against Americans and other free nations."[9]

Covering "Terror" and Uncovering "Democracy"

It is problematical—and downright un-American—to be against democracy. The brilliance of the Bush administration's framing of the tactics used to fight the "War on Terror" as the fostering of global democracies was that it was difficult for American media—whatever their platform—to find fault with such an approach, not only in the short, minute-thirty video packages favored by network and cable news programs and the 700-word-long opinion pieces in newspapers and magazines (neither of which allows for much context or nuance) but also in the unlimited time and space of online news sites.

Mainstream U.S. media have always emphasized the policy directives of the White House, but after 9/11 the Bush administration raised secrecy and information control to a level never before seen in Washington.[10] As a consequence of the administration's clever news management, reporting on the President up through the 2003 push to Baghdad amplified the administration's voice even more than political coverage had in the past. In front-page and top-of-the-news stories, the media led with White House statements. When alternative perspectives were presented as part of the coverage, that evidence and analysis tended to be buried.[11] In 2004, Robert Fisk, the leftist journalist for the *Independent* of London cattily observed that the *New York Times* should rename itself "American Officials Say."[12]

Most mainstream media outlets abdicated their independent role; they capitulated to the White House demand that they fall in with the "patriotic" message. Within a year after 9/11, for example, most had docilely accepted President George Bush and Secretary of Defense Donald Rumsfeld's linkage of terrorism and Iraq and weapons of mass destruction. Most did not report evidence that might have helped readers, listeners, and viewers to challenge the Bush administration's argument that weapons of mass destruction were inseparably part of a global terrorism matrix or its suggestion that there were direct links between al Qaeda and Saddam Hussein's regime.

There were lone voices out there, however. In the case of the coverage of WMD, for instance, Barton Gellman, Walter Pincus, and Dana Milbank of the *Washington Post*, Bob Drogin of the *Los Angeles Times*, and David Johnston and James Risen of the *New York Times* provided perspective or challenged information, as did Warren Strobel, Jonathan Landay and John Walcott of Knight Ridder. These reporters and a few others demonstrated a consistent level of skepticism in their coverage of WMD events and issues. They avoided stenographic coverage of White House statements. They worked to include more voices, articulating different policy options, higher up in their stories. In the admittedly difficult WMD beat, they didn't roll over on their coverage of intelligence or report verbatim, without qualifiers, the contentions of anonymous sources, including Iraqi exiles and defectors. They occasionally identified for their audiences the limitations and probable skew of stories when the main sources were anonymous. They at times explained the inherent uncertainties of intelligence gathering and distinguished between intelligence collection and intelligence analysis. Their stories made clear that evaluating a country's WMD status with incomplete data was both an intelligence problem and a policy problem.[13]

By the President's "Mission Accomplished" speech on May 1, 2003, declaring an end to major combat operations in Iraq, more journalists than just these few were seeking independent confirmation of the White House's and Pentagon's pronouncements. Still, the press, as a whole, continued to show by how they reported the Iraq war and other policy issues that the administration's set of priorities was still the dominant narrative. Even after the disastrous 2006 midterm elections for the Republican party, the Bush White House's characterization of a particular event was likely to be repeated by the media. The lesson here: when the White House (any White House) ignores an international story (or a particular angle on a story), the media are likely to do so as well.[14]

Yet the US mainstream media, while not aggressive in looking beyond the international agenda laid out by the administration, did, especially in the buildup to and since the 2006 elections, become more outspoken in critiquing the attempts to "build" and "sustain" foreign democracies. A survey of just a single month of newspaper editorials from November 2006, found mainstream media willing to challenge the tactics and rhetoric of "democracy" as a foreign policy goal.

• *USA Today* noted in several editorials about Iraq that "democracy" should be distinguished from "stability."[15]
• A *Los Angeles Times* editorial called for plain speaking on the viability of democracy in Iraq, rather than for camouflaging "lowered expectations in the language of "victory": "Bush continued to define 'victory' in utopian terms: a democratic Iraq 'that can defend, govern and sustain itself, and [be] an ally in the war on terror.'"[16]
• A *New York Times* editorial exposed willful ignorance: "In Mr. Bush's world, America is making real progress in Iraq. In the real world . . . the index that generals use to track developments shows an inexorable slide toward chaos. In Mr. Bush's world, his administration is marching arm in arm with Iraqi officials committed to democracy and to staving off civil war. In the real world, the prime minister of Iraq orders the removal of American checkpoints in Baghdad and abets the sectarian militias that are slicing and dicing their country."[17]

• A *Washington Post* editorial pointed up hypocrisies in U.S. foreign policy: "Does Mr. Bush regret having given so much support to a leader [Russian President Vladimir Putin] who has dismantled his country's nascent democracy and whose opponents keep turning up in hospitals and morgues?"[18]

• A *Miami Herald* editorial challenged the best tactics to encourage open dialogue necessary for peaceful transitions to democracy: "lifting U.S. restrictions on travel and remittances to Cuba would do far more to promote democracy in Cuba than any U.S. aid program. . . . Such contacts with the outside world show goodwill and break the regime's information blockade."[19]

"Without Fear or Favor"

Elite print media are no as longer quiescent as they were in the months following 9/11, and the Bush administration has not liked the new scrutiny. The president's sentiments in November 2006 in Indonesia—"Look, I applaud a society where people are free to come and express their opinion"—did not translate to the administration tolerating media coverage of information that it did not want released. In the summer of 2006, the White House went on the attack against the mainstream media—most specifically, the *New York Times*—for disclosures in the *New York Times*, the *Los Angeles Times*, and the *Wall Street Journal* that the U.S. government had been secretly monitoring overseas financial transactions as part of the "War on Terror." The three papers almost simultaneously disclosed news of the secret program on their Web sites, and the following day the *Washington Post* published an account in its later print editions.

In the midst of public speeches by the president calling for greater democracy abroad, came White House condemnation of these papers' publication of information about how U.S. officials tapped records of the Society for Worldwide Interbank Financial Telecommunications, or SWIFT, an international banking cooperative owned by nearly 8,000 banks in more than twenty countries. The news articles reported that the U.S. Treasury Department used administrative subpoenas—which do not require issue by a judge—to search for transactions by known terrorists.

The *New York Times* became the main target of attack first by the administration, then by Republicans in Congress and the right-wing blogosphere, in part because the paper had been the leader in investigating the story and because it had disclosed the secret National Security Agency telephone surveillance program the previous year.

"The disclosure of this program is disgraceful," charged President Bush in rer to reporters at the White House. "We're at war with a bunch of people who v hurt the United States of America, and for people to leak that program, ₹ newspaper to publish it, does great harm to the United States of America.'

Vice President Dick Cheney said at a Republican fundraiser in Nebraska, "What is doubly disturbing for me is that not only have they gone forward with these stories, but they've been rewarded for it, for example, in the case of the terrorist surveillance program, by being awarded the Pulitzer Prize for outstanding journalism. I think that is a disgrace."[21]

House Homeland Security Committee Chairman Peter King, R-N.Y., called for the *New York Times* to be prosecuted for violating the 1917 Espionage Act: "We're at war, and for the *Times* to release information about secret operations and methods is treasonous."[22]

In response, on June 25, 2006, the *New York Times* ran an open letter from Executive Editor Bill Keller:

It's an unusual and powerful thing, this freedom that our founders gave to the press. Who are the editors of the *New York Times* (or the *Wall Street Journal*, *Los Angeles Times*, *Washington Post* and other publications that also ran the banking story) to disregard the wishes of the President and his appointees? And yet the people who invented this country saw an aggressive, independent press as a protective measure against the abuse of power in a democracy, and an essential ingredient for self-government. They rejected the idea that it is wise, or patriotic, to always take the President at his word, or to surrender to the government important decisions about what to publish. . . .

The press and the government generally start out from opposite corners in such cases. The government would like us to publish only the official line, and some of our elected leaders tend to view anything else as harmful to the national interest. For example, some members of the Administration have argued over the past three years that when our reporters describe sectarian violence and insurgency in Iraq, we risk demoralizing the nation and giving comfort to the enemy. Editors start from the premise that citizens can be entrusted with unpleasant and complicated news, and that the more they know the better they will be able to make their views known to their elected officials. Our default position—our job—is to publish information if we are convinced it is fair and accurate, and our biggest failures have generally been when we failed to dig deep enough or to report fully enough.[23]

One great irony in the denouement of the story was that exactly thirty-five years previously the Pentagon Papers case about the secret history of the Vietnam War had been argued before the Supreme Court. In that case, the Court voted 6-3 against the Nixon administration's efforts to prevent publication. In the opinion handed down by the court, Justice Potter Stewart wrote for the majority: "In the absence of the governmental checks and balances present in other areas of our national life, *the only effective restraint upon executive policy and power in the areas of national defense and international affairs may lie in an enlightened citizenry—in an informed and critical public opinion which alone can here protect the values of democratic government.*"[24] (emphasis added)

The *Seattle Times* seconded that sentiment in its editorial written 35 years later, two days before July 4th, 2006:

The muddy stew of American democracy has four main ingredients: the judiciary, Congress, the executive and the press.

The Bush administration's booming rhetoric leaves the impression that all this nation needs is a strongman at its head. That is dangerous talk for a country at war, the temptation to bend rules intense.

The administration needs to stop its tired attack on the press for reporting on secret programs used in the war on terror. The debate should not be about the role of the press, but about the alarming lack of oversight of the executive.[25]

Democracy, Justice Stewart effectively argued, needs the media to report the news, without "fear or favor." Citizens need to know what the government is doing; the press needs the freedom to tell them. Historically, American reporters have not jeopardized the lives of servicemen or given away secrets of military operations, covert or overt ones. No respectable news organization has any interest in endangering soldiers or intelligence agents, much less compromising national security. Democracy is better served now that media—some media at least—are reassessing the assumption made in the immediate aftermath of September 11th: that reporting in an era of terrorism necessitates allowing the government a de facto veto on the contents of news stories. Only a news organization that bravely reports what it knows, rather than what it is told is acceptable to say, can act as a check on government. That is why the news media breaking of such stories as the 2005 National Security Agency telephone surveillance program and the 2006 U.S. Treasury Department tapping of the SWIFT financial transactions is good news for a reinvigorated American democracy.

Do Mainstream Media Usually Act as a Fourth Estate?

There is a distinctive divide between how journalists think of their relationship to government and how the courts have generally upheld it—and how the public considers it. A May 2005 study from the University of Pennsylvania's Annenberg Public Policy Center found that only 6 percent of journalists said that the government "sometimes" has the "right to limit the right of the press to report a story." No surveyed journalist said that the government "always" had that right. Yet 37 percent of the public said that the government "sometimes" had the right, and 14 percent of the public said the government "always" had the right—a total of 51 percent.[26]

Sydney Schanberg, who won a Pulitzer Prize for his reporting for the *New York Times* of the fall of Cambodia, has made the press's role in democracy his own cause. Schanberg has been on a campaign to get the American media to "clean up its house and vigorously fight for its traditional role in this democracy."[27] "We haven't gotten across why people need us or why what we do is important to the functioning of a free nation. We haven't effectively gotten our readers to understand that if they get lied to by their government or other power centers, and we—or some other watchdogs—

don't quickly show them the lie, bad things can happen. . . . Wars can happen and people can die."[28]

The SWIFT financial case was, unfortunately, an aberration. As Schanberg argued, journalists themselves have too often been culpable in not only ceding the news agenda to government but also in ceding their own power to illuminate key issues.

Even as the digital revolution enhanced reporters' fact-finding abilities and produced better investigative, serious journalism, the profession in other ways allowed itself to grow softer and looser. Gossip and celebrity chitchat crept into the news sections. . . . The press's proprietors and editors (some of the latter, to their credit, winced as they participated) told us that this was the necessary path to the future if we were to survive financially. They said we had to enliven newspapers and news on television so we could capture those 18- to 49-year-olds and thus draw the big advertisers who yearned to sell them things. . . . Almost without noticing, the press began losing its memory about its crucial adversary role.[29]

In addition to the lack of independence often shown by mainstream media, there have been a series of self-inflicted blows—the flurry of plagiarism cases, the spectacular fabrications of Jayson Blair, Stephen Glass, and Jack Kelley, and, later, CBS News' circulation of the forged Bush-National Guard documents. These demonstrated a laxity about the editing process, a complacency about the work done by "star" reporters and columnists, and a hubris about the need of major media institutions to rigorously demand adherence to stated news standards.

A 2005 report by the Pew Research Center for the People and the Press discovered, perhaps unsurprisingly, that 45 percent of Americans polled said they believed "little or nothing of what they read" in their daily newspapers. In a 2005 Harris poll, only 12 percent of the public reported "high confidence" in the media—ranking it only ahead of law firms. And a 2003 Pew poll found that 32 percent of those surveyed considered news organizations to be immoral.[30]

What Are the Problems?

Public attitudes will be hard to turn around—and perhaps impossible if the media themselves do not reexamine their behavior. Why have mainstream media been so weak in their response to these external and internal threats to their own authority and integrity? There are a number of causes:

The Business of Media Is Profit Not News in the Service of Democracy   Due to mergers and the consequent demand that news operations see profit and not public service as their bottom line, broadcast and even print news outlets are increasingly part—and understood to be part—of the entertainment circus that the "media" business has become. In a speech to Columbia University in February 2007, former CBS news anchor Walter Cronkite warned that media companies that look to profits rather than public service threaten American values and freedom by leaving people less informed. Today, "the need for high-quality reporting is greater than ever," he argued. "It's not just the journalist's job at risk here. It's American democracy."[31]

24/7 Means What Just Happened "Now"—Right Now   There is no media anymore that can afford to be truly deliberative always. The public demands its news "now," anytime, around the clock. As Schanberg states, the new technology and the ubiquity of the Internet has on one hand augmented investigative reporters' ability to rapidly locate facts and draw information from a broad range of sources, but that same pace too often turns hysterical, blurring solid reporting with rumor and rants into an indistinguishable and, at times, toxic slurry. Most media are in the rather more facile business of repackaging news, not discovering or investigating it. It is still newspapers and a handful of magazines—the *New Yorker,* the *New York Review of Books,* the *Atlantic,* and so forth—that do the majority of the investigative reporting in the United States, but actually very few media on any platform undertake the expense of in-depth investigative reporting.

Daily iterative journalism, much less hourly or minute-by-minute, instant journalism, is wholly inadequate to tackle the complicated nuances of life-and-death events. Prioritizing "breaking" news over other genres as occurs on headline news programs and from news feeds and Google and Yahoo news aggregators unavoidably curtails the ability of an audience to get background, history, context or multiple alternative perspectives.

Technology Goes Only as Far as Those Who Use It   The real-time ability of journalists to take high-resolution color images from Kirkuk in northern Iraq or from the beach of a tsunami-wracked Aceh and send them instantly around the globe has helped to feed the 24/7 beast. The live coverage has addicted its global audience to "being there"; it has given a new look to a world formerly covered by journalists who used to have to stop, set-up, broadcast, and break down every time they filed a report. Correspondents can now report on the fly. But they can still only see what is in front of their faces.

New Media—The Good News   The blogosphere, as Schanberg and other critics have observed, is doing "valuable and admirable work keeping mainstream journalism on its toes," and it performs invaluable service by linking to excellent coverage of events and issues so that coverage doesn't get entirely forgotten after the news cycle in which it appeared. But, Schanberg also noted, investigative reporting is "labor-intensive and time-consuming and therefore requires large amounts of money and health benefits and pensions. The blogosphere has plenty of time, but as yet none of the other items."[32]

That is not to say that terrific, award-winning sites do not perform remarkable services. Global Voices Online, for example, is an innovative international media project, launched after an international bloggers' meeting held at Harvard in 2004 and now run from the Berkman Center for Internet and Society at Harvard Law School. Global Voices aggregates what the they call "bridge bloggers,' people who are talking about their country or region to a global audience." As the site itself notes: "At a time when the international English-language media ignores many things that are important to large numbers of the world's citizens, Global Voices aims to redress some of the inequities in media attention by leveraging the power of citizens' media. We're using a wide variety of technologies—weblogs, wikis, podcasts, tags, aggregators and online chats—to call attention to conversations and points of view that we hope will help shed new light on the nature of our interconnected world."[33]

"Old" Media—The Not-So-Good News   Only scant number of U.S. newspapers still maintain international bureaus: the *Chicago Tribune*, the *Christian Science Monitor*, the *Los Angeles Times*, the *New York Times*, *USA Today*, the *Wall Street Journal*, the *Washington Post*, and McClatchy newspapers. At the close of 2006 and the beginning of 2007, a handful of others announced they were bringing home their last foreign correspondents: the *Baltimore Sun*, the *Boston Globe*, *Newsday*, the *Philadelphia Inquirer*, the *Dallas Morning News*.

According to longtime reporter Pamela Constable, a similar story is playing out in TV. "Although more than 80 percent of the public obtains most of its foreign and national news from TV," she wrote in the *Washington Post*, "the major networks are also closing down foreign bureaus, concentrating their resources on a few big stories such as Iraq. In the 1980s, American TV networks each maintained about 15 foreign bureaus; today they have six or fewer. ABC has shut down its offices in Moscow, Paris and Tokyo; NBC closed bureaus in Beijing, Cairo and Johannesburg. Aside from a one-person ABC bureau in Nairobi, there are no network bureaus left at all in Africa, India or South America—regions that are home to more than 2 billion people."[34]

Audiences Are Changing, Aging, Splintering   Audiences are shrinking, if not disappearing for traditional news outlets. Fifty-three percent of adults in the United States read a daily newspaper, down from 62 percent in the late 1980s. The total number of viewers on the three networks of ABC, CBS, and NBC has declined 28.4 percent since 1991—some watchers have moved over to cable outlets such as Fox News Channel, CNN, and MSNBC, while others—especially younger audiences—have been lost, content to grab their news via Web servers, blogs, and e-mail alerts, and the narrowcasting channels of satellite radio.[35]

Agenda-Setting—by Government, by Mainstream Media, by "Citizen-Journalists"   Cable and the Internet have made mass communication exponentially faster and exponentially more accessible to anyone who cares to speak out. As a result, traditional media are less in control of the news agenda than ever before. There are various ways in which the president can speak directly to the American public, for instance, and many of them are end runs around traditional media and traditional platforms.

Yet the freedom that allows an administration to marginalize a major media institution if it so chooses has also brought marginal players into the center of major events and issues. Digital cameras, photo phones, and such Web sites as YouTube and Flickr have put the means of direct communication into the hands of terrorists in Karachi, soldiers at Abu Ghraib, tourists in Phuket, commuters in London.

Trickle-Up "I-Guess-You-Could-Call-It" News   In lieu of a substantive accumulation of facts or reasoned thought or veteran authoritative perceptions, media outlets, especially cable news and the Web have moved towards unedited, impulsive, often stream-of-perhaps-you-could-call-it-consciousness talk. A rumor becomes something to report: "People start to talk about it," said CNN anchor Aaron Brown, "and then Fox News talks about it, and all of the sudden something that has absolutely no basis in fact becomes part of a story." That is, of course, what often makes those outlets interesting. But that is also what makes those outlets destructive, when their product is confused with the more collaborative product (of reporter, editor, producer, etc.) at more "traditional" media institutions. "Today," said Brown, "we just kind of vomit out information—I mean the Net does—and it seeps its way into broader media coverage dangerously."[36]

Sources—Who Are They? No, Really, WHO Are They?   Sourcing of stories is a huge problem. On the one hand there are Web sites that have no sources, beyond the eponymous bloggers. On the other hand there are the nightly news programs that trot out their "official" experts who are predictably white and male—especially when the topic is foreign affairs, and especially when the medium is cable news.[37]

And then there's the ubiquitous unnamed "expert" even in the mainstream media. The *New York Times* has estimated that half of the front-page stories in leading newspapers rely on anonymous sources.[38] Daniel Okrent, former public editor at the *New York Times*, has railed against their use. Sometimes they add "useful wisdom or perspective," he has written. In many other cases, they achieve "the opposite of what the writers intended"—they make readers wonder whether they are "being conned."[39] The problem is "deniability." "Welcome, in other words, to Washington," he wrote, "where 'senior State Department officials,' 'White House aides' and other familiar wraiths can say what they want without ever being held accountable for it."[40]

Who Cares About the Darfurs? Who Knows About the Darfurs? Citizens care about the news when it is about something that they have a prior connection to—their neighborhood, their school, their workplace, their sports team, their country of ancestry. As a result, the Darfurs of the world slip between the cracks. There is a temptation especially online to surf to sites that speak specifically to one's own areas of interest and that serve to confirm one's own political opinions. As a result there is often little opportunity for serendipity: for turning the page and seeing a story that one wouldn't have looked for, but upon a quick glance appears to deserve further investigation.

Why Look at Reality? Taking Responsibility Through Seeing What's Out There American comprehension of the human costs of war and disaster is minimal and easily set aside. In early 1938, in its coverage of the Spanish Civil War, *Life* magazine introduced a photoessay by already famed photographer Robert Capa with these words:

Once again *Life* prints grim pictures of War, well knowing that once again they will dismay and outrage thousands and thousands of readers. But today's two great continuing news events are two wars—one in China, one in Spain. . . . Obviously *Life* cannot ignore nor suppress these two great news events in pictures. As events, they have an authority far more potent than any editors' policy or readers' squeamishness. But *Life* could conceivably choose to show pictures of these events that make them look attractive. They are not, however, attractive events. . . . Americans' noble and sensible dislike of war is largely based on ignorance of what modern war really is. . . . The love of peace has no meaning or no stamina unless it is based on a knowledge of war's terrors. . . . Dead men have indeed died in vain if live men refuse to look at them.[41]

As the United States staggered through the opening years of World War II, *Life* magazine continued to run grim photographs. In the late summer of 1942, *Life* published images taken in the Western Desert. Readers wrote in to complain. "I have just purchased the Aug. 31 *Life*," one woman wrote, "and will destroy it, having seen the pictures which are disgusting in their graphic portrayal of the horrible side of the life our soldiers are forced to lead." In response, *Life* reiterated its statement from the 1938 issue: "'Dead men have indeed died in vain if live men refuse to look at them.' *Life* still maintains that position."[42]

Today, over sixty years later, as wars and disasters continue to convulse the globe, most American media have caved into their audiences' demand to go lightly on the "depressing realism," whether from Abu Ghraib, Aceh, Darfur, or Baghdad. The *Los Angeles Times* analyzed six months of print media coverage from Iraq—from September 1, 2004, through February 28, 2005—a timeframe that included the U.S. assault on Fallujah and the violence before the January 2005 election. Despite the considerable number of casualties, seven publications—the *Atlanta Journal-Constitution, Los Angeles Times, New York Times, St. Louis Post-Dispatch, Washington Post, Time* and *Newsweek*—did not publish a single picture of a dead U.S. serviceman during that time. The *Seattle*

Times ran a photo three days before Christmas of the covered body of a soldier killed in the mess hall bombing. Over that same six months, both the *New York Times* and *Los Angeles Times* published ten pictures of wounded in the war zone, an average of one every two and a half weeks. The other six publications ran a total of twenty-four photographs of American wounded.[43]

There is a "squeamishness about the carnage that is war's chief byproduct," *New York Times* media critic David Carr earlier wrote in explaining the U.S. media's hesitancy to show Iraqi civilian casualties:

During an era when popular culture is filled with depictions of violence and death, and the combination of technology and battlefield access for reporters has put the public in the middle of a shooting war, the images that many Americans are seeing are remarkably bloodless. The heroic narrative is shaped in part by what editors and producers view as a need to maintain standards and not offend their audience. But some cultural critics say that the relatively softened imagery has more to do with a political need to celebrate victory without dwelling on its price.[44]

There's Never a Point Where One Should Cry "Enough!"   Not only do Americans shy away from the "disgusting" in favor of the "heroic," but even when they do engage, compassion fatigue can set in. In a June 2005 *Washington Post* editorial calling for international support for the United Nations' appeal for more aid money to stop the genocide in Darfur, the editors observed—with detectable frustration—that the need for greater aid is "simple": "The Darfur crisis, which threatens to slide off the radar screen as people grow tired of hearing about it, is quietly getting worse."[45]

Sometimes It's Less About Facts and More About Framing   Americans' knowledge of the world is dramatically different than that of citizens of Europe, the Middle East, and countries elsewhere around the globe. In their coverage of the Iraq War, for example, the U.S. and Arab media emphasized radically different concerns.[46] On American television, the Iraq War's mission was paramount—it was about "regime change," it was a "war of liberation," part of the "War on Terror." Al Jazeera, together with other Arab satellite channels—the professed more detached and fact-driven Abu Dhabi, Al Arabiya, and Al Hayat/LBC networks—adopted a Tarantino-esque perspective on the fighting: violence was the defining element of the conflict. Not only did Al Jazeera and the others not flinch from the showing of wailing mothers and close-ups of wounded children, but the aesthetics of the telling, the shots that lingered on the injured and dead, were essential to the story they unfolded.

Transparency in All Things Would Be a Good Thing   If the U.S. media persist in a Pollyannish framing of global news, how can the American public understand what is at stake in the world—much less in a democracy? No matter what media on all platforms are covering, no matter where the home outlet of a media outlet is, there needs to be greater transparency as to that outlet's selection of news and its coverage of it.

That is also how media can regain the trust of their audiences. The above quoted letter by *New York Times* Executive Editor Bill Keller after the paper's reporting of the secret SWIFT program demonstrates how much the back story and a news outlet's rationale for covering—or not covering—an event or issue adds to the audience's understanding of that coverage and content.

Just as print news stories begin with a byline and a dateline, and on-air reporters identify themselves at the end of the pieces by name and location, there should be other identifying information, easily accessible—in italics at the bottom of an article or on a linked Web site. It would add to the credibility of a news story if readers or viewers were told how long the reporter had had to gather the material—there are different sets of expectations for a piece batted out on a one-hour deadline or a piece that was reported over a number of days. It would add to the credibility of a story if the audience knew whether the reporter was an eyewitness to the event or was retooling information reported by another outlet. It would be helpful to learn about problems in access, and about the politics of language used ("terrorists," "militias," or "insurgents," for example). In short, just as reviewers for scientific and other academic journals gauge the credibility of submitted articles by examining their research methodology, so too would journalists gain from exposing the parameters of their reporting.

The Tsunami as an Exception . . . It Was Big and There Were All These Pictures . . .

Most mainstream media outlets do not daily concern themselves with their role in democracy because it's not a line item on a profit-and-loss statement. Educating citizens, providing a public service, is a distant second to looking after their stockholders. News is a kind of virtual merchandise to be sold to fickle audiences who select what news to consume from an exhaustive menu of choices—from tragic disasters to celebrity breakups. News is what attracts an audience—an audience that can be delivered to advertisers.

It's all about business models. For example, those media in the business of making profit do not consider international crises and disasters holistically. When relief workers look at crises and see crises, for example, media look at crises and see news. Other professions—engineers or health workers, for instance—might consider the same crises and see the needs of a global community or of individual victims. Viewed in this light it is possible to understand why media institutions do not have any inherent business instincts to cover even major disasters beyond the initial cataclysm.

Take the tsunami as a case study. The tsunami, which struck Asia on December 26, 2004, dominated news coverage well into 2005. But even given its magnitude, commentators and even relief agencies have been uncertain why exactly the tsunami captured the media and world's imagination to the extent that it did. "Only the Christmas before last, the Iranian city of Bam was razed by an earthquake killing nearly 60,000 people, many of them children," mused Yasmin Alibhai-Brown in the London newspaper, *The Independent*. "The rest still live in the ruins, broken-hearted and destitute, trying to raise the will to rebuild their lives slowly. Outside Iran, no one is interested. Of course there are no beach resorts in Bam, no bikinis, hotels, pleasure palaces. Is that why? Gujarat heaved on 26 January four years ago, burying tens of thousands, but outside India, they are now erased from international memory."[47]

What does the tsunami coverage say—in terms of the world having access to a diversity of voices, in terms of democratizing who is heard, who is cared about? Ted Koppel, anchor of ABC's "Nightline," opened his program on January 11, 2005, with these words:

We humans are a curious, if not bewildering, bunch of creatures. What is it that allows us to turn away from any number of tragedies, say Rwanda, Congo, Sudan, while opening our hearts and checkbooks to the victims of the tsunami in Indonesia, Thailand, Sri Lanka and India? You will hear any number of theories over the next half hour.

We are, it seems, put-off by tragedies that involve both the heroics and villainies of war and politics. A giant tsunami, a natural disaster on the other hand, is nonjudgmental. By that standard, though, we should have flooded Iran with aid and generosity last year, after its devastating earthquake in Bam. We didn't. We haven't. Nor has the world community made good on its promises of aid following Turkey's terrible earthquake.

Maybe race and religion have something to do with it. All those Blacks in Africa and those Muslims in Turkey and Iran. But Indonesia is the world's largest Muslim community, and many people in Sri Lanka and India are just as dark as the Tutsi in Rwanda.

As for the numbers of victims, the ongoing tragedies in Congo and Sudan, have killed millions and continue to kill at a horrifying rate.[48]

Journalists themselves have argued that the media covered the story in part because of its terrible scale. As *New York Times* columnist Nicholas D. Kristof noted: "If you were going to make a movie, then you would make it about this kind of tsunami sweeping down all around the world. It's a disaster movie, only it's real life."[49] "It was a natural disaster like no other," noted Jan Egeland, the UN's Undersecretary-General for Humanitarian Affairs and Emergency Relief, "in the sense that 230,000 people, roughly, died in a minute."[50]

Equally important was that the disaster was so telegenic—and that images of the event itself as well as the aftermath were available. Stacy Palmer, editor of the *Chronicle of Philanthropy*, observed that in most disasters media are only able to transmit photographs and video after the fact. "Here we saw the water coming," said Palmer.[51]

Newsday reported that the tsunami images were in such demand that media outlets went to airports seeking video from returning vacationers.[52]

The plethora of international satellite channels as well as the Internet helped move the images more widely, more quickly. Reporter Chris Bury of ABC News' "Nightline" observed that "New digital technology allowed news organizations to zap those dramatic videos, nearly all shot by people caught up in the disaster, around the world at the speed of light."[53] Reports on the horrifying disaster were globalized, instantaneous, interactive and available 24/7. The intensity of this layered communication created a sense of humanitarian solidarity, motivating many to care about those in harm's way. Before the tsunami, the largest amount collected by the American Red Cross for an international disaster had been $50 million. In the United States alone, the American Red Cross collected $556 million for tsunami relief.[54] That amount suggests a tremendous audience was following the story.

"The media is a huge factor in getting people to be generous," said Oxfam's funding manager, Orla Quinlan, quoted in the *Guardian*. "If they're visually engaged, that brings it home and makes it real to them."[55] The relief community knows well the direct connection between media attention and donations, especially for neglected crises. The media cover crises; members of the public respond. They give money, AND they become better informed citizens. "The media is to political and public attention what other technological "force multipliers" are to the military," noted Pamela von Gruber, publisher of Defense and Foreign Affairs publications.[56]

When Jan Egeland appeared in December 2005 on the "Charlie Rose Show" for the one-year anniversary of the tsunami, he spoke about the role media play in disaster relief: "We asked for $1 billion in the tsunami," he said. "We got 90 percent in no time." By comparison, the lack of media attention to Niger, Egeland argued, was the cause for the lack of donor response there. "We saw it was coming up as an emergency. My people on the ground appealed December of last year [2004] for money. We didn't get anything. We . . . appealed again in March [2005], in April. Then in May, it was really bad. And I told in big press conferences that now, soon, children will start dying. Still didn't get money. And then the BBC World Television did its images, and then suddenly we got more in 10 days than we had in the previous 10 months." "Seeing suffering is a powerful incentive to give," agreed host Charlie Rose.[57]

It is for those reasons that Médecins Sans Frontières (MSF) annually publishes a list of the top ten "Most Underreported Humanitarian Stories." A March 2005 survey by Reuters AlertNet, a news network created to feature humanitarian issues, that analyzed news coverage in 200 English-language newspapers found that the Asian tsunami attracted more media attention in the first six weeks after it struck than the world's top ten "forgotten" emergencies did over a whole year.[58] According to Andrew Tyndall, publisher of *The Tyndall Report*, the ten stories highlighted by MSF for 2005 accounted for just twenty two minutes of the 14,529 minutes on the three major U.S. television networks' nightly newscasts. Two-thousand five had an unusually high amount of international coverage, but according to Tyndall only six minutes of American week-night network newscasts were devoted to the Democratic Republic of the Congo and two minutes to Chechnya. The AIDS crisis received fourteen minutes of coverage. The remaining stories highlighted by MSF's "Top Ten"—conflicts in Haiti, northeastern India, Colombia, northern Uganda, Ivory Coast, Somalia and southern Sudan—were not covered at all.[59]

. . . And the Tsunami's Tragedy Was Clear-Cut (and Not Morally Suspect) . . .

Natural disasters, such as the tsunami, lend themselves better to short news packages because there is a presumption that it is evident what happened and what is needed. Resolution of the tsunami, for example, seemed straight forward: send money and in-kind aid to rebuild the homes and infrastructure of the devastated regions. Five million across the zone lost basic services, housing, schools and jobs. Commentators noted that this wasn't another Somali famine where the cause looked like simple drought, but turned out to be that food was being used as a weapon of war. Most argued that the tsunami was an instance where aid donations could resolve the devastation, not just put a temporary Band-Aid over a suppurating wound.

There was little controversy, aside from some minor coverage of criticism of the lack of an Indian Ocean early warning system, of cautions that climate change was in part to blame, and of concern over whether relief would be well-handled in the conflict zones of Banda Aceh and parts of Sri Lanka. Long-running crises in the regions struck by the Indian Ocean tsunami, such as the fighting in Banda Aceh and Sri Lanka, were either decoupled from the disaster or their importance was minimized. *Newsweek*'s Web-exclusive article titled "Aceh's Phantom Rebellion," for example, had as its subhead: "With the insurgents that Jakarta is so worried about nowhere in sight, behind-the-scenes peace talks are underway. Could peace be a silver lining in Indonesia's awful tsunami crisis?"[60] Eric Burns, host of Fox News Channel's "Fox News Watch," a weekly half-hour program that "covers the coverage," observed that "it was a story that had no political controversy attached to it. The media could give it a lot of time without anybody being too critical."[61] The perceived lack of moral ambiguity and the breaking-news angle encouraged coverage across the political spectrum.

Over the last several years coverage of the tsunami's distinctive destruction and of the war in Iraq has sucked much of the oxygen out of newsrooms for international reporting in general and war reporting specifically. "The world's obsession with Iraq has pushed to the margins many other scenes of mass violence," said Gareth Evans, the head of the Brussels-based International Crisis Group thinktank.[62] "One television news producer we met in the U.S. summed up the situation since spring 2003 this way: 'Look, we've got three foreign news priorities these days: Iraq, Iraq, Iraq' . . . And Iraq is not simply an American obsession. We've heard a similar refrain from news producers and newspaper editors again and again throughout Europe and elsewhere."[63]

Gripping still and video images, manageable access, breaking news (rather than chronic) events, innocents (preferably children) who need to be rescued. Lives lost, substantial property destroyed, key security interests at stake, violence and/or scandal and/or corruption. Even "gee-whiz" stories, like the rescue of an Indonesian man, Rizal Shahputra, eight days after the tsunami, found floating on tree branches 100 miles from shore. These are the elements that command media coverage of disasters and crises, but there is no spreadsheet that can calculate the degree of commitment of media to a story, even when these are present. Not only are the individual variables infinitely mutable, but there are other, external components at play. Is there a major news event already being covered that is "closer to home": a presidential election, a shooting war with American soldiers, even a sensational criminal trial? Has the White House put the disaster story high on its agenda? Do Americans (or just the U.S. government) actually like these people—do Americans really want to give dollars to Iran, for example, despite the devastation of Bam?

Even the highest death tolls, tales of unthinkable violence, images that wrench at one's heartstrings, are not necessarily enough to guarantee sufficient attention to get an event onto the global news agenda and generate a critical mass of coverage. Jan Egeland at the UN argues that the world's disaster victims are caught up in "a kind of humanitarian sweepstakes." "They are in a global lottery, really. And they play every night to seek our attention and our support. And every night 99 percent of them lose. And one percent win."[64]

For journalists, it is an article of faith that the needs and the solutions for disasters that are ongoing—nations caught in wars or famines such as the Congo or Niger—or for chronic emergencies such as AIDS and TB are less obvious than those for natural disasters. Crises in stasis are more complex to cover, and often far more dangerous. In addition, it isn't easy for audience members to see how they can contribute to a positive and permanent resolution of such thorny and tragic situations. Mark Melia, director of annual giving and support for Catholic Relief Services, said that a tragedy like Darfur is "very complicated. It's hard to understand people who are doing horrible things. . . . It's very hard to understand why and what can be done to stop it."[65]

Newsrooms also have difficulties making long-running humanitarian crises sound fresh. As Mark Jones, editor of Reuters AlertNet, remarked, "If I tried to sell you the story of Congo, you might say it could wait until tomorrow, or the next day, or the next decade."[66] And tight budgets and logistical problems with visas and travel itineraries also discourage news editors from even assigning reporters to cover these drawn-out stories. "The story is always the same," said Lindsey Hilsum, the international editor of Channel 4 TV news. "It induces despair. It's expensive and dangerous, and one feels that there are no solutions and no end to it all."[67] In an AlertNet poll, more than 100 relief experts and other leaders were surveyed as to why they thought some emergencies were "forgotten." "The challenge of distilling a complex crisis down to simple soundbites . . . and finding a thread of hope to help audiences empathise" were mentioned as key variables.[68]

This sad observation is a recognition of the fact that when media consider what stories to put on their news budget, elements often far removed from the intrinsic "importance" of a crisis matter. Media worry over what's "new," what's photogenic, what directly affects their audience, what can be told in a minute-thirty or 700 words. The elements of a crisis are disaggregated and evaluated quite dispassionately, often by media accountants with priorities and expectations far different than that of government officials, policy wonks, NGO specialists, insurance executives or even news junkies. All media are capable of initiating that critical mass of attention—think Matt Drudge and Monica Lewinsky's blue dress online, think the *Washington Post* and Watergate in print, think CBS *60 Minutes* and the Abu Ghraib photos on air. The initiating venue almost doesn't matter any more. But someone, somewhere has to report the story, and someone, somewhere else (and often many people in many places) has to see that coverage and think, "Aha! This we need to cover."

With Those as Priorities, Do Media Aid in Building Democracy?

Media build democracy both when they cover the world—not just small bits of it—and when they take up the cudgels of the Fourth Estate by questioning authorities' framing of events. Media foster democracy when they themselves become more accessible and more accountable, when they put out more information and when they work hard to ensure accuracy. The proliferation of new voices on the Web (even the most strident or partisan) and the increasing practice of even "dead tree" media to use their Web sites to break major stories (hence getting the news out faster to more people)—such as the 2006 story on the SWIFT secret program—means that the opportunity exists for democracy-building, even if that opportunity is only fitfully seized.

"There is a consensus in the media industry that the tsunami was covered better than any previous disaster," wrote reporter Ruth Gridley on the Reuters AlertNet site. In part that was because more media covered the story: print, broadcast, radio, online. In addition, many were more careful about their coverage. "Journalists said they'd been good at avoiding usual pitfalls of journalists parachuted into disaster zones," noted Gridley, "they dispelled myths about bodies causing disease . . . also argued against well-meaning but misguided international adoptions of newly orphaned babies, and tried to persuade people to donate cash instead of inappropriate old clothes."[69]

But poor habits remained. In large measure, mainstream media were still heavily reliant on parachuting journalists, rather than on local journalists or observers on site. Tim Cunningham, an executive producer for Sky TV, for example, admitted he had never been to Sri Lanka before the tsunami. "My knowledge consisted of a couple of print-outs. I'd been told I was going 30 minutes before." Sky TV sent fifty journalists from London to cover the tsunami in Asia, but had just one reporter in Africa.[70]

Most mainstream—especially television—media are locked into the business model they have; establishing country bureaus or even regional bureaus is not seen as financially feasible. Media have to scale up for coverage of a major event, and in the hours after an event breaks, deadline pressure operates against any specific training of those mobilized to go. With the closing of foreign bureaus, most of those sent are skilled in crisis coverage, not educated in the politics, culture and language of a region. Ted Koppel, writing in January 2006, at the end of his ABC *Nightline* career, observed:

The networks' foreign bureaus have, for some years now, been seen as too expensive to merit survival. Judged on the frequency with which their reports get airtime, they can no longer be deemed cost-effective. Most have either been closed or reduced in size to the point of irrelevance.

Simply stated, no audience is perceived to be clamoring for foreign news, the exceptions being wars in their early months that involve American troops, acts of terrorism and, for a couple of weeks or so, natural disasters of truly epic proportions.

You will still see foreign stories on the evening news broadcasts, but examine them carefully. They are either reported by one of a half-dozen or so remaining foreign correspondents who now cover the world for each network, or the anchor simply narrates a piece of videotape shot by some other news agency. For big events, an anchor might parachute in for a couple of days of high drama coverage. But the age of the foreign correspondent, who knew a country or region intimately, is long over."[71]

If we define "democracy" (as President Bush did) as a global civic imperative, then the lack of international coverage is a problem. Most media are second-level sources. Even for the elite media, the pressure of reporting for "the 24-hour media machine" means that when covering crises parachuting reporters need others to give them context (not to mention pictures), and help them find ways to give history and background. Many mainstream media hire local stringers, fixers and translators, rely on NGO expats working overseas to provide perspective, and even use international relief flights as their primary way of getting around.

But not all media are retreating; , some mainstream news outlets continue to cover global news with regularity and depth. The major American newspapers—the *New York Times*, the *Washington Post*, the *Los Angeles Times*, the *Chicago Tribune*, the *Christian Science Monitor*, and the *Wall Street Journal* prominent among them—

continue to make substantial commitments to overseas reporting, and the American Associated Press, (AP), the British Reuters and French Agence France Presse (AFP) remain the resources from which most news outlets get their international coverage.

The networks' abandonment of a broad menu of international news has created opportunities and reasons for other broadcast media—most notably Spanish-language television, public radio, and foreign news sources (such as the BBC and Al Jazeera) to bring global news to an American audience.[72] And audiences familiar with surfing to YouTube to watch the two Chinese guys lipsynch to the Backstreet Boys or to watch which country has the newest version up of Numa Numa, can, with a simple search, find video of news events from around the world. The Web offers on-the-ground citizen observers almost from anywhere—evidence for this? A YouTube-like site for human-rights videos, witness.org, whose motto is "See it. Film it. Change it."

The ease and availability of the Internet as a publishing platform has prompted many NGOs, long frustrated by the mainstream media's peripatetic coverage that doesn't match the objectives of the relief agencies themselves, to move to become their own media outlets. World Vision, a leader in the relief business, is sophisticated in the creation of media packages to keep aid flowing after the mainstream media have turned their attention elsewhere. "Within days of the tsunami," noted *Nightline* reporter Chris Bury, "World Vision had its own camera crews on the way to the scene. Its own production teams package and update the material to give donors a stake in the relief efforts." "Within 24 hours," said World Vision president Richard Sterns, "we can have e-mail in the hands of half a million people. And that e-mail can have a situation report, photographs and even streaming video."[73] The targeted audience for these emails receives news, therefore, not from the mainstream media, but from another "news" source—an NGO with its own clear agenda, but also with a greater commitment both to a geographic area and to the issues of development and humanitarian relief than the media could ever make. What role does this new media play in a "democracy"?

At the World Electronic Media Forum, held in Geneva in December 2003, UN Secretary General Kofi Annan noted that "broadcasting leaders from all the world's regions adopted a declaration in which they pledged to do their part for development and social cohesion."[74] Information and the media are as vital in crises as food, water, shelter and medicine. Mainstream media outlets are late in coming to recognize media and NGOs share an interest in information and communication technologies (ICTs)—even while their agendas may be different.

There are some intriguing attempts by international organizations, relief agencies, NGOs, and the philanthropic community to create technologically innovative Internet experiments where information on crises can get out, can be shared, can be contextualized. Prominent among them is the Reuters Foundation's AlertNet, the portal that aggregates the Reuters news feed to feature current and potential "health, sudden onset, food-related, and conflict" crises, with special attention to "emergencies that, for a variety of reasons, receive only sporadic coverage elsewhere in the media— so-called 'forgotten' or 'hidden' emergencies." AlertNet has a network of more than three hundred contributing humanitarian organizations and allows those contributors to post news from crisis zones directly to the site. The chief limitation of the portal is stated upfront on the site itself:

AlertNet focuses its resources on covering fast-moving humanitarian emergencies and on the early warning of future emergencies. In so doing we provide relatively little on economic development which is a closely related subject and makes up the majority of the work of AlertNet member NGOs.

The reason for this focus is that Reuters has traditionally been strong in handling fast-moving information and that our chosen medium—the online world—is particularly well-suited to alerting services.[75]

A growing role for the site is as a tool and resource to help compensate for broadcast and print media's shortcomings. MediaBridge, a component of Reuters AlertNet, is now a place for journalists reporting on humanitarian crises to find background facts, tips on breaking stories, and information on relief agencies.[76]

Similar to AlertNet is a site created by the UN Office for the Coordination of Humanitarian Affairs (OCHA): ReliefWeb, a global hub for time-critical humanitarian information that also emphasizes the coverage of "forgotten emergencies." And other organizations have identified more discrete needs. The French organization, Télécoms Sans Frontières, modeled in part after Médecins Sans Frontières (MSF) and Reporters Sans Frontières, is supported by the European Commission Humanitarian Office (ECHO). TSF specializes in setting up telecom lines in disaster zones both to get information out and to coordinate aid efforts.

In the last months of 2005, a consortium of Internet resources came together under an umbrella area of activity labeled "ICT for Peace" or, as it is known online, "ICT4Peace." The UN ICT Task Force at the World Summit on the Information Society in Tunis in November 2005 released a report giving examples of how ICTs are being deployed. In addition to Reliefweb and TSF, the report mentioned MapAction, an NGO that uses satellite earth imaging, data processing, and locally deployed mapping teams to supply real-time maps to relief operations and journalists, and Martus, a software tool developed by the Silicon Valley–based non-profit Benetech, that collects, safeguards, organizes and disseminates information about human rights violations from small NGOs on the ground as well as large international groups.[77]

These entrepreneurial, problem-oriented ventures are emerging to compensate for the professional disinclination and the structural inability of most mainstream media to deliver the kind and depth of information that many in the global audience need.

As a result—and made possible through the Internet and digital and satellite technologies—mainstream media no longer have a near monopoly on the dissemination of international information.

The international ICT arena confirms that the "news" business is not only growing larger, but trying to meet the needs of more people in more ways. Technology offers the means to get more information, of more kinds, to more people, when they need or want it. Consumers—individuals, communities, institutions, entire regions—are redefining news as far more than the information that can be found in The *New York Times*.

We live in an age of extraordinary marvels, of achievements in technology that seemingly were only fiction mere years, months, days, even hours ago. New media, whatever their platform—have the ability to bring the world to our fingertips. In times of crisis, getting accurate information out fast is imperative. Getting information back in can be life-saving.

But not all crises are signaled by a tsunami wave, a hurricane, or an earthquake. Some crises—like the SWIFT financial transaction story—are silent and secret, and one only knows about them because someone—usually a journalist—dug long and deep to uncover the story.

Despite their at times crucial failures, there is still no group better equipped than traditional journalists—whatever their journalistic platform—to ask the tough questions: of politicians and scientists, of corporate executives and social workers, of the military and of doctors, of academics and of children. There is still no group better equipped than traditional journalists—whatever their platform—to cover the big stories and to find the hidden crises. "My guess is that while serious reporting may not be delivered as often on paper made from trees," agreed Sydney Schanberg, "it will nonetheless live long and contribute to democracy in other delivery forms. This is so because it will always be propelled by abuses of power—and abuses of power are everlasting."[78] The "democracy" that is just a rhetorical political flourish and even the "democracy" that is signaled by more people from more places being online are both rather hollow applications of the word. "Democracy" is more than an ideological rapier or a motley if broad collection of people. "Democracy" is a system in which everyone has a voice and all voices are heard. The Internet is not by itself "democracy's" savior. The need for a vital, aggressive, independent fourth estate remains.

Notes

An earlier version of this chapter appeared in two articles: "Trends in U.S. Media," *The Media–Public Opinion–Public Policy Nexus in German-American Relations* (American Institute for Contemporary German Studies [The John Hopkins University], 2005): 9–15; and " 'Regarding the Pain of the Others': Media, Bias and the Coverage of International Disasters," in "The Globalization of Disaster," *Journal of International Affairs* 59, no. 2 (Spring/Summer 2006): 173–196. http://www. aicgs.org/Publications/PDF/25628%20AICGS_GAI5%20FINAL.pdf. Thanks to both periodicals for allowing the use of material from those essays.

1. http://www.whitehouse.gov/news/releases/2006/02/20060209–1.html.

2. The following are formal statements made by President George W. Bush:

To the President of Poland, in the Oval Office, February 9, 2006: "I told the President, it's amazing to be sitting with somebody who knows the difference between living in a society that is not independent, and not free, and one that—and now he's the President of a free country. I thanked the President and the Polish people for their support ofdemocracy movement in Iraq" (http://www.whitehouse.gov/news/releases/2006/02/20060209-1.html).

To the President of Afghanistan, in Kabul, March 1, 2006: "One of the things I told the President, and told the members of your team and your cabinet and the government, is that people all over the world are watching the experience here in Afghanistan. I hope the people of Afghanistan understand that as democracy takes hold, you're inspiring others. And that inspiration will cause others to demand their freedom. And as the world becomes more free, the world will become more peaceful" (http://www.whitehouse.gov/news/releases/2006/03/20060301.html).

To the Prime Minister of India, in New Delhi, March 2, 2006: "The relationship between our two nations is strong and it rests on a firm foundation. We share common interests rooted in common belief that freedom can change lives and transform nations. Today our two democracies have formed a strategic partnership to bring the benefits of liberty to others, to expand global prosperity through free and fair trade, and to confront the challenges of our time" (http://www. whitehouse.gov/news/releases/2006/03/20060302-16.html).

To the Prime Minister of Slovakia, in the Oval Office, March 13, 2006: "Mr. Prime Minister, welcome. Thank you for coming. I always enjoy being with you because you're an optimistic, upbeat believer in the people of your country and the possibilities to work together to achieve peace. . . . We discussed a lot of issues. I thank the Prime Minister for his contributions to helping young democracies succeed, democracies in Afghanistan and Iraq" (http://www.whitehouse. gov/news/releases/2006/03/20060313-1.html).

To the President of Azerbaijan, in the Oval Office, April 28, 2006: "We've just had a really interesting visit. And we talked about the need to—for the world to see a modern Muslim country that is able to provide for its citizens, that understands that democracy is the wave of the future. . . . We, obviously, talked about Iran. I assured the President of my desire to solve this problem diplomatically and peacefully. I appreciate so very much the government's contribution of support in troops to the new democracy in Iraq" (http://www.whitehouse.gov/news/releases/ 2006/04/20060428.html).

To the President of Hungary, in Budapest, June 22, 2006: "Listen, I'm thrilled to be here, Mr. President. Thank you for your hospitality and thank you for your personal contribution to your country's democracy. . . . I bring greetings from thousands of Hungarian Americans who are very proud of their homeland and their heritage. I also bring greetings from a nation that admires your courage and your desire to continue to do the hard work necessary for democracy to take hold" (http://www.whitehouse.gov/news/releases/2006/06/20060622-3.html).

To the President of Georgia, in the Oval Office, July 5, 2006: "First, Mr. President, welcome. I reminded the President about what a fantastic visit I had to Georgia. . . . It was a fantastic trip.

"It was made fantastic because my friend not only was a good host, but he is a man who shares the same values I share. He believes in the universality of freedom. He believes that democracy is the best way to yield the peace. The Georgian government and the people of Georgia have acted on those beliefs. I want to thank you for your contribution in Iraq, to help the Iraqi people realize the great benefits of democracy. It's hard work, but it's necessary work" (http://www.whitehouse.gov/news/releases/2006/07/20060705-4.html).

To the President of Slovenia, in the Oval Office, July 10, 2006: "Mr. Prime Minister, thank you for coming. It's been a really fascinating discussion we've had. First, I want to thank you for your friendship. I thank you for your leadership. I really appreciate the fact that you have made the courageous decision to help two young democracies, Afghanistan and Iraq, succeed. Your contributions in Afghanistan and Iraq will make a difference in achieving peace" (http://www.whitehouse.gov/news/releases/2006/07/20060710-2.html).

To the President of Romania, in the Oval Office, July 27, 2006: "The President and I are friends. . . . We talked about the international scene and how we can work together to promote democracy and peace. . . . We've got a lot on our agenda because we're friends. I do want to thank the people of Romania for their strong support to the young democracy in Iraq and Afghanistan" (http://www.whitehouse.gov/news/releases/2006/07/20060727-5.html).

To the President of Iraq, in New York City, September 19, 2006: "President Talabani, you and your colleagues here have given us time so we can strategize together to help you succeed, help you become a democracy, a country that can sustain itself and govern itself and defend itself, in the heart of the Middle East. . . . So Mr. President, thank you for coming again. I appreciate your time. I appreciate your long-standing courage and support for freedom and liberty. History will judge you kindly, Mr. President, when they look back and realize that under your leadership a new democracy began to flourish in the heart of the Middle East, called Iraq" (http://www.whitehouse.gov/news/releases/2006/09/20060919-10.html).

To the President of Kazakhstan, in the Oval Office, September 29, 2006: "We've just had a very important and interesting discussion. We discussed our desire to defeat extremism and our mutual desire to support the forces of moderation throughout the world. I thanked the President for his contribution to helping a new democracy in Iraq survive and thrive and grow. I thank very much the President for his concerns about Afghanistan's democracy, and his willingness to help in Afghanistan" (http://www.whitehouse.gov/news/releases/2006/09/20060929-5.html).

3. http://www.whitehouse.gov/news/releases/2006/03/20060313-3.html.

4. http://www.whitehouse.gov/news/releases/2006/10/20061027.html.

5. http://www.whitehouse.gov/news/releases/2006/03/20060322-3.html.

6. "Foreign Aid, Revised," *New York Times*, November 25, 2006.

7. http://www.whitehouse.gov/news/releases/2006/01/20060123-4.html.

8. http://www.whitehouse.gov/news/releases/2006/04/20060410-1.html.

9. http://www.whitehouse.gov/news/releases/2006/02/20060224.html.

10. In a column written in April 2005, Schanberg noted that "Bush was asked about his administration's secrecy controls … in a question period after his speech to the American Society of Newspaper Editors meeting in Washington. … . he contended that all his secrecy policies were made necessary to keep from 'jeopardizing the war on terror,' in order not to 'put somebody's life at risk.' This was about as bald a falsehood as any president could tell. The public record shows that much of his information lockdown has to do with politics and with domestic issues that have no relation to terrorism or homeland security." Sydney H. Schanberg, "A Time for Disobedience," *Village Voice*, April 19, 2005.

11. For further details of the U.S. and U.K. media coverage of the Iraq War and especially their coverage of WMD, see Susan D. Moeller, "Media Coverage of Weapons of Mass Destruction," in *CISSM Report* (College Park, MD: Center for International and Security Studies (CISSM), University of Maryland, March 9, 2004). http://www.cissm.umd.edu/papers/display.php?id=32.

12. Daniel Okrent, "The Public Editor: Paper of Record? No Way, No Reason, No Thanks," *New York Times*, April 25, 2004.

13. See Moeller "Media Coverage of Weapons of Mass Destruction."

14. Moeller, "Media Coverage of Weapons of Mass Destruction."

15. "Rumsfeld's Exit Ushers in Hope for Iraq Policy Shift," *USA Today*, November 9, 2006; and "Thanksgiving Thoughts," *USA Today*, November 22, 2006.

16. "Exit Strategy," *Los Angeles Times*, November 9, 2006.

17. "The Great Divider, *New York Times*, November 2, 2006.

18. "Political Poison," *Washington Post*, November 21, 2006.

19. "U.S. Plan Ineffective by Design," *Miami Herald*, November 19, 2006.

20. Quoted in http://www.cjog.net/documents/The_Media_Response.pdf.

21. Ibid.

22. Ibid.

23. Quoted in full in ibid.

24. http://caselaw.lp.findlaw.com/scripts/getcase.pl?court=US&vol=403&invol=713.

25. "War Is No Excuse to Steamroll Press," *Seattle Times*, July 2, 2006.

26. Joe Strupp, "Study: Journos, Public Hold Divergent Views on Media," *Editor & Publisher*, May 24, 2005.

27. Sydney H. Schanberg, "Show of Farce," *Village Voice*, May 24, 2005.

28. Sydney H. Schanberg, "A Time for Disobedience," *Village Voice*, April 19, 2005.

29. Schanberg, "Show of Farce."

30. Patrick Healy, "Believe It: The Media's Credibility Headache Gets Worse," *New York Times*, May 22, 2005.

31. Pamela Constable, "Demise of the Foreign Correspondent," *Washington Post*, February 18, 2007.

32. Sydney H. Schanberg, "If Old Journalism Dies . . . Where Will New Media Get the News?" *Village Voice*, November 29, 2005. http://www.villagevoice.com/news/0548,schanberg,70452,6.html.

33. http://www.globalvoicesonline.org/top/about-global-voices/.

34. Pamela Constable, "Demise of the Foreign Correspondent," *Washington Post*, February 18, 2007.

35. Jason Fry, "Intel CEO Extols Patience," *Wall Street Journal*, May 25, 2005; The Journal Report: Technology, "How Old Media Can Survive in a New World," *The Wall Street Journal*, May 23, 2005.

36. Dan Gilchrist, "The Man in the Chair," *Rake*, June 2005.

37. "The Gender Gap," Project for Excellence in Journalism Report, May 2005. http://www.journalism.org/resources/research/reports/gender/default.asp.

38. Jonathan Alter, "A Big Source of Frustration," *Newsweek*, May 30, 2005. http://www.msnbc.com/id/7937019/site/newsweek.

39. Daniel Okrent, "The Public Editor: Analysts Say Experts Are Hazardous to Your Newspaper," *New York Times*, October 31, 2004.

40. Daniel Okrent, "The Public Editor: An Electrician From the Ukrainian Town of Lutsk," *New York Times*, June 13, 2004.

41. "The Worlds's Two Wars: Teruel Falls and Tsingtao Burns," *Life*, January 24, 1938, 9.

42. Letters to the Editors, *Life*, September 21, 1942, 4.

43. Ibid., "Unseen Pictures, Untold Stories," *Los Angeles Times*, May 21, 2005.

44. David Carr, Jim Rutenberg, and Jacques Steinberg, "Telling War's Deadly Story at Just Enough Distance," *New York Times*, April 7, 2003. "The sense that many observers have that American media shy away from showing the human costs of war was borne out by a team of researchers at George Washington University's School of Media and Public Affairs. The researchers analyzed 600 hours of Iraqi War coverage on CNN, Fox News Channel, and ABC from the start of the war on March 20 to the fall of Baghdad on April 9. They examined both the morning shows and afternoon and evening coverage, but, as they noted: 'Instead of including every story they ran during that time (which would make percentages of casualty stories look artificially low because many stories weren't about fighting) we only examined stories that included images of battles (including artillery firing and bombs falling on Baghdad), casualties of any sort, or both.'

"Of 1710 stories the team analyzed, only 13.5 percent included any shots of dead or wounded coalition soldiers, Iraqi soldiers, or civilians. 'And even when the dead were shown,' wrote one of the lead researchers, 'they were more likely to be hidden inside a coffin, under a sheet, or represented by some surrogate image such as a shoe.' 'In truth,' the researcher wrote, 'rather than showing viewers' 'the price' of the Iraq war, television instead transformed a war with hundreds of coalition and tens of thousands of Iraqi casualties into something closer to a defense contractor's training video: a lot of action, but no consequences, as if shells simply disappeared into the air and an invisible enemy magically ceased to exist." Sean Aday, "The G-Rated War," *The Gadflyer*, April 29, 2004. http://gadflyer.com/articles/print.php?ArticleID=90.

45. "The Donors and Darfur," *Washington Post*, June 20, 2005.

46. For example, Mohammed el-Nawawy, "Whose 'Truth' Is Being Reported?" *Christian Science Monitor*, April 8, 2003.

47. Yasmin Alibhai-Brown, "Today's Pity Is Worthless If We Forget," *Independent* (London), January 10, 2005, Comment section.

48. ABC News, "The Sympathy Gap," *Nightline*, January 11, 2005.

49. ABC News, "The Sympathy Gap," *Nightline*, January 11, 2005.

50. *Charlie Rose Show*, PBS, December 22, 2005.

51. Kathleen Megan, "Friends in Need: What Is It about the Tsunami Disaster that Has Made Americans So Generous?" *Hartford Courant*, January 20, 2005.

52. Antonia Zerbisias, " Will we still care when media leave?" *Toronto Star*, January 6, 2005, Opinion section.

53. ABC News, "The Sympathy Gap," *Nightline*, January 11, 2005.

54. Stephanie Strom, "Figures Reveal Dynamics of Disaster Giving," *New York Times*, October 23, 2005.

55. Julia Day, "How the Tsunami Hogged the Headlines," *Guardian Unlimited*, March 11, 2005 (on the Guardian Unlimited wire at 8 a.m.).

56. Pamela von Gruber, "Special Report: Emergency Disaster Response: The Impact of the Media, the Military, and Time," *Defense & Foreign Affairs Special Analysis*, June 16, 2005.

57. *Charlie Rose Show*, PBS, December 22, 2005.

58. Day, "How the Tsunami Hogged the Headlines."

59. Medecins Sans Frontieres "PanAfrica: MSF Issues List of the 'Top Ten' Most Underreported Humanitarian Stories of 2005," *Africa News* (wire report), January 12, 2006. http://www.doctorswithoutborders.org/publications/reports/1999/top10.cfm.   http://www.doctorswithoutborders.org/publications/reports/2002/top10.html. http://www.doctorswithoutborders.org/publications/reports/2006/top10_2005.html.

60. George Wehrfritz and Joe Cochrane, "Aceh's Phantom Rebellion," *Newsweek web exclusive*, January 15, 2005.

61. Fox News network, "Quick Takes on the Media," *Fox News Watch*, January 15, 2005.

62. Day, "How the tsunami hogged the headlines."

63. Ruth Gidley, "Brutal Conflicts Get Scant Attention. Three 'Forgotten Emergencies' Take a Back Seat to Iraq and the Tsunami in Coverage by Media," *Houston Chronicle*, March 10, 2005.

64. ABC News, "The Sympathy Gap," *Nightline*, January 11, 2005.

65. Megan, "Friends in Need."

66. Ben Flanagan, "Media: Don't Let Disaster Get in the Way of a Real Story: The Media Sometimes Makes Bad Judgments on Humanitarian Crises. But Help Is at Hand," *The Observer*, December 18, 2005.

67. Day, "How the Tsunami Hogged the Headlines." Due to mergers and the consequent demand that news operations see profit and not public service as their bottom line, broadcast and even print news outlets are increasingly part—and understood to be part—of the entertainment circus that the "media" business has become. News media geared to overnight ratings and quarterly stockholders reports fail to see the percentage in covering long-running disaster stories or static—even if horrific—crises, if they ever did. *Cf.* Moeller, "Trends in U.S. Media."

68. Day, "How the Tsunami Hogged the Headlines."

69. Ruth Gidley,"Debate: Has Tsunami Carved a News Niche for Disasters?" *AlertNet*, March 11, 2005. http://www.alertnet.org/thefacts/reliefresources/111056581462.htm.

70. Gidley, "Debate." The BBC, rival to British Sky Broadcasting, sent 25 correspondents and crew to the region on the day of the disaster and had over 100 in place at the height of its coverage. Tim Burt, Joshua Chaffin, Hannah Costigan and Justine Lau, "Media Accused of Too Much Coverage after Slow Beginning," *Financial Times*, January 8, 2005, Asia edition.

71. Ted Koppel, "And Now, a Word for Our Demographic," *New York Times*, January 29, 2006.

72. One significant area of growth in American media has been the incursion of the BBC and *The Economist* into the U.S. market. Public Radio International's 10-year-old radio program "The World," a co-production of PRI, the BBC, and WGBH, is an award-winning daily program that reaches over 2 million listeners a week. It is, however, the only hour-long program of international news on TV or radio. It is no coincidence that "The World" and the BBC's radio programming, "The BBC World Service," which reach 5 million Americans a week, operate on different—noncommercial—business models.

73. ABC News, "The Sympathy Gap," *Nightline*, January 11, 2005.

74. Kofi Annan, "Opening Statement," World Electronic Media Forum, Geneva, December 10, 2003, in *The World Summit on the Information Society: Moving from the Past into the Future* (ICT Task Force Series 8) (New York: United Nations Information and Communications Technologies Task Force, 2005).

75. http://www.alertnet.org/aboutus/.

76. Flanagan, "Media: Don't Let Disaster Get in the Way of a Real Story."

77. http://www.ictforpeace.org.

78. http://www.villagevoice.com/news/0548,schanberg,70452,6.html.

7 Democracy on the Airwaves: An Interview with Amy Goodman

Amy Goodman is the host and executive producer of *Democracy Now!* She is coauthor of the national best-seller *The Exception to the Rulers: Exposing Oily Politicians, War Profiteers, and the Media that Love Them*, written with her brother David Goodman. The book was named as one of the top 50 nonfiction books of 2004 by the editors of *Publishers Weekly*. In 2006, she coauthored again with David Goodman *Static: Government Liars, Media Cheerleaders, and the People who Fight Back*.

Democracy Now! is a national, daily, independent, award-winning news program airing on over 500 stations in North America. Pioneering the largest public media collaboration in the United States, *Democracy Now!* is broadcast on community, Pacifica, and National Public Radio stations, public access cable television stations, satellite television (on Free Speech TV, channel 9415 of the DISH Network), shortwave radio, and the Internet. This interview was conducted in a coffee shop in New York City on March 3, 2007.

Megan Boler: The purpose of this book is to pose questions about how access to distribution and production through the Internet is or is not changing the face of democracy. There's a lot of hype around these questions of democratization. Do you have any thoughts on these debates, particularly in terms of access and production online?

Amy Goodman: I think the Internet is extremely important as a grassroots globalizing force; it's a way that we can communicate with people around the world. There's still the digital divide, which we have to defeat. But it's the answer to corporate globalization, and it's much more powerful, grassroots globalization. Which is why we have to keep the Internet free—equal access to the Internet.

For *Democracy Now!* it's been extremely important. From the beginning, our show has been online everyday. We stream online; our broadcast is online in MP3 and video. We were doing audio podcasts even before the word podcast was used. It's the way people access us all over the world, and in terms of the means of production, it's also the way we produce the show. Once we're done with our broadcast, we close caption for the deaf and hard of hearing. Then we take that transcript and an army of

Figure 7.1
Goodman filming demonstration

volunteers—a different group everyday, someone in Hawaii or Taiwan or China or Germany or Sweden or Alaska or New York—put the MP3 online. We divide it up in kind of a pie, send it out as closed caption, which is sort of an imperfect transcript of the show, and then they perfect that transcript and we put it online.

And the corporate media has come to depend on it. We call it trickle-up journalism. We're one of the most content-rich Web sites online. Because of the transcript, it's a daily, global, grassroots, unembedded, independent international news hour. It's so rare.

Just drawing on international media makes a difference. We live in a globalized world, but we are so isolated when it comes to getting information in this country.

MB: Do you want to say something about the role of blogging in journalism? Particularly, do you draw on blogs as a source for your broadcasts? Are they a source of information, and has that changed for you in terms of being an increased source?

AG: Yes. First of all, it's not just me, it's a whole team of producers, and everyone in the producing team does that. Also, it's a way of pointing arrows. Someone is pointing to something that they found interesting. In the past you had one set newspaper, or several big corporate newspapers. We critique them all the time. But now people have access to other means of information, and given that these large newspapers are really just perspectives on things that are happening—well, that's what the blogs are too.

And it's very interesting to get other perspectives. Of course in the corporate media, much that is offered is just a perspective we don't agree with on a news event—or they don't cover the event we are reporting. And so with this stratification of sources, you get increased and diverse access to much more that is happening.

And it's not just blogs. You know, it's e-mail, it's visiting other people's Web sites all over the world and having access to those. To be able to quote international media outlets—it's important what they're saying, but also just to say that they're there and to cite these other sources as open windows on the world.

MB: You write a column, and I was also curious how you and your producers have elected so far in your Web presence not to have a blog.

AG: Oh, we're developing a new Web site and it'll have a blog. It's a project we've been working on for over a year now, for our new Web site. It's a work in progress.

The column is a regular weekly column that newspapers pick up around the country. They pick it up every week, and after they run it, I just post it online.

MB: So the blog format on your new site, will that be multiply authored, collaborative?

AG: We're seeing. We're just deciding right now.

MB: In an era of democracy promotion, as in U.S. imperialism, how do you make the notion of democracy resonate differently?

AG: For one thing, in the United States, we talk about the different movements for equality and democracy: the environmental movement, the antiwar movement, the gay and lesbian movement, the racial justice movement. All of these movements are part of a prodemocracy movement. I think people all over the world have a strong desire to be fairly represented, to determine their own future. I don't think one administration can corrupt that.

When you hear the voices on *Democracy Now!* from all over the globe, at the grass-roots, it just represents something very different. I hope we can model through media the idea that it's not just a small circle of pundits, who know so little about so much explaining the world to us and getting it so wrong, who are the ones to be heard. That people are experts in their own lives. And that's the power of it. That's when people take hope. I always find it amazing, in the most difficult situations we cover, that people feel hopeful. They don't get overwhelmed by it. But there's something about hearing about someone doing something about something—it's not just about the problem, it's about how people are responding to it—that ultimately is hopeful.

And that's the desire for democratic media to open up, to break the sound barrier. I think that challenges what they represent in Washington.

MB: In an interview that I listened to online with you and Bob McChesney, on *Media Matters*, you said, "media is more powerful than any bomb."

AG: Media are the most powerful institutions on earth: more powerful than any bomb, more powerful than any missile. And the Pentagon has deployed the media, and we have to take it back. Information is power. It is the greatest power. Knowing where we stand, knowing what's happening out there, are the necessary steps to knowing where we want to go. That's why it is absolutely critical that the media be independent, be powered by people, not profits, not the Pentagon.

The push for war in the United States was not only about circling the wagons, getting the soldiers overseas, manufacturing the bombs and the weapons and the planes—it was about manufacturing consent, as Noam Chomsky says. That was still essential in the United States, that the public support the war. And that came from a very concerted effort to convince the American people that they should be afraid, that they were threatened, that there was this imminent threat.

George Bush could not have done it alone if he stood on the steps of the White House with a little megaphone saying "weapons of mass destruction, weapons of mass destruction." He would have convinced a few people, but he would not have convinced the majority of Americans. He had something much more powerful and that was the American media, bombing us daily with misinformation, with lies, with the idea that Americans, their families, could be destroyed by this smoking gun that was a mushroom cloud. And it wasn't true. All the media did it. And that is what also would have stopped Bush, if the media continually questioned—as we did and independent media did—that drumbeat to war.

See, it's not enough to have one exposé in one paper, or one story in the nightly newscast, which they'll always point out to you: "See, we asked a question!" What matters is the daily coverage, the drumbeat, that sinks into the consciousness of the American people, and that was "You are under imminent threat."

Then the invasion begins and the Pentagon develops its names for a simple direct word—*invasion*. They come up with "Operation Iraqi Freedom," and that's carefully researched to have the most galvanizing effect. Actually they came up with another before that, which was "Operation Iraqi Liberation," but they couldn't use it because the acronym was O-I-L. So Operation Iraqi Freedom. And instead of the media saying, OK, and acknowledging that's what the Pentagon called it, they named their coverage "Operation Iraqi Freedom," which is just unacceptable. MSNBC, NBC, CNN—Operation Iraqi Freedom. They never used the word *invasion* as was used in the international press.

And when you have that kind of coverage—or I should say covering up—you have to ask, if we had state media, how would it be any different? My brother David and I wrote this book called *Static*, and we wrote it because we live in a high-tech digital age, with high-definition television and digital radio, and yet all we get is static: that veil of distortion and lies and misrepresentations and half-truths that obscure reality, when what we need is a different kind of media. We need the dictionary definition of static: we need criticism, opposition, unwanted interference.

We need a media that covers power, not covers for power; a media is the fourth estate, not for the state, and a media that covers the movements that create static and make history. That is very important. The media denigrates movements unless they're in other countries and they're supporting our government. The famous picture of Yeltsin in Russia standing in the streets with a thousand people. But here we're talking about half a million people and it rarely gets coverage. It may get a photograph or a small article. Movements are what change history, and we need a media that covers those movements. Instead in this country—I should say, the Pentagon—Victoria Clarke said the embedding process was a "spectacular success." They have perfected this, and it's brought the media to an all-time low. Reporters embedded in the frontlines of troops. Where are the reporters embedded in Iraqi hospitals, in the peace movements around the world, to show the real effects of war? And what's astounding is that before the invasion half the people were opposed to it even when the massive amount of information that was coming out was in the other direction.

FAIR [Fairness and Accuracy in Reporting] did a study of the four nightly news stories in the United States before the invasion, around Colin Powell giving his push for war at the UN on February 5, 2003. Four major nightly newscasts—ABC, NBC, CBS, and the PBS Newshour with Jim Lehrer—and in those two weeks, there were 393 interviews done around war. Only three were with antiwar leaders, 3 of almost 400. This is no longer mainstream media. This is an extreme media beating the drums of war.

MB: I have to jump in here because this is something I think about a great deal, and I've spent extensive research time looking at how the media covers antiwar movements. So this book [*Digital Media and Democracy*] actually opens with a story of when I was at Virginia Tech. Tim Russert came to speak there in early 2003 before the invasion of Iraq and performed what he called a fair and balanced evaluation of how the media was covering this. And his conclusion was that, given the media's coverage of whether we should or shouldn't invade Iraq, the Bush administration was justified in its invasion.

I had been doing research for a Web site called Critical Media Literacy in Times of War that looks at international news sources and compares contradictory stories. At the Russert event I was first at the Q & A–there's 2,000 people in the auditorium, and this is a very conservative, partially military school. I confront him and say, "You seem to have neglected all international news sources," and then I listed facts and arguments that had been cited in international news sources that he hadn't mentioned, that were opposed to invasion, about what might happen, why it might be a bad idea. He turned red in the face, he started shouting at me that I had no right to be a professor given my version of the facts. People cheered him. When I started to try to respond—this is February 2003—people booed and hissed me back to my seat, and I thought I was going to be attacked.

So imagine my frustration. I should have written him a letter and asked him to apologize, or sued him for libel. What gets me is the swing of the pendulum. You were talking about the importance of the media, media being more powerful than a bomb, that it would make a difference if the media covered social movements. I would like to agree with that, and yet as I try to understand analytically that the popular pendulum has shifted and the media now covers these issues slightly differently, how did that change come about and what difference would it even make if the media did cover social movements? Let's just say, it's sometimes difficult to maintain hope in the power of the media to counter bombs. But in February 2003, that was the largest international antiwar movement in history. NPR and the *New York Times* finally had to apologize for the misrepresentation of numbers.

Yet sometimes I think that even if the media did represent that—if Bush just calls the largest international antiwar movement in history a focus group, what difference does it make?

AG: Because people would hear an echo of their own views, it would further validate them. The fact is that half the people even then were opposed to the invasion. Could you imagine if they could actually hear an echo of their own thoughts in the media?

That story you told is extremely important because here are all these very same journalists who are saying to the politicians, how did you get it so wrong? But it was the media who were powerful, and they were the ones who decided who would be in the studios and be interviewed and who would be iced out. The classic example is the *New York Times* with Judith Miller and Michael Gordon coauthoring these pieces on weapons of mass destruction—the now disgraced reporter Judith Miller—on the front page, month after month. And why it matters—well, it's not just out of historical curiosity for professors to look at. It matters now. You drop the q and add an n and you've got Iran. And you've got Michael Gordon writing this piece several weeks ago on the front page of the *New York Times* coupled with the unusual news conference in Baghdad, where reporters were not allowed to bring in their cameras and they were not allowed to name the people who were briefing them, talking about Iran being the source of weapons that are killing U.S. soldiers. And they're at it again. And it's got to be stopped, because when you're talking about the networks, I mean Russert on NBC, they're using *our* airwaves. ABC, NBC, CBS, these are not the private property of these corporations, Westinghouse, General Electric which owns NBC, and Viacom which owns CBS, and Disney which owns ABC. This is not their private property. These are the public airwaves; they are a national treasure. And if they're not used responsibly. . . . These corporations should have their licenses revoked.

When you look at the Persian Gulf War, CBS was owned by Westinghouse, NBC was still owned by General Electric. Two of the major nuclear weapons manufacturers making most of the parts for most of the weapons in the Gulf War. Is it any surprise that most of what we watched on television was a military hardware show? And this equation of dissent and treason—to ask questions is to be unpatriotic—just has to be rejected out of hand. And that's what silences. You're a professor in a room of 2,000. Journalists experience that same kind of pressure. They know what will marginalize them and what will move them up the ranks. And when you say, "I want to cover the peace movement" or you start asking critical questions, these politicians, as the Scooter Libby trial has shown, have total access to these journalists. And you know, behind the scenes, unnamed sources, that's how they cultivate them. I call it "The Access of Evil"—creating truth for access. The journalists get their own quote from the president or vice president. You know, you ask these softball questions until you get the access. It's not worth it. The politicians need the journalists more than the journalists need the politicians.

And to see these same journalists, wringing their hands on television—"how did we get it so wrong?"—continuing to ask themselves this on television and not bringing

Figure 7.2
Goodman interviewing Aristide. Photo by K. Keane

in those who got it right. That's why the media democracy movement is so important in this country.

MB: Do you feel any new hope, given the increased access to production and distribution?

AG: Oh, absolutely. The fact that *Democracy Now!* has grown so big is amazing. We were on a couple of dozen community radio stations in 1996, eleven years ago. And then we branched out into television in 2001, went out on MNN, Manhattan Neighborhood Network, that's just down the road here, because they had a link to the place we had gone to, a video link. And then we started broadcasting on public access TV stations. And these are stations that were wrested from the media monopolies, the cable companies. These companies get the right to cable a town because they have to dig up the roads. And because they get the monopoly, media activists fought for a few public interest channels. So in every community there is public access TV where people can make their own media. And that's where we started. We would FedEx out our VHSs to all these different stations. Then we went on the two TV satellite networks on FreeSpeech TV, which is on Dish Network in the United States, and on Link TV, which is on Direct TV and Dish. And always on the Web. Then NPR stations started picking us up, and PBS stations. It was making money hand over fist for these stations because the public responded to our broadcasts. When you hear authentic voices, you respond. I don't care if you're a conservative, Republican, progressive, Independent, Democrat, you hear something authentic, it's humanity responding to humanity. And I think that's the power of independent grassroots media.

The story you told is so important. Is that recorded anywhere? Did anyone record that event? This was VMI?

MB: No, Virginia Polytechnic Institute and State University in Blacksburg. I don't know if his speech was recorded. The newspaper reported that exchange between us—the college newspaper. So that's the only official record I have.

AG: Really, isn't that interesting that it's only the college newspaper that reports it.

MB: I've looked and I can't find any public recordings, or texts, or transcripts of talks he gave during that time at universities. I would love to have a record of his position in 2002–3. And remix is so good right now. We're able to do remix because we can get sound bites and show, "here's what Bush said then and here's what he says now." It's fantastic. I would love to have Russert "before and after." Because a year later, he's saying to Bush, "How'd you get this wrong?" . . .

AG: But Bush's response should be, "Because you let me."

MB: But on this question of media being more powerful than a bomb, I do appreciate what you're saying, and I tend to agree.

However, I wonder about the people who are being affected by the bombs that we're talking about. Why would they agree that media is more powerful than any bomb? The pen is mightier than the sword—that's the evocation. But there's a materialist part of me that thinks, no—it's important to people like you and me who are interested in the power of the media, but for people who are being impacted by that . . .

AG: But the people who are being impacted, the people who are having the bombs dropped on them, there is something that happens that paves the way for that. That's what the media does. It manufactures consent for war. That's what it's about. The bomb doesn't just happen in one day.

The president knew he had to galvanize the people here. The media paves the way. That's why it's important. It is a part of the process. It doesn't just come afterwards and cover what happened. It makes it happen. It allows it to happen.

MB: One more question around media and democracy. I'd like to understand more about your vision of media within a highly politicized context. Notions of fairness and accuracy imply to me and to many that objectivity in news is possible. Given your sophisticated analysis of media and power, can you help me understand what you mean in your writing and on your Web site and in your broadcast by "fairness and accuracy"?

AG: As journalists we have to be fair and accurate: give people a chance to speak, be as accurate as we can be in gathering the information, and that's our responsibility. Journalists have opinions, I mean, turn on television—you're watching opinions espoused every minute of every day. When journalists want to marginalize, or the media establishment wants to marginalize journalists, they'll say "That journalist has an opinion." They're just saying, that journalist doesn't share our opinion.

So journalists can be free to express their opinion, but we have to be fair and accurate.

MB: Is there a way to be a journalist that doesn't have a political stake? Do you have a vision of journalism as potentially not having a political stake?

AG: What do you mean by political?

MB: Well, we often hear that journalism needs to be fair, objective, accurate. And that tends to imply . . .

AG: I didn't say objective, I said fair and accurate.

MB: I'm pushing that question of whether fairness and accuracy implies that there's not a political agenda.

AG: No. I mean we have to represent people fairly. You don't have to agree with someone to let them speak. And though we live in a very politicized world that has real impact on people, and especially in a time of war, it's absolutely critical that we have media that's honest, that's authentic, that breaks the sound barrier, that opens the microphones to people who are not usually heard.

The media should be a sanctuary of dissent. That's what makes this country healthy. That's what would have saved so many lives. We're talking in this country, U.S. soldiers, over 3,100 killed now [referring to the number killed between 2003 and time of interview]. For Iraqis, we're talking perhaps over 650,000 Iraqis. I mean, even that number, from the Johns Hopkins study published in the British magazine *The Lancet*, has hardly gotten any attention in this country. There was a recent poll that says most people think that less than 10,000 Iraqis have died. It's not because Americans are stupid and they don't care. It's because they don't hear it or see it in the media. The media is the way we learn about the world. If we don't learn about it personally and learn it from our own direct experience, it's through the media. And we've got to bring out this information and then let people make up their own minds.

That's also why the media democracy movement and independent media and Indymedia online is so important. Because people realize the American media got it wrong now. Not finding the weapons of mass destruction exposed more than Bush. It exposed the American media. And I think that's also why *Democracy Now!* has grown so vastly from a couple of radio stations to over 500 radio and TV stations, low power, NPR, Pacifica, Public Access, PBS, the satellite networks, online video and audio podcasting. Every week, two to three new stations pick us up, and they're publishing our headlines now in Spanish. Because people realize they did not get accurate information from those media behemoths, and so they're looking elsewhere. And we're there.

MB: I find this debate really interesting. For example, McChesney doesn't express much optimism about the microlevel interventions that we're seeing. He focuses on the large-scale policy and legislation. Many of the voices in this book are less optimistic, perhaps, than you or I about the potential impact of these kinds of interventions at the level of content.

AG: But once people hear something at a low-power FM station they're never the same. And a lot of that is hearing something in their community, people expressing a different point of view. When media is a sanctuary for dissent, it makes it safer for all of us. So that when you walk to the water cooler, when you hear this person say something different, you don't look up in shock. You say, "Oh, I've heard that." It's not perceived as dangerous. I mean, it is dangerous to the status quo, what you're hearing. It threatens to crack and fracture this edifice that has been constructed by the state and what you could sometimes call the state media, when the two go together. It's very frightening—that kind of unified front is very hard to beat. But it has been beaten down because the facts came out. And then people look, and they are critical and say, you didn't tell us this. And it's not just preaching. It's about bringing out all those voices that were there from the beginning at the highest levels of military and intelligence, saying no, the evidence doesn't add up, and giving voice to that.

And I think it is a blooming of a thousand flowers all over the country. I mean the policy and the smaller institutions do interact with each other, of course. Grant licenses for low-power FM stations, and they grow up all over the place—we started growing them! There are lots of low-power FM stations all over the country, challenging the bigger stations: *Why aren't you broadcasting any of this information?* I mean, our transcripts are brought to the Pentagon and to the White House and to the press briefings. And by the way, we're talking just this week, when it's been announced Helen Thomas is having to leave her front seat at the White House press briefing, and occupy the second, being replaced by Fox. So Fox now occupies the front row of the press and the podium. Because Tony Snow is the former Fox news anchor who is the White House press spokesperson.

But I do have hope, because people are hungry for information. And we don't really have a choice. We have to fight at the policy level to ensure equal access to media, to the Internet. And I agree with Bill Moyers when he says we have to come up with a better term than *Net neutrality*. That term means nothing to anyone. It's about *equal access*. The media is too important to be controlled by a few rich, media mega-moguls. It's got to be media run by the people—by the people, for the people. And that resonates in this country, with Americans everywhere, from conservative to progressive. They understand the idea "of, by, and for the people."

MB: Where do you see the recent launch in November, of Al Jazeera English, within this landscape you've just talked about?

AG: It's very important. That whole idea of the insularity of American media—it's very instructive that they can't get on a broadcast outlet in the United States, but they're still there, and you can see them online. And it's not just about Al Jazeera. Again, here we are, the most powerful country on earth in a globalized world, yet we are so isolated, and the way they can maintain this blockade on information is by keeping media outlets away from reaching the mainstream. But they can't do that for long with the Internet. It's as simple as that.

Al Jazeera International is just another example of this. Every which way we have to break the sound barrier and they're attempting to do that as well.

I went to a conference at Doha, and they were concerned about how Al Jazeera will change because of Al Jazeera International, that in order to eventually be accepted they will change their content and mirror the media in the United States. And, you know, we will see.

MB: It seems like it's in a really interesting formative phase right now, where people are leaving BBC and working for Al Jazeera International, and there simply isn't advertiser pressure yet, there isn't ownership pressure, from what I can tell. And I'm really wondering if that will change in six months. I don't know if you have any thoughts about that.

AG: Everything will change, but we'll see what happens.

MB: I'm going to shift now. I was going to ask you some general questions about the role of satire as a kind of commentary in the media landscape—and then I happened to watch you on *Colbert Report* last night!

AG: Last night?

MB: I watched it last night, but you were on in October 2006?

AG: How did you watch it last night?

MB: Online. One of my favorite sites is www.onegoodmove.org. I'm doing this other research project on digital dissent and how people are using online media to produce dissent. And I just interviewed the author of onegoodmove, this fellow who lives in a fairly unpopulated Western state, it's a good story . . .

AG: So tell me his story.

MB: The story with onegoodmove, which streams QuickTime clips of *The Daily Show*, impressed me as an example of technological determinism. Norm Jenson, who runs this blog, (who by the way describes himself as "older, I'm into my 60s now") switched from using a PC to a Mac. And the only way to watch clips on *Comedy Central*, especially in the early years, was if you had a PC. So if you had a Mac, you were screwed, because Macs had trouble interfacing with the *Comedy Central* site due to the proprietary software *Comedy Central* uses.

So this guy got a Mac and decides, just as a service, I'm going to TIVO clips of *The Daily Show* and put the best political segments online. Lo and behold, he gets this huge international progressive following on his Web site. This excited me because I've been studying *The Daily Show* and its effects, musing whether satire has any political effect at all or if it's just people laughing their way into doomsday. And here is a blogger who witnesses through his comments section and extensive online communication with his viewers, that they have become activists as a result of watching *TDS*. Anyway, that's another story, but that's where I watched you on Colbert.

I was impressed by how you held your ground with Colbert. I have respect for Colbert, especially his 2006 White House Press Correspondents speech. But in his interviews, his parody of O'Reilly is especially obnoxious and makes it very hard for people to do a good interview. But you held your own, managed to get a lot of airtime in there, and not let him cut you off.

Do you have any general comments about your experience with Colbert?

AG: You know what they tell you: just imagine yourself speaking to a drunk in a bar—that's what his producers tell you for talking to Mr. Stephen Colbert. I also knew how many people watch this, and how important it was to get out information and not waste the moment. So just to give out information with a smile. And to show the appreciation of the venue, and what he was doing, but also, every minute on the air—the airwaves are a national treasure—is an awesome responsibility. And it was about breaking the sound barrier around dissent and who is saying no to war.

And I chose that moment to talk about soldiers, because they are the most threatening to the establishment. They're *their* soldiers, fighting their war, but they don't share their beliefs. And how brave they are. You know, like the soldier in Utah, who came home, was the editor of the *Anaconda Times*, an Iraq newspaper, spoke to thousands of soldiers, said they're overwhelmingly opposed to war—so he came home and walked across Utah and put up a Web site called "A Soldier's Peace." It showed soldiers' boots, and I talked about him. I talked about Augustine Aguayo who this week will be court martialed in Germany, who tried to become a conscientious objector, was approved by his Investigating Officer, but the military said no, said he had to return to Iraq.

After I did this interview, I was making my way to some place in Oregon, and I was at the San Francisco airport waiting for yet another delayed plane. At San Francisco airport I know where every socket is to plug in my computer and dying phone—in every one of their terminals, I know where to go. My phone was dying as usual, I had just found the plug, plugged in the phone and it rang, and there's this crackly voice: "I cannot believe you said my name on the *Colbert Report*." And I said, "Where are you?" And he said, "I'm in Utah, walking across the state to get that kind of national attention and recognition."

I mean Augustin Aguayo is a remarkable young man, an immigrant in this country who doesn't believe war is right. Who refused to carry a gun in Iraq for a year. This other soldier was an army medic, even though it endangered him. What scared him more than dying himself was killing someone else.

These are unbelievably brave people. And I felt this was an opportunity to talk about them. This is not about being for or against the military. I would argue that the administration may profess to be for the military, but they're opposed to the soldiers. They're endangering the soldiers. And so that's what I chose to do at that moment.

MB: It was really well done. I wonder, do you have any more general comments about the popularity of parody, irony, and satire right now?

AG: People respond to satire in these crazy times. Anything that pokes fun at, pokes holes in, exposes this edifice of lies that has been built is very important.

MB: Do you have any thoughts about the use of satire as a tool in general? For example, your mode of reporting—I suppose there are moments when you might have a tinge of irony for sure, but that's not a primary rhetorical device or tool that you use. What stops you from going there more often yourself? Has it every occurred to you, wow, we could sell a lot more sound bites if we got really witty? How did you decide to go for what you might call sincerity rather than satire?

AG: Just delivering it straight. But that's no disrespect to other people doing it in their own way. And I think it takes everything. This is a very strong edifice that needs to be deconstructed, because it's a threat to a democratic society.

MB: What do you see as pressing primary issues that face media in general at this time?

AG: Media consolidation. Media concentration. It's a tremendous threat. The more radio stations and TV stations that are owned by just a few corporations—that is the greatest threat to a democratic society. Because they're controlling the airwaves: what goes on it. The Clear Channeling of America has to be challenged. They own over 1,200 radio stations in the United States, sponsored prowar rallies. They're being sued by the South Carolina Broadcaster of the Year because she dared to express an antiwar point of view and was thrown off the air.

People learn about the world through the media. Unless they come from a particular place, they learn about it through the media. And it cannot be about just one lens. The stakes are too high. And the way we break down barriers is letting people speak for themselves. You know, when you hear a Venezuelan grandmother, or a Palestinian child, or an Israeli aunt, or a Lebanese uncle, or an Iraqi cousin, you say, "Oh my God, they sound like my bubba or my baby." There is a power that is immeasurable in hearing someone speak for themselves. So I don't say, "The mother's voice cracked when she spoke about her daughter." You just hear the mother talking about her daughter, and there's so much subliminal, so much that is there, in that voice, that accent, in that emotion and that passion. And that's why the airwaves are so critical. They are oxygen for a democracy, and it's got to be free for all, open to all, accessible to all.

MB: Last thing, do you see your work as investigative journalism? Or amplifying others' investigative journalism?

AG: Everything. It's all of those things. We do our own investigations, we give a forum to those who do investigations. Just having someone describe their own experience, being there, can be the most powerful segment of all, a forum for artists to be able to speak. The music that we choose has a tremendous effect on the show, and we particularly try to bring out the music of independents. Listeners send in the music that they love. We're showing video from around the world, and for radio audiences, telling them they can go to our Web site. Building different media platforms for older people for whom the Internet is not familiar terrain and helping them navigate it—that can be revolutionary for someone. "You can go to our Web site at democracynow. org" . . . "What did they say? Democracy?"

Just yesterday, we had the most amazing show. A man who's been in Louisiana at a prison called Angola, a plantation prison named for a country in Africa from where people were brought here and enslaved. The Angola prison is one of the worst prisons in the United States. He's been in prison there for thirty-two years. He was on death row, then Louisiana overthrew the death penalty, and he was in solitary confinement for eleven years and just remains there. We had his mother and sister on in New Orleans. And we had Bob Herbert who did a series of columns on him and told his story, imprisoned when he was 17, now 49. And I said at the end to his mother, "Is there anything else you'd like to share with our listeners?" And she said "You could go to the Web site at freegarytyler org dot co." She clearly was not familiar herself, but I thought there was so much power just in that. And then after the show, you saw that more than a thousand people had signed their online petition. What a difference it makes when a person is locked up. It's information that can set him free.

And that kind of exposé is needed more than ever. Even though there's a plethora of ways to get information and a multiplicity of channels, what matters is who owns those channels and what kind of information is allowed out. So to be able to navigate through all of this is important. It's important to reach people not just through radio but through television, which is where most people get their information. And that's what we're trying to do, through video images of people all over. And we're trying to help them navigate that place they may not be familiar with.

Linking all of this so it's not inaccessible to anyone, bringing everyone up to a level of media literacy so that they can get this. Because it is through information that people can change the world.

MB: Are there ways that you envision alternative media doing an even stronger job of shifting agenda setting? And that might be connected to another question: in your wildest dreams, given new media and all the money you would need, and all the necessary infrastructure, what would be your ideal media structure or platform?

AG: I think it's everything connected. We're not in a separate place right now. I think it's bringing it all together. And people having access to make their own media and for many people to access it. One of the things *Democracy Now!* does is—you're talking about blogs or interesting sites—it's letting people know about these.

We did a piece on doctors participating in the death penalty—this was a while ago, a few years ago, with Physicians for Human Rights, I think it was called. They had been featured on *60 Minutes*. And they said they were absolutely astounded by the response from *Democracy Now!* I mean, *60 Minutes* maybe then reached many more, and we couldn't even measure how many people were listening to *Democracy Now!* because we were in all these places that are not measured by your standard measures of a network. I mean, you can measure a network, but we're linking together many different ones. Millions, we know, access in very different ways all over. But they could not believe the difference in our response. People calling and e-mailing and writing for their reports—they'd never had anything like it. *Crain's New York*, a business publication in New York, did an article saying that *Democracy Now!* launches bucks, because people are looking for alternative forms of information. It's very much below the corporate media radar. But it is bigger than MSNBC, bigger than these networks that get talked about—their little buzz, their little world. And people are getting access to it whom we don't even know about, in the most rural areas, on satellite television, and in other parts of the world, of course, through the Internet. Just to continue that work and to continue to challenge this edifice that is endangering us all, that is the corporate media stranglehold on information. We've got to storm the Bastille.

MB: So, what keeps you going every morning when you wake up?

AG: A coffee?

The voices of the people that are able to get out and get so much hope. The mother whose son has been imprisoned for thirty-two years unjustly who says she really does believe that he's going to be freed. The people in East Timor—the young man who brought us to his backyard furtively, and dug in the sand until he pulled out a piece of newspaper about a congressional resolution three years before that had been passed in the United States, he's on the other side of the world, saying did you know about this? This young man who in our world would be considered illiterate, who held such store in the American people knowing what was happening in his country, and he knew more than Americans did about a congressional resolution. People in Haiti who've experienced coup after coup who believe their country can become democratic, that their country can have a leader who the United States will not overthrow. People right here in New York who are fighting the media monopoly. We're in the media monopoly capital of the world. And the fact that you're doing this—that you take it so seriously and understand that we're at a point where looking at the media as the message itself can happen. And how important it is that you can be writing a book on this, and talking to all these different people, and that it's become a field in itself. Because the media are the most powerful institutions on earth, and people are recognizing this.

8 Alternative Media Theory and Journalism Practice

Chris Atton

In this chapter I argue that the academic study of alternative media is dominated by an approach that focuses on their political value and, in particular, on the capacity of alternative media to empower citizens. Central to empowerment is the opportunity for ordinary people to tell their own stories without the formal education or professional expertise and status of the mainstream journalist. This approach tends to celebrate alternative media and its achievements while paying little attention to how alternative media are produced. When academics act as ideological advocates for alternative media they are likely to miss important perspectives. For example, researchers seem to know why alternative media producers do what they do but less about what they do or why they do it in particular ways. Existing studies lack examinations of what can be best termed *industrial practice*. Despite its connotations from studies of the mass media, this term *industrial practice* encourages us to consider alternative media practices as work. As I shall show, the study of the working practices of alternative media is absent from most research in the field. The study of "work" in alternative media includes social and political processes such as decision-making processes, the structure of editorial meetings, and ideological disputes. I will also need to examine the ways in which people work. How do they learn to become journalists or editors? How do they identify and choose their stories? How do they select and represent their sources? Are alternative journalists truly independent, or are their working methods influenced by the practices of mainstream journalists? These questions about media practice require an understanding of its practitioners: their values, motivations, attitudes, ideologies, history, education, and relationships. In other words, this is to examine what Pierre Bourdieu terms *habitus* (Bourdieu 1993). The habitus of practitioners plays an important part in how they participate in the social arena of media production (Bourdieu's *field*). I have argued that it is possible to conceptualize alternative media production as a field in its own right (Atton 2002), but it is important to consider that the habitus of alternative media practitioners might be developed from their experience of mainstream media. I shall argue that contextualized accounts of media production, which take into account these issues, form an important, though at present largely absent, part of research into alternative media.

Later in this chapter I shall give examples of the types of research I have in mind. Prime among these is the study of audiences; we currently know very little about who uses alternative media and for what purposes. This is odd, considering the social and political claims made for alternative media. I go on to propose explorations of alternative media as news, in particular their representation of sources, as well as examinations of their reliability and credibility. I also argue for studies that recognize the relationship between alternative and mainstream media practices. For example, alternative media often employ populist methods of presentation that resemble the practices of tabloid journalism. At the same time, however, alternative media challenge conventional notions of expertise and authority, particularly in their foregrounding of ordinary people as sources of news. This foregrounding is not without its problems, though: who is to say that these sources might not be used ideologically? However novel their content might appear, alternative media are not as independent of mainstream media ideologies and practices as we might think.

First, I outline the origin of the celebratory approach to alternative media, which has impeded the study of media practices. I believe that its roots lie in critical media scholarship—that is, the study of the ideological basis of the mass media. Critical media scholarship developed as a response to an earlier tradition of "administrative" research. The critical tradition might be thought of as starting as far back as Adorno. There are far too many examples to list here, but of particular relevance to the study of alternative media are Bagdikian (2004); de Jong, Shaw, and Stammers (2005); Downing, Mohammadi, and Sreberny-Mohammadi (1995); and Herman and McChesney (1997). Administrative research was primarily conducted for the benefit of media organizations and public relations companies to enable them to function more effectively (key studies include Hovland, Lumsdaine, and Sheffield 1949; Lasswell 1948; Lazarsfeld, Berelson, and Gaudet 1948; and McCombs and Shaw 1972). Critical media scholars argued that administrative research was simply at the service of media power. The role of academics, they argued, was not to serve that power: it was to challenge it.

Critical Media Studies

There are two broad approaches to critical media studies. The first, exemplified by the Glasgow University Media Group (GUMG), looks at how media texts (news reports, television bulletins) are constructed and how they represent different social groups. The GUMG examined BBC television news reports to reveal its bias towards elite groups in society (politicians, business leaders, law and order professionals). It also showed how workers and trades unions were regularly marginalized and demonized (e.g., Glasgow University Media Group 1976, 1980). The GUMG's work challenges the BBC's claim that it is objective and impartial by showing how facts and values are routinely combined to favor one group in society over another (Eldridge 2000). GUMG argued that this represented a hierarchy of media access where professional journalists uncritically presented the ideologies of elite groups to the public. Journalists present the worlds of politics, society, economics, and culture through the narrow, ideological lens of what Stuart Hall termed *primary definers* (Hall et al. 1978).

The second approach attempts to identify a complete structure to explain the ways in which the mass media function. Herman and Chomsky's (1988) propaganda model is perhaps the best known of these structural accounts. In addition to the routine use of elite sources as primary definers, Herman and Chomsky argue that news is *filtered* by the concentrated power and ownership of the mass media; a reliance on advertising; a desire to avoid the displeasure ("flak") of powerful interest groups; and a systemic anticommunist or anti-left-wing bias. Many alternative media projects have used the propaganda model as a framework for their critiques of mainstream media (it appears in work by Indymedia, Fairness and Accuracy in Reporting, and MediaLens). Analyses derived from Herman and Chomsky's model tend to be highly deterministic. Studies (such as those at www.medialens.org) typically begin with a detailed textual analysis of news reports and editorials, which are used to produce generalized accounts of mass media power. These accounts tell us little about how journalists work with their sources or about how journalists work with their editors and with other journalists (as Schlesinger [1989] has shown). Critical media scholars such as GUMG and Herman and Chomsky portray the mass media as monolithic and unchanging. The power of the mass media marginalizes ordinary citizens: not only are they denied access to its production; they are marginalized in its reports. This portrayal becomes the background against which media researchers place alternative media.

Alternative Media and Media Power

Nick Couldry (2000) has argued that alternative media offer opportunities for "ordinary" people to become media producers (Dickinson 1997; Duncombe 1997; Harcup 2003; Kim and Hamilton 2006; and Platon and Deuze 2003, among others, indicate the scope of these opportunities). We can think of these media as more democratic. Contributors do not necessarily require prior education or training. They do not need to be professionals. We have become so used to the commercialized and professionalized mass media that we consider it as a natural status quo. Couldry believes that alternative media projects encourage the denaturalization of the media. People who had previously considered themselves only as audiences of the media can become producers of the media. They can only do this, however, by understanding that the natural state of the mass media is not the only possible form of media. Media power does not always have to lie with professionals and experts within institutions. Indymedia's news and comment from around the world attests to the knowledge and expertise that comes from direct experience of, for example, racism or police brutality. Contributors to Wikipedia come from a far wider pool of "experts" than the traditional encyclopedia, which typically draws only from academics affiliated to universities and other research institutions.

It is not difficult to see why alternative media such as Indymedia and Wikipedia should be celebrated; they offer participation in media production. They encourage amateurs and recognize the knowledge and expertise of those amateurs. In sharp contrast, the critiques of the Glasgow University Media Group and Herman and Chomsky present the mass media as elitist organizations that recognize only professional and institutionalized knowledge. They largely ignore the experiences of ordinary people, except as material for "vox pop" interviews and to tell stories of human tragedy or of people who achieve remarkable results in the face of adversity (Langer 1998). Alternative media challenge the structures of the mass media; they appear more democratic and socially inclusive. They contest the concentration of institutional and professional media power and challenge the mass media's monopoly on producing symbolic forms. Pierre Bourdieu (1991) has argued that symbolic power is the power to construct reality. Alternative media construct a reality that opposes the conventions and representations of the mass media. The value of alternative media, according to some scholars, does not end here. Alternative media can also make important contributions to the social and political life of amateur media producers by developing communities and active citizenship. The work of John Downing (1984, 2001) and Clemencia Rodriguez (2000, 2003) shows this to good effect. But their studies also show significant limits, in particular about how alternative media producers work.

Radical Democracy and Citizens' Media

For John Downing, alternative media play an important role in shaping the political consciousness of dissident groups in society. He distinguishes these groups from established political institutions and political parties. These groups operate collectively, not hierarchically; they are not formal institutions. In many cases they are loose networks of individuals and small organizations that come together on a larger scale for common ends: in other words, they become social movements. Downing (1984, 2001) argues that the media of these movements are important not only for what they say but for how they are organized. What he terms "rebellious communication" does not simply challenge the political status quo in its news reports and commentaries, it challenges in the ways it is produced. If the aim of radical media is to effect social or political change, then it is crucial, Downing says, that they practice what they preach. He calls this "prefigurative politics" or "the attempt to practice socialist principles in the present, not merely to imagine them for the future" (Downing 2001, 71). An example of this is the network of collectives that make up Indymedia. Local groups make up this network, and decision-making mostly operates at this local level. These independent, self-managed nodes in a network are examples of democratic, noncorporate media. Organizationally, they are quite different from the hierarchical structures of the mass media of western democracies.

Like Downing, Clemencia Rodriguez (2000) argues that alternative media enable ordinary citizens to become politically empowered. For her, when people create their own media they are better able to represent themselves and their communities. She sees these "citizens' media" as projects of self-education. Rather than relying on the mass media to set the boundaries of political involvement (Dahlgren, 2000), citizens use their own, self-managed media to become politically involved on their own terms (Norris 1999). For Rodriguez, however, to become a producer of citizens' media seems at times to be more important than what is being produced. To become an active participant in the process of media production is a political education in itself. She is claiming a significant ability for such practices. How do these practices come about? How do people make them happen? We know very little about this.

Her account of the Chilean community radio station Radio Estrella del Mar, for example, offers few answers (Rodriguez 2003). Describing the contribution of two kids to a Fathers' Day broadcast, she emphasizes their self-expression and a freedom from the norms of radio production: "No one told them what to do; no one suggested a different way to do things" (184). While she notes the presence of an engineer in the control booth, we have no sense of how his norms and practices relate to those of the boys behind the microphone. This underlines my initial observation that those who study alternative media tend to ignore the analysis of work. Working practices are obscured: in this case, the young boy's broadcast seems to take place in a vacuum where its value for their own self-representation and expression occurs magically, free from history, circumstance, and ideology. Rodriguez seems to acknowledge issues of media power, access, and control, but these too seem to be magically resolved once "communication, expression, networking, and information needs . . . are intelligible" (191). How communication needs are made intelligible is not addressed. This approach exemplifies the stress on "participation in the media" as if it were the sole end of such media practices. She approvingly quotes a respondent: "It's more important to get five new people to participate than to get a thousand new listeners" (191). For Rodriguez, self-empowerment and self-education are all: audiences seem irrelevant. Perhaps this explains the enduring absence of audience studies in this area (Downing 2003).

Such studies exemplify the kind of discourse found in critical media studies that emphasize media participation as a good in itself. One of the characteristics of this discourse is to adopt "an often self-consciously radical perspective" (Macek 2006,

1031). This form of critical media scholarship typically entails, as Macek points out, "an overt, although not unreflective sympathy, for the aims of various movements for progressive social change" (1032). The consequence of this is to generate "solidarity" with particular movements and their aims. It is unfortunate that a long-standing move away from administrative research ends up in a similar form: uncritical and empiricist. Critical media research that identifies too closely with its objects of study performs a double disservice. First, it runs the risk of abandoning its very ethos (the critique of media power). Second, it will fail to provide critical accounts of alternative media that might be useful to alternative media producers. In its rush to praise and support alternative media, critical media research appears reluctant to examine them too closely.

From Celebration to Critique

The celebratory approach to alternative media claims that organizational methods, political practices, self-management, and participation are enough to demonstrate the political value of alternative media. The celebratory approach is a problem because the ways in which alternative media connect to other aspects of social and cultural life are left obscure. Downing and Rodriguez show us how alternative media connect with political struggle and political empowerment, but they do not show us how alternative media producers *develop their skills*. What impact does the habitus of Rodriguez's young broadcasters have on their production? How do they position themselves in relation to the field of broadcasting? What experiences and ideologies come into play when they become broadcasters? What is their sense of audience? Is it as marginal as Rodriguez would have it? We do not know, since her observations about their "empowerment" exclude all these questions; they appear to exclude the boys' own reflections, too.

Just as the propaganda model of Herman and Chomsky tells us little about how professional journalists work, Rodriguez's model of citizen's media tells us hardly anything about how citizen journalists "empower" themselves and their communities. What are missing are contextualized accounts of actual journalistic production.

Elsewhere in this volume, Renzi argues that "sociologically oriented approaches" to the study of tactical media are deficient to the degree that they examine the groups involved in these practices as if they were "definable entities" that remain stable and observable, and thus available for "taxonomic dissection." Renzi's point, that such approaches miss the specific and dynamic processes that take place within media production, reiterates the problem with Downing's macroperspective on the radical media of social movements: that the media serve movements that are largely fixed and identifiable and that represent a collective identity. Similarly, Carroll and Hackett (2006) warn against emphasizing a static notion of collective identity. Their interviews with media activists reveal "intersecting social circles" (Carroll and Hackett 2006, 93) in which activists produce media. What these activists do, how they do it, and how they relate to each other all tend to be in flux. Carroll and Hackett consider the practice of alternative media as "a reflexive form of activism that treats communication as simultaneously means and ends of struggle" (96). This practice not only enables the building of identity (whether individual or collective), it is also directed at audiences (though they acknowledge that media activists are "especially prone to 'getting stuck' at the first stage . . . with its own inherent satisfactions"; 98). Unlike Rodriguez, both Carroll and Hackett and Renzi are as interested in what Renzi calls the "circulation of ideas and work" through alternative media, as they are in the value of alternative media for its practitioners' own self-development. This brings us to an important missing element in alternative media studies: audience research.

We can think of circulation as a search for audiences, but who are these audiences? Audiences for alternative media will differ according to their political commitment, their social and cultural background, and their media literacy. How can alternative media speak to audiences beyond the already-committed activist? The British research group Comedia (1984) argued that alternative media would only reach wider audiences by adopting mainstream (that is, commercial) strategies of organization, economics, and distribution. I have criticized this argument elsewhere (Atton 2002) on the grounds that it positions alternative media in a "ghetto" of its own making. Comedia was writing at a time when alternative media were overwhelmingly *printed media*. In Britain (as in the United States), it was impossible for these marginal publications to broker deals with national distribution companies. The only way to achieve this would be to transform both the form and content of a publication so radically as to be unrecognizable. Over twenty years later, alternative media production has largely shifted to the Internet. Distribution no longer depends on a small number of companies; no longer do alternative media need to "mainstream" themselves to gain public exposure. Nevertheless, this form of independence does not guarantee exposure, nor does it guarantee circulation. When alternative media enter a public sphere beyond that of the "micropublic" in their immediate environment, the value and purpose of that independence become crucial.

An emphasis on the independence of alternative media can blind us to the relationship between alternative media and mass media (Couldry and Curran 2003). Studies of alternative media have illuminated the complex, hybrid nature of alternative media in relation to its mainstream counterparts (Hamilton 2003; Hamilton and Atton 2001). While social movement theories might explain the role of alternative media in constructing collective identity, they do little to help us explain alternative media as communication. If we consider alternative media as "ways of going on within journalism" (Atton 2004, 159), then we may ask: Where do alternative media practices come from? Where do alternative media practitioners learn to practice? By linking theories

Figure 8.1
SchNEWS proclaims its "mission statement"

of alternative media with those of journalism studies, we might develop models of alternative media to deal with the norms and means of media practice as well as with "empowerment" and identity. We need to develop a multiperspectival approach that takes into account all of these issues.

At the beginning of this chapter, I asked some questions that could form a starting point for researching the "industrial practices" of alternative media. There is not the space to address all these questions here. Instead I shall focus on the questions of sourcing and representation. I shall show how one paper, the British alternative newspaper and Web site *SchNEWS* (www.schnews.org.uk), constructs its stories around the voices of "ordinary" citizens and marginalizes elite groups, which are the dominant voices in mainstream media. I shall then explore the impact of this practice on audiences. How do audiences judge the credibility and reliability of alternative media? To answer this question I shall draw on recent research on blogs.

Sourcing

Whereas mainstream media make extensive use of members of elite groups as sources (these are Hall et al.'s [1978] *primary definers*), alternative media offer access to a much wider range of voices. These often include members of local communities, protesters, and activists: ordinary voices compared to the privileged voices of elites. A study of the British activist newspaper *SchNEWS* shows this in action (Atton and Wickenden 2005). Where the mainstream media employ the view of "experts", *SchNEWS* employs ordinary people to provide expert knowledge. These people do not need to have high status in society. They appear in *SchNEWS* to illustrate issues and perspectives with which *SchNEWS* is sympathetic and that it wishes to promote. For example, a story about the harassment of local residents by violent gangs uses extensive quotes from residents to argue for the power of local community problem-solving "without the help of apathetic police, archaic laws or an out-of-touch government." *SchNEWS*'s use of ordinary people as sources for its news stories is very different from the mainstream media's use of "vox pop" interviews. The typical vox pop gathers brief opinion; *SchNEWS* presents local people as capable of action, who are able to identify problems and provide solutions. In this example, *SchNEWS* reports that it is local residents, not government officials, who are taking action. The paper does not ignore elite sources, but it does not tend to quote them directly. Instead, it presents their arguments in order to show their inadequacies and failings. Elite sources tend to be treated with suspicion. In a report of a wildcat postal strike in the United Kingdom, *SchNEWS* quotes striking postal workers at length. Their words not only describe and justify their actions; they also provide information and commentary about the economic situation of the postal company. In mainstream journalism, we would expect economic analysis from managers of the company or from independent experts. By contrast, *SchNEWS* uses the voices of ordinary people to set the terms of reference by which its readers are encouraged to understand issues and events.

The representation of ordinary people in alternative journalism does not set them apart as heroes or victims, but as voices that have as equal a right to be heard as do the voices of elite groups (as we learn from Fernandes's experiences with Wake Up Call and People's Production House, elsewhere in this collection). Storytelling by those who are normally actors in other people's stories challenges the expert culture of both the news journalist and the expert columnist. When reporting on other communities *SchNEWS* does not take the approach of what David Spurr (1993) has called the "colonizing journalist" but employs members of those communities to speak for themselves.

This approach to news construction appears to confirm Rodriguez's (2000) notion of citizens' media, through which communities are able to represent themselves and tell their own stories (once more, we see this in Fernandes's account). However, there is evidence to suggest that these stories are used by *SchNEWS* to promote its own ideology. In its coverage of the harassment of a local community, the only residents quoted are those who are disillusioned by local government officials and the police. They have placed their faith in local community action that fits well with the paper's aim to provide "weekly snapshots of the phenomenal rise of positive direct action" (*SchNEWS* editorial, cited in Atton 2002, 85). Similarly, the paper displays its broadly anarchist philosophy in its report on striking postal workers. It portrays the postal workers' union as a hierarchical institution that has been "fumbling" and "frightened." It is the rank and file membership, not their leaders, who have "crushed" the management. In these ways, *SchNEWS* fits the "ordinary" discourse of its sources to its own politicized discourse.

Do the sources used by *SchNEWS* share the paper's ideology? What does it mean for the paper to claim solidarity with their ordinary sources? The hierarchy of access to the media is inverted by *SchNEWS*; it provides greater access to its pages for ordinary people and less access for elite groups. But do its ordinary sources have any more control over how their words are used than they do as vox pops in the mainstream media? To what extent does *SchNEWS* employ these sources for its own ideological ends, which might not be shared by the sources themselves? The conventional hierarchy of access might be inverted, yet perhaps in its place is a further hierarchy, where the ideology of the media producers dominates the expression of their "ordinary" sources.

Alternative media such as *SchNEWS* present their ideas in a populist manner that resembles tabloid journalism. Tabloid styles are normally employed in mainstream media to maintain conservative news agenda; the radical populism of *SchNEWS* subverts this norm (Atton 2002). This radical form connects historically with earlier, radical forms of journalism, which predate the commercialized and capitalized forms of journalism and are normally considered as the origins of tabloid journalism (Williams 1970). In the United Kingdom, the Radical press of the eighteenth and the nineteenth centuries may be considered as a precursor of papers such as *SchNEWS*. Radical journalism aims to produce a communicative democracy based on a media commons, rather than on a segregated, elitist, and professionalized occupational activity. The notion of communicative democracy challenges the dominant criteria by which audiences judge the credibility and reliability of journalists and their sources, criteria based on formal education and professional status. Research into mainstream news media has found that the interaction between the media and the audience (or the lack of it) has a significant impact on the audience's understanding of the news—and its trust of that news (Hargreaves and Thomas 2002). Ideally, communicative democracy brings together media producers and audiences in a far closer relationship; it can be argued that this more intimate interaction between the working methods of the journalist and the needs of the audience is able to replace expert-based notions of credibility and reliability.

Credibility and Reliability

I have already noted that there has been little detailed research into audiences of alternative media. One of the few studies is by Matheson and Allan (2003), who studied bloggers and their reception by audiences during the war in Iraq. The bloggers included professional journalists as well as military personnel and Iraqi citizens. They presented first-hand accounts of their experiences and thus are less mediated than the experiences of the people used by *SchNEWS*. These accounts raise questions about credibility and reliability, and how audiences judge them.

Matheson and Allan found that even blogs written by professional reporters tended to eschew the established standards of objectivity and impartiality, preferring instead a style of address that has more in common with "native reporting" (Atton 2002). That is to say, the professional journalists wrote from direct, personal experience and emphasized their independence from organizational or administrative constraints. From their interviews with professional journalists who maintained blogs during the last Gulf War, Matheson and Allan found that it was these aspects that the reporters believed resonated with their readers. It was the direct, authentic account of personal experience that counted in journalists' blogs, particularly when their newspaper reports were limited by their situation as embedded journalists.

Matheson and Allan argue that the readers trusted the bloggers because their methods were transparently subjective. Journalists did not appear to present their eyewitness reports as fact; they did not use their professional authority to present a definitive version of events. Readers did not consider the blogs as absolute truth. Instead, they understood the war blogs as a set of accounts told from different perspectives. Moreover, readers were able to participate in the construction of these accounts. Allan cites freelance journalist Christopher Allbritton, who argued that his readers "trusted me to bring them an unfettered view of what I was seeing and hearing" (Allan 2006, 109). Allan argues that Allbritton's readers "shap[ed] his reporting" by asking questions and suggesting leads, "each one of them effectively serving as an editor" (109). These practices challenge both the journalistic ideal of objectivity (the separation of "facts" from "values") and the status of journalist as the recognized expert in representing the world to readers. We can understand the work of bloggers and its reception by readers as recognition of the moral and political nature of objectivity. The blogs examined by Matheson and Allan challenge the central assumptions of objectivity: that it is possible to separate facts from values and that it is morally and politically preferable to do so.

We have already seen how the radical populism of some alternative media has its roots in earlier, precommercial and preprofessional radical media. These earlier publications were "preobjective," that is to say, they were produced before objectivity became an established norm in professional journalism (for example, the English Radical press of the late eighteenth and early nineteenth centuries; Boyce, Curran and Wingate 1978; Curran and Seaton 1997). As we saw earlier, the Glasgow University Media Group have demonstrated how journalism that considers itself objective can be just as value laden as the earlier forms it sought to replace. Contemporary alternative media tend to arise in order to provide a counter to what alternative journalists consider an already-biased set of reports. Skeptical of what counts as balance in the mainstream media, they seek to set up their own counterbalance. Their radical journalistic practices offer moral and political correctives to the supposedly fact-centered techniques of the mainstream media.

Audiences play an important role in these practices. Readers of blogs are able to encounter multiple interpretations of a single event. They are, however unwittingly, experiencing the limits of objectivity that Edgar has argued is found in all forms of journalism: "Journalism cannot be objective, for that presupposes that an inviolable interpretation of the event as action exists prior to the report" (Edgar 1992, 120). For Matheson and Allan, writers and readers of blogs share a personal experience that is emblematic of a "new" journalism. This journalism is less focused on the journalist as professional; instead, it proposes a relationship between writer and reader that re-imagines the status of journalism and its practitioners. Alternative media suggest new ways of thinking about and producing journalism, a focus on what kinds of knowledge are produced and how readers and writers may come together to make sense of them.

Conclusion

I hope that these examples have shown why we need to bring the news practices of alternative media into alternative media theory and to take into account news framing, representation, discourse, ethics, and norms. We need to consider these media practices as socially situated work, as well as processes of political empowerment. To consider alternative media practices from both these perspectives is to move away from the limits of the celebratory approach. Alternative media practices might be drawn from mainstream practices, from history and from ideology, just as they might challenge those practices or effect "new" forms of communication. As I mentioned earlier, research needs to be multiperspectival. To develop a rigorously critical approach to our studies, we need to emphasize the connections between alternative and mainstream and underline the challenges that alternative media offers. We will then be better equipped to explore how alternative media practices connect to audiences and to produce work that is relevant to alternative media projects and their audiences. However provisional, transient, or slippery alternative media might be, it is inadequate to consider them as free from the influence of existing practices. The position of the researcher as ideological advocate needs to be sacrificed for the sake of properly critical media research.

References

Allan, Stuart. 2006. *Online news: journalism and the Internet*. Maidenhead: Open University Press.

Atton, Chris. 2002. *Alternative media*. London: Sage.

———. 2004. *An alternative internet: radical media, politics and creativity*. Edinburgh: Edinburgh University Press.

Atton, Chris, and Emma Wickenden. 2005. Sourcing routines and representation in alternative journalism: a case study approach. *Journalism Studies* 6(3): 347–359.

Bagdikian, Ben. 2004. *The new media monopoly*. Boston: Beacon Press.

Bourdieu, Pierre. 1991. *Language and symbolic power*. Cambridge: Polity Press.

———. 1993. *The field of cultural production: essays on art and literature*. Cambridge: Polity Press.

Boyce, George, James Curran, and Pauline Wingate, eds. 1978. *Newspaper history from the seventeenth century to the present day*. London: Constable.

Carroll, William K., and Robert A. Hackett. 2006. Democratic media activism through the lens of social movement theory. *Media, Culture and Society* 28(1): 83–104.

Comedia. 1984. The alternative press: the development of underdevelopment. *Media, Culture and Society* 6: 95–102.

Couldry, Nick. 2000. *The place of media power: pilgrims and witnesses of the media age*. London and New York: Routledge.

Couldry, Nick, and James Curran. eds. 2003. *Contesting media power: alternative media in a networked world*. Lanham: Rowman and Littlefield.

Curran, James, and Jean Seaton. 1997. *Power without responsibility: the press and broadcasting in Britain*. 5th ed. London: Routledge.

Dahlgren, Peter. 2000. Media, citizenship, and civic culture. In *Mass media and society*, ed. James Curran and Michael Gurevitch, 310–328. London: Arnold.

de Jong, Wilma, Martin Shaw, and Neil Stammers, eds. 2005. *Global activism, global media*. London: Pluto Press.

Dickinson, Robert. 1997. *Imprinting the sticks: the alternative press outside London*. Aldershot: Arena.

Downing, John. 1984. *Radical media: the political experience of alternative communication*. Boston: South End Press.

———. 2001. *Radical media: rebellious communication and social movements*. Thousand Oaks, CA: Sage.

———. 2003. Audiences and readers of alternative media: the absent lure of the virtually unknown. *Media, Culture and Society* 25(5): 625–645.

Downing, John, Ali Mohammadi, and Annabelle Sreberny-Mohammadi, eds. 1995. *Questioning the media: a critical introduction.* 2nd ed. Thousand Oaks, CA, and London: Sage.

Duncombe, Stephen. 1997. *Notes from underground: zines and the politics of alternative culture.* London: Verso.

Edgar, Andrew. 1992. Objectivity, bias and truth. In *Ethical Issues in journalism and the media,* ed. Andrew Belsey and Ruth Chadwick, 112–219. London: Routledge.

Eldridge, John. 2000. The contribution of the Glasgow Media Group to the study of television and print journalism. *Journalism Studies* 1(1): 113–127.

Glasgow University Media Group. 1976. *Bad news.* London: Routledge and Kegan Paul.

———. 1980. *More bad news.* London: Routledge and Kegan Paul.

Hall, Stuart, Chas Critcher, Tony Jefferson, John Clarke, and Brian Roberts. 1978. *Policing the crisis: mugging, the state, and law and order.* London: Methuen.

Hamilton, James. 2003. Remaking media participation in early modern England. *Journalism: Theory, Practice and Criticism* 4(3): 293–313.

Hamilton, James, and Chris Atton. 2001. Theorizing Anglo-American alternative media: toward a contextual history and analysis of U.S. and U.K. scholarship. *Media History* 7(2): 119–135.

Harcup, Tony. 2003. "The unspoken—said": the journalism of alternative media. *Journalism: Theory, Practice and Criticism* 4(3): 356–376.

Hargreaves, Ian, and James Thomas. 2002. *New news, old news.* London: ITC/BSC.

Herman, Edward S., and Noam Chomsky. 1988. *Manufacturing consent: the political economy of the mass media.* New York: Pantheon.

Herman, Edward S., and Robert W. McChesney. 1997. *The global media: the new missionaries of global capitalism.* London: Cassell.

Hovland, Carl, Arthur A. Lumsdaine, and Fred D. Sheffield. 1949. *Experiments on mass communication.* New York: Wiley.

Kim, Eun-Gyoo, and James W. Hamilton. 2006. Capitulation to capital? *OhmyNews* as alternative media. *Media, Culture and Society* 28(4): 541–560.

Langer, John. 1998. *Tabloid television: popular journalism and the "other news".* London: Routledge.

Lasswell, Harold D. 1948. The structure and function of communication in society. In *The communication of ideas,* ed. Lyman Bryson, 37–51. New York: Harper.

Lazarsfeld, Paul F., Bernard Berelson, and Hazel Gaudet. 1948. *The people's choice.* New York: Columbia University Press.

Macek, Steve. 2006. Divergent critical approaches to new media. *New Media and Society* 8(6): 1031–1038.

Matheson, Donald, and Stuart Allan. 2003. Weblogs and the war in Iraq: journalism for the network society? Paper presented at the Digital Dynamics conference, November 6–9, in Loughborough, U.K.

McCombs, Maxwell E., and Donald L. Shaw. 1972. The agenda setting function of the mass media. *Public Opinion Quarterly* 36: 176–187.

Norris, Pippa. 1999. *Critical citizens: global support for democratic governance.* Oxford: Oxford University Press.

Platon, Sara, and Mark Deuze. 2003. Indymedia journalism: a radical way of making, selecting and sharing news? *Journalism: Theory, Practice and Criticism* 4(3): 336–355.

Rodriguez, Clemencia. 2000. *Fissures in the mediascape: an international study of citizens' media.* Cresskill, NJ: Hampton Press.

———. 2003. The bishop and his star: citizens' communication in southern Chile. In *Contesting media power: alternative media in a networked world*, ed. Nick Couldry and James Curran, 177–194. Lanham: Rowman and Littlefield.

Schlesinger, Philip. 1989. From production to propaganda? *Media, Culture and Society* 11(3): 283–306.

Spurr, David. 1993. *The rhetoric of empire: colonial discourse in journalism, travel writing, and imperial administration.* Durham, NC, and London: Duke University Press.

Williams, Raymond. 1970. Radical and/or respectable. In *The Press We Deserve*, ed. Richard Boston, 14–26. London: Routledge and Kegan Paul.

9 Community Radio, Access, and Media Justice: An Interview with Deepa Fernandes

Andréa Schmidt and Megan Boler

Deepa Fernandes is a journalist, media activist, and media trainer. She is currently the host of *Wakeup Call* on WBAI, part of the Pacifica Radio Network. She has worked in communities around the world to produce award-winning documentaries, and her work has appeared regularly on the ABC and BBC World Service and across the Pacifica Network. Deepa's first book, *Targeted: Homeland Security and the Business of Immigration,* addresses the repression and exploitation of migrant workers and the rise of domestic security in the United States after 9/11. Deepa is also the founder and codirector of People's Production House, a media justice training and production institute for youth and immigrant workers.

This interview was conducted in person in New York City on March 4, 2007.

Megan Boler: You've reported and produced radio documentaries all over the world for mainstream media institutions including the BBC and ABC. What made you decide to host a show for a community radio station in New York instead of focusing on working as a producer or reporter for more mainstream institutions?

Deepa Fernandes: That was a really hard decision, because at the point when I was offered the job to host *Wakeup Call*, I was also offered two other jobs that paid double as much. But none of them had what *Wakeup Call* had, which was that in the biggest media market in the country, we could have a social justice–based news show going out for three hours every morning. And the *amazing* people who had been doing it, Sharan and Errol *and Leslie*, would stay around, and that there would be new energy too, the new generation at WBAI, myself, Kat Aaron, a young woman called Leanne, and some of the folks from Free Speech Radio News—it was just a coming together. It seemed like the possibility of "We can really do something amazing here with the media."

And it was collaborative. It wasn't like "Oh I'm going to be the host of this show, and it's me." With this crew of people who I really share so many dreams and visions and philosophies with about what the media can be, we can make this happen.

So in some ways it was a big honor to be in that position, to say yes, let's take this show on, and let's make it the kind of radio that we want to listen to. Those folks that

Figure 9.1
Fernandes interviewing in Haiti. Photo by Sacajawea Hall

I named, we're all kind of news junkies, we're all in the world of using media to try and effect social change. And we're not shy to say it either. We're not the kind of media makers who think that we have to be objective, or think that there are two sides to every story and they need to be equally represented. And that was pretty much my experience coming out of the mainstream media, the BBC particularly. I didn't want to have to toe lines. Maybe I can just give you an example.

When I was in Venezuela, when the large shutdown of industry was happening by the business and political elites—mainly the business elites, but pre-Chavez, they had also been the political elite—the way it was getting represented in the press outside was that it was a strike. And I went to Venezuela—I was then the host of *Free Speech Radio News*—to cover what was happening. I went for a month. We had decided at FSRN that we needed to cover this for a month. So I had my job, but because I was only half time, I decided I needed to string for a few people. So I reached out, and the BBC said, "Of course we want somebody down there. Yes, please contribute reporting."

And the first thing I noticed when I arrived in Venezuela was this is not a strike. A strike is when workers refuse to go to work. This is a lock out. All the workers I was meeting wanted to go to work, but they couldn't because their bosses had shut down the industries that they worked in. A very different story, right? And it was one of those instances where you step back and you say wow, this is really being represented as if it has mass support, as if it is worker led, when indeed it's the captains of industry being able to say, "We are powerful enough to sustain an economic hit to try and bring about a change in political power, because we'll benefit in the long run." And that was clearly the story that I was getting.

Now for FSRN on a daily basis, I could report different angles on that story, and it wasn't hard. I just had to go out into the streets because people weren't working. They wanted to work but they weren't. That was at the time when there were long lines at the gas station, just to fill your car up with gas. And you'd go and wait at a gas station and you'd get a cross section of Venezuelan life, from academics to bus drivers to street vendors, because every kind of life requires in some way to have access to gasoline.

So, I start putting together some pitches for the BBC, pretty much along the lines of the kinds of stories I'm covering for FSRN. And I get an e-mail back from the producer who I work with at that particular show at the BBC, and she says "You know Deepa, maybe you can—how about a story where you just leave the politics out of it?" Those were her words. And I remember sitting in an Internet café reading her e-mail thinking, "Leave the politics out of it? This is *all* political. Every single person here, this is about politics." So I e-mailed her and said this is really all about politics. Every person who you meet puts this into a political context. There isn't any kind of nice fuzzy story to tell here. So then she wrote me back and said something to the effect of, "You can go out there and find a story. Maybe try this. Go and sit in a café and just observe life as it's passing by." And this was really instrumental to me, because it really helped me to understand, you know talk to the lady who's just walking by, talk to the lady who's just coming in to get her . . . that didn't exist in Venezuela. The only place it existed was in the very elite neighborhoods where people operated outside of that, but that was a such a small percentage. You weren't going to get regular Venezuelans in that area.

So I wrote her back and said, "That's not a story I can tell. I don't have that kind of access. And furthermore, it's not really a story. It's not representative of what's going on here." And we agreed to disagree, and I didn't file for them.

This keeps happening. When I was in Chiapas, in Mexico, there was a massacre of indigenous people. And I was right there, and I'd been in the community for a little while, and I immediately pitched; I had all these powerful indigenous voices. And the BBC producer wrote back to me—and I'm just giving you some of the extreme examples here because I've filed many other stories where I didn't have to deal with this but—he wrote back to me and said, "You know that's great, but now we want you to go out and get the Mexican military voices, and the Mexican government." And I wrote back and said, "Get another reporter to do that. Because this story is about the voices who are most affected." And it was kind of the pull and push, back and forth. And he wrote back to me and he said, "Look those are powerful voices, but it's only one side of the story, you have to get the Mexican military."

And I couldn't be in that community and have the trust of those people, who into my microphone poured pain and passion, and speak with the military. They'd just lost their loved ones in a brutal massacre that I had witnessed the end of—not the actual killing, but I'd witnessed the aftermath of what that did and had no reason to doubt these people. They weren't making it up. Yet the BBC wanted me to tell the story in a very particular way. And at that point, I was lucky because I was able to say, you know what, I don't need to tell this story for you. And I had contact with producers at WBAI, particularly Mario Murillo who hosted a show called *Our Americas*, and I said I'm going to tell the story for him. And he took my tape, and he didn't try to edit me. He put it on the radio.

That was instrumental for me to be able to see—here are the ways in which an editorial process really does try to control what the story is. And I'm not saying that happens all the time, and I'm not saying that in my experience there's a bigger goal of trying to serve a particular interest, say in Venezuela, of trying to shut Chavez's government down. I think in some ways it's very limited, and people fall into working a certain way, and they don't see that every story needs to be told in its own way, as opposed to one size fits all, as in, "We should be objective. There are two sides to every story. There's a good guy and a bad guy." . . . these kinds of very simple molds that tend to fit on top of stories.

MB: That is a good segue into the next question of how you would define mainstream media. Do you use that term? Do you use the term *dominant media*?

DF: Actually I like to define it more in terms of who owns it. So I call it *corporate media*. Mainly because I think *we* are the mainstream. Not that I'd necessarily call us the mainstream media, and I think it's easy to use that term from time to time. But the more correct term is to define it as the people who own it—so we are community media, we're owned by the community, and corporate media is owned by corporations—just because it doesn't let us forget that.

I think it's too easy to forget or just not think about why news is being produced. And for the most part news is being produced for profit motive. We call ourselves a social justice news show. We're not afraid to say that social justice is why we're producing news. So let's just be real about the corporate media. They're producing media for profits—as well as very laudable objectives about doing good journalism. I don't want to say that everyone who works for corporate media is part of that agenda. (There are very good journalists and very good editors and very good photographers and sound recorders who believe in making news and telling a story for the right reasons. They just happen to work for the corporate media.) But I think from our end, we very much tell stories that are from the mainstream. I guess I consider mainstream something that many people would be interested in or want to listen to, would want to learn from. And it's just how you tell it and how you present it.

MB: I was having a conversation with some friends about what the public wants to look at. Somebody who's working eight hours a day, is exhausted, has a family, one can understand perhaps why they would want to watch Anna Nicole Smith. So one argument would be that CNN delivers what people want to watch. I have a lot of difficulty with that analysis because the reasons we come to want what we want are so complex. So when you talk about corporate media, how would you articulate the relationship of corporate profit interest to ideology to the question of what then gets created in terms of public demand for news?

DF: I think the very simple analysis, which I also reject, is that the American public has been dumbed down by the media, that we've come to expect nothing more than Anna Nicole Smith, and that that in fact translates to what we want. But I also reject the view that people don't consume media for entertainment purposes, or don't want to have their news in formats that do reflect where the media has brought us, that do reflect the times and how we've come to a certain place.

I guess I'll couch that in an example. With Kat Aaron and Saki Hall and Sylvia Guerrero, we work in middle schools and high schools with young people, and one of the exercises that we do in teaching about the media is to analyze certain media outlets. And the last couple of years we've done the hip-hop station here in New York, Hot 97. Now Hot 97, if you've listened to it, is all entertainment and rich people news and things that really are out of the sphere of real community-based content. There really isn't any. But one of the things that I've come to learn is that if we hope to bring about change in our media, we can't just reject that as not being valid. Because in young people's lives it absolutely is. And to do that, you're threatening the very ground that they stand on, and we're losing the battle by just saying that the "corporate media sucks." It doesn't work.

Especially in youth communities, and in communities of color, which are particularly targeted by media outlets and resold the images of people of color as criminals, and of youth as violent offenders, I think what we need to do is take what works and what we like from that and let that help us make the kind of media with the messages that we want for our communities. In some ways we're in an interesting position, because if we hope to be the mainstream media, meaning have an impact as broadly as possible, I think we have to be really honest about the fact that most of our communities, like you said, just turn the TV on and watch that kind of media. How do we then begin to build that knowledge and understanding in our communities of the harmful effects? We need to know more than Anna Nicole Smith. We need to know when the agenda is being switched up on us because there's probably something else going on.

I think Katrina is a great example. Why hasn't there been more mass outrage across the United States about what has happened to people from the Gulf Coast? And I think very specifically we can look at our media for that because the media has not stayed on the story, it has not rammed it home to us, and the Bush administration has very successfully been able to talk about a whole lot of other things.

So I think the question becomes, how much do we drive agendas, and potentially use the tactics of the mainstream media, like the slick production of MTV? Cause we need the slick production of MTV to win over all our highschoolers. They're not going to sit back and listen to someone on a soap box preaching about how Bush should have done this and that. For us, we really want to look at a media that—I guess we are oppositional, but we want to broaden our tent. We want to bring more people in, and I think that's what we're trying to do with *Wakeup Call*.

When you're very underresourced, which community radio is—and especially WBAI and our particular show—three hours of live radio everyday, with two point five staff people, to host, engineer and produce is ridiculous, right? So with very limited resources, how can we build a media castle so that we're not just having to do the run of the mill, so that we can actually push ourselves and the way we make radio, and keep it moving and keep it interesting so we attract more people? And then hopefully you'll hear the messages that come out.

MB: How do you decide what is worth covering on your show each morning, and how would you say that differs substantively from corporate radio agenda setting?

DF: WBAI is 99.5 and it's right in the middle of the dial in New York. Maybe not so much now because most people have digital radios. But the point is, some people still do turn the dial, and when you actually have to turn the dial, you have to go through BAI all the time, just to get to either side of it. And that's the power that we have, that we need to take advantage of. We don't have the funding, we don't have the ability to have mass PR campaigns and SUVs in the street with 99.5 on the side going out and handing out free stuff. But what we do have is this ability to hold people when they cross us. So I think our goal on a daily basis is to make radio that people just aren't hearing.

I'll give you an example from just last week. We decided we wanted to do a series on Ghana, because this week, this Tuesday, is Ghana's 50th independence anniversary. And we thought about it and we were like, "Well, we'll cover it next week because that's the anniversary." And then we were like, "Hang on, what do we know about Ghana? Do you know—like yeah, there was this guy called Kwame Nkrumah, he was this freedom fighter, I think he fought the British, he was anticolonial." Hmm. Maybe if we don't know—and we kind of use ourselves as yardsticks, because we have a very diverse team, intergenerationally, ethnically, genderwise—so if all of us put together just know the basics, that's probably a pretty good representation that most people, unless you're from Ghana or you're an Africanist, probably don't know that much about it. So then we said, "Let's do a Ghana 101. Let's hit Ghana every single day this week and try and build some knowledge so that when we get to next Tuesday, people actually have an appreciation of just what independence means for Ghana over fifty years."

So one of the things that we did was go to the Pacifica archives, and one of our producers, Selina, found this great tape of Kwame Nkrumah speeches. Now I don't know if you've ever heard Kwame Nkrumah—I hadn't. And I'd read a little bit about him. So we started each show that week with an excerpt from a Kwame Nkrumah speech. And it was riveting.

Usually that first section of the morning at 6:10 is when there's so much to still be doing for the show that we play something on tape so that I can be gathering, doing whatever I have to do, flipping through the *New York Times*, making sure I'm up on all the news. I couldn't do anything, because this man had riveted me. And I think that's one of the things we hope to do. We hope that you'll be flipping through and you'll say, "Who is this person speaking? What is this accent? Hold on, what's he saying?" And you might just stop and listen for a minute. And then later on in the program, we interviewed various people and we just tracked. We started on day one with who is Kwame Nkrumah and what did he do? What happened after Kwame Nkrumah was overthrown? Talk us through the period of military coups.

So if you listen on a regular basis, you might actually find yourself building knowledge in a cumulative way. And that's really what the media should be about. So yes, we're a daily show, and one of the things that's frustrating about that is you just sort of hit and quit. You cover something when it breaks, and then . . . But I feel like in a broader sphere, we're building a community of people who understand things in particular ways, and we're not saying, "This is what Kwame Nkrumah said and we all have to agree," but "This is what Kwame Nkrumah said and let's think about that. Do we agree with it? Does it apply today? How radical was that at the time?" So hopefully it facilitates discussions.

Those are some of our aims, as well as very concretely, prioritizing the voices of those who are affected most. I think there's also a tendency in community media to kind of make a platform for the most often heard voices on the Left or in progressive communities. And that's very important, and we absolutely need that because in some way they're the leaders on this side. But we also just need to hear from regular ordinary people living what's going on, and who might not have the savvy media training, or the PhD, or be able to frame it the way . . . they can just talk from their heart. So I think it's always trying to balance those kinds of things. Because the other thing, really, is that if you're flipping through the dial and you hear someone who sounds like you, maybe that will be an incentive to keep listening.

MB: You just published a book called *Targeted* about the repression and exploitation of migrant workers and the rise of the domestic security industry in the United States after 9/11. How important, in your mind, is investigative reporting for democracy in the United States right now?

DF: It should be mandatory for all journalists.

I wanted to do investigative journalism for that book. And I went to my friend Prathap Chatterjee, who I think is one of the best investigative journalists in this country, to learn how to do it. And he very patiently walked me and some of the other folks who were doing research for my book through the various processes of how to do it. It's a skill that you have to learn. I think especially what I was finding was that this government is turning more and more into a secrecy state. It's just impossible to get information. And I don't say that lightly. It really is impossible to get information from the government. And even when you do Freedom of Information Act requests, you get a little bit of information, and then if you want more, they charge you for it. And given the FOIA requests I did, I don't have that kind of money to continue accessing.

So I think to some degree, we who have very few resources as journalists need to figure out smart ways of doing investigative journalism. It costs money. It doesn't pay. If you're doing some investigation, it's a long-term thing. And that's where I really feel like the corporate media absolutely needs to be held responsible for not doing more of it. Because look at the history of this country! Some of the biggest exposés by corporate media have led to dramatic political changes.

It's hard for community journalists, because it's really a question of resources. It's not something that happens quickly; you need to spend time on it. And I really do believe that in terms of a healthy functioning democracy, we absolutely need to have information about what our government is doing in our name, and how it's happening. And not just our government: what corporations are doing, and how the two are working together. And once we have that information, people will be much better informed to actually call for changes in policy.

MB: I have a quote from an interview between Amy Goodman and Robert McChesney. She said, "The media is more powerful than any bomb." And in fact Al Jazeera English is using that as one of their promo things right now. What thoughts do you have about that—the "pen is mightier than the sword" philosophy?

DF: We look around the world and see people who actively participate in their democracies, and yet it's the United States that actively works to export democracy around the world. I think one of the problems that we have even and especially in progressive communities is that we think we have everything to teach and nothing to learn.

And you can look at various Latin American countries and see what democracy really means. What is democracy, and how do we participate in making a better society, or making a society that we want to live in? Because at the end of the day, to me, that's as simple as it is. How do we create the kind of community that best serves all of us? And I don't mean that in some sort of a utopian sense, that there's some sort of perfect community out there where everybody's going to be smily and happy and love their neighbor. But how do we go about really, truly participating in making that happen? And in Latin America, it's very commonly referred to by people like you and me as *participatory democracy*. And what's surprising to me is that that term and concept is not really used here at all, and it's not even really understood.

Very recently, I discovered the first African American newspaper in this country as I was beginning to do some research. It was born right in Brooklyn. And one of their philosophies, along with a white abolitionist William Lloyd Garrison, who picked up after *Freedom's Journal*, was of having an inclusive media. The word *participatory* was used. And it made me think, well what did they mean by that?

What does participatory journalism mean? Well, for me, actually, participatory media is something that *is* what will make our democracy healthy and functioning. Because we're not at a place in this country where we're instantly going to begin doing the varied actions that a participatory democracy requires, that are happening in local communities in Venezuela, and that are happening in local communities around the world that actively participate in the running and the governing of their local communities.

But I think we can achieve that with media. And I think they go hand in hand. If we could have a participatory media, that would be one of the most concrete steps to impacting the community we want to live in and how our community functions. So what does a participatory media mean or look like? I don't know. I don't have the answers to that. But I think it's for the creating.

I think to me it means that *Wakeup Call* on WBAI every morning is more of an interchange between the people who are on the program, the people who make the program, the people who listen to the program. So it doesn't become an elitist institution as well, whereby I'm the host, and I get to sit up here and look at all of you, and report on all of you, and tell you all what to think. No. That is just repetitive and mimicking the very structures of the media that don't allow for participation in democracy. And hopefully, I have just as much to learn from you as you have to learn from me.

It doesn't mean we all have to go out there and be journalists, it doesn't mean we all are going to turn into TV news anchors. But what it means is that we are players in a circle that allows for ideas to be circular, rather than to be top-down.

MB: And do you feel that the kinds of access to production and distribution that have been made possible through digital media such as blogging, YouTube, MySpace, do these represent possibilities for the kind of participatory media you envision? Is there more hope for you now for this vision than there might have been in your mind ten years ago?

DF: Yes and no. I think the reality is that low-income communities and communities of color do not have access even to Internet in the way that those who—they don't have access to not only just computers but also to Internet. So in terms of uploading to YouTube—what's the difference in speed between uploading and downloading, and who has access to that? Do we even know the answer to that question? And do we even know that there's a difference? Funny, our policy director Josh Breitbart was just teaching me about all this stuff!

And in the communities where we live, how much are we paying for Internet access, which makes it impossible for some of us to have that kind of access?

So it continues to lock out a large amount of people. And I guess where our work centers at Peoples' Production House is really in looking at the very question you just asked: at issues of access. And so we look at something like digital access, or to put it simply, just access to the Internet.

It's a question that requires us to get involved really quickly, because Net neutrality, which is what many people are very concerned about, us included, doesn't matter if we don't even have access. And that's not to say "Oh there's a whole bunch of people who are way too poor to afford it." No, as PPH codirector Kat constantly says, Communication is a right. So there are cities in this country, and there are countries in a world, whereby governments invest in fiber optic cables which have a long life, which will provide Internet at a speed we can't even imagine. We need to be pushing for that. We don't want this fight to be between Time Warner and Road Runner. Because actually, that's not where the struggle's at. What we want is a municipal wireless, which is funded by the government, and which makes access for all our communities possible. We don't want a simple program whereby we'll set up here in Harlem, where I live, a community center which has twenty computers so that you can all come and use it when you want it. No, that doesn't allow us to be part of moving forward and expanding digital communication and digital media to everybody.

It's almost about taking a step back, and really looking at not only who has access but who even talks about access. Because it's not a conversation that's happening in any of our communities.

So for example, our excellent journalist, Mitch Jeserich, heads up a program we run that works with groups of street vendors and domestic workers. They're average workers who on a daily basis could incredibly benefit from having access to, say, digital technology, be it through their cell phones, be it through computer technology. How could that help them? Why do we have to settle for the mold that's being imposed on us right now when we're creative people? Let's really think about how media can play that role in creating that community that we want.

I do feel much more hopeful now than I have in a long time, because there are some spaces that are open that many people are not thinking about. My dad once told me, "When things seem tough, and you walk into a room and the door's closed, and you can't get out, look for that tiny window. Look up. Look around. Maybe it's underneath. But find that window." And I feel like that analogy is where we're at today in terms of making an impact mediawise. Because yes we're losing to the big Tel Cos. Yes the big Tel Cos are steamrolling us in many ways. But there is that window—all we need to do is find it and begin to climb through it, and then the sky is ours.

If we can bring that vision to people in low-income communities and in communities of color, in youth communities and immigrant communities, to actually dream about how this could be possible, that's a strong constituency of people who will stand up for and demand something a hell of a lot better than they have now.

MB: And it seems, when you're describing that window, that you see radio as a medium that can assist more readily than some of these other platforms that are getting so much hype about their democratizing potential right now. Is that right?

DF: Absolutely. Because Internet access is still quite elitist. And that includes the middle class. I mean we're sitting in my apartment right now, we're in Harlem. And obviously I have my computer at home, and we have Internet access here, but just using this as an example, I get kicked off the Internet every e-mail I send. I can't stream online, I can't listen, I can't download a big file. Is that technological redlining? Is that particular communities being shut out?

MB: It's the Internet Service Provider that you are able to purchase here?

DF: The access that we have is terrible. And yes, you pay good money for it.

Where is that happening? If you look at the Upper West Side, which is a wealthier white community, what's the Internet access like there? Wall Street? That's where there's free wireless! Why is there free wireless downtown in a business district, and why isn't there up here? So there are fundamental questions of fairness.

Now I could go out and advocate for myself and say, "I need better Internet. Ok, there's a price, I'll pay it, what does that cost?" as people in this neighborhood are doing as it gentrifies more. Just on my computer everyday, you see a new connection popping up, that's locked because it's somebody else's. There's also a lot of people in this neighborhood who don't have any access. So how do we begin to look at those issues, not from a position of charity, of oh, everybody deserves access to the Internet, but from a position of empowerment and basic rights, to get the community organized to demand that right? And to have them dreaming about what is possible?

And I think what goes along with that is also having ideas of hyperlocal media that we've so forgotten, that aren't part of our landscape anymore. One project that my brother-in-law, Mike, and I talk about all the time and would love to work on in the future is a hyperlocal health Internet radio program, so that people can share health information, can hear from doctors and physicians, and can get up-to-date information on this and that; they can call in and ask questions. Because obviously health is a huge issue. We can look very locally and ask, "What issues actually affect this community right here?" Well, obesity affects this community right here, diabetes affects this community right here. We're not dealing so much with x, y, and z, we're dealing with a, b, and c. So why should this community have to listen to x, y, and z when our issues are a, b, and c? Let's deal with that.

We've forgotten that media can be used for that. But before we build and create this amazing health Internet radio twenty-four hour . . . we have to make sure people in the community actually can access it, know about it, want it. So part of that is about organizing in communities. It's not about imposing it on people. It's about getting their buy-in, getting them excited, and then listening to what they want. So it's not a top-down process, it's a community-generated process.

To me, that is participatory media. Because from the ground up, you're doing the organizing. People buy in. They see that they have a stake, they get involved, they lead the process, they get others involved, they create the agenda that they want. And we're doing this all together, so it's not me saying well, I have all this experience in media, and I've been a radio host and I've been a reporter in all these countries, so I'm going to tell you how it is. It's about listening and sharing. And hopefully I grow as a journalist and people feel empowered that they can demand something from their media rather than just passively have to intake it.

MB: What you were talking about made me think about how I was introduced to your voice, and that was at the 2007 conference in Memphis on Media Reform in the United States. I had been sitting in session after session, and aware that there was quite a bit of diversity of media interests there. There were journalists, there were policy makers, there were some academics, there were community activists. But the overarching umbrella was media reform. And pretty much everyone was white, also.

DF: It was a lot more diverse than the last one. [laughs]

MB: What I really appreciated, when you got up and gave one of the keynote addresses on Saturday night, was that you made a call not for reform, but for media justice. And that was really thrilling to me, because I had been very frustrated at the lack of attention to pirate possibilities, or tactical media. Could you say a bit more about the difference between media reform and media justice, and what was important to you that night about making that distinction?

DF: Well thank you. That means a lot.

Maybe the simplest way for me to explain the difference between media reform and media justice is an analogy I've heard made to the environmental movement. You can look at "Save the Trees," "Save the Air," "Save the Whales," as part of an environmental call that's critically important. We need that. But then particular communities, especially communities of color, began to say, but what about our communities? We're living in the path of polluting industries. Isn't that an environmental issue? And it changed from environmentalism to environmental justice. And I think that in some ways the analogy works for the media reform movement. Saying that yes, the media right now is not serving our communities. But the media reform movement harkens back to some golden day of the media that we need to take back. And for many of our communities, that didn't exist. When was that time? When was there a truly participatory media?

We don't only need to work on simply taking media out of corporate hands. It's so much broader than that. Because simply taking it out of corporate hands means that we'll most likely fall into elite white hands. And that doesn't bring in the huge diversity that exists, that is actually what we need. How do we have any guarantee that our communities will be any better served by a media that's simply not owned by corporations?

So my understanding of the media justice movement is that we're a very diverse movement. At People's Production House, we see it as a three-pronged approach. It's that we build, in our own communities, strong, powerful journalists, that we learn the art and the craft of telling stories. We learn how to be creative and be good quality reporters. Just because we're in community media doesn't mean that anything goes. So we build communities. We build in our communities good, intelligent, powerful

Figure 9.2
Deepa Fernandes and Rootz Radio peer trainer Kyra Joseph. Photo by Sacajawea Hall

reporters, storytellers, documentarians, bloggers, whatever it is. We focus on training ourselves to be good media makers. That's one part of it.

The second part of it is that we fight like hell for access. Because what good does it do to train ourselves, and have this really powerful community of great media makers, when we don't have anywhere to put it? And the reality of the struggle is that we're losing that really quickly. So while a media reform movement might just fight for Net neutrality, we want to go way beyond that.

And I particularly have learned so much from one of our crew, Josh Breitbart, who always says we want to go beyond. And that to me encapsulates what media justice wants to do. We want to go beyond what's out there right now, so we don't just want Net neutrality, because that implies that we all have equal access. We want small community, local media to be able to, when it's googled, come up equal to the *New York Times*. And why should it be anything less? We want to think creatively about how we can bring hyperlocal media to our communities.

So access is critically important. And it's not just about wresting it from the hands of the corporate media. It's about dreaming big and pursuing those dreams, so it actually works for our communities.

And then the third part is that corporate media is not going to go away over night. And it's going to continue to be dominant for a while to come. And so we learn the skills of being able to watch, listen, read, and analyze and then hold accountable that media and tell them it's not OK to represent our communities like this. To say, we listen to Hot 97. And we will keep doing it. But please, you can't do this. Or how about having some more community voices on, or how about introducing a segment of youth voices, seeing how youth listen to you so much. How about not mocking poor people all the time, because so many of us who listen to you are low income? We would love to be rich like Beyoncé, and fine, keep covering Beyoncé because we love Beyoncé and we want to hear what's going on in Beyoncé's life. But please don't end your coverage of people who receive welfare.

So I think that when those three strategies are working together, that's what I understand media justice to be.

MB: And you said earlier that the notion of media reform implies that the existing structure works. What I heard you do really clearly that night in Memphis was call attention to the limits and assumptions built into political notions of reform, and highlight the power and potential of what is happening at the groundlevel, at the hyperlocal as you put it. You know, it's important that media revolution include all of these points of attack, so yes, the policy level of the FCC is very important. But there's a way in which that frustrates me as it doesn't always seem to attend to the microlevel interventions of something like community radio or The Yes Men managing to get on the BBC.

DF: But it can, absolutely.

Just to keep going with the example of this community right here, and access to the Internet. Imagine if this community got mobilized around all the issues that we struggle with: housing issues, gentrification, access to good public transportation, access to jobs—all of these are critical issues that in some way are much more immediate than media. But imagine if in this community right here we could build awareness and have community meetings and talk about all those issues that I just mentioned—housing, food, jobs—we might have more of a chance of affecting good public policy change by actually having them represented more fairly in the media.

Now one way of course is to write the *New York Times* every day and say, "Your coverage of this is unfair."

Another way is to have people empowered at the community level to go to the FCC and say "We need x, y, z change to media policy so that we can make our own media, be it community radio, be it . . . we need that spectrum opened up. We need to have more licenses at an affordable cost for our communities. We need you to mandate local governments to put fiber optic cables in." And some of these might sound completely ridiculous. But whatever it is that the community decides, that is a critical step. It's like a tool. The media is a tool in the box for organizers of changing public policy, so that we might be able to win back Section 8 housing rights, or we might be able to keep a certain percentage of housing in this community for low-income families, which is a critical issue. But we need access to the media. So I think from that perspective, media policy and the arcane FCC regulations are critically important to our communities.

MB: I keep going back to what you said about challenging corporate media. Some people in the media reform movement envision competitive public media, so there would be more NPRs and more PBSs, but I think about what you said about the possibility that such media could still fall into the hands of simply a bit more diverse white elite, which is a genuine concern. And it seems that what you're talking about in terms of community-level intervention would be the only way to have a different vision. Do you have any broad thoughts on government broadcasting stations?

For example, I moved to Canada three and a half years ago, and I talk about critical inquiry into media a lot with students at the university. These are people who are going to be teachers. And in one class, after they'd spent a lot of time studying a site I made called Critical Media Literacy in Times of War, and we were talking about media bias, somebody said, "Well at least we have the CBC, which is neutral and objective." And it was really interesting for me to hear that after all of the time we'd spent talking about this, that these students would think about the CBC as neutral and objective. And I've spent a lot of time thinking about what it means to fight for increased funding to the CBC. There's really no youth programming, there's very little indigenous programming. It's a very big issue.

DF: I think about my experience with the ABC [Australian Broadcasting Company], where I first started and it was a very encouraging home for me, and I got to make a documentary on arranged marriages in the Indian community in Australia and I got to interview my family. I got a start with producers at the ABC who in some way saw a storyteller in me and wanted to encourage that to come out. And I'm sure they fought battles on my behalf that I didn't even know about. I made a one-hour documentary for the ABC on six Cuban women, after living in Cuba for almost a year, who were my best friends. And the story that went out on the ABC was a very pro-Cuba story. That was the first documentary I ever made. It was purely from the voices of six Cuban women. Different generations, black, white, mulatta, women talking about the struggles of living in Cuba, but essentially the overarching message was the revolution was the best thing to ever happen.

And I agree. Sometimes I get nostalgic, when I'm here in New York, in the United States, I get nostalgic for the ABC. And honestly, I don't know what it's like in terms of the broader vision I have now for the media.

But I think there needs to be a bit of everything. I think that's the beauty of our communities, is that we are very diverse, and we do take in media in different ways. So you have people who will get everything they want to know in an MTV-style format, you'll have people who get everything they want to know in a shock jock–type format, which is where Air America has filled a void on the progressive, liberal side. If there's anything that the media reform movement says that I do agree with, it's just that it needs to be opened up more. But where we go further is saying, let's be very creative and demanding in how far we take it. Let's not just settle for less corporate ownership. The struggle is much bigger than that.

MB: What are the most inspiring media initiatives that you know of right now?

DF: I think of the Youth Media Council in Oakland. While they're not particularly making media, they're really radically changing up the way in which we think about a media landscape and participatory media, and holding the media accountable, and making people realize that we are powerful, and we can demand things, and we can affect change, on the one hand. And then on the other hand, really truly bringing to light how the media's working in certain communities. And what is the impact of Clear Channel owning x amount of stations around the country. And I know I've learned so much from the Youth Media Council; it's been critical to my work. So I can only just wait to see where they're going with their work.

I guess in the area of a radio, I would really hope that we at *Wakeup Call* can, bit by bit—and it's a question of resources obviously—but that we can really begin to break new ground, just in terms of how we do it. So we had an idea of doing something like radio blogging. Let's set a topic and have people call in and let's blog on the radio about this—just kind of shaking up the way we do radio, and thinking about the medium more, and how people listen.

I mean, we think about it, and it's early in the morning, and people are making coffee and taking a shower and getting the kids ready. People don't just listen in the morning, they're not just focused on their radio. So it's almost even more pressure to like—Bam! you've got to catch people, you've got to stop people in the middle of the screaming kids and shower running and toast burning to make them actually want to keep listening.

So I think that's one of the challenges for us, and there aren't that many examples out there. So it's exciting on the one hand, because we want to create it.

And for us, in some ways, the really exciting example is what *Democracy Now!* has been able to achieve. That you can take a radical message, and you can reach millions of people. We're running a local show. And we want to stay local. But that we can do that on a local level, and we can really reach out to all these communities who don't have a voice, we can bring them in, and *Wakeup Call* and WBAI can be as much theirs as they are ours.

And the Pacifica Radio Network is really precious in that media landscape. And I know, I'm in there on a daily basis, we've got this reputation of always fighting each other and having this extreme democracy at every level that makes it so hard to do anything. But at the end of the day, being a foreigner, coming to the United States, and seeing the power of community media, that we can have this network, that we can have these archives that have a social history of the United States for the last fifty years, that we can have five stations around the country and that we can come together on minimal resources—that's powerful.

I really feel like Pacifica is on the verge of a new wave, because there are young people at every station right now. If you look around the network, three of the morning shows from LA to Berkeley to New York, are hosted by young women of color. That's huge. Followed by Amy and *DemocracyNow!* on each one of the stations. So you have this powerful women's presence that kicks off the majority of Pacifica stations in the morning. I think we really are poised to make some serious change, and to do it in a creative and inclusive way. And that's exciting to me.

MB: I was in Berkeley when the Pacifica lockout was happening. And the amount of people willing to go to the streets for that was major. We took over the streets to fight that.

DF: And the fact that at the national level we won back the board—I mean , that's participatory media right there. People took back the board. They had concerted organizing campaigns. And if people can feel that level of ownership over a radio station, imagine if we could broaden that out to other forms of media too. It's exciting. That's what the other side doesn't have on us. Who's going to go out and stand up to protest in favor of CNN? We build that kind of an active participation! That's what participatory media is: that you'll stand up and defend media that speaks to you and of which you're a part.

Note

The interview questions were developed by Andréa Schmidt, with additions from Megan Boler.

10 Gatewatching, Gatecrashing: Futures for Tactical News Media

Axel Bruns

Prologue: A Tale of Two Tiers

1980: In response to the shortcomings in journalism's coverage of current events that he has identified in his research, journalism scholar and visionary Herbert Gans outlines a new model of news media, where the mainstream

> central (or first-tier) media would be complemented by a second tier of pre-existing and new national media, each reporting on news to specific, fairly homogeneous audiences. . . . Their news organisations would have to be small [for reasons of cost]. They would devote themselves primarily to reanalysing and reinterpreting news gathered by the central media—and the wire services—for their audiences, adding their own commentary and backing these up with as much original reporting, particularly to support bottom-up, representative, and service news, as would be financially feasible. (Gans 1980, 318)

The ultimate aim of this two-tiered media system is to provide a more multiperspectival coverage of news and current events. However, in the absence of media formats that can ensure a broad audience reach without requiring significant financial backing, Gans struggles to identify pathways to realizing that vision.

Fast-forward to late 2005: U.S. President George W. Bush nominates his personal counsel and long-time friend and (as would be revealed soon, occasionally all-too-enthusiastic) follower Harriet Miers as candidate for Supreme Court Justice. Both sides of U.S. politics are critical of the nomination, which is widely seen as an instance of favoritism. In its coverage of the debate, CNN repeatedly devotes airtime to quite literally reading out "what the bloggers think"—presenting a selection of views from news and politics blogs as a kind of twenty-first-century updated version of the vox-pop interview.

Miers eventually withdraws from the nomination, but that is not important here—and neither is the extent to which blogs played a role in the demise of her candidacy. Instead, what is more interesting is the way in which CNN and other news organizations accepted bloggers' voices as an obvious part of the U.S. mediasphere, a natural indicator of public opinion on the nominee. Compared to the traditional vox-pop (often a relatively cynical task conferred to junior reporters: "get me one in favour and two against"), however, there is a significant difference here: blogs are publications in their own right, and citing blog posts in the television news points viewers to a different media form, and to the second tier that Gans had predicted. No matter how news organizations select the blogs they quote on air, no matter whether views are presented accurately or out of context, audiences are able to access these and other blogs for themselves, gauge public opinion, even comment and post their own views in the blogosphere and on alternative news sites. Bloggers and other forms of participatory online journalism by citizens for citizens have gatecrashed the previously so-closed party of the mainstream news media; they have added a second tier of news media that comments on, critiques, and regularly corrects the mainstream news, much as Gans had proposed. As Rushkoff suggests, "In an era when crass perversions of populism, and exaggerated calls for national security, threaten the very premises of representational democracy and free discourse, interactive technologies offer us a ray of hope for a renewed spirit of genuine civic engagement" (Rushkoff 2003, 16). Though still in its infancy, the emergence of citizen journalism points to the potential of a reinvigoration of discussion, debate, and deliberation on political matters, beyond the polarized and polarizing coverage of mainstream news media.

It is worth noting that such views, and my own, are explicitly opposed to those of Jodi Dean, for whom "conflict and opposition [are] necessary for politics" (chap. 3, this volume). Dean's approach essentially regards politicization and polarization as synonyms, and in doing so aligns itself with a long-established model of the journalism industry that postulates that any "proper" news story must take the form of a conflict-based narrative. If understood as a perennial conflict between opposing forces, however, such politics is inherently incompatible with democracy in its purest sense: a true "rule of the people" can only be established if a broad societal compromise and consensus is established through productive debate and deliberation; it cannot be reached through entrenched political antagonism.

Where mainstream journalism has interpreted its underlying ideals of objectivity and unbiased reporting to mean simply that a strictly bipartisan coverage must be achieved on any given issue (that is, giving airtime or column space in equal measure to representatives of Reps and Dems, Labour and Tories), it has already oversimplified the political process: reality is multipartisan, complex, and multifaceted, and any reduction to simplistic left/right schemas fails the democratic process. The polarized, conflict-based model of democracy, which Dean appears to champion and which ultimately manages opposing views simply through a periodic exchange of government and opposition roles, is fundamentally flawed and provides no credible alternative—it is itself what threatens "the very premises of representational democracy", using Rushkoff's phrase.

Mainstream journalism has been a key contributor to this polarization of politics in many developed nations—but the intrusion of new forms of (online) journalism may well swing the balance back toward a more discursive, deliberative approach. (Indeed, many of these new forms have arisen in response to the lack of nuanced reporting in mainstream news coverage, of course.) If so, the key question that arises, and that we will examine here, is how such new forms of journalism can grow beyond their beginnings as tactical media linked to specific causes and temporary actions, and how they may establish themselves as a permanent fixture in the news mediascape. As we will see, some parallels can be drawn between this process and another process of transition from short-term tactics to longer-term strategies: the rise of the European Greens from extraparliamentary activists to established political force.

The Gatecrashers

A range of related, but differing descriptions (that are not necessarily mutually exclusive) can be applied to the new forms of news media that are at the core of this challenge to mainstream journalism. Like Gans's two-tier model, most such models initially pit two sides against one another and must therefore themselves be examined critically as potential oversimplifications—what becomes crucially important in the current media environment is to investigate the potential for productive connection and even cooperation *between* these two camps. A likely result of such cooperation is that both sides will change shape to some extent, and it is in such metamorphoses that the most innovative models for citizen involvement in mainstream journalistic processes can be found. But let us begin by reviewing some of the key descriptions of the dichotomy between mainstream and off-mainstream news media.

Two Tiers

For Herbert Gans, the two tiers of news organizations describe different levels of journalism—one that today we would likely situate within the global media industry conglomerates, and one that describes a range of alternative services that would also strive for a broad citizen involvement: "I would argue that like other professionals, journalists should share their responsibility with others." (Gans 1980, 323). Emerging from his study of mainstream news media processes in the 1970s, Gans's focus is especially on the reanalysis and reinterpretation of first-tier media content, leading to the addition of alternative views in pursuit of a more multiperspectival coverage of news and current events—but such value-addition services need not be the only purpose of off-mainstream news media. Some citizen media projects, like the Korean *OhmyNews* or the Al Gore–backed *Current.tv*, focus instead on the creation of original content by users for users (in the case of *OhmyNews*, with the help of paid editorial staff).

That said, there certainly is good evidence for processes of content reappropriation by the second tier—rather than producing original reports and/or acting as gatekeepers in a traditional journalistic sense, for example, some of the most active news bloggers and participatory journalism contributors of present-day, second-tier media forms engage predominantly in what we can describe as *gatewatching*: the observation of the output gates of first-tier news organizations as well as of primary sources. These practitioners are watching out for material passing through those gates that is relevant to their own audience's interests and concerns and introduce it into their own coverage of news and current events; often, they combine and contrast the coverage of a number of mainstream news organizations in order to highlight differences in emphasis or interpretation and thus point to political bias or substandard journalistic handiwork. If through a recombination and reconsideration of existing materials such coverage produces compelling new insights previously overlooked by the first-tier media, it offers a means to reintroducing alternative viewpoints into first-tier media debates (see Bruns 2005). Again, this is in line with Gans's conception that clearly describes first- and second-tier news media as responding to and engaging with one another.

Alternative Media Production

Other descriptions tend to reduce conflicting interpretations of the news to a struggle of activists against the mainstream and point to the early successes of alternative news sites like *Indymedia* as examples. Such descriptions "place the emphasis on the production, rather than the consumption, of media texts. And they stress the conversational dimension of the Net as the creation of DIY media, rather than just as a means of debating the writings of others" (Meikle 2002, 87). Where such focus on content production leads to a comparative absence of discussion and debate, however, it will ultimately undermine the activist project: sites which do little more than *publish* content are in danger of becoming mere PR tools for oppositional groups, simply containing press releases for the latest cause. In such cases, any real engagement between opposing viewpoints is undermined. Today's *Indymedia* Web sites might serve as an example here: since its initial successes in the 1999 "Battle of Seattle," many sites of the IMC network have failed to match the high standards set during the glory days, and the *Indymedia* newswire has now turned to a mere clearinghouse for activist press releases.

The overall end result is then a mere shouting match between mainstream and alternative Web sites, where the relative visibility of arguments, rather than their argumentative force, is expected to influence audience opinions, and where alternative news sites therefore do whatever they can to have their content seen. While a Gansian approach enables practitioners to introduce their views into the mainstream media by skill, through careful and considered examination of and engagement with opposing views, a merely alternative approach puts its emphasis on a gatecrashing by force—on creating so much DIY media content that some of it must eventually make it into the mainstream. (Alternatively, some activist media sites may be content to preach only to the already converted, distributing information to fellow activists yet doing little to spread the message beyond that group.)

Tactics and Strategies

Perhaps most enduring and popularly recognized, however, is the description of off-mainstream media outlets as tactical media, in opposition to the strategists of mainstream media forms. As Meikle notes, we must understand that such "tactical media are different from . . . alternative media in important ways. Media tacticians don't try to consolidate themselves as an alternative. . . . Instead, tactical media is [sic] about mobility and flexibility, about diverse responses to changing contexts. It's about hit-and-run guerrilla media campaigns. . . . It's about working with, and working out, new and changing coalitions. And it's about bringing theory into practice and practice into theory" (Meikle 2002, 119–120). Such descriptions owe a great deal to Michel de Certeau's work on strategies and tactics, and they describe tactical media practitioners as tricksters, as poachers, as temporarily reversing flows of power. In their much-cited "ABC of Tactical Media," for example, Garcia and Lovink speak of such media as "always provisional. What counts are the temporary connections you are able to make. Here and now, not some vaporware promised for the future" (Garcia and Lovink 1997, n. pag.).

Tactical media, in this description, are profoundly temporal and temporary, then—guerrilla attacks that may leave lasting marks in popular consciousness but are themselves ephemeral and conducted from temporary, shifting bases rather than a more permanent location. Tactical media, especially in a journalistic context, can therefore also be seen as exploiting an adoption lag: the period between the emergence of new media technologies and their utilization by the mainstream, during which time tech-savvy media tacticians have an advantage over the strategists in media organizations who are still developing their ideas for how to use new technological tools safely within a corporate environment. (*Indymedia*'s early successes were due in good part to taking place during this moment, in fact.) Tactical media practitioners, in other words, do not so much gatecrash as exploit alternative entries into the mediasphere that have not (yet) been secured against unauthorized entry. They are aligned with alternative causes but pick their targets more wisely and carefully than merely alternative media; like Gans's second tier, they incorporate gatewatching practices and a discursive engagement with the mainstream but combine this with a more explicit and specific political purpose.

Most importantly, however, they operate from a temporary, shifting, and not so much deterritorialized as fundamentally aterritorial basis. While in her contribution to this collection (chap. 2, this volume), Alessandra Renzi takes Graham Meikle and others to task for overly highlighting this aspect in their description of tactical media (thus creating highly orthodox definitions "that automatically exclude any project or action that is long lasting,"), it is difficult to escape the centrality of this—inherently *tactical*—aspect of tactical media, and even Renzi herself repeatedly returns to a focus on the temporary character of tactical media actions. By contrast, Renzi's own somewhat tautological definition of tactical media "not as a movement or a practice but as a space where 'tactical things' happen" must also be problematized further: it is crucial to keep in mind that the space of a tactical media action is never its own, but only ever temporarily appropriated from others. (Renzi's later description of tactical media as "contact zones" is therefore more accurate, pointing as it does to the tactical superimposition of a temporary zone *over* a pre- and postexisting space.) Indeed, as we will see, the point at which tactical media groups acquire a basis of operations of their own marks the moment that they transmogrify into an altogether different, and no longer purely tactical, beast.

That said, it could be suggested that even now, well into the online age, much of the second-tier online news media forms still live off that temporary advantage over their first-tier cousins and to that extent are tactical media. Even relatively progressive mainstream news organizations are still struggling to come to terms with blogs, wikis, and other collaborative content management systems, and with a reconceptualization of their users not as audiences but as equal partners and collaborators in the news process—that is, with a move from journalism as lecture to journalism as conversation, as Dan Gillmor has described it (Gillmor 2003, vi). The second tier, by contrast, already has systems and approaches in place that address this shift. However, as these approaches solidify and become widely practiced, they are no longer simply temporary tactics—instead, they become stable, established strategies for the practice of new forms of journalism.

Gatewatching itself demonstrates this transition. Emerged from tactical backgrounds, it embodies a conversational, active, and productive engagement with existing mainstream media content—gatewatchers draw on news reports and official publications but frequently use journalists', politicians', and corporate actors' own words against them by creatively (but, ideally, truthfully) reappropriating, repurposing, recombining, recontextualizing, and reinterpreting such content to show a very different conception of reality. Each time news bloggers and other citizen journalists point to omissions, misrepresentations, or biases in mainstream media content by contrasting news stories, press releases, and other background information, they use the news media's own tools and resources against it. Hartley describes such practices as redaction: "bringing materials together, mixing ingredients to make something new—a creative practice in its own right" (Hartley 2003, 83). He notes that "redactional journalism is not dedicated to the same ends as public-sphere journalism inherited from previous media; it doesn't have the same agenda-setting function for public affairs and decision-making as does traditional editing by editors (which is why I am avoiding the more familiar term)." Instead, with the adoption of redactive practices, "even as its representative democratic function is superseded, journalism itself massively expands" (Hartley 2000, 44). Redaction is the "new media" counterpart to "old media" editing and relates to it much as media mashups are related to audiovisual production: as a practice that paradoxically both undermines its predecessor and uses the outputs of the older model as its own sources. It is temporary tactic turned contemporary strategy.

Whether described as tactical, alternative, or second-tier media, recent years have seen some notable successes for off-mainstream media forms. Some occurred by design—here we might note the role played by gatewatchers in the WMD debate, Trent Lott's resignation, or the Rathergate scandal, for example. At a time when any domestic media criticism of the U.S. administration was equated virtually with treason, alternative media led the way in questioning the existence of weapons of mass destruction as a reason for the war on Iraq and ultimately became visible enough to have their questions recognized and discussed; similarly, when Bush-bashing had become the fashion, second-tier media critiqued this biased stance and uncovered the unquestioning acceptance of falsified documents by seasoned journalists. Lott's demise, on the other hand, can be seen as the success of a tactical strike aimed at removing a controversial politician: the successful reintroduction of key facts into the public consciousness at a time when most mainstream news media had long decided U.S. Senate Republican Leader Lott's support for one-time segregationist presidential candidate Strom Thurmond to be a nonissue.

Other successes for off-mainstream news media were more coincidental and exploited the very temporary advantage (or, more often, disadvantage) of being a technologically equipped ad hoc citizen news reporter at the scene of world events before the world media had had a chance to scramble their crews—this was the case, for instance, with the instant coverage of events from 9/11 to the Boxing Day tsunami and the 7/7 London bombings. Yet others exist in areas where the mainstream media dare (or, more likely, care) not tread—in the coverage of local and microlocal issues that do not register on the impact scale of larger news organizations, or that reporters coming in from the outside would be hard-pressed to cover with any accuracy. This supports Gans's notion that "one of the purposes of the second tier is to continue where the central media leave off: to supply further and more detailed news for and about the perspectives of the audiences they serve. In the process, these media would also function as monitors and critics of the central media, indicating where and how, by their standards, the central media have been insufficiently multiperspectival" (Gans 1980, 322).

If there remains a significant temporary, tactical aspect to the operations even of the second tier of news media organizations at present, then, the question of how to ensure long-term sustainability for such media forms becomes all the more crucial. How, in other words, may they move beyond tactics and carve out a permanent space in the news mediasphere for themselves?

Beyond Tactics: Citizen Journalism

It is possible that

these alternative information sources are being given more attention and credence than they might actually deserve, but this is only because they are the only ready source of oppositional, or even independent thinking available. Those who choose to compose and disseminate alternative value systems may be working against the current and increasingly concretised mythologies of market, church and state, but they ultimately hold the keys to the rebirth of all three institutions in an entirely new context. (Rushkoff 2003, 18)

However, this points to a serious structural problem for second-tier media if they are to be conceptualized as inherently "tactical": are they, *should they be* engaged in this process and project of rebirth that Rushkoff outlines, a project which aims at no less than the reconfiguration of society itself for the twenty-first-century network-driven environment? Renzi notes that tactical media "are characterized by the lack of an ultimate identity or goal." If so, the information sources described by Rushkoff can no longer be seen simply as tactical; they are now involved in a longer-term struggle that requires strategies as well as tactics. Tactical media in the traditional sense are at a crossroads, then—they can choose to remain simply tactical and temporary, or must aim to develop approaches to ensure the long-term sustainability of the second tier of news and orchestrate its engagement with the first tier.

Tarleton provides a useful outline of the problem in his discussion of *Indymedia*. "As a product of the anti-corporate globalization movement," he notes, *Indymedia* "shares both its strengths and weaknesses. It is defiant, angry, hopeful, chaotic, creative, generous and, at times, painfully naive. It is a voluntocracy that operates mostly on youthful enthusiasm. And in true anarchist fashion, it is decentralized and highly participatory. All decisions are made by consensus" (Tarleton 2000, 55). *Indymedia* (or more accurately, the many Independent Media Centres that constitute the IMC network) may choose to maintain that structure, harking back to the now almost mythical golden age of the 1999 Battle of Seattle, which saw what was perhaps *Indymedia*'s finest hour as it provided one of the few issues- rather than conflict-based accounts of events, tactically exploiting the myopia of mainstream news coverage—yet any random sample of the current *Indymedia* newswire shows at least as much activist aggrandizement and knee-jerk fundamental opposition to all things corporate and capitalist as it does insightful commentary and coverage of events.

The tactical origins of *Indymedia* have given way for the most part to a merely alternative and oppositional stance that no longer engages with its enemies and prefers instead simply to rail at them; indeed, *Indymedia*'s malaise is the malaise of tactical media and its close cousin, culture jamming, overall. At their best, "jammers use the media to draw attention to issues and problems with those same media. What makes jamming more than just juvenile trespassing is its *media literacy* emphasis. Culture jamming turns familiar signs into question marks" (Meikle 2002, 132). Yet jamming is used just as often to merely shout back at the media, in a highly visible and disruptive, yet ultimately unproductive way.

What distinguishes productive engagement from merely disruptive culture jamming or tactical media is the existence of an overarching sense of purpose, of underlying aims, of longer-term goals—and this distinction is also at the heart of Henry Jenkins's critique of culture jamming, as he takes to task one of the leading theorists of this media form, Mark Dery, for "describing all forms of DIY media as 'jamming.' These new technologies would support and sustain a range of different cultural and political projects, some overtly oppositional, others more celebratory, yet all reflecting a public desire to participate in, rather than simply consume, media" (Jenkins 2006, 150). Against this, Jenkins positions his "cultural poachers": "Culture jammers want to 'jam' the dominant media, while poachers want to appropriate their content, imagining a more democratic, responsive, and diverse style of popular culture. Jammers want to destroy media power, while poachers want a share of it" (Jenkins 2006, 150).

The problem for tactical media, however, is that such approaches are no longer purely tactical. Jenkins's cultural poachers, with their vision of a better style of culture and their ambition to share in media power, employ tactical action in the pursuit of strategic goals: sharing media power is only a possibility for those who move beyond a fully deterritorialized, tactical stance. To share power necessarily means to establish one's own space, one's own basis of operations, in the mediasphere—a move beyond guerrilla tactics operating in enemy territory and toward a homeland of one's own.

As Lévy put it in 1997, "until now we have only reappropriated speech in the service of revolutionary movements, crises, cures, exceptional acts of creation. What would a normal, calm, established appropriation of speech be like?" (Lévy 1997, 171). One answer may today lie in a beginning shift of focus from purely tactical (news) media (operating on an issue-to-issue basis and in guerrilla strikes on the mainstream) to citizen journalism (pursuing the idea of a more democratic form of journalism that operates systematically from a strong base of its own). The return of citizen involvement to what through most of the twentieth century has been an increasingly industrialized journalistic field would do much to claim back a share of media power, as postulated by Jenkins. As Heikkilä and Kunelius note, "democracy requires open access to public institutions and resources for knowledge. This holds for journalism, too, for it is a public institution regardless of its ownership. Therefore, access to journalism should be open to all citizens. . . . The variety of voices in journalism is thus the measure of its 'publicness'" (Heikkilä and Kunelius 2002, n. pag.).

Citizen journalism is inspired by the positive ideas to emerge from the *Indymedia* experience—the coverage of nonmainstream themes and topics, and the open debate of issues that does not inherently privilege any one participant. Such journalism is focused not on the mere provision of "facts" as determined by a small group of journalists and editors, but instead highlights the discursive, dialogic, and even deliberatory nature of public engagement with the news. Phenomena found by Chan in her study of the participatory technology news site *Slashdot* translate across to citizen journalism overall: "Highlighting the expertise of users and the value of their participation, news reading shifts from an act centred on the reports and analyses of news professionals and designated experts, to one often equally focussed on the assessment and opinions of fellow users on the network." (Chan 2002, n. pag.). The core approach here is a collaborative one, as *Kuro5hin* operator Rusty Foster notes—"first, in the sense that a lot of people collaboratively write and help edit the site. But second, . . . in the sense that the story itself is not the final product, it's just the starting point, because ultimately the goal of every story is to start discussion, to start a lot of other people saying what they think about it" ("New Forms" 2001, n. pag.).

This collaborative, dialogic, deliberative engagement between site participants, who in the process act both as users and producers of the site—in short, as a hybrid *produser*, engaged in produsage rather than simply production or consumption (see Bruns, 2006*a*)—ultimately leads to the realization of Gans's goal of multiperspectival news coverage: as he put it in 1980, "ideally . . . the news should be omniperspectival; it should present and represent all perspectives in and on America. This idea, however, is unachievable. . . . It is possible to suggest, however, that the news, and the news media, be multiperspectival, presenting and representing as many perspectives as possible—and at the very least, more than today" (Gans 1980, 312–313). Citizen journalism, conceptualized in this manner, is positioned as an alternative and a corrective to the first, mainstream tier of the news media but no longer stands in fundamental opposition to it, as the perspectives expressed in that tier have a valid role to play in public debate as well. Instead, it engages those "mainstream" perspectives and (where appropriate) debunks them as the views of individual political and lobby groups, think tanks, and news proprietors rather than as representative for a more diverse range of societal views, values, and beliefs. Or, as Gans described it in his 2003 update on his multiperspectival vision,

Ideally, multiperspectival news encompasses fact and opinion reflecting all possible perspectives. In practice, it means making a place in the news for presently unrepresented viewpoints, unreported facts, and unrepresented, or rarely reported, parts of the population.

To put it another way, multiperspectival news is the bottoms-up corrective for the mostly top-down perspectives of the news media. (Gans 2003, 103)

The most crucial question for citizen journalism, then, is no longer one of tactics, that is, of how to gain the best short-term impact on the media and public consciousness. Instead, it becomes more important to ensure a place for multiperspectivality in the mediasphere and, thus, for citizen journalism itself, for the long term. Most importantly, this means increasing the visibility of citizen journalism projects and, in doing so, redressing the balance between the first and second tiers of the news media. As James Carey put it (though writing before the rise of online citizen journalism to public recognition), "what we need in this circumstance is to revive notions of a republican community: a public realm in which a free people can reassemble, speak their minds, and then write or tape or otherwise record their extended conversation so that others out of sight might see it" (Carey 1997, 14).

Citizen journalism, then, provides a pathway for off-mainstream news sites as they progress beyond a purely tactical stance, avoid the simplistic oppositional posturing of alternative media, and develop into a fully formed second tier of news media. Such questions of moving beyond the temporary gains available from tactical action and into the establishment of permanent bases for new ideas and approaches are not new, however: they have been faced by a variety of other initially tactical groups in the past. For example, useful comparisons might be drawn here between the present situation of off-mainstream news media and the dilemmas faced by another originally tactical and oppositional movement, the Greens (particularly, perhaps, in their Western European forms), during the 1970s and 1980s. Emerging from a fundamentalist, autonomist, extraparliamentary community that had some loose connections with, or at the very least stated sympathies for, the European anticapitalist radical and terrorist groups of the 1960s and 1970s (such as Brigate Rosse and the Baader-Meinhof Gang), the Greens also faced a choice between continuing on a tactical path and remaining in a position of fundamental opposition to the political establishment or moving toward the adoption of longer-term strategies and an involvement in the mainstream political process. Ultimately, in most cases, a split into "fundies" and "pollies" ensued; some leaders continued engaging in alternative grassroots campaigns while some took up parliamentary posts and political office (with some attempting the uncomfortable option of continuing on both paths simultaneously). Few political figures embody this shift better than Germany's Joschka Fischer, who morphed from stone-throwing, antiestablishment street protester in the 1970s into member of state parliament in the 1980s, and later became one of the first Greens ministers in Europe; he concluded his political career as a Vice Chancellor and Foreign Minister of Germany in 2005. Equally respected even by political enemies, and criticized by fellow travelers for selling out, Fischer symbolizes the possibilities as well as the dangers inherent in moving beyond the relatively comfortable familiarity and predictability of temporary

tactical responses and into participation in established and enduring political environments. (The degree to which such participation is open to initially tactical agents is
determined in part also by contextual factors, of course—in dictatorial regimes, for
example, there may be little opportunity for nontactical forms of involvement by
opposition groups. When such involvement does become possible, however, it is
important that tactical groups do not dismiss this opportunity outright, out of a false
sense of traditional allegiance to tactical action.)

Toward a Post-Gansian Mediasphere

A wide variety of such post-tactical citizen media Web projects have emerged today—
ranging from the better news-related blogs to dedicated citizen journalism Web sites
like *Kuro5hin*, and from pro-am publications like *OhmyNews* (combining professional
editors and amateur gatewatchers, now also in its Japanese and international versions)
to citizen multimedia efforts such as *Current.tv* (which, in addition to its Web site, also
operates a U.S. cable TV channel broadcasting the best of its user-submitted content).
However, it remains true that "a crucial use of the Internet is to attract attention from
other media" (Meikle 2002, 61): much citizen media remains in a parasitical, or at best
symbiotic, relationship with the mainstream. At the same time, first-tier news organizations are also expressing increasing interest in what has made some citizen journalism projects successful and are beginning to replicate those citizen-led approaches
in a corporate framework, with varying degrees of success. As Lasica writes, "all of this
begs the question: Will forms of participatory journalism and traditional journalism
complement each other, or collide head on? It may be a bit of both." (Lasica 2003*b*,
n. pag.).

Whether complementation or collision, what is evident is that the Gansian two-tier
model may be an increasingly inaccurate description of the multifaceted relationships
between industrial and citizen journalism (and that, indeed, any description that
builds on a dichotomous, binary division between two entrenched sides is no longer
sustainable). As noted already, there is a limited embrace of second-tier media by the
mainstream, which looks at such journalism alternatives "not through a limited lens
of a political-economic anti-globalisation channel but through the professional lens
of a 'competitor-colleague' journalism which may yet prove to be the crucible for new
ways of reconnecting journalism, news and media professionals with ideals of sharing
access and participatory storytelling in journalism" (Platon and Deuze 2003, 352). At
its most basic, this has occurred through the adoption of bloggers' views as a better
alternative to the vox-pop interview, and the cooption of key bloggers as expert
pundits into news and current affairs reporting. Further, we have seen the emergence
of genuine blogger-journalists from Glenn Reynolds to Margo Kingston (but also the
appearance of journalistic "faux bloggers" that adopt the title, but run their sites as

little more than traditional op-ed columns and have no interest whatsoever in engaging in a constructive dialogue with their audience). Beyond this, it remains to be seen how the more systematic embrace of blogs and other citizen journalism technologies will play out: for example through BBC Online's blogs, or in the wake of Rupert Murdoch's stated position that in a participatory, Web 2.0 media environment, journalists "must challenge—and reformulate—the conventions that so far have driven [their] online efforts" (Murdoch 2005, n. pag.).

Beyond this direct engagement between industry and citizen forms of journalism, however—crashing each other's gates, as it were, and intertwining the tiers—we can also make out the shape of altogether different models for online journalism produsage. In the first instance, they are situated at a kind of "tier 1.5", intermediaries between the ends of the journalistic spectrum, but in the process they might undermine the tiered structure of the news mediasphere altogether. Predecessors and precedents for such sites exist for example in the New York–based *MediaChannel*, which facilitates and moderates the engagement between the multiple perspectives expressed in news reportage—as editor Danny Schechter puts it, he "hoped that our evolving space could become a home for much more diverse content and in-depth reporting than is found in the increasingly entertainment-oriented mass media, as well as in staid media reviews" (Schechter 2000, 38)—and in the Australian *Online Opinion*, a site of public intellectualism that serves as a neutral ground upon which government ministers, politicians, intellectuals, academics, journalists, *and* citizens can engage in debate and dialogue. Both sites are clearly nontactical: they are spaces in their own right, not temporarily superimposed tactical zones in someone else's territory. In their dealings with both mainstream news media and off-mainstream activist and oppositional groups, however, they still exploit temporary opportunities for engagement and impact—yet they do so in the pursuit of long-term strategic aims of increasing media transparency and improving public debate. This intermediate stance enables them to maintain the respect of and attract participation from both establishment and activist camps, as well as involve contributors from the wider populace.

Such sites point to the possibility of a greater range of hybrid industry/citizen journalism approaches conducted on a "pro-am" basis (see Leadbeater and Miller 2004)—a model for which *OhmyNews* provides perhaps the most successful example to date: here, upon submission by its tens of thousands of participating citizen journalists, "all stories are fact checked and edited by professional editors" (Kahney 2003, n. pag.). While not yet as sophisticated as *OhmyNews*, other news operators are beginning to take notice, realizing that "when some media outlets start making participatory media work effectively, media companies that dig in their heels and resist such changes may be seen as not only old-fashioned but out of touch" (Bowman and Willis 2003, 50). BBC News Online and *The Guardian Online* both engage with and link directly to the blogosphere and other citizen journalism sources, for example, and more such connections are emerging rapidly. Beyond this, the development of a project like the Al Gore–backed *Current.tv* will be interesting to track as well—not only as a means of gathering citizen-produced media content and harvesting the most highly rated content for a cable TV channel but also specifically for the quality of the DIY television news content that may emerge through it.

In the process, the role of journalists—and even more crucially, that of editors—changes fundamentally: they are no longer arbiters (or gatekeepers) of what points of view, what descriptions of news are relevant or appropriate, but instead focus more strongly simply on ensuring the technical quality and factual accuracy of published contributions. As Gans describes it, "story selectors would continue to set aside personal values, for their prime value would be perspectival diversity. In the process, the journalists' enduring values would no longer play a major supporting role in story selection, although commentators could continue to apply them. Even so, these values would not disappear; rather, they would be expressed in and by the new diversity of sources" (Gans 1980, 315). The *evaluation* of information and viewpoints, on the other hand, takes place through users' discursive and deliberative engagement on the news site itself: as Clay Shirky famously puts it, "the order of things in broadcast is 'filter, then publish.' The order in communities is 'publish, then filter.' . . . Writers submit their stories in advance, to be edited or rejected before the public ever sees them. Participants in a community, by contrast, say what they have to say, and the good is sorted from the mediocre after the fact." (Shirky 2002, n. pag.).

However, even this reversal of the editorial process is unlikely to be the end point of developments. It is already evident from current trends that the days of the dedicated news *site* as the key point of access to news reports may be numbered: today, multitudes of users combine first- and second-tier RSS newsfeeds in their Web browsers and newsreaders, using these for off-site (and even off-line) headline and news blurb browsing even without ever visiting the originating news site—and certainly without regular visits to any one news Web site. RSS scraping services even provide feeds for sites that do not offer such feeds of their own volition, and overall, the bundling and aggregation of news feeds from vastly different origins in combined listings both in user clients and on aggregator sites from *Syndic8* to *Technorati* and *Google News* significantly undermines the recognition and relevance of established news brands. In a networked environment, the news is becoming increasingly viral, and the role of a handful of global news organizations as international news leaders may be in decline: a random glance at *Google News* will show the *New York Times* alongside the *Malaysia Star, Aljazeera.net, Chosun Ilbo*, the *Macon Telegraph, Salon, The Guardian Unlimited, Monsters and Critics.com, The Council on Foreign Relations*, and *Blogcritics.org*, for example. Which source is chosen by users who are interested in a specific story may be influenced more by the recency, headline, or indeed the loading time of individual reports than by the brand name associated with it.

Beyond this, of course, such news reports are further distributed or diffused through full or partial reposts, links, and commentaries on blogs and citizen journalism Web sites, regardless of whether this practice is authorized or encouraged by the originating news agency, further removing reports, once published, from the control of their publishers. In essence, this approximates what could be described as a kind of news-sharing in analogy to filesharing—an unruly flow of information and commentary between the news media tiers and through the gates of various publishing organisations (see Bruns 2005).

Toward Alternative Story Forms

Such observations support Alleyne's view that "the ability of new technologies to drastically enhance the quality and velocity of information and to personalise the distribution of such information has deposed the old concept of 'news.' News media have derived power from their ability to determine the definition of news. . . . The new technological capabilities have undermined the news media's authority in this area" (Alleyne 1997, 33). They point to the potential of developing new forms and formats for news reporting—a process that could lead simultaneously into a number of different directions. On the one hand, the new forms of engagement with news reports through RSS feeds and other forms of off-site access to story blurbs could be seen to point to a need to condense the traditional journalistic inverted-pyramid writing style even further, reducing news reports to snappy blurbs that will catch the attention of casual browsers. On the other hand, it is exactly this long-standing reductionist standard in news reporting, with its attendant tendency to focus on easily representable conflict narratives, which has contributed to the rise of citizen journalism as a means of correcting the overly simplistic and stereotypical tropes common to much of industrial journalism.

An alternative direction, then, lies in the pursuit of discussion, debate, and deliberation as an essential element of journalistic coverage. As Heikkilä and Kunelius describe it, "deliberative journalism would underscore the variety of ways to frame an issue. It would assume that opinions—not to mention majorities and minorities—do not precede public deliberation, that thoughts and opinions do not precede their articulation in public, but that they start to emerge when the frames are publicly shared" (Heikkilä and Kunelius 2002, n. pag.).

Jodi Dean and other critics might question the extent to which such public deliberation can truly take place, and they describe an environment in which isolated groups deliberate among themselves without having a wider impact; this is what Dean describes as the "fantasy of participation" in her chapter in this volume. However, such views exaggerate the isolation of individuals and groups: instead, the structures of the Net (and indeed the wider social patterns of communication within which

Internet use is embedded) are such that they more accurately resemble a vast number of more or less extensively overlapping spheres of conversation and deliberation that *are* able to implicitly influence and explicitly speak to one another. Renzi's description of tactical media as constituting "counterpublics" or "dynamic spaces of discourse" (also in this collection) is much closer to the mark.

Participation *is* a fantasy if we take the extreme view that it must mean participation by all netizens in all discussions at all times; it is anything but a fantasy if we view it more realistically as a distributed form of engagement from which shared understandings emerge that are in turn introduced into yet other discussions and deliberations. The structure of deliberative communication in this model has moved away from the centrally moderated communication forms of face-to-face group meetings (or their more formalized counterpart, parliamentary debate), and toward a decentered, distributed, networked model that operates on a more flexible, ad hoc basis that is better suited to the environments of online communication.

At any rate, a more deliberative, participatory form of journalism is highly compatible with the Gansian call for multiperspectivity in journalistic coverage, of course. At a time when agency reports, the statements of officials, and research reports are increasingly publicly available by default, such journalism works by compiling these sources into news dossiers that stimulate public debate, rather than into supposedly definitive reports of fact which stifle it. In this framework, the all-too-often institutionalized disdain of journalists for their readers and viewers has no place—"the journalist does not work in 'splendid isolation,' partly because of the sheer abundance of information and the fact that publics are perfectly capable of accessing and providing news and information for/by themselves. Institutional players (profit, governmental, non-profit, activist) are increasingly geared towards addressing their constituencies directly instead of using the news media as a go-between" (Bardoel and Deuze 2001, 98).

No longer a conduit for the messages of these players, journalism's role, then, becomes the contextualization of the content of such direct addresses. The journalists' service to the public is now no more the production of content in the form of news reports itself but the provision of the value-added service of acting as a guide through what is already available material—a gatekeeper of information no longer, the journalist becomes a gatewatcher (Bruns 2005), but this role can be played by citizen journalists as well as by members of the traditional journalism industry. Further, beyond the gatewatching process itself, journalists can engage as knowledgeable but no longer specifically privileged participants in the discussion and debate of public issues that must necessarily follow from the publication of the initial source materials, and their contextualization through (citizen-) journalistic processes.

At the same time, it should be noted that the apparent rise of "expert" punditry, especially in broadcast news coverage, is also an outcome of this shift. Such pundits are similarly positioned as knowledgeable participants in a public debate, but, contrary to the open engagement in citizen journalism environments, the limitations of the broadcast medium make it largely impossible for a truly *public* debate to take place and for the "users" of television to respond in kind and on equal footing with the talking heads of the "experts." Indeed, the standard pundits of broadcast and print news are often chosen not so much for their insightful views but instead for representing opposed party-political positions and thus providing what is considered by producers to be "hard-hitting," "confrontational," and "entertaining" television, radio, or print content. However, they may ultimately serve to polarize rather than promote public debate—or, as satirist Jon Stewart unequivocally put it to the hosts of "left versus right" CNN talk show *Crossfire*, "you're hurting America" (Stewart 2004). Television's use of pundits to embody differing political opinions and serve as representatives for a society-wide public dialogue would be legitimate if such pundits did indeed accurately represent major groups in society, but, in reality, the personalities chosen are more often selected for their predictable or, in fact, predictably stereotypical, performances than for their ability to show a nuanced deliberative engagement with opposing views.

By contrast, the best citizen journalism aims to construct a "deliberative situation [where] expert knowledge has no privileged position. All the participants are experts in the ways in which the common problem touches their everyday lives. Thus, opinions and knowledge expressed in deliberation articulate the experiences of the participants" (Heikkilä and Kunelius 2002, n. pag.). In other words, in this environment, exponents of the news industry have no competitive, brand advantage (one of the reason why they tend to shy away from such fully open engagement with their audiences). Worse yet, the highly controversial presenters, pundits, and op-ed writers of traditional journalism (from Bill O'Reilly in the United States to Andrew Bolt in Australia) do indeed often have a particularly poor track record of participation as equals in a public debate: much of their work depends on the context of a pulpit-style delivery that allows no direct response from those it addresses. As Kovach and Rosenstiel describe it,

The press has [helped] create a new class of activist pundits: loosely credentialled personalities who often thrive on being provocateurs. These people are treated as authorities, but they actually are neither news sources nor journalists. They lack the expertise to offer informal analysis. They also have no responsibility for impartiality or even accuracy.... The argument culture may be undermining the reporting culture, and news organisations are helping encourage the process as they increase the range of programming and material they produce. (Kovach and Rosenstiel 1999, 21–22)

Against this, citizen journalism sites offer the potential and the place for a more open, multiperspectival, democratic debate; this is further augmented by the distributed, decentralized discussions of the blogosphere. Traditional journalism cannot afford to ignore this space for long, as even Rupert Murdoch has noted, unless it wants its conflict-based, dyadic narratives to be seen as increasingly old-fashioned and out of step with public perception. (At the same time, it is important to realize that citizen journalism is not a zone entirely free of power structures, either; opinion leaders and key debatants emerge here, too. Additionally, the relative disempowerment of traditional experts in citizen journalism environments may not be entirely desirable. However, citizen journalism offers the potential at least for a partial reshaping of the traditional positions of power in discursive engagement: discursive power is allocated here mainly according to the individual merit of participants' contributions, rather than based simply on their institutional affiliations.)

Futures for Tactical Media

Dialogic and deliberative engagement with news and current events presents a clear and important opportunity for off-mainstream media forms to move beyond the tactical moment and develop longer-term strategies for a post-Gansian mediasphere. As Rushkoff puts it, "While it may not provide us with a template for sure-fire business and marketing solutions, the rise of interactive media does provide us with the beginnings of new metaphors for cooperation, new faith in the power of networked activity and new evidence of our ability to participate actively in the authorship of our collective destiny" (Rushkoff 2003, 18). Nonetheless, the playing field remains markedly uneven, and opposition from the journalism industry establishment is unlikely to diminish soon. Further, as Meikle points out, few citizen journalism activities "are effective without the eventual participation of the older media" (Meikle 2002, 5).

In order to move beyond a second-tier, tactical existence, citizen journalism can choose from a variety of strategic options. On the one hand, it can vigorously pursue a gatecrashing approach: reformatting its stories for easier pickup by the mainstream journalism industry and, thus, taking on the industry on its own terms. With this approach, "one way to measure the success of many of the projects . . . is to ask how effectively they can use the Net to force their cause onto the agenda of the mainstream media" (Meikle 2002, 8). However, this also risks the loss of a distinct identity and loses the gains possible through a more debate-driven, deliberative model of news coverage. The notable stagnation of *Wikinews*, nominally a citizen journalism project, but one that has all but outlawed the *discussion* of news and current events in favor of its dogged pursuit of the mythical journalistic ideal (or mirage) of objectivity, sounds a clear warning here (see Bruns 2006*b*). By contrast, citizen news sites that *are* successful at the mainstream journalism industry's game may be just as likely to be swallowed up by it (future developments surrounding *OhmyNews* will require close scrutiny in this context): sites that produce quality, traditional-style journalistic content while using citizen volunteers as authors and editors must no doubt make very attractive takeover targets for Murdoch's Newscorp and its competitors.

A second strategy could focus on building close ties with the key news aggregators such as *Google News* and *Technorati*—the conduits for emerging newssharing networks. However, their mostly automated approach, and their basis on standard journalistic story formats, could again push citizen news toward a further reduction to such formats, again losing the benefits of debate and deliberation; *Google News* is an effective tool for discovering the latest news headlines from around the world but provides little indication of where the most insightful and engaging discussions and evaluations of the meanings and implications of news events might be found. Additionally, in such aggregated environments, it is as hard for citizen journalism sites to develop brand awareness and keep control of their content as it is for the outlets of the mainstream journalism industry.

Instead, then, perhaps the most promising strategy is to remain true to those aspects of their operations that set the best exponents of citizen journalism and tactical media apart from the journalism industry. As we have seen, industrial journalism produces tightly filtered statements of "fact" that are claimed to be objective and complete and command acceptance rather than encouraging critical examination. Against this, citizen journalism must highlight the need to interpret, discuss, and debate stories, and therefore positions news as inherently subjective and incomplete. Industrial journalism aims to reduce its stories to what are believed to be the core elements and conflicts, where citizen journalism should remain mindful of the wider contexts within which any one news story must be placed. Therefore, one of the core challenges for citizen journalism "is to develop ways of telling stories which are issues-focused, without replicating the conflict-based narrative structures of the established media" (Meikle 2002, 99)—stories which instead provide the basis for debate, discussion, and deliberation. Such projects can be pursued in partnership with progressive members of the industry, blending the best of traditional journalism (for example, skills in story writing and investigative reporting) with the gains made through citizen journalism's more participatory approaches; as Lasica describes it for news blogging, "instead of looking at blogging and traditional journalism as rivals for readers' eyeballs, we should recognize that we're entering an era in which they complement each other, intersect with each other, play off one another. The transparency of blogging has contributed to news organizations becoming a bit more accessible and interactive, although newsrooms still have a long, long way to go." (Lasica 2003*a*, 73) An *Ohmy News*-style pro-am approach provides one possible pathway into the future for such intersections, then. As Bowman and Willis put it, "If journalism is indeed about informing the community and lifting up our fellow citizens, we need to evolve. We need to tell better stories and, while doing so, we need to engage the world" (Bowman and Willis 2003, 60).

Conclusion: The South Korean Joschka Fischer of Journalism?

OhmyNews is certainly not the only interesting model for future post–tactical citizen media, and, certainly, it is not without problems of its own. However, it represents an iconic example for the possibilities of citizen journalism. Writing in 2003, Bowman and Willis observed that "with the help of more than 26,000 registered citizen journalists, this collaborative online newspaper has emerged as a direct challenge to established media outlets in just four years" (2003, 7), and it has since spawned Japanese and English-language subsidiaries. Indeed, " 'OhmyNews is as influential as any newspaper,' a South Korean diplomat told the paper [*The Guardian*, in 2003]. 'No policy maker can afford to ignore it. South Korea is changing in ways that we cannot believe ourselves.' " (Kahney 2003, n. pag.).

At least in the South Korean context, *OhmyNews* can be seen as an example of tactical media moving beyond the temporary tactical moment, adopting longer-term strategies, and becoming "respectable". While "calling itself a 'news guerilla organization'—and adopting the motto, 'Every Citizen is a Reporter' " (Kahney 2003, n. pag.)—it is now nonetheless a major and established news outlet in the country and can therefore no longer be considered "tactical" in any traditional sense of the word; in the South Korean mediascape, it has claimed a space of its own as a basis for its operations. Its success lends credence to Rushkoff's assertion that "we are heading not towards a toppling of the democratic, parliamentary or legislative processes, but towards their reinvention in a new, participatory context. In a sense, the people are becoming a new breed of wonk [*sic*], capable of engaging with government and power structures in an entirely new fashion" (2003, 63–64)—and it is perhaps no surprise that this phenomenon has emerged from one of the most wired nations on earth.

In a journalism context, then, the site's founder, Mr. Oh, could be described as a South Korean equivalent of Greens leader Joschka Fischer, from a number of perspectives. On the one hand, he has blazed a trail beyond a merely tactical response to the political and journalistic establishment in his country, moving well past a temporary, guerrilla-style engagement and toward positioning his model as a highly credible and visible alternative option for the long term. On the other hand, however, as a veteran journalist himself, Oh also showed a pathway away from the oppressive environment of a highly conservative South Korean news industry and toward the more deliberative citizen journalism model espoused by *OhmyNews*. Where Fischer made the German Greens movement and party acceptable, respectable, and, ultimately, electable into government for a very wide cross-section of society, so Oh has turned citizen journalism in South Korea into a form of news that a large part of the population is ready to take seriously, trust, and, most important, is willing to participate.

Much as has been the case for Greens parties throughout the Western world as they have come to terms with their newfound place in the political process since the 1980s, what happens next for *OhmyNews* (and for other examples of post–tactical citizen journalism) will be crucial. Will *OhmyNews'* citizen journalism fundamentally affect and alter the journalistic traditions of the South Korean mediasphere—has it successfully infiltrated its target, able now to change the system from within? Or will it suffer subsumption into the day-to-day news cycle, its differences from the journalistic mainstream gradually worn down until it is little different from its existing competitors? Analogies for both processes can be found in the recent political histories of the tacticians-turned-strategists of the Greens movement and in other domains beyond this. On the one hand, *OhmyNews'* enduring success could continue to show that the processes of mainstream Korean journalism are no longer compatible with life in one of the world's most wired nations; much as the Greens helped highlight the shortcomings of the political establishment of their time and, thus, became a factor in its rejuvenation, *OhmyNews* could position itself as a more appropriate model for Korean journalism in the twenty-first century. On the other hand, however, the greater contact with the older models that is also a result of such success could also serve to influence *OhmyNews* in turn: as it develops, *OhmyNews* may be forced to work more directly to the continuing beat of the traditional journalism industry (returning, say, to more conflict-based narratives in order to make its content more compatible with that of other news outlets); it may find that it has to reach compromises just as the political arm of the Greens movement had to compromise in order to operate within existing parliamentary environments, and some of these compromises may be difficult to accommodate.

As regards *OhmyNews*, and the citizen journalism movement overall, it is as yet too early to make any definitive judgments on how this process of negotiation with the older models of journalism will play out, and it is thus all the more important to keep track of developments here. It is, however, appropriate to note that citizen journalism provides us with what Rushkoff describes as "an opportunity for renaissance: a moment when we have the ability to step out of the story altogether. Renaissances are historical instances of widespread recontextualisation. People . . . have the ability to reframe their reality. Renaissance literally means 'rebirth.' It is the rebirth of old ideas in a new context. A renaissance is a dimensional leap, when our perspective shifts so dramatically that our understanding of the oldest, most fundamental elements of existence changes. The stories we have been using no longer work" (Rushkoff 2003, 32–33).

At the same time, what the renaissance image points to is also that this is a process that is unlikely to have an end point and, indeed, may be cyclical instead: if and when citizen journalism assumes its new role in a posttactical, post-Gansian mediasphere, we may soon thereafter see the emergence of a new generation of tactical media activists who in turn will be in opposition to both industrial *and* citizen journalism, will develop their own journalistic models, and will subsequently themselves undergo a further posttactical transformation.

References

Alleyne, Mark D. 1997. *News revolution: political and economic decisions about global information.* Houndmills, U.K.: Macmillan.

Bardoel, Jo, and Mark Deuze. 2001. "Network journalism": converging competencies of old and new media professionals. *Australian Journalism Review* 23, no. 3 (December): 91–103.

Bowman, Shane, and Chris Willis. 2003. *We media: how audiences are shaping the future of news and information.* Reston, Va.: The Media Center at the American Press Institute. http://www. hypergene.net/wemedia/download/we_media.pdf (accessed 21 May 2004).

Bruns, Axel. 2005. *Gatewatching: collaborative online news production.* New York: Peter Lang.

———. 2006a. Towards produsage: Futures for user-led content production. In *Proceedings: cultural attitudes towards communication and technology 2006*, eds. Fay Sudweeks, Herbert Hrachovec, and Charles Ess, 275–284. Perth: Murdoch University.

———. 2006b. Wikinews: The next generation of online news? *Scan Journal* 3 (no. 1). http://scan. net.au/scan/journal/display.php?journal_id=69 (accessed Oct. 31, 2006).

Carey, James. 1997. Community, public and journalism. In *Mixed news: The public/civic/communitarian journalism debate*, ed. Jay Black, 1–15. Mahwah, N.J.: Lawrence Erlbaum.

Chan, Anita J. 2002. Collaborative news networks: distributed editing, collective action, and the construction of online news on Slashdot.org. MSc thesis, MIT. http://web.mit.edu/anita1/www/thesis/Index.html (accessed 6 Feb. 2003).

Gans, Herbert J. 1980 *Deciding what's news: a study of* CBS Evening News, NBC Nightly News, Newsweek, *and* Time. New York: Vintage.

———. 2003. *Democracy and the news.* New York: Oxford University Press.

Garcia, David, and Geert Lovink. 1997. The ABC of tactical media. *Subsol.* http://subsol.c3.hu/subsol_2/contributors2/garcia-lovinktext.html (accessed Nov. 2, 2006).

Gillmor, Dan. 2003. Foreword to *We media: how audiences are shaping the future of news and information*, by Shane Bowman and Chris Willis. Reston, Va.: The Media Center at the American Press Institute. http://www.hypergene.net/wemedia/download/we_media.pdf (accessed 21 May 2004).

Hartley, John. 2003. *A short history of cultural studies.* London: Sage.

————. 2000. Communicative democracy in a redactional society: the future of journalism studies. *Journalism* 1 (no. 1): 39–47.

Heikkilä, Heikki, and Risto Kunelius. 2002. Access, dialogue, deliberation: experimenting with three concepts of journalism criticism. *The International Media and Democracy Project*, July 17. http://www.imdp.org/artman/publish/article_27.shtml (accessed Feb. 20, 2004).

Jenkins, Henry. 2006. *Fans, bloggers, and gamers: exploring participatory culture.* New York: New York University Press.

Kahney, Leander. 2003. Citizen reporters make the news. *Wired News*, May 17. http://www.wired.com/news/culture/0,1284,58856,00.html (accessed June 3, 2004).

Kovach, Bill, and Tom Rosenstiel. 1999. *Warp speed: America in the age of mixed media.* New York: Century Foundation Press.

Lasica, J.D. 2003*a*. Blogs and journalism need each other. *Nieman Reports*, Fall. http://www.nieman.harvard.edu/reports/03-3NRfall/V57N3.pdf (accessed 4 June 2004): 70–4.

————. 2003b. Participatory journalism puts the reader in the driver's seat. *Online Journalism Review*, August 7. http://www.ojr.org/ojr/workplace/1060218311.php (accessed Feb. 20, 2004).

Leadbeater, Charles, and Paul Miller. 2004. *The pro-am revolution: how enthusiasts are changing our economy and society.* London: Demos. http://www.demos.co.uk/publications/proameconomy (accessed Nov. 2, 2006).

Lévy, Pierre. 1997. *Collective intelligence: mankind's emerging world in cyberspace.* Cambridge: Perseus.

Meikle, Graham. 2002. *Future active: media activism and the Internet.* New York: Routledge.

Murdoch, Rupert. 2005. Speech by Rupert Murdoch to the American Society of Newspaper Editors. News Corporation. http://www.newscorp.com/news/news_247.html (accessed Nov. 2, 2006).

New forms of journalism: weblogs, community news, self-publishing and more. 2001. Panel on "Journalism's New Life Forms," Second Annual Conference of the Online News Association, University of California, Berkeley, Oct. 27. JDLasica.com. http://www.jdlasica.com/articles/ONA-panel.html (accessed 31 May 2004).

Platon, Sara, and Mark Deuze. 2003. Indymedia journalism: a radical way of making, selecting and sharing news? *Journalism* 4 (no. 3): 336–355.

Rushkoff, Douglas. 2003. *Open source democracy: how online communication is changing offline politics.* London: Demos. http://www.demos.co.uk/opensourcedemocracy_pdf_media_public.aspx (accessed April 22, 2004).

Schechter, Danny. 2000. Independent journalism meets business realities on the Web. *Nieman Reports* (Winter): 37–40.

Shirky, Clay. 2002. Broadcast institutions, community values. *Clay Shirky's writings about the Internet: economics and culture, media and community, open source*, September 9. http://www.shirky.com/writings/broadcast_and_community.html (accessed 31 May 2004).

Stewart, Jon. 2004. *Crossfire*, CNN, October 15; see, e.g., http://youtube.com/watch?v=11TaDDUVcGQ (accessed Nov. 2, 2006).

Tarleton, John. 2000. Protesters develop their own global Internet news service. *Nieman Reports* (Winter): 53–55.

11 Tempests of the Blogosphere: Presidential Campaign Stories that Failed to Ignite Mainstream Media

D. Travers Scott

Informational stories—be they news, fiction, sensationalism, or mere factoids—are of central importance to citizens' informed decision making, according to most participatory, liberal democratic theory. Habermas's conception of the space of information exchange and debate as the public sphere has been a rich subject of critique and elaboration, generating variants such as counterpublics (Brouwer 2001; Fraser 1992; Warner 2002) and sphericules (Gitlin 1998). Conceptualizations of this space as a *mediated* public sphere have been particularly useful for analysis of tactical media interventions (Bennett & Entman 2000; Couldry & Curran 2003). Mediation foregrounds the notion of civic deliberation taking place primarily in the realm of electronic communication technologies.

This chapter starts from the "Memogate" controversy of the 2004 U.S. presidential race, when bloggers purportedly upstaged corporate media through collective fact-checking of a broadcast news story central to the campaign. Memogate was touted as an exemplar of tactical media intervention within the mediated public sphere. It was widely celebrated, not only by those who reaped its political benefits, but also by proponents, producers, and observers of online tactical media, particularly blogging. I will work from this celebratory triumphalism surrounding Memogate to make several interconnected points: in the first half of this chapter, I will describe and historicize ongoing technological triumphalism, particularly that which trumpets the democratic potential of communication technologies. Following a brief history of blogging up to and including Memogate, I will then counter the triumphalist blogging narrative exemplified by Memogate through an analysis of several "blogflops," blogging stories that did not have a similar impact on dominant media. I stress that these are not presented as disproof of the power and potential of blogging and other tactical media, but as counterexamples intended to temper and call attention to the dominant, triumphal blogging narrative. These counterexamples, along with other supporting research, will provide evidence of Memogate as exceptional, rather than the norm for blogging. In the second half of this chapter, I will use the previous topics to argue for a "suprarational" conception of the mediated public sphere—one that incorporates both rational and emotional elements. Such emotional cognizance, I argue, has dual benefits: a suprarational perspective recognizes both the utility of harnessing emotion in tactical media and the danger of succumbing to it. It allows for better tactical deployment of emotional elements, such as the basic storytelling techniques I see blogflops as lacking. It also supports a healthy skepticism toward the emotional appeal of triumphalist narratives that can obscure rhetorical tactics and material relations— and perhaps limit political engagement: if things are so good, the impetus for change may be diluted. In sum, this chapter argues that, as creators, proponents, and critical scholars of tactical media, we not only can write better stories, but we must also be vigilant in our skepticism of stories written about us.

Triumphalism and Communication Technologies

After the 2004 U.S. presidential election, a *Wall Street Journal* editorial celebrated the involvement of bloggers in fact-checking CBS News and pushing star anchor Dan Rather into retirement. Comparing it to Henry V of England's 1415 defeat of France's much larger army at Agincourt, Memogate was proclaimed "a great historical development in the history of politics in America" (Noonan 2004, ¶16). By year's end, Merriam-Webster announced that "blog" had been 2004's most requested definition in its online dictionaries (From blogs . . . 2004). ABC News named bloggers their People of the Year (People of the Year: Bloggers 2004). My conservative Christian, FOX News-fan parents told me that my choice of blogs as a research topic surely had been divinely inspired.

This tendency toward what bloggers commonly term "blog triumphalism" is indicative of the demystification often required when approaching technological analyses. Despite its apparently straightforward, mechanistic subject matter, technological discourse often can be far from rational. Futurists' breathless prognostications, hyperbolic advertising and marketing, fictional narratives, and popular news panics regarding technologies can all be suffused with cultural projections or sublimations. Jodi Dean articulates in her chapter how technological fantasies of abundance and democratic participation materialize as a technological fetishism in which communicativity replaces actual communication; "the intense circulation of content in communicative capitalism forecloses the antagonism necessary for politics" (Chap. 3, this volume). Other cultural historians of technology identify a pattern of recurrent irrationality, both utopian and dystopian, and around emergent communication technologies (Carey 1989; Jones 2006; Mattelart 1996; Robins and Webster 1999; Spigel 2001; Winston 1998, 2006). Miller (2006) outlines a history of similar cultural excitements related to communicative technologies, ranging from typography's heretical menace to video games' threat to childhood innocence—a pattern we see recently around social networking sites such as MySpace. Stern (1999, and Handel, 2001) traces how

Internet panics related to addiction as well as availability of sexual content are familiar patterns with emergent communications media. Several scholars explore the spectacular and supernatural associations related to the very lifeblood of contemporary communications technology, electricity (Marvin 1990; Milutis 2006; Sconce 2000; Simon 2004). Cultural scholars examine technological discourse as the site of displaced social anxieties around topics such as gender (Balsamo 1996; Easlea 1983), nation (McClintock 1995) and family structure (Banet-Weiser 2004). Such attitudes of technology as sui generis suggest not only misconception of technologies as discrete, independent forces shaping culture, but also an ahistorical focus on the present, attitudes that Rosalind Williams (2004) reminds us continue to lurk in most discussions of new media— regardless of protestations to the contrary. Indeed, she notes that the concept of "technology," understood as a "semi-autonomous, dominant agent of historical and social change, the force with the most 'impact' on our lives, the one that defines our historical period," did not emerge until after World War II (p. 437). Nye notes as well that such technological determinism, even if banished in the academy, "in public life remains a vigorous and misleading idea, one that tells citizens they have no agency" (2006, 615). Mattelart (1996) argues that triumphal, utopic enthusiasm goes beyond discussions of communication technologies and is recurrent in the history of the very concept of communication itself.

Thus, whether to guard against blinding fantasies, distracting panics, or narcotizing determinism, a skeptical, critical stance is crucial for discussions of communication technologies, particularly those strategizing for tactical media interventions. An archer cannot hit a target in fog.

Democratic-potential Triumphalism

Optimistic ideas of the culture-shaping power of technology have had various expressions, a common one being that of increased democratic potential. Particularly in regard to communication technologies, the ability of various media to reach new, wider, or niche audiences has been lauded, as has their ability to be used by new, wider, or niche producers. Communicative agency, expanded through technology, allows more individuals to better join the mediated public sphere and thereby participate in civic deliberation.

Debate over such expanded democratic potential is an indefatigable strain of Internet studies. Over the last decade-plus, there has been much focus on Internet-era civic stories and informative journalism. Early writing waxes utopic over the Internet providing citizens with higher quality information while circumventing big media and government (Barlow 1996; Negroponte 1995; Rushkoff 1994). Others, such as Lessig (2001), caution that this could merely be a historical moment if corporate and governmental spoilers are not kept at bay. Some assure us that technology will keep a step ahead of the dark side, whether through the open-source "liberation technology" (Unsworth 2004) or programming-inspired philosophies of "Extreme Democracy" (Ratcliffe and Lebkowsky 2004). Intermediate opinions hold that the Internet complements rather than displaces other media, neutering utopian and dystopian visions, and serves merely as a self-reinforcing, ideological echo chamber (DiMaggio et al. 2001). For many, this is now conventional wisdom, despite some contradictory research (Cole 2004; Pew Internet and American Life Project 2004). Finally, others suggest a cautiously optimistic compromise in which online technologies do not solve all the problems of U.S. political communications, yet an influential subset of hyperengaged online citizens provide a vital new check and balance (Baker 2002; Institute for Politics, Democracy, and the Internet 2004).

A recent keynote address to the Association of Internet Researchers gushes, "Everyone can create their own work and publish it, via MySpace, YouTube, Flickr and other platforms. While most such work is circulated among small groups or communities of interest, the *potential* is always there for someone's bright idea, performance or personal charm to win an audience of millions—it happens regularly" (Hartley 2006, "Consumer co-creation . . ." section, ¶3–4, emphasis mine).

Potential is a tricky thing and the often overlooked fulcrum in such discussions. My first communications instructor was quick to temper our paradigm-shifting claims for digital media with the reminder that each new medium was merely that: a CD-ROM was no more inherently revolutionary than a piece of paper. Yes, audiences of millions *can* be reached (with the resultant social change implied), but how *likely* is it? What impediments lie in its path? How does one compete in the viral sweepstakes online with drunken celebutantes, passionate sing-a-longs, and virtuoso light-saber demonstrations? If successful, to what ends? In trumpeting mere potential, such rhetoric elides the audience-gathering realities of competition and sensationalism, the challenge of being heard above the din of so many voices. As Dean relates, participation in the mere proliferation of messages is by no means necessarily engaging others in antagonistic, productive, political debate. Furthermore, her technological "fantasy of participation" parallels such recurrent belief in technological change as an agent in advancing democracy, equality, and justice. Yet, as she and Rebecca Statzel note in chap. 18, this volume, often overlooked is that such democratic potential includes nonegalitarian ideologies. The cultural roots of this blind spot go deep. MacDougall's analysis of "wire thrillers," early twentieth-century pulp novels centered around deployment of the telephone network, finds a "combination of awe and even subjugation toward technological change with a paradoxical faith in individual agency [that] would become the default rhetoric for talking about communication technology in the twentieth and twenty-first centuries" (2006, 738). Nye (1994) argues that a sense of "technological sublime" is inherent to foundational myths of American progress and divine exceptionalism. Fleetwood (2006), in her analysis of the role of technology in making Hurricane Katrina a media event, similarly sees technological determinism as a national motif. Furthermore, Williams writes that, "In current raptures about the Internet, we still hear faint echoes of the Enlightenment and its conviction that a new phase of history is nigh, thanks to the universal circulation of information accumulated through reason-based inquiry" (2004, 442). Technological progress continues to be linked with a belief in inevitable historical progress, she notes, despite such evidence to the contrary as atomic weaponry, world war, or public health collapse in Africa.

I counter that, within discussions of the Internet technology du jour, these democratic progress narratives still resonate loudly. Already blogging may be old news, but the 2006 midterms were proclaimed the "YouTube election." Naming YouTube one of its top ten Entertainers of the Year for 2006, *Entertainment Weekly* asked, "Is there a website that more richly fulfills the populist promise of the Internet than YouTube?" (Vary 2006, 58). The "you" of this and other Web 2.0 interactive technologies was anointed *Time* magazine's Person of the Year (2006/2007). Bearing this triumphal context in mind, I will now turn to a brief history of blogging and an overview of political blogging leading up to and including Memogate.

Blogging History, 1999–2004

The democratic-potential debate regarding the Internet was foundational to blogging's spread, framing much discourse around the new medium. The impact of bloggers' stories on democracy and journalism was of particular note within academia, the newsroom, and the blogosphere. Although blogs most certainly did play a role in one of the most visible and possibly influential moments of the 2004 U.S. presidential campaign, this narrative of technological triumphalism exhibited familiar features, such as a deterministic view of a communication medium (and its agents) acting autonomously, an ahistorical focus on the present, and a utopic conflation of technological and democratic progress. All of this reminds us that technological discourse is often anything but self-evident, rational, and straightforward.

Originally known as web logging, blogging content ranged from bloggers' diaries and self-promotional musings to highly personalized real-time news coverage and analysis. After blogging's "big bang" in September 1999 with the release of Pyra Labs' software application *Blogger*,[1] blogging spread beyond the technological elite with steadily increasing adoption (Jensen 2003; Kennedy School ... 2004; Pew 2005b; Welch, Jensen, and Reeves 2003). This process was facilitated by point-and-click Web-publishing software that required no detailed knowledge of HTML authoring, and RSS applications for outgoing content syndication and incoming personalized aggregation. Current events drove adoption as well, such as the September 11, 2001, U.S. terrorist attacks and the Iraq War (Kennedy 2004; Whelan 2003). In 2002, Blogger's registered users reached over 970,000 (Kennedy 2004) and online behemoth Google acquired the company (Gill 2004). A 2003 survey (Perseus Development Corporation 2003) measured 4.12 million total blogs online, although only 1.4 million were active. Although Internet users in massive numbers had not yet embraced blogs, some blog proponents pointed out that they had become influential with niche audiences such as politicians or media critics (Glaser 2003, "With the rise..." section, ¶4; Richards 2004). Meanwhile, the medium evolved to incorporate photography, video, audio, satellite positioning, and mobile technologies (Glaser 2004b; Lasica 2003). Conferences, university courses, and media feted bloggers, spawning celebrities such as Baghdad Blogger Salam Pax, whose collected postings Grove Press published (Pax 2003), Glenn Reynolds of InstaPundit and Markos Moulitsas of Daily Kos, both of whom were subjects of mass-media profiles. Fields as varied as library science (Thomsen 2002), education (Embrey 2002), demographics (Whelan 2003), and medicine (Brown 2003) noted, debated, and dabbled with blogging.

Scholars, observers, and practitioners of journalism were particularly interested in blogging, debating the nature, functions, practices, and meanings of blogging, as well as their implications for journalism. Journalists blogged; bloggers gathered and critiqued news. It was argued that blogs threatened traditional media gatekeeping (Regan 2003) by permitting "citizens to challenge the media monopoly in determining what counts as newsworthy and what the narrative frame for those stories is" (Glaser 2004b, Do you consider... section, ¶2). Situations in which blogs were purported to have in some way influenced, supplanted, surpassed, or scooped mainstream news media accumulated into a familiar litany. These included:

- The Trent Lott scandal (Gill 2004; Kennedy 2004)
- Microsoft's deceptive "Switch" ad campaign (Gill 2004)
- The Iraqi prison abuse scandal (Richards 2004)
- E-voting risks (Andrews 2003)
- The 2003 State of the Union Iraq-Africa uranium retraction (Andrews 2003)
- The September 11 attacks (Andrews 2003; Pew 2002)
- The Santa Monica Farmers Market car crash (Regan 2003)
- *New York Times* Editor Howell Raines's resignation (Regan 2003)
- The Rhode Island nightclub fire (Lennon 2003)
- Paul Bremer's Iraqi farewell speech (Leo 2004)

News bloggers were variously dissected and described as citizen-journalists putting the power of the press in the hands of the people (Outing 2003; Williams 2003), critical observers in one-on-one "adopt-a-journalist" relationships that were something like individual ombudsmen (Glaser 2004a), fact-checkers and ideological watchdogs that added a new layer of check-and-balance to the news media's power (Glaser 2004b), and mainstream journalists exploring a medium that offered them a chance to stretch their professional norms with more immediate, speculative, or opinionated reporting (Weintraub 2004). Frequent disregard for traditional journalistic neutrality was lauded for injecting voice and personality (Grossman 2004) into "a media world that's otherwise leached of opinions and life" (Jarvis, quoted in Welch, Jensen, and Reeves 2003, What's the point section, ¶1–2). News bloggers received press credentials to the 2004 Democratic (Weiss 2004) and Republican National Conventions (Grossman 2004), and some acquired readerships larger than the circulation of The *Chicago Tribune* (Lasica 2004). A few joined mainstream media (MSM), as when Kevin Drum's Calpundit.com, rechristened Political Animal, became a part of *Washington Monthly* (Grossman 2004). In the first half of 2004, *Time* declared "a golden age of blogging" (Grossman 2004) and researcher Alex Halavais suggested that news blogging hadn't "even come close to a tipping point yet" (in Glaser 2004b, last ¶). Soon, the point would tip.

By the time 2004 drew to a close, with the U.S. presidential campaign dominating news stories, the "Memogate" scandal broke, effectively silencing any debate as to whether blogs significantly affected mainstream media. On September 8, the CBS News television program *60 Minutes II* aired a story on long-standing questions over President Bush's fulfillment of obligations to the Texas Air National Guard. CBS presented damaging memos purportedly written by Lt. Col. Jerry B. Killian, Bush's supervisor in the guard (Wallsten 2004a; Wasserstein 2004), copies of which they had delivered to the White House that same morning. Nineteen minutes into the program's broadcast, "TankerKC" noted on the conservative message board FreeRepublic.com that the memos were "not in the style that we used when I came into the USAF" (Wallsten 2004a, ¶7). Only four hours later "Buckhead" posted that the memos were written

In a proportionally spaced font, probably Palatino or Times New Roman. . . . The use of proportionally spaced fonts did not come into common use for office memos until the introduction of laser printers, word-processing software, and personal computers. . . . They were not widespread until the mid- to late '90s. Before then, you needed typesetting equipment, and that wasn't used for personal memos to file. Even the Wang systems that were dominant in the mid '80s used monospaced fonts" (Wallsten 2004b, ¶s 17–18)

Buzz about the memos' questionable veracity spread through conservative blogs and discussion forums such as Power Line and Little Green Footballs, sparking a flurry of research, and then counterresearch among liberal blogs. The story leapt to gossip site The Drudge Report, talk radio, cable news, and, ultimately wide dissemination in mainstream broadcast and print (Wallsten 2004a; Wasserstein 2004). The story resonated with key themes of the campaign. In the first presidential election since the 2001 terrorist attacks, military leadership was crucial. The CBS news story and its suspect documents supported the image of Bush as a cowardly child of privilege who not only avoided combat in the Vietnam War by receiving a preferential appointment to the Texas Air National Guard, but who also then did not even fulfill his commitments there, leaving early to work on a political campaign. In contrast, Kerry was a decorated veteran (and early, influential critic of) the Vietnam War, yet the highly visible Swift Boat Veterans for Truth attack ads accused him of lying about the extent of his service.

On the right, CBS News's use of possibly forged documents and decision to broadcast the story mere weeks before the election were taken as a paradigmatic example of leftist media bias and elitist intervention in democratic politics. Among technophiles of varied politics, bloggers' trumping of the premier U.S. broadcast newsmagazine marked an unprecedented shift in the hierarchy of media power. Buckhead, however, turned out to be no mere concerned citizen typography expert but Harry W. MacDougland, an Atlanta lawyer with strong conservative Republican ties, including having helped draft a petition for the Arkansas Supreme Court to disbar former Democratic President Clinton (Wallsten 2004b). A prominent Republican fundraiser turned out to be the owner of one of the Memogate's top attack blogs; other blogs in the fracas had been fed information from the conservative Media Research Center and Creative Response Concepts, a public relations agency that had also promoted the Swift Boat Kerry attacks (Peim 2005). The exposure of such connections stopped neither the blogging narrative nor the apology and subsequent retirement of CBS' longtime star anchor, Dan Rather. After an internal investigation, CBS dismissed four top journalists from their news division (Steinberg and Carter 2005).

After years of debate, the bloggers had arrived, and spectacularly so. Savvy citizen muckrakers of the blogosphere, it was heralded, had brought the powerful establishment to its knees, heralding a new era of insurgent democracy and fulfilling the promise of e-democracy. If there had been any questions about whether bloggers were influencing mainstream news agendas or shaping public discourse, they were now answered. After the election, this media narrative continued, with bloggers credited in Howard Dean's election as Democratic National Committee Chair (Lizza 2005), the resignation of CNN executive Eason Jordan (Bauder 2005), the exposure of the identity and background of White House reporter Jeff Gannon (a.k.a. James Guckertt) (Strupp 2005), and even exposing safety flaws in Kryptonite bicycle locks (Fillion 2004).

By early 2005, Pew (2005a) found that 27 percent, or 32 million online Americans, read blogs—a 58 percent increase over the course of 2004—and 9 percent of online Americans had read political blogs frequently or sometimes during the 2004 presidential campaign. In September of that year, CDS Books published *Blog!: How the Newest Media Revolution is Changing Politics, Business, and Culture,* coauthored by Dan Burstein, whose previous book had been *Secrets of the Code: The Unauthorized Guide to the Mysteries Behind* The Da Vinci Code. With sensationalist ahistoricism, popular media collapsed this six-year blog evolution into an overnight success story: "Blogs have gone from obscurity to ubiquity in a blink," reported the *New York Times* (Schwartz 2005, ¶11).

Memogate Counterexamples: Blogflops

During the final months of the 2004 campaign, while conducting a content analysis of four leading political blogs, I noticed several stories that tickled bloggers into a tizzy. Almost weekly a new scandal was uncovered. Immersed in research, I was receiving more news from blogs than mainstream sources and was surprised how often my friends and colleagues knew nothing of these seemingly urgent, groundbreaking stories. Even as Memogate unfolded, it became clear to me that not all blog-based stories reached mainstream media. I grew curious about those that didn't. What could such "blogflops" reveal about this latest medium of the political communications system? I will now describe several blogflops observed while reading thousands of posts from four leading political blogs.

In October 2003, former National Security Advisor Sandy Berger came under criminal investigation for improperly removing copies of documents relating to the Clinton administration's antiterrorism activities from the National Archives. This story resonated off Republican accusations that Clinton had been soft on terror, distracting from the Republican motivations for the Iraq War and reinforcing their position of moral superiority. Glenn Reynolds, main blogger of InstaPundit, a somewhat jokingly, self-proclaimed "liberal" blog that exhibits a more conservative-libertarian ideology, treated this as a hot topic. During my period of observation, InstaPundit posted on the story 34 times, which, as "one of the most prominent bloggers in terms of links and traffic" (Drezner and Farrell 2004, 19), should have exerted considerable effect[2] on the blogosphere and conventional media. Amid much big-media bashing, Reynolds fumed, "I don't know what's more appalling—the thought that Berger is covering up some dreadful failing, or the thought that the man in charge of national security for much of the Clinton administration is utterly incompetent at handling supersecret national security documents" (Reynolds 2004a, ¶5). Yet fellow conservative blog Daily Dish only covered the story in 7 posts, and liberal blog Talking Points Memo only addressed it 12 times. The liberal collective blog Daily Kos never addressed the story. The mainstream media covered the story when it broke, with numerous stories in late July. However, although Reynolds continued to address the story until late November, blogosphere buzz did not give the story mainstream "legs." The *New York Times* ran only two articles on the case in July (LexisNexis 2005g); *USA Today* addressed the story in five articles in July and August (LexisNexis 2005h). The story of potentially conspiratorial document theft, with its important national security implications, always-popular Clinton connection, and humorous details of stuffed socks or pants, seemed ripe with potential, yet Reynolds's continued interest never pervaded conventional media.

On September 7, gossip Web site The Drudge Report claimed that Democratic candidate John Kerry was shown posing in a photo op with a rifle, the model of which he had voted to ban in earlier gun-control legislation. This story had potential to support the Republican portrait of Kerry as an indecisive "flip-flopper," bereft of core convictions, as well as a hypocritical, antigun elitist merely aping Bush's more authentic, populist masculinity. Reynolds picked up the item with an InstaPundit post headline that read, "Drudge offers a Kerry Gun Flip-flop Report: 'Kerry Cosponsored Bill Banning Gun He Waves'" (Reynolds 2004c, ¶1). Six updates followed, for a total of 923 words on the subject, including links to other blogs, quotes from the proposed legislation, a photograph, a debate on the definition of "pistol grip," and a rifle photograph, all in an effort to affirm that the rifle fit the definition of "assault weapon" in the proposed legislation. A follow-up post on September 20 linked to another blog claiming Kerry had returned the rifle. The only major newspaper to mention the incident, however, was the London *Daily Telegraph*—as a minor reference in an article detailing sleazy tactics in the U.S. presidential campaign (LexisNexis 2005e).

On October 3, video surfaced from one of the presidential debates that appeared to show Kerry with a cheat sheet in his pocket (fig. 11.1). Exposure of such an explicit violation of the official debate rules would have not only undercut popular perception of Kerry winning the debates, but also deflated Kerry's perceived character advantage over Bush. A cheat sheet would had provided more evidence of a character tainted by dishonesty—dishonesty charged in the Swift Boat ads and dishonesty purportedly exhibited in the forged documents used by the Kerry-colluding CBS News. InstaPundit, with Drudge and other conservative blogs, circulated this scandal rumor. After seven updates to the post within the same day, it was confirmed that the cheat sheet was merely a pen. The only major mainstream newspaper to pick up the story was the Cleveland *Plain Dealer*, which did not use the rumor to challenge Kerry's character, as blogs had, but instead used the story's 24-hour wax and wane to frame an article on blogs' influence on the mainstream media (LexisNexis 2005d). "And now the accusation," claimed the article, "cooked up online, has hit print" (Seper 2004, ¶4).[3] On October 24, news broke of the disappearance of explosives in Iraq. The story was significant as it not only illustrated the Bush administration's ineptitude in managing the war, but also refuted the use of weapons of mass destruction as justification for the war, because, in this case, the threat became worse after the U.S. forces arrived. Talking Points Memo blogged, "This has been rumored in Washington for several days. And now the Nelson Report has broken the story. Some 350 tons of high explosives (RDX and HMX), which were under IAEA seal while Saddam was in power, were looted during the early days of the US occupation" (Marshall 2004c, ¶1–2). Main *TPM* blogger Josh Micah Marshall continued to blog almost exclusively on the subject, posting over

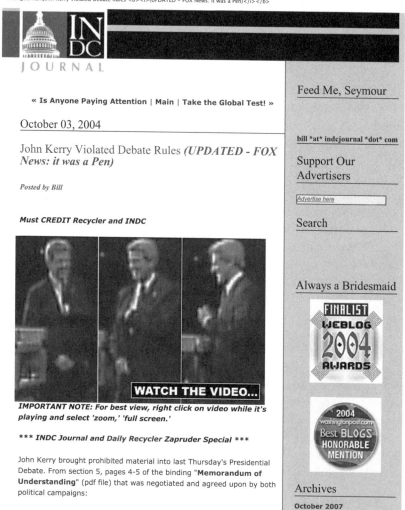

INDCJournal: John Kerry Violated Debate Rules (UPDATED – FOX News: it was a Pen)

INDC JOURNAL

« Is Anyone Paying Attention | Main | Take the Global Test! »

October 03, 2004

John Kerry Violated Debate Rules *(UPDATED - FOX News: it was a Pen)*

Posted by Bill

Must CREDIT Recycler and INDC

WATCH THE VIDEO...

IMPORTANT NOTE: For best view, right click on video while it's playing and select 'zoom,' 'full screen.'

*** INDC Journal and Daily Recycler Zapruder Special ***

John Kerry brought prohibited material into last Thursday's Presidential Debate. From section 5, pages 4-5 of the binding **"Memorandum of Understanding"** (pdf file) that was negotiated and agreed upon by both political campaigns:

Feed Me, Seymour

bill *at* indcjournal *dot* com

Support Our Advertisers

Advertise here

Search

Always a Bridesmaid

FINALIST WEBLOG 2004 AWARDS

2004 washingtonpost.com Best BLOGS HONORABLE MENTION

Archives

October 2007

http://www.indcjournal.com/archives/001054.php (1 of 43) [10/4/07 4:19:31 PM]

Figure 11.1

The purported Kerry debate cheat-sheet video, from the archives of *INDC Journal*

19,000 words in 50 posts over six days, until the release of an Osama bin Laden videotape eclipsed the story. Marshall focused on the story as a case study in the administration's deception and the media's acquiescent manipulation. When video from an embedded local TV film crew revealed footage of the explosives after the occupation, Marshall wrote, "Game. Set. Match. They got caught with a screw-up, their response was to lie, smear, obfuscate and bamboozle. And now the unimpeachable evidence is out. It captures the administration's whole record on Iraq, only fast-forwarded and telescoped into four days as opposed to four years" (Marshall 2004d, ¶1–3). The more vehemently liberal blog Daily Kos only covered the story in 10 posts, bested by conservative blogs Daily Dish, with 14, and InstaPundit, with 17. However, right-wing blogs took the story in another direction, spurred on by conservative columnist and mainstream media figure William Safire. Safire pointed out that CBS News had planned originally to hold the story until 36 hours before polls opened, presumably to influence the election against Bush, but bloggers covering the story had forced the network to run it earlier. "It is absolutely intolerable," blogged Reynolds, "for a news organization to hold on to a story for the purpose of breaking it so close to an election as to prevent a fair investigation and response" (Reynolds 2004d, ¶1). Mainstream coverage of this story did occur, but it did not match the frenzy of Marshall's cross-analysis of media reports, transcripts, and records. More significantly, although bloggers on both the right and left framed the explosives story as contradictory illustrations of media bias and/or administration deception, the mainstream media predominantly framed the story as an example of mudslinging. The *New York Times* ran 17 articles on this story between October 24 and 29, including editorials referencing it (LexisNexis 2005a). The bulk of these, however, were not about the explosives per se but about the political use of the story: "Iraq Explosives Become Issue In Campaign," ran a typical *Times* headline (Sanger 2004), as charges and countercharges involving them flew between Bush and Kerry. *USA Today* and the *Washington Post* each ran 14 stories, which were evenly distributed between addressing the issue itself and its political use in the campaign (LexisNexis 2005b, 2005c).

Prior to the campaign, Rocco Martino, an Italian businessman, had supplied forged documents that formed the basis of President Bush's infamously deceptive "16 words" regarding Iraq's attempts to acquire uranium from Africa. These purported attempts, asserted in Bush's 2003 State of the Union address, had been a crucial part of a central argument for war with Iraq. During the campaign, details of Martino's role became known, and Marshall, a working and respected journalist, smelled another scandal. Marshall posted ten times on the subject, suggesting there was more to the story.

The Bureau may well be looking to interview Martino now that they've been put on the spot. But are they really willing to take "no" for an answer from the Italians?

And more to the point, if it's really a jurisdictional issue, why didn't they try to interview Martino last month when he was in New York?

Or if not then, how about when he flew here in June?

The White House is now saying that it's imperative to get to the bottom of who's behind the CBS Memo forgeries. And they're right. But the US government has never made any serious effort to find out who is behind the Niger uranium forgeries.

Why not? (Marshall 2004b, ¶1–8)

Although, as Marshall noted, falsely supported claims were addressed in *Newsweek*, no major newspaper in the United States addressed the implications of Martino during the campaign's final months (LexisNexis 2005f). Although Marshall intoned ominously that "everything we'd learned reporting on the Niger uranium case told us that this was a story the US government did not want to get to the bottom of" (2004a, ¶18), Martino as a crucial link in falsely building a case for war never ignited mainstream coverage.

In August, the members of several collective blogs and online forums developed a story questioning the validity of Bush's Texas Air National Guard (TANG) medals, potentially adding support to claims that Bush had received preferential treatment in TANG, where he was kept safely out of combat during the Vietnam War (fig. 11.2). The story was significant as a counter to the Swift Boat Veterans for Truth accusations that Kerry's medals in Vietnam had been undeserved. During this, the first election after the 911 terrorist attacks, military service and qualifications to be commander-in-chief were of paramount importance. The Democratic Underground discussion forums featured a 275-post thread titled "George W. Bush was Photographed Wearing a Ribbon He did not Earn" (Starr 2004), which linked to a related 122-post thread also on DU. Daily Kos followed this thread with a 640-word, triple-updated post assessing the validity and meaning of the medals. Using pictures of Bush, his discharge papers, medals sported by Bush and Kerry, and primary Daily Kos blogger Markos Moulitsas's own discharge papers, the *Kos* post concluded that there was a disparity between Bush's medals and discharge papers, supporting theories that he did not serve completely. "We must start the echo chamber. Start pounding the drums" read the first of 148 reader comments, indicating the intent to influence other blogs and mainstream media coverage (Moulitsas 2004, Comments section, ¶3). However, of the other blogs I studied, only InstaPundit mentioned the issue, in an August 28 update to a longer post on Kerry's military record, noting a different blog, Stop the Bleating, was covering the medals issue (Reynolds 2004b). Reynolds rather dismissively spun the issue, denigrating a different liberal blogger for using Democratic Underground as a source and complaining that the issue was receiving more investigation from liberal blogs than Kerry's Christmas-in-Cambodia claims. The story of Bush's medals did not gain coverage in major U.S. newspapers (LexisNexis 2007).

Walt Starr ☆ (1000+ posts) 📧 🖼 🔖 🔖
George W. Bush Wore a Ribbon He Did Not Earn

Thu Aug-26-04 07:50 PM
Original message

Edited on Thu Aug-26-04 08:03 PM by Walt Starr

This is a photograph published on the Presidential Library site of George H.W. Bush. We can clearly see that in this photograph, George W. Bush is wearing an Air Force Outstanding Unit Award (AFOUA) and a Small Arms Expert Marksmanship Ribbon (SAEMR) just below his pilot wings, however, on line 24 of his NGB22 National Guard discharge form dated October 1, 1973, George W. Bush has no awards listed.

Figure 11.2
The Bush TANG medals controversy in Democratic Underground

During the campaign, both Kerry and vice presidential candidate John Edwards publicly pointed out the lesbianism of Mary Cheney, daughter of the vice president and director of vice presidential operations for the reelection campaign. These not-so-subtle stabs at the Cheneys's apparent conflicts with the Republican anti-gay-marriage platform were potential character attacks and alerts to Republican voters. Andrew Sullivan, gay author of the conservative Daily Dish, pounded on the issue for 30 posts over 7 days, dissecting Republican hypocrisy and opportunistic exploitation of constituent homophobia. In contrast, Talking Points Memo addressed it in only three posts, Daily Kos in two, and InstaPundit in one. Only the second mention of Cheney's lesbian daughter, by Kerry, garnered heavy coverage in mainstream media, and it was primarily using the Republican frame of Kerry having intruded into the Cheneys' personal matters, rather than the hypocrisy of the Cheneys' politics attacked by blogger Sullivan.

Memogate as Exceptional: Further Evidence

It is difficult to draw broad conclusions from these admittedly anecdotal descriptions of blogflops. Nevertheless, I will summarize a variety of research that supports blog-flops's suggestion that the dominant blogging narrative of Memogate was in actuality exceptional. Only two months after Memogate, a study found that 62 percent of U.S. Internet users did not even know what "blog" meant (Pew 2005a). In a study of college students—bear in mind how often youthful rhetoric is deployed in new media discussions, from McLuhan's generational appeal to fragrance CK N2U's marketing to "technosexual" youth—Hargittai (2006) found 64 percent had never visited a blog, discussion forum, or other site where they could interact with others regarding politics, economics, law, or policy. Only 34 percent reported keeping a blog or Web journal. Usage of blogging sites Blogger and LiveJournal was in the single digits. Finally, less than 2 percent had ever visited some of the most popular and publicized blogs, such as Instapundit, DailyKos, and BoingBoing. BoingBoing was also involved in high-visibility blogging after the 2004 tsunami, in which bloggers intimated that their faster information networks could have saved lives that broadcast media chose to disregard (Diana 2004; Jardin 2004; Le Meur 2004; Phil 2004; Top weblog posts 2004).[4]

However, The *New York Times* assessed the conspiracy theories of many bloggers as undermining legitimate attempts at citizen-journalist coverage of the tsunami (Schwartz 2005). In this volume, Susan Moeller examines the tsunami as an exemplary, if flawed, case of *mainstream* news coverage. Indeed, Moeller concludes that traditional journalists are still those best equipped to break stories, assigns bloggers to a relatively minor contributory status. In a separate study, Hargittai (2007) found that online media consumption patterns for adults actually tended to match offline ones.

A Pew Internet Project blogger survey (2006) found that American bloggers did not generally consider themselves journalists or blogging a public effort. Bloggers' primary topic was their own lives, with only 11 percent blogging about politics, government, or public life. The conservative opposition to Supreme Court nominee Harriet Miers was portrayed in the media as a blog-fueled tidal wave, yet successive opinion polls revealed only minority discontent, with only a slight increase during the tidal wave, particularly once conservative pundits in mainstream media joined the fray (Dunham 2005).

Furthermore, the content analysis I conducted during this same period (Scott 2007) found that four major political blogs differed from the Memogate blogging narrative in several ways. The blogs conducted very little original newsgathering, bias-busting, or fact-checking research but mainly surveyed the media environment, and this was predominantly mainstream print media, rather than any alternative news media. The power of digital technologies to manipulate source material for investigative or interpretative purposes, such as replicating documents (as in Memogate), enlarging photographs, or posting audiotapes of phone calls, was rarely employed. Furthermore, the valorized multimedia capacity of the Web was hardly ever utilized. The most basic participatory calls to action, such as get-out-the-vote efforts and voting instructions, were extremely rare—and this was among four of the most prominent political blogs. To their credit, the blogs were not found to be ideological echo chambers; their editorial responses were almost evenly split between agreement, disagreement, or mixed. These various studies, together with the blogflops previously described, suggest that cases such as Memogate were exceptional.

A Suprarational Perspective on the Mediated Public Sphere

The blogging narrative of Memogate, I have argued, is exceptional rather than representative of political blogging, in contrast to triumphalist blogging narratives. Such an emotional narrative of a communication technology fits within a previously described pattern of hyperbolic and irrational perceptions of communication technologies, one flavor of which valorizes a technology for enabling radically increased democratic participation. Because of the vital importance for media tacticians to discern media function from hyperbole, and potential from actual use, I urge media scholars and producers to conceive of the mediated public sphere as far from an exclusively rational place. However, I avoid the term *ir*rational as negative, exclusionary, and binaristic and point out the tendency for "irrational" to refer to any debate, not necessarily dominated by, but often merely containing a drop of other-than-logical reasoning. Neither exclusively sensationalistic circus nor reasoned debate, I suggest considering the mediated public sphere instead as *supra*rational: more than merely rational, inclusive of logical, fact-based information *and* emotional, narrative, or illogical elements.

I now turn to describing a dual benefit of a suprarational perspective. First, I will suggest that the lack of a suprarational perspective may account for the failure of blogflops. Better cognizance of the emotional power of basic storytelling elements may have served to more effectively ignite mainstream media. I will also argue that not only does a suprarational perspective allow for better incorporation of emotional elements into tactical media creation, but it also provides a stronger critical perspective essential to tactical media analyses. A suprarational eye is more attuned to the emotion that can serve to obfuscate rhetorical tactics and material relationships. In sum, we must not only create better stories, we must also not get swept up in the emotions of stories written about us.

Emotional Oversight: Blogflop Narrative Analysis

Theories from two public-sphere scholars suggest that what the blogflops lacked were the suprarational, emotive qualities of basic storytelling. Bennett (2004) conceives of three media strata: the *conventional* layer of mainstream, mass media; the *middle* layer of prominent blogs, webzines, advocacy groups, and so forth; and the *micro* layer of e-mail, mailing lists, and personal blogs. Activity at micro or middle layers does not guarantee impact on the conventional layer, as seen in the rise and fall of Howard Dean's campaign for the Democratic presidential nomination (Bennett 2004). One strategy for breaching the conventional layer lies in Bennett's theory of indexing (2003), in which *conflict* between elite political actors is crucial for a story to be deemed conventionally newsworthy. Like gods in classical drama or celebrities in contemporary tabloids, it is elites who are of interest, not common persons. Elites possess an emotional investment that supercedes rational self-interest. In addition, Gamson (2001) theorizes an exception to indexing, articulating rare circumstances under which ordinary citizens may drive an issue into the conventional media layer, even without elite political involvement. Citing examples of citizen collective action around issues such as abortion and nuclear power, he develops a theory of "collective action frames." Gamson proposes that the stories most likely to breach conventional mass media will contain a morally offensive, emotion-laden *injustice*, an apparent *agency* as the route via which change is possible, and a protagonist or *identity* with which viewers can empathize (ideally in opposition to a specified opponent) (2001, 58–59). This final element, viewed in terms of Bennett's indexing, then, would be an empathetic protagonist who is also an elite of some type.

What do these theories suggest about blogflops? In the Berger story, the story did index as newsworthy due to having elite political players, yet they were not in direct conflict. In terms of collective action frames, there was a somewhat clear injustice, yet neither Berger nor the National Archives were subjects with whom readers could empathize or identify. Kerry's gun flip-flop and debate cheat-sheet both lacked conflict, empathy, and any kind of clear injustice. The missing Iraqi explosives and, more important, their framing as an illustration of administration duplicity and/or media bias, possessed conflict between elite players but lacked clear injustice against a victim with whom readers could identify or a specific antagonist perpetrating that injustice. Despite the popular villainizing of mainstream media—even in conventional outlets such as FOX News—it is more potent when attached to a specific human face, such as Dan Rather. Even more vague was the Italian businessman behind the uranium documents. Although he sounded like a shady character, he was far from a political elite and not in any direct conflict, and it was never clear exactly what was the larger injustice to which Marshall seemed to allude, and whom it hurt. Bush's medals had a clear, politically elite villain in the president, but he was not locked in conflict with anyone over the issue. Furthermore, both the exact injustice—was it intentional or an oversight?—and the victims of it were diffuse. The Mary Cheney fracas did possess political elites in conflict, but Sullivan's unsuccessful framing of it can be attributed to lacking empathetic victims of injustice as potent as the parents who had their personal lives exposed on television. Finally, an element lacking from all stories was agency: readers were not given a route through which to do something about the injustice.

This examination of blogflops, when stripped of theoretical concepts, boils down to a rudimentary lesson in storytelling. Hero, villain, conflict, audience identification with characters, emotional appeals, and happy endings are all elements of popular storytelling. Journalism, even at its most elevated level of political discourse, is still about storytelling. The blogflops discussed anecdotally here all lacked one or more of these basic storytelling elements. This was exacerbated by their reliance on dissecting other media, rather than original storytelling. These blogs diluted the emotional potency of their stories. The heroes and villains, if present, became primarily second-hand, distanced, and therefore less potent. The lack of agency further sapped them of immediacy, direct application to readers' lives, and a vision of a potential happy ending. The personal, subjective nature of blogs has long been lauded by the medium's champions (Blood 2002), yet it is precisely this element that is lacking from the blogs' stories from the U.S. presidential campaign. Instead of telling their own stories, blogs retold the stories of others and did not suggest much to do about them. This may help account for the finding at the time by the ten-year Digital Future study that the Internet was "not yet perceived as a medium that can help users gain political power or more say in what government does" (Cole 2004 17).

Emotional Obfuscation: Rhetorics of Marginalization and Material Relationships

Conceiving of the mediated public sphere as suprarational helps alleviate blind spots to emotional rhetorical tactics. From a suprarational perspective, blog triumphalism is not inconceivable alongside the rhetoric of marginalization often used by the political right. Conservatives bemoan their oppression as persecuted Christians and domination by a liberal media. Not only does this encourage solidarity and urgency in the face of attack, it obscures the fact that the right has been running the country practically unchallenged for years. Statzel (chap. 18, this volume) describes how white supremacist Web site Stormfront "represents tactical media at its finest" in its political mobilization of affect, harnessing emotional attachments to subjectivities perceived as threatened in order to spur political engagement. In July 2006, prominent conservative bloggers perceived a deliberate attempt by the liberal media to assist terrorist assassins in a *New York Times* travel story on the vacation homes of Vice President

Dick Cheney and then-Secretary of Defense Donald Rumsfeld (Greenwald 2006). Such rhetoric of marginalization is used by some political blogs in their own mythmaking, as in the Memogate narrative of tackling the dreaded MSM (mainstream media). More recently, ThinkProgress called McCain's proposed extension of content provider liability to blogs a "war on blogs" (Amanda 2006). The Belmont Club used similar language of siege and assault in its popular article, "The Blogosphere at War," writing that "anyone who wants to know whether the blogosphere can help outflank the MSM during a pubic diplomacy crisis can do a systems check to observe how it works in normal times. . . . Understanding and exploiting the characteristics of [the] blogosphere will become a key skill in any information warrior's manual of arms" (Wretchard 2006, "How to optimize . . ." section, ¶4). Such rhetoric appeals simultaneously to American foundational myths of venerated individualism, such as the frontiersman, the iconoclastic outsider, and the lone inventor genius, as well as to technological progress narratives discussed previously. Furthermore, rhetoric of marginalization can function somewhat similarly to Foucault's repressive hypothesis of sexuality. The constant bleating of past repression—whether of sexual expression or media access and representation—can serve to normalize the present and validate the status quo as naturally better: *of course* we are so much more liberated than those Victorians; *of course* the blogosphere is so much more liberating than that bad ole' MSM.

The danger in this is that, if our story is one of triumph, it implies that the conflict is over, that we have won. Reminiscent of the lack of agency in the blogflop narratives I described, Williams writes that, "When hope for progress is invested in technology, then humanity looks not to great deeds and actions but to great inventions as the basic story line. Technology becomes the substitute for history itself. But the possibility of effective historical action diminishes as people assume that the story is about technology, not them" (2004, 446). Such sentiments hearken back to the "narcotizing dysfunction" of early communications scholarship, which theorized that media-fed knowledge of events substituted for action and involvement (Lazarsfeld and Merton 1949). More recently, Seigel expressed this in the *New Republic Online*, writing, "You have the impression of bloggers who are so pacified by shouting their rage—and so appeased by smugly shared sentiments—that they turn off their computers at night and go to sleep feeling empowered and relaxed. No wonder, several years after the blogosphere allegedly became a people powerhouse, the country is mired even deeper in Iraq and successfully distracted by one false public alarm after another. Catharsis is for art, not politics" (2007, ¶ 4).[5] UK communications scholars Robins and Webster (1999) have detailed how optimistic rhetoric of the democratic potential of technologies occludes the conservative social practices those technologies—developed with military, commercial, and government imperatives—actually reproduce. An example can be seen here in the United States when a Republican congressman from Texas in

2005 crowed, "The newest battlefield in the fight to protect the first amendment is the Internet. . . . The Internet is a marketplace of ideas. . . . It is one of the most democratic forms of speech that we know today. . . . The Internet, Mr. Speaker, is the new town square" (Hensarling 2005). This democratic rhetoric was used to introduce a bill exempting bloggers from campaign finance laws.

Rhetorical insight is not the only critical benefit of a suprational perspective. Mythic narratives of technology, such as triumphalism, as with Dean's technological fantasies, can hide material relationships. Examples abound in contradiction to the emotionally appealing story of triumphant, upstart, citizen bloggers. Hargittai (in press) found that the online content people find and use is heavily influenced by systemic factors companies with great resources can influence, such as search engine results, portal sites' layouts, and directions of user movement. *Forbes* advised companies criticized by bloggers to "bash back" using sympathetic bloggers who will attack their attackers. By one account, half of commercial blog attacks come from corporate rivals (Lyons 2005). The *New York Times* reported that, during the '06 midterm election, candidates hired, underwrote, or consulted bloggers, with varying degrees of disclosure (Glover and Essel 2006). A Portland, Oregon software company was found to be paying bloggers $800 a month to post on the company (Lyons 2005). Microsoft gave influential bloggers Christmas gifts of high-end laptops (Aspan 2007). Andrew Sullivan, the previously mentioned iconoclastic conservative who denounced Bush, has been a longstanding exemplar of blogger challenge to mainstream media. Yet, in 2005, an ad on his blog declared, "The blogger you read reads *The Financial Times*." These days David no longer shills for that particular Goliath—his blog is now a part of *Time* magazine online.

In sum, the examples I have presented illustrate rhetorical tactics and material relations that can be obscured by emotional narratives—narratives a solely rational model of a mediated public sphere overlooks. Ultimately, a suprational perspective toward technological discourse reminds us of I.C. Jarvie's fundamental distinction between technology and science. Whereas science has the goal of truth,[6] the goal of technology is simple instrumentality or a means to an end (cited in Hyde 1982, 7). Such pragmatic instrumentalism is rarely straightforward or exclusively rational.

Conclusion: Suprational Savvy, Seductive Stories

Tactical media require tactical messages. I urge creators of tactical media to be savvy and think suprationally. Mere fact-based truth alone may not set everyone free. Embracing a suprational, mediated public sphere will create more compelling content that pays mind to emotional elements of storytelling and—dare I say?—marketing. For even the juiciest blog story, in our current networked digital communications systems (or Dean's communicative capitalism), marketing, advertising, eyeballs, or mindshare are increasingly essential. Subversion of broadcast models is insufficient; subversion of marketing models needs to be addressed. How do you get people to encounter tactical media? How does a political viral meme compete with an exploding whale? We know successes when we see them but, like Memogate, how exceptional and complex are they? How many messages remain unheard? At times progressives exhibit a distaste for thinking in terms of ratings, numbers, brand, or advertising, but that leaves unanswered the question: once all this great media is created, who sees it? Capturing large audiences *is* possible—think back to ACT-UP's blatant and effective media-whoring.

Bloggers, file-sharers, video viralists, and other media tacticians have done amazing things. However, I urge media scholars, critics, and policymakers—in addition to authors—to bear in mind the irrational myths and narratives that suffuse technological discourse. We are not only storytellers but also the subjects of stories. We must be savvy in our deployment of emotional, narrative elements, and cautious of being swept up in them. Tales of triumph and marginalization are, each in their own way, heroic narratives, and it is hard to be critical of stories in which we are heroes.

Notes

1. Technically not the first coding-free Web-publishing application, but the first widely adopted.

2. Although it should be noted Reynolds frequently disavows what he considers the overestimation of his blog's impact.

3. However, the article did not name any other newspapers actually carrying the story, nor could I find any mainstream print mention of it other than in a humorous column published the following day—in the same paper (Heaton 2004; LexisNexis 2004d).

4. On December 27, 2004, French blog Philsland claimed to have received a U.S. Geological Survey earthquake alert via e-mail three hours before the tsunami hit (Phil 2004). This was translated and posted on the blog of Loïc Le Meur, (2004) the executive vice president and European managing director for the prominent blogging software firm Six Apart. In the post, "A blogger was alerted three hours before the tsunamis," Le Meur wrote, "In three hours thousands of casualties could have been avoided if they were warned earlier. Now Internet is everywhere and especially where the tourists were staying, we could have avoided many deaths" (2004, ¶3). A comment by Diana noted that, "I just read in the *Daily Mail* that in fact this warning had been passed on to broadcasters but fears of damaging the tourism economy with alarmist predictions took precedence and the warning was under-emphasized. Typical" (2004, ¶1). The inference clearly was that of the superiority of blogospherian communication speed, alertness, and values: Bloggers could've saved the lives the mainstream media let die. Le Meur's post was quoted and linked to at Boing Boing, a widely read and influential U.S. blog, where Le Meur drove the point home, stating, "We could have saved thousands of people's lives if information had moved

faster" (quoted in Jardin, 2004, ¶3). Daypop measured the Boing Boing post as the 14th most popular blog post, based on number of links to it, on December 29, 2004 (Top weblog posts 2004). Of course, knowledge of an earthquake does not correlate to knowledge of where and even if a tsunami will hit, as some comments to the Le Meur post pointed out. One in particular, Derek, noted that the tsunamis hit between 30 minutes to 2 hours after the earthquake, making three-hour foreknowledge of the tsunamis impossible (Derek 2004).

5. The virulent and distracting online debates criticized by Siegel turned out to be something in which he was deeply invested. He was suspended from writing for the *New Republic* after it was discovered he was involved in posting pseudonymous comments supporting himself and attacking his detractors in the magazine's online feedback forum (Foer, n.d.).

6. Epistemological debates duly noted.

References

Amanda. (2006, December 13). John McCain's war on blogs. ThinkProgress. Retrieved February 22, 2006, from http://thinkprogress.org/2006/12/13/mccain-war-on-blogs/.

Andrews, P. (2003). Is blogging journalism? [Electronic version]. *Nieman Reports* 57, 3, 63–64. Retrieved May 23, 2004, from http://www.nieman.harvard.edu/reports/03-3NRfall/V57N3.pdf.

Aspan, M. (2007, January 1). Costly gift from Microsoft becomes invite to blog. *New York Times*. Retrieved January 2, 2007, from Proquest database.

Baker, C. E. (2002). *Media, markets, and democracy*. New York: Cambridge University Press.

Balsamo, A. (1996). *Technologies of the gendered body: Reading cyborg women*. Durham, NC: Duke University Press.

Banet-Weiser, S. (2004). Surfin' the net: Children, parental obsolescence, and citizenship. In M. Sturken, D. Thomas, and S. J. Ball-Rokeach, (Eds.), (2004). *Technological visions: The hopes and fears that shape new technologies*, 270–292. Philadelphia: Temple University Press.

Barlow, J. P. (1996). A declaration of the independence of cyberspace. Electronic Frontier Foundation. Retrieved December 4, 2004, from http://homes.eff.org/~barlow/Declaration-Final.html.

Bauder, D. (2005, February 11). CNN executive Eason Jordan quits. ABC News. Retrieved February 12, 2005, from http://abcnews.go.com/Entertainment/wireStory?id=492860.

Bennett, Lance W., and Robert M. Entman. (2000). Mediated politics: an introduction. In L. Bennett and B. Entman (Eds.), *Mediated politics. Communication and the future of democracy*, 1–33. Cambridge: Cambridge University Press.

Bennett, W. L. (2004). Political communication, *Citizenship and democracy: From the mass society to personal information networks*. Presentation slide show distributed by author.

———. (2003). *News: The politics of illusion*, fifth edition. San Francisco: Longman.

Blood, R. (2002). *The weblog handbook: Practical advice on creating and maintaining your blog.* Cambridge: Perseus Publishing.

Brouwer, D. C. (2001). "ACT-ing UP in Congressional Hearings." In Robert Asen and Daniel C. Brouwer (Eds.), *Counterpublics and the State.* Albany: State University of New York Press.

Brown, H. (2003, April 26). Netlines. *British Medical Journal* 326, 7395:938. Retrieved February 23, 2004, from Proquest database.

Carey, J. W. (1989). *Communication as culture: Essays on media and society.* Boston: Unwin Hyman.

Cole, J. (2004, September). Surveying the digital future: Year four. Ten years, ten trends. USC Annenberg School Center for the Digital Future. Retrieved September 25, 2004, from http://www.digitalcenter.org/pages/current_report.asp?intGlobalId=19.

Couldry, N., and J. Curran. (2003). Introduction. In N. Couldry and J. Curran (Eds.), *Contesting Media Power.* Lanham, MD: Rowman and Littlefield.

Derek. (2004, December 30). I'm rather skeptical. . . . Loïc Le Meur blog. Retrieved January 31, 2007, from http://www.loiclemeur.com/english/2004/12/a_blogger_was_a.html#c3278088

Diana. (2004, December 29). I just read . . . Loïc Le Meur blog. Retrieved January 31, 2007, from http://www.loiclemeur.com/english/2004/12/a_blogger_was_a.html#c3274589.

DiMaggio, P., E. Hargittai, W. R. Neuman, and J. P. Robinson. (2001). Social implications of the Internet. *Annual Review of Sociology* 27:307–336.

Drezner, D., and H. Farrell. (2004, July). The power and politics of blogs. Presentation to the 2004 American Political Science Association. Retrieved August 15, 2004, from http://www.utsc.utoronto.ca/~farrell/blogpaperfinal.pdf.

Dunham, R. S. (2005, October 19). Miers: More Foes, but More Fans, Too. [Electronic version] *BusinessWeek.com.* Retrieved October 19, 2005, from 2.businessweek.com/print/bwdaily/dnflash/oct2005/nf20051019_3684_db038.htm?chan=db.

Easlea, B. (1983). *Fathering the unthinkable: Masculinity, scientists, and the nuclear arms race.* London: Pluto Press Limited.

Embrey, T. R. (2002, December). You blog, we blog. *Teacher Librarian* 30(2):7. Retrieved February 23, 2004, from Proquest.

Fillion, R. (2004, November 1). Tracking the blogs. [Electronic version] *Rocky Mountain News*, p. 1B. Retrieved February 10, 2005, from LexisNexis database.

Fleetwood, N. R. (2006). Failing narratives, initiating technologies: Hurricane Katrina and the production of a media weather event. *American Quarterly* 58(3):767–789.

Foer, F. (n.d.). An apology to our readers. *The New Republic Online.* Retrieved February 22, 2007, from http://www.tnr.com/suspended.mhtml.

Fraser, N. (1992). Rethinking the public sphere: A contribution to the critique of actually existing democracy. In C. Calhoun (Ed.), *Habermas and the public sphere*, 109–142. Cambridge, MA: The MIT Press.

From blogs to cicadas: 2004's most looked-up words. (2004, December 1). [Electronic version] *Boston Herald*. Retrieved December 14, 2004, from LexisNexis database.

Gamson, W. A. (2001). Promoting political engagement. In W. L. Bennett and R. M. Entman (Eds.), *Mediated politics: Communication in the future of democracy*, 56–74. New York: Cambridge University Press.

Gill, K. E. (2004). How can we measure the influence of the blogosphere? Presentation to The Thirteenth International World Wide Web conference, Workshop on the Weblogging Ecosystem: Aggregation, Analysis and Dynamics. New York, May 18, 2004. Retrieved May 25, 2004, from http://faculty.washington.edu/kegill/pub/www2004_blogosphere_gill.pdf.

Gitlin, T. (1998). Public sphere or public sphericules? In T. Liebes and J. Curran (Eds.), *Media, ritual and identity*, 168–174 New York: Routledge.

Glaser, M. (2003, November 18). Media critics rave (and kvetch) about the Internet's impact. *Online Journalism Review*. Retrieved November 23, 2003, from http://www.ojr.org/ojr/glaser/1069197815.php.

———. (2004a, February 11). "Watchblogs" put the political press under the microscope. *Online Journalism Review*. Retrieved February 16, 2004, from http://ojr.org/ojr/glaser/1076465317.php.

———. (2004b, May 11). Scholars discover weblogs pass test as mode of communication. *Online Journalism Review*. Retrieved May 25, 2004, from http://www.ojr.org/ojr/glaser/1084325287.php.

Glover, D., and M. Essel. (2006, December 3). New on the web: Business as usual [Electronic version]. *New York Times*. Retrieved January 12, 1007, from http://www.nytimes.com/2006/12/03/opinion/03glover.html?ex=1322802000&en=e8518da36332c7c9&ei=5088&partner=rssnyt&emc=rss.

Greenwald, G. (2006, July 1). Conservative pundits reveal murderous plot by the Travel Section of the NYT! Unclaimed Territory. Retrieved January 12, 2006, from http://glenngreenwald.blogspot.com/2006/07/conservative-pundits-reveal-murderous.html.

Grossman, L. (2004, June 21). Meet Joe Blog. *Time* 163(25):65–70.

Hargittai, E. (2006). Just a Pretty Face(book)? What College Students Actually Do Online. Presentation at Beyond Broadcast 2006, May 12–13, 2006, Berkman Center for Internet and Society at Harvard Law School. Retrieved June 14, 2006, from http://results.webuse.org/uic06/HargittaiBeyondBroadcast06Web.pdf.

———. (2007). Content diversity online: Myth or reality? In Philip Napoli (Ed.), *Media diversity and localism: Meanings and metrics*, 349–362. Mahwah, NJ: Lawrence Erlbaum.

———. (2004). The changing online landscape: From free-for-all to commercial gatekeeping. [Electronic version]. In Peter Day and Doug Schuler (Eds.), *Community practice in the network society: Local actions/global interaction*, 66–76. New York: Routledge. Retrieved September 19, 2007, from http://www.eszter.com/research/c03-onlinelandscape.html.

Hartley, J. (2006, October 23). Facilitating the creative citizen. *On Line Opinion*. Retrieved February 22, 2007, from http://www.onlineopinion.com.au/view.asp?article=5036.

Heaton, H. (2004, October 8). A method to Martha's madness and other Answer Man musings. [Electronic version]. *Plain Dealer*, Friday! section, p. 3. Retrieved February 12, 2005, from Lexis-Nexis database.

Hensarling, J. (2005, November 2). Online freedom of speech act. *Congressional Record*. [Electronic version]. Retrieved January 21, 2007, from http://frwebgate2.access.gpo.gov/cgi-bin/waisgate .cgi?WAISdocID=764238251307+1+0+0&WAISaction=retrieve

Hyde, M. J. (1982). The debate concerning technology. In Michael Hyde (Ed.), *Communication, philosophy and the technological age*, 1–10. Tuscaloosa, AL: University of Alabama Press.

Institute for Politics, Democracy and the Internet. (2004, March). Political Influentials Online in the 2004 Presidential Campaign. Retrieved March 3, 2004, from http://www.ipdi.org/ UploadedFiles/political%20influentials.pdf.

Jardin, X. (2004, December 27). Tsunami blog coverage: update. Boing Boing. Retrieved January 31, 2007, from http://www.boingboing.net/2004/12/27/tsunami_blog_coverag.html.

Jensen, M. (2003). A brief history of weblogs. [Electronic version]. *Columbia Journalism Review* 42(3):22. Retrieved May 23, 2004, from Proquest database.

Jones, S. E. (2006). *Against technology: From the Luddites to neo-luddism*. New York: Routledge.

Kennedy School of Government Case Program. (2004). "Big media" meets the "bloggers": Coverage of Trent Lott's remarks at Strom Thurmond's birthday party. Cambridge: Harvard College.

Lasica, J. D. (2003). Blogs and journalism need each other. [Electronic version]. *Nieman Reports* 57(3):70–74. Retrieved May 23, 2004 from http://www.nieman.harvard.edu/reports/03-3NRfall/ V57N3.pdf.

———. (2004, May 5). Surf's down as more netizens turn to RSS for browsing. *Online Journalism Review*. Retrieved May 11, 2004, from http://ojr.org/ojr/workplace/1083806402.php.

Lazarsfeld, P. F., and R. K. Merton. (1949). Mass communication, popular taste and organized social action. In W. Schramm (Ed.), *Mass communications*, 459–480. Urbana: University of Illinois Press.

Le Meur, L. (2004, December 28). A blogger was alerted three hours before the tsunamis. Loïc Le Meur blog. Retrieved January 31, 2007, from http://www.loiclemeur.com/english/2004/ 12/a_blogger_was_a.html.

Lennon, S. (2003). Blogging journalists invite outsiders' reporting in. [Electronic version]. *Nieman Reports* 57(3):76–79. Retrieved May 23, 2004 from http://www.nieman.harvard.edu/reports/03-3NRfall/V57N3.pdf.

Leo, J. (2004, July 19). Blogging the watchdogs. *U.S. News and World Report* 137(2):6.

Lessig, L. (2001). The Internet under siege. [Electronic version]. *Foreign Policy* 127:56–66.

LexisNexis. (2005a, February 12). Search of online database by author for string "Iraq" + "explosives" in General News, Major Papers, full text, date range 10/24/04–11/05/04, publication title: New York Times.

———. (2005b, February 12). Search of online database by author for string "Iraq" + "explosives" in General News, Major Papers, full text, date range 10/24/04–11/05/04, publication title: USA Today.

———. (2005c, February 12). Search of online database by author for string "Iraq" + "explosives" in General News, Major Papers, full text, date range 10/24/04–11/05/04, publication title: Washington Post.

———. (2005d, February 12). Search of online database by author for string "Kerry" + "debate" + "cheat" in General News, Major Papers, full text, date range 07/20/04–11/05/04.

———. (2005e, February 12). Search of online database by author for string "Kerry" + "gun" in General News, Major Papers, full text, date range 07/20/04–11/05/04.

———. (2005f, February 12). Searches of online database by author for string "Niger" + "document" + "fake" or "Niger" + "document" + "forge" in General News, Major Papers, full text, date range 07/20/04–11/05/04.

———. (2005g, February 12). Search of online database by author for string "Sandy Berger" in General News, Major Papers, full text, date range 07/20/04–11/05/04, publication title: New York Times.

———. (2005h, February 12). Search of online database by author for string "Sandy Berger" in General News, Major Papers, full text, date range 07/20/04–11/05/04, publication title: USA Today.

———. (2007, March 25). Search of online database by author for string "Bush" + "medals" + "guard" in General News, Major Papers, full text, date range 07/20/04–11/05/04, publication title: USA Today.

Lizza, R. (2005, February 4). The outsiders. *The New Republic Online*. Retrieved February 10, 2005 from http://www.tnr.com/doc.mhtml?pt=GC1nbWBk1KawulpqPq3uRR%3D%3D.

Lyons, D. (2005, Nov. 14). Attack of the blogs. [Electronic version] *Forbes*, 176, 10, p. 128. Retrieved October 31, 2005, from http://www.forbes.com/business/forbes/2005/1114/128 .html?_requestid=1050.

MacDougall, R. (2006). The wire devils: Pulp thrillers, the telephone, and action at a distance in the building of a nation. *American Quarterly* 58(3):715–741.

Marshall, J. M. (2004a, September 19). In recent days . . . Talking points memo. Retrieved February 8, 2005, from http://www.talkingpointsmemo.com/archives/week_2004_09_19.php#003506.

———. (2004b, September 22). In Newsweek this afternoon . . . Talking points memo. Retrieved February 8, 2005, from http://www.talkingpointsmemo.com/archives/week_2004_09_19.php#003506.

———. (2004c, October 24). This has been . . . Talking points memo. Retrieved February 8, 2005, from http://www.talkingpointsmemo.com/archives/003777.php.

———. (2004d, October 28). Game. Set. Match. Talking points memo. Retrieved February 8, 2005, from http://www.talkingpointsmemo.com/archives/week_2004_10_24.php#003835.

Marvin, C. (1990). *When old technologies were new: Thinking about electric communication in the late nineteenth century.* New York: Oxford University Press.

Mattelart, A. (1996). *The invention of communication.* Minneapolis: University of Minnesota Press.

McClintock, A. (1995). *Imperial leather: Race, gender and sexuality in the colonial contest.* New York: Routledge.

Miller, T. (2006). Gaming for beginners. *Games and Culture* 1:5–12.

Milutis, J. (2006). *Ether: The nothing that connects everything.* Minneapolis: University of Minnesota Press.

Moulitsas, M. (2004, August 23). Bush's medals. Daily Kos. Retrieved February 8, 2005, from http://www.dailykos.com/story/2004/8/23/113152/124.

Negroponte, N. (1995). *Being digital.* London: Hodder and Stoughton.

Noonan, P. (2004, November 4). So Much to savor. [Electronic version.] *Wall Street Journal.* Retrieved November 10, 2004, from LexisNexis database.

Nye, D. E. (1994). *American technological sublime.* Cambridge, MA: MIT Press.

———. (2006). Technology and the production of difference. *American Quarterly* 58(3):597–618.

Outing, S. (2003, October 15). Advancing citizen blogs on news sites. Editor and Publisher. com. Retrieved May 23, 2004, from http://www.editorandpublisher.com/eandp/columns/stopthepresses_display.jsp?vnu_content_id=2002027.

Pax, S. (2003). Salam Pax: The clandestine diary of an ordinary Iraqi. New York: Grove Press.

Peim, C. (2005). Blog-gate. [Electronic version] *Columbia Journalism Review.* Retrieved on February 17, 2007, from http://www.cjr.org/issues/2005/1/pein-blog.asp.

People of the Year: Bloggers. (2004, December 30). ABC News. Retrieved February 12, 2005, from http://abcnews.go.com/WNT/PersonOfWeek/story?id=372266andpage=1.

Perseus Development Corporation. (2003, November 26). The blogging iceberg: Of 4.12 million hosted weblogs, most little seen, quickly abandoned. Retrieved June 17, 2004, from http://www.perseus.com/blogsurvey/thebloggingiceberg.html.

Person of the year. (2006, December 25/2007, January 1). *Time* (168):26.

Pew Internet and American Life Project. (2002, September 15). One year later: September 11 and the Internet. Retrieved June 16, 2004, from http://www.pewinternet.org/pdfs/PIP_9-11_Report .pdf.

———. (2004, October 27). The Internet and democratic debate. Retrieved October 27, 2004, from http://www.pewInternet.org/PPF/r/141/report_display.asp.

———. (2005a, January 12). Data memo: The state of blogging. Retrieved January 12, 2005, from http://www.pewinternet.org/PPF/r/144/report_display.asp.

———. (2005b, January 25). A decade of adoption: How the internet has woven itself into American life. Retrieved January 29, 2005, from http://www.pewinternet.org/PPF/r/148/report_display .asp.

———. (2006, July 19). Bloggers: A portrait of the internet's new storytellers. Retrieved July 22, 2006, from http://www.pewinternet.org/pdfs/PIP%20Bloggers%20Report%20July%2019%20200 6.pdf.

Phil. (2004, December 24). Choquant. . . . Philsland. Retrieved January 31, 2007, from http:// philsland.blogs.com/philsland/2004/12/choquant.html.

Ratcliffe, M., and J. Lebkowsky. (2004). What is extreme democracy? Retrieved August 23, 2004, from http://www.extremedemocracy.com/about.html.

Regan, T. (2003). Weblogs threaten and inform traditional journalism. [Electronic version]. *Nieman Reports* 57(3):68–70. Retrieved May 23, 2004 from http://www.nieman.harvard.edu/ reports/03-3NRfall/V57N3.pdf.

Reynolds, G. (2004a, July 20). What's in Sandy Berger's Pants? InstaPundit.com. Retrieved February 10, 2005, from http://instapundit.com/archives/016650.php.

———. (2004b, August 28). W a Lot of People Emailed Me . . . InstaPundit.com. Retrieved February 10, 2005, from http://instapundit.com/archives/017430.php.

———. (2004c, September 7). Drudge Offers a Kerry Gun Flip-Flop Report: "Kerry Cosponsored Bill Banning Gun He Waves". InstaPundit.com. Retrieved February 8, 2005, from http:// instapundit.com/archives/017663.php.

———. (2004d, October 26). I've Never Read a Code of Journalistic Ethics. InstaPundit.com. Retrieved February 10, 2005, from http://instapundit.com/archives/018678.php.

Richards, A. (2004, May 20). Interview. *The Larry King Show*. Transcript retrieved May 25, 2004, from http://www.cnn.com/TRANSCRIPTS/0405/20/lkl.00.html.

Robins, K., and F. Webster. (1999). *Times of the technoculture: From the information society to the virtual life*. London: Routledge.

Rushkoff, D. (1994). *Cyberia: Life in the trenches of hyperspace*. London: Harper/Collins.

Sanger, D. (2004, October 26). Iraq explosives become issue in campaign. [Electronic version] *New York Times*. Retrieved February 21, 2007, from Proquest database.

Schwartz, J. (2005, January 3). Myths run wild in blog tsunami debate [Electronic version]. *New York Times*. Retrieved January 31, 2007 from http://www.nytimes.com/2005/01/03/international/worldspecial4/03bloggers.html?ei=5088&en=199bb268d4abd66e&ex=1262494800&partner=rssnyt&pagewanted=print&position=

Sconce, J. (2000). *Haunted media: Electronic presence from telegraphy to television*. Durham, NC: Duke University Press.

Scott, D. T. (2007). Pundits in muckrakers' clothing: Political blogs and the 2004 presidential election. In M. Tremayne (Ed.), *Blogging, citizenship and the future of media*, 39–57. New York: Routledge.

Seigel, L. (2007). Blogofascism and the quality of Internet discourse. *New Republic Online*. Retrieved August 23, 2006, from http://www.tnr.com/doc.mhtml?i=20060807&s=diarist080706.

Seper, C. (2004, October 7). For good or ill, blogs make waves. [Electronic version.] *Plain Dealer*, A1. Retrieved February 12, 2005, from LexisNexis database.

Simon, L. (2004). *Dark light: Electricity and anxiety from the telegraph to the x-ray*. Orlando, FL: Harcourt Books.

Spigel, L. (2001). *Welcome to the dreamhouse: Popular media and postwar suburbs*. Durham, NC: Duke University Press.

Starr, W. (2004, August 23). George W. Bush was photographed wearing a ribbon he did not earn. Democratic Underground. Retrieved February 8, 2005, from http://www.democraticunderground.com/discuss/duboard.php?az=view_allandaddress=132x654437.

Steinberg, J., and B. Carter. (2005, January 11). CBS dismisses 4 over broadcast on Bush service. [Electronic version.] *The New York Times*, section A, p. 1. Retrieved February 10, 2005, from LexisNexis database.

Stern, S. E. (1999). Addiction to technologies: Asocial psychological perspective of Internet addiction. *CyberPsychology and Behavior* 2:419–424.

Stern, S. E., and A. D. Handel. (2001). Sexuality and mass media: The historical context of psychology's reaction to sexuality on the Internet. *The Journal of Sex Research* 38(4):283–291.

Strupp, J. (2005, February 11). Gannon' interview: No Plame subpoena, no tie to White House, he says. [Electronic version.] *Editor and Publisher*. Retrieved February 13, 2005, from http://199.249.170.220/eandp/news/article_display.jsp?vnu_content_id=1000799182.

Thomsen, E. B. (2002). Internet column: Blogging, anyone? *Collection Building* 21(2):76. Retrieved February 24, 2004, from Proquest database.

Top weblog posts. (2004, December 29). Daypop. Retrieved January 31, 2007, from http://mon.daypop.com/archive/posts/2004/12/29/1845.

Unsworth, J. M. (2004). The next wave: Liberation technology. *The Chronicle of Higher Education* 50:21. Retrieved December 9, 2004, from http://www.hewlett.org/NR/rdonlyres/3888CB00-0689-4680-8F7A-26D2E982FB75/0/chronicleunsworth.pdf.

Vary, A. B. (2006, December 29). The entertainers: YouTube. *Entertainment Weekly* 913/914: 58–59.

Wallsten, P. (2004a, September 12). The race to the White House; No disputing it: Blogs are major players. [Electronic version.] *Los Angeles Times*, section A, p. 22. Retrieved February 10, 2005, from LexisNexis database.

———. (2004b, September 18). The race to the White House; GOP activist made allegations on CBS memos. [Electronic version.] *Los Angeles Times*, section A, p. 18. Retrieved February 10, 2005, from LexisNexis database.

Warner, M. (2002). *Publics and counterpublics*. New York: Zone.

Wasserstein, B. (2004, September 19). Bloggers' "moment" doesn't make for a revolution [Electronic version.] *Los Angeles Times*, section M, p. 1. Retrieved February 10, 2005, from LexisNexis database.

Weintraub, D. (2004, January 14). Politics and beyond: An inside look at The California Insider. *Online Journalism Review*. Retrieved June 12, 2004, from http://ojr.org/ojr/workplace/1074119409.php.

Weiss, J. (2004, May 10). Blogs colliding with traditional media: Convention credentials expected for Web logs. [Electronic version.] *The Boston Globe*. Retrieved February 10, 2005, from LexisNexis database.

Welch, M., M. Jensen, and J. Reeves. (2003). Blogworld and its gravity. [Electronic version.] *Columbia Journalism Review* 42(3):20–26. Retrieved May 23, 2004, from Proquest database.

Whelan, D. (2003). In a fog about blogs. [Electronic version.] *American Demographics* 25(6):22. Retrieved May 23, 2004, from Proquest database.

Wretchard. (2006, December 28). The blogosphere at war. The Belmont Club. Retrieved February 22, 2007, from http://fallbackbelmont.blogspot.com/2006/12/blogosphere-at-war.html.

Williams, L. (2003, October 10). The blogger as citizen journalist. Cadence90. Retrieved November 24, 2003, from http://www.cadence90.com/blogs/2003_10_01_Nixon_archives.html#106580374740640747.

Williams, Rosalind. (2004). Afterword: An historian's view on the network society. In Manuel Castells (Ed.), *The Network Society: A Cross-cultural Perspective*, 432–448. Cheltenham, UK: Edward Elgar Publishing Limited.

Winston, B. (1998). *Media and technology: A history from the telegraph to the Internet*. New York: Routledge.

———. (2006). *Messages: Free expression, media and the west from Gutenberg to Google*. New York: Routledge.

12 Al Jazeera English: An Interview with Hassan Ibrahim

Nathalie Magnan, Megan Boler, and Andréa Schmidt

Hassan Ibrahim is a "third-generation BBC-er" and Sudanese journalist. Born in England, Hassan was raised in Saudi Arabia where he was a classmate of Osama bin Laden, attended American universities, and headed the BBC Arab News Service before joining Al Jazeera. During his career Hassan has covered a wide range of conflicts in the Middle East and Africa as well as in Panama, Nicaragua, Honduras, Colombia, and Brazil, making him a well-respected voice in the region. He covered the Iran-Iraq war as a young reporter, following the conflict from both the Iranian and the Iraqi fronts, a life-changing experience. While reporting on the wars in his native Sudan, he managed to make it twice to the Southern Sudan and Darfur. He was featured as Al Jazeera's senior producer in the major motion picture documentary *Control Room*, in 2004. The interview was conducted by telephone between Cairo and Toronto on April 30, 2007.

Context of Al Jazeera English

Al Jazeera English, launched in November 2006, is part of the Al Jazeera network. The network includes a documentary channel as well as the flagship channel Al Jazeera Arabic, which began broadcasting in 1996 and whose estimated viewership is now 100 million worldwide. Access to information through media and especially television is now understood as a central weapon in what can be called the "information war." Al Jazeera English, with an estimated 40 million viewers, is the first channel to broadcast in English from the Middle East and represents one player in a field of channels of varying ambitions, powers, and finances, many of which have been launched only in the past few years. Among these are France 24, the pan-European EuroNews, and Deutsche Welle, all of which are competing with the more established BBC World and CNN to deliver the news in corporate hotel rooms around the globe as well as in countries that do not have the means to own local news services.

Al Jazeera English is distributed worldwide via satellite and is available through satellite (and in some cases cable) in many European countries including Britain, as well as to many other countries around the globe. However, in the United States and Canada it is not available by satellite or by cable.

In 2004, the Canadian Radio-television and Telecommunications Commission (CRTC), Canada's broadcast regulatory body, approved cable distribution of Al Jazeera Arabic in Canada.

Figure 12.1
Hassan Ibrahim, *Control Room* (2004), directed by Jehane Noujaim

However, 500 of the over 1200 public submissions received by the CRTC during a highly polarized comments process complained that Al Jazeera Arabic "has a pattern of broadcasting hate propaganda during its programming, largely targeted at Jewish people." Although the CRTC itself found that the citations of hate speech were "dated" and cited by opponents "out of context"—and although Al Jazeera English is widely available in Israel—the CRTC placed conditions on the Arabic service of Al Jazeera that effectively make it impossible for cable operators to make the channel available in Canada. A cable operator broadcasting Al Jazeera would have to record and monitor the channel for anything deemed "abusive" under Canada's hate laws and allow enough of a delay to be able to delete the offending material before it hit the airwaves. Tony Burman, editor-in-chief of CBC news at the time of the decision, commented that "This type of 'condition' is like holding your local newsstand owners responsible for the editorial content of the 200 newspapers and magazines sold at their corner store." So far, Al Jazeera English has not made a new application to the CRTC for licensing in Canada.

In the United States, Al Jazeera English launched without reaching a deal with a major cable or satellite carrier. Spokespeople for the cable networks claimed it was because there was no significant U.S. market for the new channel. And although observers and insiders alike speculated that no major carrier wanted to take the political risk of broadcasting it because of perceptions of the Arabic language channel as "anti-West" and "pro-Al Qaeda," Nigel Parsons, managing director of Al Jazeera English, demurred. "The cable companies say, 'you're a news and current affairs channel and Americans aren't interested in news and current affairs'," he told the *Guardian*, in November 2005. By July 2007, Al Jazeera English had negotiated distribution with Globecast in the United States but had still not secured a deal with any large U.S. cable network. The *Financial Times* reported that Parsons "blamed political opposition to [Al Jazeera English's] Arabic sister company" for major cable networks' reluctance to carry it.

It is remarkable then that less than a year after Al Jazeera English launched, U.S. viewers make up 60 percent of the channel's online audience. Indeed, in the United States there are more than 20,000 subscribers to the channel online, where North American viewers left in the lurch by satellite companies and cable providers can access it by paying $8.95 a month for a subscription delivered by web-streaming services like JumpTV and VDC. The primary "free" accessible option for the high-bandwidth viewer is at present through YouTube (http://www.youtube.com/AlJazeeraEnglish). Indeed, YouTube offers the same level of access to Al Jazeera as it does to the BBC. However, what is accessible through YouTube is only a selection of TV broadcasts.

There is need for a detailed analysis of this information war and research about the question of the relationship between the "war on terror" and the control of public access to news sources like Al Jazeera. The following interview provides one window into the Al Jazeera network and its recent launch of Al Jazeera English.

Megan Boler: The first questions have to do with your sense of the vision of Al Jazeera—Al Jazeera Arabic and now Al Jazeera English. From your point of view, as you've joined the international team, what's the difference between Jazeera original and Jazeera English?

Hassan Ibrahim: I would say that language, with all its complexity, is the major difference. With language, on Al Jazeera English, you are targeting a different viewership, and that entails a lot of modifications to how news is presented and how programs are produced because you are reaching a wider audience. You are compelled in Al Jazeera English to cater to the four corners of the globe, because English is a global language, while with Al Jazeera Arabic, your main concern are the Arab-speaking populations either in the Arab world or in diaspora. That's the major difference.

And the other difference is: you'll find that with Al Jazeera English you are compelled to actually grapple with the various aspects of the English culture. You have Indian English–speaking culture, you have English English–speaking culture, Canadian, U.S., Australian, so that is a major concern, definitely.

MB: What is the relationship between the two "channels" or networks (I don't know how you refer to them)?

HI: The network—Al Jazeera is a network with various branches. Al Jazeera Arabic is part of it, Al Jazeera English is part, Jazeera Sports, Jazeera Children, and now Jazeera Documentaries. There is a board of directors that govern all these various outlets. Of course Al Jazeera Arabic and Al Jazeera English are twenty-four-hour news services, so there is coordination on various levels: the managerial level, editorial level, they exchange information, they exchange tapes, they exchange priorities, they sit and coordinate. You know, we are in the first stage of this coordination, so you have the teething pains and the culture differences, but it's getting there.

MB: Would you say that there are clearly defined agendas, or that the agendas of each aspect of the network are distinguishable from each other?

HI: I wouldn't say different agendas. I would say different approaches to news, different focuses. But the news remains the news. The priorities remain the same. Jazeera Arabic is mainly concerned with Arab issues, and other issues as well, but Jazeera English is claiming to be the voice of the South. And our aim is to enable people from the four corners of the globe to express their own problems, to express their own news, culture, and outlook equally on our channel. So while the first one is a news machine, the second one is claiming to be a multicultural platform.

MB: What is your vision of what Al Jazeera English does and could do?

HI: Al Jazeera English can be a very, very useful tool in reaching out to the outside world. I mean, this is an English-speaking Middle Eastern channel. The personnel come from various parts of the world, but it remains a Middle Eastern channel. I would really like the world to see the problems of the Middle East and the South mainly, India, the subcontinent, Africa, the Arab World and the rest in a different light, to see the complexities. I would like our bulletins and our programs to express that diversity. I worked for BBC for many years, but to be honest with you, I don't really see them scratching deeper than the surface, and I would like to go deeper than that.

MB: That's a good segue to this question. Al Jazeera is thought of by some as the "CNN of the Middle East," and many staff are coming from the BBC or even ABC [the Australian Broadcasting Corporation] like you were saying. How should we see this new entity of Al Jazeera English, and which format do you think Al Jazeera is or is not like?

HI: I don't like the term "CNN of the Middle East" because CNN is a private enterprise, but having said that, CNN sometimes appears to be the mouthpiece of the American administration or the American culture or the American people, in a sense. I see CNN as a very vibrant news outlet, but I don't see it as a generic model that I aspire to become. I aspire for Al Jazeera to become a true voice of the people, a place where diversity can be expressed freely and free of intervention of the attempts of some to use a news service to serve political goals. Having said that, Al Jazeera is not free of agendas and free of special interests. But because Jazeera is not a money-making operation—it doesn't aspire to make money, it aspires to make news and programs and is funded by the government of Qatar—we don't have various corporations pulling us left and right, and that's the element of stability in Al Jazeera that is very rare on CNN.

MB: Friends of Al Jazeera—in a statement one of us found online—write that "Al Jazeera is a case of empire writing back" and Nigel Parsons says, "We want to set a different news agenda." Could you tell us a little more about this new agenda setting?

HI: In terms of Al Jazeera, Friends of Jazeera does not represent Al Jazeera—it's basically a bunch of journalists from England and other places writing about us. And it's a very destructive Web site to be on, honestly, because some people are attacking and hiding behind the anonymity of the site, and people use pseudonyms for their input, and it does not really represent Al Jazeera at all. It is not a Jazeera site.

But the agenda of Al Jazeera International is to become the voice of the South. And that is our main aspiration. Is that an agenda? I don't know. It's not an agenda per se—we're reaching out. We're making people see what the South is really like.

That's all. That is all. It's as simple as that.

MB: We've heard that there was a debate over whether to call the new network Jazeera International or Jazeera English—and apparently the term *English* won out. Do you know what the substance of that debate was, and do you think the ultimate decision was significant?

HI: I believe it was a wise decision. Calling the English-speaking arm of Al Jazeera International in a way implies that the other was not, while Al Jazeera Arabic for the past ten years became one of the most influential brands in the world. And it is an international brand. So the name *international* stuck for the first few months, and then they decided that it is wise to call—since Al Jazeera had become a network and this was an English-speaking venture—to call it Al Jazeera English. It didn't take long at all, by the way; it wasn't a lengthy debate. It was just a meeting and then the name was decided.

MB: In your mind, does it say something about the perspective or presumed audience of the new network?

HI: It sure does, because it targets an English-speaking population.

MB: I don't know if you saw the *Frontline* program with Greg Barker, a PBS *Frontline* documentary on the "Arab media revolution." In it they were talking about the audience being 50 million people and primarily made up of English as a second language speakers. Is that correct?

HI: I didn't watch that.

MB: Do you know if the assumed audience is English as a second language speakers?

HI: Of course we're airing to the subcontinent, we're airing to Malaysia, Indonesia, parcels of Asia and Africa where English is a second language. And we have, I believe, a wide viewership in those parts, so the figure doesn't surprise me.

In the States we're not on cable yet, and not in Canada—in Canada it's just Internet. So that limits our broadcasts to countries where English is a first language.

MB: How would you say that journalists and producers of Jazeera English think about audience as they're coming up with content? More specifically, when you do your reporting and writing, who are you actually picturing as your audience? And how does that shape your stories, if at all?

HI: That's a brilliant question. For example, I did a six-part on Sudan. And I wanted to explain to the outside world the complexity of Sudan, of one million square miles, to an audience that is fairly illiterate about Sudan. They only know Darfur and the conflict in the South. So I wanted to show the diversity of that. So you need to be—not ultrasimplistic, but you have to stick to the basics, because people just don't know the Sudan, and take it from there. You should assume that your audience is not that educated about what you're writing about. That's why you should do more explaining—probably your packages must be longer, and your programs must concentrate more on fact. At the risk of sounding like an almanac or *National Geographic*, you have to really be careful to explain basics.

MB: I was just looking this morning at the views expressed on the Web site, the public comments. Do you tend to look at those? Are those a source of feedback that you . . .

HI: Religiously. Of course, religiously.

MB: What do you get from reading those?

HI: I get criticism, I get praise, I get suggestions, and I gauge the mood of the public and the concerns of certain elements and people of specific cultural backgrounds. I'm trying to cater and be clearer and more succinct in what I present and write.

MB: It's really a striking cross section of people. I mean the international representation of those comments and also the political perspectives there was a much wider range than I would have expected.

In addition to those comments on the Web site, would you want to say anything else about the international reception of your stories, or of the network?

HI: Let me give you an example. When I did my report on Sudan, the last episode was aired in late January. And I received personal phone calls from people and places as far away as New Zealand, Israel, South Africa, the Arab world, India. It was just amazing.

MB: How do you see the shift in which, I understand, Israel's satellite provider YESTV dropped BBC World in favor of the newly launched Al Jazeera English?

HI: Al Jazeera is the favorite channel of the Israelis—people don't realize that. I have been to universities and various institutions of learning in Israel. They do like Al Jazeera because a lot of Israelis know Arabic. Even before the launch of the national channel. And they also like Jazeera because they believe it tells the truth—many Israelis who are very anti-Arab like Al Jazeera because they believe it is more truthful than their own news media.

MB: I understand that there are some new English news channels that appeared this year. Among them are France 24 and the German DW World. Are you aware of those?

HI: Yeah. I'm not that aware of them but I know they exist.

MB: I'm just wondering if you have any thoughts on what might be considered an "air-wave battle to capture an English-speaking public"—the competition among different networks for this audience?

HI: In a way we're unique because we're a Middle Eastern–based English-speaking network. The fierce competition would come from Al Arabiya, our major Arabic language competitor, and they are launching a Middle Eastern–based English-language satellite channel this year.

The competition is there, there is a battle for the airwaves. And I believe that is good, because when you think you've "cornered" a concept, complacency follows.

MB: What do you expect to be the differences in content and perspective between Al Arabiya and Al Jazeera?

HI: Al Arabiya as a news channel has all the ingredients of success, but they are very limited by the restrictions of Saudi media—conservative, and they cannot rock the boat. As far as Arabs are concerned, it's always safe to talk about Israel, South Africa, Barbados, and the moon, but not their own countries. [laughs] But on Al Arabiya, you have that Wahabi element where certain topics cannot be expressed, and you have the interests of Saudi Arabia as a huge country with distinct political interests, while Qatar is a small country, and they don't have the same concerns of Saudi Arabia. That's why the feeling is higher in Al Jazeera than in Al Arabiya. And that is our major point of strength.

Having said that, again, complacency can really hurt Al Jazeera if people say, "Oh, Al Arabiya can never compete with them." Of course they can! It requires us to be better and finish our—to be more prepared, and move forward.

MB: In this documentary that I mentioned I was watching last night, the channel Al Hurrah . . .

HI: Washington-based.

MB: They claim they have 20 million viewers. And in the documentary it says well, no, at best they have a tenth of that. Do you have any questions about what they're trying to do and/or whether it's related at all to the rapid response unit that the United States engages to monitor international media?

HI: The problem with the U.S.-based media, especially—in the past, in the '60s and the '70s, they had the Voice of America in Arabic. And they thought it was successful, but they could never compete with the BBC World Service. And Al Hurrah shot itself in the foot from the first day of broadcasting. They launched the channel, and the first broadcast was a speech by George Bush. The message that sent to the Arab world was, "We are the official spokesperson of the American administration." And they will never recover from that. Never.

MB: Do you or do people at Al Jazeera—are you aware of the rapid response unit, or do you care that the military and the U.S. administration is doing this kind of monitoring of media?

HI: Oh yeah. We monitor media as well. We monitor about 140 channels as part of our monitoring service, so everybody monitors the news. The largest monitoring service in the world is the BBC monitoring service, which is larger than CNN. It's a huge operation, outside London. It's much more ambitious than any rapid response unit the American Army would ever think of creating because they've existed since the 1930s, since World War II.

As far as I'm concerned, the rapid response unit of the United States is also constrained by the ideological cloud over their eyes. If you cannot be objective, then you cannot really monitor, because you will be seeing things, but you'll be seeing them through your ideological glasses. You will not be able to objectively see things. And that's the problem with all American rapid response units.

MB: Speaking of American responses, in this PBS *Frontline* news show that I mentioned, which is titled, "War of Ideas: Inside the Arab Media Revolution," the narrator and journalist Greg Barker says "Al Jazeera is used by extremist groups." Do you have a comment on that *Frontline* representation?

HI: I was asked the same question by ABC New York, and I said proudly, "We are a news medium. Of course there is a political message that can be aired, and is worthy of being broadcast and viewed." The United States tried to vilify Al Jazeera for airing Bin Laden tapes. Yet they were buying the same tapes and airing parts of them at the cost of 100,000 dollars a minute. It's absurd. The accusation is simply absurd, because if we don't air them, it's censorship; if we air them, its being used by the extremists. It's an unwinnable war of words. We evaluate news on newsworthiness. And that's the bottom line.

MB: I'm going to shift now to some questions about the format and delivery of Jazeera English. Do you see the primary audience of Jazeera English being via broadcast or Web-based delivery? And how does this affect distribution of the network?

HI: Well it's broadcast. But certain countries will not allow it on the air, and there it's Internet. And no, it doesn't affect our delivery at all.

MB: One thing that Jazeera English does, one could argue, is to normalize the Middle East for the Western viewer as, among other things, a feasible business location or vacation destination through the format, the ads, and the news format. This choice of streamlining certainly allows for a recognizable form for the global viewer. In terms of representing a new format, Al Jazeera English may not be as radical as the early CNN or the new MTV, but it does depart from the classical format in many subtle ways. And I wonder if you have any comments about the selected format for delivery?

HI: To be honest with you, it was born of necessity. Our main ambition was to—yes we have our own Web site, and we would love that our broadcast would be received on cable and people would log on to our Web site, just like any other news channel. But we've been forced to streamline our broadcasts to avoid a lot of censorship of Al Jazeera in certain Western countries, the United States and Canada, where certain lobbies are basically blocking Al Jazeera from being on cable. And that is really regrettable, but we've been forced to do that. Maybe it's a blessing in disguise, because the future is the Internet, you know, so if people are used to logging on to Al Jazeera, to me that is not all that bad.

MB: I'm interested in this phrase "forced to." I'm outraged that in Canada they allow Fox News but not Al Jazeera—and really, it's not a matter of allowing, it's actually permitted to broadcast Al Jazeera, but the lobby was so strong that no channel is willing to pick it up. So when you say "forced to do that" do you mean "forced to use a Web-based delivery"?

HI: Yes.

MB: One of us writing the questions said, to play devil's advocate, "Why choose such a well-tested format when the content of Al Jazeera, at its best"—in her opinion—"is when it's irreverent and a little bit outside of the usual"?

HI: Well, irreverent and outside of the usual sells. I mean why would you want to be—our journalism has always been described as irreverent, and I'm very proud of that stigma! Why would you want to be just like everybody else? What's the point?

MB: Another way to put that question is "Does cross-cultural communication—to the extent that Al Jazeera English is attempting cross-cultural communication—have to look like an American format?" Does it have to have that familiar feel for certain audience members?

HI: Well, you need to broadcast to people the easiest way to ensure accessibility. Whether that is Internet, cable, satellite depends on the country. It's cheaper for an African to go to the neighborhood club where there's one satellite dish and people are watching Al Jazeera International. Or people of means can have a satellite dish in their own home. So certain countries have cable, and we have deals to broadcast Al Jazeera through cable in Indonesia, Malaysia, Philippines, but in places where we are banned, we use the format where people log onto the Internet alone. They can log on and watch Al Jazeera streamlined—why not?

MB: Any comments about blogs and what role they play for you in shaping news agendas?

HI: Bloggers for me are a breath of fresh air. They're quick, they're daring, but unfortunately in most cases aren't very reliable. We stick to our policy of double-sourcing news items. With a blogger, they can write serious news of Elvis being spotted in a parking lot in Pennsylvania. So you have to be very careful, you need to sift through plenty and plenty of bloggers to get a news item right.

Still, some of the blogs are really more respectable and more in depth than major newspapers and publications and news agencies. I use them a lot.

MB: Do you have any thoughts on "OhMyNews" in South Korea? It's a show based on citizen journalism—they've corralled hundreds of citizen journalists to produce content for this site.

HI: Oh yeah. I like all innovations. But—if they write analysis, that's fine. But when they post the news, I just fear that it will be an explosion of innuendo and rumors and the fantastic . . . that we'll fall into the trap of one of these bloggers to our detriment. Still, any news outlet, any utilization of the Internet to promote openness and promote free access is good.

MB: Picking up on the question of the feel, of the sort of style of these different formats, Al Jazeera has a grassroots, trans-roots, alternative tone at times, especially through the jingles, the little promo videos. How would you describe the difference between Jazeera English and other grassroots media?

HI: Well I can only compare Jazeera English to Jazeera Arabic, because they represent two branches of the same organization. I find the jingles on Al Jazeera English are faster, the pace is quicker, probably because some of the editors and some of the designers come from very refined technical backgrounds, while on the Arabic side, I find it a little bit sluggish. But now that we are a network, I believe both sides will benefit from each other. As far as other news, grassroots outlets, I'm not that cognizant of a major difference, really.

MB: I don't know if you'll have thoughts about this next question then. Is Jazeera consciously co-opting the feel of those jingles to make it appear grassroots, or is there actually a commitment from the network or the journalists to be accountable to people's movements in the reporting, to broadcast citizen journalism? In other words, is there just a feel, or . . .

HI: That's a very difficult question, because again it goes right to the heart of our message. Our message is to represent people, whether they are individuals or movements or political entities, but you would be risking your journalistic integrity if you appear sympathetic to a particular point of view or an angle from which you represent the cause, because you'll find other organizations, also grassroots, also basically batting for the same team, disagreeing with you. So you need to maintain your objectivity. Jingles should represent a meaning that is acceptable by all, rather than a meaning that is adopted by a specific group or groups.

MB: How do you define *independent media*, and is that a term that you would use to describe Jazeera English?

HI: Independent media . . . oh my god! That's so difficult. Bloggers are probably the only independent media providers in the world. Because they're basically individuals or a group of individuals who are using a very affordable means to broadcast a message.

But it's different. And when you say Jazeera is not an independent network, than it sounds pejorative, you know? And I don't mean that. It's just difficult to define what is independent media.

MB: Jazeera Arabic has been known for integrating feedback along the lines of citizen journalism, for example providing people with phones to report. Do you have any comments about this new hybrid form that combines classic TV with Web-based digital media?

HI: It's a revolution. It's a revolution because for the first time an average human being walking down the streets of Jakarta, New York, or Khartoum, or Darfur can actually pick up the phone and dial a number and report what they see—you're recruiting journalists from all over the world, people who know nothing about the secrets of the trade, of the industry, but they just saw something, and they want to report it. And that's a revolution, when you have millions and millions of reporters around the world.

MB: What role is Al Jazeera English playing in this hybrid news broadcast streaming?

HI: Al Jazeera English is going through some teething pains—I mean we just launched in November 2006, so give us some time. Hopefully when we're fully operational and we have our 24-hour service, we'll start perfecting our techniques and our message and take it from there.

MB: I think it is already. It's certainly having a big impact on most of the audience I've talked to.

What sort of relationship do you—or Al Jazeera—cultivate with political movements, particularly those in the Arab world who make use of mobile phone video, photos, home video, to supplement your news production? What relationship do you see cultivated there?

HI: Well, from my own experience with Jazeera Arabic, I can tell you about Bahrain for example. In Bahrain, for a very long time, we weren't allowed to operate, and prior to 2000, before the reconciliation between the royal family and the opposition, there were lots of demonstrations, people were imprisoned, tortured, and we had no access to that. So the opposition in Bahrain would smuggle tapes to us, and we would air them. That's one example.

In terms of Saudi Arabia, kingdom of silence, we had the first footage of demonstrations inside Saudi Arabia, again from political activists who smuggled tapes to us. It is not a structural relationship, where there is a department called "Department for Foreign Movements," but I mean we encourage people from various organizations and individuals and movements to send us their footage.

Having said that, you have to sift through it and authenticate its content. Or sometimes exercise some sort of editorial authority, because some of the stuff is really gruesome; you cannot show on television decapitated heads and all that nonsense. And sometimes, some tapes are clearly doctored. So it's not always safe to have a relationship with a political entity.

MB: Is Jazeera English using that kind of relationship to sources in the same way as Jazeera Arabic?

HI: I believe we haven't come across that yet. I mean we just launched in November.

MB: So what you were speaking about just has to do with Al Jazeera Arabic?

HI: Well, with Al Jazeera as an organization. I don't know what the policy of Al Jazeera English will be.

MB: It's a huge question of what constitutes accuracy and objectivity. I've been talking to different journalists, as I mentioned to you, like Amy Goodman and Deepa Fernandez. But given the risks of how Al Jazeera can be perceived, as the guy in the documentary that I quoted to you shows, how does Jazeera make decisions on sources and content in terms of the political perception?

HI: It can take hours to answer that! In a nutshell, when we evaluate the political content of the message, you need to satisfy certain criteria. Number one: newsworthiness. Authenticity. Value to the audience. I mean if someone sent to me a report about a mosque collapsing in a remote village in Thailand, it wouldn't really be on top of my agenda ahead of a Bin Laden or a Zawahiri tape. But even a Bin Laden tape or Zawahiri tape is screened for political worthiness. We have at least ten or twelve Bin Laden tapes that were not fit for broadcast because they contained no political message whatsoever; it's the same rantings and ravings and a few lines of poetry and advice—so you don't broadcast that. There is no value, there is nothing new in that.

When you deal with the Palestinian Arab-Israeli conflict, the pivotal topic for the Middle East, again you have to exercise editorial control and air what is newsworthy worldwide, rather than a news item that would be fit for a domestic Palestinian agenda. I wouldn't worry that much about a cabinet reshuffle in the Sudan because that happens every other weekend, but I would worry about the Sudanese government's response to the UN over the issue of Darfur, for example. That type of thing—you have to exercise your judgment based on certain criteria.

MB: Moving now to some questions about content: since Jazeera English hardly speaks of the region in which it is produced, how would you describe the position Jazeera is speaking from?

HI: It's always been a sore point for Al Jazeera reporters. Because contrary to common belief, the actual sponsors of Al Jazeera encourage Al Jazeera to do stories about the country itself—Qatar and the countries in the region. But I don't know if it's self-censorship—people worry that they're going to upset the pay masters—or not, but to be honest with you, I sat with the leadership of Qatar and they would love to see stories about Qatar. From their point of view that would help them plan better for Qatar. And as long as it's double-sourced, that shouldn't be a problem.

Having said that, Al Jazeera Arabic over the years has reported human rights violations from Qatar, have reported when there was a coup attempt against the Emir in 2001, and the culprits in the conspiracy were captured and put on trial and Al Jazeera showed them, and they paraded their wounds in front of the camera. So stuff like that happens, but rarely, and we need more about the region.

One problem about those societies is that they are very conservative societies. They don't open up easily. Out of six GCC members—Gulf Corporation Council Members, Qatar being the center—we cannot operate in Saudi Arabia, we can't operate or do anything political in Oman, we can't do most political items from Kuwait. So that's one of the major concerns about where we broadcast from. I would love to see more about the Gulf being broadcast on Al Jazeera.

MB: Although it is state funded and run through a private company, are there ways in which Jazeera journalists or editors feel constrained by the funders?

HI: I can tell you this. I joined Al Jazeera three weeks after they started broadcasting in 1996, and we were told one rule: if you double-source any news item, you are free to air it. And I can tell you that over the past eleven years, not a single Qatari official has tried to interfere in the way I wrote or reported on a news item, even when Qatar and Bahrain were going to the International Court at the Hague over the Island of Hawar and the gas fields. I wrote the report. The only request came from the managing director, and he said he would delay broadcasting my report until after the ruling of the court, because that would make more sense. That's that.

In 1998, as Qatar mediated between the Sudan and Eritrea and the Sudanese president and the Eritrean president came to Doha to settle their differences, I went to the managing director and said, listen, I want to write something about Qatari diplomacy. And he kind of cringed and said, we don't want to start praising Qatar, and the wisdom of this and the wisdom of that. And I said, no, the report is about the suspicious role of Qatari diplomacy. And he looked at me and said, do it and let's see. I remember he came with the board of directors and the editor-in-chief and we played the report—it was four minutes long. And both of them looked at the editor-in-chief and asked him, "Is this congruent with Al Jazeera standards?" He said yes. And they said, "Air it," and we did.

MB: That's really impressive. Because some people would say, "How independent can a network be, given that it has state funding?" and in saying that I'm also referring to BBC, CBC, PBS . . .

HI: But can I tell you one thing? Qatar is a small country, defined in diversity. They've always had good ties with both sides of a conflict. They had good ties with Saddam, and good ties with the United States; good ties with Hamas and good ties with Fatah;

good ties with the Israelis and good ties with the Palestinians. Even when Saddam was alive, it was one of the few countries with embassies in Baghdad. So they cannot afford to make enemies, and they thrive on that diversity. And that in essence is Al Jazeera. Al Jazeera succeeded because it broadcasts from a tiny, rich Gulf state that needs diversity to exist.

MB: So you don't actually encounter final editorial control—which lies with the board of directors—that often, is that what you're saying?

HI: Not really. The board of directors really meets once a month to decide on matters of policy and give the outlines of running Al Jazeera and all that. But the philosophy of Al Jazeera since 2000 has been decided in a conference that is held annually; it's called the Al Jazeera Forum. It's actually being held during these days in Doha. And they invite journalists from all over the world to evaluate Al Jazeera and to engage in discussions with Al Jazeera staff. It's really useful, and it's multilingual, and hundreds of journalists and personalities and writers from all over the world are invited. It's a good dialogue. And I believe that these forums help in shaping Al Jazeera's outlook for the year to come. It happens every year.

MB: One of my colleagues, Nathalie [Magnan], mentioned that right now, with the English launch, viewers can have the feeling that there's this wonderful sense of independence. I know you were questioning before just how we define independent media, but there's a sense that people can be irreverent here. She told me she watched one story about a leader's birthday, and so while it was apparently a feature story about someone's birthday, it actually became a political story, but through the back door. Is that only going to last a little while? Is this a window of opportunity that will change as the ownership increases its control over time?

HI: The leadership in Qatar needs Al Jazeera and believes Al Jazeera to be independent. The minute they interfere or start directing Al Jazeera or veering in one direction or another, they will start losing Al Jazeera. And they're very aware of that.

MB: And when you say losing Al Jazeera, what do you mean?

HI: They will lose Al Jazeera as a channel with a backbone.

MB: Lose journalists? Lose audience?

HI: All of the above.

MB: So you think that they'll remain committed to this diversity?

HI: Yes, they need it.

MB: Apparently it is difficult to get advertisements on the channel, and Jazeera has been kicked out of several countries, which raises this question: Can you tell us about the fine line between integrity versus sustainability?

HI: As far as financial considerations, then yes, that issue is important. But as far as Al Jazeera is concerned, Saudi Arabia threatens anyone who works on Al Jazeera, because Saudi thinks of Qatar as a wayward state and they would love to control Al Jazeera because they're the only channel that criticizes the Saudi royal family and the shenanigans of Saudi diplomacy and all that. As for sustainability, that applies to a channel that is cashed out or that needs the backers to continue. Our backer is the government of Qatar, and it is very wealthy, and it's bankrolling Al Jazeera, no problem, and no questions asked.

MB: Do you think that Al Jazeera's coverage was changed in any way when the United States kicked Al Jazeera out of Iraq in 2004?

HI: Of course it did, because we lack real access. Now we function through our stringers in Baghdad, Iraqis, and companies working with Al Jazeera. That is not like working directly with the people. And of course, because of the security situation in Iraq, even our lone correspondent in Baghdad, Hoda Abdel-Hamid, is confined to the Green Zone, and that is not Al Jazeera–style journalism but that is the best we can do these days.

MB: And that makes me think of a question I had in my mind, which is what has changed in the media landscape in the time between the filming of *Control Room* and the present?

HI: With the war in Iraq and the American occupation and the disintegration of Iraq, we have an extra hundred and twenty-five Arab channels and the style of reporting has become more ideological. You'll find even the most respected American and British journalists are becoming more interested in "Hail to the Leader" and saluting the flag than real journalism. And the same goes for Arab journalists who are either supporting the resistance or supporting the fundamentalists or opposing the fundamentalists or are progovernment or whatever you might call it. All these factions have become more ideological, more factionalized and the credibility of the media has suffered tremendously.

MB: How would you describe the differences in Jazeera's journalism, compared with CNN and BBC, besides the obvious interests they both carry? You've been talking about newsworthiness, double-sourcing—what would you want to say more particularly about the different kinds of journalism you're seeing on these networks?

HI: Can I be blunt?

MB: Yes!

HI: At Al Jazeera, we are not arrogant. We are not going to a country and looking at its inhabitants as if we're touring the Bronx Zoo. And that's what I feel when I see BBC journalists in Darfur. I am Sudanese; I am deeply offended by their style of reporting. They don't scratch the surface. They actually even try to put words into people's mouth. For example, there was a report recently about the use of rape as a weapon. And they went to this refugee camp, and they were interviewing a woman, and they asked her about rape and the translator deliberately used a very classical expression in Arabic that no layperson in Darfur would understand. And she said "yes" as if she was coached. And to me that was the ultimate insult. And places in Darfur where rape is actually being used, no one ventures there because it is just too dangerous. Only Al Jazeera went there and interviewed some of the actual rape victims, and we used the vernacular or slang to make people understand the meaning of what we were saying.

We need to—I remember when the Israeli guns bombed a family on the shores of Gaza, just strolling on the beach, a sunny day in Gaza, and Israeli tanks fired at the beachgoers. The report on Al Jazeera went to the family house, interviewed the parents, we humanized the story, so there was a Palestinian element to the story. When the BBC reported, not a single Palestinian name was mentioned. And I was sitting next to a colleague of mine, a Palestinian from Gaza, and I could see tears in his eyes, tears of rage.

That style of reporting is no longer acceptable by the third world. When you go to the Congo and make mistakes in the names of the ethnic groups fighting and side with one group over the other as if there is an innocent party in the struggle over the Congo, as if Mr. Bemba is less criminal than Mr. Kabila, and you report that as fact— well, that style of journalism is no longer acceptable. And it's making people very angry; it makes me very, very upset.

MB: I'm wondering if you'd want to say a little more about the political implications of that kind of arrogance that you're describing in journalism, in terms of public opinion. What would be your main worry or concern?

HI: I was born in England. I'm a third-generation BBC-er. And the way that this arrogance and lack of consideration for cultural diversity is really galvanizing people against the West and against liberal democracy . . . A dream of mine is to see my country going back to a real parliamentary system and real liberal democratic traditions. That has become unrealizable now. I mean it just couldn't exist: people are so anti-West, and they look at these journalists, and to them these journalists have become the enemy, as troops at the service of the enemy. And they look at each humanitarian gesture coming out of New York, London, or Toronto as either hostile, arrogant, or an attempt to subjugate a people.

I mean, honorable people like Mr. Clooney and Mr. Glover who demonstrate for Darfur have so missed the point that they've become an object of ridicule in the Sudan. Not among the perpetrators of the crimes but among the victims themselves, because they just miss the point: the issue of Darfur is so complex. Just the term *Janjaweed*, attaching that to the Arabs is so infantile, so irresponsible, and so untrue. *Janjaweed* is an expression in Darfur—it's not even an Arabic expression, it's an expression in Darfur language that means "gangster on a horse," and that includes African tribes, Arab tribes, Fur people, leaders of the nation of Darfur, the Zaghawa tribe. I mean there are at least twelve tribes in Darfur fighting, and the government is a culprit, and then you have militias thrown against the government. And not to see that happening is just so—and to see the misrepresentation on CNN and BBC is making people very angry. And that will precipitate terrorism.

What scared me—the other day I was sitting with a bunch of Sudanese kids who are so secular—but all of them, all of them, at least eight, said "Well, we understand why Mr. bin Laden committed these crimes in 2001." I never thought I would hear that from an average Sudanese, people who are so anti-Islamist and anti-Wahabi, just to say that because they are so pissed off at the West because they see CNN and BBC as the representatives of Western culture and Western civilization. When they see themselves so misrepresented it makes them crazy.

MB: It reminds me of a quote from Amy Goodman that I challenged, and I wonder what you think about it. She said in an interview, "The media is more powerful than any bomb." What do you think about that claim?

HI: Well, of course it is. Of course it is. And I'll give you an example of an Al Jazeera mistake. When the second Intifada erupted in 1999, one of our reporters mistakenly reported that the Israelis had declared a curfew in Ramallah. He misheard the Hebrew message. And the program on the radio was an analytical program that was using examples from the first Intifada. So the Al Jazeera reported on this fraud curfew in Ramallah. People rushed to get their kids from school to bring them home before curfew. And there was huge crowding in the streets, and three people died trying to get to their kids. That's a small example of what the media can do to people—especially if you have a credible news outlet, people believe you and what you say is gospel truth. And if you get it wrong, then people get it wrong.

MB: I want to think as well about your vision for how Jazeera provides new hope for the relationship between media and democracy for people in the West. Just now the example you gave was the effect of the media in particular regions that are under siege; what would you want to say about Jazeera working to inform citizens in the West? What's your best hope for that?

HI: My best hope is—let's say the election in 2008—that people will be watching Al Jazeera to get the real, or at least the unbiased, view on certain candidates from a diverse range of experts, activists, and reporters, and it will be a vision that is not tainted by special interests—a vision that is independent. By the 2008 elections, an average viewer in Iowa or Arizona or Mississippi would be watching their candidates being critically analyzed by experts who wouldn't normally have access to ABC, CBS, NBC, and CNN, but people who are brilliant with sharp views and different visions. It would add a different dimension to the democratic process.

MB: I had a question for you as someone who has been doing this work for a long time. I wonder what you think about notions that journalists like yourself might

Figure 12.2
Hassan Ibrahim, *Control Room* (2004), directed by Jehane Noujaim

perhaps experience secondary trauma in terms of being in these kinds of war zones. And I'm wondering on a personal note how you sustain yourself through this long career.

HI: Well, I have my own escape routes. My favorite one is to always, always arm yourself with reading and practice some form of release mechanism. I paint, I write for the theater. Just take your mind off this rigamarole of war and death and destruction and conflict. You have to have a respite to take a step back and look at it from outside the situation. You have to take time off. Without that, you'll be repeating yourself, and you'll find yourself stuck in a very dark corner. Because war is dark. Conflicts are not pleasant experiences. And in order to survive those, you need to take a step back. That is a must.

MB: I have one last question. What example of news coverage that you've been involved in has given you the most hope recently?

HI: I was in southern Sudan last September, and meeting young, vivacious former warriors now going to school and playing basketball and singing in choirs, chanting in the streets, and digging ditches and building hospitals gave me real hope for that part of the world.

MB: Is there anything else on your mind that's important to you that I haven't touched on in these questions?

HI: One thing that I notice happening with greater frequency: journalists who are pushed to areas of conflict by their networks without arming them with the necessary knowledge of the complexity of the situation. You see the reporters being flat, boring, and lacking in depth. If we don't rectify that, we risk further alienation of people.

MB: That's a warning you would want to issue to other news networks?

HI: Yes.

MB: Is it in terms of the language, to begin with?

HI: Knowledge of the region. It's not enough to say, oh, I'm going to report on the Muslims of Northern Thailand, without knowing the ethnic configuration of Northern Thailand, the differences between them and the people of the Mekong Valley, the history of Thailand, the religions. Without knowing that, you'll go and give people basically a very flat, one-dimensional report.

MB: I suppose that warning and that challenge should be extended not only to journalists but to the leaders of the American nation.

HI: To leaders of all nations. To be honest with you, it is disconcerting to see not just American officials but even Middle Eastern officials getting it wrong about America and the West. I don't know . . . The Internet has become a mixed blessing. Sometimes it's a curse in disguise because some people say, "I read on the net that such and such and such is the case," and they don't really bother to dig deeper and compare sources and go to libraries. Nothing can replace a good book. Nothing.

MB: In addition to background knowledge, it seems the other thing that you've stressed is this question of double-sourcing as the way to ensure fairness and accuracy. Are those terms you would use? What are the terms you would use to describe good journalism?

HI: I would say accuracy. You need to be accurate. I remember my former mentor at the BBC said to me: we don't need to get it fair, but we need to get it right.

Note

These interview questions were developed collaboratively by Nathalie Magnan, Andréa Schmidt, and Megan Boler.

1. http://english.aljazeera.net/NR/exeres/BB13080C-E34D-4E06-9F68-161E032FF957.htm

III   Tactics in Action

13   Media Interventions and Art Practices: Interview with Shaina Anand

with Alessandra Renzi and Megan Boler

Shaina Anand is a filmmaker and media artist who works collaboratively with video and televised media. She is the founder of ChitraKarKhana.net (picture factory/artist food), a fully independent unit for practical media based in Mumbai. ChitraKarKhana's media interventions employ cheap and accessible do-it-yourself (DIY) video and editing hardware skills to produce on-site televised media.

In this interview Anand discusses media and information politics in global and local context, grounded in her media art projects of experimentation and critiques of video as a documentary form. Four of Anand's projects are referenced in this interview.

Rustle TV (2004) was a temporary TV channel set up inside Russell Market, Bangalore. The market presented a microcosm of the real world, over which was forced an idealistic utopia; the people in the market became the clients, the stars, and the primary audience, while a group of students performed in the service of the community and delivered programming.

The project World Information City TV (2005) transmitted programming to 3,000 homes in and around Shivaji Nagar, Bangalore, through an existing informal local cable channel. Local programming generated daily was spun off from the world-information.org conference held in Bangalore in November 2005. WI City TV was an intervention in the World Information conference itself and a response to the conference themes and participants, but more important, it pushed outward into the immediate neighborhood of spaces, languages, and infopolitics.

Khirkee Yaan (2006) is an open-circuit TV system, a local area network communication and feedback device. It employs cheap security apparatuses, otherwise used for surveillance of the community at large. In this project on site, public access to video feedback in real time encourages experiments in community networking, performance, and automated storytelling and filmmaking.

"Recurrencies: Across Electricity and the Urban" (2007), with Ashok Sukumaran, documents a number of electrical public works primarily based in Mumbai. The project highlights alternative media currencies, altered circuits of information infrastructure from the bottom up, foregrounding issues of contemporary power, information flows, and property and control relationships.

In Anand's work, these sites of intervention become players in the creation of autonomous media, generated for their own use. This negotiation is at each step tenuous, made possible by person-to-person interaction. The intervention is self-organized, messy, gray, and at all times collaborative.

This interview was conducted by telephone between Toronto and Mumbai in March 2007.

Figure 13.1
Real-time communication interface through surveillance cameras during the Khirkeeyaan project

Alessandra Renzi: First, I was wondering, how did you come to media activism?
Shaina Anand: I came to media activism from filmmaking. My early training as a film student was probably instrumental in shaping a political worldview, mainly through an exposure to world cinema from Latin America, Europe, North America, and East Asia, and what we called parallel cinema, a movement we had in India in the '60s and '70s outside of the industry of mainstream *Bollywood*. We had a realist cinema, we had socialist cinema, and so on. Filmmaking did, in a sense, shape an early world-view, what we call *Nazariya*, a way of seeing.

   An early mentor of sorts was Saeed Mirza, a filmmaker I worked with while I was still in my teens—a lot of my early political thinking came from him. I used to write fiction then. But I began thinking very closely about issues of power, power dynamics, and power structures within the politics and processes of filmmaking exactly ten years ago in '97. I was assistant director on a documentary with the same director I mentioned. We traveled the country, all of India, by road for six months nonstop making a serialized documentary: *A Tryst with the People of India*.

Our intentions were noble—a very sensitized director, politically aware, politically correct. The agenda for this documentary was to speak to the ordinary Indian—to give representation to that subaltern voice, analyze what went wrong in fifty years since a democratic India, and so on and so forth. This journey shifted my preoccupation with the medium, a turning point where I questioned my career choice and our filmmaking practice: issues about the technology, the methodology of filmmaking or film craft, an acute awareness of the machinery of a film crew—Beta cameras, big mic, boom operator, assistant cameraman, sound recordist, camera and recorder attendants. A crew of six handling the gear and a director asking the questions, and three assistant directors who would butt in, there would be a cameraman who would be angry when lighting was not beautiful, a sound recordist who would be bugged when a baby in the village would cry midinterview. I began questioning where the agency came from and what happens to all this footage and experience in the face and veneer of a thirty-minute episode. And mind you, this is India: four large jeeps going down roads where cars have not been, again and again through the vast and brutally diverse country. At twenty-one, this journey stayed with me. I began rewatching the footage and writing critically about it, asking others and myself about documentary aesthetics and ethics, grappling with the idea of India in the '90s.

GATT has happened. We had entered the new trade order, rather belligerently and happily because we have the largest democracy in the world. We went nuclear on May 12, 1998. A bunch of colleagues—we called ourselves the *Indian People's Media Collective*—started organizing talks and screening films on nuclearization and militarism in colleges. Those were very deterministic times; there was almost no nuclear debate in the mainstream media in the subcontinent, just like there had not been any globalization debate. This same decade had witnessed a sweeping rise of majority communalism. Urban campuses were politically insipid. Authorities would not allow screenings. We had to maneuver around, build our networks from the inside via sensitized professors, and sustain the campaign. We even organized students and musicians and activists and pulled off a huge twelve-hour concert on Hiroshima day. Back then, we were just grappling with the violent '90s. There was naivete and not much for the youth to hold on to as precedent. The left had gotten left behind in a dark hole. Then technology got cheap and got DIY.

I come from privilege: educated, middle class, the Internet-access generation in Bombay, center of the TV industry, of Bollywood, financial capital, and all of that. I thought the digital revolution would herald radical cinema. Cheap technology for alternative media would change things. Soon I thought otherwise. But these were my early inroads into media activism, though I am never comfortable calling it that.

AR: So basically what you are saying is that it was part of a generational shift. This is certainly your personal experience, but is it also a kind of broader phenomenon in India, where there is a generation now that has more access to these forms of technology and is more politicized through the '90s?

SA: Good question, though I am not sure I could validate that. A decade ago we were all getting stoned and thirsting for radical cinema, young and cynical, believing no one will fund it. And three years later, certainly, no one needed to fund it. We could do it together, by ourselves. But strangely, I felt alone in that space. It seemed so easy to say, "Let's get up and do it, let's not complain, but try." I did not see it happening as much as I thought it would. We still waited for our budgets, we still waited till an NGO wanted to fund it, we still waited till there was a better camera, we still needed an XLR mic for sound, so there was always something lacking. I do not think that media, DIY media, really caught on as fast as I thought it should have.

Megan Boler: So how did access to resources affect this era of this media activism?

SA: Soon enough, many people could access the technology. A telling point was how quickly all our TV channels started exploiting the resources while we were still paying commercial fees to go to editing studios, which, of course, by then were using souped-up PCs or consumer Macs. Everyone was shooting mini-DV and you needed to watch news on TV here to know how they were on top of things, just like now they are using phone videos, hidden cameras, and broadband if they need to—any kind of technology. But us independent practitioners—we were a little behind.

I still joke, being so aware of tactical media, about the *Sangh Parivar*—the Hindu Rights think tank's strategies in the '90s when we had this rise of majority communalism—how effectively and locally their networks masterminded hate: flyers, pamphlets, boycotts, all-India rallies spreading hatespeech on a mythical, air-conditioned chariot, the *Rath Yatra's*. They were appropriating mailing lists and electoral databases to send you propaganda videotapes in your mailbox, they would telejam via local cable networks, cut out ads and insert their propaganda, CDs slipped inside news magazines. So, DIY and tactical media strategies were being claimed much faster by either mainstream media or by political parties and their cultural wings. Also, in the wake of liberalization, we had quickly moved into that post-Marxist phase where activists—all with integrity—began working for the sudden proliferation of NGOs flush with funds, because "they had to." They could not sustain their struggle—the left was decimated. So a decade goes by caught amid liberalization, the technological moment, and the possibilities are missed by one generation on the field.

Having said that, we do have a strong documentary film movement. A lot of politically motivated filmmakers continue to make relevant films, and a shared-footage collective formed after the Gujarat riots marked an interesting turn. But its use and strategy was caught up in self-righteous and proprietary zeal. Also, they do not question the form. They provide some political context and alternative, rarely a political critique of the form or process.

AR: I would say that that is probably not just a problem in India. That is very common with filmmakers everywhere.

I found interesting what you were saying about the NGOs. I am not aware of many projects here in Canada for instance, or the European countries I am familiar with, which are affiliated with NGOs. It is usually independent activist groups that may recur to media activism to further their cause. But I find it interesting because a lot of NGOs are also connected to bigger structures and institutions; so in a way it is a funny link between independent media-making and some kind of institutions.

SA: Yeah, it is a funny link. But it is something that is here to stay. And we cannot sit high on exclusive autonomy. Yet, an acute awareness of being coopted, of using funding—this social capital that in one sense is systemic to maintaining status quos or adjusting social conditions—needs to inform our practice. Tactics and strategies have to evolve around these dilemmas. In most of my interventions, I begin by conceptually interrogating the funding source and then carefully positioning the project, be it for an alternative information conference, a workshop, or an artist residency.

Despite an NGO or more for everything, our public culture is in abject poverty. This is also perhaps why I shift from "break the bank and end the war" to what I see as micropolitics, or more correctly, interventions into political ramification of everyday life. And yes, I am cynical of a lot of NGO-driven community-based stuff in India that begins and ends with power politics: the "we are giving things to you and we are telling you what's good for you" kind of approach.

MB: Are there specific examples of NGO funding that radically reshaped the work of independent media/tactical media artists? Or is your concern more generally that when there is NGO funding, it can predetermine what the artist or activist wants to produce, or engender self-censorship?

SA: I would have to think about it; I am not sure I have a particular example. But I can be categorical of the fact that most independent media practitioners or activists pacify their politics when funded. Large progressive cultural organizations posture more, preach a little, and do much less when funding increases.

With video and documentary, I think my grouse is basically with the kind of media that is generated. It is often either very top down or repressed in its aesthetics and rendering of a politically correct picture, or it sits on a higher fence of which I am often critical.

AR: That is what I was wondering. What is the link between NGOs and local media, and how do the two elements interact, and what kind of product comes out?

SA: It is also subjective. There of course are positive effects if you are thinking broadly about alternative media. For example, certain films made after the Gujarat riots were crucial in talking about the pogrom and the fury of hate that had ruptured. Thanks to NGOs, there were sustained screening campaigns that managed to convey to an unpoliticised audience a lot of facts on the riots and state terrorism that the mainstream media would not tell you about.

In my own works, I see this collaboration (and calibration) very transparently. Other than community-driven or peer/self-organized initiatives, appropriating small amounts of culture funds is one "survive and flourish" strategy. Small funding, but yet the kind of product that comes out is by no means modest. And to me, video does not lie. That is the good and bad part about video. To critical eyes it reveals a lot. As a filmmaker, I am always looking at the products and asking, where is the agency? Where is the power reversal for these people who have become your subjects?

A little aside, to bridge the gap between my cynicism with video and its use in my current work processes: on 9/11, I started working on what began to look like an epic—it was a film called *Tellavision Mumbai*. I was at home with my video camera in hand, watching those Twin Towers being hit and coming down, filming it over and over again for over two hours. In the weeks that followed this moment of reckoning—this supposed end of America's "holiday from history"—factions and remnants of our completely fractured left started popping out of virtual oblivion. E-mails, demonstrations, street plays, public meetings—interventions were sorely needed. We have the second largest Muslim population in the world, there was fear of persecution, but there was also hope that groups would come together to counterbalance the war spin.

I began this very systematic documentation of what I ironically saw as the invisible public culture of the city: trade union solidarity meetings, ultra-left demonstrations, citizens action groups, journalist networks, Muslim cultural organizations, Gandhians, human rights activist groups, a sole reporter with a camera. Back home I would watch and film TV off the screen. From *infinite justice* to *enduring freedom*, the building up of the global coalition and the war in Afghanistan, I followed the timeline in a contrapuntal manner: ambient TV and direct DV. Each chronological event was preceded by a physical journey through the postindustrial and postliberalized landscape of Bombay, into the heart of a street play or public meeting, and then journeying home on that timeline, back into fishbowl of global TV, war, and entertainment. Through all these episodes, I was trying to cull and stitch together a holistic discourse, a chronicle, a global media critique, a city searching for an articulation of a vision—and the reality: an ultimate critique of our public culture.

Watching a rough cut, a fellow activist filmmaker warned me that I should not be coopting one faction of the ultra left with another more moderate one. But that was the whole point. They were all to be coopted, and represented as presenting their information, which is what they are trying to do anyway. The film with its mega-narrative was never completed, even though each chronological event was made into a short film, countered and interpreted with the help of restless TV surfing bites. I thought I should mention it, as this zero-budget project did corroborate my disillusionment with straight-up video with empirical narratives, and shifted my focus to micropolitics and very local effects in recent works.

MB: Might you just say in a brief form, in a sound-bite form, what it was that you wanted to convey in this project that you didn't get a chance to finish?

SA: The title said it, quite ambitiously: *Tell-a-vision Mumbai.* A public consciousness had mutated, been manufactured and realigned with global spin—9/11 was a media event with far-reaching effects like no other, and *Tellavision Mumbai* was an attempt to cast our vote, to inform and be informed and be counted in, but also to look into ourselves, the city, and subcontinent for symptoms and scars of this clash, of "us and them" politics. It was countering an almost private and invisible space of public dissent with the public, ubiquitous face of private TV—trying to immerse and inform the viewer through this altered mediascape.

MB: What was the nature of the conversation at those protest events in India after September 11? What were people talking about, and how was that related to reactions to mainstream media or corporate media representation of the events in the United States?

SA: Well, corporate media and mainstream media, and the *Bharatiya Janta* Party (right-wing Hindu fundamentalist party) that was in power then just picked up where George Bush, the Republicans, and mainstream media in America left off. The government willfully and jingoistically replicated Bush's "good against evil," "us vs them," dividing the world—the clash of civilization speak.

Afghanistan is contiguous to India; America's overt war was close by. The demon face of Osama and the Taliban, the projected crisis and partisan generalization of Islam and terrorism was eerily global, yet its effects were mirrored nationally and locally. CNN and BBC were the mainstay global news channels; we also had three or four Indian satellite news channels and state and regional channels. The educated Indian middle class surfed through all these channels, and the rhetoric was essentially the same. In the meetings I documented, the conversations sought to throw light on history, the cold-war years, America's covert war in Afghanistan, its support of corrupt dictators of Islamic nations, its interventions, coups, and CIA operations across the globe. Voices would caution and speak of reinstilling our secular democratic fabric that had been ruptured often through the violent '90s, and was being fueled to blow up again. Activist journalists critiqued media monopolies, abridged Chomsky, and localized manufacturing consent. The Muslim intelligentsia and organizations came out strongly against fundamentalism and terrorism of all kinds. Peaceniks spoke about the cost of war—or what Arundhati Roy called the "algebra of infinite justice." They called on the UN and Kofi Annan to "deserve" their 2001 Nobel peace price, to stand up to America. Neighborhood *Mohalla* committees talked and worked to prevent riots. Human-rights groups protested against the introduction of a new Prevention of Terrorism Ordinance that came into force soon after 9/11. The Marxists talked of empire and neoliberalism, people like Medha Patkar retracted from rhetoric and brought our attention to the real war of power against people, their land, and livelihood by the state or transnational empire. People gleaned texts from political theorists and alternative sites on the Net, localized and translated them. Yet, the voices were minuscule; local alternative media was ineffective, reaching and preaching only to the converted, and lacking in action, living in the nostalgic days of the '70s when the left had the streets in the heart of the industrial city. I did feel my documentation and chronicle were valid, but the truth was in the video: there was an aching gap between people's movements and the people.

The buildup to Iraq was different, a semblance of awareness, debate, moderation, and total helplessness prevailed in the world, and in India, dissent had almost run out of the urge for renewal through decentralized, nonpolitical party politics that characterized it in 2001. The 9/11 and Afghanistan blitzkrieg was extreme in how it divided people. The *Vishwa Hindu Parishad* (World Hindu (cultural) Organization) whipped up the communal hate with global justification, and in March 2002, a pressure valve was upped and opened: the torching of a train carrying Hindu pilgrims by terrorists and a widespread massacre of Muslim families in Gujarat carried out by party workers, police, and educated middle-class neighbors. The right-wing Hindu hate sites outnumbered independent or politically leftist sites.

Even Indymedia was a casualty in India. It was around during September 11 but its energy was short-lived, so that during the World Social Forum in Bombay people from all over the world were checking it out and its last entry was from two years earlier. There were enough urban youth and activists with Internet access then, yet besides some individuals, there was no community network.

We do not have a precedence of Net art or Net activism; we did not have access to the Net on a broader level. Now of course, educated youth have access to computers—a recent survey said Net users in Bombay totaled two million. That is a sizable 12 percent of the city's population, and some of our newer collaborative projects include building an online video footage archive, and an alternative community wireless mesh intranet and information repository. Still, most of my works now intervene into physical space in India, where the ubiquitous information mass-media devices everybody has are passive TVs and radios.

And yes, I still use video, like I was telling you—it does not lie to critical eyes. A while ago I read a very early essay by Critical Art Ensemble, maybe it was from *The Electronic Disturbance*[1], it was the chapter on video resistance. It is a nasty chapter against documentary, saying it was born in a crisis and the technological invention of video, its instantaneity changed nothing in the retrograde tradition of documentary film. Come to think of it, all critique of documentary and its technology, all seminal shifts happened in the film medium before video. Video technology is about feedback, instant broadcast—the TV is versatile unregulated hardware capable of receiving things in the air—and the moment comes with cheap accessible DIY. These cameras have screens on them—just flip the screen around—and for me that is projection, that is broadcast. Carry eight hundred meters of cable, if you have to, and there are things one can do with wireless—illegally temporarily—to occupy the air. Alternative media has to look actively beyond the antiwar Web site or documentary. There is more than enough of that, and it is not breaking a bank or ending the war. Like Jodi Dean says in her essay, there is all this circulation of content; it is all mainstream. Arundhati Roy says it in a recent essay: "the information is out there; it is just going nowhere." I think my tactical media practice has therefore shifted; it has moved into the generation of micromedia. It has developed by harvesting or claiming resources, and it is not necessarily events but everyday life and embedded politics that you dirty your hands with and respond to.

AR: This is one of the things I find most interesting—the way you trouble the idea of resources and the distribution of resources—not only media, but also electricity distribution in your new project. Can you tell us something more about that project and what kind of ideas are behind it?

SA: The project is called "Recurrencies—Across Electricity and the Urban," where we are looking at "electronic commodities" that have become smoothly marketable closed systems. It is collaboration with my partner, Ashok Sukumaran, whose installations and works have stretched across the fields of contemporary computer-based art, cinema, and architecture, imagining various kinds of "publicness." With Recurrencies, we begin with electricity—that prefigured new media, cold media as McLuhan called it (as opposed to hot media with content). We are exploring alternative media currencies, altered circuits of information infrastructure from bottom up, making technology newly curious about contemporary power, information flows, and property and control relationships, with today's ability to look back at the digital. For example, electricity is fundamentally "open source." It is not hidden or encrypted, it does not take a serious hacker to break some code to modify it or steal it or tap into any stream at any given point. So, imagine a simple system: a switch could potentially trigger anything, breach boundaries, share networks, offer more participation, posit other informal utopian states. . . . We intend to do several "acts," installations around public infrastructures, and slowly shift media as well—video, airwaves, wireless, the future of so-called embedded or pervasive computing—then open up the project as it goes, begin to grow wild with some of these currencies, with local communities—across the open.

AR: I especially like the play with "recurrencies" because the guiding thread of electricity can transversally connect to so many other different issues. You had as tags on your Web site, "sharing," but you also had "different spaces." One of the things that struck me the most when I was watching the videos and your descriptions of the games was the way electricity can create a space where people come together and interact more. For instance, the project in the student quarters where all these families were connecting is a very beautiful and simple way to trouble different notions of community and to create something new.

SA: You said it just like I was thinking about it. But we are also looking hard at interactive art and trying to unpeel notions and theories of relational arts and dialogical arts, community art—participatory art is the new buzzword again. We want to look at these things as critically and as meaningfully as one can. Look at the public history of technology and leak out from the holes that remain open. There are tags like "sharing," "gift," "distance," "switch"—kinds of economy or currency that one can imagine. While these might be conceptual ideas, once they play out in a physical context or place, there are also all sorts of embedded politics there that we want to shift or temporarily hijack. In many ways, these works state possible technologically reorganised futures. The essential free soul or tactical heart behind it is integral to how we see things and what we do.

MB: You just used the term "participatory art" and you said it has a new popularity. Could you say something about how you envision these projects concretely? Do you feel that the conception of the project itself is a participatory engagement? Who is the audience that you imagine directing those participatory actions to or with, and what kinds of communities are you participating with?

SA: Participatory—that hype around Web 2.0! I would not bandy that word around too much. It sometimes has too happy a veneer of sharing and democracy around it that often does not exist. In my own work, the conception has not been participatory in that sense at all. Of course the projects themselves are about the involvement, cooperation of a number of people.

In Rustle TV, one of my earlier works, the idea was to flip or turn the usual way of video production or filmmaking on its head. The participation and collaboration involved the entire market, but the intent was laid open to the students and in the manifesto to the market: "This is your channel—it is the channel of the people of the market for the people of the market—but it is by the crew that is going to work their asses off and produce the content for you as per your desires." So participation was very much key. Conceptually, the site of the market was the public realm, its people were the audience and performers who determined the content and in turn received what the students gave them by way of their performance.

With KhirkeeYaan I wanted to push that envelope and explore how autonomous this production could get for the people that were participating in the creating and

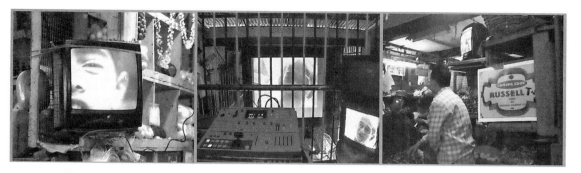

Figure 13.2
Shots from the Rustle TV project at Russell Market, Bangalore

receiving. Could the usual bunch of people who produce that content—me or the camera person or the editor, the DIY—be thrown out of the equation, and could that interaction belong to the eight, ten, twenty, forty people who are on that screen at that point? The screen comprised of a grid of four frames in different places that were networked and fed back to each other in real time. These conversations were generated in distinct spaces all within a radius of two hundred meters. Participants were performers, audiences, subjects, witnesses, etc., at the same time. So yes, participation is something that I think of from concept. Filmmaking is a collaborative process, but the nature of the normal structure of how media is produced, which is interpreted by the few people doing it on behalf of many, and so on, is questioned.

And on site, what works for me is a very careful but organic calibration of the power structures and dynamics of other forces at play. With Rustle TV I was to conduct a workshop for students, and this was part of their New Media semester called "Force" at Srishti School of Art Design and Technology. I knew it was a private arts school and that there would be ten, fifteen students who would be extremely privileged, not just in terms of their demographics or background, but also by being in this wonderful school with much access. The idea was to make a pedagogical intervention right there. They would have to learn and experience all sorts of things in the field. At the time of conception, I did not know the students or the people of the market. I had no relationship with them. I was just imagining a space where little or no media existed, especially electronic media.

KhirkeeYaan was done during an artist residency at Khoj in New Delhi where I was invited to work within in Khirkee Extension, a fragmented urban village, the neighborhood where their studios were located, a place I had not been to ever before. *Khirkee* means "window" in Hindi, *KhirkeeYaan* is the plural, *Yaan* means "vehicle." All those live episodes were generated after relationships and microcontracts were forged in the course of a couple of days with people offering TVs, electricity, their property, and participation. The stories evolved with the people who were engaging in conversation and performance via this transparent act of media production. The audience was determined by the site(s), and what they were seeing and hearing was performed by this "televisation." It was a complex mix of people residing in this neighborhood, about the length of a kilometer, and each episode represented distinct linguistic, regional, and sociopolitical states.

World Information City TV was a little different. I was thinking, "Alright, here's the alternative conference on information politics that's going to happen in Bangalore, the Silicon Valley of the East, the IT capital of India. Naturally, it's the 'in' venue for an international conference such as World Information." There was Net-base/t-01 from Vienna, Sarai from Delhi, Waag from Amsterdam, and Alternative Law Forum from Bangalore. These were some of the players organizing the conference. At the outset, the project was publicly defined as an intervention into the conference itself. It pushed outwards from this conference, its themes and participants, and channeled information to a completely different vernacular and wider audience, who in various ways were the empirical subjects of many conference themes: intellectual property, closure, regulation, access, piracy, gray markets, cinema, media. WIC TV aired to about 3,500 homes in Shivaji Nagar on their illegal channel that was hugely popular, as it showed the latest Tamil and Bollywood flicks soon after release. They were our audience, and the programming revolved around their neighborhood: its histories, trade and services, people, places, and practices—and the infopolitics discussed at the conference, without representing the talks.

Unlike Rustle and KhirkeeYaan—here our total viewers were invisible—imagined, watching a range of local content about their city, communities, neighborhood, and world in their homes. Yet, this local terrestrial, literally roof-to-roof, window-to-window network of cables through which they receive all other satellite channels for once reported from the ground. Our connection with Lokesh, the cable operator, had been formed during Rustle TV when he and his colleagues had helped us cable the market. We set up an open studio on the terrace room of Lawyers Collective, an NGO that happened to be located in the center of our ambit. A number of films were generated in the "chaorganization" of the ten days that followed, made by a voluntary crew of rookies, film students, tactical media jammers, and practitioners. Ironically, WIC TV was part of World Information City, an art exhibition curated by a group of lawyers and artists.

MB: You are talking about the importance of process or medium, which comes across more strongly than concerns about content or message. I wonder if you might want to say something about that.

SA: The process or the medium *are* the concerns about content or message. The medium alone is not the message, and the form-content tension needs to confront itself. Process, tactics, strategies, even rules are explored, emphasized. So, while the

Figure 13.3
Khirkee Yaan project in the streets of Delhi

films that aired in the market on Rustle TV were made by students, most of whom had never held a video camera before, there were rules of engagement: the few who had video skills were encouraged to flip the screen outwards, mirror the view, so that the viewfinder was no longer their privilege but the subject's as well. The students had to perform in the service of the market, their market research involved speaking to vendors in every stall. Their political naivete was bombarded by much sensory information. Indeed, in the early days of the project, emotions and zeal led some students to believe they could solve a lot of problems of the market. Quickly—it was not called Rustle TV just for fun—running along the timeline of production, their attention was shifted to their experience and the footage they had generated, which they had to confront to create a whole range of programming. People had sung songs, recited prose and poetry, brought tapes with their favorite songs, and danced in the aisles, in the aquarium, in the open courtyards. Movie scenes were reenacted, talents and skills displayed. A range of serialized programming was generated, and it included, apart from remixed music videos, film spoofs, talent and comedy shows, short features and portraitures about the old folk, the young, the women, the kids who worked in the market, time-lapsed shorts about the twenty-four-hour cycle of the market and its environs, photo essays, promos, signature tunes, and animations in more than four languages. Interestingly, no adverting was generated, even though this service was available and stated in the manifesto stuck on all the notice boards and gates of the market. When the channel went on air inside the market exactly fifteen days into the project, we included live events, quiz shows, checkers tournaments, open forums, open stage, and even "tele-jammed" between cricket and pirate cinema. There was festivity, serendipity, irreverence, and joy in the market—at least this content *did* something for all us involved. Video became the site, place became the media for a feedback mechanism of shared memories and experiences. I would also like to believe that it was a fruitful case of radical pedagogy for the students, as was WIC TV.

KhirkeeYaan's process was more subjective. While the system allowed for real-time collaborative conversation that was happening in local time—the episodes themselves simulated and represented a range of contexts: labor, urban migration, caste politics, gender bias, communal anger, the violent redevelopment of New Delhi. In episode one, we just wanted to take the device to the street and see what would happen. It was instantly claimed by the children of the four streets it connected together. Within a minute they transformed this four-way network into their own *Indian Idol* talent show. We connected the homes of four women from Nepal, some of whom were very recent immigrants, living close by but not in a community. For over two hours they chatted with each other in their native language, exchanged personal narratives and journeys, wisdom, and warmth. In one episode we networked labor under four distinct basement sweatshop owners for an entire eight-hour shift—quite ironical, since we used surveillance gear. A leatherworks unit, two hand-embroidery units, and one tailoring unit worked the drudgery away with some passive play. A polyglot network—common hometowns, districts, and languages were discovered; friendships were forged with promises to meet outside, in person. Barters and exchanges were struck, music and cricket scores were piped from different locations.

Here is a sampling of the films made and aired by our motley crew during WIC TV: a thirty-minute film that personalizes Elgin Cinema, its loyal workers and clients. This is Bangalore's oldest cinema house, (and possibly India's oldest—more than a hundred years old), now rundown, with the cheapest ticket prices in the world, a Shivaji Nagar icon—with its reruns and B-grade Hindi and Tamil cinema, a dark cool escape for menfolk who throng here after a hard shift's work. There was a film about the old car junk market, another looking at the demolition of old markets to make way for malls. Then a true story about of how one of our crewmembers broke his camera and got it repaired for 3.33 euros in thirty minutes through local connections despite the Canonauthorized service center telling them it will take a week just for the estimate. A sideways look at the digital ecology of the area, IP, and piracy, featuring many interviews, including a strong case in support of piracy primer in Hindi by legal theorist Lawrence Liang. We learned of a local Urdu channel called *Suroor TV* (pleasure TV) that a young entrepreneur had tried to run from his family home. To air to Shivaji Nagar residents, his linguistic target audience, he had negotiated a set of complicated hurdles that revealed the messy control wars and misplaced laws from top to bottom. His channel could not survive and had to shut down despite being extremely popular. We shot an uncensored talk show in their studio room, featuring local cable operators and the *Suroor TV* crew in conversation with a panel of conference speakers whom we invited as guests. Of course the content is important, but this is practice and not theory.

MB: I wonder if you would want to speak a little bit about the different kinds of access to technology in the areas you have been working with. Who has access and what are the important questions around access?

SA: Even the poorest slum has TV. And that is the first device that everybody has. It is not even radio; I think I can fully say it is TV. This is an access point for me. It is a largely uncontested piece of hardware, with relatively open standards built into the system. Inside Russell Market only one TV with cable existed, though most vendors had TVs at home. For Rustle TV, we rented out a dozen TV sets at three dollars each and cabled them to receive the feed from our studio desk upstairs. In Khirkee, most shops and homes, including the small tenements and squats for migrant labor, had TVs. In case we needed some, we rented them from the half a dozen shops in the lane,

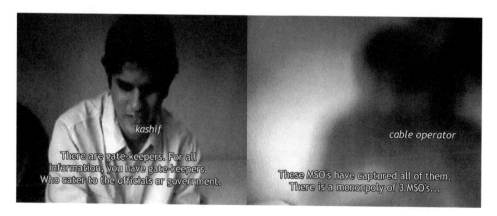

Figure 13.4
WIC TV talk show: cable operator discussing the monopoly of MultiService Operators who provide him satellite feed

which assemble and sell their own TV sets—a tube, a tuner kit, and a chassis with some obscure brand.

The interface device for KhirkeeYaan was connected using the cheapest consumer level CCTV and CATV equipment: Taiwanese surveillance cameras, a generic Chinese quad splitter, locally manufactured RF modulator, audio mixer, and meters of hardy coaxial cables that I bought from Mumbai's electronics market. None of these places had a density of computers or distributed Internet penetration.

WIC TV's entire cable infrastructure already existed; we collaborated with the cable operator. He had offered to air our programming on his network: "local programming, everyone will watch." These interventions claimed and tweaked the social understanding and acceptance of TV as a way of life. Most of my works are situated in places where almost no local or autonomous media exists.

There are many questions around access, and importantly around access to systems of technology. Where there is an even field access to ICTs, like, for example, Internet and wireless routers in Bandra where I live, we are working to harvest these resources through participation and sharing. We want to create a mesh network and community wireless intranet that through wider collaboration and support would spread citywide, become an offline, maybe even legal, local Internet—if we manage to tactically posit it and skirt around the laws. Software, knowledge, and media repositories, open and closed, black, white, and gray could be claimed and shared; media could also be very localized.

With Recurrencies, the intent is to look hard at technological commodities, use and imagine differently organized states, while looking to the past and future. Bombay City has been the essential modernist example of India in the West and nationally. This modernity in the real-time global world is getting closed in seemingly one-way loops, and this refers to the mass culture of consumption and worldview down here that systemically mimics its Western democratic counterparts. I am more interested in the heterogeneous urban spaces, where there are diverse and hydra-headed ways in which small economies function. There is an inherent squatting or hacker intent for survival and function, whether they are on the edge of gray or downright illegal.

I find the flow of information in these places can be extremely interesting, and not just because I like to romanticize them, but because that is where I see freedom—the future and potential for alterations and practices that we could even be aware of, but cynical or distanced from, in our cloning, liberalized times. In fact, unlike the West we are not such a regulated information society—as yet. There are a lot of gray practices that can happen, do happen, and function even as new internal laws are being formed. With our socialist-democratic modernity past and the privatized and transnational present, it is fair to worry about how closed and repressive the State will become, is becoming already.

AR: I was wondering about two things. What is the reception of your work in India, because, in a way, it seems to be very original. Do you ever hear the criticism that your work is too short-lived, that it does not have an effect, or that your interventions do not necessarily leave any structures for people? Or, some people may overlook that you are concentrating on the process more than creating content, and what kind of effects these processes have? So, I was wondering what people think about your work and how useful they think it is, and *how* useful you think it is.

SA: The second question first. A lot of projects by way of process have exposed the under use of existing infrastructure or displayed quite transparently the potential for newer network and communication zones. And they have done this by small examples, locally on the ground in a short and economical period of time, ironically as workshops or art events, with negligible budgets. Of course, there will always be that criticism of these being temporary and short-lived, or not permanently resulting in shifts, especially when seen as tactical media. Our tactics are informed by a host of practices, and beyond critical self-awareness and clarity of practice, I am looking hard for some contextual peer review here. Yet I have to say, media alone is never going to bring about shifts in power. It can never fundamentally do so, unless it is a piece of video that is clinching evidence in court or something. Seizing and producing temporary shifts in power motivates my individual practice. I guess I am hardwired that way.

With Recurrencies however, we are looking purely at the structures that make up our electric realm. So far, the projects have sought to articulate practical, tactical, and equitable, and even spectacular usable things. Since this is a longterm project, where we are also building relationships with the people in the neighborhood, we are also looking at alternative community infrastructures that could result. It is natural to think of how to make these circuits more meaningful, sustainable, and instrumental to changes.

And that said, I do have a cynicism in the permanent thing, because the permanent thing needs to follow the currency of commerce or social capital, and that for me brings back into focus what we talked about earlier: a power dynamic. If I had to run things permanently, it would not be autonomous, it would be autocratic. It would change the nature of things and it would happen to the best of people, unless there are tactical and colluded collaborative ways something can happen.

I live very close to the art world and the film world, just by virtue of living in Bombay, and ironically my work has gained some recognition as art practice, and not as filmmaking. But what I feel I would really like is peer recognition and peer interaction in more fearless and collaborative ways, so that there is give-and-take and urgent critique. Ashok and I are looking at the new art boom here, artists using new media technologies in galleries, and we just get bored with it because one has seen enough of this in the last decade anyway. To suddenly encounter derivations of it in India in the midst of a huge art-market hype and boom—it is a serious boom—is such a lost cause that it's not even worth contesting. Our peers will not be found there. So, I am not sure how people see us, because we have not been able to belong somewhere entirely. Definitely we are art practitioners, and that is what we will always do. For the time being, art is what legitimizes what we do, and I like that. I like the fact that I can just walk down the street and say, well, it is an art project so we are taking electricity from the park, and for a while nobody knows what to say. So, art and even pedagogy allows you to justify doing things.

We find ourselves working more and more with people who are advocating alternative technologies like wireless, micro-FM, FLOSS. People who are doing very interesting research on Knowledge and Culture Commons, on intellectual property law, and issues of piracy. Ashok and I are committed to set up a kind of base for what we call CAMP: Critical Art and Media Practices. As of now, there is no money to back this, there is no immediate, organized framework, but I believe it will change.

India is no longer a developing country; we are "second world" now. The big boosterist monster is trampling over the real estate in the city, crushing and uprooting people and livelihoods, countering this vision of a global city. It is also democracy boomtime; the middle class and intelligentsia think they have rights they can claim and exercise. Everybody is talking that rights-based discourse. It was nauseating to see the mass of NGO's eloquence in every tent at the World Social Forum. There are millions for whom there is no fundamental concept of a right, be it labor, livelihood, housing, land. We are all riding this wave that India is soon going to become the richest country in the world, never mind the fact that six hundred million people will *not* be rich, but dare you say anything negative at this moment. It is such a gung-ho time. With Web 2.0 and YouTube and social networking, young people are back in start-up mode, in venture mode.

MB: Do you have any thoughts about the buzz around the democratization of media that is surrounding formats like YouTube, which you just mentioned?

SA: On the face of it, it is great. Why should I complain? In much the same way I would not complain about my two-GB storage on my G-mail account. I am just hoping and looking for slightly better bandwidth so that I can download more videos. But I am not buying the "you're the broadcast yourself generation" and all of that. And on very basic levels, YouTube is Google, Murdoch is MySpace, eyeballs mean money. You know, Creative Commons India launched a couple of weeks ago, and it was almost eerie. You had this guy, Joichi Ito, who is a venture capitalist, who runs the World of Warcraft Guild, and is the head of Creative Commons worldwide—Lessig is the other head. Ito is more the operating head and he gave his spiel about buzz marketing, how free downloads and Pepsi and iPods can work together. There is this idea that free culture will happen if we build it. So, "creativity builds on the past," but the past starts on the day that free culture thinks it starts, or a Creative Commons license legitimizes its presence.

I am sure if I lived in America or in Europe I would be endorsing CC and licensing my own work and my own films, but living here in India I could never take a very critical and vocal stand against piracy, quite the contrary. I mean that *is* access here. It might come from software or movie piracy, but for me it is the best, cheapest, most localized, fastest superefficient distribution of information. If anything, I have a little cynicism about many things democratic at the moment.

MB: To conclude, do you want to say something about what the grandest vision of dissemination and distribution would look like, imagining you had no issues with resources? What would your more ideal form of distribution be?

SA: Fiction film. Really, it does not get more ideal than that, and in all forms of distribution, from being aired on TV and cinemas to it being streamed and pirated on YouTube in ten-minute segments, torrented, sold in black, whatever. You know, there is just beauty and joy in telling happy stories about people. But it is not all like that, so one must continue doing what we do. Did I answer that, or did you want me to give a more serious answer?

Notes

www.chitrakarkhana.net, www.recurrencies.net, http://world-information.org/wio/program/bangalore

1. http://www.critical-art.net/books/ted/

14 The *Gambiarra*: Considerations on a Recombinatory Technology

Ricardo Rosas

The street finds its own uses for things.
—William Gibson, *Burning Chrome*

Two contemporary facts: on March 11, 2004, bombs exploded in metro and train stations across Madrid, killing hundreds of civilians. In São Paulo, between May 12 and 16, 2006, a wave of attacks against various targets, coordinated and commanded by cell phone by the PCC—*Primeiro Comando da Capital* (First Command of the Capital)—spread panic across the city. In both cases, we see actions that terrorized society and wreaked profound havoc on the daily life of these cities.

However, besides their obvious association as acts of urban terrorism, there is another common factor in these events—an element that was perhaps essential in their modus operandi, without which they would never have worked—an element that has perhaps gone unnoticed, having been a subliminal and imperceptible component of the acts, but nonetheless crucial in their execution: both were most likely carried out using limited and precarious resources, improvised devices, in other words, *gambiarras*.[1]

Many of the cell phones used in our prisons before, during—and perhaps since the PCC attacks—were stolen devices adapted with similarly stolen chips, a common cloning practice. The bombs that went off in Madrid were made of dynamite and nitroglycerine strapped to cell phones.

And yet, luckily, it's not all bad news. At the same time we see the *gambiarra* being used in bombs, we also see its use as a solution provider, as in the recycling of the scrap metals, other materials, and technologies discarded by our consumer society, and even in works of art.

After all, what does *gambiarra* actually mean? The Portuguese word *gambiarra* immediately conjures images of the clandestine electricity hookups so often seen in slums and shantytowns, and this is precisely the first sense of the word as defined by the dictionary *Houaiss*.[2] However, *gambiarra* also means something far more akin to the English term *makeshift*, referring to any improvisation of an expedient substitute when other means fail or are not available. In other words, "making do."

In Brazil, the term carries an especially strong cultural weight, being used to define any quick-fix solution made with whatever happens to be at hand. This sense of the term has not been lost on the art scene, and features in various creations in the field of the visual arts. Indeed, it is from this harvest in particular that we can identify further and revealing concepts behind the *gambiarra* and its symbolic/cultural meaning. In an essay on the theme of the *gambiarra* in Brazilian art, *O malabarista e a gambiarra* (The Conjurer and the *Gambiarra*), Lisette Lagnado suggests that the *gambiarra* is an item around which a certain type of discourse is now gaining momentum. Pieced together of articles expelled from the functional system, the *gambiarra*, "taken as a concept, involves transgression, fraud, and jiggery-pokery—though without relinquishing order, albeit a very simple one."[3] However, for Lagnado, the *gambiarra* mechanism carries a political stress beyond its aesthetic emphasis. As a response to a lack of resources, "*gambiarras* are not made without nomadism and collective intelligence."

The *gambiarra* also comes very close to the concept of bricolage formulated by Claude Lévi-Strauss in *The Savage Mind*. Considering the *bricoleur* as "he who works with his hands, but using indirect means, if compared with the artist,"[4] his materials are not definable in terms of a project, like those of the engineer, but merely by their instrumentality as items collected and stored because they "might come in handy." The *bricoleur* creates in the absence of a preconceived plan, removed from all standard technical processes and norms, using only fragmentary, readymade materials; and his creations always come to a new arrangement of elements the natures of which are only modified by the manner in which they feature in the instrumental assemblage or the final structure. The distinction Lévi-Strauss draws between the *bricoleur* and the engineer is essential to understanding the *gambiarra*, this freewheeling creation that goes beyond user manuals and projectual restrictions, being essentially a practice of bricolage.

Above all else, in order to understand the *gambiarra* not merely as a practical creative endeavour, but as art and intervention in the social sphere, there are certain ever-present elements that must be borne in mind: the precariousness of the means; the improvisation; the inventiveness; the dialogue with the surrounding or local reality and the community; the possibility of sustainability; the flirtation with illegality; the technological recombination in the reuse or new use of a given technology, among other factors. These aspects need not necessarily appear together or even always be present. But one thing is certain—some will always arise for one reason or another.

In addition, there is always that tinge of unpredictability, as things can indeed be what they seem, or not. Added to that, as we shall see later, are the present technological conditions, which infinitely multiply the range of possible recombinations of the technologies, apparatuses, and artefacts that surround us, dilating still further the concept and definition of what the *gambiarra* is and is not.

Let us turn to some particular creations. For reasons of space, and given the immense number of works to choose from, we shall limit ourselves to Brazilian and Latin American productions.

A good place to start is with the classical *gambiarra*, the kind we see in the streets. The *gambiarra* is undeniably vernacular in nature and origin. It is born from the meanderings of spontaneity, from daily improvisation as a means of survival, sometimes even crossing the threshold into piracy and illegality, sometimes adding an extra flash of creativity to the quotidian of chaos and poverty. The scope is immense, but we can begin with a still incipient cartography of apparatuses and configurations: among the many possible examples, we could cite the clandestine hookups (or "Cats," as they are known in Brazil), whether of electricity or cable TV; the bicycles rigged with loudspeakers for advertising in the streets of Belém do Pará, the so-called electric bikes; the "Little Yellow Tricycle" of *seu* Pelé in Rio de Janeiro, which, according to Gabriela de Gusmão Pereira,[5] boasts a three-in-one stereo, TV, spotlight, batteries, rain canopy, alarm clock, and Christmas-tree lights; the already established *trios elétricos*, carnival trucks rigged with sound systems; or the sound tables mounted at the funk balls in Rio, which look more like spaceship control panels than anything else.

Some production in the sphere of art presents a portrait of vernacular *gambiarra*-ing, whether by approaching it from the perspective of design, as with the photos by Gabriela de Gusmão Pereira (Figure 14.1) and reports by Christian Pierre Kasper, or in the photos and videos by Cão Guimarães.

Subtle and sophisticated reinterpretations of the realm of vernacular technological *gambiarra*-ing have been made, for example, by the Brazilian group BijaRi (Figure 14.2), which reuses much of this popular repertoire in research with street vendors, junk collectors, and *gambiarras*, most notably their current research on technologies of resistance.

Likewise, we cannot fail to mention certain common practices in the digital arena and catalogue such actions as digital piracy, cracking and wardriving (invading unprotected wireless networks), using, for example, Pringles potato chip tubes. The same reasoning extends to the growing community of free and open-source software developers. Working within a vast exchange network of information and code, these developers are always creating and improvising configurations, inventing new modalities of use and application, veritable code *gambiarras*, open to meddling and tweaking by whoever has the skill.

Another type of *gambiarra*-ing is that done by artists and activists who recreate, alter, or pervert machines and their uses. The connection between art and the invention/alteration of machines is nothing new. Contraptions imagined or produced by artists

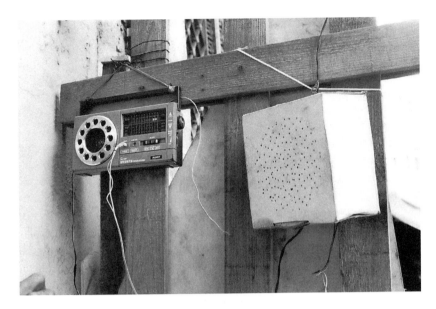

Figure 14.1
Rue dos inventos—caixa de som, 2002. Photo by Gabriela Gusmão

Figure 14.2
Arquitetura de resistencia, 2005. Photo by BijaRi

have long dwelled in the human imagination. One thinks of such creators as Leonardo da Vinci or Athanasius Kircher, to name just two rather distant examples.

An interesting machine, albeit with no guarantee of proper functioning, is the *Brain Decooder* (sic) *Plus* created by Moacir Lago (Figure 14.3), an artist from Recife. Ticketed as a "thought decoder," it is an invention licensed to the company Obsoletch Brasil, another of the artist's creations. This machine purports to do what technology has not yet achieved: decode what is most intimate and personal in us, namely our thoughts and desires. Using irony as an approach, Lago wants to stimulate reflection on the issue of ethics in science and technological progress, as well as the relationship between technological artifacts and people's everyday lives. For Lago, technological inventions instill new consumer desires, such that, faced with the launch of new, more modern products, people come to regard as obsolete the equipment they already possess. In addition to investigating the use of technology in art and vice versa, the artist raises for discussion the appropriation and democratization of knowledge, as much by the sciences as by art. In order to question the way galleries legitimize art, he transformed both wings of Recife's Fundação Joaquim Nabuco gallery into Obsoletch showrooms.

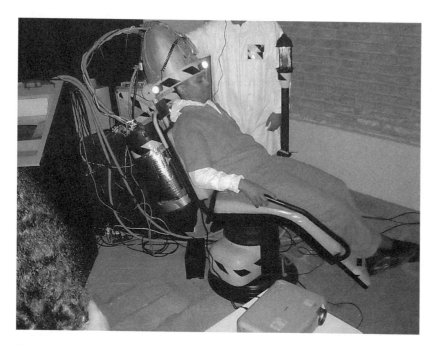

Figure 14.3
Brain Decooder Plus (Projeto Trajetorias), 2005. Photo by Moacir Lago

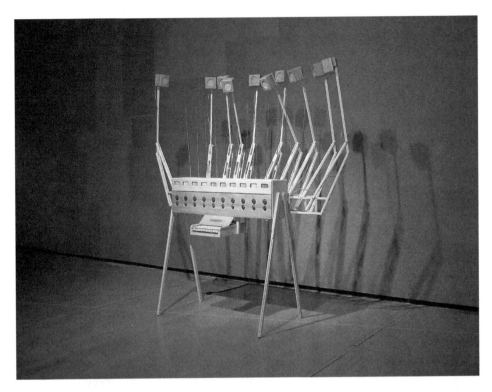

Figure 14.4
Decabraquido radiofonico, 2006. Photo by Paulo Nenflidio

More involved in sound studies, Paulo Nenflídio (Figure 14.4) creates sound contraptions and gadgets that mix novel and surprising materials, such as his wind-powered musical instruments or digital *berimbau* (a single-string instrument used to accompany capoeira performances), rigged with a mouse and doorbell bobbin. One of his most notable creations in terms of public intervention is undoubtedly the *Bicicleta maracatu*, in which a device strapped to the back of a bike produces a *maracatu* rhythm on an *agogô* rattle when pedaled. Other examples of *gambiarra* soundwork are the installations and presentations of the group of musicians/artists Chelpa Ferro, including the sound machine *Jungle*, which consists of a plastic bag attached to a motor that produces a jungle-like rhythm, and the installation *Nadabhrama*, which mechanically ruffles dry, seed-bearing tree branches.

Lucas Bambozzi, an artist who started out in media art, turns every now and then to transgressions in the technological sphere. Of special interest is his recent creation *Spio Project* (Figure 14.5), an automated Roomba vacuum cleaner equipped with high-sensibility wireless infrared CCTV cameras and a light emission diode (LED) for night-

Figure 14.5
Spio Project, 2005. Photo by Lucas Bambozzi

vision tracking. *Spio* transmits real-time images captured from the robot's perspective, like a kind of continuous generator of images void of human authorship, seen as the robot's autonomous movements are filmed by two attached cameras. Partly preprogrammed short circuits cause the robot to behave and move erratically, while simultaneously irritating the visitors. One of the intentions behind the project is to discuss the almost unnoticed invasion of our houses by apparently innocent devices that could easily be rigged with surveillance or remote positioning equipment. *Spio* alludes to emergent practices in digital culture, such as sampling and remixing, the ineffectiveness of intention in interactive works, the changes in the notion of authorship, and the continuous transit between high and low technologies. Obviously, *Spio*'s prime target is the surveillance increasingly pervading our routine, here translated into a good-humored and dysfunctional parody in the form of a captivating (or irritating) little gadget representing the archetype of the electronic eye in our surveillance society.

Without fanfare, Etienne Delacroix is the artist who incorporates, perhaps more than any other, many of the issues discussed thus far. Belgian, though resident in Brazil, he inhabits an indistinct borderland between engineering and art, technological inclusion and creativity, bricolage and design, cultural activism and education, appropriation and reinvention, theory and practice. A computer *bricoleur*, he is much more an artist of process than product. With a degree in physics, he has passed through MIT, where he tried to set up his "nomadic workshops," behind which the basic idea was to create a low-cost interface between the gestuality of the traditional artist and the fundaments of the sciences of IT and electrical engineering. Bringing together students of engineering, computing, the arts, communication, design, architecture, and music, and a growing mass of computer scrap, the project only really started to take off when he moved to the Universidad de La República in Montevideo. At his studio there, scrapped computers are taken apart in order to select the still functional components, which are then reused not only to assemble new computers, but also in huge art installations. What we have here is not simply a brand of machine recycling for the purposes of social or digital inclusion—though that is certainly a part—but more essentially a fundamentally experimental deportment, a technical processuality that involves a more complex sensibility.

There would be nothing new in stating that the *gambiarra* is endemic to Brazil. That being so, why, even today, do we still lack a theory that deals with this praxis? This text is just a first step in that direction. Perhaps we can find the reasons for this by looking at the contexts in which theories on technology, electronic art, art and technology, or media art are generated in Brazil. We therefore need to pay more attention to what goes on around us in the streets as opposed to merely keeping up with trends in the United States and Europe. Moreover, perhaps a true engagement with the idea of technological *gambiarra*-ing also demands that we abandon the presuppositions, bad habits, and prejudices that still prevail over some of these scenes. Above all, we need to open our eyes to a possible excess of complacence, a snobbery toward more vernacular practices. As with "art by art," the creations of art and technology also run the risk of being ostracised by "art by technology."

In the meantime, we have closed our eyes to the phenomena that abound not only in the arena of the popular repertoire, on the streets of our large cities and small towns, among the stalls of street vendors, or on shantytown corners, but also those equally widespread, though perhaps under other names, throughout geek culture, in the increasingly creative and abundant production of the new media, or in the machinations of media activists and the practitioners of tactical media.

In relation to geek culture, how can we not notice the practices disseminated through programming, systems installation, trials with new programs in the free software community, for example, all products of continuous reinvention and experimentation? Not to mention the growing number of user-modified devices, customizations, and the hacking of games and robots, among other manifestations.

Gambiarra-ing is undoubtedly a political activity—political not only in the sense of activism (or a support for activism), but because the very practice itself is a political statement. And, whether consciously or not, *gambiarra*-ing can often negate the productive logic of capitalism, stop a gap, fill a lack, balance the precarious, reinvent production, offer utopian glimpses of a new world, stir a revolution, or simply try to heal the open wounds of the system, bringing comfort or a voice to the dispossessed.

The *gambiarra* is itself a voice, a cry—of freedom, of protest—or simply of existence, the affirmation of an innate creativity.

However, *gambiarra*-ing—as a process, a work in progress—does not necessarily guarantee a finished product. In fact, perhaps the process is even more important, precisely because the *gambiarra* is never final; there is always something to add or improve. And yet, there is something else here. If we turn, for instance, to pirate radio or the *gambiarra* screenings, such as Cine Falcatrua's digital practices, *gambiarra*-ing is also a method. It is a mode, modus operandi, a stratagem, a guerrilla tactic, a plan of action, transmission, dissemination. This can be observed not only in the way the media activist groups function, but also in the practices of alternative local art groups and networks. Alternative forums throughout Brazil, like the Casa de Contracultura in São Paulo, the now defunct Gato Negro, Espaço Insurgente, Espaço Impróprio, and Espaço Estilingue are not just meeting places, but, as if through a kind of anarchic processual *gambiarra*-ing, provide residencies, occupations, exchanges, and self-sustainable strategies to keep themselves afloat while facilitating interchange among artists, activists, and groups. This *gambiarra*-ing process both enables exchange in the southern circuit (examples are the interchanges among such groups as BijaRi and A Revolução Não Será Televisionada (*The Revolution Will Not Be Televised*) and Argentinian counterparts like the Callejero Theater Group), and opens up new prospects of mobility for these groups and artists, thus breaching the frontiers of the art world, something that would not otherwise occur. The same can be said of the work method, which implies collaboration, the formation of networks, the use of new (and old) technologies. These networks are already highly visible on the horizon of Brazilian activism and art. One thinks of the exchanges brought about by such lists as *Corocoletivo*, *mídiatática*, *digitofagia*, or even the festivals these groups have held over recent years: events promoted with hardly any financial support, just with the participants' will to collaborate and take part.

The current technological conditions have fueled a growing proliferation of apparatuses, connection possibilities, and convergences, and on- and off-line networks that are becoming more and more interconnected, where mobile, wi-fi, remote positioning devices, global positioning systems (GPS), radio frequency identification devices (RFID), and other systems engage in dialogue and allow for a mixing of analogical and digital technologies, low- and high-tech, in what the theorist Giselle Beiguelman has dubbed "cybrid culture."[6]

In the area of new media and art and technology, this intense technological convergence has, in turn, coincided with a veritable boom in the practice of invention (or reinvention) using preexisting instruments and apparatuses, thus generating a host of *gambiarras*, gizmos, and contraptions of the strangest possible order and for the most varied ends, ranging from new forms of communication to new activist strategies, from hitherto unthought of ways of handling urban space to innovative attempts to adapt to an unlikely ubiquity of computational machines. These conditions have, in a certain way, erased the limits between the artist and the engineer, something the Russian productivists could only dream of, and confused the staunch notions Lévi-Strauss formulated to separate the *bricoleur* from the engineer, on the one hand, and from the artist on the other. This set of circumstances opens future perspectives that are almost unforeseeable to the practitioners and creators of the *gambiarra*. We could perhaps dabble in futurist speculation on what the *gambiarra* has in store for us, and in so doing we may turn to someone who has, in a certain way, already envisaged a future landscape for the contraptions that surround us—the science fiction writer Bruce Sterling, who has recently been writing on the objects and apparatuses of today and tomorrow. Exercising a form of speculation he calls "design fiction", a more designed form of science fiction, Sterling imagines our future on the basis of our relationship with these objects. In his most recent book, *Shaping Things*, a lampooning of sustainable design for the future, he claims that we are in danger "because we design, build, and use dysfunctional hardware."[7] Sterling sensibly points out that the present form of domination by the ruling classes relies on archaic forms of energy and materials that are both finite and toxic. A regime that destroys the climate, poisons the population, and generates wars over resources is a futureless one.

In his singular style, Sterling attempts to demonstrate along evolutionary lines how mankind, at a certain point in the course of its technological development—somewhere around the fall of the Mongol Empire—switched from producing and using artifacts to using the machines that substituted those artifacts, thus turning users into clients. Centuries later, after World War I, these clients transformed into consumers, as the machines became *products* by agency of distribution, commercialization, and anonymous, uniform mass production. This evolution implied specialization in the manufacturing and use of things, specialization that was to sharpen in the stage that followed, beginning, according to Sterling, in 1989. This, he claims, was the year that saw the emergence of gizmos (contraptions, gadgets) and the transformation of consumers into the end users of the "New World Disorder" in which we now live. These gizmos are, we are told, highly unstable, user-alterable, tremendously multifunctional, and generally programmable. They also have a short life cycle. These gizmos have so much functionality that it is usually cheaper to import new functionalities for the object than to try to simplify it. The next evolutionary phase is what Sterling calls *spime*. Technically, *spimes*—a neologism of the author's making—do not yet exist as such, but he envisages them as interactive, new, inventive, manufactured objects the framework of which supports such a wealth and volume of information and data that they effectively amount to materializations of an immaterial system. *Spimes* will basically be data from start to finish: sustainable, improvable, each with its own unique identity, and made of substances that can be returned to the productive chain for use in future *spimes*. For Sterling, "*Spimes* are information melded with sustainability."[8]

Even though Sterling does not directly mention its DIY-style production, and despite the fact that *spime* incorporates data from the history of the object itself (among other forms, from the RFID system) and that sophistication is largely something one would not associate with the *gambiarra*, it is impossible not to see in his description of *spime* something of the multifunctionality, the ever-present possibility for recreation, alteration, and modification that defines the recombinatory character of the *gambiarra*. In an almost biological way, to think of Gilbert Simondon or Bernard Stiegler, the technical object (the appliance, the apparatus, or whatever else it may be) can improve over time, generating composites and transforming, perhaps even evolving. And on these terms, the *gambiarra* could well be a riskier, more creative sister of the gizmo, that is, a precursor of the *spime*. Then again, could it be that, with its constant updatings and reupdatings, the *gambiarra* isn't already just that—a *spime*?

Notes

This essay was originally published in *Caderno Videobrasil 02—Arte Mobilidade e Sustentabilidade* (Art Mobility and Sustainability) © Associação Cultural Videobrasil 2006.

Special thanks to Andre Mesquita for his assistance in finalizing this chapter. Ricardo was in the process of revising this essay for this book but unfortunately died before finishing it. His passing is a tremendous loss to many, including the international communities of tactical media activists and artists.

1. The artist Cao Guimarães gives a nice definition of *gambiarra* in his interview for the Singapore Film Festival Web site (http://www.sfs.org.sg/2005/10cao-g-interview.html): "*Gambiarra* is a word we have in Brazil, which means something like 'solving problems in alternative ways' or 'giving different functions to different objects'" (my translation).

2. Houaiss, Antônio, *Dicionário Houaiss da Língua Portuguesa*, 1st ed. (Rio de Janeiro: Editora Objetiva, 2001), p. 1423.

3. Lagnado, Lisette, "O malabarista e a gambiarra," in *Revista Trópico*, http://p.php.uol.com.br/tropico/html/textos/1693,1.shl.

4. Lévi-Strauss, Claude, *O Pensamento selvagem* (Campinas: Papirus, 1989), p. 32.

5. Pereira, Gabriela de Gusmão, "Sobreviventes Urbanos," in *Terreno baldio*, www.terreno.baldio.nom.br.

6. Beiguelman, Giselle, "Admirável Mundo Cíbrido," http://www.pucsp.br/~gb/texts/cibridismo.pdf#search=%22admir%C3%A1vel%20mundo%20c%C3%ADbrido%22.

7. Sterling, Bruce, *Shaping Things* (Cambridge, MA: MIT Press, 2005), p. 54.

8. Sterling, p. 43.

15 Where the Activism Is

Trebor Scholz

You may have watched some of the 180 episodes of LonelyGirl15 and thousands of comments on YouTube.[1] MySpace, the giant social networking site, may have made you curious. Or, perhaps you set up a Facebook page.[2] It's likely that you read articles on Wikipedia, and maybe you even wrote or edited an entry yourself. If you are daring, you may have even set foot into Second Life, a virtual online world.[3] You are clearly getting it.

Just call it "Read/Write Web," Network Culture, Web 2.0, Participatory or Convergence Culture.[4] I refer to it as the "social Web"—the platform of platforms with much potential for social life. Out of all single sites on the Web, Americans spend the most time, by far, on MySpace. There are over one hundred million people who mingle on MySpace and more than eighteen million who enjoy a kind of ambient intimacy on their Facebook profile pages. That's 15 percent short of including all American students. Add some six million people in Second Life and you'll see that social life on the Web has to be reckoned with.

This text gives an overview of the current activist media landscape. Activism is more than action in favor of social or political change—in support of, or opposition to, one side of a controversial argument. It extends beyond street protest, riots, direct action, singing protest songs, organizing strikes, attending town hall meetings or demonstrations, donating money, motivating colleagues to vote, volunteering for a campaign, or writing letters to Congress.

It now includes also the toolbox of the social Web. Claims about its potential need to be balanced between the proclamations of the click-happy techno-positivists and neo-Luddite refuseniks. In addition, the debate has to go beyond the Web 2.0 ideology, the widespread fetish of American participatory consumer culture, and the Che Guevara mutiny rhetoric of Californian radicality. Today, that has nothing to do with the radical politics of the Argentinean medical doctor who took off into the Congo and later the Bolivian jungle. This traditional thinking in terms of friend and enemy does not work anymore. That does not mean, however, that judgment is not possible or needed.

Cultural practice in this arena takes faith. You have to believe that gestures mean something, that they have a kick in real life. Tactical media projects, often deeply indebted in the belief that information will alter the way things are, have in fact, and with few notable exceptions, caused little concrete change. Today, there is hardly any autonomous zone, not even a temporary one. Instead, millions socialize on the turf of corporate context providers. Life itself is put to work, is monetized; community is the product and the message. This also includes the workers in the Amazon.com warehouses.

The social Web can be defined in terms of creativity, collaboration, courage, collective intelligence,[5] and content as well as commodification, control, consumption, and crisis, as Jose van Dijck of the University of Amsterdam pointed out.[6] To be able to open the participatory toolbox of the social Web, activists need to have the necessary skills. Without media literacy the Web-based possibilities remain a mystery that is best deflected with generalizing arguments that have little basis in specific technologies.

Today, in the economically developed world, activists are fond of the blogosphere with wikis and one hundred million weblogs. In the developing world, activists find neat ways of using mobile phones for activist purposes. The tools that we are using shape our way of life as much as the politicians who rule our countries.

Arguments relating to technology require examples of actual tools, devices, or platforms. Without such specificity and historical comparison, claims remain unfounded ideology. While specific instances of the social Web may disappear, these participatory phenomena will only gain importance.

In mid-2007, the Anglophone social Web is losing the race for online influence.[7] Now, the BRIC countries (Brazil, Russia, India, and China) are taking the lead. China reported that it had almost twenty-one million bloggers in 2006. Did you ever visit even one of the three Chinese sites that are among the ten highest traffic Web sites on the World Wide Web (e.g., QQ)?[8]

With few remaining places for social life in the public sphere, networked organization of activist events, electoral fundraising, cultural self-expression, and public speaking on the Internet are on the rise. More and more people spend more and more time online.

In the economically developed world, the disappearing public sphere plays people into the hands of the social Web. Where can you meet face to face except in a noisy cafe, a transitory undifferentiated mall, or a parking lot? The French philosopher Marc Auge adds highways, airports, and hotels to this list and calls them "non-places." Where do you go and play as a (sub)urban kid when your parents are too scared to let you explore the deep dark woods? Add a dose of the American culture of fear and American individualism and it's not just youth that is affected.

Kids have the reputation of taking quickly to technology. They start text messaging with their friends, or they meet in online spaces to hang out, play, share their lives online, or get creative. The lack of face-to-face interaction is not something that they like. It would be ludicrous to condemn these "social patches" because they offer at least some way of addressing what went wrong in the process of corporatizing anything that was meant to be public in our cities.

This dilemma makes a much-needed complex critique of the corporate social Web more difficult. There must be a space to question the turf on which so many of our friends, kids, and neighbors socialize. The core sites of the social Web are *using* the people who contribute to them. Their wealth is created on the backs of the very many people who create profiles, flirt, chat, and learn on sites like MySpace. Networked publics contribute content, enjoy each others creations, but hand over most rights to the platform owner. How can this ownership be fairly shared in proportion to the original contribution? And also as part of this conversation let's not forget that there is a substantial difference between a mom-and-pop store that struggles to stay open and the global media giant NewsCorp, for example.

How productive is cocky all-out rejection of everything capitalist today? People who make an argument for the end of capitalism have good reasons, but the end is nowhere in sight. Without turning into corporate apologists whose goal it is to fine-tune corporate tools, making them more fun and useful, let's dig deeper and point out what really does not work about the corporate social Web and let's build ethical alternatives.

Teens are not the only ones squeezed between a rock of suburbia and the hard place of the Internet when it comes to getting their voices heard in public. The failed war in Iraq, the disaster of Darfur, the world AIDS crisis—all these many struggles call for our engagement beyond the cathartic couch experience of watching blockbuster films like "An Inconvenient Truth."

Today, many North Americans spend hours commuting to work. Life is work. We are fighting off the onslaught of information and it is not just the disappearing public sphere that makes true political engagement difficult. In the United States, people work endless hours. How do you squeeze in activism in this precarious situation? The Internet makes it in many ways easier to engage.

Politics and dissent are very much about affect, and cultural resistance keeps that flame going; both writing texts and making artworks contribute. "EA Spouse," for example, was a widely circulated anonymous letter of the spouse of an employee of the games company Electronic Arts (EA) mounting an emotional critique of the labor practices at EA.[9] It could be a fictional letter, an artistic intervention, written from the perspective of the spouse of an EA employee. Read all across the World Wide Web, this letter seriously impacted the public image of EA. Match that, union negotiators!

Or, remember Kanye West's remix, "George Bush Don't Like Black People."[10] West took the scandal of the blatant nonresponse of the G.W. Bush administration to the

Katrina disaster, and the implicit racism in the response to the looting, and made this remix that kids started whistling in the street. Kanye West's song became so popular that George W. Bush feel a need to respond to the song in order to adjust his public image.

The young Parisian designer Alex Chan produced the film "The French Democracy," explaining the deep-rooted racism in France that led to the riots in 2005. The thirteen-minute, nine-second-long work uses *machinima*,[11] and is based on the simulation game, "The Movies." Chan produced the piece within one week on his laptop, and soon many thousand people downloaded it online.

The found footage remix lip-synched love song between George W. Bush and Tony Blair by the art group U.S. Department of Art & Technology is a hit on Archive.org and YouTube.[12] The superbly talented text pieces by Young-Hae Chang Heavy Industries are another example.[14]

MoveOn.org sponsored a popular video contest to produce thirty-second advertisements putting President Bush on the spot.[15] Also the works by 0100101110101101.org intelligently knock on the door of "passive-aggressive capitalism."[16] Sites like Homeland Security Threat Monitor and the political-satire site Whitehouse.org work on the level of humor.[17] But at the same time, and perhaps more importantly, they share a sense of dissatisfaction and opposition. People send a link with a new clip criticizing policy, thus sharing their disagreement with the decisions of the current administration. The Homeland Security Threat Monitor builds on the strong and widespread impression that threat-level warnings were strategically used by the White House to instill fear and thus guide the elections in favor of those who appear to be strong on security.[18] (Traditionally, the Republican Party managed to convince more U.S. Americans that they are strong in this domain.)

Citizen media became known in 1999 when the World Trade Organization met in Seattle, and IndyMedia was launched. The idea was simple: citizens send in their news stories to the site that would indiscriminately post them. Over the years and despite high traffic, IndyMedia failed to become a real challenge to mainstream media.[19] In 2004 bloggers stepped to the podium with full force causing a hype. Today, blogs like the "Daily Kos" have up to 500,000 readers per day.[20]

Short Message Service (SMS), also referred to as "text messages," has become an organizing tool for spontaneous protests, and all over the economically developing world mobile phones are deployed to document and report human rights violations. In March 2004, for example, text messages alerted thousands of people to antigovernment protests in Spain following the Madrid bombings. SMS has served as political tool in the process of governmental change in the Philippines and the number of mobile-phone lines in Africa increased drastically. South African women in the rural KwaZulu-Natal province, for example, use mobile phones to report on violations of their human rights as well as to assert constitutional rights. Despite intensive efforts by authoritarian governments, bloggers in Bahrain, Hong Kong, Iran, Nepal, and the United Arab Emirates have broken their news monopoly.

GlobalVoices founder Ethan Zuckerman describes how an anonymous Bahrani activist created a set of maps and distributed it as a .pdf file.[21] The highlighted maps contrasted the cramped urban neighborhoods with the spacious palaces built for members of the ruling family.[22] Bahrain's government temporarily blocked GoogleMaps following this incident.[23]

In 2001 massive protests in the Philippines, coordinated by text messaging, were credited with ousting President Joseph Estrada. In 2005 the "Hello Garci!" scandal marked a new electoral crisis in the Philippines.[24] Wikipedia describes the event "that involved incumbent president Gloria Macapagal-Arroyo, who allegedly rigged the 2004 national election in her favor." In June 2005 audio recordings of a phone conversation between President Arroyo and Virgilio Garcillano allegedly talking about the rigging of the 2004 national election results, were released to the public. Consequently, the audio recording "Hello Garci!" became a popular mobile-phone ring tone that led to the creation of over thirty remixes, now hosted on the site of The Philippine Center for Investigative Journalism.[25]

In 2004 in the United States, the Institute for Applied Autonomy developed TxtMob in the context of the Democratic National Convention in Boston and the Republican National Convention in New York. TxtMob is a free service that lets you easily broadcast SMS text messages to a group of people.[26]

The examples from the Philippines and the United States show that text messaging can be a valuable tool to initiate and coordinate dissent. The ring-tone remix activism in the Philippines works on an affective level and makes it easy to distribute a political message—for example, the elections are rigged—in a creative and humorous way. However, low-tech interventions can also be highly effective: the e-mail with an attached .pdf file of the GoogleMap image of Bahrain outraged the poor villagers. The example from the South African women in the rural KwaZulu-Natal province showed that text messaging can in fact aid people in geographically isolated locations by giving them an opportunity to report human rights violations.

An editor of Channel NewsAsia, Joanne Teoh (Singpaore), says that a recent World Bank survey among those living on less than one dollar a day found that when asked, most of them responded that "access to voice" would make the biggest difference in their lives.[27] In China, for instance, issues addressed by grassroots media include poverty, minority unrest, and corruption. The Beijing blogger Li Yuanyuan posted a story about Gong Jinghong, a young orphan of migrant workers.[28] The blog post received tens of thousands of comments; it galvanized the community, and the girl became a poster child for migrant politics.

In the United States, distributed research is another activist approach. The project "WhoDies?" by the Committee to Help Unsell the War, for example, summarizes lies of the Bush administration about both Gulf wars. It addresses the cost of war on U.S. civilians and soldiers as well as Iraqi civilians and soldiers. The IraqBodyCount project tracks Iraqi casualties of war by crosschecking news accounts, listing a minimum of 62,770 dead in May 2007.[29]

The Internet is not just a valuable environment to publicize research but also a useful platform for fundraising and organizing. On February 15, 2003, about ten million people took to the streets in over six hundred cities around the world to protest the U.S. invasion of Iraq. On February 26, 2003, MoveOn's "virtual march" on Washington D.C. mobilized thousands. In June 2003 Howard Dean used a site called Meetup (a free service that organizes local gatherings) to coordinate 23,000 people in nearly five hundred cities.[30] Another important example is Craigslist, started by Craig Newmark in 1995. Craigslist is an ethical business that offers local classifieds and forums to fifteen million people per month in 450 cities worldwide—community moderated, and largely free.

In March 2006 students in Los Angeles organized a large-scale protest on MySpace. Finally, sites like Protest.net inform about upcoming protests,[31] and Campaigns Wikia links people to ongoing political campaigns.[32]

Not a protest site but an important example of ad-hoc activist work in the United States appeared after August 29, 2005 near the coastlines of Louisiana when Hurricane Katrina hit the shores, causing massive human tragedy. The Katrina PeopleFinder Project was developed quickly as a central site to find missing people. Craigslist, Yahoo! and the Red Cross had put up sites, but they were scattered. The Katrina PeopleFinder Project was used by more than 650,000 people to post entries regarding their whereabouts. Over one million people searched for loved ones by entering their zip codes and names.

Kiva.org lets you loan money to small businesses in the developing world.[34] Throughout the course of the loan, you can receive e-mail updates from the business you have sponsored.

Surveillance on the social Web is one-to-many, many-to-many, and many-to-one. Platforms like MySpace are infiltrated by police and other governmental groups in search of illegal activity. What are new modes of surveillance and how can we learn to address them critically? Lateral survei/lance (everybody knows that all others are watching) now has the added component of unwilling, invisible watchdogs. Employers check the MySpace pages of potential employees, who are often young and don't expect such intrusion into their private life. Now, surveillance is a goddess with many arms. People don't even suspect being watched. Just check out the privacy details in the small print of companies like Yahoo! and Ebay. There you will find that Yahoo! is not shy to point out that all content a user produces (including e-mails and instant messages) can be read by Yahoo! employees."[35] EBay says that it "may collect information about your e-mail address, physical contact information, IP address, and standard

Web log information; financial information, such as credit-card or bank-account numbers."[36]

The Electronic Frontier Foundation reacted to problems of communication privacy online. It developed "Tor," a toolset for a wide range of organizations and people that want to improve their safety and security on the Internet.[37] Tor users can anonymize their Web browsing, publishing, and instant messaging.

The project Wikileaks faces the challenges to anonymity by offering an uncensorable platform for untraceable mass document leaking and analysis.[38] It combines the protection and anonymity of cutting-edge cryptographic technologies with the transparency and simplicity of a wiki interface.

Steve Mann, of the Department of Electrical and Computer Engineering at the University of Toronto, proposed to turn the tables by monitoring authority figures with the same technologies of surveillance that they use to watch us.[39] He calls this "sousveillance."

Metavid is a Web-based sousveillance project.[40] It allows citizens to keep a close tab on the Senate. It takes C-SPAN feeds of public-domain video of our government in action, strips out the copyrighted material, and makes it all searchable by indexing the close captioning provided by the government.

Web-based virtual worlds have been in the media limelight for a while now. Critics are quick to point out that activism in virtual worlds like Second Life (SL) only detracts from real life activism. Entering Camp Darfur in SL users may have something like a cathartic experience that leaves them with the impression that they have actually done something about the issues when in fact they were simply sucked into computer screens for hours. In addition, people need a fairly lucrative first life to afford Second Life. Critics are too quick, however, to dismiss all of SL as spooky cultural and political regression.

Just take the Avatar Action Center (AAC).[41] The AAC is a virtual educational center in Second Life dedicated to real-world social change. If you ever spend time in Second Life, you may find it pathetic to see avatars marching from left to right (of your screen) holding up banners. Due to its novelty factor, such initiatives draw media attention by the BBC and others that also aid the motivating political causes.

Activism, however, does not just mean holding up a banner or raising a fist. Intellectual and ethical rigor matter, and flag-waving activist rhetoric gives us all a rush, but who listens? It's time for complexities and radical hybridity. Let's not mistake that for the academic exercise of accurately describing the object of study without judging the gained information. It is not sufficient to pack your rucksack and venture out to mingle among the Facebook kids, however important that may be. Defending the "Generation Me" against a society that does not care about youth (except in their function as consumers) is worthwhile, but the observation needs to turn into critique that is inclusive of the deep-rooted social causes for what went wrong.

Forty percent of the page views on the World Wide Web are being attributed to only ten Web sites. Good old capitalism is also responsible for the social architecture of the Web. We need to look at the edges and borders of the social Web and not just smack in the middle where the corporate giants feast over all that collective intelligence.

The defense of our rights over the content that we created and uploaded to big corporate platforms is an additional crucial site for activism. There needs to be complete transparency with regard to privacy. What does NewsCorp do with 170 million MySpace profiles? Activists need to develop an acute awareness of what we are giving away on the social Web. This is where we need activism. Where is the fair share of the corporate profits generated from our attention and networked social life? How fair and transparent is this relationship? Such literacy, such grammar of the social Web is an important site of activism. Transparency of the rules of the sociable media game is part of this literacy. Who owns our content? Who profits from our online social life? What happens with our profiles (our birth date, favorite music, movies, and books and all that info about our friends and how we met them, and whom we date, and where their sites are, and what our schedule is . . .). Tell us how much money you make from our attention. Tell us. MySpace was bought by NewsCorp for $583 million and now has a predicted market value of $15 billion by 2008. Content creators want a fair share. Again, it needs a close look at the small print of the social networking sites to understand the concerns that this chapter brings forward.

"MySpace can use or edit your content."[42] YouTube says that "you retain the copyright for your content, but by submitting it to YouTube you are giving YouTube the right to use the material in any form that it may desire."[43] "Anything you put on Orkut becomes the Orkut property to copy or distribute."[44] "If you post any content or submit material on Amazon, you are giving Amazon a free, perpetual, irrevocable, and transferable right to use or publish it."[45] ITunes says that it has the right to use the content submitted by you in any way it likes without paying you.[46]

The "keep up, shut up, or leave" attitude cannot be easily applied to social networking sites like MySpace, as people are largely a *captive community*. Their content (blog entries, videos, music, photos) cannot be easily moved (exported) to another forum and it's especially hard to move an entire group of friends to a new platform. It's also harder to become a star on Bebo.com than on YouTube.[47]

Throughout this chapter, I introduced many domains of activism. The social Web offers easy gateways for people with the intention to actively engage with politics. Sites like Change.org make it simple to connect individuals with nonprofit organizations that support causes that they feel strongly about.

Text messaging has been shown to be valuable in the coordination of political dissent in the Philippines. In the United States, a specifically designed application for text messaging helped protesters at the Republican convention to coordinate the movement of groups of people in response to the actions of the police. SMS was used to report human-rights violations in South Africa, and GoogleMaps showed villagers in Bahrain that the land behind the tall walls of the ruler's palace could house hundreds of families.

The social Web also became a vast distribution platform for activist research. Examples like WhoDies and IraqBodyCount are significant and often quoted in the mainstream media. Like anybody else, activists share knowledge online. They build how-to repositories and share bibliographies.

In July 2006 the blogosphere and the video-sharing site YouTube were full of citizen accounts from Israel and Lebanon. One prominent, widely circulated case was that of the Lebanese mobile phone video of the burned out Lebanese villages. These accounts, documenting the devastation of this war, were brought forward with urgency, viral affect, intimacy, and care that mainstream media cannot match. They were out-cooperated.

A complex critique of the social Web itself, including issues of labor, privacy, transparency, and property on the social Web is also part of contemporary activism. This includes the struggle for the wealth of public goods on the Web. Keep them free and keep the Net neutral. Net neutrality should be the frontline of media activism today. It means defending the Internet as a place that is not owned by anybody (mind you, the hardware is private but the TCP/IP protocol is nonproprietary). Which protocol dominates, however, has a lot to do with real power and money. Everybody with a connection and the necessary hardware can use it. Anybody can add services and tools to it without extra charge (the rule of common carriage).

The social Web is not merely about social networking. It's not merely about machines and cables, but about networking humans through technology. Ask your daughter to show you Facebook and MySpace, or Mixi[48] and Nearbie.[49] Youth has acclimatized to instant messaging (for them e-mail is only used to talk to the Man), chat groups, peer-to-peer sharing, and multiplayer online games. They swap videos and music with ease. You can probably teach them about open source and media monopoly. Tell them about Murdoch and the idea of introducing news feeds into MySpace. Join Flickr, edit a page on Wikipedia. Create a video clip for YouTube and also upload it to BlipTV,[50] Bebo,[51] and Archive.org.[52] Get your hands dirty on the social Web turf.

Activism has become increasingly dependent on social skills, more reliant on technological competence and mobile devices. It is more geographically dispersed. Activists now brainstorm new ideas, envision projects, and coordinate them on wikis. They don't leave the playing field to the corporate executives, who understand collective intelligence and distributed creativity fairly well. Use your imagination. Don't launch a Web site, start up a community. Step out of the digital wilderness; change the world.

Notes

1. http://www.youtube.com/profile?user=lonelygirl15

2. http://facebook.com

3. http://secondlife.com

4. http://www.collectivate.net/journalisms/2006/5/26/against-web-20.html

5. Collective intelligence is a quality that emerges from the collaboration, mutual aid, or competition of many individuals.

6. http://home.medewerker.uva.nl/j.f.t.m.vandijck/

7. http://australianit.news.com.au/articles/

8. http://www.sina.com.cn, www.baidu.com, and www.qq.com

9. http://ea-spouse.livejournal.com/274.html

10. http://www.youtube.com/watch?v=UGRcEXtLpTo&mode=related&search=

11. http://www.machinima.com/films.php?id=1407

12. http://ia300131.us.archive.org/0/items/bush_blair/bush_blair.mov

13. http://www.carbondefense.org/

14. http://www.yhchang.com/THE_STRUGGLE_CONTINUES.html

15. http://www.bushin30seconds.org/

16. http://0100101110101101.org

17. http://whitehouse.org/

18. http://hewgill.com/threat/

19. http://www.indymedia.org/en/index.shtml

20. http://www.dailykos.com/

21. http://www.globalvoicesonline.org

22. http://flickr.com/groups/bahraingoogleearth/

23. http://ethanzuckerman.com/blog/?p=1085ap/

24. http://en.wikipedia.org/wiki/Hello_Garci_scandal#_note-10

25. http://pcij.org/blog/wp-files/ringtones.php

26. http://www.txtmob.com/

27. http://lyep.blog.sohu.com/41877269.html

28. http://globalvoicesonline.org/2007/04/china-community-embraces-orphan/

29. http://www.iraqbodycount.net/

30. http://dfa.meetup.com/

31. http://protest.net/

32. http://campaigns.wikia.com/wiki/Campaigns_Wikia

33. http://www.change.org/

34. http://www.kiva.org/

35. http://www.wikisummaries.com/Yahoo_Terms_of_Service

36. http://www.wikisummaries.com/EBay_Terms_of_Service

37. http://tor.eff.org/

38. http://wikileaks.org/faq

39. http://wearcam.org/

40. http://metavid.ucsc.edu/

41. http://www.avataraction.org/twiki/tiki-index.php

42. http://www.wikisummaries.com/MySpace_Terms_of_Service

43. http://www.wikisummaries.com/YouTube_Terms_of_Service

44. http://www.wikisummaries.com/Orkut_Terms_of_Service

45. http://www.wikisummaries.com/Amazon.com_Terms_of_Service

46. http://www.wikisummaries.com/ITunes_Store_Terms_of_Service

47. http://Bebo.com

48. http://mixi.jp/home.pl

49. http://www.nearbie.com/start.html

50. http://blip.tv/

51. http://www.bebo.com/

52. http://archive.org

16 Whacking Bush: Tactical Media as Play

Graham Meikle

The great archetypal activities of human society are all permeated with play from the start.
—Johan Huizinga

Rarely is the question asked: is our children learning?
—George W. Bush

Bushwhacked?

In 2003, President George W. Bush's State of the Union speech staked out some distinctive positions:

Mr. Speaker, Vice President Cheney, members of Congress, distinguished citizens and fellow citizens. Every year, by law and by custom, we meet here to threaten the world. The American flag stands for corporate scandals, recession, stock market declines, blackmail, terror, burning with hot irons, dripping acid on the skin, mutilation with electric drills, cutting out tongues, and rape. Our first goal is to show utter contempt for the environment. . . . And this year, for the first time, we must offer every child in America three nuclear missiles. . . . Secretary of State Powell will plant information to incite fear about Iraq's links to terrorist groups. And tonight I have a message for the people of Iraq—go home and die. Trusting in the sanity and restraint of the United States is not a strategy and it is not an option.

Anyone reading a book about tactical media may well be familiar with the four-minute video from which this is extracted: "Bushwhacked," which circulated widely online in 2004.[1] Created by UK satirist Chris Morris, the "Bushwhacked" video was assembled from footage of Bush's actual State of the Union speech, cut with audio samples from this and other speeches, and remixed to create an arresting new hybrid. This video, while an accomplished satirical intervention, was far from unique. In 2004 it looked at times as though more people were remixing Bush than were voting for him.

Scores of such mash-ups are posted on the video-sharing Web site YouTube: Bush singing U2's "Sunday Bloody Sunday"; Bush and UK Prime Minister Tony Blair dueting on Diana Ross and Lionel Richie's "Endless Love," or Electric Six's "Gay Bar," among others. In one of the most elaborate examples, Australian artist Wax Audio created "Imagine This," a sophisticated mash-up of John Lennon's "Imagine" and "Give Peace A Chance," with a painstaking assemblage of authentic snatches of Bush speeches sequenced to have the president "perform" the songs http://www.waxaudio.com.au. Moreover, some of these remixes and mash-ups were coordinated: in one example, the Web site of virtual band The Bots organized a contest for remixes of Bush speeches set to original music, to be made using its George W. Bush Public Domain Audio Archive, http://www.thebots.net/GWBushSampleArchive.htm. This archive offers mp3 and .wav files of Bush speeches, as well as named samples of individual phrases (such as "freedom is beautiful" or "go home and die") The complete archive runs to 15,000 samples: enough data to fill three DVDs.[2]

Of course, Bush had generated such remix interventions in his first presidential campaign too. For example, ®™ark's gwbush.com Web site, which cloned and subverted Bush's official georgewbush.com page and provoked the Bush campaign into registering for themselves dozens of such addresses as bushblows.org and bushsucks.com. The official Bush campaign set these up as aliases to the candidate's real site, thus blocking anyone else from registering them and joining the satirical fray (Meikle 2002: 117).

"Reality," James Carey once argued, "is a scarce resource"—one which people compete to control (1989: 87). In the digital era, this competition remains fierce, but the raw material is no longer in such short supply. Defining reality, carving up and exploiting that resource, is one of the central phenomena of the media. As President, Bush not only occupies the paramount position in electoral politics, but he is also a symbol at the heart of a burgeoning activist participatory culture, one which manifests itself by, among other things, creating and circulating remixes, mash-ups, and subverted texts and imagery of all kinds. As president, Bush exercises and is implicated in the political power of government, the coercive power of the military and the law, and the economic power of corporations—but he also exercises and is implicated in symbolic power: what John B. Thompson characterizes as the capacity "to intervene in the course of events, to influence the actions of others, and indeed to create events, by means of the production and transmission of symbolic forms" (1995: 17). Thompson is here building upon the work of Bourdieu, who characterized symbolic power as "a power of constituting the given through utterances, of making people see and believe . . . an almost magical power which enables one to obtain the equivalent of what is obtained through force" (Bourdieu 1991: 170).

This chapter is concerned with particular expressions of symbolic power: those that can be usefully understood as tactical media. Tactical media practice trades in symbolic power—and increasingly this is not just the domain of quasi-professional groups such as ®™ark http://rtmark.com, but of dispersed amateurs as well. These are, of course, unequal power relations, which could perhaps be classed with what anthropologist James C. Scott identifies as "the ordinary weapons of relatively powerless groups: foot dragging, dissimulation, false compliance, pilfering, feigned ignorance, slander, arson, sabotage, and so forth" (Scott 1985: 29). "A tactic," as Michel de Certeau put it, "is an art of the weak" (1984: 37). However, while it would be a mistake to overstate or romanticize such tactics, such "weapons of the weak," it would also be a mistake to dismiss them. This chapter first reviews some of the key definitions of the elusive discourse of tactical media, before developing an account of its key characteristics through the use of an extended example: the "Revolution: USA" project. It goes on to argue that tactical media can be productively analysed through a number of concepts of play.

Tactical Media?

Tactical media mix creative subversion and subversive creativity. The manifesto of the discourse, "The ABC of Tactical Media," by David Garcia and Geert Lovink (1997), opens with the following definition:

Tactical Media are what happens when the cheap "do it yourself" media, made possible by the revolution in consumer electronics and expanded forms of distribution (from public access cable to the Internet) are exploited by groups and individuals who feel aggrieved by or excluded from the wider culture.

Tactical media has been both theorized and practiced at the series of "Next 5 Minutes" (N5M) events held in The Netherlands. The third of these, in 1999, offered the following definition:

The term "tactical media" refers to a critical usage and theorization of media practices that draw on all forms of old and new, both lucid and sophisticated media for achieving a variety of specific noncommercial goals and pushing all kinds of potentially subversive political issues (cited in Critical Art Ensemble 2001: 5).

The history of the term includes the "tactical television" emphasis of the first N5M in Amsterdam in 1993, which brought together Western artists, intellectuals and activists with their counterparts from the former communist countries of Eastern Europe (Critical Art Ensemble 2001; Lovink 2002; Rushkoff 1994). The emphasis on TV and the camcorder was broadened for the subsequent N5M in 1996 (Lovink 2002: 255; Critical Art Ensemble 2001: 4).

Tactical media, writes Internet critic and activist Geert Lovink, one of the concept's key theorists, is "a deliberately slippery term, a tool for creating 'temporary consensus zones' based on unexpected alliances. A temporary alliance of hackers, artists, critics, journalists, and activists" (Lovink 2002: 271).[3] Tactical-media use is characterized by flexibility and mobility (some situations might be best tackled by making a Web site, others by making a phone call), by novelty and reinvention, and by a certain transient and temporary dimension—"hit and run, draw and withdraw, code and delete," as Lovink and Schneider put it (2001). It emphasizes the technological, the transitory, and the collaborative—qualities exemplified in the "Revolution: USA" project, which is introduced in the following section.

Revolution: USA

"Revolution: USA" was a 2004 tactical-media project coordinated by UK electronic music act Coldcut and Canadian art duo NomIg. In 2001, Coldcut had released a track called "Re:volution," a metal/drum-and-bass collision which used as its hook a sample of UK Prime Minister Tony Blair announcing that "the lunatics have taken over the asylum." Coldcut themselves created the accompanying video clip using the VJAMM video-mixing software http://www.vjamm.com, which they had developed with multimedia firm Camart http://www.camart.co.uk, compiling a collage of political samples and newspaper headlines ridiculing both major UK political parties in the lead-up to the 2001 general election.

"Revolution: USA" extended this premise into an open access participatory project. For the 2004 Presidential election, Coldcut and NomIg created the "Revolution: USA" Web site to encourage others to remix Coldcut's original track with new U.S. content http://www.revusa.net/main.php. The site offered an enormous collection of samples, both audio and audio-visual, for use in remixes (see fig. 16.1). A 300-megabyte library of audio samples of the original "Re:volution" recording was available, including extended and a capella mixes and samples of each individual instrumental track.

The "about" page of the "Revolution" Web site states the project's aims as follows:

to incite the public to assemble their own protest-ant [*sic*] magic from Coldcut's vast multimedia archive, including content uploaded by public contributors. The site also contains free audio loops and tracks created by Coldcut, which are available for use in would-be artist mixes. The aim is to build a digital A/V library replete with work that unearths the veiled wasteland of U.S. politics, in order to invoke social change, and to create a new forum for meaningful artistic interactivity. (http://www.revusa.net/subnavs.php?act=a)

The main page of the site featured a timeline of major U.S. political events, scandals, and international interventions dating back to 1960. Rolling the mouse over an item on the timeline would call up a brief descriptive text, accompanied by external links for further background reading and a selection of audiovisual samples, for the most part consisting of snatches of speeches or media appearances by political figures involved in the events in question. For example, Arnold Schwarzenegger's successful 2003 campaign to become governor of California is represented on the timeline by a fifty-word text, links to coverage archived at Fox News and CNN's Web sites, and

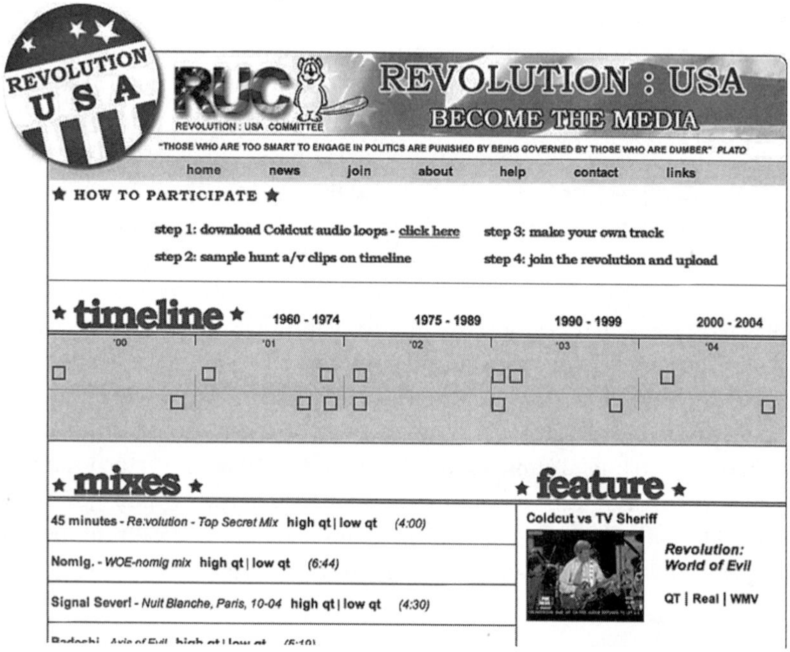

Figure 16.1

Revolution: USA main page. http://www.revusa.net/main.php.

two brief QuickTime movies of Schwarzenegger describing Democratic Party candidates as "girlie men," which could be downloaded for remixing and recontextualization. Unsurprisingly, the more recent events on the timeline generally had more accompanying video clips, while earlier events often had none, although users were able to upload clips of their own to expand the database: so, for example, there were more than twenty video clips of Bush, Colin Powell, and others proclaiming the existence of Iraqi WMDs, but no samples to accompany the entry on the Bay of Pigs.

"Revolution: USA" was launched on September 11, 2004. When the project closed on election day, November 2, 2004, thirty-six user-submitted remixes were available from the front page. Some emphasized military and civilian deaths in Iraq; others drew contrasts between spending on defence and spending on foreign aid. Some concentrated on reworking footage of the Bush/Kerry presidential debates; others traced connections between the elder and younger Bush's Iraq interventions. Some were banal and unimaginative; others were downright inspired, such as Outerbongolia's collage of moments of Bush lost for words at press conferences over the Pixies' *Surfer Rosa* cut "Where Is My Mind?," or the footage of the VJAMM Allstars' fifteen-minute live audio-visual mixing session, which climaxes with the main riff from Nirvana's "Smells Like Teen Spirit" mixed in with samples of dancing troops and Darth Vader's light-saber battle with Obi-Wan Kenobi. A featured piece was "World of Evil" by TV Sheriff, which subsequently aired on MTV. "World of Evil" drew on the full repertoire made available on the site, such as video samples of Richard Nixon ("the office of president will always be suspect") and Ronald Reagan ("government *is* the problem"). It also cut up samples to produce, for example, Madeleine Albright promising that "As President, John Kerry will lead Nazi storm troopers to defeat and destroy the world."

The entry selected as the winner by Coldcut and NomIg was a Flash project by a design group called Future 3 http://www.future3.net/bush. The interface combined a selection of computer keys, a cartoon image of five musicians, and a screen area on which video loops played (fig. 16.2). Clicking on each of the musicians triggered a loop of guitar, bass, keyboards, drums, or vocals, as well as triggering video samples showing images of death and destruction in Iraq. Clicking on one of the keys shown below triggered video loops of Bush, saying: "Freedom is beautiful, beautiful, people love freedom, freedom, we're corporate criminals, criminals, you're free, free, special

Figure 16.2
Future 3 remix page. http://www.future3.net/bush/

evil, evil, money." The user can mix these either with a mouse or by typing, to produce new combinations of Bush declaring, for example, "Freedom is money, money is evil," or "people love criminals freedom," and so on, layered over the other available combinations of the music loops.

"Revolution: USA" as Tactical Media

The "Revolution: USA" project illustrates all the major characteristics of tactical media. First, it exploits the potential of new communications technologies. Second, it is built around remixing and reworking found material. Third, the project is satirical, and while not every tactical media project could be described as satirical, it is almost always an element. Fourth, "Revolution: USA" works on the tactical principles of mobility, reinvention, temporariness, and novelty. The project is ephemeral, a moment in a participatory activist culture: its traces remain as a Web archive, but its energy and participants have since moved elsewhere. This section addresses these four points in turn.

First, "Revolution: USA" illustrates how tactical media are inseparable from new media technologies. Tactical-media practice involves, in Lovink's words, "taking full advantage of the free spaces in the media that are continually appearing because of the pace of technological change and regulatory uncertainty" (2002: 265). The precursor concept of tactical television revolved around the possibilities of camcorders and of new distribution possibilities such as cable and video. The discourse of tactical media subsequently emerged at the same time as the Net was establishing itself in the popular imagination.

"Revolution: USA" was entirely a product of the convergent media environment. It depended on the convergence of computers, media content, and telecommunications at all stages of its production, distribution, and reception. It was built around the possibilities of sampling (the audio files provided to remix the "Re:volution" track; the video archive of political speeches and soundbites), of remixing, and of the Web as a distribution platform for dissonant perspectives. One distinguishing characteristic of tactical-media practice is such use of new communications technologies to circumvent the established media, to create new channels for the circulation of images, arguments, and stories, each of which has in turn been created and manipulated by other new media technologies.

For example, Wax Audio's Bush-sings-"Imagine" recording made use of a karaoke version of the Lennon song, while its Bush samples came from the George W. Bush Public Domain Audio Archive. The resulting "Imagine This" text is distributed free as part of a download-only minialbum from the Wax Audio Web site, but has been featured on radio stations around the world—a tactical media strike. The ways in which "Imagine This" or any of the remixes generated through "Revolution: USA" were created are of more significance here than the content of the recordings themselves;

what count are the possibilities that were used in the production—the taking advantage of moments of creative opportunity afforded by technological adoption and adaptation.

Second, "Revolution: USA" invited participants to remix existing texts, to subvert found material. It was not a songwriting contest, but one which asked people to rework an existing Coldcut track. It did not ask people to write or shoot film, but to remix and repurpose existing video samples. It was a project built around tactical principles of remixing, collage, Situationist detournement.[4] Detournement can be thought of as "a politics of subversive quotation, of cutting the vocal cords of every empowered speaker" (Marcus 1989: 179). It describes the sampling of texts or images from one context and their embedding in a new one; the creation of a synthesis that calls attention to both the original context and the new result. It is the "reversal of perspective," in the Situationist Raoul Vaneigem's terms: "to stop seeing things through the eyes of the community, of ideology, of the family, of other people. To grasp hold of oneself as of something solid, to take oneself as starting point and centre" (Vaneigem 1983 [1967]: 144). Detournement is the reshaping of familiar signs into question marks.

The Situationists were a small band of writers, activists and artists whose membership churned constantly around the pivotal figure of Guy Debord. Active from the mid-1950s until the early 1970s, they sought to undermine what Debord called the spectacle: the integrated, commercialized cultural space in which "Everything that was directly lived has moved away into a representation" (1987 [1967]: section 1). The society of the spectacle, Debord wrote, drew together five phenomena: "incessant technological renewal; integration of state and economy; generalized secrecy; unanswerable lies; an eternal present" (1988: 11–12). Against this matrix of forces, the Situationists argued for art as revolutionary, and revolution as artistic—"the possibility of a life of playful opportunity in which the satisfaction of desires, the realization of pleasures, and the creation of chosen situations would be the principal activities" (Plant 1992: 2). Debord best illustrated the Situationist synthesis of art and activism in his account of how a band of Venezuelan student revolutionaries stole some paintings from an exhibition of old masters and attempted to exchange these for the release of political prisoners. The paintings were retrieved in a shootout, only for the students to hurl bombs at the police van taking the artworks away: "This is clearly an exemplary way to treat the art of the past," wrote Debord, "to bring it back into play for what really matters in life" (2002 [1963]: 161).

The Situationists had their precursors too—the creative destructions of Dada (Richter 1965), the deliberate derangements of Surrealism (Alexandrian 1970). But while the practice of detournement could be traced back beyond the Situationists themselves, it is from their promotion of the concept that its contemporary influence largely flows. The influence of the Situationists often surfaces in projects that fall within the tactical media orbit. It is, for example, very clear in the work of Adbusters, for whom Debord in particular functions as something of a patron saint. Another example would be DJ Spooky's touring video project *Rebirth of a Nation*, in which he remixes Griffith's film *The Birth of a Nation*—a film which, on the one hand, maintains its status as one of the foundational works of cinema, while on the other hand, it operated as a Ku Klux Klan recruiting film until the 1960s, if not beyond (Miller 2004: 84). DJ Spooky's project of detourning Griffith's film to subvert its racist dimension was explicitly proposed by the Situationists, who used the example of *The Birth of a Nation* to explain detournement in 1956 (Debord and Wolman 1981 [1956]).

Détourner is to remix and, as Manovich (2006) argues, the remix aesthetic has become the fundamental logic of all cultural production. Cultural commentators as diverse as Richard Florida (2002) and DJ Spooky (Miller 2004) emphasize creativity as a matter of remixing, reworking, restating, recombining. As Miller puts it, "play and irreverence toward the found objects that we use as consumers and a sense that something new was right in front of our oh-so-jaded eyes" (2004: 45).[5]

Third, "Revolution: USA" was satirical. Satire is an underemphasised element of media activism and is central to tactical media in particular.[6] While not every tactical media project could be best described as satirical, satire is almost always an element. Satire is art on the attack; it aims to ridicule and provoke. "The most potent weapons known to mankind," as the community organizer and tactical theorist Saul Alinsky wrote, "are satire and ridicule" (1971: 75). Satire is inherently subversive.[7] Like other forms of activism, satire asks questions about power and influence. Satirists and activists each make judgments about social, cultural, and political standards and failings. Both satire and activism are, among other things, forms of cultural criticism. Satire and activism are both means of resistance to various forms of power, including symbolic power—and both attempt to draw attention to things which are often otherwise ignored, underplayed, or taken for granted.

Of those projects most frequently discussed as tactical media—®™ark's various impersonations, including as the Yes Men; the Electronic Disturbance Theater's virtual sitins; the "Twelve Days of Christmas" campaign against online retailer etoys.com—each uses satire as part of its approach. Even the deadly serious struggles by Belgrade independent radio station B92 to circumvent censorship by the Milosevic regime (Lovink 2003) involved satirical interventions: for example, banned repeatedly from broadcasting, B92 at one point banned itself for a day, pretending to have been taken over and turned into a state propaganda outlet (on the B92 example see Collin 2001: 57; on each of these examples see Meikle 2002).

Fourth, "Revolution: USA" emphasised tactical media qualities of temporariness, mobility, novelty, and reinvention. Tactical-media projects, as Critical Art Ensemble note, are usually ephemeral (2001: 9). They depend, suggests Lovink, on "the art of getting access" and on "disappearing at the right moment" (2002: 260). Such emphases are where the debt of tactical media theory to Michel de Certeau is most apparent, building on his distinction between strategies (the exploitation of space, the privileging of place over time) and tactics (the exploitation of moments of opportunity and possibility made possible as cracks appear in the evolution of strategic place). This distinction underpins the concept of tactical media, which revolves around de Certeau's characterization of the tactic:

It operates in isolated actions, blow by blow. It takes advantage of "opportunities" and depends on them, being without any base where it could stockpile its winnings, build up its own position, and plan raids. What it wins it cannot keep. This nowhere gives a tactic mobility, to be sure, but a mobility that must accept the chance offerings of the moment, and seize on the wing the possibilities that offer themselves at any given moment. It must vigilantly make use of the cracks that particular conjunctions open in the surveillance of the proprietary powers. It poaches in them. It creates surprises in them. It can be where it is least expected. It is a guileful ruse. (de Certeau 1984: 37).

But Does It Work?

The emphasis on this conception of the tactical in so much media activism raises real questions. For example, as Wark (2002) asks, how can networks be built and sustained on practices which favor hit-and-run media gestures, temporary coalitions and disappearances? Conversely, does the very popularity of the term mean that tactical media risks becoming frozen as a particular set of gestures and actions—the detourned advertisement, the overidentified press release, the pie-struck politician—with the impulse toward reinvention being underplayed? Moreover, what do tactical-media interventions really accomplish? George W. Bush, one need hardly point out, was reelected in 2004. Should one conclude that Republican party activists were getting out the vote, while tactical-media activists were at home remixing old Coldcut tunes? Or that tactical media and the wider activist participatory online culture displace energy that is needed for old fashioned organizing? This latter tension has long been felt and continues to be voiced (see for example, Dean, chap. 3, this volume). The second part of Lovink and Garcia's tactical media manifesto, "The DEF of Tactical Media," framed it as "Simulation vs. Real Action":

For many, the urgency of some of the questions we are facing generate an angry scepticism around any practice that raises art or media questions. For real actionists the equation is simple, discourse = spectacle. They insist on a distinction between real action and the merely symbolic. From this perspective media tacticians are accused of merely talking not doing anything. By focusing on the media question we are accused of just creating more empty signs. (Garcia and Lovink 1999)

Social movement scholars might explore this tension as one between instrumental and expressive activism: "the activities of social movements are in part expressive;

in part instrumental; in part directed at their own members; in part designed to transform the external environment" (Della Porta and Diani 2006: 196). On the instrumental side, activists have tangible goals, changes they wish to effect, laws they wish to change, outcomes they hope to achieve. On the expressive side, communicating these objectives to the wider public often demands media gestures, stunts, and gimmicks. What's more, as Della Porta and Diani note, such gestures can be directed at participants as much as (or even more than) this wider public. Stacked up against the problems of the day, the expressive activism of cultural activities such as remixing video clips of George Bush can seem hopelessly unreal, misguided, ineffective, or pointless. However, such activity of course has its own goals and objectives, its own value. For example, as Maddison and Scalmer point out, expressive activism can communicate an idea to the wider public, it can draw attention to issues and raise questions, it can create a space in public debate for activist perspectives, it can challenge complacency (2006: 72). The next section pursues this direction in further detail.

Tactical Media as Play

An instrumental activist assessment of tactical media, then, would ask, in essence, Does it work? This chapter proposes instead that a more interesting question is Does it play? To ask of the "Revolution: USA" project, Does it work? would be to tap into such questions as, Has it raised public awareness and support? Has it affected government policy? Is there a tangible political outcome? However, to ask instead, Does it play? would be to tap into quite different sorts of questions—questions that point toward the creators or participants and toward the users of the project, rather than toward the policymakers, governments, and corporations, which are the usual targets of contemporary activist interventions. Tactical media provokes creative engagement with media texts and media technologies, and it does so in the context of a burgeoning participatory culture. In this context, then, it is possible to move beyond the Does-it-work question and instead ask questions of creativity and engagement.

To ask, Does it play? would be to open up such questions as, Is it creative? This is an interesting question in relation to activism; after all, as Richard Florida points out, creativity is inherently subversive, as it disrupts existing patterns of living and thinking (2002: 31). Does it encourage the user, the audience, to be creative? What would count here, as Walter Benjamin said in the 1930s, would be the transformation effected on the audience: "readers and spectators into collaborators" (Benjamin 1978 [1934]: 233). Does it use humor? "A good tactic," Saul Alinsky suggested, "is one that your people enjoy. If your people are not having a ball doing it, there is something very wrong with the tactic" (1971: 128).

An important resource for thinking about such questions of play is Brian Sutton-Smith's book *The Ambiguity of Play* (1997).[8] Sutton-Smith explores the range of ways in which play is understood and expressed, and identifies seven different rhetorics—or discourses—of play. First, the discourse of *play as progress*, through which ideas of play as central to learning and development are expressed. Second, *play as fate*, the discourse of play as gambling, luck and chance, the belief in a controlling destiny. Third, *play as power*, the rhetoric of contests and sport: "the use of play as the representation of conflict" (1997: 10). Fourth, *play as identity*: in Sutton-Smith's analysis, this discourse is "usually applied to traditional and community celebrations and festivals . . . when the play tradition is seen as a means of confirming, maintaining, or advancing the power and identity of the community of players" (1997: 10). Fifth, *play as the imaginary*—the language of play as it relates to creativity, innovation, imagination, and improvisation. Sixth, *play and the self*, a discourse of personal experience and satisfaction, of self-fulfillment and relaxation. Finally, *play as frivolous*: the discourse that can be set against the work ethic (cf. Kane 2004), and applied to "historical trickster figures and fools, who were once the central and carnivalesque persons who enacted playful protest against the orders of the ordained world" (Sutton-Smith 1997: 11).

Each of these discourses of play (with the possible exception of *play as fate*) opens up possibilities for considering tactical media. Each suggests different questions that could be asked of a project such as "Revolution: USA," questions that move past the instrumental "Does it work?" For example, situating tactical media within the discourse of *play as progress* would make it possible to ask what opportunities are presented for learning and development—as activists, as citizens, as people involved in mediated communication, as individuals, as members of a group or community. To situate tactical media within the discourse of *play as imagination* would offer different perspectives, suggesting such questions as: to what extent does the project offer resources for participants to improvise with or to improve? Does it draw upon the imaginative resources of its users? Does it encourage its users to use their imaginations? And to situate tactical media within the discourse of *play as frivolity* might open up such deceptively simple questions as: Is it enjoyable? Is it engaging? Is it something that people will enjoy doing, above and beyond whatever political merits the project may or may not have?

As an example, we might take further just one of Sutton-Smith's discourses of play, that of *play as identity*. This involves conceptualizing play as a form of bonding, of community formation and maintenance and renewal, of play designed around "potentially cooperative identity" (1997: 100). In this conception of play as expressed in festivals and celebrations, in the creation and sustaining of community, one might hear echoes of Bakhtin's account of medieval carnivals and their elision of the distinction between participant and spectator (1984: 7). Or one might see the outlines of more contemporary temporary autonomous zones (Bey 1991) such as Reclaim the Streets (Jordan 1998).

From this perspective of play as identity, what would it mean to ask of "Revolution: USA," Does it play? To ask this would be to draw attention to, among other things, the limited time span of the project, an eight-week festival of participatory video, and an opportunity for pleasurable and/or satirical participation in the final phase of the election campaign. It would also be to draw attention to the project not as an instrumental Web site for the provision of information, for the cause-and-effect delivery of messages and recruitment of voters, but rather as a space for the creation and maintenance of a community, a point of view, a shared context—ritual communication, in Carey's terms (1989). From this perspective, "Revolution: USA" is significant not for its capacity to influence policy but for the resources it offers users to collaborate, to create their own media, to participate in the debates, and to act as citizens as well as audiences—with citizenship defined at least in part here in terms of symbolic power, of participation in mediated conversations. Most of all, it is significant in its creation of a space for participants to come together and recognise in each other at least a fleeting commonality.

Conclusion

This chapter began by discussing tactical media as manifestations of symbolic power, something which cannot help but sound serious, even grave, and it ended by proposing tactical media as forms of play. This is not bathos, because play is a deadly serious business. The chapter has also referred to satire more than once, and so is subject to the statutory requirement to invoke Jonathan Swift: it is, then, a modest proposal that the discourses and practices of tactical media, as manifestations of symbolic power, might best be approached by asking not, Does this work? but rather, Does this play?

Notes

1. The "Bushwhacked" video is a remix of the second of two audio files, both also titled "Bushwhacked," which Morris posted online at http://www.thesmokehammer.com and on the Web site of Warp records. The video is also included as an extra on the DVD release of Morris's 1994 BBC TV series *The Day Today,* a six-part surrealist news satire.

2. Also important here was the "Bush in 30 Seconds" contest sponsored by MoveOn.org: this contest invited advocacy, parody, and outsider TV commercials to feed into the 2004 presidential election campaign (http://www.bushin30seconds.org). More than a thousand ads were submitted, although many were not remix-based and so are beyond the focus of this chapter. The winning entry, "Child's Pay," by Charlie Fisher, was rejected for broadcast by CBS, although it

of course spread across the Net. Many of these ads, including "Child's Pay," can also still be viewed online at http://www.archive.org among other places.

3. There is a certain unresolved quality to the definition of *tactical media* that is itself part of the discourse (and part of its power). See for example the catalog of definitions maintained online as part of NYU's Virtual Casebook project, at http://www.nyu.edu/fas/projects/vcb/definingTM.html.

4. The term *detournement* is generally not translated from the French, but rather anglicized. Plant suggests that the best English equivalent would fall "somewhere between 'diversion' and 'subversion'" (1992: 86).

5. Miller contributed to an interesting online discussion of remix culture on the e-mail list of the Institute for Distributed Creativity in April 2006; archived at http://mailman.thing.net/pipermail/idc.

6. One could go further, as Paul Lewis does in *Cracking Up*, arguing that satire and humor are central to contemporary political discourse, at least in the United States, which is the site of his study.

7. The fact that satire is inherently subversive made it all the more striking when, in February 2007, Rupert Murdoch's Fox News aired pilots of a "conservative satire" show intended as a deliberate counter to Jon Stewart's *The Daily Show*. One trailer for the Fox Show (*The Half Hour News Hour*) featured the right-wing broadcaster Rush Limbaugh as U.S. president in 2009, with the conservative columnist Ann Coulter as vice president. "Stay tuned," said Limbaugh to the viewer. "And if you don't," added Coulter over a laugh track, "we'll invade your countries, kill your leaders, and convert you to Christianity." But was this satire? Or a restatement of actual foreign policy positions? After all, Coulter's line came from her own column of 13 September 2001. However, the fact that Fox perceived a need for such a show with a right-wing slant underscores the political significance and potential influence of satire.

8. I was led to *The Ambiguity of Play* by Pat Kane's book *The Play Ethic*, which also uses Sutton-Smith's analysis. Kane, however, makes much larger claims than does the present chapter, seeing in concepts of play an entire ideology, the values of which include "play as a source of human energy; as a perpetual engagement with the world; as a mentality capable of living with uncertainty and risk; as an attractive form of collective identity; as an imaginative, symbolic freedom; as a spirit of honesty and integrity; as a saving sense of humour and subversion" (2004: 257). Other important attempts to take play as seriously as it deserves include: Huizinga's *Homo Ludens* (1950); Richard Neville's *Play Power* (London: Jonathan Cape, 1970); McKenzie Wark's *GAMER THEORY* (Cambridge, MA: Harvard University Press, 2007).

References

Alexandrian, S. 1970. *Surrealist Art*. London: Thames and Hudson.

Alinsky, S. D. 1971. *Rules for Radicals*. New York: Vintage Books.

Bakhtin, M. 1984. *Rabelais and His World*. Bloomington: Indiana University Press.

Benjamin, W. 1978 [1934]. "The Author as Producer." In *Reflections*, pp. 220–238. New York: Harcourt Brace Jovanovich.

Bey, H. 1991. *T.A.Z.: The Temporary Autonomous Zone, Ontological Anarchy, Poetic Terrorism*. New York: Autonomedia.

Bourdieu, P. 1991. *Language and Symbolic Power*. Cambridge: Polity Press.

Carey, J. 1989. *Communication as Culture*. New York: Routledge.

Collin, M. 2001. *This Is Serbia Calling: Rock 'n' Roll Radio and Belgrade's Underground Resistance*. London: Serpent's Tail.

Critical Art Ensemble. 2001. *Digital Resistance: Explorations in Tactical Media*. New York: Autonomedia.

De Certeau, M. 1984. *The Practice of Everyday Life*. Berkeley: University of California Press.

Debord, G. 1987 [1967]. *The Society of the Spectacle*. Exeter: Rebel Press.

———. 1988. *Comments on the Society of the Spectacle*. London: Verso.

———. 2002 [1963]. "The Situationists and the New Forms of Action in Politics or Art." In Tom McDonough, ed., *Guy Debord and the Situationist International: Texts and Documents*, pp. 159–166. Cambridge, MA: MIT Press.

——— and G. Wolman. 1981 [1956]. "Methods of Detournement." In Ken Knabb, ed., *Situationist International Anthology*, pp. 8–14. Berkeley: Bureau of Public Secrets.

Della Porta, D., and M. Diani. 2006. *Social Movements* (second edition). Malden, MA: Blackwell.

Florida, R. 2002. *The Rise of the Creative Class*. New York: Basic Books.

Garcia, D., and G. Lovink. 1997. "The ABC of Tactical Media." Posted to the Nettime list on 16 May. http://www.nettime.org/Lists-Archives/nettime-l-9705/msg00096.html.

———. 1999. "The DEF of Tactical Media." Posted to the Nettime list on 22 February. http://www.nettime.org/Lists-Archives/nettime-l-9902/msg00104.html.

Huizinga, J. 1950. *Homo Ludens: A Study of the Play-Element in Culture*. Boston: Beacon Press.

Jordan, J. 1998. "The Art of Necessity: The Subversive Imagination of Anti-Road Protest and Reclaim the Streets." In George McKay, ed., *DiY Culture: Party and Protest in Nineties Britain*, pp. 129–151. London: Verso.

Kane, P. 2004. *The Play Ethic*. London: Macmillan.

Lewis, P. 2006. *Cracking Up: American Humor in a Time of Conflict*. Chicago: University of Chicago Press.

Lovink, G. 2002. *Dark Fiber: Tracking Critical Internet Culture*. Cambridge, MA: MIT Press.

———. 2003. *My First Recession: Critical Internet Culture in Transition*. Rotterdam: V2_Publishing/ Nai Publishers.

——— and F. Schneider. 2001. "New Rules of the New Actonomy." Posted to the Nettime list on 25 June. http://amsterdam.nettime.org/Lists-Archives/nettime-l-0106/msg00114.html.

Maddison, S., and S. Scalmer. 2006. *Activist Wisdom: Practical Knowledge and Creative Tension in Social Movements*. Sydney: UNSW Press.

Manovich, L. 2006. "Generation Flash." In Wendy Hui Kyong Chun and Thomas Keenan, eds., *New Media Old Media: A History and Theory Reader*, pp. 209–218. New York, Routledge.

Marcus, G. 1989. *Lipstick Traces: A Secret History of the Twentieth Century*. London: Picador.

Meikle, G. 2002. *Future Active: Media Activism and the Internet*. New York: Routledge.

Miller, P. D., aka DJ Spooky That Subliminal Kid. 2004. *Rhythm Science*. Cambridge, MA: MIT Press.

Plant, S. 1992. *The Most Radical Gesture: The Situationist International in a Postmodern Age*. London: Routledge.

Richter, H. 1965. *Dada: Art and Anti-Art*. London: Thames and Hudson.

Rushkoff, D. 1994. *Media Virus!* Sydney: Random House.

Scott, J. C. 1985. *Weapons of the Weak: Everyday Forms of Peasant Resistance*. New Haven: Yale University Press.

Sutton-Smith, B. 1997. *The Ambiguity of Play*. Cambridge, MA: Harvard University Press.

Thompson, J. B. 1995. *The Media and Modernity*. Cambridge: Polity Press.

Vaneigem, R. 1983 [1967]. *The Revolution of Everyday Life*. London: Rebel Press and Left Bank Books.

Wark, M. 2002. "Strategies for Tactical Media." *Realtime*, October. http://www.realtimearts.net/ rt51/wark.html.

17   *The Daily Show* and *Crossfire*: Satire and Sincerity as Truth to Power

Megan Boler with Stephen Turpin

The most holy function of comedy is to speak truth where truth is not present. It is a holy burning sacrament, people, and it shall make you free. And whereever there are pundits bloviating, there are billowing clouds of mistruths and a need for the sweet salvation of satire.
—TC's Ministry of Propaganda, March 21, 2005

Our standards for what passes as real journalism are, collectively, at such a stupifying, mind-boggling, all-time low in the United States that it takes the words of a jester to cut through the bullshit and strike a chord with the general populace.
—Comment posted to Joi Ito blog, October 19, 2004

Isn't it kind of sad that we get more substance from a comedy show than from the news media?
—Google group alt. Slack comment, 2004

Salvation through Satire

For those invested in the ideal that a news press should serve the democratic function of informing its citizenry, Jon Stewart's nightly-broadcast news parody *The Daily Show* (*TDS*) offers a touchstone of sanity. The glimpse of a reality more in tune with the experience of many Americans stands in sharp contrast to the otherwise surreal media coverage by 'mainstream' media sources (MSM).[1] Since 9/11, corporate media coverage ranges from shockingly uncritical perspectives even in the so-called liberal media, to ultraconservative propaganda such as Fox news, to purveyors of Bush administration press briefings. Jon Stewart's "court-jester" critiques not only offer a much-needed antidote, but they also represent a niche of media convergence for news content as well as circulation. In 2004, the top-cited blogosphere media story (www.BlogPulse, Year in Review) was the appearance of Jon Stewart on CNN's *Crossfire* talk show. Over 600,000 people watched the television broadcast and millions watched the online streaming of Jon Stewart skewering the talk show hosts for debasing journalism in the name of political debate. Refusing to be the hosts' funny "monkey," Stewart instead appealed for "civilized discourse," a "responsibility to public discourse," and to "stop hurting America" with partisan hackery and theater that masquerades as news on CNN. Stewart drops his smirking satire and instead makes a heartfelt, pleading appeal for media's civic responsibility. Overnight, this public cry spread through the blogosphere like wildfire.

This landmark moment illustrates not only the soaring lack of faith in media serving democracy, but also the increasing use of online communications to construct a counterpublic sensibility and reality check about the insanity that is supposed to represent news. As one fan proclaims, "Jon Stewart is the voice of sanity." (Posted by Orville Redenbacher, October 15, 2004 09:06 PM http://talkleft.com/new_archives/008312.html)

The *Crossfire* phenomenon (like Stephen Colbert's keynote at the White House Press Correspondent's Dinner in 2006[2]) deserves the attention of those interested in the mutations of contemporary news media, primarily as it is an unusually populist political event—both because of the comedic status of satirists like Jon Stewart and Stephen Colbert and the consequent response from viewers ranging from sports fans to myriad others who do not fit the profile of radical media critics. Bloggers and those who were posting recognized it as a watershed moment as it was happening: "My prediction: This will be a liminal (threshold) moment that will not fully be appreciated by the political hacks until it's too late." (http://talkleft.com/new_archives/008312.html) And six months after the event, it was being referred to as "the now legendary appearance of Jon Stewart on *Crossfire*." (TC's Ministry of Propaganda, March 21, 2005: http://

Figure 17.1
Jon Stewart on *Crossfire*, October 14, 2004

cheever.typepad.com/tc/2005/03/a_reading_from_.html). It continues to receive regular reference in news media stories and blogs as a milestone moment in media criticism history.

Further, the *Crossfire* episode merits attention as a phenomenon of media convergence, in which the Internet functions as a tool for amplification, alternative broadcast, and public engagement in discussion that is not possible through traditional, unidirectional journalism or media formats. This cable show is watched as much online as through broadcast, and generates extensive online discussion, evidencing the degree to which news readers not only turn to online formats for news consumption but also create alternative online public spaces and networks of political engagement.

Digital media's challenge to MSM is illustrated not only in the numbers who were able to view the *Crossfire* episode online and discuss it in the blogosphere but also in the rise of independently produced multimedia memes and viral videos—political movies and animations circulated on the Internet. This analysis of *The Daily Show* is situated within a larger research project titled "Rethinking Media, Democracy and Citizenship: New Media Practices and Online Digital Dissent after September 11," a three-year study funded by the Canadian Social Science and Humanities Research Council that investigates discourses of truth and lies in media by studying the motivations of online authors, bloggers, meme and viral video artists of digital dissent. My interest in digital dissent developed from my close study of independently produced blogs and digital media in the years following September 11, 2001, studies that led me to observe a persistent and increased public demand for truthful accounts from the media and politicians. The perception that the media are failing democracy is potently evidenced across the four sites of online production studied in my broader research project.[3]

In this chapter, I illustrate through analysis of online discussions about the *Crossfire* episode a renewed demand for truthfulness and accountability expressed by consumers of U.S. news media.[4] I begin by offering a description of *The Daily Show* and its significance in contemporary political context. I then discuss the ways in which Jon Stewart as court jester represents the contemporary form of political satire that speaks "truth to power." I detail the public response to Jon Stewart's appearance on *Crossfire*, with an analysis of how his critiques of the function of the press represent a widely shared concern about the state of democracy in the United States.

In addition, I wish to situate the appeal of political satire and its role in constructing new counterpublics within our larger theoretical frame on ironic citizenship.[5] Thus before moving into detailed discussion of the *Crossfire* event, I briefly outline our theorizations about the appeal of irony as context for understanding contemporary public discourses about truth and lies against the backdrop of spectacle and complicity.

Coping with Complicity in Spectacular Society

In the *Crossfire* episode, the court jester switches from satire to sincerity to voice the widely felt demand for media's responsibility to democracy. The desire expressed by the public for politicians and media to tell the truth is held in paradoxical contradiction to the postmodern sensibility that all narratives are constructed, that all the world's a fiction. The paradoxical desire for truth alongside awareness of truth's impossibility is a hallmark of this stage of spectacular complicity: "no one really believes the spectacle" (Debord, Comments, 1988, 60). This postmodern sensibility might also be described as a widely shared skepticism toward authority as it attempts to exert control through spectacle. Thus an overarching argument that frames this analysis of *Crossfire* recognizes irony as a distinctive contemporary strategy for coping with complicity in the spectacular society. Notably, whether satiric or sincere, the court jester frankly admits complicity with spectacle.

The appeal of satire and irony[6] is in large part the *frank admission of complicity* with the spectacle. Beginning with the self-assignation of "fake news" (*The Daily Show* is known as "the most trusted name in fake news"), both Jon Stewart and Stephen Colbert insistently assert that their shows are merely comedy and not news, have no partisan agenda, and do not claim to be outside of the spectacle of commodity.[7] They assert this complicity in the following ways: by referring to their corporate owners; by dismissing their own authoritative claims; by recognizing the immediate contradiction of the very fact that they exist and appear through broadcast at all ['I would not exist but for the corporation that feeds me']. Then, on this plane of contradiction,

Figure 17.2
Stephen Colbert addressing the White House Press Correspondent's Dinner, April 29, 2006

they unfold myriad layers of ironic and satirical nuance that begin to satisfy the craving for what we might call, with a nod to Foucault, an "effective history of the recently past."[8] The shared frustration and consequent appeal of irony, we suggest, is best described as the challenge of "coping with complicity in spectacular society." Networked cultures and practices of dissent represent a plurality of activities that demonstrate how we cope with and productively recuperate our complicity in spectacular society. Because we tend to recognize, experientially and thus intuitively, the immense planetary problems created through the structures of global capitalism and its attendant state institutions (not to mention the media itself), our reality is inevitably one of complicity. However, this complicity, when accompanied by an ironic approach to truth and politics, engenders a correlative critique of spectacular relations[9] and offers the potential for thinking new possible relations within the social and political registers.

The levels of irony are multiple, existing within form, content, and between the performative characters and their real-life appearances or interventions in real political discourses, which is the focus of this essay. Within their four-times weekly broadcasts, these multiple layers range from the ironic statements about other news media, to the parodic character of Colbert himself being a parody of Bill O'Reilly from Fox news. But another level of meta-irony is communicated when they step outside of their usual broadcasts and perform "interventions" such as on *Crossfire* and the White House Press Correspondent's Dinner.

These questions of irony, complicity, and spectacle will be expanded in the chapter's conclusion following a close discussion of Jon Stewart and the *Crossfire* appearance.

The Phenomenon of *The Daily Show*

The Daily Show (*TDS*) with Jon Stewart is transmitted four nights a week in the United State and Canada on cable television. The format of this highly popular news satire is to use real news clips from mainstream media—generally about Washington D.C. politics—with Stewart's satirical and ironic commentary about the media representations as well as about the actions and speech of politicians. Aired in Europe through CNN in a half-hour, once weekly version, *TDS* is also available on Comedy Central's official site and selected excepts can be found through mirrored independent streaming. Jon Stewart became host of *The Daily Show* in 1999, with a steadily increasing audience currently at 1.7 million television viewers, a wide audience who view TDS online, and a larger segment of age 18–31 viewers than any other U.S. nightly news show (Friend 2002, 28).[10] The increasingly international familiarity with Jon Stewart is evidenced by a recent example in which *The Australian* spiced up a story about George W. Bush's latest plan for "border control" by using Jon Stewart's humorous coverage of Bush's speech ("Borderline support strategy: Cheap labour v job

Figure 17.3
The most trusted name in fake news

protection?" by Geoff Elliott May 20, 2006 http://www.theaustralian.news.com.au/story/0,20867,19190332-28737,00.html).

Central to the popularity of TDS and the *Crossfire* event is the widely-shared frustration and perception that the news media is failing democracy.[11] Public and populace outrage about U.S. news media is powerfully illustrated in the remarkably extensive online discussion of Jon Stewart's ambush of the left/right talk show *Crossfire*. "Stop hurting America," he pleads on *Crossfire*, decrying the lack of civil discourse and partisan hackery that passes for news. As a *Newsweek* columnist noted at the time,

There are no unscripted moments in American politics anymore, certainly not seven days before the presidential election. That's why the talk of Washington last week was a few minutes of spontaneous unrehearsed drama–among TV personalities, not politicians. Comedy Central's Jon Stewart, host of the wicked political satire *The Daily Show*, had gone on CNN's *Crossfire* as a guest and complained about the show. "It's hurting America," Stewart said, explaining that "*Crossfire*" and programs like it were not discussion shows but theater." ("TV, Money and '*Crossfire*' Politics," Fareed Zakaria, *Newsweek*, November 1, 2004, 35)

The frustration expressed by Stewart clearly resonated with the sentiments of thousands of viewers who were keenly grateful that Jon Stewart had the status and authority to represent the "average citizen" and broadcast their views. Stewart's demand of *Crossfire* represents a longing articulated in many circles, though given the fragmentation of media it is in fact rare to have a text shared by 4 million. Whether in sincere or satiric delivery, this critique of the spectacular relations of media is a running theme in the content and rhetorical address of *The Daily Show*. Stewart himself refers to the *Daily Show* as reflecting what he calls "a quaint idealism." Stewart is described as a court jester who cares (Jeffrey Jones, *Entertaining Politics*, 2005). After the 2000 election and World Trade Center attacks on 9/11, the news media coverage of these events solidified "Stewart's court jester persona" (Jones 2005, 108). Competition among news channels had changed what counted as news in the 10 years leading up to 2001; secondly, after 9/11 these changes became more pronounced with patriotism packaging of channels like Fox. "Stewart was dismayed. In regard to cable news reporting, he says, 'They've so destroyed the fine credibility or the fiber that was the trust between the people and what they're hearing on the air. . . .' *The Daily Show* took it as its patriotic duty, so to speak, to parody and ridicule these constructed falsities" (Jones 2005, 109). In Jon Stewart's words, "'I represent the distracted center. . . . My comedy is not the comedy of the neurotic. It comes from the center. But it comes from feeling displaced from society because you're in the center. We're the group of fairness, common sense, and moderation. . . . We're clearly the disenfranchised center . . . because we're not in charge'" (Stewart, quoted in Jones 2005, 114–115).

The appeal of *The Daily Show* and its political strategy is founded on a membership imagined as "the group of fairness, common sense, and moderation. . . . Jon Stewart's approach is not a 'rant' . . . [but] instead he simply asserts a smirking disbelief," often used to expose contradiction and the outright lies of politicians (Jones 2005, 110).

Moreover, Stewart's voice carries legitimacy because he holds this position as commonsensical fellow citizen. "Stewart seems to be speaking for a lot of people who would much rather see something substantial and informative on OUR airwaves. He went on that show as a fellow citizen and did us all a favor. Patriotism at its best" (comment posted to Media Matters Web site, October 16, 2004, http://mediamatters .org/items/200410160003?offset=60#comments).

Another post proclaims, "Jon Stewart . . . is credible simply because he mirrors the critical observations of viewers" (comment posted to PressThink, October 23, 2004, http://journalism.nyu.edu/pubzone/weblogs/pressthink/2004/10/23/strain_pol.html). The perception of Jon Stewart as a caring citizen allows him to occupy the status of hero for truth. "Stewart cares far more about what journalism is for than either Begala or Carlson, but for some reason they either didn't grasp this ahead of time, or never thought Stewart would demonstrate it to them on their own show. Not only did Stewart prove the vacuousness of much of the media's coverage of politics, but the very fact that they were clueless about Stewart's convictions about journalism also shows just how out of it they really are" (http://talkleft.com/new_archives/008312. html).

These comments are echoed throughout the blogosphere discussion of his appearance on *Crossfire*, reiterating again and again the notion of Stewart "representing the feeling of most Americans": "Stewart IS the face of most of America . . . confused about what the real issues are, in desperate need of honest discourse about the issues and the hope of honest compromise" (Comment posted to Dave Matthews Discussion Group, October 16, 2004, http://groups.google.ca/group/alt.music.dave-matthews/ browse_thread/thread/2c7f07a286c15a56/251d52d948f0a05e?lnk=st&q=*Crossfire* +truth+honesty+stewart&rnum=1&hl=en#251d52d948f0a05e).

I would argue that TDS functions as an anti-gaslighting measure. Defined by *Webster's New Millennium Dictionary, gaslighting* is a slang verb dated to 1956, which means "to manipulate someone into questioning their own sanity; to subtly drive someone crazy." *TDS* counters the sense that one is being gaslighted by the Bush Administration and the media's lapdog role: someone—in this case the court jester, Jon Stewart—is offering a reality check in the otherwise apparently absurd theater of media and politics. "There's a magic moment in that interview where Stewart pulls back the curtain surrounding the political machine and the manipulation of the media" (comment posted to Dave Matthews Discussion Group, October 16, 2004, http://groups.google.ca/group/alt.music.dave-matthews/browse_thread/thread/ 2c7f07a286c15a56/251d52d948f0a05e?lnk=st&q=*Crossfire*+truth+honesty+stewart&rnum =1&hl=en#251d52d948f0a05e).

The irony, satire, and parody of *The Daily Show* and *The Colbert Report* offer a reality check and also hold appeal through their frank admission of complicity, which stands in stark contrast to corporate news media's assumed relationship to "truths." Traditional broadcast and print news not only uphold a naive-seeming correspondence notion of truth, but any such correspondence theory (through its discourse of fairness and facts) assumes an overly simplistic morality of right and wrong that insults postmodern sensibilities of complexity and contradiction which the spectacle itself cannot help but make obvious. In short, attempts to hide the spectacle do not sell, and many audiences are so savvy that in PR and advertising, truth and sincerity are "in": for example, on YouTube ads are praised only when they are not posted by the advertisers as ads selling a product; rather, their critical acclaim occurs when they are posted by users as contributions to the recognized media spectacle.[12] This sense of insult when complicity is unrecognized loses readers/viewers by the droves (creating the problem of media literacy as commonly conceived and the near impossibility of a pedagogy of media to suit current sensibilities). The irony and satire of fake news suit this particular user best: we would rather follow the empty square than fill it in simplistically or deterministically; but we risk losing faith, hope, and optimism and falling into the second accident of structuralism—apathy. As Deleuze explains in a 1967 article "How do we recognize structuralism?", the empty square is the location of a *problematic*. The empty square is the very possibility of forming a problem that intersects a variety of different planes or registers (government, the family, race, gender, class, etc.)—without falling victim to an apathetic passivity nor filling in the square of meaning with any final determinant (the desire to fix cause and thus determine course of action too simply). MSM fixates on either of these options, creating a discourse of truths and final solutions that makes any critique within their own discourse or on their own terms all but impossible.

Satire such as *TDS* and *CR* is the salvation for many in North America and increasingly for other English-speaking audiences, because at its best it allows an ambiguity of meaning that resonates with our lived experience of hypercontradiction. Satire allows one to embrace both/and: we disagree with the current order, with the current regime, with the current administration, but the complexities of our reality prevent us from articulating—as Fox News might demand of us—a perfectly honed and sound bite–ready answer to these problems.

Truth to Power: The Function of Satire

A great deal of *TDS* viewer's pleasure comes from having a public figure speak "truth to power." Commenting on the pleasure derived from *TDS*, this posting observes:

Y'know, I consume a lot of media, probably like you do. A lot of it is pretty smart, like stuff from NPR. However, I'm finding that the best commentary these days isn't from serious sources. I watch *The Daily Show* on Comedy Central, with Jon Stewart. Turns out, the "fake news" there is really good. The guy is funny, yet the commentary is deeper and smarter than any other commentary I consume. As a kid, I read the usual Shakespeare, and almost the only thing I remember is the idea of the "wise fool" usually in the form of a court jester. The deal is that such a guy can say what he wants, because he's not intended to be taken seriously. The fool can speak truth to power. I guess that's what Stewart's doing on the show, and it sure works for me. (Craig, Craigblog, September 13, 2003, http://www.cnewmark.com/archives/000055.html)

The wise fool, or court jester, is commonly the figure who speaks truth to power in the tradition of political satire. In times marked by the stifling of dissent and narrowing of press freedom and bandwidth, political satire thrives. Political satire's roots are traditionally traced to Juvenal and Horace, two Roman writers, who used sharp wit to expose the evils and weaknesses of those in power. The tradition of satire is also marked by the work of Twain, Swift, and Cervantes. Satire makes its point by use of parody, irony, travesty, and grotesquery, and is characterized by reduction or exaggeration and use of wit. A significant question often posed by satirists is whether there is a protagonist, and if so, what tone and methods does the protagonist adopt to critique those in power? Traditionally, protagonists have often been divided into different roles: court jester, clown, buffoon, and so on.

As one blogger describes the role of the court jester and satire, "Comedy makes fun of the particulars of a situation; satire makes fun of the opinions of a situation. By definition, neither takes opinionated peoples' opinions seriously. That's a key function of comedy and has been since the days of the court jester—really, in fact, the entire point of a court jester" (TC's Ministry of Propaganda, March 21, 2005, http://cheever. typepad.com/tc/2005/03/a_reading_from_.html). In the case of *The Daily Show*, "Stewart gets to play the fool by using the words of those in power against them, revealing 'truth' by a simple reformulation of their statements" (Jones 2005, 113).

Much could be said about the history of political satire moving up to current "fair use legislation," which legally protects those who perform parody, one subset of satire. A more general comment on the relation of humor to politics offers context for the relationship of satire to contemporary political transmissions.

Humor . . . helps one only to bear somewhat better the unalterable; sometimes it reminds both the mighty and the weak that they are not to be taken seriously. . . . One's understanding of political jokes obviously depends on one's understanding of politics. At one level, politics is always a struggle for power. Along with persuasion and lies, advice and flattery, tokens of esteem and bribery, banishment and violence, obedience and treachery, the joke belongs to the rich treasury of the instruments of politics. We often hear that the political joke is an offensive weapon with which an aggressive, politically engaged person makes the arrangements or precautions of an opponent seem ridiculous. But even when political jokes serve defensive purposes, they are nonetheless weapons. (Speier 1998, 1352)

However, in line with my argument that there is a new expression of demand for truthfulness, Jon Stewart is not simply the classic court jester. A recurring theme in the online discussions is that, in the current climate, truth can *only* be achieved through this kind of humor: "Jon Stewart and the excellent writers of *The Daily Show* have also given anyone paying attention an essential piece of strategy: sometimes the truth can ONLY be delivered through comedy. While 'real' news shows refuse to check political claims against reality, it has taken a 'fake' news show to do actual research necessary to prove many of the lies politicians tell" (Global Dialog Project, Web site, http://www.global-dialog.org/mvd/Humor.JonStewart.html).

In particular, *TDS* is appealing in large part because it is seen as more real or more truthful than the MSM news.

The *Crossfire* appearance goes straight to the reason of why Stewart and *The Daily Show* are so popular. With the corporate journalism organized around flattering the politicians, instead of challenging them—no matter how outrageous the lies or how bloated the rhetoric—Stewart's "fake news" ends up being more truthful about the reality of U.S. politics than all the *Crossfire*s and *Hardball*s piled up in a great steaming heap. (http://www.counterpunch.org/maass10282004 .html)

In online discussion, there is frequent commentary on how Stewart's fake news is more effective than so-called real news. "The comedian parades around as a fake journalist. But his fake journalism is far superior to anything else out there. Stewart doesn't make up fake news. The satire is in the jokes and the way Stewart adds humorous commentary to real news. The news is real. The reporting is fake" (Sara Looten, The Daily Toreador, webpage, November 4, 2004, http://www.dailytoreador.com/vnews/display.v/ART/2004/11/04/4189876febb55).

The function of political satire as saying what is otherwise unsaid within a given political climate combines as well with people's individual sense of being unheard. *TDS* fulfills both functions—saying the unsaid, and saying it for the unheard populace: "Thank you, Jon Stewart, for saying what I would have liked to say to infotainment hosts more interested in pleasing their bosses and their political patrons than providing information to the viewer" (Snarkcake, October 19, 2004, http://www.snarkcake.com/archives/2004_10.html).

Hence we come to the *Crossfire* moment as watershed: the most trusted name in fake news speaks for the masses. "The moments in which something real and genuine occurs on *Crossfire* are few and far between. It was an absolute joy to witness nearly thirty. Stewart delivered a message long overdue. Do they not realize that he was speaking for the masses?" (comment posted to Media Matters website, October 16, 2004, http://mediamatters.org/items/200410160003?offset=60#comments).

Crossfire

Stewart's naked appeal to his hosts to "please stop, stop, stop. Stop hurting America," had a loopy, apocalyptic power. It burned a hole in the screen, like Peter Finch as the crazed anchorman in *Network*, bellowing, "I'm mad as hell and I'm not going to take it anymore."
—Dana Stevens on *Slate*, October 18, 2004, http://www.slate.com/id/2108346/

Overnight, Jon Stewart's appearance on *Crossfire* offered a shorthand for the failings of contemporary news media. While such critiques have been made with much greater depth by media critics such as Bill Moyers, Robert McChesney, Arundhati Roy, Paul Krugman, and Lewis Lapham among others, the *Crossfire* moment dominates bandwidth with its populist appeal, and has become part of the vernacular for many TV and online audiences unfamiliar with these other established media critics.

The following offers a brief glimpse of how this event comes to qualify as the "top cited media event in the blogosophere in 2004." A google search for "jon stewart *Crossfire*" yields 366,000 hits. If one adds the word "blog," the number is 191,000. On many blogs that addressed the *Crossfire* event, there are extensive comments and postings made by blog readers. For example, on media matters there are 295 posts in response to the transcript of *Crossfire*. Talk left closed its comments after 97 comments were posted in the five days following October 14.

Slate writer Dana Stevens offers a good summary of the media event (I quote her at length to give a sense of the tone and context that surrounded the reporting of the event):

Boy, I'm telling you. You spend one weekend in the boonies, visiting some crunchy friends with no TV set, and you miss out on the biggest television story in months: something *actually happens* on a political talk show! Moral of story: never go anywhere, and watch as much TV as possible. But meme time be damned: I just have to say a few words about Jon Stewart's live freakout on *Crossfire* last Friday. Well, perhaps not so much "freakout" as "searing moment of lucidity."

Hosts Tucker Carlson and Paul Begala had invited Stewart on the show to "take a break from campaign politics" (Carlson's words), have a few laughs, and promote his new book, *America (The Book)*. Too bad for them that the host of *The Daily Show* had another agenda in mind. Within less than a minute, the interview degenerated (or ascended, depending on your point of view) into an encounter of the sort not often—OK, never—seen on the talk show circuit. Stewart was like the cool college roommate you bring home for Thanksgiving only to spend the evening squirming as he savages your parents' bourgeois values. "Right now, you're helping the politicians and the corporations," he told the dueling pundits. "You're part of their strategies. You are partisan, what do you call it, hacks."

Things quickly escalated into a full-scale food fight. Carlson accused Stewart of being John Kerry's "butt boy" and "sniffing his throne." Stewart parried by making fun of Carlson's signature bow tie and calling him a "dick." (Think I'm kidding? Watch the clip yourself.) When Carlson goaded Stewart to "be funny. Come on, be funny," Stewart responded, "I'm not going to be your monkey." (October 18, 2004, http://www.slate.com/id/2108346/)

During his appearance on *Crossfire*, Jon Stewart expressed three central ideals for news media: (1) to "stop hurting America" with partisan hackery and theater; (2) a "responsibility to public discourse," and (3) the need for genuine debate, referred to at one point as "civilized discourse." A further key issue is whether a comedy show like *The Daily Show* can be held accountable to the same standards of journalistic integrity that Stewart is demanding of CNN's *Crossfire*.

Arguably the most often quoted, signature line of the exchange is Stewart's plea: "Stop, stop, stop, stop hurting America. . . . See, the thing is, we need your help. Right now, you're helping the politicians and the corporations. And we're left out there to mow our lawns" (As of May 21, 2006, we found 49,800 hits on Google for "stop hurting America crossfire blog.") The point that follows his plea is his critique that *Crossfire* is engaging in theater, rather than the kind of debate important to journalism:

Stewart: So I wanted to come here today and say. . . . Stop, stop, stop, stop hurting America. . . . See, the thing is, we need your help. Right now, you're helping the politicians and the corporations. And we're left out there to mow our lawns.

Begala: By beating up on them? You just said we're too rough on them when they make mistakes.

Stewart: No, no, no, you're not too rough on them. You're part of their strategies. You are partisan, what do you call it, hacks.

Despite the CNN hosts trying to derail him from this point, Stewart returned to the issue of news as theatre:

Stewart: But the thing is that this—you're doing theater when you should be doing debate, which would be great.
Begala: We do, do. . . .
Stewart: It's not honest. What you do is not honest. What you do is partisan hackery.

Halfway through his *Crossfire* appearance, Stewart made the next central point, which is also referred to frequently in the online chatter:

Stewart: You know, the interesting thing I have is, *you have a responsibility to the public discourse*, and you fail miserably.
Carlson: You need to get a job at a journalism school, I think.
Stewart: You need to go to one.

In an attempt to reverse the attack, Carlson tries to turn the tables and flogs Stewart for not asking hard enough questions of presidential candidate John Kerry.

Stewart: It's not honest. What you do is not honest. What you do is partisan hackery. And I will tell you why I know it.
Carlson: You had John Kerry on your show and you sniff his throne and you're accusing us of partisan hackery?
Stewart: Absolutely.
Carlson: You've got to be kidding me. He comes on and you. . . .
(Crosstalk)
Stewart: You're on CNN. The show that leads into me is puppets making crank phone calls.
(Laughter)
Stewart: What is wrong with you?
(Applause) Carlson: Well, I'm just saying, there's no reason for you—when you have this marvelous opportunity not to be the guy's butt boy, to go ahead and be his butt boy. Come on. It's embarrassing.

Finally, Stewart reflects:

Stewart: You know, it's interesting to hear you talk about my responsibility. . . . I didn't realize that—and maybe this explains quite a bit.
Carlson: No, the opportunity to . . .
(Crosstalk)
Stewart: . . . is that the news organizations look to Comedy Central for their cues on integrity. . . .
  But my point is this. If your idea of confronting me is that I don't ask hard-hitting enough news questions, we're in bad shape, fellows.

Stewart attempts to point out that if "news organizations look to Comedy Central for cues on integrity . . . we're in bad shape." Interestingly, in online discussions this particular concern is not often expressed—rather, people feel that indeed, *TDS* sets a new standard for journalism, by essentially doing a better job as the quotes throughout this chapter indicate.

Within online discussions, appreciation is often expressed to Stewart for making these key points about media responsibility. But some of the reasons for the emotional impact of Jon Stewart's appearance have more to do with the sincere tone of his remarks. This points to a phenomenon I find curious: part of the power of the *Crossfire* event is the illusion of authenticity—the real Jon Stewart has stood up. This is not the tongue-in-cheek satirist Jon Stewart but Jon Stewart the sincere and caring citizen. "Stewart . . . went on that show as a fellow citizen and did us all a favor. Patriotism at its best" (Comment posted to Media Matters Web site, October 16, 2004, http://mediamatters.org/items/200410160003?offset=60#comments).

The perception of Stewart's sincerity is tied to the perception of his *honesty* in choosing to speak truth to power in this context. One sees this appreciation of honesty in these three comments from different threads:

Why was this interview so shocking? Honesty. (comment from Dave Matthews Discussion Group, October 16, 2004, http://groups.google.ca/group/alt.music.dave-matthews/browse_thread/thread/2c7f07a286c15a56/251d52d948f0a05e?lnk=st&q=*Crossfire*+truth+honesty+stewart&rnum=1&hl=en#251d52d948f0a05e

He went on to accuse them of being theater, not debate, of being dishonest and partisan hacks. It was honest, it was funny, it was brutally frank, and it was accurate. (Tony Iovino, A Red Mind in a Blue State, blog, October 20, 2004, http://redmindbluestate.blogspot.com/2004/10/jon-stewart-v-*Crossfire*.html)

I just watched the video and have an even greater respect for Stewart. What he did took a lot of courage, but it really needed to be said. He made the most honest and relevant remarks I've heard on cable news for months. (comment posted on Media Matters, by Rob, October 15, 2004, http://mediamatters.org/items/200410160003?offset=60#comments)

A key appeal, then, is that Stewart switched roles. Stewart gets credit for using humor to speak truth to power on *The Daily Show*, but in this instance, it is his refusal to be the "funny man" that gives him credibility. "It was an amazing segment. Carlson and Begala thought they had a funny man today and he gave them the truth" (comment posted on Media Matters, by Jamato, October 15, 2004, http://mediamatters.org/items/200410160003?offset=60#comments).

As another blogger writes,

Some might say, well, he was booked as a comedian so he should have been funny. And I would say, no. He was booked as a comedian, so he did precisely what any good comedian does: used comedy as a vehicle to speak truth. Watch the piece closely; he is clearly serious about his intent but starts out delivering it with a funny angle until Begala and Carlson start in on the "I thought you were supposed to be funny" harangue. (TC's Ministry of Propaganda, March 21, 2005, http://cheever.typepad.com/tc/2005/03/a_reading_from_.html)

We experience the profound sincerity of the court jester and satirist as most trust-worthy when—with values consistent with their nightly critiques of the spectacle of politicians and media—they express calls for democracy, justice, fairness of representation, and public responsibility of media and politicians within the ironic stage of the real. This occurs when the court jester steps from his usual stage into another "real" staged context—for example, Jude Finisterra of The Yes Men on BBC; Jon Stewart on *Crossfire*; or Colbert at the White House Press Correspondent's Dinner. When these demands for accountability are made in public forms that reveal the emperor's nakedness with *tactics that get play*, the de-naturalizing critique gains teeth and its bite becomes effective—revealing the complicities of the spectacle in public to the public. Too much sincerity depresses and won't sell; but strategic sincerity builds on trust. To the extent that sincerity is used it says, "it could get worse." This is perhaps the closest that satire comes to a call to action: playing on the sincerity that it demonstrates through the prior admission of complicity and the platform of an impossible truth ("fake news"), contemporary political satire at its best forms an effective history.

Another central focus of online discussion is the question of whether a comedian (Jon Stewart) should or can be expected to play the role of a serious journalist. As I have tried to show, part of the reason for Stewart's popularity is that people feel a fundamental lack of trust in mainstream news media, and Stewart's comedy validates the reasons for this mistrust: "Jon Stewart, with his fake news show and honest look at government, is much closer to being a journalist than the whole sorry pack at CNN. And the talking heads at CNN and the rest of the television media, indolent, pampered, out of touch and VERY well cared for by their corporate masters, are much closer to being clowns" (Zepp Jamieson, Zepp's Political Commentaries, October 23, 2004, http://www.zeppscommentaries.com/Sociology/stewart.htm).

The following comment illustrates not only my point about *TDS* being a touchstone of sanity, but the frequently expressed gratitude that the comedic host is able to morph into a sincere and not parodic critic:

I've heard people talk about "The Daily Show" as an oasis of sanity, a public service. I couldn't agree more. Stewart's appearance on *Crossfire* was another public service. He went on and acted as if the show's purpose really was to confront tough issues, instead of being the political equivalent of pro wrestling. Given a chance to say absolutely what he thought, Stewart took it. He accomplished what almost never happens on television anymore: He made the dots come alive. ("The War Room," by Tim Grieve, *Salon* http://www.salon.com/politics/war_room/index .html?blog=/politics/war_room/2004/10/15/*Crossfire*/index.html)

Conclusion: Desiring Truths, Living Contradictions

The popular appeal of the *Crossfire* moment lies in the perception of Stewart's courage to speak the truth, to confront politician's lies and MSM spin with an antidote of honesty. The viral popularity of Stewart's skewering of *Crossfire* offers a window into the phenomenon that underlies this essay: the sincere demand for truthfulness and accountability that occurs against a culturally understood backdrop of "all-the-world's-an-image," the spectacular society in which we recognize our inevitable complicity.

Within the complex and contradictory discourses of truth and lies, honesty and sincerity, and irony's appeal through its frank admission of complicity in spectacular society, what sense does one begin to make of the increasingly widespread appeal of "fake news," of political satire that uses comedy to take questions of politics and democracy extremely seriously?

As one conclusion, we suggest that the post-2001 media landscape is but the confirmation of the necessity of a "contradictory" life—the spectacle of terrorism and the abuses of the exportation of democracy represent the modulation of foundational ideologies from previous epochs as they shift into postmodern landscape of oligarchies and corporations. Within this landscape, the premise of the news "telling the truth" has lost all credibility as we recognize the impossibility of noncontradiction. This is well exemplified in an exchange between Stewart and Bill Moyers in 2003: "I do not know whether you are practicing an old form of parody and satire . . . or a new form of journalism. Stewart replies, "Well then that either speaks to the sad state of comedy or the sad state of news. I can't figure out which one. I think, honestly, we're practicing a new form of desperation" (Bill Moyers interview of Jon Stewart, on Public Broadcasting Service, July 2003). This new form of desperation is precisely the creation of a gap, or affective moment of satirical performativity that allows a space for thinking the empty square, or of unfolding the problematic of politics on new terms (not just "Leave Iraq or Stay," but how do we actually conceptualize the subtleties of this war and on what terms should we engage with its illegitimacy—*not* on the terms of the MSM!).

Foucault argues for the importance of effective history, stating that this method of historical knowledge production "deprives the self of the reassuring stability of life and nature, and it will not permit itself to be transported by a voiceless obstinacy toward a millennial ending. It will uproot its traditional foundations and relentlessly disrupt its pretended continuity. This is because knowledge is not made for understanding; it is made for cutting."[13] If knowledge is made for cutting, we can see the development of political satire as a potent breach, break, or fracture in our spectacular mediascape that occasions a shift in our concepts of politics and truth that lingers after the punchline, beckoning us to reconsider the complexities that populate our daily lives and experience. Without giving up hope on solutions, we are encouraged, with often biting irony, to follow the empty square and complicate the discourses of the MSM.

There is hope provided by what we term an *effective history of the recently present*: longer sound bites, creation of a pause and a gap, context, engendering of reflection as a practice that occurs as part of the process of both watching and/or producing news/facts,[14] and creating a counterpublic or viral rhizomatic rupture in which the

Figure 17.4
Stephen Colbert popularizes "Truthiness"

spectacle is revealed in new light through watershed moments of public and counter-hegemonic critique. Through the offering of effective history, the spectacle's exhausting evacuation of history is channeled into mutated remix that creates conditions for different social relations within the contradictions of the spectacle.

In this sense, the contradictory elements foregrounded by postmodern satirical practices cannot be resolved through any dialectical synthesis, but instead reveal the complexity of the overlapping networks of power and our participation within them. A major media intervention such as that represented by Jon Stewart on *Crossfire* is but one example of how media convergence, satire, spectacle, and complicity increasingly blur the boundaries of what satisfies the deep affective longings for truthfulness and certainty with a highly uncertain political landscape and future. But whether sincere or satiric, the interventions always recognize their spectacular complicity.

Political satire cannot be dismissed simply as a medium complicit with the monstrous media power that sustains it, because it is precisely this often-stated complicity with power that makes the truth of the fake news so effective. Without any pretense to easy solutions, and without suggesting that turning away from our political realities will make them go away, an ironic citizenship can help engender new effective histories that allow us to better navigate the complexities of our own complicity within spectacular society. In sum, perhaps the satirical cut of "truthiness"[15] is now a necessary tool for critique, because, as Foucault says, "Nothing is more inconsistent than a political regime which is indifferent to the truth; but nothing is more dangerous than a political system which pretends to prescribe the truth."[16] Political satire and fake news balance on this fence between indifference and prescription, precariously juggling the inherent dangers that accompany our longing for truths and certainty.

Notes

While this chapter represents a revised version of an essay I published in 2005 (*Scan Journal of Media Arts Culture* 3, no. 1 [summer 2006] http://scan.net.au/), I have integrated in this version portions of recent theoretical analyses developed collaboratively with Stephen Turpin, who has been working with me on the funded research project "Rethinking Media Democracy and Citizenship" since 2005.

1. The terms *mainstream* and *corporate* media are often used interchangeably. However, Fernandes (chap. 9, this volume) makes a useful distinction: "I like to define it more in terms of who owns it. So I call it corporate media. Mainly because I think *we* are the mainstream. Not that I'd necessarily call us the mainstream media, and I think it's easy to use that term from time to time. But the more correct term is to define it as the people who own it—so we are community media, we're owned by the community, and corporate media is owned by corporations—just because it doesn't let us forget that. I think it's too easy to forget or just not think about why news is being produced. And for the most part news is being produced for profit motive."

2. In this chapter, I address data our research team gathered in 2005–06, just prior to Stephen Colbert's equally significant public intervention on April 29, 2006. In 2006, Stephen Colbert was an invited keynote speaker/performer at the Washington, D.C., annual White House Press Correspondent's Dinner. Colbert's masterful parodic performance delivered a scathing critique of George W. Bush and his administration—with Bush himself sitting three feet away from Colbert, and in front of hundreds of White House and other political figures. There was an extensive corporate media blackout covering the event, but it has become a second watershed moment in recent public media and political critique. One Web site of the many various official and unofficial fan sites for Colbert is dedicated to thanking him simply for this speech, the site itself called thankyoustephencolbert.org with 64,386 "thank yous" posted on this site as of July 27, 2007.

  While there are interesting differences between the role and character each plays and their comedic strategies, both events represent interesting ruptures—or continuations—within their comedic political landscape of media critique, in terms of adding a level of reality. Stewart's intervention on *Crossfire* is notable for its sincerity, while Colbert's intervention at the WHPC Dinner is noted perhaps for its sheer guts. In both instances, the jester moves from his usual "faux news anchor set" into a "real" stage: in the case of Stewart, the stage is CNN's news show *Crossfire*, and in the case of Colbert, the stage is the White House Press Correspondent's Dinner broadcast through C-Span (both events by now watched by millions online). The bottomline realness of issues addressed combined with the ironically real stage magnifies the effective rhetorical power of their scathing critiques of media and the Bush administration.

3. For more extensive research findings from this project, see www.meganboler.net.

4. The material analyzed in this chapter is representative of the hundreds of discussion threads, blog posts, and blog comments about Stewart's appearance on *Crossfire*, gathered primarily by research team members Catherine Burwell and Mark Renneson in 2005–2006. Although we originally set out to analyze more generally blogs and online discussion of *The Daily Show*, it was quickly apparent that most links led to discussion of Stewart's appearance on *Crossfire*.

5. By "our" and "we" in this Chapter, I refer to collaboratively produced work theorizing complicity, spectacle, and irony with Stephen Turpin.

6. To define these terms in brief, *satire* is commonly understood as literary, dramatic, or visual art intended to critique vice, folly, or abuse. While frequently comedic and using humor and wit, its primary intent—particularly, and in its best instances I would argue in the case of political satire—is to call attention to the wrongs committed by those in power. Satire uses various devices, ranging from irony to buffoonery, derision and grotesquery. Many argue that satire is set apart from other comedy by its clear moral outrage—the attempt to point out vice or abuse through the stated or implied measure of what is morally right or a value that should be strived for by those who are targeted in the satirist's critique. *Parody* at its simplest is a stylistic imitation that serves to call attention to and ridicule the original style. In skillful parody, the original style is so aptly imitated and pushed to its extreme, that the viewer sees not merely a silly imitation but a scathing critique of the satirist's target (Stephen Colbert's comic adoption of Fox News personality Bill O'Reilly's character is a clear example of an extraordinarily skillful parody). *Irony* is one style used within satire, generally understood as the use of language to say one thing and mean another. Irony is frequently the aspect of satire in which one finds discussions about the necessity of shared cultural meanings in order to "get" the joke or play on words and meaning. We are interested not only in this basic sense of irony, but also in cases that exemplify where "the most complex forms of irony intensify contradiction; they do not clearly contradict the true or the logical in order to present themselves as in opposition to what is said; they do not allow for a truth or sense behind the speech act. The speech act produces a conflict of sense, expressing both sides of an assertion with equal force" (Colebrook 2004: 166–67).

7. *TDS* and *CR* stand in distinct contrast to Linda Hutcheon's description of television as primarily "commodified complicity" and in lacking the critique that characterizes her notion of postmodern paradox: "Most television, in its unproblematized reliance on realist narrative and transparent representational conventions, is pure commodified complicity, without the critique needed to define the postmodern paradox" (Hutcheon 1989:10).

8. Michel Foucault, *Language, Counter-memory, Practice*, translated by Donald F. Bouchard and Sherry Simon (Ithaca, New York: Cornell University Press), 1980.

9. "The spectacle is not a collection of images, but a social relation among people, mediated by images" (Debord 1967, section 4).

10. Viewers of Jon Stewart's *The Daily Show* and Stephen Colbert's *The Colbert Report* rank number 1 in the "best informed American public."

"The six news sources cited most often by people who knew the most about current events were: 'The Daily Show' and 'The Colbert Report' (counted as one), tied with Web sites of major newspapers; next came 'News Hour With Jim Lehrer'; then 'The O'Reilly Factor,' which was tied with National Public Radio; and Rush Limbaugh's radio program (Katharine Q. Seelye, *New York Times*, "Best-Informed Also View Fake News, Study Says," April 16, 2007).

In counterpoint, see also the academic study that purported the "daily show effect"—that watching *TDS* will cause cynicism in young people with respect to electoral politics: "Although research indicates that soft news contributes to democratic citizenship in America by reaching out to the inattentive public, our findings indicate that *The Daily Show* may have more detrimental effects, driving down support for political institutions and leaders among those already inclined toward nonparticipation" (Jody Baumgartner and Jonathan Morris, "The Daily Show Effect: Candidate Evaluations, Efficacy, and American Youth," *American Politics Research* 34, no. 3 (2006): 341–367).

11. Key questions that underlie this phenomenon include what counts as "democracy" and "truth," questions that cannot be taken up here given space limitations.

12. These points were underscored at a panel discussion titled "Meet the Insiders: Candid Conversations with the Advertising Industry" hosted by the Association of Media Literacy, May 2, 2007, at the National Film Board in Toronto. Participants included Dan Pawych, Creative Director of Downtown Partners; Phillipe Garneau, Creative Director of GWP Brand Engineering; and Nancy Vonk, Creative Director of Ogilvy.

13. Foucault, *Language, Counter-memory, Practice*, p. 154.

14. Hutcheon's definition suits this reflexive function of satire and irony as a window that opens onto the effective history of the recent past: "This is the confrontation that I shall be calling postmodernist: where documentary historical actuality meets formalist self-reflexivity and parody. At this conjuncture, a study of representation becomes, not a study of mimetic mirroring or subjective projecting, but an exploration of the way in which narratives and images structure how we see ourselves and how we construct our notions of self, in the present and the past." (1989: 7)

15. "Truthiness" was popularized through Stephen Colbert's invocation in 2005, making it one of the top words of the year in 2006. "Truthiness is meant to 'describe things that a person claims to know intuitively, instinctively, or "from the gut" without regard to evidence, logic, intellectual examination, or actual facts" (Wikipedia).

16. Michel Foucault, *Dits et Écrits II—1976–1988* (Paris: Éditions Gallimard, 2001), p. 1497.

References

Colebrook, Claire. 2004. *Irony: the New Critical Idiom*. New York: Routledge.

Debord, Guy. 1967. *Society of the Spectacle*. Michigan: Red and Black.

Debord, Guy. 1988. *Comments on the Society of the Spectacle*. New York: Verso.

Deleuze, Gilles. 1967/1998. "How do we recognize structuralism?" In *The Two-fold Thought of Deleuze and Guattari*, Charles J. Stivale, ed. New York and London: Guilford Press, 1998, pp. 258–282.

Foucault, Michel. 2001. *Dits et Écrits II – 1976–1988*. Paris: Éditions Gallimard.

Foucault, Michel. 1980. *Language, Counter-memory, Practice*, translated by Donald F. Bouchard and Sherry Simon. Ithaca, New York: Cornell University Press.

Hutcheon, Linda. 1989. *The Politics of Postmodernism*. New York: Routledge, 1989.

Jones, Jeffrey. 2005. *Entertaining Politics*. Lanham, MD: Rowman Littlefield.

Speier, Hans. 1998. "Wit and Politics: An Essay on Laughter and Power." *American Journal of Sociology* 103(5):1352–1401.

18 Cybersupremacy: The New Face and Form of White Supremacist Activism

R. Sophie Statzel

In 1994, ex-Grand Wizard of the Ku Klux Klan Don Black foresaw the coming of two revolutions and placed himself firmly in the midst of both. The first revolution he correctly foresaw as the rise of the Internet and its impact on everything from social movements to media transmission. Black's dream and life mission, however, was geared to his second imagined revolution, that of white nationalism and the creation of an international movement successfully rearticulating racial politics on a national and global level. Attempting to harness the power of the cyber-revolution to fulfill the promise of the white nationalist one, Black created stormfront.org, transmitting "White Pride World Wide" and successfully, continually increasing membership and reach.

While the cyber-revolution is in full force, the white nationalist movement has slowly fomented and expanded, though far less publicly. Since its founding as a tiny electronic bulletin board connecting a handful of dedicated, entrenched white supremacists, Stormfront has grown into a global electronic meeting ground and achieved a level of activity placing it in the top 1 percent of all Internet sites. In January 2007, they boasted over one hundred thousand white nationalist cyberactivist members with an average of more than seventy new members joining daily. Just over half of the membership is located in the United States with the rest spread out over a dozen countries (see figure 18.1). These membership numbers, though striking, actually fail to reflect the real popularity and use of the site; at any given time there are likely a few hundred members and often thousands of guests perusing the bulletin boards. Featuring fifty separate subcategories from "Dating Advice" and "Stormfront South Africa" to "Philosophy and Ideology," tens of thousands of people visit the bulletin boards each day, reading posts and publishing comments to the million-plus threads that explore everything related to white nationalism.

When I first encountered Stormfront I understood it as a highly marginal fringe group, and as an antiracist scholar I became interested in studying the site not out of a fear of any real threats posed by the site itself, but out of an interest in studying the white supremacist fringe as a strategy for better understanding broader white

Stormfront White Nationalist Community - Discussion Board for Activists

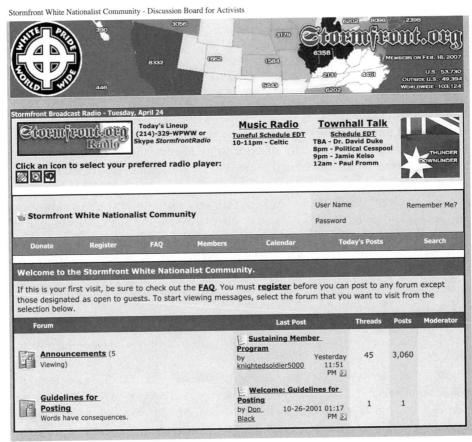

http://www.stormfront.org/forum/ 4/24/2007 6:03:32 PM

Figure 18.1
Stormfront.org main page

supremacy. Yet, as I've seen the site expand in membership numbers and organizing savvy, I've come to understand the Stormfront as posing a serious threat of possible political futures, both in its ability to galvanize and organize a certain type of discontent among white folks as well as what this success reveals about broader political trends on- and off-line.

In this article my intention is to use Stormfront as a case study to better explore the limits and possibilities of democratic practices online, particularly tactical media. As such, this article is not simply a study of a radical group, but an analysis of a particular online nationalist mobilization that also attends to the theoretical questions and challenges this movement poses to democratic theory and our understandings of tactical media. By exploring the political implications of white nationalist online organizing, my aim is to problematize the common assumption that resistance to dominant modes of power is intrinsically connected with democratic principles and practices or desires for liberation. I argue that Stormfront is an example of tactical media, and therefore the movement frames itself in opposition to dominant modes of power. Yet clearly the oppositional vision mobilized on Stormfront fails to invite democratic possibilities or redress inequalities, attempting instead to affirm a racial hierarchy. This is accomplished through the mobilization of racial sentiments and subjectivities in the protection of a perceived morally superior white identity that is threatened by the current dominant social and cultural order. As a nationalist movement, white nationalism focuses on constructing and policing an imagined community defined by exclusion. It is a community or public that only engages in antagonistic politics. A significant aspect of the white nationalist political project is precisely this creation of a shared, racial, imagined community, tactically constructed and connected through a tapestry of online and off-line practices. While some of the practices are defined as traditionally political, such campaigns and mobilizations targeting specific people, policies, or corporations, we need to expand our understanding of the political to include the imaginative frame from which political practices emerge. Recognizing political praxis as stemming from historically located cultural imaginaries and passions, and not from a precultural rationality, means the inclusion of imaginative frames within our definition of the political. Tactical interventions and pedagogies that influence this imaginative frame are thus part of broader political mobilizations.

The two revolutions imagined by Don Black—white nationalism and the transformation of politics and publics through the new media possibilities in cyberspace—are best understood when analyzed together. The contemporary white nationalist movement is dependent on new media for its success and its existence and can only be understood through an analysis of the movement's engagement with tactical media. On the other hand, I argue that exploring the political passions that steer the white nationalist movement increases our understanding of the limitations and possibilities of new media and political activism. Exploring the relations between these two imagined revolutions is actually productive in attempting to understand both. Though "the 'Internet' revolution may be over,"[1] there is far less consensus as to the nature and impacts of this revolution. Has it provided a rupture with or extension of previous political forms and identities? Does it divert or enhance democratic potential? Are new identities and publics produced through computer-mediated communication or are off-line identities reinforced through online practices? While often seen in binary or potentially oppositional terms, the distinction between "the real world" and "virtual reality" is often actually quite blurred. And, when it comes to questions of "power, politics, and structural relations" it is argued that "cyberspace is as real as it gets."[2]

While tactical media is defined as opposing interventions of power into the intimate realm, there are multiple understandings of what constitutes undesirable interventions of power and simultaneously vast number of forms that such opposition takes. There seems to be a tension in understanding tactical media: does the mobilization of passions, the creation of new social relations, and the nurturance of oppositional subjectivities count as political activity or do these act as diversions away from the real of political engagement? When applied to antiliberatory activism this raises provocative questions. It is important to take heed of Jodi Dean's (chapter 3, this volume) caution about the possibility of allowing a fantasy of political participation obscure a reality of circuitous, self-contained transfers of information which the Web can facilitate. However, Stormfront highlights another reading of the possibilities of tactical engagements of new media. To appreciate these politics requires rethinking how we actually understand the political. Jodi Dean quotes Shirkley, writing on the disparity between Howard Dean's on- and off-line campaign success: "When you're communing with like-minded souls, you *feel* (emphasis in original) like you're accomplishing something by arguing out the smallest details of your perfect future world, while the imperfect and actual world takes no notice, as is its custom" (Dean, chap. 3, this volume). Yet, this emphasis on *feeling* takes on new significance when considering a cyber-supremacist online community as opposed to the online dimension of a political campaign, where the mobilization of sentiments creates imagined worlds as its politics.

From this perspective it appears that "communicative capitalism," Dean's description of the communicative and political implications of the current economic order, may facilitate easier political mobilizations for antidemocratic aims which are organized specifically around sentiments and subjective attachments. I assert that the politics articulated on Stormfront consist not of specific campaigns or demands for change, but in this tactical stirring of racial sentiments for the purposes of constructing an imagined white public which must band together against racialized and sexualized others who fall outside the purview of the imagined political community. The white nationalist movement is a clear example of a Schmittian politics of the mutual construction of friend and foe. While the racialized public or imagined community of Stormfront is a radical vision for our contemporary moment, the vision is a historically precedented one. Exploring the historical role of race in riving political imaginaries and practices raises important questions about the very possibilities of democratic politics today. Between a Schmittian vision of the antagonistic politics of friend and enemy and a liberal vision which fails to recognize the importance of struggle and disagreement in political practice, Chantal Mouffe articulates the importance for democratic practices to engage in agonism, where difference is seen in the language of opposition and struggle and not enmity and war. Yet, exploring the construction of the nationalist public complicates Mouffe's call for agonistic politics for it shows that the idea of the public sphere requires a simultaneous construction of an imagined public, constituted through practices and media representation. Race constructs the boundaries of the imagined public sphere not only in white nationalism, but also hauntingly shapes many conservative and liberal understandings of the public. Through this exposition of Stormfront as a site of tactical media I explore several questions about the role of tactical media, race, and political passions in the construction of publics and politics. This exploration of the tactics used and the racial sentiments mobilized within the white nationalist movement provides insights for progressive, prodemocratic activists and scholars to counter their success and better understand the possibility of tactical media and political resistance.

Stormfront as Tactical Media

Don Black contends that Stormfront is not a supremacist Web site, arguing instead that it is focused on racial pride, yet it is solidly the product of a supremacist history. When describing his decision to leave the KKK and start Stormfront, Black admits that the Klan has "a reputation for random and senseless violence that it can never really overcome, and we could never on any large scale attract the kind of people that we wanted."[3] Along with other ex-KKK leaders such as David Duke, Black has worked to reframe white supremacist activism in a more palatable form. Instead of focusing on explicit white supremacy, movement members use the term "white pride" to describe their politics, as though their movement is simply about pride and not supremacy. When asked if his views on race had changed since being in the KKK, Black responded, "Well, everybody's views change somewhat, but, no, my basic ideology and philosophy is pretty much the same. My views are essentially the same as they were in the seventies. The tactics, however, are different."[4] This tactical shift includes changes in message and medium, however the heart of white nationalist organizing remains consistent with the goals of traditional white-supremacist organizing.

Stormfront is itself an established Web site with over a dozen-year history and was created by activists as a strategy for building and expanding the white nationalist movement. Though part of a movement and thus part of a broader political strategy, the site is organized as a tactical space for building an imagined political community. It is thus a constructed space of tactical media, a networked space where discourse circulates and tactical things happen. The site represents tactical media at its finest. It is a space where the medium is perfectly meshed with the possible strategies available to the movement. As a senior moderator of Stormfront writes to a member across the country, "It is the White man's friend ... the World Wide Web ... that makes it possible for me in Louisiana to talk to you in California through a server administered in Florida in order to get Mr. Duke's works to you and share this experience with our kinsmen all over the world."[5] As the connectivity of cyberspace diminishes the significance of physical distance, white nationalists have succeeded in connecting a variety of local disparate groups into the beginnings of an international movement.

A key aspect of the site is its role as an alternative new venue. Black describes the goal of Stormfront as follows: "Our mission is to provide information not available in the controlled news media and to build a community of White activists working for the survival of our people."[6] The white-nationalist strategy is not geared to immediate political campaigns, for leaders know that they currently lack the political base to realistically impact the political process. This has not always been the case. Stormfront traces its origins to a dial-up bulletin board started in 1990 to facilitate David Duke's Louisiana senate campaign coordination (where he won over 60 percent of the white vote according to exit polls, yet lost the election). As the Internet has expanded, developed, and become more accessible to a larger audience, Black and others have helped to continually reshape the site to maximize its potential to both reach more people and to create a political base.

Stormfront leaders recognize that because of changes in public consciousness in the post–Civil Rights era traditional white-supremacist tactics including the open advocacy of racial violence will likely fail. To create a more viable message, Stormfront is a place for members to coach each other on a reworked approach to white supremacy. Site leaders are well aware of their marginality, unpopularity, and of the continual surveillance they are under from law enforcement agencies and watchdog groups. In Black's "Guidelines for posting," a photo of a business-suit-clad Black accompanies instructions to members on how to professionalize the image of the movement. He coaches members to "avoid racial epithets," to "make an effort to use proper spelling, grammar and capitalization (no ALL-CAPS posts)," and to otherwise keep the conversation as professional as possible. Often using racially coded language and photos attached to stories of violent crime, members play on racist fears of violence by people of color and feelings of racial superiority by whites while often restraining from using racial expletives and calls for violent action. If a member disobeys these rules and posts a comment that either calls for overt violence or illegal activity, the post is deleted by a moderator within a short time.

This strategy of toning down extreme messages and expanding a base through the use of new media is historically precedented in the rise of National Socialism, an ideology prominent on Stormfront. It seems clear that many of the leaders of the movement have studied Hitler's ascent to power and are attempting to apply his strategies. Hitler himself praised the invention of the loudspeaker for its ability to increase one man's audience from hundreds to tens of thousands and stated, "Without the loudspeaker we would never have conquered Germany."[7] He also learned to drastically tone down the anti-Semitism at the core of his ideology and shifted focus to praising and defending the Volk while simultaneously working with others to change public consciousness to accept anti-Semitism. White nationalists are employing similar strategies, utilizing the most advanced technology to reach the most members while shifting their language and ideas to best match their audience.

In arguing that Stormfront is an example of tactical media I am also arguing, given Renzi's definition, that it is resisting certain modalities of power, particularly power which acts on "people's innermost sense of individuality" (chapter 2, this volume). As a supremacist movement, it seems counterintuitive to make the argument that it is also mobilizing against power, but this indeed is my position. First, central to the white nationalist imaginary is the classic anti-Semitic conspiracy that Jews are in control of the media and the government. White nationalist training begins with an introduction to ZOG, white supremacist shorthand for Zionist Occupation Government, a powerful conspiracy that argues that the government and the mainstream media are under the control of an ideologically cohesive Jewish supremacy. In addition to this conspiracy of marginality, awareness of being under constant surveillance by the FBI and the fact that many of their leaders are currently residing in jail is used as evidence that the movement is fighting a racist power structure which oppresses whites.

In this conspiracy, the popular media are operating under an anti-white mission. A prominent article on the site "Who Rules America?" begins: "There is no greater power in the world today than that wielded by the manipulators of public opinion in America. No king or pope of old, no conquering general or high priest ever disposed of a power even remotely approaching that of the few dozen men who control America's mass media of news and entertainment."[8] A persuasive argument is laid out about how the mass media create "our image of the world and then tell us what to think about that image."[9] The article concludes that all of this massive influence is really controlled by a handful of Jews. The most popular section of Stormfront is consistently "Newslinks and Articles" where TV and newspaper stories are circulated and commented upon with a white nationalist spin. The most popularly circulated thread in this section is the "Ethnic Crime Report," where news stories are circulated about violent crimes purportedly committed by people of color against whites. Consistently throughout this thread members post stories and comment on the race of victims and perpetrators, including pictures whenever possible to bolster racial stereotypes. These pictures and stories provide the "evidence" circulated on the site that a race war is already in effect, where people of color are consistently and randomly maiming, murdering, and attacking whites. This thread has been in development for five years and is updated daily. Additional news links cover a broad array of what appears in the popular press, but respun with a white-nationalist flair. In this way members are consistently communing with each other and broader society as they are appropriating images and narratives circulating in the dominant press in ways that bolster their conspiratorial ideas about white racial persecution.

Throughout the site it is argued that the popular media devalue white identity, fostering white guilt and racial shame. In the active participation in constructing white-empowered media, either through discourse with other members or appropriating and commenting on stories from the popular media, members are constantly defending and constructing a newly empowered racial self. Participation on this site, with the construction of their own media commentaries within this broader cyber community, is a way for members to assert a new racial subjectivity. And race in these chat boards means far more than phenotype alone. Members articulate a set vision of the white nation as a moral community in their chat, connecting strict, heterosexual gender roles, a focus on childrearing and the patriarchal family, with a white racial identity. Members comment that feminists and homosexuals are not welcome on the site or in the movement.

Growing Threats

Although it may be comforting to think of this movement as a marginal, nonsensical group of radical haters, the reality is that they are a group daily *increasing* in numbers. When I first began monitoring Stormfront in July of 2004, the Web site had recently celebrated its achievement of reaching a membership of 34,000. Today the site has almost three times as many members and additional daily readers in the tens of thousands. Two years ago the record for most site observers at one time was 865 users, today that number is 4,500 and it is common to have over fifteen hundred users perusing the site at any given time. The movement is successfully harnessing the power of the Internet not only to share information but also to increase membership. The successful, continual expansion of Stormfront's membership counters early assessments that online recruiting had little potential for extremist groups.[10]

Concomitant to the rise of white nationalist online organizing has been a surprising increase in off-line activism as well. The Ku Klux Klan actually succeeded in making a rebound in 2005, with new chapters forming in almost every region of the United States. It is noteworthy that this new organizing facilitates rapid increases in membership of new groups as well as increasing similarities between the various white supremacist groups, with KKK, neo-Nazi, and racist skinheads sharing ideological orientations, aesthetic styles (music and dress), and cooperating together.[11] The broad circulation of anti-immigrant discourse in the popular press and political debate is certainly fueling this movement, but the increasing collaborations across ideologies and group affiliations off-line seems to correlate with the sharing of information and strategies online. This paper is based solely on monitoring online activity and thus cannot definitively assess this relationship between on- and off-line practices and politics. This relationship, however, remains a question of ongoing concern and calls for further studies.

While several organizations track the activity on white nationalist and white supremacist Web sites, this does little to uncover and challenge the racial stereotypes built up over generations of white supremacy. Particularly when national debates fuel racist sentiments, challenging white supremacy is a difficult task. Since the September 11 attacks on the World Trade Center and the subsequent targeting of Muslims as terrorists or threatening outsiders, racist Web sites and organizations have grown exponentially. A 2005 study by the Southern Poverty Law Center documents more than eight hundred hate groups operating in the United States, a rise of over 30 pre cent since 2000.[12] Additionally, national Republican-led anti-immigration debates have done much to blame economic instability on Latino immigrants, inflaming xenophobia. And, when the president of the United States takes over six years to meet with the country's largest civil rights organization, treating people of color as a fringe political group, we are far from a national dialogue on racism that will do anything to make white-supremacist organizing more difficult.

Welcome to Stormfront

Those unfamiliar with this emerging movement will be surprised at the diversity of members and interests represented. Die-hard National Socialists, Christian Identity enthusiasts, Hitler brides, young skinheads, Pagans, housewives, computer nerds, rural farmers, and city dwellers are all united by the feeling that whiteness and white people are imperiled. Across a great divide of ideology, religion/spiritual practices, class positions, ages, and actual locations the bulletin boards of Stormfront house a plethora of arguments and insecurities about the changing nature of racial politics and identity in the contemporary West (see figure 18.2).

The Web site has numerous simultaneous functions: (1) an international electronic meeting ground for a diverse group of white supremacist/separatist/nationalist activists to discuss philosophy and strategy, (2) an alternative news venue to distribute news of interest, a recruitment, outreach, and educational tool, and (3) a place to vent animosity at those who disagree with the movement (one of the most popular sections of the site is consistently the "Opposing Views" forum, where members argue their cause with those dubbed "antis," a term covering anyone who disagrees with the movement). Members create signature quotes that end their posts with links to all of the major white supremacist organizations and regional white nationalist groups, including: http://www.sigrdrifa.net/, National Socialist links, and links about Hitler, the white power organization Blood and Honor, various Ku Klux Klan sites, and every other major and most minor white supremacist/separatist sites. Members thus represent a wide variety of racist organizations and ideologies.

Stormfront is also much more than a loosely organized set of bulletin boards. The site is not organized for an anonymous, presumed audience, but carefully calculates

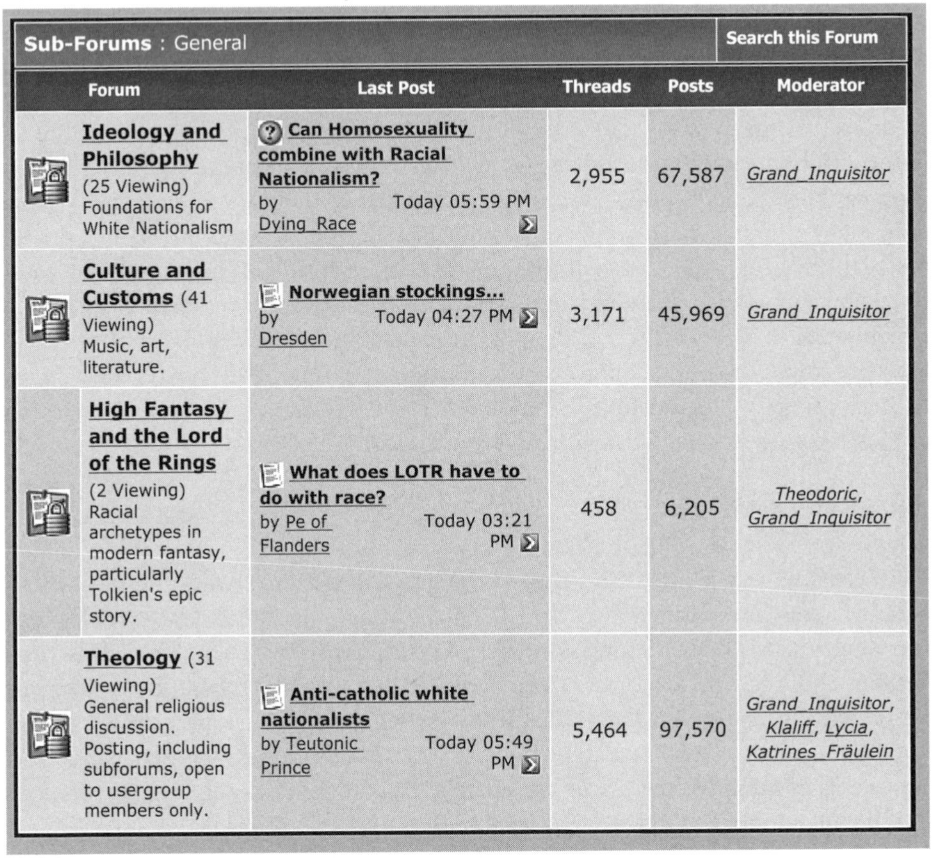

General - Stormfront White Nationalist Community

Sub-Forums : General				Search this Forum
Forum	**Last Post**	**Threads**	**Posts**	**Moderator**
Ideology and Philosophy (25 Viewing) Foundations for White Nationalism	⑦ **Can Homosexuality combine with Racial Nationalism?** by Today 05:59 PM Dying_Race ▶	2,955	67,587	*Grand_Inquisitor*
Culture and Customs (41 Viewing) Music, art, literature.	**Norwegian stockings...** by Today 04:27 PM ▶ Dresden	3,171	45,969	*Grand_Inquisitor*
High Fantasy and the Lord of the Rings (2 Viewing) Racial archetypes in modern fantasy, particularly Tolkien's epic story.	**What does LOTR have to do with race?** by Pe of Today 03:21 Flanders PM ▶	458	6,205	*Theodoric, Grand_Inquisitor*
Theology (31 Viewing) General religious discussion. Posting, including subforums, open to usergroup members only.	**Anti-catholic white nationalists** by Teutonic Today 05:49 Prince PM ▶	5,464	97,570	*Grand_Inquisitor, Klaliff, Lycia, Katrines_Fräulein*

http://www.stormfront.org/forum/forumdisplay.php/general-7.html 4/24/2007 6:08:02 PM

Figure 18.2
Stormfront.org forum threads

and tracks readership and documents exactly what and who is popular, read, and responded to. The entire site is carefully orchestrated for maximum tactical effect for both transmitting information and building community. Through self-selected avatars, signature quotes, and the posting of their location or region of residence, members are able to create cyber-identities which do not feel anonymous even as they retain anonymity. Members can create cyber-identities which convey information about their personalities and interests while not disclosing their actual names or places of residence. The site also incorporates a variety of efforts to create the feeling of a community. It tracks numbers of postings by member, allows members to rank the quality

Stormfront White Nationalist Community - Discussion Board for Activists

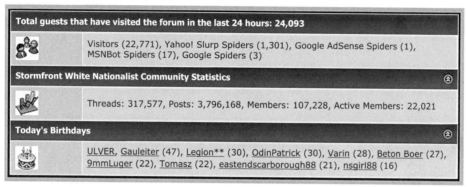

Total guests that have visited the forum in the last 24 hours: 24,093

Visitors (22,771), Yahoo! Slurp Spiders (1,301), Google AdSense Spiders (1),
MSNBot Spiders (17), Google Spiders (3)

Stormfront White Nationalist Community Statistics

Threads: 317,577, Posts: 3,796,168, Members: 107,228, Active Members: 22,021

Today's Birthdays

ULVER, Gauleiter (47), Legion** (30), OdinPatrick (30), Varin (28), Beton Boer (27),
9mmLuger (22), Tomasz (22), eastendscarborough88 (21), nsgirl88 (16)

http://www.stormfront.org/forum/ 4/17/2007 4:24:02 PM

Figure 18.3
Stormfront.org community statistics

of a thread (noted by a series of stars along the thread), and shows the number of
views for each thread. The main page is consistently updated to show total membership numbers, overall page hits, and the number of people currently viewing each
section of the site, demonstrating to members and visitors that they are not alone in
their searches, readings, and ramblings (see figure 18.3). The main page also includes
"Today's Birthdays" which lists individual members and often the age they are turning.
They are connected to an online radio station that airs music as well as five white-
nationalist news and talk shows each day, including regular commentaries by David
Duke. Members can keep "buddy lists" that display which members on their lists are
currently online and also provide instant private messaging between members. The
site is thus geared toward constructing an imagined community for its members. The
site also serves to connect with off-line practices in a variety of ways, including a
thorough "activist" section discussing strategies and tactics, postings of local events,
a popular dating section, and announcements of national and regional conferences
and gatherings.

Take for instance the exchange between "Zoe" and "fightforwhitey" shown in figure
18.4, which demonstrates many of the tactics used on Stormfront to foster an online
community. We can see several things happening here. First, the avatars chosen by
each member convey an idealized racial image that also serves to personalize the posts,
making their screen presence highly personal. We also see when each became a
member, how many posts they have authored, either their physical location or some
coded description of their location, and whether or not they are currently online.
Within their posts members can easily include a variety of *smilies* and vbcode to add
emphasis and set the tone of the text. The signatures further personalize the posts as

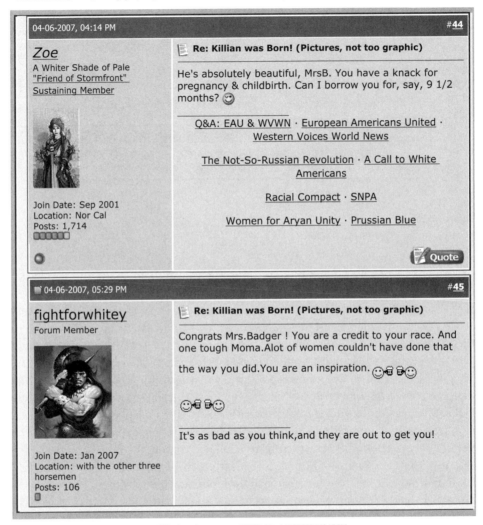

Figure 18.4
Stormfront.org signatures and avatars

they provide information about the individual's passions or politics with quotes or links to various organizations. This exchange was part of a thread that began with photos of another member's (Mrs. Badger) birth and new baby. In less than one month this thread received over sixty posts which all echo the highly congratulatory tone of these two, praising Mrs. Badger's strength and commenting on how beautiful her family is. This is far from an anonymous exchange.

The Web site succeeds in creating a personalized space where members can create actual connections with each other, even while retaining their anonymity if they so desire. This potential anonymity on the Internet provides white-supremacist groups with a significant boon as it lessens the pressure for self-censorship common today for whites around expressions of racist thought. An unintended consequence of the dominant culture of liberal multiculturalism's stigmatization of racism is the foreclosure of honest discussion by whites about their fears and concerns associated with shifts in racial identity and privilege. The lack of broader conversations about race and racism sadly leaves anonymous online spaces such as Stormfront as one of the few spaces where whites can openly grapple with their concerns about race without fear of personal stigma or embarrassment. This leaves Stormfront as a space ideally suited for educating others and gaining new recruits for a cause typically scorned in the broader public. While it is commonly asserted by scholars that most whites espouse some amount of white nationalist sentiment,[13] the dominant "color-blind" discourse on race today ensures that white nationalist activists must often help other whites develop a racial consciousness to gain new recruits. "Racially aware" is Stormfront shorthand for describing the development of a white-nationalist consciousness. Members frequently discuss their "awakening," which also provides the title of David Duke's famous autobiography, *My Awakening*. The site is a space of education, not only through the sharing of information, but also through the mobilization of residual racist sentiments, making participation in a racist community seem desirable. This is a sentimental education that emphasizes feelings and subjective attachments that fuel the site. It must not be seen as a displacement of off-line politics, but a tactical use of online media to build the possibility of achieving off-line political impacts for a community of political interests that currently lacks viability, visibility, and cohesion. Given the difficulty of politically mobilizing a set of ideas as stigmatized as white nationalism, it is significant that a precursor to effective political engagement is validation, education, and consolidation of a political base.

The Cyber Revolution: Reality and Virtual Reality

Numerous utopian visions frame cyberspace as transcending the divisions that structure our "real world" relations, though off-line positionality often frames online activity. Regarding questions of race, the "internet is a place where race happens: even in the absence of users of color, images of race and racialism proliferate in cyberspace."[14] Much of the cyber-studies literature fails to address this. Mark Hansen argues that the Internet allows for racial passing. He writes, "the suspension of the social category of visibility in online environments transforms the meaning of race in a fundamental way. . . . it also permits a certain play with racial signifiers that, in my opinion, can and does yield something positive."[15] Yet all too often experiments with fluid subjectivity online result in racialized appropriations through the use of racialized avatars in chatrooms and bulletin boards and the playing out of racial fantasies in online gaming.[16] Such dreams of online sociality and identity as divorced from racialized processes only helps to obscure the ways that these inscriptions are constantly carried into cyber-activity. Even in attempts at creating nonracist spaces (McPherson 2000) or at challenging racism (Gonzalez 2000), racist patterns and relations tend to structure the attempts at subverting them. Although the Internet surely provides the possibility of interpellating, or "hailing into being," new identities and subjectivities, we do not lose our real-world histories and identities when we go online. As Tara McPherson writes of white Southerners' investments in neo-Confederate Web sites, they "seem relatively unconcerned with the prosthetic nature of cyber-communication."[17] She writes, "For these cyber-rebels, reconstructing Dixie and its citizens is not about play at all; rather, it is a very serious battle over demands of place, race, and identity."[18] Asserting racial identities online in this case is then an explicitly political act. Similar to Dean's argument that the imaginary of the global serves to dismiss political differences, subsuming race under the banner of a new globalism or "virtual ethnicity" belies the trenchant nature of race and racism. Arguments that cyber-practices create identities no longer tied to the body obscure the way that race and racism continue to structure cyberspace not only in white-supremacist Web sites but often in attempts at creating nonracist and antiracist spaces.

Cyber scholarship is now increasingly recognizing that "the Internet is not growing apart from the world, but to the contrary is increasingly embedded in it."[19] Wilson and Peterson (2002) go so far as to challenge "that the distinction between real and imagined or virtual community is not a useful one," and instead assert that the analysis should focus on "contextualized identities" that recognize contingent and historically situated relations shape online identities.[20] In noting the ways that off-line identities shape their cyber counterparts, they list the continued influence of the state in censuring data and structural inequalities in constraining access. However, when thinking about the relations between on- and off-line political mobilizations it is also important to consider the limitations of real-world constraints on political imaginaries. Specifically regarding race, while the abstracted nature of computer-mediated communication allows for the creation of cyber-communities not demarcated by race, can our political sensibilities be radically transformed when our material reality is still organized by race? While the civil rights movement has changed the discourse on race and succeeded in stigmatizing racism, segregationary and other racist practices have been scarcely changed and at present the United States has achieved virtually the same levels of de facto residential racial segregation by choice and economics as it once did under Jim Crow laws.[21] With our post racial imaginary we are able to perceive equality as the norm while in real terms the racist system hasn't changed as drastically. Particularly in the construction of cyber-communities, preexisting structures, style communication, and "systematic social meanings . . . enable participants to imagine themselves as a community."[22] Political attachments online are embedded in our off-line contexts. In order to understand the imaginary mobilized on Stormfront we need to delve through the historical debris that shapes the affective ties that frame the movement.

Race, Passions, and Public Imaginaries

Stormfront represents a particular form of passionate politics (Mouffe 2002) that demonstrates that the affective terrain of sensation and instinct that helps shape imaginaries is not inherently libratory. This is contrary to optimistic accounts, such as one by Mark Hansen, which argues that affectivity is prepolitical or preindividual, and exists as bodily sensation that can be mobilized in revolutionary resistance to subjectivity and individuation. Engaging with the work of Mark Poster, who argues that the disembodied nature of computer-mediated communication transforms racial and ethnic identity,[23] and the philosophy of Giorgio Agamben, Hansen sees the Internet as providing a space of awareness and disruption between social categories and subjectivation. In this view resistance against racial subjectivation will take the form of "collective individuation rooted in the exposure of the affective basis of life, the excess of bodily life in relation to itself."[24] Assuming that affectivity is not affected by subjectivation is problematic in that affective life is clearly shaped by our interpellated subjective attachments. While the rupture provided by the Internet between social categories and our interpellation into them certainly has the potential to lead towards a post-identitarian subject, we must also theorize the limitations that impede this possibility. In the case of white nationalist cyber-activists on Stormfront, they are clearly motivated by their subjective attachments to bolster their social categories for highly emotional ends. This also complicates an understanding of the democratic possibilities of tactical media. While the mobilization of affect may not inherently lead to political action, it is imperative to understand the links that tie affect to political engagement. Regarding white nationalism, movement members are fighting against the possible desubjectifying trends in global capitalism, its challenges to the nation-state and its national imaginaries. The mobilized imaginary of Stormfront utilizes the Internet to reinscribe meanings on bodies that are no longer conclusively achieved through inter-pellation by national media and the nation-state, bolstering perceived social divisions that foreclose the possibility of democratic engagement.

My argument is that the concepts and their associated sentiments mobilized in the white nationalist movement are historical products of modern Western nationalism, now mobilized against the challenges to the nation-state under neoliberalism. While the Internet provides a space for radical rearticulations of political possibilities and subjectivities, Stormfront members instead advocate rearticulations of deeply histori-cal subject positions. While the temptation is great to study such a movement as deviant, in actuality white nationalism draws on significant, dominant Western con-cepts of race and nation and the subjective identities these concepts create.[25] The type of subjectivation that occurs through participation in the site is not libratory or new, but instead is deeply historical and connected to broader regimes of power.

Such an analysis challenges the simplistic optimism present in certain analyses of new media in an emerging, post national world. Certainly new media create the pos-sibility of new imaginaries given the decline in the nation-state under neoliberal globalization. Yet Stormfront shows us that our contemporary moment is not free of historical debris. If we read our current moment and its possibilities with a more nuanced understanding of historical epochal change, such as that articulated by Raymond Williams (1977), we have a clearer understanding of the possibilities afforded our current moment. Williams argues that epochal change does not occur through ruptures, but any given time contains emergent, residual, and dominant cultural ele-ments, signaling possibilities of the present and thus of the future. While Arjun Appadurai's (1996) claim that movement towards postnationalism can free the imagi-nation to construct communities no longer bound by national borders and exclusive imaginaries, this will not always be the case. The diasporic public spheres imagined by Appadurai are certainly proliferating, but so are other public spheres that bolster various regimes of power. Residual elements of the national era exist as structures of feeling of our previous time and can be mobilized in new, antidemocratic ways. The movement to postnationalism certainly does not come with a clean sociopolitical or cultural slate.

Appadurai's analysis of the movement to postnationalism is based on Benedict Anderson's *Imagined Communities*, where Anderson argues that nations are imagined political communities whose emergence is related to the development of print capital-ism. I think it useful to engage another study of nationalism, that of Etienne Balibar.[26] Balibar argues that national imaginaries serve to construct the "people." Given that "(n)o modern nation possesses a given 'ethnic' basis," then "(t)he fundamental prob-lem . . . is to produce the people. More exactly, it is to make the people produce itself continually as national community."[27] The "people" of the modern nation-state can also be described as the "public," a construct which, like the people, requires elaboration. This took a very consistent form in the modern nation. Through their interpellation as subjects, simultaneous groups are constructed through the subordination and relativization of differences between the "citizens" "in such a way that it is the symbolic difference between 'ourselves' and 'foreigners' which wins out and which is lived as irreducible."[28] Implicit within this production of the people or the public is the reproduction of its form, with the enemy or outsider consistently serving to consolidate the people within a "fictive ethnicity" of language and race.

Balibar's writing provides two significant cautions to this current analysis on white-nationalism and tactical media. The first is that the "public" is historically constructed not simply as a space of exchange of discourse and political engagement, but also on a false shared assumption of similarities in relation to external others outside the bounds of political engagement. Key to my analysis is that the historical and institutional practices of racializing private spaces have helped to secure a racially segregated imagined public sphere. In the United States, the securing of segregation under Jim Crow laws and the national implementation of redlining practices through the Federal Housing Act and through countless antimiscegenation laws helped to construct a national polity that could be imagined by whites as a white polity. The private segregation of people of color by whites correlated with a fantasy of the nation as white, or at least controlled by whites. This racially privileged citizenship was only expanded after significant antiracist struggle. Given the centrality of race in historically shaping the imagined public sphere, it is interesting that much political theory treats race as a nonissue regarding political practice. Carl Schmitt articulated this tension when he stated that the political is sensible "only in the context of ever present possibility of the friend-and-enemy groupings," a conceptualization that liberalism fails to observe or understand in its inability to grapple with collective identities.[29] Chantal Mouffe (2002) argues that to challenge this antagonistic opposition that forecloses the possibility of democratic engagement, we must keep political divisions in the realm of the political, and not slip into moral condemnation or perceptions of enmity. Instead she calls for the fostering of agonistic relationships based on recognizing different positions that are capable of struggling with and against each other. For Mouffe, this requires maintaining an oppositional politics of left and right and not collapsing political beliefs into moral oppositions. If we include in this challenge the recognition of the structuring role of race in dividing political identities and imaginaries, agonistic politics requires building multiracial, antiracist political identities that disrupt the relationship between whiteness and an exclusive public, creating the possibility of antiracist political identification.

The second caution Balibar provides us with is that the production of the public involves creating the conditions for its internal reproduction. While Anderson highlights the role of the national media in constructing the imagined national community, Balibar argues that the production of "the people" includes their instruction to reproduce themselves and the idea of their unification as a national community. While old media work to produce the public, the participatory nature of new media does not ensure the end of exclusive national imaginaries. Even as new media and changes in the geopolitical order are creating the possibilities of new interpellations and breaks with the bodily inscriptions of race, nation, and gender, the people can continue to reproduce themselves. This can occur through the continued embrace of a particular ideology, but more so through the interpellation as citizen-subjects that involves a sentimental education to invest in the national imaginary. As this interpellation functions at the sentimental and subjective levels, it makes sense that these restrictive national imaginaries continue to find articulation online, the people tend to reproduce themselves even as they face the possibility of imagining themselves anew.

As Balibar elaborates, this internal reproduction of solidarity is facilitated by the mutual production of external enmity. The people, or public, prove their solidarity through the continual emphasis on the division between "us" and "them." This raises a provocative question, virtually ignored in liberal political theory: Does the public need an enemy? This indeed has traditionally been the case and race has consistently served this function of marking insiders from outsiders or citizens from subjects or enemies.[30] While this logic is clearly evident on Stormfront, this analysis raises questions about how widespread racial citizenship actually is. While Stormfront articulates an explicitly racialized understanding of citizenship, we should ask: In which other movements and mobilizations is the public imagined (though likely unacknowledged) as racialized and exclusionary? The discourse of the citizen almost exclusively fails to acknowledge its reliance on the imagined community of the nation as the context for constricting and constructing the public sphere and its multiple exclusions.

White-nationalist online organizing provides a clear example of how well cyber-activism can serve in the production of an enemy, giving further credence to Dean's argument that the imaginaries produced online can avoid democratic forms of engagement, instead creating segmentary bubbles of likemindedness against which enemies must be imagined and constructed. Stormfront is tactically and ideologically organized to limit the possibility of any opposition to white-nationalism. As mentioned above, one of the most consistently popular forums is "Opposing Views," the section of the site dedicated to white-nationalist critics to voice their opinions. A posting to the site by one of its opponents includes the following statement: "The world doesn't need a bunch of clinically insane paranoids spreading the word of hate. Enjoy your site while it lasts because some day this hate site will be shut down for good and hopefully all WN members end up where they belong . . . in jail."[31] Although the responses vary, they tend to follow two themes. One theme focuses on the First Amendment's protection of free speech. However, the majority of the responses tend to discount this comment by racializing the writers, whether or not the authors gave indication of their own racial identification. Members respond through explicitly labeling the opponent as racialized ("I'll see you when I get there negro")[32] or through racially coded insults ("Why are you posting here? Did you lose your basketball?").[33] This theme is echoed throughout the site in a racial tautology where any criticism of white nationalism will be assumed to come from a Jew or person of color and is systematically discounted.

In my study of this nationalist community I have had to grapple with the relationship among politics and publics, morality and imagined communities. At least in my reading of U.S. political history, the polity has always been organized and riven by race, which complicates an understanding of the possibility of democratic politics. How does this challenge our conceptions of political antagonism and the possibilities of democracy? As nationalism and democracy are both products of the modern era, has democratic practice not always been defined by and limited to the national imaginary, originally overtly excluding those dubbed racially other and inferior?

Concluding Thoughts and Democratic Possibilities

Currently, the white nationalist movement remains peripheral. Its impact on the majority of citizens in the West is miniscule, its rampant anti-Semitism and thinly veiled racism are marginalized, and its membership is comparatively small. However, the movement's current insignificance should not be taken as a sign of comfort. One only has to look back to Germany in 1920 and the way that an ambitious, young anti-Semite began to work steadfastly to bring his radical ideology to mainstream Germany to understand the potential threat of even a highly marginal group. Perhaps it seems extreme and overwrought to compare the potential of radical racist movements to Hitler and the Nazi party and I hope this is indeed an extreme comparison, but I don't think it is unwarranted. As Carol Swain writes, "Mass movements . . . often begin with small fringe groups, but grow and eventually become part of the mainstream."[34] In 1920, the Nazi party was a peripheral political group with only 6 percent public support. With the synergistic mix of Hitler's charismatic ability to speak to crowds, the successful tapping into German fears and insecurities posed by the post–World War I economic downturn and loss of international political power, and the strategic accumulation of political, educational, and organizational reach, the Nazi party slowly worked its way into political power. While the imagined community being built on Stormfront is not currently focused on creating immediate political change, it is providing the resources, imagination, information, and relationships which can easily be tapped into for more overt political projects in the future. They are reconstructing a racial public imaginary which can serve as the basis for a variety of types of political engagements. Therefore, although it is hard to imagine the white-nationalist movement gaining a national political presence, the increasing membership numbers on Stormfront promises the continued presence of dispersed racial conflict and potential violence.

The tactical mobilization of racial sentiments on Stormfront gives us caution about the continued existence of nationalist imaginaries even through new media communications that provide the possibility for liberatory politics and imaginaries. This continuation of nationalist sentiments and subjectivities should challenge our thinking about political agency as it is expressed through various political engagements, including tactical media. Political agency shapes our civic engagements; agency and the subjective attachments that spur agency are thus a site, *the* site, of the protection or destabilization of power, even if it is machinations of power which structure our subjective identities. Democratic potential depends on "constructing new locations of struggle, vocabularies, and subject positions that allow people in a wide variety of public spheres to become more than they are now."[35] Racism and its nationalist practices have historically functioned to construct publics that rest on exclusionary imagined communities that preclude the possibility of political engagement with other publics. Successful democratic politics rests on our ability to construct nonexclusionary publics. This can only be accomplished by addressing the political passions that move people and by thinking through tactical interventions that allow people to question and subvert power.

Such questions about race, passions, agency, and media mobilizations rarely emerge in new media theory. While the trend in cyber-studies literature is to theorize the Internet as a postracial space, the Internet itself seems to be employed to do the opposite. There is also an incredible lack of applied tactical interventions on the Internet countering the messages of Stormfront and the hundreds of other racist and neo-Nazi Web sites currently in operation. This lack of antiracist theory and practice, in contradistinction to the organizing savvy of the white-nationalist movement, leave the playingfield of cyberspace tilted toward the success of conservative and white-supremacist organizing. To counter this tendency we must ground our political analysis with an understanding of how people are making sense of their identities and positions and the political possibilities which stem from them.

The Internet holds huge sway over how future politics and race relations will unfold. In our increasingly globalized, interconnected, and diverse world, the hope is that cyberspace will be a place where the centuries-old prejudices that have kept communities apart can finally be breached. The reality, sadly, is that currently the supremacists are winning this race for the future, although my hope is that we can reverse this trend.

Beyond the specific fears of increased white nationalist organizing, this analysis provides two cautions to theorizing tactical media and political mobilizations more generally. The first is on the role of passions in motivating political engagements and the historical-cultural influences or interpellations which can be understood as entrenched in affective life. Tied to this is the need to link studies of political mobilizations to imaginaries that are drawn on, changed, and constituted through political practice. While the imagination can function ideologically, creating an illusion of political participation while sustaining practices that fail to impact the political realm, we should not discount the workings of the imagination in political life. While it is tactical practices that create political change, practices themselves are spurred by a combination of affect, imagination, and relations, to political ideologies, movements, organizations, or the like. Part of the work of the imagination is in constructing the public or political realm that one's practices seek to change and to which *one belongs*. The construction of an imagined community not only provides the basis and frame for political action but simultaneously provides the needed sense of belonging to a social collective or community. Imagined communities thus provide both political and social purposes. They also inspire great significant emotional attachments. One Stormfront member's signature quote demonstrates the significance of affect in white nationalism in a quote attributed to Hitler: "The doom of a nation can be averted only by a storm of flowing passion, but only those who are passionate themselves can arouse passion in others."[36] This desire for and valorization of imagined communities is a political act in defining who belongs within and who remains outside.

New and tactical media, in tandem and often in opposition to old media, work not only to engage in official political processes, but also to create the illusion of a community of belonging. It is my argument that such shaping of the imagination is a political project. Stemming from this is a challenge to our understanding of the goals of prodemocratic, liberatory, tactical, and political interventions. While the difficult political work is to tactically interject and work to change political processes (the United States will not simply end its Iraq war because enough people desire it, but when they demand it), tactical interventions that change, free, or expand the imagination should be seen as part of the political realm. While stirring residual sentimental attachments has proven so successful for conservative movements, can we progressives learn to broaden our political tactics through a recognition that political identities are based as much on passion and affect as on rational intent? What would progressive political tactics look like that focused on mobilizing affect and responding to our needs for group identity and community? Our ability to mobilize emergent identities and imaginaries of inclusion will certainly determine the possibilities of our political futures. To move beyond exclusive imaginaries of race we have to challenge racism and its structuring role in our on- and off-line identities, communities, and political affinities.

Notes

1. Lisa Nakamura, *Cybertypes: Race, Ethnicity, and Identity on the Internet* (Routledge: New York and London, 2002), xi.

2. Kolko, B., L. Nakamura, and G. Rodman, "Race in Cyberspace: An Introduction," in *Race in Cyberspace*, ed. B. Kolko, L. Nakamura, and G. Rodman (New York and London: Routledge, 2000), 4.

3. Quoted in Carol M. Swain and Russ Nieli, *Contemporary Voices of White Nationalism in America* (Cambridge University Press, 2003), 161.

4. Ibid.

5. Charles A. Lindbergh, "How Did It Start for You?" 20 July 2004, http://www.stormfront.org/forum/showthread.php/did-start-you-127184p5.html?highlight=How+did+it+start+for+you.

6. Don Black, "Guidelines for Posting," 26 October 2001, http://www.stormfront.org/forum/showthread.php/welcome-guidelines-posting-4359.html.

7. Hitler quoted in Claudia Koonz, *The Nazi Conscience* (Cambridge, MA: Belknap Press of Harvard University Press, 2003), 18. Koonz traces how, although violent anti-Semitism remained central to Hitler's ideology throughout his political career, as a strategist he understood that to gain public credibility he must veil the core of this belief until the opportune moment. While his speeches remained focused on saving the *Volk* and were only occasionally peppered with the use of "Jew" as an epithet, he worked, through academics, scientists, propagandists, and educational programs, to successfully mainstream his radical views.

8. Research staff of *National Vanguard* magazine, "The Alien Grip on Our News and Entertainment Media Must Be Broken: Who Rules America?" 1 July 2001, http://www.stormfront.org/jewish/whorules.html.

9. Ibid.

10. Beverly Ray and George E. Marsh II, "Recruitment by Extremist Groups on the Internet," *First Monday*, February 2001, http://firstmonday.org/issues/issue6_2/ray/index.html.

11. "Ku Klux Klan Rebounds," Anti-Defamation League reports, 06 February 2007, http://www.adl.org/learn/ext_us/kkk/intro.asp?LEARN_Cat=Extremism&LEARN_SubCat=Extremism_in_America&xpicked=4&item=kkk.

12. "Hate group numbers top 800," *SPLC Report*, March 2006, http://www.splcenter.org/center/splcreport/article.jsp?aid=187.

13. See Carol M. Swain, *The New White Nationalism in America: Its Challenges to Integration* (Cambridge: Cambridge University Press, 2002), and Jessie Daniels, *White Lies: Race, Class, Gender, and Sexuality in White Supremacist Discourse* (New York and London: Routledge, 1997).

14. Nakamura, *Cybtertypes*, xii.

15. Mark B. N. Hansen, "Digitizing the Racialized Body or the Politics of Universal Address," *Substance 104* (vol. 33, no. 2, 2004), 108.

16. Nakamura, *Cybtertypes*, xv.

17. T. McPherson, "I'll Take My Stand in Dixieland," in *Race in Cyberspace*, ed. B. Kolko, L. Nakamura, and G. Rodman (New York and London: Routledge, 2000), 119.

18. Ibid.

19. P. Agre, quoted in Wilson and Peterson 2002, p. 451.

20. Wilson and Peterson 2002, p. 456.

21. Jeff R. Crump, "Producing and Enforcing the Geography of Hate: Race, Housing Segregation, and Housing-Related Hate Crimes in the United States," in *Spaces of Hate: Geographies of Discrimination and Intolerance in the U.S.A.*, ed. Colin Flint (New York and London: Routledge, 2004), 227.

22. Nancy K. Baym, "The Emergence of On-Line Community," in *Cybersociety 2.0*, ed. Steven Jones (Thousand Oaks, CA: Sage Publications), 38.

23. Mark Poster, "Virtual Ethnicity," in *What's the Matter with the Internet?* (Minneapolis: University of Minnesota Press, 2001), 148–170.

24. Mark B. N. Hansen, "Digitizing the Racialized Body or The Politics of Universal Address," *Substance 104* (vol. 33, no. 2, 2004), 107–133.

25. See G. Mosse, *Nationalism and Sexuality: Middle-Class Morality and Sexual Norms in Modern Europe* (Madison and London: University of Wisconsin Press, 1988).

26. Etienne Balibar, "The Nation Form: History and Ideology," in *Race Critical Theories*, ed. Philomena Essed and David Theo Goldberg (London: Blackwell, 2002), 220–230.

27. Ibid, 221.

28. Ibid, 222.

29. Schmitt, quoted in Mouffe 2002, p. 6.

30. Though talking about "society" and not the public, Michele Foucault makes a similar point in his lectures published in *Society Must be Defended*. There he articulates the role of race as traditionally serving to secure the notion of the society through its protections from the imagined threats of racial outsiders. See, *"Society Must be Defended": Lectures at the College de France, 1975–76* (New York: Picador, 1997).

31. Wildcat01, "Stormfront should be shutdown for good," 5 April 2007, http://www.stormfront.org/forum/showthread.php/stormfront-should-shutdown-good-378009.html?t=378009&highlight=stormfront+should+be+shutdown+for+good.

32. WhiteEnglishRocker, "Re: stormfront should be shutdown for good," 5 April 2007, http://www.stormfront.org/forum/showthread.php/stormfront-should-shutdown-good-378009.html?t=378009&highlight=stormfront+should+be+shutdown+for+good.

33. Canadian Caucasian, "Re: stormfront should be shutdown for good," 5 April 2007, http://www.stormfront.org/forum/showthread.php/stormfront-should-shutdown-good-378009.html?t=378009&highlight=stormfront+should+be+shutdown+for+good.

34. Carol M. Swain, *The New White Nationalism in America: Its Challenges to Integration* (Cambridge: Cambridge University Press, 2002), 338.

35. Ibid, 132.

36. Nailedn2place, "Re: Tales of the Holocaust," 19 January 2007, http://www.stormfront.org/forum/showthread.php/tales-holocaust-354283.html?p=3811779.

References

Anderson, Benedict. 1983. *Imagined Communities: Reflections on the Origin and Spread of Nationalism*. New York and London: Verso.

Appadurai, Arjun. 1996. *Modernity at Large: Cultural Dimensions of Globalization*. Minneapolis: University of Minnesota Press.

Gonzalez, Jennifer. 2000. "The Appended Subject: Race and Identity as Digital Assemblage." In *Race in Cyberspace*, ed. B. Kolko, L. Nakamura, and G. Rodman. New York and London: Routledge, 37–50.

Hage, Ghassan. 2000. *White Nation: Fantasies of White Supremacy in a Multicultural Society*. New York: Routledge.

McPherson, Tara. "I'll Take My Stand in Dixieland." In *Race in Cyberspace*, ed. B. Kolko, L. Nakamura, and G. Rodman. New York and London: Routledge, 117–132.

Mouffe, Chantal. 2002. "Political Passions: The Stakes of Democracy." Centre for the Study of Democracy, London.

Williams, Raymond. 1977. *Marxism and Literature*. Oxford: Oxford University Press.

Wilson, S., and L. Peterson. 2002. "The Anthropology of Online Communities." *Annual Review of Anthropology* 31 (October), 449–467.

19 Re-Visioning the State of the Media: Concluding Interview with Brian Holmes

with Megan Boler

Brian Holmes is an art critic, cultural theorist, and activist, particularly involved with the mapping of contemporary capitalism. Since the Carnival against Capital in the city of London in 1999, he has taken part in and written about many of the large demonstrations against corporate globalization around the world. He is the author of *Personality*, and has recently also published an anthology of essays, *Hieroglyphs of the Future* (Zagreb: Arkzin/WHW, 2003). This interview was conducted through e-mail correspondence during April 2007.

BH: Hello Megan, greetings from Valdecaballeros. Your questions come at a perfect time! An unusual moment of reflection in a busy life. I am presently in Extremadura, one of the most isolated regions in Spain, so far out of the loop that the inhabitants jokingly call it "Siberia." It's springtime, everything is green with tiny white daisies popping up out of the meadow grass all around. We're beneath a geodesic dome, on an open field dotted with olive trees, with an empty nuclear power plant in front of us, its construction halted in the late seventies by a successful antinuclear movement. Nearby is parked the Psand.net van, which is a live-in rolling media lab. They've set up a satellite link for the Internet connection, offering the capacity to hook into the GISS cooperative of streaming servers. A curious and lively group of active and inquiring people have converged from the region, from Spain, from all over Europe, for a week-long festival called "Emergent Geographies." The tactical media group Hackitectura has organized this event in collaboration with their long-term friends, interested participants from the area, architecture students from Seville and Lisbon, and also the Karosta media lab far away in Latvia, which over the last eight years has been established as a cultural experiment in a town left half-empty by the withdrawal of the Soviet army. It's quite a network, an intricate geometry of people and ideas. If you wanted me to sum up this whole thing in a few words, I'd say we're here to think about how to replay the twentieth-century modernities that failed, that were not able to give people what they needed or desired. We're here to put another myth into circulation, to tell a different story about the world and build it at the same time. But suddenly it's kind of hard to think, let alone go on writing, with all these kids crawling around!

Picture this: about twenty or thirty kids just arrived walking across the field, dressed in semitransparent, white overalls, like hygienic suits, maybe for entering an unknown territory. But there's two kids stuffed into each overall! It's an educational group, part of the festival, led by young people with a lot of funny ideas. So you can imagine there is an incredible tumult, an uproar of laughter and pleasure as these kids move step by step together in twos across the muddy grassy field, then arrive at the platform and look at all the computers set up in a circle like a kind of mock control room. Now the kids are stripping out of their double suits and the volume level is going down a notch as one of the group leaders says in Spanish, "I'm going to tell you about a good idea. We're sitting right beneath a good idea. And you can play with it!" He gestures as he talks, holding a ball up in the air and spinning it around on his fingertip. It's an ordinary soccer ball, so it has hexagons and pentagons traced on it, forming a sphere. He retraces them in blue felt pen on the ball, then starts sketching in the triangles that nest inside the pentagons composing the steel-framed dome above our head, all the while telling the kids about the project. See it, draw it, and speak it. "Cooperation, no? And discovering good ideas, no? That's what we're here for," says the guy with the ball, spinning it around, showing the kids and everybody else how they can use their imagination to play with the space.

Curiously enough, a man from the provincial government in Extremadura has just arrived, dressed in a conventional suit with a name tag, and he has been explaining to me over the last few minutes how they established their public network starting in 2002, using free software. They have set up access points for free in every town in the province, using a Debian system that seems to work pretty well. This connection with a progressive part of the local government is part of the reason why the festival is happening, because Hackitectura is pretty much based on free software development and the larger, fuzzier idea that you can transform the urban space from below, through experiments in thinking and living that are developed by people working together, making different kinds of interventions: political, cultural, architectural, technological. I'm pretty interested in the free software stuff myself, since I finally got out of the commercial racket and into something a little more inspirational. Hopefully I will go to a workshop later on this afternoon and see how the public software program functions in reality.

Anyway, this is a perfect introduction to the things I will have to say in answer to your questions. This is the place from which I am speaking—right now, anyway. So let's take it from here, *tranquilo tranquilo*, I'm going to think a little about your concerns and also about what's going on here, and then we will see what the idea of tactical media has to offer in the present.

MB: Brian, how do you respond to Jodi Dean's argument and pessimism? "Why, at a time when the means of communication have been revolutionized, when people can contribute their opinions and access those of others rapidly and immediately, why has democracy failed?"

BH: Well, I'd say Jodi Dean is understandably dismayed about the state of democracy. She has good reason. In the United States in particular, September 11, 2001, was followed by a tremendous degree of censorship and self-censorship, especially within the major communications media, but also in the educational and cultural institutions. The result was to give Bush and his administration free rein. Only during the last, lame-duck years of his presidency have congressional representatives and former administration officials openly characterized his policies as antidemocratic and positively dangerous for the American people, and, I would add, for the world. However, to attribute this genuine failure of democracy to "communicative capitalism" is quite misleading. The first observation one could make is that the emergence of the Internet very quickly was accompanied by an impressive result: the networked protests at the World Trade Organization meeting in Seattle in 1999. In their wake came the very effective, deeply democratic questioning of the WTO's economic agenda, and of the IMF / World Bank structural adjustment policies, which were convincingly shown to be dictated by criteria of corporate profit. In this case, the increase in communicational capacities that marked the 1990s immediately led to the taking of very principled ethical positions in the public sphere. However, I would also have to observe that from the very start, this protest movement was heavily repressed by the police, especially in the United States and especially after September 11. I'm talking about preemptive attacks by the police, the confiscation and destruction of dangerous things like video cameras and giant puppets, along with arrests for blocking traffic on the sidewalk, that sort of thing. The new-found capacity for people from all walks of life to inform themselves about complex issues and to organize themselves in such a way as to make their voices heard and to compel public officials to respond was not cultivated and encouraged, as one could hope for in a democracy, but vigorously opposed and stifled. This reaction to the new possibilities of grassroots political communication does not seem to have been taken into account in Jodi Dean's argument.

Why then, one could ask, did the citizenry at large allow such constructive criticism to be stifled? Was it because they were fascinated by their blogs and Web sites? The problem of passivity in democratic societies is not new. Throughout the world, the former function of political parties—namely, to be information-gathering systems able to relay opinions, needs, and desires from the grassroots to the upper levels of representation—has been replaced by the PR formula of a telegenic candidate mouthing messages crafted on the basis of statistical polls and focus groups. What gets lost are the local debates and the experience of lower-level party membership that at least gave a few people a concrete experience of the political process. Meanwhile, another characteristic of the 1990s, in addition to the emergence of the Internet, was the extreme concentration of media ownership in the United States and throughout the world. Now, innumerable critics have studied the ways that commercial media train their spectators for passive acceptance, cynicism, individualistic opportunism, and the reflexes of consumerism. To claim, as major advertisers still do, that advertising has no proven effect on human behavior, is worse than naive. It recalls the denial of the health problems associated with asbestos, with tobacco consumption, et cetera. Let's be serious. If democracy is going to work, it has to be carefully cultivated by public institutions. Processes of self-education have to be encouraged, forums of debate have to be supported, with a continuous respect for the divergence of opinions that makes a democracy real. All of this requires a subtle balance between government and civil society, which can never be attained once and for all but must instead be open to continuous reformulation as generations change and fresh challenges arise. What we have seen instead is the sweeping privatization of the institutions of culture, communication, and education, and their realignment to fit commercial priorities, to the point where the health of all the world's democracies is now gravely endangered.

In the face of this privatization process, many people have seized the new communications technologies in attempts to organize processes of self-education and political organization. The impulse comes from the grassroots. That's exactly what's happening here in Valdecaballeros—and without all this voluntary effort, there wouldn't be anything going on here today. But here, at least you have a modicum of public support. I don't mean to romanticize it. The region of Extremadura is the poorest in Spain, and if they got interested in free software, it's because free software offered a possibility to extend a far greater range of services to the public than they could otherwise afford. Necessity, as the saying goes, is the mother of invention. Poverty can be a great stimulus. But the big question is how to arrive at a different kind of wealth than the one which is massively proposed to us today: because policy is conducted in the name of poisoned wealth, like nuclear power whose very existence literally engenders huge amounts of poison. The ecological and social problems of the overdeveloped societies are accumulating fast, too fast. At this point, necessity could well become the mother of a great democratic invention. Because if it doesn't, given the level of tensions in the world today, given the competition for scarce resources, given the looming ecological problems, the chances for truly democratic governance do not look particularly good.

MB: How then do we begin to understand the contradictions of proliferation (of access to production, circulation, expression), alongside the rigid coordination of political, corporate, and media institutions? Where do we turn for a useful theorization of "virality" (viral circulation) as a way to understand the modes of communication and their relationship to capitalism?

BH: I believe these two phenomena are connected. From the viewpoint of those who organize and govern, the proliferation of communications results in a dramatic rise in uncertainty. Multiple opinions, diverse sensibilities, divergent analyses, all these present risks to organizational continuity, to the predictability of behavior. One response is even more rigid coordination. Every message is vetted, every communication is monitored. The phenomenon of the embedded reporter is the quintessence of this. An institution as vast as the U.S. military believes it has the resources to take over the communication process entirely, to internalize it, to absorb the news media within its own structure. Oil companies like Shell have done very similar things, inventing their own ecological groups in the wake of serious protests (made possible because of the Internet, by the way). But then what happens? The Iraqi bloggers, the Abu Ghraib photos. Viral circulation is actually rather natural, just as the name suggests. Information itself doesn't want to be free, but people certainly do, and curiosity is only increased through prohibition, orchestration, and control. Curiosity becomes contagious. The question is, Can we place our faith in sheer "virality"?

You ask in the same breath about capitalism. It's true that capitalism is wonderfully opportunistic. Recent years have seen the rise of "viral marketing," which depends on people's desire to spread slogans, jokes, images, lightweight media such as stickers, tee-shirts, video clips on YouTube. I'm not going to complain about enthusiasm. Nothing yet shows that viral marketing has in any way overcome or demeaned the rather magical experience of throwing an idea or an image or any other creation out into the public realm, and watching it proliferate and spread. That's a viable mode of distribution today, no question. But I think to lay too much emphasis on such small miracles is imprudent. It can also become a form of mysticism, flourishing in the face of general despondency and lack of wider perspectives.

The democratic question, today as always, is how to organize free cooperation? How to find meeting points between reliable structure and open desire? Every time that society's complexity goes up another notch, this question emerges anew. Now, with the security panic that has gripped the world, we are once again entering a phase of increasing rigidity. In the 1960s, during the Cold War, one of the great social responses to that was sheer spontaneity, playful anarchy, the liberation of sexuality with all its disruptive consequences. The problem is, most of those strategies have now been absorbed by capitalism, and also very well studied by the state. Never have I heard of a more convincing proof of this than in the way that the very creative and radical direct-action protests surrounding the G8 summit in Gleneagles, Scotland, in 2005, were totally eclipsed by the massive fanfare around the "Live 8" concerts in support of the campaign to "Make Poverty History." The problem here is that this is a totally formatted behavior: the utopian mass rock concert, featuring all the names and hits of the 1960s. People come away from such an event having learned almost nothing about how to change their daily lives. As for its effect on politicians, well, it's easy to make promises. But I have not yet seen any moves to make poverty history! The question is how to find an intermediate scale, in between the small, radical protest and the massive, neutralizing media event.

To tell you the truth, I am less preoccupied with virality than with social institutions like universities. Why have there been so few student movements, why have professors not taken a more active role in questioning the agendas of American policy? Maybe one answer is that disciplines are now so narrowly conceived, and success in those disciplines is now so vitally important for students who are obliged to take out such gigantic loans. The old Marxists drone on about commodity fetishes. But in our business-obsessed societies, what you see most often are professional fetishes. In our field, that means media technologies, strategies, styles. They are important, but they're not the whole cookie. What you say matters along with how you say it. Messages spread like wildfire when people are prepared to hear them, to act on them. What we need are compelling ideas that take the risk of different strategies, different styles, different media.

MB: What might be the significance of the fact that scholars express more despair and tempered hope about media and democracy than do those working on the profession of journalism?

BH: Well, what could be more natural? Scholars have to look at facts, they have to look at statistics, they have to look at determinisms. Fortunately they do, because that's a reality check and I still want to be part of the reality community. But the thing about facts, statistics, and deterministic forces is that they always point in the same way, they don't allow you to imagine anything different. Whereas journalists, or even more so, activists and artists, always find fresh resources in cooperation and contact with other people. That's why I take the time and energy to go to places like Valdecaballeros, to check out the emergent geographies. It's not too often that you come back disappointed. The idea of tactical media was always "do it anyway," send out the dissenting message, even though CNN will still have wider distribution. I think that attitude goes a long way; the same thing has inspired guys like Jon Stewart, who are getting national and international audiences. They're building new forces in the media just because they can't stand the ones that are already out there. And that's tremendously important in a world where media concentration has so drastically limited the range of what's acceptable to say in public.

The real problem is right there, in my opinion. Huge numbers of people have doubts about what's going on in the world today, but most need an outside figure, a public figure, to formulate that same doubt and make it legitimate. Once you've heard the basic idea, you can add things, you can embroider. This is what we need to offer people. The mediated message is a key to embodied speech. That's why it's so important to take hold of the media when you have something to say—not just for your own satisfaction, but to make speech possible for everyone. And if the perfect medium doesn't come knocking at your door, then it might be time to invent it. For me, nothing is more interesting than experimentation, than invention, particularly when you keep the facts right there on the table as a reality check. With one hand you point back to an empty shell, a dead end, an abandoned future. And with the other you invite people to discover a territory that might be worth living in.

Contributors

Shaina Anand is a filmmaker and media artist based in Mumbai. She is the founder of ChitraKarKhana.net (picture factory/artist food), a fully independent unit for practical media.

Chris Atton is a reader in journalism at the School of Creative Industries, Napier University, Edinburgh, Scotland. His books include *Alternative Literature* (Gower, 1996), *Alternative Media* (Sage, 2002) and *An Alternative Internet* (Edinburgh University Press, 2004).

Megan Boler is a professor at OISE/University of Toronto and earned her PhD at the History of Consciousness Program at the University of California Santa Cruz. Her books include *Feeling Power: Emotions and Education* (Routledge, 1999), and an edited volume *Democratic Dialogue in Education: Troubling Speech, Disturbing Silences* (Peter Lang, 2004). Her Web-based projects include Critical Media Literacy in Times of War.

Axel Bruns lectures in the Creative Industries Faculty at Queensland University of Technology in Brisbane, Australia. He is the author of *Gatewatching: Collaborative Online News Production* and the editor of *Uses of Blogs*, with Joanne Jacobs, and is currently developing *From Production to Produsage: The Rise of Collaborative Content Creation*, forthcoming in 2008.

Catherine Burwell is a teacher and a PhD candidate at the Ontario Institute for Studies in Education, University of Toronto. Her interests include public broadcasting, participatory cultures, and interactive technologies.

Jodi Dean is professor of political science at Hobart and William Smith Colleges in Geneva, New York. Among her eight authored or edited books are *Publicity's Secret: How Technoculture Capitalizes on Democracy* (Cornell University Press, 2002) and *Zizek's Politics* (Routledge, 2006).

Ronald J. Deibert is associate professor of political science and Director of the Citizen Lab at the Munk Centre for Internet Studies, University of Toronto.

Deepa Fernandes is a journalist, media activist, and media trainer. She is a radio features producer who has worked in communities around the world to produce award-winning documentaries about forgotten peoples with marginalized voices. She is currently the host of Free Speech Radio News and a freelance producer for the British Broadcasting Corporation, Australian Broadcasting Corporation, and Pacifica Radio.

Amy Goodman is the host and executive producer of the daily radio, TV, and Web broadcast Democracy Now! She is coauthor of the national best-seller *The Exception to the Rulers: Exposing Oily Politicians, War Profiteers, and the Media that Love Them*, written with her brother David Goodman.

Brian Holmes is an art critic, cultural theorist, and activist, particularly involved with the mapping of contemporary capitalism. He is the author of *Personality* and a recent anthology of essays, *Hieroglyphs of the Future* (Zagreb: Arkzin/WHW, 2003).

Hassan Ibrahim is a Sudanese journalist. He was raised in Saudi Arabia, attended American universities, and headed the BBC Arab News Service before joining Al-Jazeera. Hassan has covered a wide range of conflicts in the Middle East and Africa as well as in Panama, Nicaragua, Honduras, Colombia, and Brazil, making him a well-respected voice. As a young reporter, he covered the Iran-Iraq war, following the conflict from both fronts. He was featured as Al Jazeera's senior producer in the major documentary *Control Room* in 2004.

Geert Lovink a media theorist, activist, and net critic, is author of *Dark Fiber, My First Recession* and *Zero Comments*, director of the Institute of Network Cultures at the Amsterdam Polytechnic (HvA), and associate professor of media studies, University of Amsterdam.

Nathalie Magnan is an artist and a media activist who worked both with grassroots TV as well as for Canal+. She is currently teaching at l'Ecole Nationale Superieure d'Art de Bourges in France.

Robert W. McChesney is research professor in the Institute of Communications Research and the Graduate School of Library and Information Science at the University of Illinois at Urbana-Champaign. In 2002 he cofounded, with Dan Schiller, the Illinois Initiative on Global Information and Communication Policy, and is author and coauthor or editor of seventeen books including *Rich Media, Poor Democracy*.

Graham Meikle is the author of *Future Active: Media Activism and the Internet* (Routledge 2002) and *Interpreting News* (Palgrave, forthcoming 2008). He lectures in the Department of Film, Media, and Journalism at Stirling University in Scotland.

Susan D. Moeller is the director, International Center for Media and the Public Agenda (ICMPA) and associate professor, Philip Merrill College of Journalism and

School of Public Policy, University of Maryland. Her books include *Compassion Fatigue: How the Media Sell Disease, Famine, War and Death* and *Shooting War: Photography and the American Experience of Combat.*

Alessandra Renzi   is writing her dissertation on Telestreet, an Italian network of pirate television producers, at the Ontario Institute for Studies in Education at the University of Toronto. She is a member of CAMERA (The Committee on Alternative Media Experimentation, Research, and Analysis) and a founding member of the labor-immigrant rights organization Precarity Toronto.

Ricardo Rosas   was the editor of the Rizoma e-magazine and a former member of the Midiatatica.org network. Rosas helped organize the Mídia Tática Brasil 2003 and the Digitofagia 2004 festivals in São Paulo, both of them aimed at discussing the tactical media scene, free software, and the creation of collaborative projects in art and activism involving new media. Rosas was the Net Art curator of the Prog: Me festival in Rio de Janeiro (2005) and a lecturer at the fourth edition of the Next 5 Minutes festival in Amsterdam (2003), the first international event dedicated to the mapping of tactical media.

Andréa Schmidt   is an independent journalist and researcher. She has reported from Haiti and Iraq and is currently based in Toronto.

Trebor Scholz   is an artist, activist, and professor of media studies at the State University of New York at Buffalo who writes on network culture, media art, education, and labor on the social Web. Scholz founded the Institute for Distributed Creativity (iDC) in 2004 and coedited *The Art of Free Cooperation* with Geert Lovink (Autonomedia, 2007). Scholz contributes essays and chapters to books and journals and presents his research at national and international conferences and on his blog: http://collectivate.net/journalisms.

D. Travers Scott   is a doctoral student researching technological culture and gender at the University of Southern California, Annenberg School for Communication. He is also the author of two novels.

R. Sophie Statzel   is a doctoral student in anthropology at the City University of New York. Her research interests include nationalist movements and religious mobilizations in North America and critical race theory.

Stephen Turpin   is a PhD candidate at the Ontario Institute for Studies in Education of the University of Toronto. His doctoral thesis, Assembling a Minor Architecture, maps the mutation of pedagogical concerns within modernist architectural discourse and practice as they are taken up within contemporary installation art practices. He is also editing a collection of essays on Deleuze and war and a documentary art project on the history of Semiotext(e).

Index